SIXTH EDITION

Introducing Communication Theory

ANALYSIS AND APPLICATION

Richard West
Emerson College

Lynn H. Turner
Marquette University

Mc
Graw
Hill
Education

INTRODUCING COMMUNICATION THEORY: ANALYSIS AND APPLICATION, SIXTH EDITION

2 3 4 5 6 7 QVS 21 20 19 18 17

ISBN 978-1-259-87032-3
MHID 1-259-87032-4

Chief Product Officer, SVP Products & Markets: *G. Scott Virkler*
Vice President, General Manager, Products & Markets: *Michael Ryan*
Vice President, Content Design & Delivery: *Betsy Whalen*
Managing Director: *David Patterson*
Brand Manager: *Jamie Laferrerra*
Director, Product Development: *Meghan Campbell*
Marketing Manager: *Meredith Leo*
Director, Content Design & Delivery: *Terri Schiesl*
Program Manager: *Jennifer Shekleton*
Content Project Managers: *Lisa Bruflodt, Samantha Donisi-Hamm*
Buyer: *Susan K. Culbertson*
Designer: *Jessica Serd*
Content Licensing Specialist: *DeAnna Dausener*
Compositor: *MPS Limited*
Printer: *Quad/Graphics*

All credits appearing on page or at the end of the book are considered to be an extension of the copyright page.

Library of Congress Cataloging-in-Publication Data

West, Richard L. | Turner, Lynn H.
  Introducing communication theory : analysis and application/Richard
  West, Emerson College, Lynn H. Turner, Marquette University.
  Sixth edition. | New York, NY : McGraw-Hill Education, [2019] |
  Includes bibliographical references and indexes.
  LCCN 2016059715 | ISBN 9781259870323 (alk. paper)
  LCSH: Information theory. | Communication.
  LCC Q360 .W47 2019 | DDC 003/.54—dc23
  LC record available at https://lccn.loc.gov/2016059715

The Internet addresses listed in the text were accurate at the time of publication. The inclusion of a website does not indicate an endorsement by the authors or McGraw-Hill Education, and McGraw-Hill Education does not guarantee the accuracy of the information presented at these sites.

mheducation.com/highered

Brief Contents

Contents

PART ONE   *Foundations*   001

COMMUNICATION, THEORY, AND RESEARCH

Chapter 1   Thinking About Communication: Definitions, Models, and Ethics   3

Chapter 7   Expectancy Violations Theory   119

RELATIONSHIP DEVELOPMENT

Chapter 8   Uncertainty Reduction Theory   135

THE PUBLIC

Chapter 18   The *Rhetoric*   306

Chapter 19   Dramatism   324

Preface

As we present the sixth edition of *Introducing Communication Theory: Analysis and Application*, we remain excited by its enormous success. The previous five editions demonstrate that communication theory courses are vibrant, that teachers of communication understand the importance of theoretical thinking, and that both instructors and students appreciate the consistent and organized template we employ throughout. This text explores the practical, engaging, and relevant ways in which theory operates in our lives. *It is written primarily for students who have little or no background in communication theory.* We originally wrote the book because we thought that students need to know how theorizing helps us understand ourselves, as well as our experiences, relationships, media, environment, and culture. We also wrote this book because we believe that students should have a text that relates theory directly to their lives. We felt that some books insulted the student and trivialized theory while other books were written at a level that was far too advanced for an undergraduate. In this book, we take great care to achieve the following additional objectives:

- Familiarize students with the principles and central ideas of important theories they are likely to encounter in the communication discipline.
- Demystify the notion of theory by discussing it in concrete and unequivocal ways.
- Provide students with an understanding of the interplay among theory, communication, and application.
- Introduce students to the research process and the role of theory within this process.
- Assist students in becoming more systematic and thoughtful critical thinkers.

The sixth edition of this book maintains its original focus of introducing communication theory to students in an accessible, appealing, and consistent way. We believe that students understand material best when it is explained in a clear, direct way through a number of realistic and applicable examples. Our hope is that students will take away a basic knowledge of, and appreciation for, communication theory from reading our text.

The theories in communication studies have roots in both communication and in other fields of study. This interdisciplinary orientation is reflected in the selection of the various theories presented in the text. We not only include the unique contributions of communication theorists, but also theories with origins in other fields of study, including psychology, sociology, biology, education, business, and philosophy. Communication theorists have embraced the integration of ideas and principles forged by their colleagues across many disciplines. Yet, the application, influence, and inherent value of communication are all sustained by the theorists in this text. In other words, although theories cut across various academic disciplines, their relevance to communication remains paramount and we articulate this relevancy in each theory chapter. We do not presume to speak for the theorists; we have distilled their scholarship in a way that we hope represents and honors their hard work. Our overall goal is to frame their words and illustrate their theories with practical examples and instances so that their explication of communication behaviors becomes accessible for students.

Together, we have over 60 years of experience in teaching communication theory. During this time, we have learned a great deal. *Introducing Communication Theory: Analysis and Application* utilizes and applies all that we as teachers have learned from our students. We continue to be indebted to both students and colleagues whose suggestions and comments have greatly influenced this newest edition.

The Challenges of Teaching and Learning Communication Theory

The instructor in a communication theory course may face several challenges that are not shared by other courses. First, because many students think of theory as distant, abstract, and obscure, teachers must overcome these potentially negative connotations. Negative feelings toward the subject can be magnified in classrooms where students represent a variety of ages and socioeconomic, cultural, and linguistic backgrounds. *Introducing Communication Theory* addresses this challenge by offering a readable and pragmatic guide that integrates content with examples, capturing the essence and elegance of theory in a straightforward manner. In addition, the book takes an incremental approach to learning about theory, resulting in a thoughtful and appropriate learning pace.

A second challenge associated with teaching and learning communication theory relates to preconceived notions of research: Students may view scholarship as difficult or remote. This book demonstrates to students that they already possess many of the characteristics of researchers, such as curiosity and ambition. Students will be pleasantly surprised to know that they operate according to many personal theories every day. Once students begin to revise their misconceptions about research and theory, they are in a position to understand the principles, concepts, and theories contained in this book.

A third challenge of teaching and learning communication theory is capturing the complexity of a theory in an approachable way without oversimplifying the theoretical process. To address this problem, instructors often present a skeletal version of a theory and then fill in the missing pieces with personal materials. By providing a variety of engaging examples and applications reflecting a wide range of classroom demographics, *Introducing Communication Theory* facilitates such an approach.

A final challenge relates to a theory's genesis and today's students. Clearly, in this technological age, students look for and usually crave a desire to find a "tech angle" to communication theory. Although many theories were conceptualized decades ago, in each chapter, we have provided the most recent research that represents a theory–technology framework. Further we have added questions in each chapter that are technological in nature, facilitating further student interest in the material.

Major Changes in Content in the New Edition

The sixth edition has undergone significant modification, namely in the content of the theory chapters and in the various learning aids available. EACH chapter has been updated to reflect the most current thinking. In particular, the following chapters have undergone major changes:

Chapter 2 (Thinking About the Field: Traditions and Contexts) includes the most current scholarship in each of the seven contexts of communication.

Chapter 3 (Thinking About Theory and Research) is completely reorganized to reflect both the quantitative and qualitative thinking influencing theoretical development.

Chapter 4 (Symbolic Interaction Theory) has been completely reorganized so that it disentangles the assumptions and themes of SI.

Chapter 8 (Uncertainty Reduction Theory) has been overhauled and provides a more thoughtful presentation of the various axioms and theorems related to the theory.

Chapter 12 (Communication Privacy Management Theory) has been substantively reorganized. In addition, new information on the criteria used to for developing privacy rules is discussed in detail.

Chapter 14 (Groupthink) includes new information on NASA and the Military Whistleblower Protection Act and their relationship to groupthink.

Chapter 15 (Structuration Theory) provides the newest thinking on various cautionary tales related to social integration.

Chapter 20 (The Narrative Paradigm) delineates new research and practices related to storytelling.

Chapter 21 (Agenda Setting Theory) presents a reorganization and reconceptualization of the three levels of agenda setting.

Chapter 22 (Spiral of Silence Theory) employs the legalization of marijuana as an overarching template while discussing the influence and pervasiveness of public opinion.

Chapter 24 (Cultivation Theory) includes extensive additions throughout on how technology and "mass-mediated storytelling" influence individuals.

Chapter 25 (Cultural Studies) uses both the Flint, Michigan water crisis and marriage equality to demonstrate several of the issues and themes related to the theory.

Chapter 29 (Muted Group Theory) includes a brief history of sexual harassment as computer jargon's male-centeredness to exemplify several concepts associated with MGT.

Features of the Book

To accomplish our goals and address the challenges of teaching communication theory, we have incorporated a structure that includes number of special features and learning aids into the sixth edition:

- *Part One, Foundations.* The first three chapters of the book continue to provide students a solid foundation for studying the theories that follow. This

"The first three chapters of the book continue to provide students a solid foundation for studying the theories that follow. This groundwork is essential in order to understand how theorists conceptualize and test their theories."

"Every theory chapter is self-contained and includes a consistent format that begins with a vignette, followed by an introduction, a summary of theoretical assumptions, a description of core concepts, and a critique (using the criteria established in Part One). This consistency provides continuity for students, ensures a balanced presentation of the theories, and helps ease the retrieval of information for future learning experiences."

groundwork is essential in order to understand how theorists conceptualize and test their theories. Chapters 1 and 2 define communication and provide a framework for examining the theories. We present several traditions and contexts in which theory is customarily categorized and considered. Chapter 3 provides an overview of the intersection of theory and research. This discussion is essential in a theory course and also serves as a springboard for students as they enroll in other courses. In addition, we present students with a template of various evaluative components that we apply in each of the subsequent theory chapters.

- *Part Two, Theories and Theoretical Thinking.* Updated coverage of **all** theories. Separate chapters on each of the theories provide accessible, thorough coverage for students and offer flexibility to instructors. Because of the feedback we received from the previous edition, we retained the original theories from the fifth edition This updating results in a more thoughtful, current, and applicable presentation of each theory. As noted earlier, in many cases, we have provided the most recent information of the influences of culture and/or technology upon a particular theory, resulting in some very compelling discussions and examples.

- *Section openers.* The theory chapters in Part Two are organized into six sections. We have written section openers to introduce these groups of chapters. The overviews provide students with an explanation for our choices, placing the theories in context and allowing students to have a foundation in order to see the connections between and among theories.

- *Chapter-opening vignettes.* Each chapter begins with an extended vignette, which is then integrated throughout the chapter, providing examples to illustrate the theoretical concepts and claims. We have been pleased that instructors and students point to these vignettes as important applications of sometimes complex material. These stories/case studies help students understand how communication theory plays out in the everyday lives of ordinary people. These opening stories help drive home the important points of the theory. In addition, the real-life tone of each vignette entices students to understand the practicality of a particular theory.

- A *structured approach to each theory.* Every theory chapter is self-contained and includes a consistent format that begins with a story, followed by an introduction, a summary of theoretical assumptions, a description of core concepts, and a critique (using the criteria established in Part One). This consistency provides continuity for students, ensures a balanced presentation of the theories, and helps ease the retrieval of information for future learning experiences. Instructors and students have found this template to be quite valuable since it eliminates the stream-of-consciousness frequently found in other published resources.

- *Student Voices boxes.* These boxes, featured in every chapter, present both new and returning student comments on a particular concept or theoretical issue. The comments, extracted from journals in classes we have taught, illustrate the practicality of the topic under discussion and also show how theoretical issues relate to students' lives. In a sense, this feature illustrates how practical theories are and how much their tenets apply to our everyday lived experiences.

- *Theory in Popular Press.* Students will be introduced to further applications of the various theories and theoretical concepts by examining popular press stories. Stories and articles exemplifying various parts of a theory are provided from a number of different outlets, including *Forbes, USA Today,* the (U.K.) *Guardian,* the *Chicago Tribune,* the *New York Times,* among many others.

- *Visual template for theory evaluation.* At the conclusion of each theory chapter, a criteria for theory evaluation (presented in Chapter 3) is employed. In addition, the theory's context, scholarly tradition (based on Robert Craig's typology), and approach to knowing are articulated.

- *Theory at a Glance boxes.* In order for students to have an immediate and concise understanding of a particular theory, we incorporate this feature at the beginning of each theory chapter. Students will have these brief explanations and short summaries before reading the chapter, thereby allowing them to have a general sense of what they are about to encounter.

- *Afterword: ConnectingQuests.* This final section of the book provides students with an integration of the various theories in order to see the interrelationships between theories. We believe that theories cut across multiple contexts. To this end, students are asked questions that address the intersection of theories. For instance, to understand "decision making" from two theoretical threads, students are asked to compare the concept and its usage in both Groupthink and Structuration Theory. These questions form a foundation for future conversations about communication theory.

- *Tables, figures, and cartoons.* To increase conceptual organization and enhance the visual presentation of content, we have provided several tables and figures throughout the text. Further, we have provided cartoons to provide another engaging reading option. Many chapters have visual aids for students to consider, helping them to understand the material. These visuals provide a clearer sense of the conceptual organization of the theories, and they support those students who best retain information visually.

- *Running glossary.* Throughout each chapter, a running glossary provides students immediate access to unfamiliar terms and their meanings.

- *End-of-book glossary.* Students have expressed interest in having a compiled list of definitions at the end of the text. This glossary provides easily accessed definitions of all the key terms contained in the book.

In addition to the aforementioned features, several new additions exist in the new edition of *Introducing Communication Theory*:

- **NEW** Quantitative and Qualitative Research. In Chapter 3, we have reorganized the information to make it more understandable for students. We first discuss quantitative research methods and then qualitative research methods. We also added an evaluative statement at the conclusion of each theory chapter which notes whether the theory has primarily been investigated using a framework that is qualitative, quantitative, or both.

- **NEW** Theory-Into-Practice (TIP). We include this feature to provide further application of the information contained in the chapter. We identify a conclusion or two from the theory and then provide a real-world application of the particular claim. This feature sustains our commitment to enhancing the pragmatic value of a theory.

- **NEW** Socially Significant Themes and Noteworthy Celebrities. In an effort to provide students with examples that are compelling and memorable, we make a concerted effort to illustrate points with timely topics and recognizable newsmakers. Themes such as marriage equality, social media, medical marijuana, whistle-blowing, internships, civility, among many others are woven throughout the book. Important global issues, including Black Lives Matter, climate change, the world refugee crisis, among others are woven throughout the text. Cultural figures such as Dr. Oz, Samantha Bee, Maya Angelou, Jimmy Fallon, Dr. Phil, Martha Stewart, and others are also identified at appropriate points along the way. Although we never "dumb down" the theoretical material, we feel it's important for students to read examples that are somewhat contemporary and not dated.

- **NEW** *Tech Quest*. Each chapter concludes with several Discussion Starters and a new question that probes how the theory relates to technology. Students will be asked to discuss the interface between a theory and several social media, for instance, including Twitter, Instagram, Facebook, LinkedIn, among others.

- **NEW** Cartoons. Eight new cartoons have been added to the text, providing a humorous break from the theoretical content.

- **NEW** *Incorporation of over 200 new references*. The explosion in communication research, in particular, is reflected in the incorporation of dozens of new studies, essays, and books that help students understand the theory or theoretical issue. We also provide students with easy access to a citation by integrating an APA format (the acceptable writing style of the communication field) so that they can see the relevancy and currency of a theory. When appropriate, we also have provided URLs for websites that have information which can be readily available.

- **NEW** Theoretical Thought. Each theory chapter begins with a statement made by a theorist or theorists that highlights the essence of the chapter's content. These quotations reflect further effort to honor the words of the theorist(s).

The 6th edition of *Introducing Communications Theory: Analysis and Application* is now available online with Connect, McGraw-Hill Education's integrated assignment and assessment platform. Connect also offers SmartBook for the new edition, which is the first adaptive reading experience proven to improve grades and help students study more effectively. All of the title's website and ancillary content is also available through Connect, including:

- An Instructor's Manual for each chapter with general guidelines for teaching the basic theory course, sample syllabi for quarter and semester courses, chapter outlines, and classroom activities.
- A full Test Bank of multiple choice questions that test students on central concepts and ideas in each chapter.
- Lecture Slides for instructor use in class.

Organization

Part One, Foundations, provides a conceptual base for the discrete theory chapters in Part Two. Chapter 1 begins by introducing the discipline and describing the process of communication. Chapter 2 provides the prevailing traditions and contexts that frame the communication field. In this chapter, we focus on Robert Craig's guide to the ways in which communication theory can be considered. The chapter then turns to primary contexts of communication, which frame the study of communication in most academic settings across the country. Chapter 3 explores the intersection of theory and research. In this chapter, we provide students an understanding of the nature of theory and the characteristics of theory. The research process is also discussed, as are perspectives that guide communication research. Our goal in this chapter is to show that research and theory are interrelated and that the two should be considered in tandem as students read the individual chapters. Chapter 3 also provides a list of evaluative criteria for judging theories as well as for guiding students toward assessment of each subsequent theory chapter.

With Part One establishing a foundation, Part Two, Theories and Theoretical Thinking, introduces students to 27 different theories, each in a discrete, concise chapter. Many of these theories cut across communication contexts. For example, Relational Dialectics Theory can be understood and applied in an organizational context as well as in an interpersonal context. However, to facilitate understanding, we have grouped theories into six sections according to primary focus: The Self and Messages, Relationship Development, Groups, Teams, and Organizations, The Public, The Media, and Culture and Diversity. We undertake this approach to align it with the contexts identified in Chapter 1.

It was challenging for us to decide which theories to include because there are so many from which to choose. In making our selections, we were guided by four broad criteria: (1) whether the theory is significant in the field, (2) whether it reflects the interdisciplinary nature of the field, (3) whether it is important in the context of current thinking in the field, and (4) whether it contributes to a balance of pioneering and contemporary theories in the book. In addition, we were sensitive to the need to include theories developed by a diverse group of scholars. We know that there are many theories that we were unable to include. Yet, our book provides an expansive and respectful array of theories that in the end, we believe provides an important introduction to this challenging and worthwhile area known as communication theory.

McGraw-Hill Connect®
Learn Without Limits

Connect is a teaching and learning platform that is proven to deliver better results for students and instructors.

Connect empowers students by continually adapting to deliver precisely what they need, when they need it, and how they need it, so your class time is more engaging and effective.

Connect's Impact on Retention Rates, Pass Rates, and Average Exam Scores

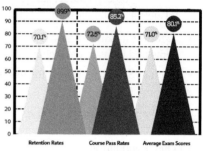

73% of instructors who use **Connect** require it; instructor satisfaction **increases** by 28% when **Connect** is required.

Using **Connect** improves retention rates by **19.8%**, passing rates by **12.7%**, and exam scores by **9.1%**.

Analytics ——————

Connect Insight®

Connect Insight is Connect's new one-of-a-kind visual analytics dashboard—now available for both instructors and students—that provides at-a-glance information regarding student performance, which is immediately actionable. By presenting assignment, assessment, and topical performance results together with a time metric that is easily visible for aggregate or individual results, Connect Insight gives the user the ability to take a just-in-time approach to teaching and learning, which was never before available. Connect Insight presents data that empowers students and helps instructors improve class performance in a way that is efficient and effective.

Impact on Final Course Grade Distribution

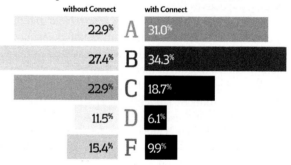

Students can view their results for any **Connect** course.

Mobile ——————

Connect's new, intuitive mobile interface gives students and instructors flexible and convenient, anytime–anywhere access to all components of the Connect platform.

Adaptive

THE **ADAPTIVE** **READING EXPERIENCE**
DESIGNED TO TRANSFORM THE WAY STUDENTS READ

More students earn **A's** and **B's** when they use McGraw-Hill Education **Adaptive** products.

SmartBook®

Proven to help students improve grades and study more efficiently, SmartBook contains the same content within the print book, but actively tailors that content to the needs of the individual. SmartBook's adaptive technology provides precise, personalized instruction on what the student should do next, guiding the student to master and remember key concepts, targeting gaps in knowledge and offering customized feedback, and driving the student toward comprehension and retention of the subject matter. Available on tablets, SmartBook puts learning at the student's fingertips—anywhere, anytime.

Over **8 billion questions** have been answered, making McGraw-Hill Education products more intelligent, reliable, and precise.

www.mheducation.com

STUDENTS WANT

SMARTBOOK®

95% of students reported **SmartBook** to be a more effective way of reading material.

100% of students want to use the Practice Quiz feature available within **SmartBook** to help them study.

100% of students reported having reliable access to off-campus wifi.

90% of students say they would purchase **SmartBook** over print alone.

95% of students reported that **SmartBook** would impact their study skills in a positive way.

Mc Graw Hill Education

*Findings based on 2015 focus group results administered by McGraw-Hill Education

Acknowledgments

Our book owes its existence to efforts made by others in addition to the listed authors, and some people who have helped with this book may not even realize the debt we acknowledge here. We would like to thank all those who have helped us as we worked our way through this large project. First, many professors and students have written to us, providing important clarification and examples.

In addition, our work rests on the shoulders of the theorists whose creations we profile in this book. We are grateful for their creative thinking, which allows us to understand and begin to predict the complexities of the communication process. We worked hard to try to capture their insights and conclusions and convert these thoughts for introductory students in theory.

Further, our insights represent the discussions that we have had with our communication theory students and colleagues over the years. Several parts of this book are based on student input at both of our institutions. Students have contributed to this book in both direct and indirect ways.

Textbook writers understand that no book is possible without the talents and commitment of both an editorial and production team. We extend our deep appreciation and admiration to those who have made our words come to life in various ways:

Jamie Laferrera, Brand Manager
Jasmine Staton, Editorial Coordinator
Lisa Bruflodt, Content Project Manager
DeAnna Dausner, Content Licensing Specialist

Finally, the development editing was handled by Erin Guendelsberger and Sowmya B. We thank both of them and the entire **ansr**source development team.

As is customary in each book he writes, Rich would like to acknowledge his mother for her continual focus on what matters in life: family, fun, and spirituality. He remains grateful for her continued positive influence. Rich would also like to thank his partner, Chris, who knows precisely when to make things less intense and more relaxing.

Lynn would like to thank her family: her husband, Ted; her daughter's family, the Spitznagles—Sabrina, Billy, Sophie, and Will; her stepdaughter's family, the Kissels—Leila, Russ, Zoe, Dylan; and her stepson's family, the Feldshers—Ted, Sally, Ely, and Lucas, for invaluable lessons in communication theory and practice. Further, she is indebted to her brother and his family, as well as all of her extended family members who helped in ways great and small as this project continued over time. And always, Lynn is grateful for the memory of her loving parents whose steadfast support and encouragement of her scholarship, and all of her interests, sustain her in every project she undertakes. Friends and colleagues provided great support and have taught her many valuable lessons about scholarship and communication theory. She also wishes to thank Marquette University; the school offered a supportive climate, research assistance, and a general tenor of encouragement.

Finally, both Rich and Lynn give a special shout out to Holly Allen. Holly, a senior editor at Wiley, was the first to believe in us in 1994. She persuaded us to think about writing a textbook, the first of which was *Perspectives on Family Communication* (now in its sixth edition/McGraw-Hill). We began this writing enterprise because of Holly and, to this day, she remains an inspiration as we celebrate the various successes we've had in textbook writing. Thanks Holly! Always.

Finally, we thank the manuscript reviewers who gave their time and expertise to keep us on track in our interpretation of the ideas of others. We are grateful for their careful reading and insightful suggestions, which expanded and clarified our thinking in many ways. Our text is a much more useful product because of the comments and suggestions of the following reviewers who have shaped this book over the past few editions:

Sixth Edition

Greg G. Armfield,
New Mexico State University

Christine Armstrong,
Northampton Community College

Shaun Cashman,
Pfeiffer University

J. Dean Farmer,
Campbell University

Javette Grace Hayes,
California State University, Fullerton

Lisa Hebert,
Louisiana State University

Juan Liu,
Wayne State University

Jimmie Manning,
Northern Illinois University

Libby McGlone,
Columbus State Community College

Robert William Wawee,
University of Houston Downtown

Fifth Edition

Michael Barberich,
University at Albany, SUNY

Martha J. Haun,
University of Houston

Bryan Horikami,
Salisbury University

Anna Laura Jansma,
University of California, Santa Barbara

Susan Jarboe,
San Diego State University

Kelly Jones,
Pitt Community College

Fourth Edition

Rebecca Dumlao,
East Carolina University

Edward T. Funkhouser,
North Carolina State University

Scott Guest,
Bowling Green State University

Anna Laura Jansma,
University of California, Santa Barbara

Anne M. Nicotera,
University of Maryland

Mark Zeigler,
Florida State University

Third Edition

Randall S. Chase,
Salt Lake Community College

Chrys Egan,
Salisbury University

Kathleen Galvin,
Northwestern University

Reed Markham,
Salt Lake Community College

Rita L. Rahoi-Gilchrest,
Winona State University

Second Edition

Sue Barnes,
Fordham University

Jack Baseheart,
University of Kentucky

Jamie Byrne,
Millersville University

Thomas Feeley,
State University of New York, Geneseo

Amy Hubbard,
University of Hawaii at Manoa

Matthew McAllister,
Virginia Tech

Janet Skupien,
University of Pittsburgh

Jon Smith,
Southern Utah University

Katy Wiss,
Western Connecticut State University

Kevin Wright,
University of Memphis

First Edition

John R. Baldwin,
Illinois State University

Holly H. Bognar,
Cleveland State University

Sheryl Bowen,
Villanova University

Cam Brammer,
Marshall University

Jeffrey D. Brand,
North Dakota State University

Randy K. Dillon,
Southwest Missouri State University

Kent Drummond,
University of Wyoming

James Gilchrist,
Western Michigan University

Laura Jansma,
University of California–Santa Barbara

Madeline M. Keaveney,
California State University–Chico

Joann Keyton,
University of Kansas

Debra Mazloff,
University of St. Thomas

Elizabeth M. Perse,
University of Delaware

Linda M. Pledger,
University of Arkansas

Mary Ann Renz,
Central Michigan University

Patricia Rockwell,
University of Southwestern Louisiana

Deborah Smith-Howell,
University of Nebraska

Denise Solomon,
University of Wisconsin

Tami Spry,
St. Cloud State University

Rebecca W. Tardy,
University of Louisville

Ralph Thompson,
Cornell University

About the Authors

Richard West is a Professor in the Department of Communication Studies at Emerson College in Boston. Rich received his BA and MA from Illinois State University and his PhD from Ohio University. Rich has been teaching since 1984, and his teaching and research interests range from family diversity to teacher–student communication. He began teaching communication theory as a graduate student and has taught the class in lecture format to more than 200 students. Rich is a past recipient of the Outstanding Alumni Award in Communication at Illinois State University and Ohio University. He is a member of several editorial boards in communication journals. Rich is also the recipient of the Eastern Communication Association's (ECA) Distinguished Service Award where he also serves as a Research Fellow. He also served as ECA's President in 2008.

Lynn H. Turner is a Professor in Communication Studies at Marquette University in Milwaukee, Wisconsin. Lynn received her BA from the University of Illinois and her MA from the University of Iowa, and she received her PhD from Northwestern University. She has taught communication theory and research methods to undergraduates and graduates in the Diederich College of Communication at Marquette since 1985. Prior to coming to Marquette, Lynn taught at Iowa State University and in two high schools in Iowa. Her research interests include interpersonal communication, family communication, and gendered communication. She is the recipient of several awards, including Marquette's College of Communication Research Excellence Award, and the Book of the Year award from the Organization for the Study of Communication, Language, and Gender for her book with Patricia Sullivan, *From the Margins to the Center: Contemporary Women and Political Communication*. Lynn is a past president of the Central States Communication Association.

Rich and Lynn, together, are coauthors of dozens of essays and articles in the communication field. In addition, the two have served as guest coeditors of the *Journal of Family Communication* a few times, focusing on diversity and the family. In addition, they have coauthored several books, including *Gender and Communication, Perspectives on Family Communication, IPC,* and *Understanding Interpersonal Communication: Making Choices in Changing Times.* The two have coedited the *Family Communication Sourcebook* (Sage, 2006; Winner of the Outstanding Book Award by the

National Communication Association), and The Handbook of Family Communication. Further, both are the recipients of the Bernard J. Brommel Award for Outstanding Scholarship and Service in Family Communication. Finally, both recognize the uniqueness and the honor to have served as president of the National Communication Association (Lynn in 2011; Rich in 2012), "the oldest and largest organization in the world promoting communication scholarship and education" (www.natcom.org).

Foundations
Communication, Theory, and Research

YOU MIGHT NOT HAVE THOUGHT ABOUT THIS, BUT each day the decisions we make, the (social) media we consume, and the relationships we experience can be enriched and explained by communication theory. Communication theory helps us to understand other people and their communities, the media, and our associations with families, friends, roommates, coworkers, and companions. Perhaps most important, communication theory makes it easier to understand ourselves.

We begin our discussion of communication theory by asking you to consider the experiences of Morgan and Alex. After randomly being assigned as roommates, the two met on "move-in day" at Scott Hall. They were both pretty nervous. They had checked out each other on Facebook, emailed each other, and talked on the phone a few times, so they knew quite a bit about each other. Once they met, they started talking. They went out for coffee the first few weeks of school, getting to know each other better. They spent a lot of time telling stories about their families and friends, and talking about what they look for in a partner. They both loved television, especially the reality shows, because they loved to see how other people dealt with their lives in times of stress. After several weeks, Morgan and Alex became closer. They were going to have to balance their desire to hang out with each other with their need to be alone. And it was going to be give-and-take because their schedules were completely opposite. Eventually, the two became great friends.

To illustrate the various ways in which communication theory functions in the lives of Morgan and Alex, let's identify important aspects of their story and see how theory provides some understanding of Morgan's and Alex's behaviors.

First, these roommates supported the research of Uncertainty Reduction Theory (Chapter 8) through their need to reduce their uncertainty about each other. They also probably self-disclosed some personal information to each other, underscoring a central feature of Social Penetration Theory (Chapter 10). Next, they discovered that they both watch television and use it to see how others live their lives, highlighting the essence of Uses and Gratifications Theory (Chapter 23). Balancing their need to be together with the need to remain private encompasses Relational Dialectics Theory (Chapter 11). Morgan and Alex also told personal stories to each other; storytelling is at the heart of the Narrative Paradigm (Chapter 20). In sum, at least five communication theories could help explain the experiences of the two roommates.

The first three chapters provide an important foundation for discussing each communication theory that follows. These chapters give you a general introduction to communication and to theory. First, to provide you some insights into the communication field, in Chapter 1 we present our definition of communication, the prevailing models of communication, and other important issues including ethics and communication. Chapter 2 is dedicated to a discussion of the various traditions and contexts of communication, two important frameworks to consider as you read the remainder of the book. We prepare you directly for understanding the intersection of theory and research in Chapter 3. In this chapter, we also present you the necessary templates to evaluate and understand each theory. The chapter provides important criteria for evaluating a theory and also includes a model for you to examine. We revisit these templates at the conclusion of each theory chapter so that you have a consistent approach from which to interpret the various theories.

CHAPTER 1

Thinking About Communication: Definitions, Models, and Ethics

I suppose all of us get accustomed to look at what we are doing in a certain way and after a while have a kind of "trained incapacity" for looking at things in any other way.

—Marie Hochmuth Nichols

The Bollens

Jimmy and Angie Bollen have been married for almost 30 years, and they are the parents of three children who have been out of the house for years. But, a recent layoff at the company where their son Eddy worked has forced the 24-year-old to return home until he can get another job.

At first, Eddy's parents were glad that he was home. His father was proud of the fact that his son wasn't embarrassed about returning home, and his mom was happy to have him help her with some of the mundane chores at home. In fact, Eddy showed both Jimmy and Angie how to instant message their friends and also put together a family website. His parents were especially happy about having a family member who was "tech-savvy" hanging around the house.

But the good times surrounding Eddy's return soon ended. Eddy brought his laptop to the table each morning, marring the Bollen's once-serene breakfasts. Jimmy and Angie's walks at night were complicated because their son often wanted to join them. At night, when they went to bed, the parents could hear Eddy talking on his cell phone, sometimes until 1:00 A.M. When Eddy's parents thought about communicating their frustration and disappointment, they quickly recalled the difficulty of their son's situation. They didn't want to upset him any further. The Bollens tried to figure out a way to communicate to their son that although they love him, they wished that he would get a job and leave the house. They simply wanted some peace, privacy, and freedom, and their son was getting in the way. It wasn't a feeling either one of them liked, but it was their reality.

They considered a number of different approaches. In order to get the conversation going, they even thought about giving Eddy a few website links related to local apartment rentals. Recently, the couple's frustration with the situation took a turn for the worse. Returning from one of their long walks, they discovered Eddy on the couch, hung over from a party held earlier at his friend's house. When Jimmy and Angie confronted him about his demeanor, Eddy shouted, "Don't start lecturing me now. Is it any wonder that none of your other kids call you? It's because you don't know when to stop! Look, I got a headache and I don't want to hear it from you guys!" Jimmy snapped, "Get out of my house. Now!" Eddy left the home, slamming the front door behind him. Angie stared out of the window, wondering whether they would ever hear from their son again.

The value of communication has been lauded by philosophers ("Be silent or say something better than silence"—Pythagoras), writers ("The difference between the right word and the almost right word is the difference between lightning and a lightning bug"—Mark Twain), performing artists ("Any problem, big or small, in a family usually starts with bad communication"—Emma Thompson), business leaders ("Writing is great for keeping records and putting down details, but talk generates ideas"—T. Boone Pickens), motivational speakers ("The quality of your communication is the quality of your life"—Tony Robbins), and even talk show hosts ("Great communication begins with connection"—Oprah). Perhaps one of the most lasting of all words came from a 1967 film (*Cool Hand Luke*): "What we have here is a failure to communicate"—a quotation that has subsequently been stated in such diverse settings as in the movie Madagascar, the song "Civil War" by Guns N' Roses, and television shows NCIS and Frasier. It's clear that nearly all cross sections of a Western society view communication as instrumental in human relationships.

In the most fundamental way, communication depends on our ability to understand one another. Although our communication can be ambiguous ("I never thought I'd get this gift from you"), one primary and essential goal in communicating is understanding. Our daily activities are wrapped in conversations with others. Yet, as we see with the Bollen family, even those in close relationships can have difficulty expressing their thoughts.

Being able to communicate effectively is highly valued in the United States. Corporations have recognized the importance of communication. In 2016, the National Safety Management Society (nsms.us/?s=communication&submit=Search) reports that industrial safety is contingent on the ability of employees and management to communicate clearly and to avoid jargon when possible. Indeed, the entire Safety Professions http://www.com.edu/gcsi/ "First and foremost, risk managers must be good communicators." Health care, too, is focusing more on the value of communication. Interestingly, as early as the late 1960s, doctor–patient communication has been a topic of concern in research (Korsch, Gozzi, & Francis, 1968). More recent literature shows that doctor–patient communication is essential for the recovery of patients (Singh, 2016). Finally, in the classroom, researchers (e.g., Bolkon & Goodboy, 2011; Titsworth, Mazer, Goodboy, Bolkan, & Myers, 2015) have concluded that affirming feedback/student confirmation positively affects student learning. And, with respect to social networking sites such as Facebook, individuals in romantic relationships report using communication (technology) as a way to check up on "status updates" on an individual's wall—from commitment to fidelity (usatodayeducate.com/staging/index.php/campuslife/the-bytes-and-the-bees-love-can-transcend-anything-even-facebook). Make no mistake about it: Abundant evidence underscores the fact that communication is an essential, pervasive, and consequential behavior in our society.

As a student of communication, you are uniquely positioned to determine your potential for effective communication. To do so, however, you must have a basic understanding of the communication process and of how communication theory, in particular, functions in your life. We need to be able to talk effectively, for instance, to a number of very different types of people during an average day: teachers, ministers, salespeople, family members, friends, automobile mechanics, and health care providers.

Communication opportunities fill our lives each day. However, we need to understand the whys and hows of our conversations with others. For instance, why do two people in a relationship feel a simultaneous need for togetherness and independence?

Why do some women feel ignored or devalued in conversations with men? Why does language often influence the thoughts of others? How do media influence people's behavior? To what extent can social media affect the communication among people? These and many other questions are at the root of why communication theory is so important in our society and so critical to understand.

Defining Communication

Our first task is to create a common understanding for the term *communication*. Defining communication can be challenging. Katherine Miller (2005) underscores this dilemma, stating that "conceptualizations of communication have been abundant and have changed substantially over the years" (p. 3). Sarah Trenholm (1991) notes that although the study of communication has been around for centuries, it does not mean communication is well understood. In fact, Trenholm interestingly illustrates the dilemma when defining the term. She states, "Communication has become a sort of 'portmanteau' term. Like a piece of luggage, it is overstuffed with all manner of odd ideas and meanings. The fact that some of these do fit, resulting in a conceptual suitcase much too heavy for anyone to carry, is often overlooked" (p. 4).

We should note that there are many ways to interpret and define communication—a result of the complexity and richness of the communication discipline. Imagine, for instance, taking this course from two different professors. Each would have his or her way of presenting the material, and each classroom of students would likely approach communication theory in a unique manner. The result would be two exciting and distinctive approaches to studying the same topic.

This uniqueness holds true with defining communication. Scholars tend to see human phenomena from their own perspectives, something we delve into further in the next chapter. In some ways, researchers establish boundaries when they try to explain phenomena to others. Communication scholars may approach the interpretation of communication differently because of differences in scholarly values. With these caveats in mind, we offer the following definition of *communication* to get us pointed in the same direction. **Communication** is a social process in which individuals employ symbols to establish and interpret meaning in their environment. We necessarily draw in elements of mediated communication as well in our discussion, given the importance that communication technology plays in contemporary society. With that in mind, let's define five key terms in our perspective: *social, process, symbols, meaning,* and *environment* (Figure 1.1).

First, we believe that communication is a social process. When interpreting communication as **social,** we mean to suggest that it involves people and interactions, whether face-to-face or online. This necessarily includes two people, who act as senders and receivers. Both play an integral role in the communication process. When communication is social, it involves people who come to an interaction with various intentions, motivations, and abilities. To suggest that communication is a **process** means that it is ongoing and unending. Communication is also dynamic, complex, and continually changing. With this view of communication, we emphasize the dynamics of making meaning. Therefore, communication has no definable beginning and ending. For example, although Jimmy and Angie Bollen may tell their son that he must

communication
a social process in which individuals employ symbols to establish and interpret meaning in their environment

social
the notion that people and interactions are part of the communication process

process
ongoing, dynamic, and unending occurrence

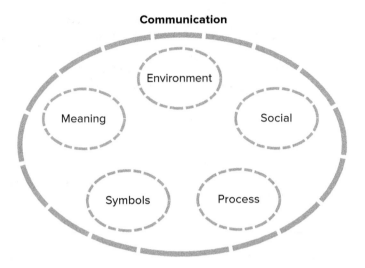

Communication

Environment

Meaning

Social

Symbols

Process

**Figure 1.1
Key Terms in
Defining
Communication**

leave the house, their discussions with him and about him will continue well after he leaves. In fact, the conversation they have with Eddy today will most likely affect their communication with him tomorrow. Similarly, our past communications with people have been stored in their minds and have affected their conversations with us.

The process nature of communication also means that much can happen from the beginning of a conversation to the end. People may end up at a very different place once a discussion begins. This is exemplified by the frequent conflicts that roommates, spouses, and siblings experience. Although a conversation may begin with absolute and inflexible language, the conflict may be resolved with compromise. All of this can occur in a matter of minutes.

Individual and cultural changes affect communication. Conversations between siblings, for example, have shifted from the 1950s to today. Years ago, siblings rarely discussed the impending death of a parent or the need to take care of an aging parent. Today, it's not uncommon to listen to children talking about nursing home care, home health care, and even funeral arrangements. The 1950s was a time of postwar euphoria; couples were reunited after World War II and the baby boom began. Today, with an ongoing U.S. troop presence around the world, Americans rarely experience the euphoria they once had. The tensions, uncertainties, and loss of life are too compelling for many people. As you can see, perceptions and feelings can change and may remain in flux for quite some time.

Some of you may be thinking that because the communication process is dynamic and unique it is virtually impossible to study. However, C. Arthur VanLear (1996) argues that because the communication process is so dynamic, researchers and theorists can look for patterns over time. He concludes that "if we recognize a pattern across a large number of cases, it permits us to 'generalize' to other unobserved cases" (p. 36). Or, as communication pioneers Paul Watzlawick, Janet Beavin, and Don Jackson (1967) suggest, the interconnectedness of communication events is critical and pervasive. Thus, it is possible to study the dynamic communication process.

To help you visualize this process, imagine a continuum where the points are unrepeatable and irreversible. Frank Dance (1967) depicts the communication process by using a spiral or helix (Figure 1.2). He believes that communication experiences are cumulative

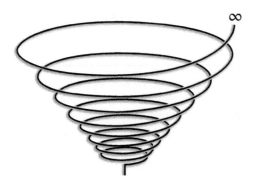

Figure 1.2
Communication
Process as a Helix
Source: Reprinted by permission of Frank E. X. Dance.

and are influenced by the past. He notes that present experiences inevitably influence a person's future, and so he emphasizes a nonlinear view of the process. Communication, therefore, can be considered a process that changes over time and among interactants.

A third term associated with our definition of communication is *symbols*. A **symbol** is an arbitrary label or representation of phenomena. Words are symbols for concepts and things—for example, the word love represents the idea of *love*; the word *chair* represents a thing we sit on. Labels may be ambiguous, may be both verbal and nonverbal, and may occur in face-to-face and mediated communication. Symbols are usually agreed on within a group but may not be understood outside of the group. In this way, their use is often arbitrary. For instance, most college students understand the phrase "preregistration is closed"; those outside of college may not understand its meaning. Further, there are both **concrete symbols** (the symbol represents an object) and **abstract symbols** (the symbol stands for a thought or idea).

Even the innocuous Twitter symbol—the hashtag has resonance in politics. Tamara Small (2011), for example, claims that in-depth political reporting and discussion is fast becoming rare in politics. Rather, the search for a condensed, 140-character tweet has supplanted efforts to investigate and interrogate sometimes called "viral politics" (Penney, 2014). So, the hashtag symbol effectively becomes a representation of a story that used to be several hundred words found in newspapers and magazines.

In addition to process and symbols, meaning is central to our definition of communication. **Meaning** is what people extract from a message. In communication episodes, messages can have more than one meaning and even multiple layers of meaning. Without sharing some meanings, we would all have a difficult time speaking the same language or interpreting the same event. Judith Martin and Tom Nakayama (2013) point out that meaning has cultural consequences:

> [W]hen President George W. Bush was about to go to war in Iraq, he referred to this war as a "crusade." The use of this term evoked strong negative reactions in the Islamic world, due to the history of the Crusades nearly 1,000 years ago . . . . While President Bush may not have knowingly wanted to frame the Iraq invasion as a religious war against Muslims, the history of the Crusades may make others feel that it is. (p. 70)

Clearly, not all meaning is shared, and people do not always know what others mean. In these situations, we must be able to explain, repeat, and clarify. For example,

symbol
arbitrary label given to a phenomenon

concrete symbol
symbol representing an object

abstract symbol
symbol representing an idea or thought

meaning
what people extract from a message

THINKING ABOUT COMMUNICATION: DEFINITIONS, MODELS, AND ETHICS

if the Bollens want to tell Eddy to move out, they will probably need to go beyond telling him that they just need their "space." Eddy may perceive "needing space" as simply staying out of the house two nights a week. Furthermore, his parents will have to figure out what communication "approach" is best. They might believe that being direct may be best to get their son out of the house. Or they might fear that such clear communication is not the most effective strategy to change Eddy's behavior. Regardless of how Jimmy and Angie Bollen communicate their wishes, without sharing the same meaning, the family will have a challenging time getting their messages across to one another.

The final key term in our definition of communication is *environment*. **Environment** is the situation or context in which communication occurs. The environment includes a number of elements, including time, place, historical period, relationship, and a speaker's and listener's cultural backgrounds. You can understand the influence of environments by thinking about your beliefs and values pertaining to socially significant topics such as marriage equality, physician-assisted suicide, and immigration into the United States. If you have had personal experience with any of these topics, it's likely your views are affected by your perceptions.

The environment can also be mediated. By that, we mean that communication takes place with technological assistance. At one point or another, all of us have communicated in a mediated environment, namely through email, chat rooms, or social networking sites. These mediated environments influence the communication between two people in that people in electronic relationships are (usually) not able to observe each other's eye behavior, listen to vocal characteristics, or watch body movement (Skype would be an exception to this, however). Clearly, the mediated environment has received a great deal of attention over the years as communication theory continues to develop.

environment
situation or context in which communication occurs

Student Voices

Janelle

The discussion in class about environment was interesting to me. I can't begin to tell you how many different types of physical environments I'm in every day. I work in a nonprofit, so I'm always in and out of the office. Our office is on the third floor of a five-story building. It's quite small, but we have a lot of fun. Sometimes, though, I have to go to a corporate office where everything is new and looks very expensive. A lot of the workers, though, seem up-tight! Then, I have to visit some people's homes and I can say that there is so much difference in the way people have arranged their home environments. And I haven't even begun to talk about how I use email and the different mediated environments. It's unbelievable!

Models of Understanding: Communication as Action, Interaction, and Transaction

models
simplified representations of the communication process

Communication theorists create **models**, or simplified representations of complex interrelationships among elements in the communication process, which allow us to

www.CartoonStock.com

visually understand a sometimes complex process. Models help us weave together the basic elements of the communication process. Although there are many communication models, we discuss the three most prominent ones here. In discussing these models and their underlying approaches, we wish to demonstrate the manner in which communication has been conceptualized over the years.

Communication as Action: The Linear Model

In 1949, Claude Shannon, a Bell Laboratories scientist and professor at the Massachusetts Institute of Technology, and Warren Weaver, a consultant on projects at the Sloan Foundation, described communication as a linear process. They were concerned with radio and telephone technology and wanted to develop a model that could explain how information passed through various channels. The result was the conceptualization of the **linear model of communication.**

This approach to human communication comprises several key elements, as Figure 1.3 demonstrates. A **source**, or transmitter of a message, sends a **message** to a **receiver**, the recipient of the message. The receiver is the person who makes sense out of the message. All of this communication takes place in a **channel**, which is the pathway to communication. Channels frequently correspond to the visual, tactile, olfactory, and auditory senses. Thus, you use the visual channel when you see your roommate, and you use the tactile channel when you hug your parent.

Communication also involves **noise**, which is anything not intended by the informational source. There are four types of noise. First, **semantic noise** pertains to the slang, jargon, or specialized language used by individuals or groups. For instance,

linear model of communication
one-way view of communication that assumes a message is sent by a source to a receiver through a channel

source
originator of a message

message
words, sounds, actions, or gestures in an interaction

receiver
recipient of a message

channel
pathway to communication

noise
distortion in channel not intended by the source

semantic noise
linguistic influences on reception of message

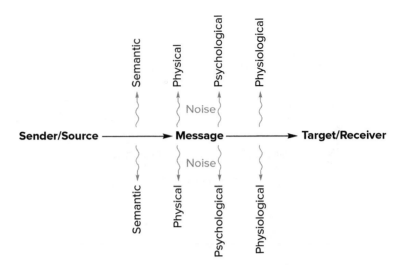

Figure 1.3
Linear Model of Communication

when Jennifer received a medical report from her ophthalmologist, the physician's words included phrases such as "ocular neuritis," "dilated funduscopic examination," and "papillary conjunctival changes." This is an example of semantic noise because outside of the medical community, these words have limited (or no) meaning. **Physical**, or **external**, **noise** exists outside of the receiver. **Psychological noise** refers to a communicator's prejudices, biases, and predispositions toward another or the message. To exemplify these two types, imagine listening to participants at a political rally. You may experience psychological noise listening to the views of a politician whom you do not support, and you may also experience physical noise from the people nearby who may be protesting the politician's presence. Finally, **physiological noise** refers to the biological influences on the communication process. Physiological noise, then, exists if you or a speaker is ill, fatigued, or hungry.

Although this view of the communication process was highly respected many years ago, the approach is very limited for several reasons. First, the model presumes that there is only one message in the communication process. Yet we all can point to a number of circumstances in which we send several messages at once. Second, as we have previously noted, communication does not have a definable beginning and ending. Shannon and Weaver's model presumes this mechanistic orientation. Furthermore, to suggest that communication is simply one person speaking to another oversimplifies the complex communication process. Listeners are not so passive, as we can all confirm when we are in heated arguments with others. Clearly, communication is more than a one-way effort and has no definable middle or end (Anderson & Ross, 2002).

Communication as Interaction: The Interactional Model

The linear model suggests that a person is only a sender or a receiver. That is a narrow view of the participants in the communication process. Wilbur Schramm (1954), therefore, proposed that we also examine the relationship between a sender and a receiver. He conceptualized the **interactional model of communication**, which emphasizes the two-way communication process between communicators (Figure 1.4). In other words, communication goes in two directions: from sender to receiver and

physical (external) noise
bodily influences on reception of message

psychological noise
cognitive influences on reception of message

physiological noise
biological influences on reception of message

interactional model of communication
view of communication as the sharing of meaning with feedback that links source and receiver

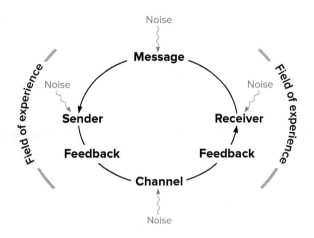

Figure 1.4
Interactional
Model of
Communication

from receiver to sender. This circular process suggests that communication is ongoing. The interactional view illustrates that a person can perform the role of either sender or receiver during an interaction, but not both roles simultaneously.

One element essential to the interactional model of communication is **feedback,** or the response to a message. Feedback may be verbal or nonverbal, intentional or unintentional. Feedback helps communicators to know whether or not their message is being received and the extent to which meaning is achieved. In the interactional model, feedback takes place after a message is received, not during the message itself.

To illustrate the critical nature of feedback and the interactional model of communication, consider our opening example of the Bollen family. When Eddy's parents find him on the couch drunk, they proceed to tell Eddy how they feel about his behavior. Their outcry prompts Eddy to argue with his parents, who in turn, tell him to leave their house immediately. This interactional sequence shows that there is an alternating nature in the communication between Eddy and his parents. They see his behavior and provide their feedback on it, Eddy listens to their message and responds, then his father sends the final message telling his son to leave. We can take this even further by noting the door slam as one additional feedback behavior in the interaction.

A final feature of the interactional model is a person's **field of experience**, or how a person's culture and experiences influence his or her ability to communicate with another. Each person brings a unique field of experience to each communication episode, and these experiences frequently influence the communication between people. For instance, when two people come together and begin dating, the two inevitably bring their fields of experience into the relationship. One person in this couple may have been raised in a large family with several siblings, while the other may be an only child. These experiences (and others) will necessarily influence how the two come together and will most likely affect how they maintain their relationship.

Like the linear view, the interactional model has been criticized. The interactional model suggests that one person acts as sender while the other acts as receiver in a communication encounter. As you have experienced, however, people communicate as both senders and receivers in a single encounter. But the prevailing criticism

feedback
communication given to the source by the receiver to indicate understanding

field of experience
overlap of sender's and receiver's culture, experiences, and heredity in communication

of the interactional model pertains to the issue of feedback. The interactional view assumes two people speaking and listening, but not at the same time. But what occurs when a person sends a nonverbal message during an interaction? Smiling, frowning, or simply moving away from the conversation during an interaction between two people happens all the time. For example, in an interaction between a mother and her daughter, the mother may be reprimanding her child while simultaneously "reading" the child's nonverbal behavior. Is the girl laughing? Is she upset? Is she even listening to her mother? Each of these behaviors will inevitably prompt the mother to modify her message. These criticisms and contradictions inspired development of a third model of communication.

Communication as Transaction: The Transactional Model

transactional model of communication
view of communication as the simultaneous sending and receiving of messages

The **transactional model of communication** (Barnlund, 1970; Frymier, 2005; Wilmot, 1987) underscores the simultaneous sending and receiving of messages in a communication episode, as Figure 1.5 shows. To say that communication is transactional means that the process is cooperative; the sender and the receiver are mutually responsible for the effect and the effectiveness of communication. In the linear model of communication, meaning is sent from one person to another. In the interactional model, meaning is achieved through the feedback of a sender and a receiver. In the transactional model, people build shared meaning. Furthermore, what people say during a transaction is greatly influenced by their past experience. So, for instance, at a college fair, it is likely that a college student will have a great deal to say to a high school senior because of the college student's experiences in class and around campus. A college senior will, no doubt, have a different view of college than, say, a college sophomore, due in large part to his or her past college experiences.

Transactional communication requires us to recognize the influence of one message on another. One message builds on the previous message; therefore, there

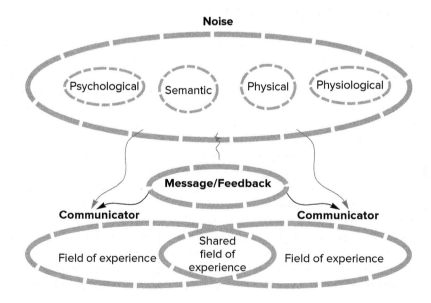

Figure 1.5
Transactional Model of Communication

is an interdependency between and among the components of communication. A change in one causes a change in others. Furthermore, the transactional model presumes that as we simultaneously send and receive messages, we attend to both verbal and nonverbal elements of a message. In a sense, communicators negotiate meaning. For instance, if a friend asks you about your family background, you may use some private language that your friend doesn't understand. Your friend may make a face while you are presenting your message, indicating some sort of confusion with what you've said. As a result, you will most likely back up and define your terms and then continue with the conversation. This example highlights the degree to which two people are actively involved in a communication encounter. The nonverbal communication is just as important as the verbal message in such a transactional process.

Earlier we noted that the field of experience functions in the interactional model. In the transactional model, the fields of experience exist, but overlap occurs. That is, rather than person A and person B having separate fields of experience, eventually the two fields merge (see Figure 1.5). This was an important addition to the understanding of the communication process because it demonstrates an active process of understanding. That is, for communication to take place, individuals must build shared meaning. For instance, in our earlier example of two people with different childhoods, the interactional model suggests that they would come together with an understanding of their backgrounds. The transactional model, however, requires each of them to understand and incorporate the other's field of experience into his or her life. For example, it's not enough for Julianna to know that Paul has a prior prison record; the transactional view holds that she must figure out a way to put his past into perspective. Will it affect their current relationship? How? If not, how will Julianna discuss it with Paul? The transactional model takes the meaning-making process one step further than the interactional model. It assumes reciprocity, or shared meaning.

Communication Models of the Future

As we move further into the 21st century, we have to ask the question: Are these models sufficient as we examine human communication? We already know that communication models are usually incomplete and unsuitable for all purposes (McQuail & Windhal, 2015). The answer is fairly complex. First, the proliferation of new social networking sites (SNS), for example, and their influence upon communication demand that communication models integrate technological discussions. Second, this integration must necessarily be thoughtful, given the plethora of SNS. Traffic to SNS has grown exponentially over the past few years with about 75 percent of online adults using social networking (http://www.pewinternet.org/fact-sheets/social-networking-fact-sheet)—up from 7 percent in 2005. The diversity of these sites—from Facebook to LinkedIn to Instagram—suggests that no simple model will be possible. We address the notion of technology in several chapters in this book and the theorist's perception of how technology affects the communication process.

We can envision a model of communication that incorporates SNS as both the sender and the receiver. We anticipate that scholars will embark upon understanding the transactional nature of such platforms as Snapchat, where a message disappears after 10 seconds.

Clearly, Shannon, Weaver, Schramm, and Barnlund could never have envisioned such technology. We're sure that in the not-so-distant future, we will have an abundance of research on the influences of these technological influences on the communication process.

You now have a basic understanding of how we define communication, and we have outlined the basic elements and a few communication models. Recall this interpretation as you read the book and examine the various theories. It is probable that you will interpret communication differently from one theory to another. Remember that theorists set boundaries in their discussions about human behavior, and, consequently, they often define *communication* according to their own view. One of our goals in this book is to enable you to articulate the role that communication plays in a number of different theories.

Thus far, we have examined the communication process and unpacked the complexity associated with it. We have identified the primary models of communication, trying to demonstrate the evolution and maturation of the communication field. We now explore a component that is a necessary and vital part of every communication episode: ethics.

Ethics and Communication

In the movie *The Insider,* which was based on a true story, the lead character's name is Jeffrey Wigand, a former tobacco scientist who violated a contractual agreement and exposed a cigarette maker's efforts to include addictive ingredients in all cigarettes. The movie shows Wigand as a man of good conscience with the intention of telling the public about the company and its immoral undertakings. Wigand clearly believed that saving lives was the right and only thing to do, and he made his actions fit his beliefs: He acted on his ethics.

ethics
perceived rightness or wrongness of an action or behavior

In this section, we examine **ethics,** or the perceived rightness or wrongness of action or behavior. Ethics is a type of moral decision making (May, 2013), and determining what is right or wrong is influenced by society's rules and laws. For example, although some may believe Wigand's efforts were laudable, others may note that Wigand apparently knew what was going on when he signed a contract prohibiting him from disclosing company secrets. Furthermore, the murkiness of ethics is evidenced when one considers that Wigand made a lot of money before disclosing what was occurring.

The United States is built on standards of moral conduct, and these standards are central to a number of institutions and relationships. Because ethical standards tend to shift according to historical period, the environment, the conversation, and the people involved, ethics can be difficult to understand. Let's briefly discuss ethical issues as they pertain to cultural institutions; a more comprehensive explanation of ethics can be found elsewhere (see MacKinnon, 2012).

To begin, George Cheney, Debashish Munshi, Steve May, and Erin Ortiz (2010) posit the following: "Communication, as both a discipline and an 'interdiscipline' or field, is poised to play a unique role in advancing discussions of ethics because the field offers an array of concepts and principles attuned to the examination of ethics" (p. 1). Their words resonate throughout this discussion.

Let's start here by asking why we should understand ethics, next explain ethics as it relates to society, and finally, explain the intersection of ethics and communication theory. As you think about this information, keep in mind that ethical decision making is culturally based. That is, what we consider to be ethical and appropriate in one society is not necessarily a shared value in another society. For instance, though many in the United States can identify with the plight of the Bollen family, you should know that in many cultures, having a son return to his family-of-origin is revered and would not pose the problems that the Bollens are experiencing.

Why study ethics? The response to this question could easily be another question: Why not study it? Ethics permeates all walks of life and cuts across gender, race, class, sexual identity, and spiritual/religious affiliation. In other words, we cannot escape ethical principles in our lives. Ethics is part of virtually every decision we make. Moral development is part of human development, and as we grow older, our moral code undergoes changes well into adulthood. Ethics is what prompts a society toward higher levels of integrity and truth. Elaine Englehardt (2001) observes that "we don't get to 'invent' our own system of ethics" (p. 2), which means that we generally follow a given cultural code of morality. And, Ken Andersen (2003) argues that without an understanding and an expression of ethical values, society will be disadvantaged: "Violating the norms of ethical communication is, I believe, a major factor in the malaise that has led many people to withdraw from the civic culture whether of their profession, their associations, their political arena" (p. 14).

From a communication perspective, ethical issues surface whenever messages potentially influence others. Consider, for instance, the ethics associated with telling your professor that you couldn't turn in a paper on time because a member of your family is ill, when such an illness doesn't exist. Think about the ethics involved if you take an idea of a coworker and present it to your boss as if it were your own. Consider the ethical consequences of going out on several dates with someone and choosing not to disclose a past felony for assault, or of posing as someone other than yourself on Match.com or Tweeting events that are deceptive. Television, too, carries ethical implications. For example, can television promote racial tolerance and harmony and simultaneously present portrayals of cultural groups in stereotypic and offensive ways? We continue our discussion of ethics by identifying some of the institutions whose ethical standards have been the subject of much conversation. Business and industry, religion, entertainment, education, medicine, politics, and technology are just a few of the many fields that have been prone to ethical lapses and have been challenged in communicating messages of integrity (Table 1.1).

Business and Industry

Perhaps no cultural institution has been under more ethical suspicions of late than "corporate America." Unethical behavior in corporations has reached proportions never before seen. In fact, many of these scandals prompted the Occupy Wall Street protest movements in 2011 and 2012, and in 2016, the rise of a (then) little known U.S. Senator from Vermont: Bernie Sanders.

Because a corporation is usually obsessed about its reputation (Carroll, 2015), companies have tried to hide costs, use creative accounting practices, commit accounting fraud, and a plethora of other ethical breaches. The examples are plentiful: The former head of the World Bank engineers a job promotion and salary increase for his long-time companion; WorldCom declares bankruptcy after the discovery of an $11 billion accounting "error"; Volkswagen, the world's biggest automaker, admits to rigging diesel emissions tests in the United States and Europe; Enron inflates earnings reports and hides billions in debt, while increasing salaries of its executives; the founder of

Table 1.1 Examples of Ethical Decision Making in the United States

INSTITUTION	EXAMPLES OF ETHICAL ISSUES
Business and industry	Should CEOs be given pay raises in companies that are not profitable?
Religion	Should the church allow priests to counsel couples who are about to be married?
Entertainment	Does viewing violence in movies prompt violence in society?
Higher education	Should student fees go to political groups on campus?
Medicine	Can pharmaceutical companies be held responsible for sample medicines?
Politics	Should political candidates make promises to citizens?
Technology	Who should monitor websites targeting children?

Adelphia Communications and his two sons commit bank and securities fraud, leading to the company's demise; and Boeing's chief financial officer inappropriately recruits a retired government official with whom he previously negotiated contracts. Finally, the Bernie Madoff investment securities scandal included Madoff bilking nearly $64 billion from over 4,500 clients. Sadly, each of these situations occurred within a 10-year period. The list of business scandals has been especially prominent. But with the advent of Corporate Ethics Statements, congressional legislation requiring public accountability, improved transparent accounting practices, and increased accountability to stockholders, most businesses have begun to improve their ethical standing. Of course, much, much more needs to be done to eliminate lingering levels of distrust.

Religion and Faith

Both Eastern and Western civilizations have stressed ethics in their moral traditions. For instance, according to Taoism, no one exists in isolation, and, therefore, empathy and insight will lead to truth. For the Buddhist, being moral requires that one use words that elicit peace and avoid gossip, self-promotion, anger, argument, and lying. From a Western perspective, many ethical issues derive from early Greek civilization. Aristotle first articulated the principle of the Golden Mean. He believed that a person's moral virtue stands between two vices, with the middle, or the mean, being the foundation for a rational society. For instance, when the Bollens are deciding what to say to their son Eddy about overstaying his welcome, their Golden Mean might look like this:

EXTREME	GOLDEN MEAN	EXTREME
lying	truthful communication	reveal everything

The Judeo-Christian religions are centered as well on questions of ethics. In fact, there is an online publication devoted solely to Religion and Ethics (pbs.org/wnet

/religionandethics/current/headlines.html). Christianity is founded on the principle of good example—that is, live according to God's laws and set an example for others. However, some believe that such moral standards are not uniquely religious. For those not affiliated with organized religion, the secular values of fairness and justice and working toward better relationships are important as well. Affiliating with a religion may also pose some ethical difficulty if a person does not subscribe to a number of its philosophies or orientations. For instance, people who believe that Catholic priests should be able to marry will have a difficult time reconciling that value with Catholic law that prohibits such marriages.

Despite efforts to retain ethicality, religious institutions have had a number of ethical challenges over the years. Ministers frequenting prostitutes, pedophilic priests, drug abuse by church leaders, and sexual immorality among parishioners and pastors are just a few of the dozens of religious scandals that have caused outrage. Fortunately, many religious bodies are now developing clear ethical statements on appropriate behavior and clarifying the consequences of ethical violations.

Entertainment

The entertainment industry has also been intimately involved in dialogues about ethics and communication. Often, a circular argument surfaces with respect to Hollywood: Does Hollywood reflect society or does Hollywood shape society? Many viewpoints are raised in these arguments, but three seem to dominate. One belief is that Hollywood has a responsibility to show the moral side of an immoral society; movies should help people escape a difficult reality, not relive it. A second opinion is that Hollywood should create more nonviolent and nonsexual films so that all family members can watch a movie. Unfortunately, critics note, films like Hostel, Kill Bill, Sin City, The Wicker Man, Rampage tend to exacerbate violent attitudes in young people. A third school of thought is that Hollywood is in show *business*, and therefore making money is what moviemaking is all about. Regardless of whether you agree with any of these orientations, the entertainment industry will continue to reflect *and* influence changing moral climates in the United States. Some might say that Hollywood leading the charge in any conversation on ethics is, in itself, a question of ethics.

Higher Education

A third cultural institution that has been charged with questionable ethics is higher education. Colleges and universities across the United States teach introductory courses in ethics, and these are required courses in many schools.

Despite this interest, many schools have lost their own moral compass. For instance, colleges and universities face an ethical choice about reporting crime statistics on their campus. Despite the fact that they are required to report campus crime via the Jeanne Clery Act (named after a Lehigh University student who was murdered in 1986), some campuses fear the bad publicity. As a result, crime is "contextualized" ("Our campus is in a large city; there's a lot of crime everywhere" or "Our campus is in a rural setting; we may have a few problems but, we're still relatively safe"). On a logistic level, another ethical decision arises when schools are required to identify the enrollment patterns for legislative and financial support. Frequently, schools report statistical increases in enrollment over a number of years when in reality the school system has simply adopted a new way of counting heads. And, in 2012, Emory University (preceded by McKenna College, Baylor University, Iona College, and many others) made front-page headlines when it was found that the school manipulated and falsified data used in the ratings used by publications that rank colleges (e.g., *U.S. News & World Report*). The institution's integrity is often called into question by engaging in such practices (Ramsey & Wesley, 2015). Clearly, although they are called institutions of "higher" learning, some would argue that many campuses have reached new "lows" in ethical decision making.

Medicine

A fourth institution concerned with ethics and communication is the medical community. Specifically, with advances in science changing the cultural landscape, bioethical issues are topics of conversation around the dinner table. Physician-assisted suicide is one example of medicine at the center of ethical controversy. To some, the decision to prolong life should be a private one, made by the patient and his or her doctor. To others, society should have a say in such a decision.

Medical decisions can become publicly debated far from the hospital bedside. Late-term abortions, human cloning, drug-enhanced athletes, medicinal marijuana, executed prisoners organ use, and physician-assisted suicide are all topics that demonstrate the interrelationship among ethics, politics, and medicine. This topic has resonated sufficiently in our society that there is an abundance of professional journals, websites, and publications dedicated to the interface of ethics and medicine. The American Society of Law, Medicine, and Ethics is one such organization dedicated to ethical decision making (www.aslme.org).

Theory in Popular Press • *Ethics and Health Care*

Howard Brody, in the *New England Journal of Medicine*, one of the most oft-cited medical journals, presents new ethical discussions taking place in the medical community. Dr. Brody evidences that 30 percent of health care costs can be considered to be "waste." That is, he contends that this waste, or what he determines to be "useless interventions, useless tests, and harmful treatments," is too frequent. He laments that this "non-beneficial medicine" is fast becoming the norm in medicine. Brody argues that an "ethics of rationing care and waste avoidance" is necessary if medicine is to be able to respond to health-related concerns. Brody posits that physicians are not prioritizing this notion of wasteful medical care and that this ignorance is contributing to higher medical costs. He also acknowledges that although there are clearly political implications to this ethical discussion, it is incumbent upon physicians to undertake this topic to "protect . . . patients from harm."

Source: Brody, H. (2012). From an ethics of rationing to an ethics of waste avoidance. *New England Journal of Medicine, 366*, 1949–1951.

Politics

It is difficult to disentangle the topic of ethics from politics. The two are often viewed as incompatible. We are living in cynical times, and opinion polls consistently show that the public's view of political leaders rates lower than the public's view of paying taxes. The scandals associated with politics relate to lobbyists, campaign financing, infidelity, deception, conflicts of interest, cover-ups, bribery, conspiracy, tax evasion. Political scandals have been in the news since, well, the beginning of politics. It may seem, however, that they have grown in number over the past few years. Whether it's the resignation of the CIA Director because of his extramarital affair, the U.S. President's sexual harassment allegations from 20 women, or the hateful Facebook postings by political candidates the list goes on and on.

The ethical problems associated with politics may never go away, despite efforts to establish ethics commissions and oversight advisory boards in state and national governments. Though many of us wish to be optimistic in thinking that we are cultivating a new generation of political leaders who are ethical beings, there are those who are not as hopeful. Still, with nonprofit organizations such as Public Interest Research Group (PIRG) and the Government Accountability Project—groups that expose ethical shortcomings in our government and its leaders—and with aptly named Government offices such as the U.S. Office of Government Ethics, there may be cause for increased confidence in the future.

Technology

Technology is at the center of many ethical debates today (van Manen, 2015). Armed with a copy of the First Amendment, proponents of free speech say the Internet, for example, should not be censored. Free speech advocates stress that what is considered inappropriate can vary tremendously from one person to another, and consequently, censorship is arbitrary. Consider, for instance, the U.S. Supreme Court decision protecting "virtual" child pornography on the Internet. Noting that the Child Pornography Protection Act was overly broad, the justices felt that banning computer-generated images of young people was unjustified. In addition, social networking sites such as Facebook, with over 1 billion global users are prone to ethical problems. How much information is too much? Teenagers letting others know where they live, blogs that divulge too much information about a family's financial situation, and would-be employers looking over the shoulders of users are just a few of the many ethical challenges characterizing the online world.

As the United States is clearly more reliant on technology than ever before, ethical issues will continue to arise. Lying about one's identity online, downloading copyrighted material, inviting young people into violent and hate-filled websites, and watching executions on the Internet are all examples of potential technological ethics dilemmas.

Some Final Thoughts

The relationship between communication and ethics is intricate and complex. Public discourse requires responsibility (Torcello, 2016). We presume that political leaders will tell the truth and that spiritual leaders will guide us by their example. Yet we know that not all elected officials are honest and that not all religious leaders set a spiritual standard. Organizations are especially prone to ethical dilemmas. For instance, whistle-blowing, or revealing ethically suspicious behavior in a company, can have lasting implications. Although some may view whistle-blowing as a courageous and morally sound act, others may view it as a violation of trust. This difference in perception usually rests on whether a whistle-blower is perceived as a disgruntled employee who may have been passed over for a promotion or as someone who is genuinely concerned about a company's ethical practices. Unethical practices do little to garner trust in people.

There is an ethical dimension to listening as well. As listeners (or readers) we have a responsibility to give a fair hearing to the ideas of others. This responsibility extends to such ideas as the communication theories presented in this book. Rob Anderson and Veronica Ross (2002) point out six important ethical strategies to consider when reading communication theory:

1. Remain open to being persuaded by the statements of others.
2. Remain willing to try out new ideas that may be seen by others as mistakes, and invite others to experiment also.
3. Accept that multiple perspectives on reality are held as valid by different people, especially in different cultural contexts.
4. Attempt to test any tentatively held knowledge.
5. Live with ambiguity, but become less tolerant of contradiction.
6. Evaluate knowledge claims against personal experience and the everyday concrete pragmatics of what works. (p. 15)

In addition to these suggestions, we add one more: If a theory is a bit difficult to understand at first, don't gloss over it. Delve into the explanation once more to gain a clearer picture of the theorists' intentions. You may feel inexperienced or unprepared to challenge these theories. Yet we offer the theories for review, application, and comment and want you to ask questions about them. Although we would like to think that all theorists are open and receptive to multiple ways of knowing, the reality remains that theory construction is bound by culture, personality, time, circumstance, and the availability of resources. As students of communication theory, we all must be willing to ask some difficult questions and probe some confusing areas.

Student Voices

Mandy

I've always thought that ethics is the most important part of communicating with other people. I don't care whether I'm in an office or in the classroom, I think we have to live using ethical standards. We need to know that lying to other people rarely makes sense. We need to know that if we don't try to understand others from their point of view, we're probably never going to understand what they mean. The media have to be ethical, too. They just can't put out whatever they want and not be held accountable. I guess the bottom line is that if we try to be concerned about others, try to understand what they are feeling, and do what we can to be honest, we are on our way to being ethical.

The Value of Understanding Communication Theory

Although we've alluded to this throughout the chapter, we'd like to emphasize the importance of communication theory to all of our lives. We realize that many of you may not be immediately aware of the value of this topic. Therefore, we want to give you a glimpse into the significance of communication theory. Remember: You can understand all sorts of issues in life (e.g., divorce, a job interview, your self-concept) through communication theory. As you read and understand each chapter, you will likely develop your own personal understanding of the importance of communication theory. That is, you'll likely develop your own theoretical lens of understanding human behavior. We encourage you to be open as you explore this exciting area.

Understanding Communication Theory Cultivates Critical Thinking Skills

One important value you glean from studying communication theory relates to your critical thinking skills. Without doubt, as you read and reflect on the theories in this book, you will be required to think critically about several issues. Learning how to apply the theory to your own life, recognizing the research potential of the theory, and understanding how a particular theory evolved will be among your responsibilities in this course. In addition, understanding communication can aid in your skill set. If only every Hollywood celebrity going through a divorce had read Chapter 11 (Relational Dialectics Theory), perhaps there would be a better understanding of relational pushes and pulls. The various decision-making groups of global governments might be more effective in-group members, read about Groupthink (Chapter 14). Even motivational speakers would find value in what Aristotle had to say (The *Rhetoric*; Chapter 18). These skills notwithstanding, as Tapas Ray (2012) notes, many theories and communication traditions have a Western cultural bias, so we need to be cautious in a universal application of the theory. These activities require that you cultivate your critical thinking skills—skills that will help you on the job, in relationships, and as you are introduced to media.

Understanding Communication Theory Helps You to Recognize the Breadth and Depth of Research

In addition to fostering critical thinking skills, being a student of communication theory will help you appreciate the richness of research across various fields of study. Regardless of what your current academic major is, the theories contained in this book are based on the thinking, writing, and research of intellectually curious men and women who have drawn on the scholarship of numerous disciplines. For instance, as you read about the Relational Dialectics Theory (Chapter 11), you will note that many of its principles originate in philosophy. Groupthink (Chapter 14) originated in foreign policy decision making. Communication Accommodation Theory (Chapter 28), you will find that many of its principles originate in cultural anthropology. And, Face-Negotiation Theory (Chapter 27) was influenced by research in sociology. As you pursue a particular degree, keep in mind that much of what you are learning is a result of theoretical thinking and this thinking is often interdisciplinary in nature.

Understanding Communication Theory Helps to Make Sense of Personal Life Experiences

Understanding communication theory also helps you make sense of your life experiences. It's impossible to find a theory in this book that does not in some way relate to your life or to the lives of people around you. Communication theory aids you in understanding people, media, and events and helps you answer important questions. Have you ever been confused about why some men speak differently from some women? Chances are that reading Muted Group Theory (Chapter 29) will help you understand why that may be the case. Do the media promote a violent society? The theory of Cultivation Analysis (Chapter 24) will likely help you answer that question. What role does technology play in society? Media Ecology Theory (Chapter 26) responds to that question. And what happens when someone stands too close while talking to you? Expectancy Violations Theory (Chapter 7) explores and explains this type of behavior. Some of you may have entered this course thinking that communication theory has limited value in your life. You will see that much of your life and your experiences in life will be better understood because of communication theory.

Communication Theory Fosters Self-Awareness

Thus far, we observed that learning about communication theory helps your critical thinking skills, informs you about the value of research across different fields of study, and aids you in understanding the world around you. One final reason to study theories of communication pertains to an area that is likely to be most important in your life—you. Learning about who you are, how you function in society, the influence you are able to have on others, the extent to which you are influenced by the media, how you behave in various circumstances, and what motivates your decisions are just a handful of the possible areas that are either explicitly or implicitly discussed in the theories you will be introduced to in this book. We are not suggesting that you should be central to whether a theory has relevance. Rather, we are stating that theories related directly to you—your thoughts, values, behaviors, and background. For instance, Social Penetration Theory (Chapter 10) will help you consider the value of self-disclosing in your relationships. Chapter 4 (Symbolic Interaction Theory) will assist you in thinking about the meaning of the various symbols surrounding you. Yet these are not "self-help" communication theories; they do not provide easy answers to difficult questions. What you will encounter are theories that will help you as you try to understand yourself and your surroundings.

You are about to embark on an educational journey that is likely new to you. We hope you persevere in unraveling the complexity of communication theory. The journey may be different, challenging, and tiring at times, but it will always be applicable to your life.

Conclusion

In this chapter, we introduced you to the communication process. We presented our definition of communication and provided you various elements embedded in that process. In addition, we identified three prevailing models of communication: the linear model, the interactional model, and the transactional model. We discussed ethics and its relationship to communication theory. Finally, we provided several reasons why it is important for you to study communication theory.

You now have an understanding of the communication process and some sense of how complex it can be. As you read the many theories in this book, you will be able to view communication from a variety of perspectives. You will also gain valuable information that will help you understand human behavior and give you a new way to think about our society. We continue this examination in Chapter 2 when we present the traditions in communication study and important contexts in which communication takes place.

Discussion Starters

TECH QUEST: We noted that technology will likely affect future communication models. Based on your use of a social media platform, construct a communication model that incorporates how technology will influence face-to-face communication.

1. What led to the blowup between Eddy Bollen and his parents? Do you believe that Eddy and his parents were trying to handle his situation in an ethical way? Why or why not?

2. Do you believe that all slips of the tongue, conversational faux pas, and un-intentional nonverbal behaviors should be considered communication? Why or why not? What examples can you provide to justify your thoughts?

3. Explain why the linear model of communication was so appealing years ago. Explain the appeal of the transactional model using current societal events.

4. Discuss the value of looking at communication theory from a variety of different disciplinary angles.

5. What are some recent ethical dilemmas related to communication? How was each dilemma resolved, if it was?

6. Comment on why so many definitions of communication exist.

7. Discuss how different family members might have different fields of experience.

CHAPTER 2

Thinking About the Field: Traditions and Contexts

Theory, in my understanding of theory, is a form of discourse.
—Robert T. Craig

Jenny and Lee Yamato

As the 18-year-old daughter of a single parent, Lee Yamato knows that life can be difficult. She is the only child of Jenny Yamato, a Japanese American woman whose husband died from a heart attack several years ago. Jenny raised her daughter in Lacon, a small rural town in the South. It was stressful being a single mom, and Jenny was sometimes the target of overt racist jokes. As a waitress, Jenny knew that college would be the way to a better life for her daughter. She saved every extra penny and worked at the children's library for several months to bring in extra income. Jenny knew that Lee would get financial aid in college, but she also wanted to be able to help her only child with college finances.

As Lee finished her senior year in high school, she knew that before too long she would be leaving to attend a public university. Unfortunately, the closest college was over 200 miles from Lacon. Lee had mixed feelings about her move. She was very excited to get away from the small-town gossip, but she also knew that leaving Lacon meant that her mom would have to live by herself. Being alone could be devastating to her mom, Lee thought. Still, Lee recognized that her education was her first priority and that in order to get into veterinary school, she would have to

stay focused. Thinking about her mom would only make the transition more difficult and could sour her first year as a college student.

Jenny, too, felt ambivalent about Lee leaving. When Jenny's husband died, she didn't think that she could raise a 13-year-old by herself. In fact, given that single moms were not looked at with a lot of respect, Jenny felt even more overpowered. However, her own tenacity and determination had paid off, and she was extremely proud that her child was going away to college. Like her daughter, though, Jenny felt sad about Lee's departure. She felt as if her best friend was leaving her, and she couldn't imagine her life without her daughter. She knew that they would talk on the phone, but it couldn't replace the hugs, the laughter, and the memories.

On the day that Lee was to leave, Jenny gave her a box with chocolate chip cookies, some peanut butter cups (Lee's favorite), a photo album of Lee and Jenny during their camping trip to Arizona, and a shoe box. Inside the shoe box were old letters that Jenny and her husband had written to each other during their courtship. Jenny wanted Lee to have the letters to remind her that her dad's spirit lives on in her. When Lee looked at the first letter, she put it down, hugged her mom, and cried. She then got into her car and slowly drove away, leaving her house and her only true friend behind.

The communication discipline is vast, and its depth is reflected in the lives of people across the United States, people like Lee and Jenny Yamato. Their relationship is obviously a close one, marked now by a common and often emotional point in a family's development: college. As the two begin to adapt to a new type of relationship characterized by distance, their communication will also take on new levels of importance. As Bethani Dobkin and Roger Pace (2006) state, "[C]ommunication has the potential to shape identities, relationships, environments, and cultures" (p. 6). The Yamato family will likely communicate with an appreciation for the full impact that communication can have on their lives. Let's begin our discussion of the communication field by looking at seven traditions in communication. We will then examine various settings in which communication occurs. These two approaches guide this chapter. The first approach (the seven traditions) is theoretical in nature; the second framework (the seven contexts) is more practical in its approach. We describe each in the following pages.

Chapter 1 provided a foundation for conceptualizing what communication is and understanding the complexity of the communication process. In this chapter, we further unravel the meaning of communication by articulating two primary ways of looking at the field of communication.

Student Voices

Trish

To be honest, I wasn't sure how to explain my communication major to my mom and dad when I went home for Thanksgiving. They had no idea why I wanted to major in it! After I talked to them about what communication is (and what it isn't!), I think they were pretty happy that I found a major that made sense to me. I know I'm more employable by understanding communication, but I also just love knowing how broad a field it is. I think I convinced some of my roommates to switch their major!

Seven Traditions in the Communication Field

Robert Craig (Craig, 1999; Craig & Muller, 2007) outlines communication theory in one of the more intellectually valuable ways, assisting people in understanding "themselves, their society, and their culture in a communicative way" (Garcia-Jimenez & Craig, 2010, p. 430). Craig believed that communication theory is an often unwieldy area of study and, to this end, provided categories to aid our understanding of it. Craig and Muller note that trying to make sense of communication theory is often complicated because of different intellectual styles in the field. A classification system for understanding communication theory, then, helps us to break down the challenges associated with understanding theory.

Craig terms the following framework as "traditions" to highlight the belief that theoretical development doesn't just occur naturally. Indeed, theorizing in communication is a deliberative, engaging, and innovative experience that happens over

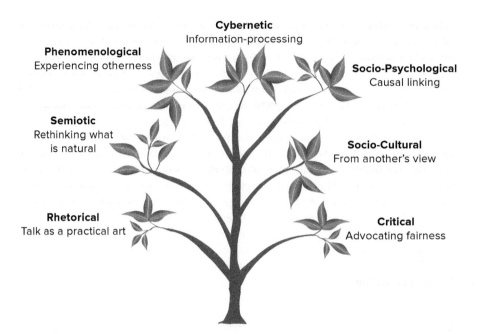

Cybernetic
Information-processing

Phenomenological
Experiencing otherness

Socio-Psychological
Causal linking

Semiotic
Rethinking what
is natural

Socio-Cultural
From another's view

Rhetorical
Talk as a practical art

Critical
Advocating fairness

Figure 2.1
Traditions in
Communication
Theory

time. As Craig and Muller (2007) point out, "[T]heorists invent new ideas to solve problems they perceive in existing ideas in a particular tradition" (p. xiii). And, although traditions suggest adhering to a historical preference, Craig and Muller are quick to point out that traditions change frequently and, like communication, are dynamic. Further, they caution that many theories are not easily categorized: "Even a theory that rebels against its tradition and rejects major parts of it can still belong to the tradition in significant ways" (p. xiv). So let's examine the seven traditions of communication theory as advanced by Craig (1999). To honor the integrity of each tradition yet avoid irrelevant detail for this section of the chapter, we will provide you an overview of each tradition. If you'd like additional details, you are encouraged to consult Craig's research. See Figure 2.1 for more information the traditions.

The Rhetorical Tradition

At the heart of the rhetorical tradition is what Craig notes as the "practical art" (p. 73) of talk. This tradition suggests that we are interested in public address and public speaking and their functions in a society. Rhetorical theory is especially valued in many Western societies because it helps us understand the influence of speech and how we can cultivate our public speaking effectiveness. This tradition also includes the ability to reflect on different viewpoints before arriving at a personal view. It is the usefulness of the rhetorical tradition that remains attractive to researchers, theorists, and practitioners.

The rhetorical tradition necessarily involves elements pertaining to language and the audience. Henry Alford (2016), for instance, discusses the linguistic challenges for many same-sex marriages. Some couples wish to avoid the "heteronormative" nature of husband and wife and instead, elect to have more unique titles, including "hersbands," "wusbands," and even "support staff." The tradition also includes a discussion pertaining to audience appeals; how do audience members respond to emotions, for example? To what extent does the power of language move people to emotional and decisive action? How are we influenced or swayed by the appeals by mass media? What role does personal example play in having others accept our point of view? What effect does speaking to a large group of people have on the perceptions or actions of that group? Or, to what extent does the rhetorical tradition challenge the common belief that "telling the plain truth is something other than the strategic adaptation of a message to an audience"? (Craig, 2007, p. 73). Answering such questions is not easy and such questions are often the domain of philosophers. Yet, they are important if we are to consider the value and historical significance of looking at the communication process from a rhetorical lens.

The Semiotic Tradition

Simply put, **semiotics** is the study of signs. Signs are part of a social life; they stand for something else. Children laughing and running around is a sign of play. A ring on the ring finger of the left hand is a *sign* of a married individual. An adult crying in a funeral home is a *sign* of sadness. Most common among these signs are words or what we generally consider language usage. According to the semiotic tradition, meaning is achieved when we share a common language. As noted in Chapter 1, people arrive at a communication exchange with various fields of experience and values placed on these experiences. Pioneer linguist I. A. Richards (1936) observed that words are arbitrary and have no intrinsic meaning. Consequently, achieving commonality in meaning is more difficult than first imagined, particularly if one is using language that is not recognized or valued by another.

semiotics
the study of signs

Semiotics suggests that what we think of as "natural" or "obvious" in public discourse needs to be considered in context. That is, our values and belief structures are often a result of what has been passed down from one generation to another (a tradition). What was considered to be a "given" years ago may simply not be that way today. Semiotics challenges the notion that words have appropriate meanings; indeed, words change as the people using those words change. Consider, for example, the use of the words *war* and *peace* in the 1940s, the 1960s/1970s, the 1990s, and today. There are also likely to be multiple meanings of these two words if, for example, someone lost a family member in one of these wars and if another person protests war on a regular basis. Consider the phrase *single parent*. In the 1950s, it did not resonate deeply in society. However, as time evolved, the divorce rate soared and marriage was not a "default" choice; being a single mom (like Jenny Yamato) or single dad is now commonplace.

The Phenomenological Tradition

Let's explore the term phenomenology, a concept derived from the field of philosophy. **Phenomenology** is a personal interpretation of everyday life and activities.

Craig (2007) believes that the phenomenological tradition is marked by communication that he contends is an "experience of otherness" (p. 79). What this means is

phenomenology
a personal interpretation of everyday life and activities

that a person tries to attain authenticity by eliminating biases in a conversation. Many phenomenologists believe that an individual's system of beliefs should not influence the dialogue taking place. As you're probably figuring out, this is quite challenging, or, as Craig points out, is a "practical impossibility" (p. 80). Consider, for example, the challenge many people have communicating with other people who have different points of view or who are from different backgrounds. Craig notes that many phenomenological ideas are especially applicable to issues pertaining to diversity, identity, class, sexuality, and religion.

The Cybernetic Tradition

Communication as information science was first introduced by Shannon and Weaver, two scholars associated with the linear model we discussed in Chapter 1. Recall that this model's fundamental shortcoming pertained to the fact that human communication is not as simplistic as linearity suggests. Nonetheless, what Shannon and Weaver advanced was the belief that communication involves noise. Cybernetics in particular looks at problems such as noise in the communication process. But it goes further. Cybernetics tries to unravel the complexities of message meaning by underscoring the unpredictability of the feedback we receive.

By advocating a cybernetic approach, communication theorists are embracing an expansive view of communication. As Craig (2007) states: "[I]t is important for us as communicators to transcend our individual perspectives, to look at the communication process from a broader, systemic viewpoint, and not to hold individuals responsible for systemic outcomes that no individual can control" (p. 82). In other words, the cybernetic tradition asks us to understand that communication is not only information processing, but also that individuals enter into communication settings with different abilities in that information processing. Fields of study which have been influenced by cybernetics include game theory, psychology, architecture, and artificial intelligence (Ashby, 2015).

The Socio-Psychological Tradition

Those who adhere to the socio-psychological tradition uphold a cause–effect model. That is, communication theory is examined from a view that holds that someone's behavior is influenced by something else—something social psychologists call a "variable." Craig (2007) believes that underlying this tradition is the assumption that our own communication patterns and the patterns of others vary from one person to another. It is up to the social psychologist to unravel the relationship among these patterns.

An early advocate of the socio-psychological tradition was Carl Hovland. Hovland, a Yale psychologist, examined attitude change and investigated the extent to which long- and short-term recall influences an individual's attitudes and beliefs. In the 1950s—long before personal computers came into existence—Hovland also was the first to experiment with computer simulations and the learning process. His work and the work of other social psychologists underscored the importance of experimental research and trying to understand causal links. It is this scientific evidence for human behavior that continues to pervade much communication theorizing from this tradition.

The Socio-Cultural Tradition

The essence of the socio-cultural tradition can be summed up this way: "Our everyday interactions with others depend heavily on preexisting, shared cultural patterns and social structures" (Craig, 2007, p. 84). The core of the socio-cultural tradition suggests that individuals are parts of larger groups who have unique rules and patterns of interaction. To theorize from this tradition means to acknowledge and become sensitive to the many kinds of people who occupy this planet. Theorists should not instinctively nor strategically "group" people without concern for individual identity.

Socio-cultural theorists advocate that we abandon the binary "you/me" or "us/them" approach to understanding people. Instead, appealing to the *co-creation* of social order/reality is a worthier goal for consideration. As people communicate, they produce, maintain, repair, and transform reality (Carey, 1989). Dialogue and interaction must be characterized by an understanding of what Craig (2007) calls "voice" (p. 84), an individual point of view that inevitably finds its way into everyday conversation.

The Critical Tradition

Individuals who are concerned with injustice, oppression, power, and linguistic dominance are those who would likely identify themselves as critical theorists. Critiquing the social order and imposing structures or individuals on that order are at the heart of critical theory. Among the theorists most known for protesting social order is philosopher and political economist/revolutionary Karl Marx. Marx believed that power in society has been hijacked by institutions that have no real concern for the working class. In his book *The Communist Manifesto*, Marx and his colleague Friedrich Engels (1848) contend that the history of a society is best understood by looking at the class struggles in that society.

Critical theorists look at language and how it creates imbalances and power differentials in society. Critical theorists also find that openly questioning the assumptions that guide a society is legitimate. In doing so, communicators expose the beliefs and values that guide their decision making and actions. As is suggested in our opening story of Jenny and Lee Yamato, Jenny felt that as a single mom, she could never achieve the level of respect afforded to other family types. Critical theorists would attempt to unravel how a society defines freedom, equality, and reason, three qualities identified by Craig (2007), in order to understand Jenny's experiences. Who or what are the principal forces on social order? How does one achieve the freedom to express one's will? These and a host of other questions are at the core of the critical tradition.

Putting It All Together

This discussion provides you one way of looking at the texture of the communication field. Communication theory, as you will discover, is not created in a vacuum. Scholars enter into the theory-building process with particular positions, some of which influence the direction of the theories they construct and refine. The preceding traditions are rooted in communication and we will consider each as we introduce you to the various theories. As we alluded to earlier, theory is not always so "clean" and therefore, there will be a hybrid of a few traditions along the way.

With this backdrop, we now wish to explore a more practical framework from which to view communication theory. We turn our attention to the various contexts, or environments, of communication from which research and theory develop.

Seven Contexts in the Communication Field

In order to make the communication field and the communication process more understandable and manageable, we now look at the various contexts of communication. What is a context? **Contexts** are environments in which communication takes place. Contexts provide a backdrop against which researchers and theorists can analyze phenomena. Contexts also provide clarity. Our discussion of context focuses on **situational contexts.** To suggest that a context is situationally based means that the communication process is limited by a number of factors—namely, the number of people, the degree of space between interactants, the extent of feedback, and the available channels.

Earlier we noted that the communication field is very diverse and offers various research opportunities. This can be a bit cumbersome, and at times even communication scholars lament the wide array of options. Still, there seems to be some universal agreement on the fundamental contexts of communication. In fact, most communication departments are built around some or all of the following seven communication contexts: intrapersonal, interpersonal, small group, organizational, public/rhetorical, mass/media, and cultural (Figure 2.2). Keep in mind, however, that communication departments in colleges and universities across the United States divide themselves uniquely. Some, for instance, include mass communication in a department of communication whereas others may have a separate department of mass communication. Some schools have a department of interpersonal communication and include every context therein. This diversity underscores that the discipline is permeable, that boundary lines among the contexts are not absolute.

Intrapersonal Communication

As you review theories in this book, keep in mind that a theory may focus on how individuals perceive their own behavior. At the root of this thinking is intrapersonal communication. Intrapersonal communication theorists frequently study the role that cognition plays in human behavior. **Intrapersonal communication** is communication with oneself. It is an internal dialogue and may take place even in the presence of another individual. Intrapersonal communication is what goes on inside your head even when you are with someone. Intrapersonal communication is usually more repetitive than other communication; we engage in it many times each day. This context is also unique from other contexts in that it includes those times when you imagine, perceive, daydream, and solve problems in your head. Intrapersonal communication is much more than talking to oneself. It also includes the many attributions you may make about another person's behavior. For instance, an employer may

contexts
environments in which communication takes place

situational contexts
environments that are limited by such factors as the number of people present, the feedback, the space between communicators, among others

intrapersonal communication
communication with oneself

CONTEXT		SOME RESEARCH AND THEORETICAL CONCERNS
INTRAPERSONAL Communication with oneself		Impression formation and decision making; symbols and meaning; observations and attributions; ego involvement and persuasion
INTERPERSONAL Face-to-face communication		Relationship maintenance strategies; relational intimacy; relationship control; interpersonal attraction
SMALL GROUP Communication with a group of people		Gender and group leadership; group vulnerability; groups and stories; group decision making; task difficulty
ORGANIZATIONAL Communication within and among large and extended environments		Organizational hierarchy and power; culture and organizational life; employee morale; opinions and worker satisfaction
PUBLIC/RHETORICAL Communication to a large group of listeners (audience)		Communication apprehension; delivery effectiveness; speech and text criticism; ethical speechmaking; popular culture analysis
MASS/MEDIA Communication to a very large audience through mediated forms		Use of media; affiliation and television programming; television and values; media and need fulfillment; effects of social networking sites
CULTURAL Communication between and among members of different cultures		Culture and rule-setting; culture and anxiety; hegemony; ethnocentrism

Figure 2.2 Contexts of Communication

want to know why an employee arrives late to work and looks disheveled each day. The supervisor may believe that the worker's tardiness and demeanor are a result of some domestic problems. In reality, the employee may have another job in order to pay for his or her child's college tuition. We all have internal dialogues, and these internalized voices can vary tremendously from one person to another.

Intrapersonal communication is distinguished from other contexts in that it allows communicators to make attributions about themselves. People have the ability to assess themselves. From body image to work competencies, people are always making self-attributions. You may have thought seriously about your own strengths and shortcomings in a number of situations. For example, do you find that you are an excellent parent, but not so excellent as a statistics student? Are there times when you feel that you are a trusted friend, but not so trusted in your own family?

Seven Contexts in the Communication Field   **31**

Although some people may believe that talking to oneself is a bit peculiar, Virginia Satir (1988) believes that these internal dialogues may help individuals bolster their **self-esteem**—the degree of positive orientation people have about themselves. Often, intrapersonal communication is difficult; it requires individuals to accept their accomplishments and confront their fears and anxieties. Looking in a mirror can be both enlightening and frightening. Of course, mirrors can also be distorting. Jenny Yamato, for example, may think that her world is over once her daughter leaves for college. The reality for the vast majority of parents, however, is that they survive the "loss." As a single parent, Jenny may think that she is incapable of moving on without Lee. Once Lee leaves, however, Jenny may find that she is more empowered living alone.

The research in intrapersonal communication centers a great deal on the cognitions, symbols, and intentions that individuals have. To this end, researchers in this area have examined attitudes toward specific behaviors and events, including dating (McEwan & Guerrero, 2012), suspicion and detection, (Kim & Levine, 2011), mother–daughter relationships (Arroyo & Andersen, 2016), stress (Wright, 2012), silence (Bisel & Arterburn, 2012), attachment (Goodboy & Bolkan, 2011), and motivation of business executives (Millhous, 2004).

Our discussion of intrapersonal communication has focused on the role of the self in the communication process. Recall from Chapter 1 that as individuals communicate with themselves, the process may be either intentional or unintentional. Intrapersonal communication is at the heart of a person's communication activities. Without recognizing oneself, it is difficult to recognize another.

Interpersonal Communication

From its beginnings, **interpersonal communication** referred to face-to-face communication between people. Contemporary views of interpersonal communication incorporate a technological lens (e.g., dating websites, etc.). Several theories that you will read about in this book have their origins in the interpersonal context. This context is rich with research and theory and is perhaps the most expansive of all of the contexts. Investigating how relationships begin, the maintenance of relationships, and the dissolution of relationships characterizes much of the interpersonal context.

One reason researchers and theorists study relationships is that relationships are so complex and diverse. For instance, you may find yourself in dozens of relationship types right now, including physician–patient, teacher–student, parent–child, supervisor–employee, and so forth. Interacting within each of these relationships affords communicators a chance to maximize the number of channels (visual, auditory, tactile, olfactory) used during an interaction. In this context, these channels function simultaneously for both interactants: A child may scream for his mom, for instance, and as she is able to calm him with her caress, she touches the child, looks in his eyes, and listens to his whimpering subside.

The interpersonal context itself comprises many related subcontexts. Interpersonal researchers have studied the family (Koerner, 2015; Turner & West, 2015), friendships (Chen & Nakazawa, 2012), long-term marriages (Hughes & Dickson, 2006), physician–patient relationships (Gordon & Street, 2016), and the organization–public relationship (Ifert-Johnson & Acquavella, 2012). In addition, researchers are

---

self-esteem
the degree of positive orientation people have about themselves

interpersonal communication
face-to-face communication between people

interested in a host of issues and themes (e.g., risk, power, teasing, gossip, liking, attraction, emotions, etc.) associated with these relationships.

Researchers have also examined the link between interpersonal communication and mass media, organizations, and the classroom (Frymier & Houser, 2002) as well as the role that social media (Facebook) and email play in establishing and maintaining relationships (Lee, Choudhry, Wu, Matlin, Brennan, & Shrank, 2016). Finally, relationships that have not been studied enough, including gay and lesbian relationships, cohabiting relationships, and Facebook friendships and computer-anchored relationships, are being investigated at a rapid pace in the communication field (Bryant & Marmo, 2012; Croom, Gross, Rosen, & Rosen, 2016; Muraco & Fredriksen-Goldsen, 2011; Willoughby, Carroll, & Busby, 2012). As you can see, researchers have framed some very diverse and exciting work within the interpersonal communication context, and studying relationships and what takes place within them has broad appeal.

Small Group and Team Communication

A third context of communication is the small group or team. Small groups are composed of a number of people who work together to achieve some common purpose. Small group research focuses on task groups as opposed to the friendship and family groups found in the interpersonal context. Communication theory centering on small groups frequently concerns the dynamic nature of small groups, including group roles, boundaries, and trust.

Researchers disagree about how many people make up a small group. Some scholars argue that the optimal number for a small group is five to seven members, whereas others put no limit on the maximum number of members. Nearly all agree, however, that there must be at least three people for a small group to exist (Poole, 2007; Schultz, 1996). For our purposes, then, **small group communication** is defined as communication among at least three individuals.

The number in a group is not as important as the implications of that number. The more people, the greater the opportunity for more personal relationships to develop. This may influence whether small groups stay focused on their goals and whether group members are satisfied with their experiences (Shaw, 1981). A classic study (Kephart, 1950) revealed that as the size of the group increases, the number of relationships increases substantially. With a three-person group, then, the number of potential relationships is 6; with a seven-person group, there are 966 possible relationships! When there are too many group members, there is a tendency for cliques to form (Kesebir, 2012). However, large numbers of group members may result in additional resources not present in smaller groups.

People are influenced by the presence of others. For example, some small groups are very cohesive, which means having a high degree of togetherness and a common bond. This **cohesiveness** may influence whether the group functions effectively and efficiently. In addition, the small group context affords individuals a chance to gain multiple perspectives on an issue. That is, in the intrapersonal context, an individual views events from his or her own perspective; in the interpersonal context there are more perspectives. In the small group context, many more people have the potential to contribute to the group's goals. In problem-solving groups, or task groups in

small group communication *communication among at least three individuals*

cohesiveness *the degree of togetherness between and among communicators*

synergy
the intersection of multiple perspectives in a small group

networks
communication patterns through which information flows

roles
positions of group members and their relationship to the group

particular, many perspectives may be advantageous. This exchange of multiple perspectives results in **synergy,** and explains why small groups may be more effective than an individual at achieving goals.

Networking and role behavior are two important components of small group behavior. **Networks** are communication patterns through which information flows, and networks in small groups answer the following question: Who speaks to whom and in what order? The patterns of interaction in small groups may vary significantly. For instance, in some groups the leader may be included in all deliberations, whereas in other groups, members may speak to one another without the leader. The small group context is made up of individuals who take on various **roles,** or the positions of group members and their relationship to the group. These roles may be very diverse, including task leader, passive observer, active listener, recorder, and so forth.

Before we close our discussion of small groups, we should point out that as with the interpersonal communication context, research on small groups spans a variety of areas. Team and small group communication scholars have studied meeting management (Rogelberg, Rhoades-Shanock, & Scott, 2012), emotional intelligence (Tajeddin, Safayeni, Connelly, & Tasa, 2012), gossip in public school classrooms (Jaworski & Coupland, 2005), conflict (Gross, Guerrero, & Alberts, 2004), creativity (Martins & Shalley, 2011), and cultural diversity (Zhang & Huai, 2016). Much theory and research today continues to underscore the fact that groups exist to meet certain needs (Adams & Galanes, 2015).

Working in small groups seems to be a fact of life in society. At times, it may seem as if we cannot go anywhere without some sort of small group forming. From peer groups to task groups to support groups, the small group experience is a ubiquitous one. Very few students can receive their degree without working in small groups. From study groups to presentations, you may feel as if you are immersed in small group activities. Company supervisors relish team approaches to problem solving. Some families have weekly or monthly family meetings, at which the group discusses such issues as vacations, sibling rivalry, and curfew.

The United States will continue to rely on teams and small groups, even as we increase our reliance on technology. In fact, this technology has found its way into group experiences, namely in the form of telecommuting and web conferencing. Still, perhaps it's because we are students of communication or perhaps it's because we understand relational development in myriad ways, we feel that person-to-person contact will never go out of style. Computers may crash, email may freeze up, and cell phones may run out of charge, but people will continue to function and communicate in small groups.

Organizational Communication

organizational communication
communication within and among large, extended environments

It is important to distinguish between small group communication and organizational communication. **Organizational communication** pertains to communication within and among large, extended environments. This communication is extremely diverse in that organizational communication necessarily entails interpersonal encounters (supervisor–subordinate conversations), public speaking opportunities (presentations by company executives), small group situations (a task group preparing a report), and mediated experiences (internal memos, email, and videoconferencing).

Organizations, then, are groups of groups. Theories of organizational communication are generally concerned with the functionality of the organization, including its climate, rules, and personnel.

What distinguishes this context from others is that a clearly defined hierarchy exists in most organizations. **Hierarchy** is an organizing principle whereby things or persons are ranked one above the other. For an example of the hierarchy in many colleges and universities, see Figure 2.3. Does your school follow the same hierarchy? Katherine Miller (2015) points out that organizations are traditionally hierarchical in nature and that there are almost uniform ideas about structure, values, and division of labor. Organizations are unique in that much of the communication taking place is highly structured, and role playing is often specialized and predictable. Employees and employers alike are clear in their chain of command. Unlike in the interpersonal context, several modes of communication can substitute for face-to-face interaction, including email and teleconferencing.

The uniqueness of organizational communication is also represented by the research and theory conceptualized in this context. Many of the present-day organizational communication theories had their origins in a series of studies conducted in the mid-1920s to early 1930s. These studies, known as the **Hawthorne experiments,** were significant influences on modern theory in that they inaugurated the human relations approach to organizations (Jung & Lee, 2015). Researchers at the Western Electric Hawthorne plant in suburban Chicago were interested in determining the effect of lighting levels on employee productivity. Interestingly, results of this research

hierarchy
an organizing principle whereby things or people are ranked one above the other

Hawthorne experiments
a set of investigations that ushered in a human relations approach to organizations

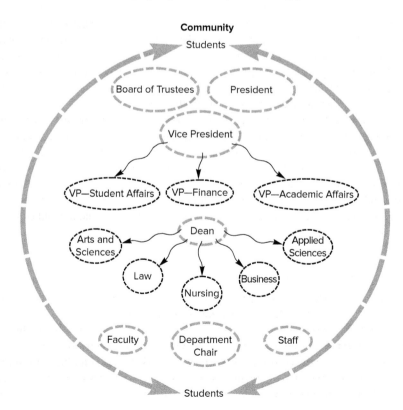

**Figure 2.3
Example of
Hierarchy in
Higher Education**

indicated that not only did the environmental conditions influence employee output, but so did the interpersonal relationships with other employees and supervisors. One conclusion arising from these studies was that organizations should be viewed as social entities; to speed up production, employers must consider workers' attitudes and feelings. These studies were among the first to put a human face on the impersonal corporate world (Roethlisberger & Dickson, 1939).

Although the human relations approach has enjoyed a great deal of theoretical and research attention, today there are a number of additional organizational orientations, including cultural systems and scientific management. Further, organizational (communication) theory and research today address various eclectic issues, including the *Challenger* disaster (Gouran, Hirokawa, & Martz, 1986), uncertainty on the job (Waldeck, Seibold, & Flanagin, 2004), whistle-blowing (Miceli, Near, Rehg, & Van Scotter, 2012), rumor (Berbary, 2012), job training (Waldron & Lavitt, 2000), sexual harassment (McDonald & Charlesworth, 2016), and workplace bullying (Akella, 2016). In addition, as with other contexts, the influence of ethnic and racial culture has also been examined (Jenkins & Dillon, 2012) within organizations.

What is important to glean from this discussion is that, like other contexts, the organizational context has a rich tradition. The Hawthorne studies of human behavior on the job have led today's researchers and theorists to expand their perspectives of organizations and organizational life.

Public/Rhetorical Communication

public communication
the dissemination of information from one person to many others (audience)

The fifth context is known as the **public communication** context, or the dissemination of information from one person to a large group. This is not a new context; speech presentations have existed since the beginning of time and continue today. Tony Robbins, Deepak Chopra, Suze Orman, Bill Gates, and Bono are just a few of the contemporary public figures who are in high demand as public speakers.

In public speaking, speakers usually have three primary goals in mind: to inform, to entertain, or to persuade. This latter goal—persuasion—is at the core of rhetorical communication. Many of the principles of persuasion—including audience analysis, speaker credibility, and verbal and nonverbal delivery of a message—are necessarily part of the persuasive process. As you reflect on your own public speaking experiences, you may be surprised to learn that in actuality you have been following rhetorical strategies rooted in early Greek and Roman days. How people have constructed their persuasive speeches has been the focus of study for more than 2,500 years.

rhetoric
a speaker's available means of persuasion

Effective public speakers owe their success to early rhetorical principles, a topic that we discussed earlier. For our purposes here, we define **rhetoric** as a speaker's available means of persuading his or her audience. This definition was advanced many years ago by Aristotle. Rhetoric has been described as an art that brings together speakers and audience (Hart, 1997). The study of rhetoric is expansive and can include the study of texts of speeches, presidential inaugural addresses, and rhetorical analyses of cultural themes and issues. Samples of rhetorical scholarship include analyses of the Spanish gay and lesbian youth on YouTube (Acevedo-Callejas, 2015), Sarah Palin's Facebook posts (Lawrence & Schafer, 2012), President Nixon's speech on Vietnam (Drury, 2016), and abolitionist Frederick Douglass (Selby, 2000). We will discuss rhetoric in much more detail in Chapter 18.

One area in the public/rhetorical context that has received significant scholarly attention is **communication apprehension** (CA), or the general sense of fear of speaking before an audience. Pioneering and valuable research undertaken by James McCroskey and Virginia Richmond, over the years, has been quite informative as the communication field tries to unpack the challenges of speech anxiety. You will recall that boundaries between and among the contexts are often blurred, and CA research is one example of that blurring. Although communication apprehension is a public speaking concern, CA focuses on intrapersonal issues. Furthermore, CA has been studied with a number of different populations, including student athletes (Stockstill & Roach, 2007), pharmacy undergraduates (Nayeem, Khan, & Mehta, 2015), employees (Russ, 2012), and those in romantic relationships (Theiss & Solomon, 2006), as well as across cultures (Hsu, 2004). In addition, researchers have advanced ways to reduce communication apprehension. Clearly, the public communication/ rhetorical context addresses the confluence of theory, research, and skills.

communication apprehension
a generalized fear or anxiety regarding communicating in front of others

Mass/Media Communication

The sixth context is the mass communication or mediated context, which targets large audiences. First, we need to define a few terms. **Mass media** refers to the channels, or delivery modes, for mass messages. Mass media include newspapers, videos, CD-ROMs, (tablet) computers, TV, radio, and so forth. **Mass communication** refers to communication to a large audience via one of these channels of communication. Although mass communication frequently refers to "traditional" venues (e.g., newspapers), we expand our discussion to include **new media,** which encompasses computer-related technology. This communication technology includes the Internet, including emailing, blogging, and texting the influence of social networking sites (Facebook and LinkedIn) on communication; cell phone usage; and high-definition (HD) television. For our purposes, we assert that mass communication pertains communication to a large audience via multiple channels of communication. The mass communication context, therefore, includes both the channel and the audience.

Like each of the preceding contexts, the mass communication context is distinctive. It allows both senders and receivers to exercise control. Sources such as a

mass media
channels or delivery modes for mass messages

mass communication
communication to a large audience via various channels (e.g., radio, Internet, television, etc.)

new media
computer-related technology

THINKING ABOUT THE FIELD: TRADITIONS AND CONTEXTS

newspaper editor or a television broadcaster make decisions about what information should be sent, and receivers have control over what they decide to read, listen to, watch, or review. Suppose, for instance, that you are an advertiser who has slotted an expensive television commercial featuring Venus and Serena Williams. You've paid the Williams sisters handsomely, and yet, to determine whether their endorsement has made a difference in sales, you have to wait for the numbers to come in. You have control over the choice of the endorsers, but the audience also simultaneously has control over what they watch and what they ultimately buy.

Some, like theorist Stuart Hall (see Chapter 25), suggest that mass media inherently serve the interests of the elite, especially big business and multinational corporations, who, Hall suggests, fund much of the research in mass communication. Many studies, however, are not underwritten by corporate sponsorship. They reflect the growing diversity of mass communication researchers and theorists. A myriad of topics using a mass media framework have been studied, including the portrayal of sex on prime-time television (Eyal & Finnerty, 2007), online dating sites (Kang & Hoffman, 2011), heroes in the movie *The Matrix* (Stroud, 2001), racist ideologies in *Orange is the New Black* (Enck & Morrissey, 2015), email (Turnage, 2007), grandparent personal websites (Harwood, 2000), and an analysis of *The Daily Show* and *The Colbert Report* (Hmielowski, Holbert, & Lee, 2011). As you can see, a wide array of research studies characterize the mass communication context.

As we write this, some of our comments may already be out of date. In fact, the rapidity of change may even render some of our technological references as obsolete! Mass communication quickly changes, and what was promised as a marvelous advance today is often considered outdated tomorrow (e.g., MySpace's value has dropped in billions, for example, because of the introduction of other sites and even Facebook and Twitter numbers have dropped among the very young because of a fear that their posts will have repercussions later in life). Because of the pervasiveness and availability of mass media in our society, media theorists will have to deal with the impact of media on the communication process itself. Some researchers (e.g., Turkle, 2015) suggest that computers help (re)define the way we conceive of ourselves. This redefinition may have an inevitable impact on the communication process. Furthermore, although a large number of homes and businesses subscribe to new technologies, a gap will always exist between those who have the resources and those who do not. Consequently, future mass communication theorists may have to rethink the universality of their theories.

Cultural Communication

The final communication context we wish to examine is cultural communication. To begin, we should define what we mean by *culture*. There are many definitions of *culture*. For our purposes, **culture** can be viewed as a "community of meaning and a shared body of local knowledge" (Gonzalez, & Chen, 2015, p. 5). **Cultural communication,** therefore, refers to communication between and among individuals whose cultural backgrounds vary. These individuals do not necessarily have to be from different countries. In a diverse country such as the United States, we can experience cultural communication variation within one state, one community, and even one block. It is not uncommon in many parts of this society, for instance, to see

culture
a community of meaning with, among other things, a shared body of knowledge

cultural communication
communication between and among individuals whose cultural backgrounds vary

two people from different cultural backgrounds speaking to each other. Urban centers, in particular, can be exciting cultural arenas where communication takes place between members of different co-cultures. **Co-cultures** are groups of individuals who are part of the same larger culture, but who—through unity and individual identification around such attributes as race, ethnicity, sexual identity, religion, and so forth—create opportunities of their own. The word, *co-culture,* is now widely accepted in the academic community as a replacement for *subculture,* a term suggesting that one culture has dominance over another culture.

co-cultures
groups of individuals who are part of the same larger culture, but who can be classified around various identities (e.g., race, sex, age, etc.)

Cultural communication is an historically important academic context, with its beginnings traced back only to the 1950s (Leeds-Hurwitz, 1990). However, much exciting work has been done since then. The growth of this area of study can be attributed to the growth across organizational cultures, with more U.S. companies doing business abroad. In addition, technological availability, population shifts, and genuine efforts to understand other cultures contribute to the growing interest and frequent conversations pertaining to this context. Some of these dialogues are still difficult, nearly 50 years after the signing of the Civil Rights Act. Some cultural events have helped jumpstart the 21st century cultural conversations (e.g., Senator Barack Obama becoming president), but these conversations are still fraught with challenges because not everyone becomes engaged with these dialogues.

The cultural context differentiates itself from other contexts in a few ways. First, as you may have determined, this context is the only context that specifically addresses culture. Although some contexts, such as the organizational context, comprise research on racial and ethnic cultures, this work is often ancillary, with culture being examined for its effects on the organization, for example. In the intercultural context, however, researchers and theorists purposely explore the interactions and events between and among people of different cultures. Second, study in the intercultural communication context means that researchers inherently accept the fact that human behavior is culturally based. In other words, culture structures how we perceive and how we act.

To give you an indication of the type of research and thinking taking place in the cultural communication context, consider the following research titles: "Connecting Community Voices: Using a Latino/a Critical Race Theory Lens on an Environmental Justice Advocacy" (Anguiano, Milstein, De Larkin, Chen, & Sandoval, 2012), "Native American Culture and Communication Through Humor" (Shutiva, 2015), "Discursive Negotiation of Family Identity: A Study of U.S. Families with Adopted Children from China" (Suter, 2008), "When Mississippi Chinese Talk," and "Growing up Together: The Internet, Cultural Knowledge, and Thai Names" (Korn, 2015).

Although this research derives from a number of different cultural perspectives, you should be aware that much of what we know and how we relate is a result of a Western model of thinking—that is, many of us interpret events and behaviors through a European (American) lens (Asante, 1987). Gonzalez and Chen (2015) state that when studying culture and communication, it's important to "invite *experience*" (p. 3) into the research arena. A great deal of intercultural communication theory and research embraces such an effort. This context is filled with opportunities to study areas that have not received a lot of attention in the past. Investigating culture and cultural groups holds continued promise as the United States grows more diverse.

Collating the Contexts

In discussing these seven contexts, we have provided you with a basic category system for dividing the broad field of communication. These seven categories help us discuss the communication process more clearly and specifically. Yet the template is not perfect, and as you have probably noted in our discussion, there is often overlap among the categories. For instance, when people belong to an online cancer support group, their communication has elements of at least four contexts: intrapersonal, interpersonal, small group, and mass communication. Thus, we caution you against viewing these categories as completely exclusive and distinctive from one another.

Finally, as alluded to earlier, technology similarly pervades each of these contexts and consequently, communication is affected. That is, one or more contexts are influenced by technology. For example, online dating sites are not always researched with a mediated lens; it is a topic that is also both intrapersonal (e.g., the personal decision to go online) as well as interpersonal (the communication between two people).

In fact, as you review these theories, you should be asking yourself whether any important questions can be asked about the impact of technology. And, despite the

---

Theory in Popular Press • Facebook Addiction Disorder

A web essay identifies something that scores of students of communication should understand but too often ignore: Facebook addiction. The article begins by acknowledging the fact that social networking sites (SNS) have value insofar as they provide connections to others, including friends, relatives, and colleagues. And, of all the SNS, Facebook is arguably the location where people have the most online activity. Yet, the essay also concludes that because Facebook has become such a huge hit, "people are actually suffering from what has been dubbed FAD, or Facebook Addiction Disorder." This addiction may seem trivial or even humorous, yet, the article provides both signs of addiction and tips to avoid the addiction. Signs that one has FAD include: (1) spending copious amounts of time on the site, (2) signs of anxiety and stress when restricted from using the site, (3) reduction of recreational activities, (4) substituting real dates for virtual dates, (5) establishing fake friends, and (6) realizing a complete addiction (e.g., pets have Facebook pages, require friends to contact you via Facebook, etc.). Ways to beat FAD include: (1) recognize a possible addiction, (2) set time aside away from browsing Facebook, (3) allocate times that are dedicated to Facebook only (brief times), and (4) be prepared to delete Facebook if the addiction becomes too powerful. Because "it is easy to get sucked in and spend hours on the site," the contents of this piece resonate to users (and nonusers) all across the globe.

Source: http://www.adweek.com/socialtimes/facebook-addiction-disorder-the-6-symptoms-of-f-a-d/61408. Retrieved February 20, 2016.

pervasiveness of technology in all of our lives, sometimes its influence is muted. As Nancy Baym (2012) and her colleagues suggest, legitimate reasons need to exist to justify the inclusion of technology and new media in research. They state that it's important for researchers and theorists to rationalize the need to study communication technology; explaining phenomena is much more important than exploring it.

Conclusion

This chapter provided you a framework to use as you try to understand the communication field. We began by exploring the seven established traditions of communication theory that are inclusive of the theories you're about to read in this book. These traditions include Rhetorical, Semiotic, Phenomenological, Cybernetic, Socio-Psychological, Socio-Cultural, and Critical. We next examined the primary contexts of communication: Intrapersonal, Interpersonal, Small Group, Organizational, Public/Rhetorical, Mass/Media, and Cultural. As various theories are introduced to you, you will see that many of them fall neatly in these divisions. Other theories will cut across traditions and contexts.

You should now be able to discern the uniqueness of the communication discipline. As you read the next chapter on theory building, you will begin to link the communication process with the theoretical process. These preliminary chapters offer important foundations to draw on as you encounter the theories presented later in the book.

Discussion Starters

TECH QUEST: We have cautioned against assuming that technology is always a relevant topic to examine as you learn about the various communication theories. First, discuss the challenges and pitfalls of placing too much attention on technology. Next, apply your responses to the various contexts that are outlined in this chapter.

1. Lee and Jenny Yamato's experiences fall across several of the contexts we identified in this chapter. Which of the contexts are in play in their story?

2. Which of the seven traditions in the communication field most appeals to you? Why?

3. Which context of communication most appeals to you? Why?

4. If you had to add another context of communication based on your experiences, what context would it be? How would you interpret the context for others? What examples illustrate the context?

5. How would you illustrate—with a picture—the overlap between and among the various communication traditions?

6. Explain how politics can influence each of the communication contexts.

7. Suppose you were asked to differentiate between a tradition and a context. What would guide your thinking in your response?

CHAPTER 3

Thinking About Theory and Research

There is nothing so practical as a good theory.
—Kurt Lewin

Rolanda Nash

Rolanda Nash hurried to class after work. She always seemed to be running late. Since she decided to divorce Anton and move from Sheridan, Wyoming, to Chicago things were confusing. After her relationship with Anton, she felt she would never trust another man again. Meanwhile, she had to complete six credits to graduate and keep the new job she had secured in Chicago. In addition to doing her schoolwork, Rolanda was working 30 hours a week for one of her professors, Dr. Stevens. Dr. Stevens was testing a theory called Communication Accommodation Theory that focused on how and when people made their own communication sound like their conversational partner's (a process of accommodation). According to the theory, when someone wants to get another's approval, there is a higher chance they'll mirror the other's talk. Dr. Stevens wanted to observe communication accommodation in an organizational setting. The professor sent Rolanda into two different organizations with a tape recorder to tape naturally occurring conversations between subordinates and managers.

It was very challenging for Rolanda to capture natural conversations. Although Stevens had obtained permission for her to record conversations in the organizations, some people recognized her and seemed to clam up when she appeared. In addition, neither of the two organizations employed many African Americans and Rolanda felt she stuck out as she walked through the hallways. But she was used to that. In most of her university classes she was the only African American woman. She was hoping Chicago would offer more diversity.

If she could get enough conversations to satisfy Dr. Stevens, she could go home to tackle her English assignment. Stevens hadn't really told her how many conversations she needed, but Rolanda was hoping 10 would be enough because that's all she had gotten in five days of taping. Dr. Stevens had mentioned last week that when Rolanda was finished taping, she would probably be sending her back to the organizations to do some follow-up interviews with the people she had taped. Rolanda wondered how that'll work out.

Rolanda is involved in theorizing and researching about complex communication interactions both in her work and in her personal life. Although not everyone does research for a living, often people wonder to themselves, or ask one another, How can we stop arguing so much? Why are we successful in communicating sometimes and not at other times? How can we be better communicators? Will social media unite us or divide us? We can provide answers to these kinds of questions with theory, because as Robert Craig and Heidi Muller (2007) observe, "[T]heorizing is a formalized extension of everyday sense-making and problem solving" (p. ix). Theories allow us to see how organizations (as well as individuals) handle crisis and communication (Liska, Petrun, Sellnow, & Seeger, 2012). Furthermore, when we make observations and compare them to theory, we're doing research. Theory and research are inextricably linked. Paul Reynolds (2015) points out that some researchers begin with theory (theory-then-research) whereas others begin with research (research-then-theory), but all researchers need to think about both theory and research.

In this book we are discussing theory and research as professionals use them in their work; yet all of us in daily life think like researchers, using implicit theories to help us understand those questions we mentioned previously. Fritz Heider (1958) referred to everyday interactors engaging in theoretical thinking as "naïve psychologists" or what we might call *implicit theorists.* Whenever we pose an answer to one of our questions (e.g., if we suggest that maybe we are really fighting over power and control and not what color to paint the living room), we are engaging in theoretical thinking.

Sometimes, an implicit theorist and a professional work in the same ways. First, as we have just mentioned, they are similar because both puzzle over questions encountered through observations and both seek answers for these questions. Both also set up certain criteria that define what an acceptable answer might be. For instance, when Ely wonders why his college roommate talks so much, he might decide on the following criteria for an answer: The answer has to apply to all communication contexts (online, face-to-face, and so forth); and the answer has to make sense (Ely wouldn't accept an answer stating that his roommate comes from another planet where talk is more highly valued than here on earth, for instance). When Ely (and social scientists) find answers that satisfy their criteria, they generalize from them and may apply them to other situations that are similar. If Ely concludes that his roommate is insecure and talks to cover up his insecurity, he may determine that others he meets who talk more than he does are also insecure. We will return to the notion of an implicit theorist a bit later in the chapter.

In all those processes, everyday communicators follow the basic outline advanced by social science. However, there are differences between them as well. Social scientists systematically test theories whereas nonscientists test selectively. Ely merely makes observations of people he knows, whereas a social scientist will try to observe some kind of systematic sample of the population. In addition, Ely will probably easily accept evidence that agrees with his theory about the relationship between insecurity and talking, and tend to ignore evidence that contradicts it. Researchers are more rigorous in their testing and are more willing to amend theories, incorporating information arising from inconsistencies to create a revised formulation of the theory.

In this chapter, we build on what you already know as an implicit theorist and prepare you for reading about the theories in the text by providing the following: (1) a definition of *theory* that maps the term onto intellectual traditions and explains how assumptions affect the process of theorizing, (2) a list of evaluative criteria for assessing a theory, and (3) a brief description of the research process.

Student Voices

Martina

When we first started talking about the "implicit theorist" idea, I thought it was kind of weird. I was pretty sure I wasn't a theorist, implicit or not! Then I started keeping track of how I was thinking like a theorist in my everyday life. It was amazing how many times I did make a theory and then tried to test it. It seemed like it happened a lot at work. When I was being considered for a promotion, I watched carefully to see what the "higher ups" in my office did and how they reacted to my work. I developed a "theory" that the men in positions of power needed to think of me as their daughter, but the women wanted me to perform as an equal. So, when I presented my work to the men, I was more deferential and asked them for advice. I never did that with the women. I decided my theory was correct when I got the promotion!

Defining Theory: What's in a Name?

theory
an abstract system of concepts and their relationships that help us to understand a phenomenon

Generally speaking, a **theory** is an abstract system of concepts with indications of the relationships among these concepts that help us to understand a phenomenon. Stephen Littlejohn and Karen Foss (2011) suggest this abstract system is derived through systematic observation. Donald Stacks and Michael Salwen (2014) suggest that theory "is like a map for exploring unexplored territories" (p. 4). Jonathan H. Turner (1986) defined *theory* as "a process of developing ideas that can allow us to explain how and why events occur" (p. 5). This definition focuses on the nature of theoretical thinking without specifying exactly what the outcome of this thinking might be. William Doherty and his colleagues (1993) have elaborated on Turner's definition by stating that theories are both process and product: "Theorizing is the process of systematically formulating and organizing ideas to understand a particular phenomenon. A theory is the set of interconnected ideas that emerge from this process" (p. 20). In this definition, the authors do not use Turner's word *explain* because the goals of theory can be more numerous than simply explanation, a point we explore later in this chapter.

In this brief discussion, you have probably noticed that different theorists approach the definition of *theory* somewhat differently. The search for a universally accepted definition of theory is a difficult, if not impossible, task. In part, the difficulty in defining theory is due to the many ways in which a theory can be classified or categorized. We'll refine our definition here by examining the components and goals of theories.

As you work toward understanding theory and the various theoretical perspectives in this book, understand that a "Eurocentric cultural bias" problem exists (Craig, 2013, p. 42). We need to frame our understanding of the current discussion with the belief that "communication research around the world has relied on Western theories and methods, and the global discourse on communication theory has been excessively one-sided" (Craig, p. 43). With this essential concern identified, we now turn our attention to defining theory via its components and various goals.

Components

To understand theory as a whole, we need to understand the component parts that make up theories. Theories are composed of several key parts, the two most important of which are called concepts and relationships. **Concepts** are words or terms that label the most important elements in a theory. Concepts in some of the theories we will discuss include *cohesiveness* (Groupthink), *dissonance* (Cognitive Dissonance Theory), *self* (Symbolic Interaction Theory), and *scene* (Dramatism). As you can see, sometimes theories are named using one of their key concepts, although this is not always the case.

A concept often has a specific definition that is unique to its use in a theory, which differs from how we would define the word in everyday conversation. For example, the concept "cultivation" used in Cultivation Analysis (see Chapter 24) refers specifically to the way media, especially television, create a picture of social reality in the minds of media consumers. This use of the term differs from using it to mean hoeing your garden or developing an interest, skill, or friendship. It is always the task of the theorist to provide a clear definition of the concepts used in the theory.

Concepts may be nominal or real. **Nominal concepts** are those that are not observable, such as democracy or love. **Real concepts** are observable, such as text messages or spatial distance. As we'll discuss later in the chapter, when researchers use theory in their studies, they must turn all the concepts into something concrete so that they can be observed. It is much easier to do this for real concepts than for nominal ones.

Relationships specify the ways in which the concepts in the theory are combined. For example, in Chapter 1 we presented three different models of the process

concepts
labels for the most important elements in a theory

nominal concepts
concepts that are not directly observable

real concepts
concepts that are directly observable

relationships
the ways in which the concepts of a theory relate to one another

www.CartoonStock.com

"I'm between theories right now. I'm very vulnerable."

of communication. In each model, the concepts are very similar. What is different is the relationship specified among them. In the first model, the relationship is a linear one where one concept relates to the second, which then relates to the next, and so forth. In the second model, the posited relationship is interactive, or two-way. The third model illustrates mutual influence (transaction), where all the concepts are seen as affecting one another simultaneously.

Goals

We can also clarify the definition of theory by understanding its purposes. In a broad sense, the goals of theory can include explanation, understanding, prediction, and social change; we are able to *explain* something (why Rolanda and Anton's marriage ended, for example) because of the concepts and their relationships specified in a theory. We are able to *understand* something (Rolanda's distrust of men) because of theoretical thinking. In addition, we are able to *predict* something (how Rolanda will respond to other men she meets) based on the patterns suggested by a theory. Finally, we are able to effect *social change* or empowerment (altering the institution of marriage so that it more completely empowers both partners, for example) through theoretical inquiry.

Although some theories try to reach all these goals, most feature one goal over the others. Rhetorical theories, some media theories, and many interpersonal theories seek primarily to provide explanation or understanding. Others (e.g., traditional persuasion and organizational theories) focus on prediction. Still others (e.g., some feminist and other critical theories) have as their central goal to change the structures of society. This means effecting social change, not simply improving individual lives. To understand the difference, think about a theory of conflict management that may help people understand how to engage in conflict more productively, thus enriching their lives. Yet, it may do nothing to change the underlying structures that promoted the conflict in the first place.

In the previous discussion, we suggest that theories act as lenses to help researchers interpret concrete experiences and observations. Janet Yerby (1995) refers to theories as "the stories we have developed to explain our view of reality" (p. 362). This line of thinking prompts us to ask what motivates a scholar to choose one theory (or lens) over another in their work. The answer to this question comes from an examination of the "approaches to knowing" that scholars bring to their work before they begin to do research.

Approaches to Knowing: How Do You See (and Talk About) the World?

Scholars (e.g., Treadwell, 2016; White & Klein, 2008; Zhou & Sloan, 2015) have discussed how researchers think and talk about the world. Most of these scholars have identified three general approaches: positivistic or empirical, interpretive, and critical. We will discuss each of these below, but remember because we wish for you to have a comprehensive understanding of each, we're presenting each approach in detail. Most researchers, however, do not subscribe to all the details we present (Stacks & Salwen, 2014).

The Positivistic, or Empirical, Approach

The **positivistic,** or **empirical, approach** assumes that objective truths can be uncovered and that the process of inquiry that discovers these truths can be, at least in part, value-neutral. This tradition advocates the methods of the natural sciences, with the goal of constructing general laws governing human interactions. An empirical researcher strives to be objective and works for **control,** or direction over the important concepts in the theory. In other words, when the researcher makes observations, he or she carefully structures the situation so that only one element varies. This enables the researcher to make relatively definitive statements about that element. As Leslie Baxter and Dawn Braithwaite (2008) observe, the researcher's task in the empirical approach is "to deduce testable hypotheses from a theory" (p. 7). In other words, the positivistic approach moves along the theory-then-research model to which Reynolds (2015) referred. Graham Bodie and Susanne Jones (2012) illustrate this process because they conducted an empirical study to test which one of three different theoretical models of supportive communication best explains their results.

positivistic/ empirical approach *an approach assuming the existence of objective reality and value-neutral research*

control *direction over the important concepts in a theory*

The Interpretive Approach

The **interpretive approach** views truth as subjective and co-created by the participants, with the researcher clearly being one of the participants. There is less emphasis on objectivity in this approach than in the empirical approach because complete objectivity is seen as impossible. However, this does not mean that research in this approach has to rely totally on what participants say with no outside judgment by the researcher. The interpretive researcher believes that values are relevant in the study of communication and that researchers need to be aware of their own values and to state them clearly for readers, because values will naturally permeate the research. These researchers are not concerned with control and the ability to generalize across many people as much as they are interested in rich descriptions about the people they study. This emphasis on rich description leads interpretive researchers to put a lot of focus on the voices of their participants and quote their comments extensively (deSousa, 2011). For interpretive researchers, theory is best induced from the observations and experiences the researcher shares with and/or hears from the respondents. We should note that many positivistic scholars have acknowledged the importance of being value-free in their thinking. Yet, most will acknowledge that the communication researcher can influence the study in many (unintended) ways. This is usually referred to as *post*-positivism.

interpretive approach *an approach viewing truth as subjective and stressing the participation of the researcher in the research process*

The Critical Approach

In the **critical approach,** an understanding of knowledge relates to power. Critical researchers believe that those in power shape knowledge in ways that perpetuate the status quo. Thus, powerful people work at keeping themselves in power, while silencing minority voices questioning the distribution of power and the power holders' version of truth. Feminists and Marxists, among others, work from this intellectual tradition. For critical researchers, it's important to change the status quo to resolve power imbalances and give voice to those silenced by the power structure. Kent Ono (2011) observes that critical theory "often emerges out of the everyday life experiences of women, people of color, and members of LGBTQ communities"

critical approach *an approach stressing the researcher's responsibility to change the inequities in the status quo*

THINKING ABOUT THEORY AND RESEARCH

Table 3.1 Three Approaches to Knowing

	EMPIRICAL	INTERPRETIVE	CRITICAL
Goal	Explanation of world	Probe the relativism of world	Change the world
Engagement of researcher	Separate	Involved	Involved
Application of theory	To generalize about many like cases	To illuminate the individual case	To critique a specific set of cases

(p. 9). Claudia Anguiano and her colleagues (Anguiano, Milstein, De Larkin, Chen, & Sandoval, 2012) provide a concrete example of Ono's statement. They examined environmental inequity using Latino/a Critical Race Theory. They wished to promote Hispanic activism around environmental justice issues, and sought, with their research "to translate theoretical knowledge into practical strategies for better policymaking" (p. 137).

Some critical theorists, notably Stuart Hall (1981), whose work we feature in Chapter 25, have commented that power imbalances may not always be the result of intentional strategies on the part of the powerful. Rather, ideology, or "those images, concepts, and premises which provide the frameworks through which we represent, interpret, understand and 'make sense' of some aspect of social existence" (Hall, 1981, p. 31), is often "produced and reproduced" accidentally. For example, this may come about when certain images of masculinity work to sell a product. When advertisers observe this success, they continue creating ads with these images. In this fashion, the images of masculinity become entrenched in society. Thus, although the powerful are interested and invested in staying in power, they may not be fully aware of what they do to silence minority voices. To have a visual understanding of the three approaches, look at Table 3.1.

Approaches to Knowing: What Questions Do You Ask About the World?

ontology
a branch of knowledge focused on the nature of reality

epistemology
a branch of knowledge focused on how we know things

axiology
a branch of knowledge focused on what is worth knowing

Each of the three approaches to knowing provides different answers to questions about the nature of reality (researchers call this **ontology**), questions about how we know things (known as **epistemology),** and questions about what is worth knowing (or what researchers call **axiology**). We'll briefly address each of these terms and suggest how the three approaches to knowing treat them differently.

Ontology is the study of being and nonbeing, or in other words, the study of reality. The word *ontology* comes from the Greek language and means the science of being or the general principles of being. Pat Arneson (2009c) states that ontology is "the study of what it means to be human, which shapes the background understanding for theorizing about human communication" (p. 697). This definition focuses on the idea that ontology gives us a certain vision of the world and on what constitutes its important features. It is called the first philosophy because it is not possible to philosophize until the nature of reality is determined. Often questions of ontology cluster around how much free will people have. Researchers who see the world from an empirical approach believe that general laws govern human interactions. Thus they also believe that people don't have a lot of free choice in what they do—people are predictable because they follow the laws of human behavior which, to a large extent, determine their actions. A researcher's job is to *uncover* what is already out there in reality. This differs from researchers with an interpretive bent, who would allow that people do have free choice, and see a researcher's job as to co-create reality with research participants. Finally, critical researchers see both choice and constraint in the power structures they wish to change.

The questions surrounding epistemology focus on how we go about knowing; what counts as knowledge is intimately related to ontology. Epistemology looks at "nature, scope, and limits of human knowledge" (Arneson, 2009b, p. 350). How researchers see the world, truth, and human nature necessarily influences how they believe they should try to learn about these things. The approach (positivistic, interpretive, or critical) Dr. Stevens took in our opening example would affect her way of collecting information, an epistemologic choice. For instance, if Dr. Stevens researched as a positivist, she would institute many more controls than we described in our opening case study. Furthermore, the number of observations would not be left to chance or to Rolanda's schedule. Dr. Stevens would have calculated the number of conversations she needed to support the statistics she'd use to test relationships among status and communication accommodation. If Dr. Stevens operated in the interpretive tradition, she would not be content with her own analysis of the conversations. She might invite the participants to read the transcripts of their conversations so that they could tell her whether they were trying to accommodate to their partners. Stevens would probably be interested in the participants' explanations for why they changed (or did not change) their speech patterns as they conversed with superiors or subordinates in the workplace. Using a critical approach, Dr. Stevens might bring some of the following questions to her research: How is the relationship between workers of differing statuses communicatively constructed? Does convergence happen unequally based on status? Are there status differences other than occupation that impact communication accommodation? How can we change the prevailing power structures to improve the inequities we observe in the workplace?

The final set of questions focuses on the place of values in theory and research. The empirical position on axiology is that science must be value free. However, most researchers do not take this extreme position and accept that some subjectivity, in the form of values, informs the research process (Merrigan & Huston, 2014). Research and theory-building are indeed, axiological efforts in that the very topic selection and the approach to studying that topic are usually value-laden undertakings. The question is not *whether* values should permeate theory and research but *how* they should.

Here we briefly present three positions on this debate that correspond to the three ways of knowing: avoiding values as much as possible in research (empirical), recognizing how values influence the entire research process (interpretative), and advocating that values should be closely intertwined with scholarly work (critical). The first stance argues that the research process consists of many stages and that values should inform some of these stages, but not others. For example, the part of the research enterprise

Table 3.2 Answers Supplied by the Three Approaches to Knowing

	EMPIRICAL	INTERPRETIVE	CRITICAL
Ontology	No free choice	Free choice	Choice restrained by power
Epistemology	Theory first. Control study	Research first. Co-create study	Critique power. Seek change
Axiology	Reduce role of values	Acknowledge values	Celebrate values

that focuses on theory choice must be informed by the values of the researcher. Scholars choose to view a research problem through the lens that they believe most accurately describes the world. Thus, some researchers choose theoretical frameworks that are consistent with an ontology of free choice, whereas others choose frameworks that are more "lawlike" and deterministic. Yet, when they test these theories (the verification stage), they must eliminate "extra-scientific values from scientific activity" (Popper, 1976, p. 97). As you can see, this stance proposes a very limited role for values.

The second position argues that it is not possible to eliminate values from any part of theorizing and research. In fact, some values are so embedded in researchers' culture that researchers are unconscious that they even hold them. Sandra Bem (1993), for instance, observes that much of the research on differences between women and men was influenced by biases existing at the time. Many feminist scholars argue that social science itself suffers from a male bias (Harding, 1987). Some scholars examining African American issues make the same observations about the European American biases that exist in much social scientific research (Dixon, 2015). Thomas Nakayama and Robert Krizek (1995) point out that communication researchers often take White for granted as the default race. Thus, the values and assumptions held by those with a European American perspective are never highlighted, questioned, or acknowledged; they simply inform a scholar's process (Gunaratne, 2010). Yoshitaka Miike (2007) takes this one step further to advocate using Asiacentric (meaning rooted in Asian thinking) theories rather than Eurocentric ones.

The final position argues that not only are values unavoidable, but they are desirable in research. Earlier in this chapter we mentioned social change as one goal of theory. Those who embrace this goal are called critical theorists. Critical theorists advocate seeing theory and research as political acts that call on scholars to change the status quo. Thus, scholars must contribute to changing conditions rather than simply reporting conditions (Table 3.2).

Approaches to Knowing: How Do We Go About Theory Building?

When researchers seek to create theory, they are guided by all of the issues we've just discussed: their general approach to knowing things (empirical, interpretive, or critical) and the answers to questions about truth or reality, gathering information, and values (ontology, epistemology, and axiology). In addition, they have some guidelines about how to create theory. We will review three traditional guidelines: covering law, rules, and systems. The covering law approach and the rules approach represent two extremes, whereas the systems approach provides an intermediate position between the extremes. Again, we caution that few scholars take the extreme positions sketched out here. Rather, these positions form benchmarks from which researchers anchor their own stances on questions of communication.

The **covering law approach** seeks to explain an event in the real world by referring to a general law. Researchers applying a covering law approach believe that communication behavior is governed by forces that are predictable and generalizable. The **rules approach,** at the other end of the ontological continuum, holds that communication behavior is rule governed, not lawlike. The rules approach differs from the covering law approach in that researchers holding the rules approach admit the possibility that people are free to change their minds, to behave irrationally, to have idiosyncratic meanings for behaviors, and to change the rules. Ultimately, their differences focus on the concept of choice. The covering law model explains human choices by seeking a prior condition (usually a **cause**) that determines the choice that is made (usually an **effect**). From the rules model, rule following results from a choice made by the follower, but does not necessarily involve antecedent conditions or any aspect of the cause–effect logic of the covering law approach.

A third view, the **systems approach,** subscribes somewhat to the beliefs of the rules approach while also suggesting that people's free will may be constrained by the system in which they operate. Further, this approach acknowledges the impossibility of achieving what the covering law approach requires: laws about human communication that are invariant and general. The systems approach proposes assumptions that are more easily met than those of the covering law approach (Monge, 1973). We now examine each of the three approaches in more detail and provide an overview in Table 3.3.

covering law approach
a guideline for creating theory suggesting that theories conform to a general law that is universal and invariant

rules approach
a guideline for creating theory that builds human choice into explanations

cause
an antecedent condition that determines an effect

effect
a condition that inevitably follows a causative condition

systems approach
a guideline for creating theory that acknowledges human choice and the constraints of the systems involved

Table 3.3 Guidelines to Communication Theory Construction

APPROACH	DESCRIPTION/EXAMPLE
Covering Law	Covering law theorists hold that there are fixed relationships between two or more events or objects. Example: Whenever Linda speaks, Bob interrupts her; this is a lawlike statement that expresses a relationship between Linda and Bob. These statements are commonly referred to as if-then statements.
Rules	Rules theorists contend that much of human behavior is a result of free choice. People pick the social rules that govern their interactions. Example: In an interaction between co-workers, much of their conversation will be guided by rules of politeness, turn taking, and so on.
Systems	Systems theorists hold that human behavior is part of a system. Example: Think of a family as a system of family relationships rather than individual members. This illuminates the complexity of communication patterns within the family and the family's relationship to society at large.

Covering Law Approach

This term was first introduced by William Dray (1957), a historian who defined *covering law* as that "explanation is achieved, and only achieved, by *subsuming what is to be explained under a general law*" (p. 1 [emphasis in original]). Some covering law explanations refer to universal laws that state all *x* is *y*. These laws are not restricted by time or space. However, as new information comes to light, even laws have to be modified. Covering law explanations do not always have to be cause and effect. They may also specify relationships of coexistence. We have a causal relationship when we say that self-disclosures by one person cause self-disclosures from a relational partner. A claim of coexistence merely asserts that two things go together—that is, when one person self-discloses, the other does, too—but it does not claim that the first self-disclosure causes the second. It's possible that social norms of reciprocity cause the second self-disclosure or that both disclosures are caused by the environment (an intimate, dimly lit bar or consuming more alcohol than usual).

hypotheses
testable predictions of relationships between concepts that follow the general predictions made by a theory

Critical attributes of covering law explanations are that they provide an explicit statement of a boundary condition and that they allow **hypotheses,** testable predictions of relationships, of varying levels of specificity, to be generated within this boundary condition. Furthermore, because the system is deductive, complete confirmation of theories is never possible. There will always be unexamined instances of the hypothesis.

The type of covering law that we have just described is considered outdated by most social scientists (Bostrom, 2004). Most researchers today recognize that this type of universal law is unrealistic. Instead, researchers might strive for "probabilistic laws," or statements we can predict with a certain degree of probability. For example, as Berger (1977) asserts, "We can predict with a certain probability that if males and females with certain eye colors have large numbers of children, a certain proportion of those children will have a certain eye color. However, we are *not* in a position to predict what the eye color of a *particular* child will be" (p. 10).

Overall, a covering law approach instructs researchers to search for lawlike generalizations and regularities in human communication. These lawlike generalizations may be culturally bound or may have some other complex relationship with culture. Covering law offers a theory-generating option that aims for complete explanation of a phenomenon. The law, in effect, governs the relationships among phenomena.

Rules Approach

This approach assumes that people are typically engaged in intentional, goal-directed behavior and are capable of acting rather than simply being acted upon. We can be restricted by previous choices we have made, by the choices of others, and by cultural and social conditions, but we are conscious and active choice makers. Further, human behavior can be classified into two categories: activities that are stimulus–response behaviors (termed **movements**) and activities that are intentional choice responses (termed **actions**) (Cushman & Pearce, 1977). Rules theorists contend that studying actions is most relevant to theorists.

movements
activities based on stimulus response

actions
activities based on intentional choice responses

Rules theorists look inside communities or cultures to get a sense of how people regulate their interaction with others (Shimanoff, 1980). Rules do not require people to act in a certain way; rather, rules refer to the standards or criteria that people use

Table 3.4 Rules Governing Initial Peer Encounters

In the first fifteen minutes of an encounter:	In the second fifteen minutes:
Politeness should be observed.	Politeness should be observed.
Demographics should be exchanged.	Likes and dislikes can be discussed.
Partners should speak in rough equivalence to each other.	One partner can speak more than another, but avoid dominance.
Interruptions and talk-overs should be minimal.	More interruptions can be tolerated, but avoid dominance.

when acting in a particular setting (Cushman & Cahn, 1985). For example, when two people meet, they normally do not begin at an intimate level of exchange. Rather, there is an agreed-upon starting point, and they will delve further into intimacy if the two see the relationship as having a future. The process of meeting another is guided by rules, although these rules are rarely verbally identified by either person. Don Cushman and Barnett Pearce (1977) believed that if the relationship evolves, the rules guiding interactions change. Rules, then, are important benchmarks for the direction of an interaction. Table 3.4 illustrates how rules guide initial encounters of peers in the United States.

Several researchers (Lull, 1982; Van den Bulck, Custers, & Nelissen, 2016; Wolf, Meyer, & White, 1982) have used a rules-based theoretical framework to study media and family television-viewing behaviors. James Lull (1982) identified three types of rules that govern family television watching. First are **habitual rules,** which are nonnegotiable and are usually instituted by the authority figures in the family. When Roger and Marie tell their children that there can be no television until all homework is checked over by one of them and declared finished for the night, they are establishing a habitual rule.

Parametric rules are also established by family authority figures, but they are more negotiable than habitual rules. For example, the Marsh family may have a rule that members can engage in extended talk only during commercial breaks when they are viewing television. Yet, if something exciting has happened to one member, they may negotiate to talk about it during the program itself.

Finally, Lull identified **tactical rules,** or rules that are understood as a means for achieving a personal or interpersonal goal, but are unstated. For example, if Rob and Jeremy are watching television together and Rob likes Jeremy, he may tune in to Jeremy's favorite show even though he himself would not have chosen that program. He follows the tactical rule of maintaining relational harmony with his partner.

Overall, a rules approach instructs researchers to discover the rules that govern particular communication contexts and construct theoretical statements around these rules. The rules perspective offers a theory-generating option that aims for a satisfying explanation of a specific communication situation. The theorist would normally begin with a typology of the rules that govern the situation and move from those to statements connecting the rules and specifying the conditions affecting the rules.

habitual rules
nonnegotiable rules that are usually created by an authority figure

parametric rules
rules that are set by an authority figure but are subject to some negotiation

tactical rules
unstated rules used to achieve a personal or interpersonal goal

Systems Approach

Systems thinking in communication is derived from General Systems Theory (GST), which is both a theory of systems in general—"from thermostats to missile guidance

THINKING ABOUT THEORY AND RESEARCH

computers, from amoebas to families" (Whitchurch & Constantine, 1993, p. 325)—and a program of theory construction. Systems thinking captured the attention of communication researchers because it changed the focus from the individual to an entire family, a small group, or an organization. This shift reconceptualized communication for scholars and helped them to think innovatively about experience and interaction in groups. Further, systems thinking replaced the stringent assumptions of covering law with more realistic ones. Systems theorists (Monge, 1973; Stroh, 2015) agreed with the rules assertion that "human communication is not characterized by universal patterns" (p. 9). Systems thinking requires systemic, nonuniversal generalizations, does not depend on inductive reasoning, separates the logical from the empirical, allows alternative explanations for the same phenomenon, and permits partial explanations (Monge, 1973).

Systems thinking rests on several properties, including wholeness, interdependence, hierarchy, boundaries, calibration/feedback, and equifinality. We will explain each of these properties briefly.

wholeness
a fundamental property of systems theory stating that systems are more than the sum of their individual parts

Wholeness   The most fundamental concept of the systems approach is **wholeness**. It states that a system can't be fully comprehended by a study of its individual parts in isolation from one another. To understand the system, it must be seen as a whole. Wholeness suggests that we learn more about a couple, for example, by analyzing their interactions together than we do by analyzing one partner's motivations or statements alone.

interdependence
a property of systems theory stating that the elements of a system affect one another

Interdependence   Because the elements of a system are interrelated, they exhibit **interdependence**. This means that the behaviors of system members co-construct the system, and all members are affected by shifts and changes in the system. Virginia Satir (1988) compares the family to a mobile to illustrate how this principle applies to families. We might expect that when elderly parents decide to sell the family home and move to a small condo, their decisions will affect all of their children.

subsystems
smaller systems that are embedded in larger ones

suprasystems
larger systems that hold smaller ones within them

Hierarchy   All systems have levels, or **subsystems**, and all systems are embedded in other systems, or **suprasystems**. Thus, systems are a **hierarchy**, a complex organization. Each of the subsystems can function independently of the whole system, but each is an integral part of the whole. Subsystems generally shift and change over time, but they may potentially become extremely close and turn into alliances or coalitions that exclude others. For example, if one parent confides a great deal in a son whereas the other talks to one of their daughters, two coalitions may form in the family, making interactions more strained and troubled. This property is mapped in Figure 3.1.

hierarchy
a property of systems theory stating that systems consist of multiple levels

boundaries
a property of systems theory stating that systems construct structures specifying their outer limits

Boundaries   Implicit in the preceding discussion about hierarchy and complexity is the notion that systems develop **boundaries** around themselves and the subsystems they contain. Because human systems are open systems (it is not possible to completely control everything that comes into or goes out from them), these boundaries are relatively permeable: They have **openness**. Thus, although the managers of a General Motors plant in Ohio may wish that their employees did not know about the strike at a General Motors plant in Michigan, they will be unable to prevent information and communication from passing through the boundary around their organizational system. And, it's fair to say that technology usually influences the boundaries in any human system.

openness
the acknowledgment that within all human systems the boundaries are permeable

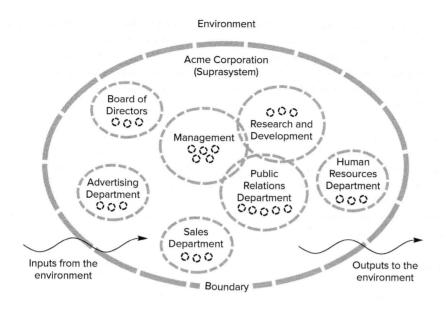

Environment

Figure 3.1
**Suprasystems,
Systems, and
Subsystems in the
Acme Corporation**

Calibration/Feedback All systems need stability and constancy within a defined range (Watzlawick, Beavin, and Jackson, 1967). **Calibration,** or checking the scale, and subsequent **feedback** to change or stabilize the system, allow for control of the range. The thermostat provides a common example illustrating this process. Home heating is usually set at a certain temperature, say 65 degrees. The thermostat will allow a temperature range around 65 before changing anything. Therefore, if the thermostat is set for 65 and the temperature is 65 plus or minus 3 degrees, nothing happens. If the temperature drops below 62 degrees, the heat goes on; if it rises above 68 degrees, the furnace shuts off. In this way, the heating system remains stable. However, if conditions change in the house (e.g., the family insulates the attic), the thermostat may need to be recalibrated or set at a slightly lower temperature to accommodate the change. After insulating, the house may feel comfortable if the temperature is set at 63 degrees.

Changing the standard (moving the temperature from 65 to 63 degrees) is accomplished through feedback. Feedback, in systems thinking, is positive when it produces change (the thermostat is set differently) and negative when it maintains the status quo (the thermostat remains at 65). When systems change they are called **morphogenic,** and when they stay the same they are called **homeostatic.**

Equifinality Open systems are characterized by the ability to achieve the same goals through different means, or **equifinality** (von Bertalanffy, 1968). This principle applies to human groups in two ways. First, a single group can achieve a goal through many different routes. For example, if a manager wants to increase productivity, he can raise wages, threaten the workers with firing, hire a consultant, or do some combination of these. There are several ways the manager can reach the goal. Additionally, equifinality implies that different groups can achieve the same goal through multiple pathways. For instance, PK Computer Systems may achieve

calibration
a property of systems theory stating that systems periodically check the scale of allowable behaviors and reset the system

feedback
a subprocess of calibration; information allowing for change in the system

morphogenic
a process that occurs when a system recalibrates (or changes)

homeostatic
a term for a stable system that isn't changing

equifinality
a property of systems theory stating that systems can achieve the same goals through different means

profitability by adopting a casual organizational culture, whereas Western Communication Systems may achieve profitability by demanding a more formal workplace.

Overall, a systems approach instructs researchers to search for holistic explanations for communication behavior. Systems thinking offers a theory-generating option that aims to model the phenomenon as a whole, admitting the possibility for change from a variety of outside influences.

Evaluating Theory

As you read the communication theories in the text, you'll need some standards for judging their value, worth, and effectiveness. Communication theory should not be viewed as "good" versus "bad" (Dainton & Zelley, 2014). All theories have unique strengths and shortcomings, therefore, we should not dismiss or embrace any theory without understanding all of its various parts. The following criteria are generally accepted as useful measures for evaluating communication theory: scope, logical consistency, parsimony, utility, testability, heurism, and the test of time. We will discuss each of them briefly.

scope
a criterion for evaluating theories; refers to the breadth of communication behaviors covered in the theory

Scope **Scope** refers to the breadth of communication behaviors covered by a theory. It is somewhat similar to the level of generality notion we discussed earlier. Boundaries are the limits of a theory's scope. Although theories should explain enough of communication to be meaningful, they should also have clear boundaries specifying their limits. The scope of some theories may change over time. Uncertainty Reduction Theory (URT), for example, which we discuss in Chapter 8, originally was bounded by initial encounters between strangers. In some ways this suggests a rather limited scope for the theory. However, although the duration of initial encounters is short, it is true that people spend a great deal of time throughout their lives meeting and conversing with new people. Thus, the scope of the theory may seem a bit broader upon reflection.

logical consistency
a criterion for evaluating theories; refers to the internal logic in the theoretical statements

Logical Consistency Simply put, theories should make sense and have an internal logical consistency so they are clear and not contradictory. The claims made by the theory should be consistent with the assumptions of the theory. **Logical consistency** means that the theory "hangs together" and doesn't contradict itself, either by advancing two propositions that are *in* conflict with each other or by failing to operate within the parameters of its assumptions.

parsimony
a criterion for evaluating theories; refers to the simplicity of the explanation provided by the theory

Parsimony **Parsimony** refers to the simplicity of the explanation provided by the theory. Theories should contain only the number of concepts necessary to explain the phenomenon under consideration. If a theory can explain a person's communication behavior satisfactorily by using one concept (such as expectancy violations), that is more useful than having to use many concepts. However, because theories of communication and social behavior are dealing with complex phenomena, they may have to be complex themselves. Parsimony requires simplicity without sacrificing completeness.

utility
a criterion for evaluating theories; refers to the theory's usefulness or practical value

Utility This criterion refers to the theory's usefulness, or practical value. A good theory has **utility** when it tells us a great deal about communication and human behavior. It allows us to understand some element of communication that was previously unclear. It weaves together pieces of information in such a way that we are able to see a pattern that was previously unseen. To a large extent, the utility criterion asks the following question: "Can real-world applications be found?"

Testability   **Testability** refers to our ability to investigate a theory's accuracy. One of the biggest issues involved in testability concerns the specificity of the theory's central concepts. For example, as we discuss in Chapter 9, Social Exchange Theory is predicated on the concepts of costs and rewards. The theory predicts that people will engage in behaviors that they find rewarding and avoid behaviors that are costly. However, the theory defines costs and rewards in a circular fashion: Behaviors that people engage in repeatedly are rewarding, and those that they avoid are costly. You can see how difficult it is to test the central prediction of Social Exchange Theory given this circular definition.

testability
a criterion for evaluating theories; refers to our ability to test the accuracy of a theory's claims

Heurism   **Heurism** refers to the amount of research and new thinking that is stimulated by the theory. Theories are judged to be good to the extent that they generate insights and new research. Although not all theories produce a great deal of research, an effective theory prompts some research activity. For example, the theory we discuss in Chapter 25, Cultural Studies, came from many diverse disciplines and has stimulated research programs in English, anthropology, social psychology, and communication.

heurism
a criterion for evaluating theories; refers to the amount of research and new thinking stimulated by the theory

Test of Time   The final criterion, the **test of time**, can be used only after some time has passed since the theory's creation. Is the theory still generating research or has it been discarded as outmoded? Deciding whether a theory has withstood the test of time is often arbitrary. For instance, if a theory was conceptualized and tested in the 1970s, but has remained dormant in the literature for over a decade and is now being reintegrated into research, has this theory satisfied the test of time? Judging this criterion is often a subjective process. Furthermore, it is not a criterion that can be used to assess a new theory (see Table 3.5 for a review of each of the seven criteria just discussed).

test of time
a criterion for evaluating theories; refers to the theory's durability over time

These criteria have been general standards for evaluating theories for some time, but our changing communication environment may require us to add to or revise this list.

Student Voices

Ray

Before reading this chapter, I never thought that I could evaluate theory. It just seemed like theory was a given. It's interesting to think about some theories being better or worse than others. I guess that's why researchers argue. It's not exactly about the facts—those are probably not all that different—but it's about whose theory is a better explanation of those facts. It helps to have some criteria to use in evaluating theory. But I bet that even with those criteria, researchers with different paradigms will disagree. It's just hard to see things the same way if one person thinks there's absolute truth out there and another thinks that everyone has his or her own truth.

Table 3.5 Criteria for Evaluating Communication Theories

CRITERIA	QUESTIONS TO CONSIDER
Scope	What are the boundaries of the theory's explanation?
Logical consistency	Do the claims of the theory match its assumptions? Do the principles of the theory contradict each other?
Parsimony	Is the theory as simple as it can be to explain the phenomenon under consideration?
Utility	Is the theory useful or practical?
Testability	Can the theory be shown to be false?
Heurism	Has the theory been used in research extensively to stimulate new ways of thinking about communication?
Test of time	How long has the theory been used in communication research?

The Research Process

Any introduction to communication theory must necessarily include a discussion of research. You already know that the two processes—theory-building and research generation—are unique. Yet, we need to provide you some sense of the research process for you to have a foundation from which to draw as we discuss each theory.

In the example at the beginning of the chapter, we illustrated how interrelated theory and research processes are, so now we'll examine the research process. Our discussion will necessarily be brief here; we know many of you will take an entire class devoted to the study of research methods, so here we simply give you an idea of how important theory and research are to one another. Although we could delve into a variety of areas in communication research, we maintain our focus on the objective (quantitative) and subjective (qualitative) efforts undertaken by researchers.

Communication Research and the Scientific Method

Conceptualizing communication theory has historically been related to quantitative thinking. That is, many of the theories you read about have their roots in experiments and the qualities related to those investigations. We will briefly address several themes related to this research orientation. Should you wish to find out more about quantitative communication research, you should look at additional information (e.g., Wrench, Thomas-Maddox, Richmond, & McCroskey, 2015). At the beginning of this chapter, Dr. Stevens's study illustrated theory-then-research. Rolanda's transcripts are used to test what Communication Accommodation Theory predicts about communication behaviors in the workplace. Dr. Stevens will see if the speculations she made based on the theory's logic hold true in the conversations that Rolanda taped. This traditional process, known as the **scientific method**, follows **deductive logic** in that Stevens moved from the general (the theory) to specific instances (the actual conversations gathered in two workplaces). If Stevens had used **inductive logic** (moving from specific to general), she would have asked Rolanda to record many more conversations. Stevens would have refrained from hypothesizing, or guessing, about what she might find in advance of the data collection. Then she and Rolanda would have listened to their tapes, trying to find some type of pattern that best explained what they heard. Finally, Stevens would have generalized based on her observations.

After Stevens hypothesized about what she will find in the workplace regarding accommodations between workers and managers based on the theory, she then must **operationalize** all the concepts. This means she needs to specify how she will measure the concepts that are important to her study. In this process, Dr. Stevens turns the abstract concepts of the theory into concrete variables that can be observed and measured. For example, status difference is a critical notion in the theoretical framework, so Stevens specifies to Rolanda how she should measure this. In this case, measurement will be based on job title. Rolanda has to discover the job title for each of the people she observes and then compare those titles to a chart Stevens has given her classifying job titles into the two categories of "supervisor" and "subordinate." This seems like a fairly straightforward means to operationalize the notion of status, but there may be instances where it is not a perfect operationalization. For instance, a lower-level employee who has worked for the company for many years might hold more status than a middle manager who has only recently arrived and is just learning the corporate culture. Additionally, women managers often report some problems with achieving the status expected from their job title. You can see how nominal concepts that are more complex and abstract, such as love and intimacy, would be even more difficult to operationalize than occupational status.

A next step in quantitative investigation and the traditional scientific model sends Rolanda into the two organizations to make **observations** and collect **data** (in this case, the conversations and the job titles). When Rolanda returns with the tapes, Dr. Stevens will have to **code** the conversations, again using operationalizations for various concepts related to the theory. Some types of data do not need extensive coding to analyze. For example, if Dr. Stevens operationalized status based on income and then provided respondents with a survey asking them to indicate the category for their salary, these data would not need the same type of coding required in the taped conversations. The income categories could simply be numbered consecutively. In contrast, the conversations have to be listened to repeatedly to determine whether a given comment converges with or diverges from the comment preceding it.

Although some researchers approach their work strictly as hypothesis testers and some approach it more as theory generators, in practice most weave back and forth between the two. Furthermore, Wallace (1983) has argued that two types of research exist: pure and applied (Figure 3.2). In **pure research,** researchers are guided by knowledge-generating goals. They are interested in testing or generating theory for its own sake and for the sake of advancing our knowledge in an area. In **applied research**, researchers wish to solve specific problems with the knowledge they or other researchers have generated. Figure 3.2 illustrates the relationship between these two types of research goals and processes.

scientific method
the traditional method for doing research involving controlled observations and analysis to test the principles of a theory

deductive logic
moving from the general (the theory) to the specific (the observations)

inductive logic
moving from the specific (the observations) to the general (the theory)

operationalize
making an abstract idea measurable and observable

observations
focused examination within a context of interest; may be guided by hypotheses or research questions

data
the raw materials collected by the researcher to answer the questions posed in the research or to test a hypothesis

code
converting raw data to a category system

pure research
research to generate knowledge

applied research
research to solve a problem or create a policy

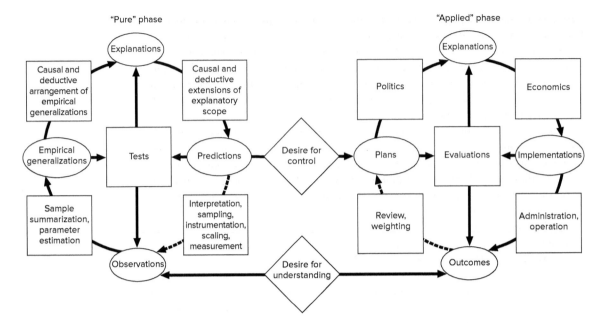

Figure 3.2 The Procedures of Scientific Analysis

In our example of Dr. Stevens's research, we see her performing pure research. If a specific organization hired Dr. Stevens to consult with them to improve employee morale, however, her research would become applied. Theory and practice are intertwined, and pure and applied research are not unrelated processes. In Figure 3.2, the arrows running between the two types of research show this interrelationship. Without each other, each type of research would be conducted in a vacuum (Pettey, Bracken, & Pask, 2016). Let's dig a little deeper into the qualitative lens in communication research.

Communication Research and the Qualitative Approach

Similar to quantitative design, we could write a great deal related to qualitative communication research. In fact, an entire journal in the communication field is dedicated to this topic ("Qualitative Research Reports in Communication"). Therefore, we necessarily truncate our discussion and focus on a number of different methods that can be undertaken using this approach, knowing that you can find further information elsewhere (e.g., Silverman, 2016). Instead of delineating all of the numerous methods related to qualitative inquiry, we focus our attention on the primary characteristics of this type of research. As a result, you will be able to see how a particular communication theory is influenced by qualitative thinking. We address four different characteristics: context-situated, inductive, emergent, and privileged-centered.

When we say that qualitative research is context-situated, similar to what we noted in Chapter 2, we are saying that individuals must be studied in their naturalistic setting and accommodate the time, space, and location. Qualitative scholars do not believe that objectivity can be achieved (unlike quantitative researchers who believe that objectivity is possible and probable). If, for instance, Marla was interested in studying roommate rivalry, she would talk to the roommates and to understand their conflict, she will have to understand conflict as it occurs organically and not presuppose any measurement or template. Marla will need to understand conflict taking into account when it happened, why, where, and with whom. In other words, she will have to examine conflict contextually.

The inductive feature of qualitative research refers to what we alluded to earlier. Researchers using a qualitative lens aim to collate individual observations, for instance, and draw some general claims about human behavior. However, in this process, every effort is made to honoring the voice of the participant, even while trying to develop some conclusions. So, let's use Marla again. If she interviewed say 15 roommates and found out that most of the sources of conflict were related to finances, she could draw a conclusion ("Roommate equity in paying bills"), but would work to report unique responses to the question on finances. She will use the data/responses to generate ideas or claims about the participants.

A third characteristic of qualitative research is that it is emergent. When we note that research is emergent we mean that as questions are posed, they must be responsive to the setting. Again, this is an organic process in that researchers must be aware of respondent reactions and manage appropriately. So, when Marla finds that a roommate she interviews decides to detail his experiences with his parents paying his college tuition, Marla will have to encourage him to be focused on the question about conflict, but also simultaneously recall this response diversion as she analyzes her results.

Embedded in many qualitative research studies is the notion that participants possess privilege. This privilege-centeredness means that answers can ramble and that any "power" differences between the researcher and the participant is diminished. You are able to see that this quality is somewhat applicable to every other quality, but it's important to highlight. Is the information that is gathered authentic? So, as Marla listens to roommates talk about their conflicts, she shouldn't look at her watch for time limits, she should avoid telling her participants to "stay focused on the question," and she must take into consideration all of the dimensions of their responses. In doing so, she will be indulging an authenticity so often sought out in qualitative research.

Student Voices

Alexandria

My uncle got back from serving in Iraq and I know very well he has PTSD. I'd like to do a study on those military people who are on "the front lines" and what happens to their relationships when they return home. My aunt and he always argue and before he left, they never yelled at all! I know it'd be stupid to study this using statistics, but I'd rather "survey his voice" to see what his experiences were and whether he feels he has some "issues" as a result of serving.

The preceding four characteristics are among many that are considered by qualitative researchers. We hope that as you review each theory, you understand that many are derived from the sorts of qualities we explained.

Let's discuss a few more points relative to quantitative and qualitative research. In conducting quantitative research, one key difference between professional researchers and implicit ones rests on the definition of two terms: reliability and validity. Researchers say that something has **reliability** when you can get the same results over time. For example, if Rolanda visited the organizations in two years and her observations there yielded the same results that they do now, her observations would

reliability
the stability and predictability of an observation

Theory in Popular Press • *Explaining the Gender Gap on Wikipedia*

The *New York Times* (online) in February 2011 asked the following question on the Room for Debate page: "Where are the women in Wikipedia?" The introduction noted that although Wikipedia had more than 3.5 million articles in English, and advertises itself as open to all to edit, less than 15 percent of the contributors are women. Following this, eight posts attempted to answer the question as to why there was a gender gap on Wikipedia. The answers ranged depending on the theoretical perspective of the poster. For instance, Susan Herring noted that differing communication styles might account for the imbalance. She observed that "it's a popular stereotype that men are believed to know more 'hard facts,' while women are better at nurturing and getting along with people." Yet, when Herring tested this stereotype she found that academic women posted slightly more factual messages online in discussion forums than did academic men. What did differ, however, was communication styles or the way men and women posted their messages. She found that "men tended to assert their opinions as 'facts,' whereas women tended to phrase their informative messages as suggestions, offers, and other non-assertive acts." Herring concludes that Wikipedia doesn't encourage women's style and rather favors a more masculine, fact-asserting, style.

Joseph Reagle argues that women's low participation on Wikipedia is based on subtle discrimination against women as seen in a culture of hackers with geeky images and argumentative styles. Further, Reagle notes that Wikipedia's openness allows misogyny that keeps women away. Others theorized that the lack of women on Wikipedia had more to do with power than gender, and others offered that the fight to make oneself "heard" might be unappealing to women. Terri Oda theorized that since women have less spare time than men, they might be discouraged by the time-consuming nature of posting on Wikipedia.

Source: nytimes.com/roomfordebate/2011/02/02/where-are-the-women-in-wikipedia/trolls-and-other-nuisances.

---

be called reliable. You can imagine many reasons reliability is difficult to obtain. For instance, if there had been a big turnover in personnel at one of the organizations, reliability would be difficult. Professional researchers conduct statistical tests to judge reliability. Implicit scientists usually operate as though their observations are reliable without ever testing for it.

Reliability is important, but validity is even more critical to the empirical research process. This is the case because observations can be reliable even if they are not valid, but the opposite is not true. To draw useful conclusions from research, observations must be both reliable and valid. **Validity** refers to the fact that the observation method actually captures what it is supposed to. For instance, Dr. Stevens is interested in communication accommodation, so she is having Rolanda listen to workplace conversations in hallways to find it. If people engage in extensive conversations where Rolanda can tape them, then probably the observations are able to measure the concept of interest. But, what if Rolanda tapes a lot of casual greetings that don't show much of anything important to the notion of communication accommodation? Would Dr. Stevens be correct in concluding that people do not accommodate their communication according to status? Maybe not, if a lot of accommodating is going on behind closed doors where Rolanda didn't go. In that case, the measurement (taped hallway conversations) was not valid because it didn't capture what the researcher was interested in. Again, professional researchers are concerned about the validity of their observations and work diligently to demonstrate validity. Implicit researchers don't think too much about validity unless they somehow discover that they have been basing their generalizations on a mistaken notion.

validity
the truth value of an observation

In qualitative research (Schwandt, Lincoln, & Guba, 2007) a different standard is applied to assess the value and rigor of a study. In particular, four areas are proposed: credibility, transferability, dependability, and confirmability. The credibility criterion requires the research participant to assess the legitimacy of the findings. For instance, if members of the "Black Lives Matter" movement were interviewed for a study on discrimination, only the members participating in the study could provide credence to the research. Transferability is the extent to which a study's results can be generalized to other settings or contexts. Qualitative researchers tend to avoid using "reliability" in their findings because they often don't find it possible to measure the same thing twice with the same results. Therefore, they often contend that dependability is more appropriate; researchers need to account for the dynamism of human behavior and that it continually changes. Finally, when research can be corroborated by others, it is confirmable, an effort to discover any challenges or modifications to the original study. Although there is some disagreement in the research community whether or not a different set of expectations should exist in qualitative research, there is value, nevertheless, in knowing that not all scholars think and act alike in their research.

Overall, the research process is similar for implicit and professional researchers, but professional researchers are more rigorous at every step of the process. Both draw conclusions based on their findings, and ultimately we are convinced by the arguments each advances about the strength of their process. When we believe that the results are based on good (reliable and valid) observations and careful logic, we accept the findings.

We have briefly outlined a discussion of the primary ways to understand human behavior. Regardless whether a quantitative or qualitative approach is embraced, there is room for a great deal of creativity in the research process. You will encounter this as you read and understand the theories in this book.

Conclusion

This chapter introduced the concepts of theory and research and discussed their usefulness for examining communication behaviors. We have provided an initial definition of *theory* as well as explored some of the goals of theory. We discussed the frameworks for theories, or three approaches to knowing: empirical, interpretive, and critical. Each of these approaches answers questions about truth (ontology), gathering information (epistemology), and values (axiology) somewhat differently. Further, we discussed how theories can be created using three different guidelines: covering law, systems, and rules. We offered a list of criteria to help with evaluating different theories. We explained the research process briefly, discussing issues of induction (grounded theory), deduction (scientific method), and an overview of qualitative thinking in communication research. As we seek to understand communication, we turn to theory to help us organize the information that research provides.

Discussion Starters

TECH QUEST: Imagine a study that explores the intersection of narcissism and Twitter. Describe how both a quantitative and qualitative researcher might go about studying this topic.

1. How do you think a theory can help us understand the communication behavior of subordinates and superiors in an organization? Use examples in your response.

2. Provide some examples of ways you think like a theorist in your daily life.

3. What is the difference between inductive and deductive logic? Give some examples of your everyday use of both induction and deduction.

4. Do you see communication behavior as being lawlike, like a system, or rule governed? Explain your answer.

5. How do a researcher's beliefs about the world actually affect the research process? Be specific.

6. How is a critical theory different from an empirical or humanistic theory? What do we learn about a theory by classifying it in terms of its approach to knowing?

7. What factors do you think should go into determining whether a study should be qualitative or quantitative in nature?

THINKING ABOUT THEORY AND RESEARCH

Understanding the Dialogue

The Self and Messages

ACHIEVING MEANING IS CRITICAL IN OUR LIVES. We can't get too far in our conversations unless we understand others and can make ourselves understood. Understanding messages and co-creating meaning is what the communication process is all about. Meaning, therefore, requires us to assess our own thinking and also to be prepared to assess how others interpret our messages. Through our conversations with others, we gain a better sense of ourselves and a clearer understanding of the messages we are sending and receiving.

How we process meaning is the cornerstone of our first section of theories, which we have labeled "The Self and Messages." Four theories highlight the prominent role of intrapersonal communication in meaning making. First, Symbolic Interaction Theory explores the interplay between the self and the society in which we live. Symbolic Interactionists argue that people act toward other people or events on the basis of meaning they assign to them. Coordinated Management of Meaning is also concerned with achieving meaning; however, the theory goes a bit further. It states that people will apply a personal set of rules to try to understand a social situation. Cognitive Dissonance Theory also looks at a person's ability to manage meaning and the discomfort people feel when their beliefs are in conflict with each other. Expectancy Violations Theory looks specifically at what happens when someone does something different than what we'd expected. The theory suggests that we will judge a violation as either good or bad and act accordingly in the conversation.

The theories associated with the self and with messages deal with the ways people work toward gaining clarity and comprehension. Before, during, and after conversations with others, we process things in our own minds to determine meaning. As you read about these theories, you will encounter a number of important topics; namely, the influence of society on attitudes, communicator credibility, decision making, conversational rules, attraction, and liking.

CHAPTER 4

Symbolic Interaction Theory

*Based on the research of **George Herbert Mead***

*Only selves have minds, that is, that cognition only belongs to selves, even
in the simplest expression of awareness.*

—George Herbert Mead

Roger Thomas

Roger Thomas stared in the mirror and straightened his tie. He gave himself a last glance and decided that he looked pretty professional. He was a little apprehensive about the new job, but he was excited, too. He had just graduated from Carlton Tech in Omaha, Nebraska, with a degree in engineering, and he had landed a terrific job in Houston. This made for a lot of changes in his life. It was a bit overwhelming. He was born and raised in central Nebraska, and he had never really been in a city bigger than Omaha until he went on his job interviews. Now he was living in Houston! It had all happened so quickly that Roger could almost feel his head spin.

Some of Roger's concern centered on the fact that he was the first person in his family to graduate from college. As far back as he could recall, his family had been farmers, and although he knew that engineering was something he loved and excelled at, he felt a little confused about how to behave off the farm and in a completely new life. It also didn't help that he was so far from home. Whenever he had felt stressed at Carlton, he had gone home to see his family, and they had usually made him feel better. He remembered one day in during his first year at Carlton when he felt impossibly out of place and uncomfortable. He really didn't know how to act as a college student. He went home for the weekend, and being in a familiar place with his family instantly gave him confidence. When he returned to Carlton on Monday, he felt much more self-assured.

Even though his parents had not attended college themselves, they respected education and communicated this to Roger. They expressed pride in him and his accomplishments. They also told him how his younger brothers looked up to him. This gave Roger confidence in himself, and he liked the idea that he was blazing a new trail for his family. Also, whenever he visited, he appreciated his parents' qualities; they were so calm and steady. As they went about their tasks, they demonstrated the peace and harmony that Roger wanted to find in his life's work. After seeing them, he always had a renewed sense of self.

Now Roger decided he would have to get on Skype, but today he had to face his new office alone. Yet even thinking about his family made him feel a little stronger. He was smiling when he got to the office. He was greeted warmly by the office assistant, who showed him into the conference room. He waited there for the other new hires to join him. By 9:05 A.M. they were all gathered, and their boss came in to give them an orientation speech. While the boss was talking, Roger looked around at his colleagues.

There were 10 new employees in all, and they could not have been more different. Roger was the youngest person in the room by at least 5 years. He was a bit alarmed when he realized that he must be the one with the least experience. He tried to calm himself down. He thought of his parents' pride in him and how his brothers looked up to him. Then he remembered his favorite teacher telling him that he was one of the best engineering students ever to go through Carlton. This helped Roger, and after the boss was finished speaking, he felt prepared to face the challenges of the job. During the break, he even had the confidence to begin talking to one of his new colleagues. He introduced himself and discovered that he didn't have less experience than she did. Helen Underwood explained that she had lived in a small Texas farming town, where she worked for the government. After working for a couple of years, she had decided to go back to school and get a degree. Roger was amazed to meet someone else who came from a farming background. Helen told Roger she was really impressed that he had graduated from Carlton. She knew it had a wonderful reputation, and its internship program was supposed to be the best in the country. Roger replied that he had been really lucky to go there and had loved working at his internship, where he had learned a great deal. Helen said she was nervous about starting out at this firm, and Roger smiled and nodded.

This conversation made him feel much better about the challenges that were ahead of him. Even though Helen was in her forties, they had a great deal in common, and they were in the same situation at the firm. Roger thought they would be friends.

As Roger goes through preparations for the first day of his new job and as he speaks with his boss and his new colleague, he is engaging in the dynamic exchange of symbols. George Herbert Mead, who is credited with originating the Theory of Symbolic Interaction, was fascinated with humans' ability to use symbols; he proposed that people act based on the symbolic meanings that are communicated in a given situation. People use language and symbols in their everyday communication with others. Symbols form the essence of Symbolic Interaction (SI) Theory, and the theory centers on the relationship between symbols (or verbal and nonverbal codes) and interactions between people using these symbols. As Lorie Sicafuse and Monica Miller (2010) observe, generally in social encounters people do not respond to stimuli directly but, rather to symbolic representations of stimuli, negotiated through interactions with others.

Ralph LaRossa and Donald C. Reitzes (1993) suggest that Symbolic Interaction Theory is "essentially . . . a frame of reference for understanding how humans, in concert with one another, create symbolic worlds and how these worlds, in turn, shape human behavior" (p. 136). LaRossa and Reitzes reflect Mead's contention about the interdependency between the individual and society. In fact, SI forms a bridge between theories focusing attention on individuals and theories attending to social forces. This is the case because of Mead's belief in individuals as active, reflective participants in their social context. Dana Berkowitz and Linda Liska Belgrave (2010) concur and use SI to frame their study examining how drag queens in South Florida take their marginalized status and turn it into something empowering.

Mead published very little during his academic career, but after he died his students collaborated on a book based on his lectures. They titled the book *Mind, Self, and Society* (Mead, 1934), and it contains the foundations of Symbolic Interaction Theory. Interestingly, the name *Symbolic Interaction* was not a creation of Mead's. One of his students, Herbert Blumer, actually coined the term, but it was clearly Mead's work that began the theoretical movement. Blumer published his own articles in a collection in 1969.

The ideas of SI have been very influential in communication studies because of Mead's emphasis on the importance of communication and social encounters (e.g., Harrigan, Dieter, Leinwohl, & Marrin, 2015; Lucas & Steimel, 2009; Poe, 2012). Communication scholars have found in SI a flexible framework allowing application to numerous communication contexts. For instance, Pamela Poe (2012) explored how older people perceive health messages using SI as a framework; Patricia Book (1996) examined family narrative influences on a person's ability to communicate about death. In addition, Daniel Flint (2006) found the theory useful in understanding marketing, Jan Fernback (2007) studied online social networking, Braden Leap (2015) discussed the interplay between the National Wildlife Refuge and SI, and Matthew Loveland and Delia Popescu (2011) extended the theory to an examination of web-based deliberations about democracy.

Several researchers observe, however, that Symbolic Interaction is a community of theories, rather than simply one theory. Many theorists refer to the Chicago School and the Iowa School as the two main branches of the theory. We can understand these branches and the overall contentions of SI by a brief examination of the history of the theory's development.

History of Symbolic Interaction Theory

The intellectual ancestors of Symbolic Interaction Theory were the early-twentieth-century pragmatists, such as John Dewey and William James. The pragmatists believed that reality is dynamic, which was not a popular idea at that time. In other words, they had different ontological beliefs than many other leading intellectuals. The pragmatists advanced the notion of an emerging social structure and insisted that meanings were created in interaction. They were activists, or critical theorists, who saw science as a way to advance knowledge and improve society.

Two different universities, the University of Iowa and the University of Chicago, employed scholars who subscribed to the ideas of the pragmatists, and at both schools, SI was advanced. At Iowa, Manford Kuhn and his students were instrumental in affirming the original ideas of the theory and added to the theory as well. The Iowa group advocated some new ways of looking at the self, but their approach was viewed as eccentric; and not universally embraced by researchers. Thus, most of the principles and developments of Symbolic Interactionism stemmed from the Chicago School.

Both George Herbert Mead and his friend John Dewey were on the faculty at the University of Chicago. Mead had studied both philosophy and social science, and he lectured on the ideas that form the core of the Chicago School. As a popular teacher who was widely respected, Mead played a critical role in establishing the perspective of the Chicago School. He focused on an approach to social theory emphasizing the importance of communication to life and social encounters.

The two schools diverged primarily on methodology (or epistemology). Mead and his student at the University of Chicago, Herbert Blumer, contended that the study of human beings could not be conducted using the same methods as the study of other things. They advocated the use of case studies and histories and nondirective interviews. The Iowa School adopted a more quantitative approach to their studies. Kuhn believed that the concepts of SI could be operationalized, quantified, and tested. To this end, Kuhn developed a technique called the Twenty-Statements Self-Attitudes questionnaire. A research respondent taking the 20-statements test is asked to fill in 20 blank spaces in answer to the question, Who am I? Some of Kuhn's colleagues at Iowa became disenchanted with this view of the self and broke away to form the "new" Iowa School. Carl Couch was one of the leaders of this new school. Couch and his associates began studying interaction behavior through videotapes of conversations, rather than simply examining the 20-statements test, although they still subscribed to a quantitative approach. Couch's innovative research studies "led many to differentiate the Iowa School as 'old' and 'new,' representing Kuhn's and Couch's respective influence during those eras" (Carter & Fuller, 2015, p. 4).

Mead's theory was rooted in a practical view of behavior (Fink, 2015). And, to be sure, in addition to the main schools of thought described above, several variations exist. In addition to these main schools of Symbolic Interaction, there are many variations. Many other theories that emphasize slightly different aspects of human interaction owe some debt to the central concepts of SI. Despite this variety, Mead's central concepts remain relatively constant in most interpretations of SI. Consequently, we will examine the basic assumptions and the key concepts that Mead outlined and Blumer later elaborated.

Theory at a Glance • Symbolic Interaction Theory

People are motivated to act based on the meanings they assign to people, things, and events. These meanings are created in the language that people use both in communicating with others (interpersonal context) and in self-talk (intrapersonal context), or their own private thought. Language allows people to develop a sense of self and to interact with others in the community.

Themes and Assumptions of Symbolic Interaction Theory

Symbolic Interaction Theory is based on ideas about the self and its relationship to society. Because this statement can be interpreted very broadly, we wish to spend some time detailing the themes of the theory and, in the process, reveal the assumptions framing the theory.

Three assumptions frame Symbolic Interactionism (Carter & Fuller, 2015; LaRossa & Rietzes, 1993):

- Individuals construct meaning via the communication process.
- Self-concept is a motivation for behavior.
- A unique relationship exists between the individual and society.

Each of these assumptions supports a number of different conclusions of SI. We discuss each assumption and the themes related to each.

First, Symbolic Interaction Theory holds that individuals construct meaning through the communication process because meaning is not intrinsic to a thing or idea. It takes people to make meaning. In fact, the goal of interaction is to create shared meaning. This is the case because without shared meaning communication is extremely difficult, if not impossible. Imagine trying to talk to a friend if you had to explain your own idiosyncratic meaning for every word you used, and your friend had to do the same. Of course, sometimes we assume that we and our conversational partner agree on a meaning only to discover that we are mistaken (Mom: "I said get ready as fast as you can." Joe: "One hour was as fast as I could get ready." Mom: "But I meant for you to be ready in 15 minutes." Joe: "You didn't say that!"), but, frequently, we can count on people having common meanings in a conversation.

Three conclusions can be derived from this assumption (Blumer, 1969; LaRossa & Reitzes, 1993). They include:

- Humans act toward others on the basis of the meanings those others have for them.
- Meaning is created in interaction between people.
- Meaning is modified through an interpretive process.

Humans Act Toward Others on the Basis of the Meanings Those Others Have for Them This assumption explains behavior as a loop between stimuli and the responses people exhibit to those stimuli. Symbolic Interaction theorists such as Herbert Blumer were concerned with the meaning behind behavior. They looked for meaning by examining psychological and sociological explanations for behavior. Thus, as researchers study the behaviors of Roger Thomas (from our beginning scenario), they see him making meanings that are congruent with the social forces that shape him. For instance, Roger assigns meaning to his new work experience by applying commonly agreed-upon interpretations to the things he sees. When he sees the age of his coworkers, he believes that they have more experience than he does because in the United States, we often equate age with experience. Furthermore, SI researchers are interested in the meaning that Roger attaches to his encounter with Helen (e.g., he is cheered up and believes they will become friends).

Meaning Is Created in Interaction Between People Mead stresses the intersubjective basis of meaning. Meaning can exist, according to Mead, only when people share common interpretations of the symbols they exchange in interaction. Blumer (1969) explains that there are three ways of accounting for the origin of meaning. One approach regards meaning as being intrinsic to the thing. Blumer states, "Thus, a chair is clearly a chair in itself . . . the meaning emanates, so to speak, from the thing and as such there is no process involved in its formation; all that is necessary is to recognize the meaning that is there in the thing" (pp. 3–4).

A second approach to the origin of meaning sees it as "brought to the thing by the person for whom the thing has meaning" (Blumer, 1969, p. 4). This position supports the popular notion that meanings are in people, not in things. In this perspective, meaning is explained by isolating the psychological elements within an individual that produce a meaning.

Mead's theory takes a third approach to meaning, one that is congruent with many communication researchers, seeing it as occurring between people. Meanings are "social products" or "creations that are formed in and through the defining activities of people as they interact" (Blumer, 1969, p. 5). Therefore, if Roger and Helen did not share a common language and did not agree on denotations and connotations of the symbols they exchanged, no meaning would result from their conversation. Furthermore, the meanings created by Helen and Roger are unique to them and their relationship. A study of how police officers symbolically construct the meaning of their jobs (Innes, 2002) illustrates this assumption by showing how the police talk about murders to the public and among themselves.

Meaning Is Modified Through an Interpretive Process   Blumer notes that this interpretive process has two steps. First, communicators point out the things that have meaning. Blumer argues that this part of the process is different from a psychological approach and consists of people engaging in communication with themselves. Thus, as Roger gets ready for work in the morning, he communicates with himself about the areas that are meaningful to him. The second step involves communicators selecting, checking, and transforming the meanings in the context in which they find themselves. When Roger talks with Helen, he listens for her remarks that are relevant to the areas he has decided are meaningful. Further, in his interpretation process, Roger depends on the shared social meanings that are culturally accepted. Thus, Roger and Helen are able to converse relatively easily because they both come from similar co-cultures.

The second assumption focuses on the importance of the **self-concept,** or the relatively stable set of perceptions that people hold of themselves. Self-concept is a motivation for human behavior. When Roger (or any social actor) asks the question "Who am I?", the answer relates to self-concept. The characteristics Roger acknowledges about his physical features, roles, talents, emotional states, values, social skills and limits, intellect, and so forth make up his self-concept. This notion is critical to Symbolic Interactionism. Furthermore, Symbolic Interaction is interested in the ways in which people develop self-concepts. The theory pictures individuals with active selves, grounded in social interactions with others (Figure 4.1). This theme suggests two conclusions, according to LaRossa and Reitzes (1993):

self-concept
a relatively stable set of perceptions people hold about themselves

- Individuals develop self-concepts through interaction with others.
- Self-concepts provide an important motive for behavior.

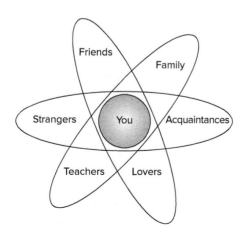

Figure 4.1
How the Self-Concept Develops

Individuals Develop Self-Concepts Through Interactions with Others   This conclusion suggests that it is only through contact with others that we develop a sense of self. People are not born with self-concepts; they learn them through interactions. According to SI, infants have no sense of an individuated self. During the first year of life, children begin to differentiate themselves from their surroundings. This is the earliest development of the self-concept. Mead's theory contends that this process continues through the child's acquisition of language and the ability to respond to others and internalize the feedback he or she receives. Roger has a sense of self because of his contacts with his parents and his teachers and his colleagues. Their interactions with him tell him who he is. Granberg (2011) notes that, in the context of identity change following weight loss, it was not enough to successfully lose weight and sustain that over time. The identity change was not effected until interactions with others validated the new identity.

Self-Concepts Provide an Important Motive for Behavior   The notion that beliefs, values, feelings, and assessments about the self affect behavior is a central tenet of the theory. Symbolic Interactionists contend that a unique relationship exists between the individual and society. Mead argues that because human beings possess a self, they are provided with a mechanism for self-interaction. This mechanism is used to guide behavior and conduct. It is also important to note that Mead sees the self as a process, not as a structure. Having a self forces people to construct their actions and responses, rather than simply expressing them. So, for instance, if you feel great about your abilities in your communication theory course, then it is likely that you will do well in the course. In fact, it is likely that you will feel confident in all of your courses. This process is often called the **self-fulfilling prophecy,** or the self-expectations that cause

self-fulfilling prophecy
a prediction about yourself causing you to behave in such a way that it comes true

"I start the morning with a warm 'Hello!' then downgrade through the day to a nod until I finally lose eye contact altogether."

a person to behave in such a way that the expectations are realized. When Roger remembers his professor's praise of his engineering abilities, he is setting himself up to make a self-fulfilling prophecy about his performance at his new job.

The final assumption pertains to the relationship between individual freedoms and social constraint. Symbolic Interactionists contend that a unique relationship exists between the individual and society. Mead and Blumer took a middle position on this issue. They tried to account for both order and change in social processes. Symbolic Interaction Theory as a comprehensive sociological theory recognizes that both social structural and personal factors influence behavior (Andersen & Taylor, 2016). Individuals are influenced in their thoughts and actions by social forces and processes, shared meanings and symbols, and by individual agency and self-motives (Mead, 1934). Donald Reitzes and his colleagues (2010) noted that because of this middle position, acknowledging the importance of both the individual and society, SI allowed them to examine how people quit smoking by providing an integrated framework of social factors and individual factors contributing to the "smoker identity."

Conclusions related to this assumption include the following:

- People and groups are influenced by cultural and social processes.

- Social structure is worked out through social interaction.

People and Groups Are Influenced by Cultural and Social Processes   This assumption recognizes that social norms constrain individual behavior. For instance, when Roger gets ready for his first day at his new job, he selects a navy suit, a white oxford shirt, and a burgundy and blue striped tie. His preferred mode of dress would be jeans and a flannel shirt, but he chooses clothing that he feels will be socially appropriate in the job context. Furthermore, culture strongly influences the behaviors and attitudes that we value in our self-concepts. In the United States, people who see themselves as assertive are likely to be proud of this attribute and reflect favorably on their self-concept. This is the case because the United States is an individualistic culture that values assertiveness and individuality. In some Asian cultures, cooperation and community are highly valued, and the collective is more important than the individual. Thus, an Asian who sees herself as assertive might feel ashamed of such a self-concept.

For example, Mary Roffers (2002) notes that a college assignment to design a personal website was very difficult for a Hmong student in her class. The student explained that talking about oneself is not approved of in his culture and putting information about himself on the website felt inappropriate. In contrast, Jenny Davis (2010) found that people in the United States enjoyed creating a personal website for the control it gave them in negotiating their self-presentation.

Social Structure Is Worked Out Through Social Interaction   This assumption mediates the position taken by the previous assumption. SI challenges the view that social structure is unchanging and acknowledges that individuals can modify social situations. For example, many U.S. workplaces have instituted "casual Fridays," when the employees wear casual clothing rather than the typical, socially prescribed office wear. In this way, the participants in the interaction modify the structure and are not completely constrained by it. In other words, SI theorists believe that humans are choice makers. In our opening scenario, Roger chooses to introduce himself to Helen; he is not bound to do so by forces outside his control. In making choices, Roger exerts his individuality and demonstrates that he is not completely constrained by culture or situation.

Student Voices
Francisco

I liked the example about casual Fridays in the workplace. When I went to work at my current job there were a lot of rules I found difficult to follow. At first, it seemed like I was going to be constrained by the structure I found on the job. But, then I started to talk to people and we were able to make a couple of changes that makes working there a lot better for me. So, I think that assumption of SI is true. People have some constraints on them because of social rules, but people also have free will and can change some of the rules. If I hadn't been able to change things, I probably would have quit—which would have been my choice, too.

Key Concepts

Previously we stated that the book outlining Mead's thinking was titled *Mind, Self, and Society.* The title of the book reflects the three key elements of Symbolic Interaction. We describe each element here, noting how other important issues relate to these basic three. It will become clear that the three concepts overlap to some extent.

Mind

mind
the ability to use symbols with common social meanings

language
a shared system of verbal and nonverbal symbols

significant symbols
symbols whose meaning is generally agreed upon by many people

Mead defines **mind** as the ability to use symbols that have common social meanings, and Mead believes that humans must develop minds through interaction with others. Infants cannot really interact with others until they learn **language,** or a shared system of verbal and nonverbal symbols organized in patterns to express thoughts and feelings. Language depends on what Mead calls **significant symbols,** or those symbols that evoke basically the same meaning for many people. Let's use the infant as an example to illustrate the concept of significant symbols. When parents coo and talk to their baby, the infant may respond, but she does not really understand the meanings of the words her parents use. As she learns language, the infant exchanges shared or significant symbols and can anticipate the responses of others to the symbols she uses.

By using language and interacting with others, we develop what Mead calls *mind,* and this enables us to create an interior setting for the society that we see operating outside us. Thus, mind can be viewed as the way people internalize society. Yet mind does not just depend on society. Mead suggests that there is a reciprocal relationship: Mind reflects and creates the social world. As people learn language, they learn the social norms and cultural values that constrain them. But they also learn ways to shape and change that social world through interaction. When children learn to talk, they may learn to say "please" and "thank you" as cultural indicators of politeness. Yet they may also create unique, personal ways of expressing politeness, like saying "mayberry" and "yes you," that become accepted phrases within a specific relationship.

Closely related to the concept of mind is the notion of **thought,** which Mead conceives of as an inner conversation. While Roger, in our opening story, prepares for his new job, he reviews all the experiences that brought him to that time and place. He thinks about his family's example and support, he remembers a favorite teacher, and he tells himself that he will be successful at this challenge. Through this intrapersonal conversation, Roger sorts out the meaning of his new situation. Mead holds that without social stimulation and interaction with others, people would not be capable of holding inner conversations or sustaining thought.

thought
an inner conversation

According to Mead, one of the most critical activities that people accomplish through thought is **role taking,** or the ability to symbolically place oneself in an imagined self of another person. This process is also called "perspective taking" because it requires that one suspend one's own perspective on an experience and instead view it from the imagined perspective of another. For example, if Helen thought about Roger after their meeting and reflected on how he must have felt to be newer and younger than most of the other employees, then she would be role taking. Whenever we try to imagine how another person might view something or when we try to behave as we think another would, we are role taking. Mead suggests that role taking is a symbolic act that can help clarify our own sense of self, even as it allows us to develop the capacity for empathy with others.

role taking
the ability to put oneself in another's place

Self

Mead defines **self** as the ability to reflect on ourselves from the perspective of others. From this you can see that Mead does not believe that self comes from introspection or from simply thinking on one's own. For Mead, the self develops from a particular kind of role taking—that is, imagining how we look to another person. Borrowing a concept originated by the sociologist Charles Cooley in 1912, Mead refers to this as the **looking-glass self,** or our ability to see ourselves in the reflection of another's gaze. Cooley (1972) believes that three principles of development are associated with the looking-glass self: (1) we imagine how we appear to others, (2) we imagine their judgment of us, and (3) we feel hurt or pride based on these self-feelings. We learn about ourselves from the ways others treat us, view us, and label us. For example, when Rachel participated in the Great Bike Ride Across Iowa, she rode a three-speed bike 523 miles, from one end of the state to the other. The ride took one week, and after about three days, she felt she could not pedal a minute longer. But just as she was about to give up, a man biked up beside her and said, "You are amazing, going on this bike ride on a three-speed bike. You are just great. Keep it up." As he pedaled off, she straightened up and thought to herself, "Well, I guess I *am* amazing. I can finish this ride!" The label the man gave her actually changed her feelings of exhaustion and made her see her accomplishments and herself differently and more positively.

self
imagining how we look to another person

looking-glass self
our ability to see ourselves as another sees us

T*I*P

Theory-Into-Practice
Symbolic Interaction Theory

Theoretical Claim: Individuals develop self-concepts through their interactions with others.

Practical Implication: Because Brianna has received ongoing supportive messages about her abilities in class, on the lacrosse field, and in the church choir, she evaluates herself as able to meet nearly any challenge presented to her.

Other researchers (e.g., Gilovich & Keltner, 2015; Ishida, 2016; Zhao, 2016) refer to the looking-glass self as *reflected appraisals*, or people's perceptions of how others see them. Joanne Kaufman and Cathryn Johnson (2004) used the concept of reflected appraisals to examine how gay men and lesbians develop and manage their identities. They argue that SI is a much better framework for understanding identity construction than the stage models often applied to gay and lesbian identity development. Kaufman and Johnson found that gay men and lesbians who experienced positive reflected appraisals (in regard to same-sex identity) had an easier time developing their identity than did those people who experienced negative reflected appraisals.

Mead's notion of the looking-glass self implies the power that labels have on self-concept and behavior. This power represents a second type of self-fulfilling prophecy. Earlier in the chapter we spoke of self-fulfilling prophecies as being self-expectations that affect behaviors. For example, Roger tells himself repeatedly that he will succeed at his job and then engages in behaviors that are congruent with his expectations of success. In turn, these behaviors will likely ensure that he will succeed. By the same token, negative self-talk can create situations where predictions of failure come true. The second type of self-fulfilling prophecy produced by labels is called the **Pygmalion effect,** and it refers to the expectations of others governing one's actions.

The name comes from the myth of Pygmalion, on which a play of the same name and the musical *My Fair Lady* were based. The main character, Eliza, states that the difference between an upper-class lady and a poor flower girl is not in her behavior, but in how others treat her. This phenomenon was tested in a classic study by Robert Rosenthal and Lenore Jacobson (1968). In their study, Rosenthal and Jacobson told elementary-school teachers that 20 percent of their students were gifted. But the names of these "gifted" students were simply drawn at random. Eight months later these students showed significantly greater gains in IQ compared to the rest of the children in the class. Rosenthal and Jacobson concluded that this was the result of teachers' expectations (and behaviors based on these expectations) toward the "gifted" children.

As Mead theorizes about self, he observes that through language people have the ability to be both subject and object to themselves. As subject, we act, and as object, we observe ourselves acting. Mead calls the subject, or acting self, the **I** and

Pygmalion effect
living up to or down to another's expectations of us

I
the spontaneous, impulsive, creative self

the object, or observing self, the **Me.** The I is spontaneous, impulsive, and creative, whereas the Me is more reflective and socially aware. The I might want to go out and party all night, whereas the Me might exercise caution and acknowledge the homework assignment that should be done instead of partying. Mead sees the self as a process that integrates the I and the Me.

Society

Mead argues that interaction takes place within a dynamic social structure that we call culture or society. Mead defines **society** as the web of social relationships that humans create. Individuals engage in society through behaviors that they choose actively and voluntarily. Society thus features an interlocking set of behaviors that individuals continually adjust. Society exists prior to the individual, but is also created and shaped by the individual, acting in concert with others (Bern-Klug, 2009; Forte, 2004).

Society, then, is made up of individuals, and Mead talks about two specific parts of society that affect the mind and the self. Mead's notion of particular others refers to the individuals in society who are significant to us. These people are usually family members, friends, work colleagues, and supervisors. We look to particular others to get a sense of social acceptability and a sense of self. When Roger thinks of his parents' opinion of him, he is deriving a sense of self from **particular others.** The identity of the particular others and the context influence our sense of social acceptability and our sense of self. Often the expectations of some particular others conflict with those of others. For example, if Roger's family wants him to work hard and be successful, whereas his friends want him to party and ignore work, he is likely to experience conflict.

The **generalized other** refers to the viewpoint of a social group or the culture as a whole. It is given to us by society, and "the attitude of the generalized other is the attitude of the whole community" (Mead, 1934, p. 154). The generalized other provides information about roles, rules, and attitudes shared by the community. The generalized other also gives us a sense of how other people react to us and of general social expectations. This sense is influential in developing a social conscience. The generalized other may help mediate conflicts generated by conflicting groups of particular others. So if your friends want you to party and your family wants you to study, your knowledge of the importance of a college degree in your culture may lead you to decide in favor of your parents' position.

Integration, Critique, and Closing

Symbolic Interaction Theory has been a powerful theoretical framework for over 80 years. The theory is derived from mostly qualitative work, although more recent applications have been quantitative in nature. The theory provides striking insights about human communication behavior in a wide variety of contexts. Without doubt, SI is well developed, beginning with the role of the self and progressing to an examination of the self in society. Yet the theory is not without its critics. As you think about Mead's theory, consider three areas of evaluation: scope, utility, and testability.

Integration

Communication Tradition	Rhetorical	**Semiotic**	**Phenomenological**	Cybernetic	Socio-Psychological	Socio-Cultural	Critical

Communication Context	**Intrapersonal**	**Interpersonal**	Small Group	Organizational	Public/Rhetorical	Mass/Media	Cultural

Approach to Knowing	Positivistic/Empirical	**Interpretive/Hermeneutic**	Critical

Critique

Evaluation Criteria	**Scope**	Logical Consistency	Parsimony	**Utility**	**Testability**	Heurism	Test of Time

Scope

Some critics (e.g., van Krieken, Habibis, Smith, Hutchins, Martin, & Maton, 2014) complain that Symbolic Interaction Theory is too broad to be useful. This criticism centers on the evaluation criterion of scope. The theory covers too much ground, these critics assert, to fully explain specific meaning-making processes and communication behaviors. It is helpful to have a theory that explains a wide variety of human behavior, but when a theory purports to explain everything, it will be vague and difficult to apply. This is the criticism leveled against the theory: It tries to do too much, and its scope needs to be refined. In response to this criticism, proponents explain that Symbolic Interaction is not one unified theory; rather, it is a framework that can support many specific theories.

Utility

The second area of criticism concerns the theory's utility. Symbolic Interaction Theory has been faulted as not as useful as it could be for two reasons (Charmaz, 2014). First, it focuses too much on the individual, and second, it ignores some important concepts that are needed to make the explanation complete. In the first case, critics observe that the theory's focus on the individual's power to create reality ignores the extent to which people live in a world not of their own making. Symbolic Interaction theorists regard a situation as real if the actors define it as real. But Erving Goffman (1974) comments that this notion, although true, ignores physical reality. For instance, if Roger and his parents agreed that he was an excellent engineer and that he was doing a wonderful job at his new firm, that would be reality for them. Yet it would not acknowledge the fact that Roger's boss perceived his skills as inadequate and fired him. Others counter by citing that the theory treads a middle ground between freedom of choice and external constraint

(Sicafuse & Miller, 2010). They recognize the validity of constraint, but they also emphasize the importance of shared meanings.

Related to this is the suggestion that the theory ignores important concepts such as emotions and self-esteem. Critics observe that it does not explain the emotional dimension of human interaction. Further, critics note that Symbolic Interaction discusses how we develop a self-concept, but it does not have much to say about how we evaluate ourselves. These deficiencies render the theory less useful than it should be in explaining the self. With reference to the lack of attention to the emotional aspects of human life, theorists respond that although Mead does not emphasize these aspects, the theory itself can accommodate emotions. In fact, some researchers have applied the theory to emotions with success. For instance, James Forte, Anne Barrett, and Mary Campbell (1996) used a Symbolic Interaction perspective to examine grief. Their study examined the utility of a Social Interaction perspective in assessing and intervening in a bereavement group. The authors found that Symbolic Interaction was a useful model. Regarding self-esteem, Symbolic Interactionists agree that it is not a focus of the theory. But they point out that this is not a flaw in the theory; it is simply beyond the bounds of what Mead chose to investigate.

Testability

With regard to testability, critics comment that the theory's broad scope renders its concepts vague. When so many core concepts are nominal (not directly observable), it is difficult to test the theory. Again, the response to this critique argues that Mead's theory is a general framework, not a single theory. In more specific theories derived from SI, such as Role Theory, for example, the concepts are more clearly defined and are capable of falsification, satisfying the criterion of testability.

Closing

Symbolic Interaction has critics, but still remains an enduring theory. It supports research in multiple contexts, and it is constantly being refined and extended. Further, it is one of the leading conceptual tools for interpreting social interactions, and its core constructs provide the foundation for many other theories that we discuss in this book. Thus, because Symbolic Interaction Theory has stimulated much conceptual thinking, it has accomplished a great deal of what theories aim to do.

Discussion Starters

TECH QUEST: SI asserts that we learn about ourselves through interactions with others. And, specifically, Cooley's concept of the looking-glass self notes that we see ourselves reflected in the gaze of others. How does it (or does it) affect the theory if the "gaze" is computer mediated? Can we learn about ourselves in the same way as the theory asserts if our interactions with others are conducted over social media sites such as Facebook, for instance?

How would (or would) the theory have to change to accommodate these types of interactions?

1. Discuss Roger Thomas's initial reactions to his new job in Houston. How do they specifically relate to his sense of self?

2. Do you believe Mead's argument that one cannot have a self without social interaction? Would a person raised in relative isolation, for example, have little to no sense of self? Explain your answer.

3. Has there been a time in your life when your sense of self changed dramatically? If so, what contributed to the change? Did it have anything to do with others in your life?

4. Do you agree with the emphasis that Mead places on language as a shared symbol system? Is it possible to interact with someone who speaks a completely different language? Explain your position.

5. One of the criticisms of Symbolic Interaction Theory is that it puts too much emphasis on individual action and not enough emphasis on the constraints on individuals put upon them by society and their social position. What do you think about this criticism?

6. Explain the difference between the concepts self-fulfilling prophecy and Pygmalion effect. How are they similar? How are they different?

7. Do you agree that Mead's theory is too broad in scope to really be considered a theory? Explain your answer.

CHAPTER 5

Coordinated Management of Meaning

*Based on the research of **W. Barnett Pearce** and **Vernon Cronen***

> *I am prepared to argue that the quality of our personal lives and of our social worlds is directly related to the quality of communication in which we engage.*
>
> —Barnett Pearce

The Taylor-Murphys

About four years ago, Jessie Taylor decided that she could not stay in her abusive marriage and left her husband, taking her two children—Megan, 13, and Melissa, 9—with her. They currently live in a small apartment, and Jessie knows that the place is too cramped for the three of them. Yet, with her upcoming marriage to Ben Murphy, Jessie realizes that her living situation will change very soon. Her work hours as a new law clerk, however, are quite long; at times, she must be in the office for 12-hour days. As a result, Jessie's children frequently require adult supervision in the early evening. Although Jessie would rather be at home with her children, she realizes that she cannot count on her ex-husband's child support payments, and she must keep her job. She hopes that her approaching marriage to Ben will help ease the financial and familial challenges.

Ben Murphy's wife died a little over a year ago. He parents his 4-year-old son, Patrick, but gets a great deal of help from both his mother and his two sisters. He feels badly about leaving Patrick but is grateful that his family is there, because his job as a state trooper is frequently unpredictable. He never really knows when he is going to be called out for an emergency or when he will be asked to work overtime. Lately, however, his sisters have made some comments, and Ben worries that the baby-sitting may be turning into a burden for them and his mom. Ben is hoping that his marriage to Jessie will ease his reliance upon his mother and sisters.

One evening, as Ben and Jessie are discussing final wedding plans, the two begin to talk about their future family. Ben is very excited about raising three children and looks forward to his son, Patrick, having new siblings. Jessie, however, is nervous about the logistics of bringing new people into her children's lives. Megan and Melissa are not pleased about their upcoming "blended" family. They have already had disagreements with Ben about a number of issues, including computer use and after-school activities.

As Ben and Jessie sit in front of the fireplace, they openly talk about the challenges, obstacles, and frustrations that they know they will experience in just a few months. Ben admits, "First, I need to tell you that I love you and that should be the most important thing right now. And I really think that the kids will come around in time—probably after we've been together for a while. A lot of families in our situation start out like this. There's a lot of chaos and then things begin to settle down. Hey, we're not all that unusual."

Jessie agrees. "Yeah, I know we're not the first family arranged this way. And I know things will work out. But when? And how are we all going to keep from screaming at each other while we work it all out? Adjusting can take some time." Her words are greeted by a warm hug from Ben.

Many people take their conversations for granted. When individuals speak to one another, they often fall into predictable patterns of talk and rely on prescribed social norms. To understand what takes place during a conversation, Barnett Pearce and Vernon Cronen developed Coordinated Management of Meaning (CMM). For Pearce and Cronen, people communicate on the basis of rules. Although we will address this later in the chapter, rules help us not only in our communication with others but also in our interpretation of what others are communicating to us. CMM helps explain how individuals co-create the meaning in a conversation. Jessie Taylor and Ben Murphy, for instance, are beginning to forge rules and patterns that will govern their new family's interaction.

For our purposes, Coordinated Management of Meaning generally refers to how individuals establish rules for creating and interpreting meaning and how those rules are enmeshed in a conversation where meaning is constantly being coordinated. Human communication, therefore, is guided by rules. Cronen, Pearce, and Harris's (1982) summary of CMM is informative here: "CMM theory describes human actors as attempting to achieve coordination by managing the ways messages take on meaning" (p. 68). And it is important to note that Pearce (2007) succinctly underscores the transactional nature of communication we identified in Chapter 1 by noting: "CMM invites you to ask, of the passing moment, 'What are we making together?'" (p. xi). Clearly, the theory requires an understanding of the co-creation of "social worlds" that Pearce believes exist. Finally, Pearce (2012) notes, "CMM does things to us; it changes in constructive ways the way we think and relate to others" (p. 17). As we discuss this theory, we will underscore a number of issues associated with it.

All the World's a Stage

To describe life experiences, Pearce and Cronen (1980) use the metaphor "undirected theater" (p. 120). They believe that in life, as in theater, a number of actors are following some sort of dramatic action and other actors are producing "a cacophonous bedlam with isolated points of coherence" (p. 121). Pearce (1989) describes this metaphor in eloquent detail:

> Imagine a very special kind of theater. There is no audience: everyone is "on stage" and is a participant. There are many props, but they are not neatly organized: In some portions of the stage are jumbles of costumes and furniture; in others, properties have been arranged as a set for a contemporary office; in yet another, they depict a medieval castle. . . . Actors move about the stage, encountering sets, would-be directors, and other actors who might provide a supporting cast for a production of some play. (p. 48)

The theorists believe that in this theatrical world, there is no one grand director, but rather a number of self-appointed directors who manage to keep the chaos in check.

Conversational flow is essentially a theater production. Interactants direct their own dramas, and, at times, the plots thicken without any script. For many people, how they produce meaning is equivalent to their effectiveness as communicators. To continue the metaphor, when actors enter a conversation, they rely on their past acting experiences to achieve meaning. How they perceive the play is their reality, but the roles they play in the production are not known until the production begins. To this end, the actors are constantly coordinating their scripts with one another.

The theatrical metaphor was later reconsidered by Pearce (2007). He noted that it was somewhat incomplete as he considered the ebb and flow of conversations and the unpredictability of dialogue. As you might imagine, conversations are frequently chaotic. Pearce and Cronen indicate that the actors who are able to read another's script will attain conversational coherence. Those who do not will need to coordinate their meaning. Of course, even agreeing upon what conversational script to follow can be difficult. Jessie and Ben, for example, may agree that achieving family harmony is essential, but may not agree on how to achieve that harmony. As Pearce (1989) observes, people may battle it out with respect to what script they will enact and then continue to argue about it.

This notion of a creative theatrical production was in stark contrast to the perspective held by other researchers when CMM was conceptualized. Early discussions of CMM centered on the need to break away from the empirical tradition that characterized much theory building at that time. To shape their theory, Pearce and Cronen looked to a number of different disciplines, including philosophy (Wittgenstein), psychology (James), and education (Dewey). Further, at the heart of CMM, according to Catherine Creede, Beth Fisher-Yoshida, and Placida Gallegos (2012), is the following question: What are we making together? Before delving into the theory's central features, we first consider three assumptions of the Coordinated Management of Meaning.

Theory at a Glance • Coordinated Management of Meaning

In conversations and through the messages we send and receive, people co-create meaning. As we create our social worlds, we employ various rules to construct and coordinate meaning. That is, rules guide communication between people. CMM focuses on the relationship between an individual and his or her society. Through a hierarchical structure, people come to organize meaning of literally hundreds of messages received throughout the day.

Assumptions of Coordinated Management of Meaning

CMM focuses on the self and its relationship to others; it examines how an individual assigns meaning to a message. The theory is especially important because it focuses on the relationship between an individual and his or her society (Philipsen, 1995). Referring back to the theater metaphor, consider the fact that all actors must be able to improvise—using their personal repertoire of acting experiences—as well as reference the scripts that they bring into the drama.

Human beings, therefore, are capable of creating and interpreting meaning. In addition to this, there are a few assumptions as well:

- Human beings live in communication.
- Human beings co-create a social reality.
- Information transactions depend on personal and interpersonal meaning.

The first assumption of CMM points to the centrality of communication. That is, human beings live *in* communication. Communication is, as noted in Chapter 1, a dynamic process that is more than talk; communication, according to CMM, is also a way of creating and doing things (Pearce, 2007). Pearce (1989) claims that "communication is, and always has been, far more central to whatever it means to be a human being than had ever been supposed" (p. 3). Further underscoring the interplay between communication and CMM, Paige Marrs (2012) advances that communication is the "substance of human community" and that CMM is an essential part of the discourses embedded in these communities. Finally, in CMM, Christine Oliver (2014) contends that communication can be identified as a "performative phenomenon" (p. 273).

We live in communication. In adopting this claim, Pearce rejects traditional models of the communication process such as the linear model to which we referred in Chapter 1. Rather, CMM theorists propose a counterintuitive orientation: They believe that social situations are created by interactions. Because individuals create their conversational reality, each interaction has the potential to be unique. This perspective requires CMM adherents to cast aside their preexisting views of what it means to be a communicator. Further, CMM theorists call for a reexamination of how individuals view communication because "Western intellectual history has tended to use communication as if it were an odorless, colorless, tasteless vehicle of thought and expression" (Pearce, 1989, p. 17). Pearce and Cronen contend that communication must be reconfigured and contextualized in order to begin to understand human behavior. When researchers begin this journey of redefinition, they start investigating the consequences of communication, not the behaviors or variables that accompany the communication process (Cronen, 1995a).

To illustrate this assumption, consider our opening story. Although Jessie and Ben believe that they have covered most of the details associated with merging their families, many more issues will appear as the families come together. Family members will create new realities for themselves, and these realities will be based on communication. Conversations will frequently be determined by what the family knows as well as what the family does not know. That is, parents and children will work through unexpected as well as expected joys and sorrows. Like many families in their situation, they may stumble upon areas they never considered. The two families will be working from different sets of conversation rules and therefore may arrive at very different conclusions as they discuss important issues.

A second assumption of CMM is that human beings co-create a social reality. Although we implied this assumption earlier, it merits delineation. The belief that people in conversations co-construct their social reality is called **social constructionism**. Pearce (2007) is clear in his social construction advocacy. He observes: "Rather than 'What did you mean by that?' the relevant questions are 'What

social constructionism *belief that people co-construct their social reality in conversations* are we making together?' 'How are we making it?' and 'How can we make better social worlds?'" (pp. 30–31). These social worlds require an understanding of **social reality**, which refers to a person's beliefs about how meaning and action fit within his or her interpersonal encounters. When two people engage in a conversation, they each come with a host of past conversational experiences from previous social realities. Current conversations, however, elicit new realities because two people are arriving at the conversation from different vantage points. In this way, two people co-create a new social reality.

social reality
a person's beliefs about how meaning and action fit within an interpersonal interaction

Sometimes, these communication experiences are smooth; at other times they are cumbersome. As we alluded to earlier and as Gerry Philipsen (1995) concludes, "Many interactions are more messy than clean and more awkward than elegant" (p. 19). Our opening example of Jessie and Ben illustrates this assumption. Although Jessie and Ben have been dating for some time and are preparing for their wedding, CMM theorists believe that they will continue to co-create a new social reality. For instance, the two will have to manage the issue of Jessie's daughters' reluctance to support the marriage. As Jessie and Ben discuss the matter in front of the fireplace, regardless of how they have previously discussed it, they create a new social reality. Perhaps some new issues will emerge—child support, Jessie's job, the age of the children, Jessie's ex-spouse, and so forth—or perhaps Jessie, Ben, or both will adopt new perspectives on their future family makeup. In any event, the social reality that the two experience will be a shared reality.

Student Voices

Alejandro

The idea that we "live" in communication was really a simple thing for me to understand. I look around me. I listen. I talk. I think about the patterns that I'm establishing with others and that others are establishing with still other people. I think about how I construct my communication realities. And, then, I begin to see part of what CMM is. We are "communication-centric," even as I think about where I came from (Mexico). I think that communication is very real, regardless of where you're born or raised. And, I like the fact that CMM puts communication at the center of all the relationships we have.

The third assumption guiding CMM relates to the manner in which people control conversations. Specifically, Pearce (2012) concluded that "communication is about *meaning*" (p. 4) and that meanings are constantly changing from interaction to interaction.

Transactions depend on personal and interpersonal meaning, as distinguished many years ago by Donald Cushman and Gordon Whiting (1972). **Personal meaning** is defined as the meaning achieved when a person interacts with another and brings into the interaction his or her unique experiences. Cushman and Whiting suggest that personal meaning is derived from the experiences people have with one another, and yet "it is improbable that two individuals will interpret the same experience in a

personal meaning
the meaning achieved when a person brings his or her unique experiences to an interaction

similar manner . . . and equally improbable that they would select the same symbolic patterns to represent the experience" (p. 220). Personal meaning helps people in discovery; that is, it not only allows us to discover information about ourselves, but also aids in our discovery about other people.

interpersonal meaning
the result when two people agree on each other's interpretations of an interaction

When two people agree on each other's interpretation, they are said to achieve **interpersonal meaning.** Cushman and Whiting (1972) argue that interpersonal meaning can be understood within a variety of contexts, including families, small groups, and organizations. They note that interpersonal meaning is co-constructed by the participants. Achieving interpersonal meaning may take some time because relationships are complex and deal with multiple communication issues. A family, for example, may be challenged with financial problems one day, child-raising concerns the next, and elderly care the next. Each of these scenarios may require family members to engage in unique communication pertaining to that particular family episode.

Personal and interpersonal meanings are achieved in conversations, frequently without much thought. Perceptive individuals recognize that they cannot engage in specialized personal meaning without explaining themselves to others. Cushman and Whiting tell us that interpersonal meaning must often be negotiated so that rules of meanings move from "in-house usage" to "standardized usage." Sharing meaning for particular symbols, however, is complicated by the fact that the meaning of many symbols is left unstated. For instance, consider a physician specializing in HIV/AIDS who discusses recent drug therapies with a group of college students. As the physician discusses HIV/AIDS, she must talk in laypersons' terms so that audience members will understand. However, despite honest efforts at avoiding jargon, it may be nearly impossible to avoid it completely. That is, as much as the physician tries, time may not permit her to fully explain the meaning of all specialized terms.

These three assumptions form a backdrop for discussing CMM. As these assumptions indicate, the theory rests primarily on the concepts of communication, social reality, and meaning. In addition, we can better understand the theory by examining a number of other issues in detail. Among these issues is the manner in which meaning is categorized.

The Hierarchy of Organized Meaning

You already have learned that the essence of communication is meaning and that "we live our lives filled with meanings, and one of our life challenges is to *manage* those meanings" (Pearce, 2012, p. 4). Therefore, according to CMM theorists, human beings organize meanings in a hierarchical manner. This is one of the core features of CMM, so we will discuss this at length. First we examine the meaning behind this claim, and then we look at the framework associated with the assumption. We have highlighted the hierarchy in Figure 5.1.

Suggesting that people organize meaning implies that they are able to determine how much weight to give to a particular message. It is true that people are constantly being bombarded with stimuli and that they must be able to organize the stimuli for communication to occur. This thinking is relevant to CMM. Imagine, for instance, Ian arriving at his new job on Monday morning. Throughout the day he will be exposed to a number of messages. From understanding company policy on medical

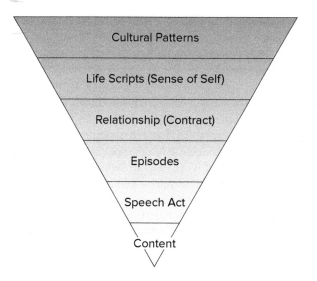

Figure 5.1
Hierarchy of
Meaning

Cultural Patterns

Life Scripts (Sense of Self)

Relationship (Contract)

Episodes

Speech Act

Content

leaves to overtime pay to computer safety, Ian must manage countless messages. As he returns home at the end of the day, he must organize the messages. In some way, he must try to coherently frame literally hundreds of messages from his day.

The process of organizing for Ian is similar to what many people experience when they speak to others. When people come together, they must try to handle not only the messages that are sent to them from others, but also the messages that they send to others. This helps people understand the full meaning of the messages. Let's consider how Pearce and Cronen (1980) illustrate the management of meaning.

CMM theorists propose six levels of meaning: content, speech acts, episodes, relationship, life scripts, and cultural patterns. As you read about the levels, keep in mind that higher levels help us to interpret lower-level meanings. That is, each type is embedded in the other. In addition, Pearce and Cronen prefer to use this hierarchy as a model rather than as a true ordering system. They believe that no true ordering is appropriate because people differ in their interpretation of meaning at various levels. Further, Illene Wassermann (2012), invoking the hierarchy of meaning, states that communication occurs at more than one level at a time and that the meaning that is created by individuals are embedded in each level of the hierarchy. CMM theorists, then, propose a hierarchy to help us understand the sequencing of meaning in different people.

Content

The **content** level specifies the first step of converting raw sensory data into some meaning. For instance, during your break at work, you may convert the symbols being observed or sent into some sort of meaning by their content. You may group information you hear about the boss in one category, information about the work-place environment in a second category, and information about the pay scale in a third category. For Ben Murphy in our chapter's opening, the words "I love you" convey information about Ben's reaction to Jessie, but the content of his words

content
the conversion of raw data into meaning

requires this additional level of meaning. Imagine the content level as a message without a context (Pearce, Cronen, & Conklin, 1979).

Speech Act

In discussing the second level of meaning, Pearce (2007) describes **speech acts** as a "class of very familiar things, such as *promises, threats, insults, speculations, guesses,* and *compliments*" (p. 105). These are actions we perform by speaking. Speech acts communicate the intention of the speaker and indicate how a particular communication should be taken. Using our earlier example of Ben Murphy, when Ben states, "I love you," to Jessie, the phrase communicates more than an assertion. The phrase carries an affectional tone because of the speech act (Austin, 1975).

Furthermore, Pearce (1994) notes that "speech acts are not things; they are configurations in the logic of meaning and action of conversations, and these configurations are co-constructed" (p. 119). Therefore, we should be aware that two people co-create the meaning of the speech act, a belief we talked about in our earlier assumption of CMM. Frequently, the speech act is defined both by the sender and by the response to what others have said or done. As Pearce concludes, "You cannot be a 'victim' unless there is a 'victimizer'" (p. 119). In addition, the relational history must be taken into consideration when interpreting a speech act. It is difficult to figure out what a message means unless we have a sense of the dynamics between the participants. And it's important to point out that speech acts don't always involve speech; Pearce acknowledges the importance of nonverbal communication, too.

Episodes

To interpret speech acts, Pearce and Cronen (1980) discuss **episodes,** or communication routines that have definable beginnings, middles, and endings. In a sense, episodes describe contexts in which people act. Irene Stein (2012) states that episodes can be small, such as discernible parts of a conversation, or large, such as the entire discussion between people. At this level, we begin to see the influence of context on meaning. Episodes vary tremendously—from picking up a hitchhiker to talking to your doctor about a diagnosis to having an affair with a coworker to fighting with your colleague over the direction of a project. Pearce (2007) states that episodes are sequences of speech acts that are "linked together as a story" (p. 132). Individuals in a communication exchange may differ in how they punctuate an episode. **Punctuation** pertains to the

process of identifying when an episode begins or ends. Episodes show how interactions are organized into a meaningful pattern. Pearce and Conklin (1979) clearly note that "coherent conversation requires some degree of coordinated punctuation" (p. 78). Different punctuation, however, may elicit different impressions of the episode, thereby creating "inside" and "outside" perspectives of the same episode. For example, Ben Murphy and Jessie Taylor may have punctuated differently their previous discussions about their future together. Ben may believe that dealing with the children will be better left until after their wedding, whereas Jessie may believe that the issue should be dealt with beforehand. Their subsequent episodes, therefore, will be partly determined by the way they handle their punctuation differences. Pearce (2005) believes that episodes are fairly imprecise because the actors in social situations find themselves in episodes that vary tremendously. He notes that episodes are also culturally based in that people bring to their interactions cultural expectations for how episodes should be executed. Finally, episodes can be highly structured within a social unit (e.g., family) that contains rituals, roles, or prescribed behavior.

Relationship

The fourth level of meaning is the **relationship,** whereby two people recognize their potential and limitations as relational partners.

Pearce (2007) expands our traditional understanding of relationship. In addition to partnerships between and among friends, spouses, and family members, he also believes that relationships can include "larger, less personal relationships such as corporations, cities, religions, and tennis clubs" (p. 200). He asserts that, in a sense, we're all "related" because of genes, language, and the planet's forces on each of us. These all coalesce to connect us, willingly or unwillingly.

Relationships are like contracts, which set guidelines and often prescribe behavior. In addition, relationships suggest a future. Few people take the time to outline relational issues unless they are concerned about their future together.

The relationship level suggests relational boundaries in that parameters are established for attitudes and behavior—for instance, how partners should speak to each other or what topics are considered taboo in their relationship. Pearce and Cronen (1980) note that boundaries distinguish between "we" and "they," or those people who are included in the contract and those who are not. The theorists use the term **enmeshment** to describe the extent to which people identify themselves as part of the relational system. Pearce (2012) further contends that enmeshment is the extent to which individuals get "caught up" in their patterns of communication. He asserts that people are enmeshed in a variety of different social systems, each comprised of various logics and meanings.

A relationship may prove invaluable as two people discuss issues that are especially challenging. For instance, there will certainly be some difficult discussions once the Murphy-Taylor family resides together. Knowing the relational boundaries and the expectations the family members hold for themselves as well as for one another will be important as they become a stepfamily. Although upcoming events will be trying for this family, they will be managed more effectively with an understanding of the contract.

Life Scripts

Clusters of past and present episodes are defined as **life scripts.** Think of life scripts as autobiographies that communicate with your sense of self. You are who you are because of the life scripts in which you have engaged. And how you view yourself over your lifetime affects how you communicate with others. Imagine the differences between Ben Murphy's and Jessie Taylor's life scripts. Their past episodic experiences will be very informative as they try to deal with their future plans together. Ben comes from a very supportive and loving family, so he may expect conversations with Jessie to be characterized by these nurturing episodes.

relationship
agreement and understanding between two people

enmeshment
the extent to which partners identify themselves as part of a system

life scripts
clusters of past or present episodes that create a system of manageable meanings with others

COORDINATED MANAGEMENT OF MEANING

In fact, it is likely that his experiences as a single father and his perceptions of parenthood are less troubled because of past episodes co-created with his biological family. Jessie, however, did not have an affirming relationship with her ex-husband. Consequently, her past debilitating episodes influence how she now communicates with Ben. Moreover, in her interactions with Ben, she may expect something very different from what Ben expects from her. We should point out, though, that life scripts include those episodes that two people construct together. So, once Ben and Jessie begin to co-create their social world, they will simultaneously co-create a life script.

Cultural Patterns

cultural patterns
images of the world and a person's relationship to it

individualism
prioritizing personal needs or values over the needs or values of a group (I-identity)

collectivism
a cultural value that prioritizes group needs or values over the needs or values of an individual (we-identity)

When discussing cultural patterns, Pearce and Cronen (1980) contend that people identify with particular groups in particular cultures. Also, each of us behaves according to the actual values of our society. These values pertain to sex, race, class, and spiritual spirituality, among others. **Cultural patterns,** or archetypes, can be described as "very broad images of world order and [a person's] relationship to that order" (Cronen & Pearce, 1981, p. 21). That is, an individual's relationship to the larger culture is relevant when interpreting meaning. Speech acts, episode relationships, and life scripts are all understood within the cultural level. This is even more paramount when two people from two different cultures try to understand the meaning of each other's words. For instance, Myron Lustig and Jolene Koester (2015) point out that the U.S. culture puts a premium on **individualism,** or the notion that the interests of an individual are put before the interests of the group. Individualism focuses on independence and initiative. Other cultures (such as Colombia, Peru, and Taiwan) emphasize **collectivism,** or the notion that the interests of the group are put before the interests of the individual. Difficulty may arise when two people representing two different orientations interpret meaning from their particular vantage point. Culture, therefore, requires shared meanings and values.

The levels of meaning espoused by Pearce and Cronen are critical to consider when conversing with another. However, keep in mind that the theorists contend that their purpose is to model the way people process information, not to establish a true ordering. Also, remember that individuals vary in their past and present interactions. Therefore, some people will have highly complex hierarchies and others will have simplified hierarchies. In addition, some people are able to interpret complex meaning, while others are not as proficient. Fisher-Yoshida (2012) succinctly summarizes the utility of the hierarchy by stating the model "reflects that communication occurs at more than one level at the same time, and the meaning we make is embedded in the contexts that went before and the contexts that follow" (p. 228). The hierarchy of meaning is an important framework in helping us understand how meaning is coordinated and managed.

Charmed and Strange Loops

The hierarchy of meaning presented earlier suggests that some lower levels can reflect back and affect the meaning of higher levels. Pearce and Cronen (1980) have termed this process of reflexivity a **loop.** Because the hierarchy cannot go on forever, the theorists propose that some levels reflect back. This supports their view that communication is an ongoing, dynamic, and ever-changing process, a topic we discussed in Chapter 1.

loop
the reflexiveness of levels in the hierarchy of meaning

When loops are consistent throughout the hierarchy, Pearce and Cronen identify them as a **charmed loop.** Charmed loops occur when one part of the hierarchy confirms or supports another level. Furthermore, the rules of meaning are consistent and agreed upon throughout the loop. Figure 5.2 illustrates a charmed loop. Note that there is consistency, or confirmation, in the loop. To illustrate, consider the following example. You hired a painter to repaint the first floor of your home. You agreed to pay the painter by the hour, and when you receive the bill you are shocked at the price. You confront the painter, stating that you observed a lot of "wasted" hours and that you are not going to pay the entire bill. The painter is prepared to challenge your judgment.

charmed loop
rules of meaning are consistent throughout the loop

This encounter between painter and client exemplifies a charmed loop. In this case, the episode, or event, is the disagreement you both have over the costs of painting your home. Because your life script is your sense of self, your life script in this encounter is consistent with your passion to stand up for what you believe. In this example, the cultural pattern suggests that the two of you—painter and client—enter the conflict with two different views of the situation. The painter wants to get paid for a service and the client wants to feel satisfied with the service. In this brief example, the loop is charmed in that there is consistency among the levels (episode, life script, cultural pattern) in the hierarchy. In other words, the encounter makes sense in that your willingness to challenge the bill is *consistent* with who you are. And the way

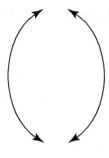

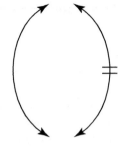

Figure 5.2   Charmed Loop   **Figure 5.3   Strange Loop**

strange loop
*rules of meaning
change within the
loop*

you communicate with the painter is *consistent* with the cultural expectations of this type of relationship (i.e., you expect efficiency). The rules of meaning in this interaction are confirmed throughout the loop.

At times, however, some episodes are inconsistent with levels higher up in the hierarchy. Pearce and Cronen have called this a **strange loop.** Strange loops usually align with *intra*personal communication in that individuals engage in a sort of internal dialogue about their self-destructive behaviors. In a basic sense, Creede et al. (2012) contend that strange loops refer to some sort of a "stuck experience" that people have when they cycle through patterns that are, well, rather oppositional. We illustrate strange loops in Figure 5.3.

To exemplify strange loops, the theorists offer the case of an alcoholic whose bouts with sobriety are followed by bouts of drinking. We present this strange loop in Figure 5.4. In this strange loop, confusion sets in. The life script of an alcoholic, for instance, suggests that drinking is out of control, so the alcoholic refuses to drink. But once the drinking stops, an alcoholic may feel a sense of control, so drinking begins again. In this example, the life script is the person's alcoholism, which manages meaning (or drinking) in particular episodes. The episodes are part of the alcoholic's life script. It's apparent, then, that the strange loop will continue to repeat itself. We call this a vicious cycle.

With this background, we now turn our attention to the issue of coordination and examine its meaning in CMM.

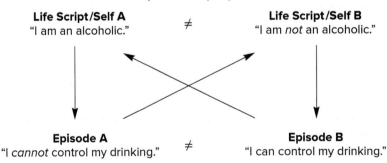

**Figure 5.4
Example of a
Strange Loop**

Cultural Pattern: It is important for people to control their behavior.

Life Script/Self A   ≠   **Life Script/Self B**
"I am an alcoholic."   "I am *not* an alcoholic."

Episode A   ≠   **Episode B**
"I *cannot* control my drinking."   "I can control my drinking."

The Coordination of Meaning: Making Sense of the Sequence

In his discussion of coordination, Pearce believes that coordination is best understood by watching people interact on a daily basis. Underscoring the first assumption of CMM, Pearce (2007) concludes that "'coordination' is probably not the first word that leaps to your mind when someone says 'communication.' Perhaps it should be" (p. 83).

Because people enter conversations with a variety of abilities and competencies, achieving coordination can be difficult at times. Coordination with others is challenging, in part because others try to coordinate their actions with ours. **Coordination** exists when two people try to make sense out of the sequencing of messages in their conversation. According to Pearce (2012), meaning is not achieved in isolation, but rather in coordination with other people. Three outcomes are possible when two people converse: They achieve coordination, they do not achieve coordination, or they achieve some degree of coordination (Philipsen, 1995). Gerry Philipsen reminds us that social reality is not perfectly coordinated, so the most likely outcome is partially achieved coordination.

coordination
trying to make sense of message sequencing

Let's look at some examples of perfect coordination, no coordination, and partial coordination by borrowing the experiences of Jessie Taylor and Ben Murphy. They are discussing an upcoming camping trip:

BEN: We need to be straightforward with the girls now. I don't see any problem with sleeping in the same tent and letting the kids sleep in their tent. Patrick can sleep with us if he gets upset.

JESSIE: I think you're right. He should have fun with the girls.

BEN: Also, they love him, which makes it easier for all of us.

JESSIE: The weekend should be a great bonding time for the families.

The two have coordinated their meanings of what to do with their children on the first family trip. Although each is entering the conversation with different experiences, Ben and Jessie have created a completed episode of meaning. Perfect coordination is attained.

However, things are not usually this smooth when discussing such complex issues. For instance:

BEN: We need to be straightforward with the girls now. I don't see any problem with sleeping in the same tent and letting the kids sleep in their tent. Patrick can sleep with us if he gets upset.

JESSIE: My girls won't like that. I'm hoping you're not saying that our feelings are more important than our kids' feelings?

BEN: I didn't say that. . . .

JESSIE: Why would you even think that? Our first trip together shouldn't be spent trying to explain why Mom and Dad want their privacy.

BEN: All I was trying to do was to let the kids know that their Mom and Dad need to have their own space.

JESSIE: And that they need to deal with their own problems?! Look, I may be over-reacting here, but . . . .

BEN: I'm sorry that I ever brought up the issue.

As you can see, this episode is quite different from the previous one. In fact, it appears that Ben and Jessie have different interpretations of what the other is saying, which prevents coordination from being achieved.

The following dialogue represents partial coordination of meaning:

BEN: We need to be straightforward with the girls now. I don't see any problem with sleeping in the same tent and letting the kids sleep in their tent. Patrick can sleep with us if he gets upset.

JESSIE: It's more complicated than that. This is the first time that we're all going to be together for a weekend.

BEN: Honey, if we don't try this right away, it'll be more difficult when we all move in together.

JESSIE: But the kids are still trying to get this situation all figured out. Separating things out this way may be more of a pain than we thought.

BEN: How about if we bought a larger tent and let the kids sleep on one side and we'll be on the other?

JESSIE: That should work.

This partially coordinated dialogue closes the episode between the two parents. Both appear to be satisfied with the compromised sleeping arrangements.

Influences on the Coordination Process

Coordination is influenced by several issues, including a sense of morality and the availability of resources. Our social worlds are essentially moral places that prescribe ways we should act and the resources we should draw upon to live our lives with dignity and honor. Pearce (2014) claims that "we only know the social world from 'inside'" (p. 9). In this section, we examine both morality and resources.

First, coordination requires that individuals be concerned with a higher moral order (Pearce, 1989). Many CMM theorists, like Pearce, explain morality as honor, dignity, and character. Moral order involves ethics, and this order is essentially an opportunity for individuals to assert an ethical stance in a conversation. CMM theorists contend that ethics is an inherent part of the conversational flow.

Each person brings various moral orders into a conversation to create and complete an episode. Pearce contends that people simultaneously perform various roles, such as sister, mother, lover, student, employee, friend, and citizen. He believes that each of these roles carries various rights and responsibilities that differ from one person to another. Difficulty arises, however, if inconsistent moral obligations exist in conversations. For instance, in some cultures, men are identified as the sole decision makers and chief protectors of their family. This may conflict with women's obligations and may affect the coordination process in their conversations. These value differences may play themselves out throughout a relationship.

resources
stories, symbols, and images that people use to make sense of their world

In addition to morality, coordination can be influenced by the resources available to an individual. When CMM theorists discuss **resources,** they refer to "the stories, images, symbols, and institutions that persons use to make their world meaningful" (Pearce, 1989, p. 23). Resources also include perceptions, memories, and concepts that help people achieve coherence in their social realities.

When resources in a conversation vary from one person to another, coordination may be challenged. To better understand this notion, consider the experiences of Loran and Wil. As a 19-year employee of a local textile manufacturer, Loran is respected by the seven employees he supervises. Although he does not have a college degree, he relishes his seniority in a company that almost shut down a few years ago. Wil, however, has a college degree and an MBA. Because the company is interested in energizing its employees with fresh perspectives on management, it is hiring college graduates with management savvy. As a result, Wil became a new supervisor in Loran's department. These changes were marked by heated discussions and a great deal of disagreement between Loran and Wil. Loran's resources—his historical understanding of the factory, his relationships with his employees, the stories shared with others, the perceptions he has of the company's goals, and so forth—seem to be secondary to Wil's resources. Wil's resources are limited, because he has little understanding of the company's history, but he does bring his college education to his job, a credential shared by few at the factory. Because an incompatibility between resources exists, Loran and Wil may have difficulty coordinating their meaning. Two important, but incompatible, sets of resources exist between Loran and Wil, and each may threaten conversation coordination.

Coordinating conversations is critical to communication. At times, coordinating with others is simple, but at other times it is quite challenging. People bring different resources into conversations, prompting individuals to respond to others based on their own management of meaning. In addition to resources, coordination relies on the rules that conversationalists follow. We now explore rules and their relationship to CMM.

Rules and Unwanted Repetitive Patterns

One way that individuals manage and coordinate meaning is through the use of rules. Earlier in the chapter we mentioned that CMM follows a rules perspective, meaning that people's dialogues include templates for how to behave. For CMM theorists, rules provide people opportunities to choose between alternatives. Once rules are established in a dialogue, interactants will have a sufficiently common symbolic framework for communication (Cushman & Whiting, 1972). CMM theorists argue that rule usage in a conversation is more than an ability to use a rule. Interactants must understand the social reality and then incorporate rules as they decide how to act in a given situation.

Rules are necessarily linked to time, place, relationship, self-concept, episode, culture, and other elements in a context (Murray, 2012). As you understand the notion of rules and their placement in CMM, keep in mind that rules are always dependent on context and that context is a multifaceted environment.

Two types of rules exist in CMM: constitutive and regulative. **Constitutive rules** refer to how behavior should be interpreted within a given context. In other words, constitutive rules tell us what types of behavior mean. We are able to understand another person's intention because of the constitutive rules in place. For example, saying "I love you" has different implications when you speak to a roommate, a lover, a family member, or even a coworker. In each of these relationships, we adopt a rule that suggests that the relationship type (contract) and the episode will determine how the statement should be received.

constitutive rules
rules that organize behavior and help us to understand how meaning should be interpreted

A second type of rule assisting coordination is the regulative rule. Constitutive rules assist people in their interpretation of meaning, but they do not provide people with guidelines for behavior. That is the function of regulative rules. **Regulative rules** refer to some sequence of action that an individual undertakes, and they communicate what happens next in a conversation. There are, for instance, regulative rules for meeting a new coworker. You generally introduce yourself, welcome your colleague to the workplace, and indicate that you're available to answer appropriate questions.

To understand the interfacing of constitutive and regulative rules, consider the following situation. A couple married 20 years is having a crisis. The wife has discovered her husband's extramarital affair and must now decide what constitutive and regulative rules to follow. She decides on a venting session because the constitutive rule tells her that such an affair is wrong in their marriage. In turn, her husband must determine how to interpret the venting (constitutive rule) and must construct some sequence of response (regulative rule). As the two engage in their discussion (and co-create their social reality), they will ultimately discover each other's rules systems. Although they have been married for two decades, this situation has not surfaced before, and consequently they may not know what the possibilities are in terms of constitutive and regulative rules. As this discovery takes place, it is likely that the coordination of the conversation will be jeopardized. That is, each person may enact different episodes along the way. They may not always agree on the rules enacted, but at least they are able to make sense out of their conversational experiences.

If the couple continue to have sustained conflict, they may engage in what Cronen, Pearce, and Linda Snavely (1979) identify as unwanted repetitive patterns (URPs). **Unwanted repetitive patterns** are sequential and recurring interpersonal conflictual episodes that are considered unwanted by the individuals in the conflict.

regulative rules
guidelines for people's behavior

unwanted repetitive patterns (URPs)
recurring, undesirable conflicts in a relationship

The individuals in a conflictual pattern feel powerless to cease the conflict (Murray, 2012). Pearce and his associates studied hostile workplace relationships and noted that although privately each worker communicated a genuine desire to be amicable and efficient, publicly their discussions were hostile and ego bruising. This verbal sparring seemed to be ripe for explanation using CMM. The researchers explained that URPs arise because two people with particular rules systems follow a structure that obligates them to perform specific behaviors, regardless of their consequences. It may seem peculiar that people believe they are obligated to act a certain way. Yet as we alluded to earlier, Pearce (1989) states that "persons find themselves in URPs . . . in which they report, with all sincerity, that 'I had no choice; I had to act this way'" (p. 39). Consider the notion of unwanted repetitive patterns this way: "Our communication has fallen into a pattern of responses that is not benefiting us" (Coleman, Deutsch, & Marcus, 2014, p. 215).

Why do two people continue to engage in URPs? First, they may see no other option. That is, the couple may not possess the skill to remove themselves from the conflict. Second, the couple may be comfortable with the recurring conflict. They

---

Theory in Popular Press • *Family Conflict as an Unwanted Repetitive Pattern*

In her blog, Elizabeth Scott contends that when families get together (over the holidays, for instance), usually everyone wants to get along. Yet, the reality is that family conflict continues to be revved up, despite our knowledge of the person or the source of conflict. Scott poses the following question: How often do we decide to be around family members, knowing very well that many of these interactions will turn out to be conflictual? Scott provocatively also asks: "Have you ever wished you had a remote control for humans, complete with pause, rewind and mute buttons?" Interviewing an expert who specializes in "using conversation to master confrontation," Scott concludes that many of our conflicts are recurring and repeated with people whom we know so well. And, despite our best efforts to the contrary, we try to "win" an argument as much as possible. We fall into these patterns because they are so familiar and because we often don't even know we've fallen victim to these unwanted repetitive patterns. Scott reports that conflict specialists recognize the importance of using "choice points," or points in a conversation where the tone can be elevated or the topic reframed. These "choice times," Scott acknowledges, are difficult, but help us to avoid reacting irrationally. It also helps the other person to rethink whether or not the conflictual episode is important enough to argue.

Source: Scott, E. (2010). Family conflict resolution solutions, stress.about.com/od/familystress/a/Family-Conflict-Resolution-Solutions.htm.

know each other and know how the other generally communicates in conflictual situations. Third, a couple may unwittingly fall into this pattern, almost instinctively and by default. Finally, a couple may simply be too exhausted to work toward conflict resolution.

Integration, Critique, and Closing

The Coordinated Management of Meaning is one of the few theories to place communication explicitly as a cornerstone in its foundation. It has both quantitative and qualitative roots. Because communication is central to the theory, many scholars have employed the theory in their writings. Among the criteria for evaluating a theory, four seem especially relevant for discussion: scope, parsimony, utility, and heurism.

Integration

Communication Tradition	Rhetorical	Semiotic	**Phenomenological**	**Cybernetic**	Socio-Psychological	**Socio-Cultural**	Critical
Communication Context	**Intrapersonal**	**Interpersonal**	Small Group	Organizational	Public/Rhetorical	Mass/Media	Cultural
Approach to Knowing	**Positivistic/Empirical**	**Interpretive/Hermeneutic**	Critical (early research) (recent research)

Critique

Evaluation Criteria	**Scope**	Logical Consistency	**Parsimony**	**Utility**	Testability	**Heurism**	Test of Time

Scope

It is unclear whether CMM is too broad in scope. Some communication scholars (e.g., Brenders, 1987) suggest that the theory is too abstract and that imprecise definitions exist. Further, Brenders believes that some of the ideas espoused by Pearce and Cronen lack parameters and beg clarification. The introduction of personal language systems, argues Brenders, is problematic and "leaves unexplained the social nature of meaning" (p. 342). Finally, M. Scott Poole (1983), in his review of CMM, notes that the theory may be problematic in that it is difficult to "paint with broad strokes and at the same time give difficult areas the attention they deserve" (p. 224).

Yet CMM theorists contend that such criticisms do not take into account the evolution of the theory and its refinement over the years (Barge & Pearce, 2004). Pearce (1995) candidly admits that during "the first phase of the CMM project, [our writings] were confused because we *could not* say what we were doing in the language of social science" (pp. 109–110). Therefore, critics should interpret the theory within the spirit of change; even theorists change as they clarify the goals of their theory. Furthermore, Cronen (1995b) admits some early problems with the concep-tualization of CMM by indicating that the way he and Pearce discussed the creation of meaning was originally confusing and "wrong-headed." Pearce, Cronen, and other CMM theorists believe that those who levy indictments regarding the scope of the theory should understand the time period in which the theory was developed.

Parsimony

The scope may be broad, but do not think that the theory has not undergone tests of parsimony. At first glance, one may conclude that the theory is too cumbersome because it "is better understood as a worldview and open-ended set of concepts and model" (Barge & Pearce, 2004, p. 25). However, illustrating difficult concepts with a visual and succinct way of looking at conversations (vis-à-vis the hierarchy of meaning), for instance, has resulted in making CMM a model that is efficient and available to theoretical consumers. The theorists posit that "there is no reason why any research method could not be used in CMM research" (p. 25). One could argue, then, that Pearce and Cronen's illustration of the hierarchy of meaning is a visual and succinct way of looking at conversations. Therefore, even cumbersome and complex conversations can be analyzed and understood.

Student Voices

Jeremy

If I analyzed a recent conversation with my supervisor, I'd say that a lot of CMM concepts apply. First, in the hierarchy of meaning, I'm French Canadian and he's Japanese American. Our conversations are definitely affected by cultural patterns. Second, my life script or view of myself as a good worker is pretty solid. I can't imagine I would ever be called in for slacking on the job. I also think that on the relationship level, he and I are pretty clear. I know that as my supervisor he doesn't appreciate joking around, and as his employee I don't enjoy "off-color" discussions. I guess this hierarchy can be applied to almost any conversation.

Utility

The application of this theory to individuals and their conversations is quite ap-parent. The practicality of looking at how people achieve meaning, their potential recurring conflicts, and the influence of the self on the communication process is admirable. CMM is one of the few communication theories that has been identified by both theorists and CMM scholars as a "practical theory" (Creede et al., 2012). In fact, Pearce was always concerned with the utility of his theory since its inception (Pearce, 2012). As well, he is direct in calling CMM a practical theory and notes that the one question guiding CMM is "How can we make better social worlds?" (Pearce, 2007, p. 45). Finally, Pearce observes that the theory has evolved along three stages: interpretive, critical, and *practical*" [emphasis added] (p. 52). Clearly, there is a pragmatic legacy with CMM.

Heurism

CMM is a very heuristic theory, spanning a number of different content areas, including examining international adoption (Leinaweaver, 2012), spirituality (Pearce, 2012), student–professor relationships (Murray, 2014), refugee communities such as the Congolese (Hughes & Bisimwa, 2015), electronic chat rooms (Moore & Mattson-Lauters, 2009), and mentoring relationships (Parke, 2011). Furthermore, researchers have incorporated the theory and its tenets to understand health care (Forsythe, 2012), high school hazing (DeWitt & DeWitt, 2012), the Presbyterian Church (Hutcheson, 2012), volunteer work (Creede, 2012), and families who have been tortured or persecuted across cultures (Montgomery, 2004).

Closing

Thanks in large part to CMM, we have a deeper understanding of how individuals co-create meaning in conversations. In fact, Ronald Arnett (2014) contends that Pearce provided a "communicative roadmap for navigating an era" (p. 6) in communication research. Further, the thinking and research of Pearce have been collated and are archived at Fitchburg State University where a certificate in CMM is available. CMM is, as Allan Holmgren (2004) says, like a Swiss Army knife, useful in many situations. The theory has aided us in understanding the importance of rules in social situations. CMM, and Pearce in particular, is credited for moving the theory into areas that have allowed for a "porous boundary" between his scholarship and his work toward social change (Lannamann, 2014, p. 257). It is clear that few can deny that CMM positioned communication at the core of human experience and remains a theory that has anchored communication as central to discourse.

Discussion Starters

TECH QUEST: Since CMM relies so heavily on the ability of people to coordinate their communication in order for meaning to be achieved, how might meaning be "interrupted" if, while communicating in person, someone began texting another person? Explain the anticipated effects and your response.

1. What types of coordination will our chapter opener's Taylor-Murphy family experience as they begin a life together? Try to identify stages that the family may experience and specific episodes of coordination.

2. How might coordination be influenced by differing cultural backgrounds of communicators?

3. Discuss enmeshment and its relationship to conversations in your family. Be sure to define the term and apply it to your family relationships.

4. Chess and poker are games requiring coordination. Discuss some of life's "games" and how they require coordination. Be creative and give specific examples.

5. What types of meaning breakdowns have you experienced in your conversations with others? Be specific and identify the context, the situation, and the conversation topic.

6. Identify and explain a strange loop that exists in popular culture or in your interpersonal relationships.

7. Discuss specific ways in which any component of CMM has practical value to you as a college student. Identify the part of the theory that has relevancy to you and reasons for its applicability.

CHAPTER 6

Cognitive Dissonance Theory

*Based on the research of **Leon Festinger***

I prefer to rely on my memory. I have lived with that memory a long time, I am used to it, and if I have rearranged or distorted anything, surely that was done for my own benefit.

—Leon Festinger

Ali Torres

Ali Torres shuffled the papers on her desk and looked out the office window. She was really bored with this job. When she initially signed on to work with the Puerto Rican Alliance in Gary, Indiana, she was so excited. The job seemed to be a dream come true. First, it offered her a chance to give back to her community—both the city of Gary and the Puerto Rican community within the city. She had grown up in Gary, Indiana, and knew firsthand how difficult it was to get ahead for people of color, especially Latinos. Latinos were a minority among minorities in this city, and it was tough to make much progress. Despite that, Ali had gotten a lot from growing up in Gary. When she was in high school, a friendly guidance counselor had offered her a helping hand and suggested that Ali consider college. Without Ms. Martinez's support, she never would have thought about college, much less actually graduated. But, Ali had finished college and now she felt strongly about giving something back. So the job had seemed perfect; it would be a way for her to give back to the community and at the same time use her major in public relations.

Yet, in the six months Ali had worked in the Alliance office, her sole responsibilities had centered on typing and running errands. She felt like a gofer, with no chance to do anything she considered important. Actually, she was beginning to question whether the Alliance itself was doing anything worthwhile. Sometimes she thought the whole operation was just a front so politicians could say something was being done to help the Latino population in the city.

Her coworkers didn't seem to mind that they didn't do much all day, so Ali wasn't getting much support from them. But it was her boss's attitude that bothered Ali the most. He was a respected leader in the Latino community; she remembered him from when she was growing up. When she found out she would be working for him, she had been delighted. But as far as Ali could tell, he hardly ever worked at all. He was rarely in the office, and when he did come in, he took long lunch hours and many breaks. He spoke to Ali very infrequently and never gave her assignments.

Ali was feeling extremely frustrated. She was on her own to develop projects or, more likely, simply to put in eight hours doing a lot of nothing. Ali had decided that she would quit this job and start looking for something where she could feel more useful, but she was having a hard time giving up on her dream of contributing to her community. She had begun this job with such high hopes. She had expected to work to persuade funding agencies to sponsor programs to strengthen opportunities for the Latino community. Ironically, now she found that the only person she was persuading was herself, as she

COGNITIVE DISSONANCE THEORY

wrestled with the decision of whether to keep working or give up on this job. Ali spoke to some of her friends, who encouraged her to do what she thought was right and quit the Alliance if she wanted to. That made her feel better, but she couldn't completely shake her memories of the auspicious beginning of the job and all her high hopes.

■

Suppose you are Ali Torres's friend and are interested in knowing how she feels about her job. You notice that she seems a little depressed when she talks about work, and lately she hasn't brought up the subject at all. Her silence about her work is especially obvious to you compared with how enthusiastically she spoke about the position when she first started at the Alliance. You could ask Ali directly how she feels, but you wonder how honest she will be with you. You know Ali doesn't want you to worry about her. You also know that Ali cares a great deal about the ideals of the Alliance and that she might not want to tell you if she is disappointed. Your problem in this situation is inferring Ali's attitudes.

The problem you would face as Ali's friend is a common one because people's attitudes cannot be directly observed; yet attitudes are believed to be excellent predictors of people's behaviors (Knobloch-Westerwick & Meng, 2009; O'Neill & Arendt, 2008). As Susan Fiske and Shelley Taylor (1984) observe, "[A]ttitudes have always been accorded star status in social explanations of human behavior by lay people and professionals alike" (p. 341). Because of their importance, many theories try to explain attitude formation, change, and the interlocking relationship among cognitions, attitudes, affect, and behavioral tendencies. Many psychologists (e.g., Rydell, Hugenberg, & McConnell, 2006) assert that the most influential approaches to attitudes come from cognitive consistency theories.

Consistency theories in general posit that the mind operates as an intermediary between stimulus and response. These theories assert that when people receive information (a stimulus), their mind organizes it into a pattern with other previously encountered stimuli. If the new stimulus does not fit the pattern, or is inconsistent, then people feel discomfort. For example, Ali Torres feels this type of distress as she reflects on the discrepancy between her desire to respect her boss and her observations of his seeming indifference to the job. In these cases, consistency theorists note that there is a lack of balance among varying **cognitions,** or ways of knowing, beliefs, judgments, and so forth.

cognitions
ways of knowing, beliefs, judgments, and thoughts

Leon Festinger called this feeling of imbalance **cognitive dissonance;** the feeling people have when they "find themselves doing things that don't fit with what they know, or having opinions that do not fit with other opinions they hold" (1957, p. 4). This concept forms the core of Festinger's Cognitive Dissonance Theory (CDT), a theory that argues that dissonance is an uncomfortable feeling that motivates people to take steps to reduce it (Figure 6.1). As Roger Brown (1965) notes, the basics of the theory follow rather simple principles: "A state of cognitive dissonance is said to be a state of psychological discomfort or tension which motivates efforts to achieve consonance. *Dissonance* is the name for a disequilibrium and *consonance* the name for an equilibrium" (p. 584). To some (e.g., Chang, Solomon, & Westerfield, 2016), dissonance is especially "acute when one of the beliefs in question relates to the individual's self-concept" (p. 268). Further, Brown points out that the theory allows

cognitive dissonance
feeling of discomfort resulting from inconsistent attitudes, thoughts, and behaviors

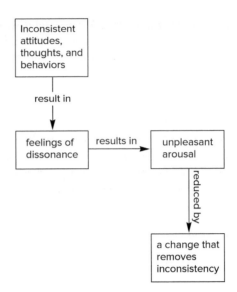

Figure 6.1
**The Process
of Cognitive
Dissonance**

for two elements to have three different relationships with each other: These relationships are called consonant, dissonant, or irrelevant.

A **consonant relationship** exists between two elements when they are in equilibrium with one another. If you believe, for instance, that health and fitness are important goals and you work out three to five times a week, then your beliefs about health and your own behaviors would have a consonant relationship with one another. Ali would have a consonant relationship if she believed that the Alliance was really making a difference in the Latino community and that her work was meaningful. A **dissonant relationship** means that elements are in disequilibrium with one another. An example of a dissonant relationship would be if a practicing Catholic we'll call Rita believes in a woman's right to choose abortion. In this case, Rita's religious beliefs are in conflict with her beliefs about abortion. In our opening story, Ali Torres is experiencing a dissonant relationship.

An **irrelevant relationship** exists when the elements imply nothing about one another. This type of relationship is illustrated by believing that the speed limit should be raised to 65 miles per hour on all freeways, and believing that women should have equal rights in the workplace. Although the two beliefs may indicate a general view endorsing individual freedoms, they basically have no relationship to each other. When beliefs are in a consonant or irrelevant relationship, there is no psychological discomfort. However, if beliefs are dissonant, discomfort results.

The importance of cognitive dissonance for communication researchers rests on Festinger's assertion that the discomfort caused by dissonance motivates change. As we see in our chapter-opening vignette, Ali Torres is feeling frustrated and uncomfortable in her job. Her initial belief about the opportunities for her to help others through this job and her prior high regard for her boss are inconsistent with her present situation. This is the point at which persuasion can occur. The theory suggests that to be persuasive, strategies should focus on the inconsistencies while providing new behaviors that allow for consistency or balance. Thus,

**consonant
relationship**
*two elements in
equilibrium with
each another*

**dissonant
relationship**
*two elements in
disequilibrium with
each other*

**irrelevant
relationship**
*two elements that
have no meaning-
ful relation to each
other*

COGNITIVE DISSONANCE THEORY

Daniel Tomasulo writes in his blog, "Ask the Therapist," that he is experiencing cognitive dissonance as a result of learning that Lance Armstrong will no longer fight allegations of doping violations during his cycling career. Further, as a result, the U.S. Anti-Doping Agency voted to ban Armstrong from competing for life and strip him of his record seven Tour de France titles. Tomasulo notes that he considered Armstrong a true hero and now he has to readjust his thinking about the cyclist. Armstrong is, in Tomasulo's view now, both a hero for what he has done for raising cancer awareness and a fraud for seemingly admitting that his victories were fueled by performing-enhancing drugs. Tomasulo states that: "In my opinion, Lance Armstrong is a survivor and a liar. He is an incredibly strong man, and an incredibly weak man. Armstrong is a source of inspiration, and a source of disgrace and embarrassment. He is both a hero and a villain. In short, he has become the modern-day example of *cognitive dissonance.*" As CDT suggests, Tomasulo observes that he has to reconcile his dissonant beliefs about Armstrong or suffer anxiety.

Source: Tomasulo, D. Lance Armstrong: Cognitive dissonance as a hero's journey ends, psychcentral.com/blog/archives/2012/08/25/lance-armstrong-cognitive-dissonance-as-a -heros-journey-ends/.

CDT offers communication researchers some explanation for persuasion, as well as providing guidelines for creating persuasive messages. Further, cognitive dissonance focuses on communication behavior as people seek to persuade others and as people strive to reduce their dissonant cognitions. For example, when Ali went to her friends to discuss her decision, she was seeking help in reducing dissonance. Her conversations with friends and her efforts at self-persuasion are examples of communication being used in the dissonance reduction process (We address the interplay between Cognitive Dissonance Theory and persuasion a bit later in the chapter.)

Theory At a Glance • Cognitive Dissonance

The experience of dissonance—incompatible beliefs and actions or two incompatible beliefs—is unpleasant, and people are highly motivated to avoid it. In their efforts to avoid feelings of dissonance, people will ignore views that oppose their own, change their beliefs to match their actions (or vice versa), and/or seek reassurances after making a difficult decision.

Assumptions of Cognitive Dissonance Theory

As we have indicated, Cognitive Dissonance Theory provides an explanation for how beliefs and behavior change attitudes. Its focus is on the effects of inconsistency among cognitions. Our introductory material suggested a number of assumptions that frame CDT. Four assumptions basic to the theory include:

- Human beings desire consistency in their beliefs, attitudes, and behaviors.
- Dissonance is created by psychological inconsistencies.
- Dissonance is an aversive state that drives people to actions with measurable effects.
- Dissonance motivates efforts to achieve consonance and efforts toward dissonance reduction.

The first assumption portrays a model of human nature that is concerned with stability and consistency. When we discuss Uncertainty Reduction Theory in Chapter 8, you will see a similar conceptualization of human nature. Cognitive Dissonance Theory suggests that people do not enjoy inconsistencies in their thoughts and beliefs. Instead, they seek consistency. This is why Ali feels uncomfortable in her job and unhappy with her thoughts about quitting the job. She is seeking consistency, yet her perceptions of her job provide her with inconsistency. Janet Meyer (2011) found that a frequent reason that people regretted messages they had sent to others had to do with dissonance.

The second assumption speaks to the kind of consistency that is important to people. The theory is not concerned with a strict logical consistency. Rather, it refers to the fact that cognitions must be psychologically inconsistent (as opposed to logically inconsistent) with one another to arouse cognitive dissonance. For example, if Ali Torres holds the cognition that "I want to contribute to my community," it is *not* logically inconsistent to also believe that the Alliance is not contributing much to the community. The two beliefs are not logically contradictory. Yet it is psychologically inconsistent for Ali to continue working for the Alliance when she believes it is doing little to help Latinos in Gary, Indiana. That is, Ali will feel psychologically inconsistent by continuing to do nothing when she wishes to be of help. Ali also feels stress related to her thoughts of quitting and her lingering hopes for what she might have accomplished in this job.

The third assumption of the theory suggests that when people experience psychological inconsistencies, the dissonance that is created is aversive. Thus, people do not enjoy being in a state of dissonance; it is an uncomfortable state. Festinger asserted that dissonance is a drive state possessing arousal properties. Since Festinger's initial conceptualization of the theory, a significant amount of research has supported this assumption (e.g., Foster & Misra, 2013; Rydell, McConnell, & Mackie, 2008). One study (Elkin & Leippe, 1986) found that physiological arousal was also related to dissonance. Therefore, Cognitive Dissonance Theory would assume that Ali would feel physically uncomfortable as a result of the psychological dissonance that she is experiencing.

Finally, the theory assumes that the arousal generated by dissonance will motivate people to avoid situations that create inconsistencies and strive toward

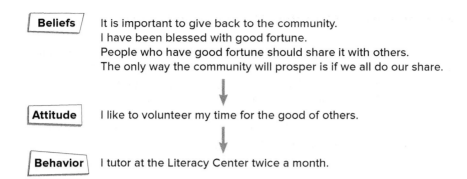

Beliefs It is important to give back to the community.
I have been blessed with good fortune.
People who have good fortune should share it with others.
The only way the community will prosper is if we all do our share.

Attitude I like to volunteer my time for the good of others.

Behavior I tutor at the Literacy Center twice a month.

Figure 6.2
Consistency in Beliefs, Attitudes, and Behaviors

situations that restore consistency. Thus, the picture of human nature that frames the theory consists of seeking psychological consistency as a result of the arousal caused by the aversive state of inconsistent cognitions (Figure 6.2).

Concepts and Processes of Cognitive Dissonance

As the theory developed over the years, certain concepts were refined and other concepts were added. For example, the following scenario illustrates a situation where dissonance would arise: If Juan believes that relationships should be completely harmonious (a cognition) and yet he argues a great deal with his partner (a conflicting behavior), the theory predicts that Juan will become tense and suffer discomfort. When dissonance theorists seek to predict how much discomfort or dissonance Juan will suffer, they invoke many concepts, which we will discuss further.

Magnitude of Dissonance

The first concept is **magnitude of dissonance,** which refers to the quantitative amount of dissonance a person experiences. Magnitude of dissonance will determine actions people may take and cognitions they may espouse to reduce the dissonance. The theory differentiates between situations producing more dissonance and those producing less dissonance. A peculiar relationship sometimes exists with respect to dissonance and beneficial events. For instance, in one study, when people thought they were candidates for an "unpleasant medical screening," even though the screening had medical value, they reported less favorable perceptions about the screening than those who were deemed ineligible (Ent & Gerend, 2015).

Three factors influence the magnitude of dissonance a person will feel (Zimbardo, Ebbesen, & Maslach, 1977). First, the degree of **importance,** or how significant the issue is, affects the degree of dissonance felt. If, for example, Juan has many friendships and activities outside his relationship and his partner is not critically important to him, the theory predicts that his magnitude of dissonance will be small. But if Juan finds much of his identity and social interaction in his

magnitude of dissonance
the quantitative amount of discomfort felt

importance
a factor in determining magnitude of dissonance; refers to how significant the issue is

COGNITIVE DISSONANCE THEORY

relationship with his partner, then the magnitude of dissonance should be greater. The same could be said for Ali Torres. If she does a great deal of volunteer work in the community and her job is not the main source of her identity, then the magnitude of her dissonance is not as great as if her job is critically important to her.

dissonance ratio
a factor in determining magnitude of dissonance; the amount of consonant cognitions relative to the dissonant ones

Second, the amount of dissonance is affected by the **dissonance ratio,** or the amount of dissonant cognitions relative to the amount of consonant cognitions. Given Juan's propensity to argue with his partner, he probably has many cognitions that are relevant to that behavior. Some of these cognitions are consistent with his behavior; for example, "It is good to get feelings out in the open." "It is positive to feel you can really be yourself with your partner." "Sometimes arguing allows you both to see problems in a creative way." Several of his cognitions are dissonant with conflict behavior, however. For example, consider: "If we really loved each other, we wouldn't argue so much." "We spend so much time fighting, we never have any fun." "Our fights are so repetitive, we never solve anything." "My parents never argued with each other; we must not be very sensitive to each other." "I didn't picture my relationship like this." Because Juan has more dissonant cognitions than consonant ones, the ratio is negative. Thus, Juan is likely to feel that there is inconsistency, and the discomfort of dissonance will result. If the ratio were more balanced or weighted toward the positive, Juan would feel less dissonance.

rationale
a factor in determining magnitude of dissonance; refers to the reasoning employed to explain the inconsistency

Finally, the magnitude of dissonance is affected by the rationale that an individual summons to justify the inconsistency. The **rationale** refers to the reasoning employed to explain why an inconsistency exists. The more reasons one has to account for the discrepancy, the less dissonance one will feel. For instance, if Juan and his partner have just moved, changed or lost a job, purchased a home, or experienced any other stressor, Juan may be able to justify the conflicts as being a result of the stress he is feeling and thus probably a temporary situation. In this case, it is likely that the dissonance he feels will be much less than if he is unable to come up with any rationale explaining his behaviors (Matz & Wood, 2005).

Coping with Dissonance

Although Cognitive Dissonance Theory explains that dissonance can be reduced through both behavioral and attitudinal changes, most of the research has focused on the latter. Many ways to increase consistency are cognitively based, and the theory suggests several methods Juan may use to reduce his dissonance. First, Juan could add or subtract cognitions to change the ratio of consonant to dissonant cognitions. In Juan's case, this might mean adding the fact that his friends Albert and Don fight a lot but seem to be happy, and subtracting the idea that he didn't picture his relationship as full of conflict. Alternatively, Juan might try to reduce the importance of the dissonant cognitions. He might think about the fact that children do not know much about their parents' relationship, so the fact that he did not think his parents fought a lot might not weigh too heavily in the equation. Finally, Juan could seek out information that advocates conflict in relationships and stresses the benefits of open communication between partners. He might discredit the information that suggests conflict is not good for a relationship by believing that it comes from an unrealistic, overly optimistic point of view. In sum, we can cope with dissonance by (1) adding to our consonant beliefs, (2) reducing the importance of our dissonant beliefs, or (3) changing our beliefs to seemingly eliminate the dissonance in some way. With reference to the third option, Katie Dunleavy and Matthew Martin (2010) found that students expressed that nagging an instructor to obtain a better grade was more acceptable behavior than their instructors did. The researchers speculated that students might have reduced their dissonance about performing a negative behavior (nagging) by transforming their beliefs about the behavior's negative impact. Teachers, on the other hand, did not perform the behavior, so they had no need to change their beliefs.

Cognitive Dissonance and Perception

As Juan engages in any of these strategies to change his cognitions and reduce his feelings of dissonance, perceptual processes come into play. Specifically, Cognitive Dissonance Theory relates to the processes of selective exposure, selective attention, selective interpretation, and selective retention because the theory predicts that people will avoid information that increases dissonance. These perceptual processes are basic to this avoidance.

Selective exposure, or seeking consistent information not already present, helps to reduce dissonance. CDT predicts that people will avoid information that increases dissonance and seek out information that is consistent with their attitudes and behavior. In the example of the conflictual relationship, Juan might seek friends who also fight a great deal yet seem to be happy in their relationships.

Selective attention refers to looking at consistent information once it is there. People attend to information in their environment that conforms to their attitudes and beliefs while ignoring information that is inconsistent. Thus, Ali Torres might read favorable articles about the Alliance in the newspaper while overlooking articles that suggest contrary views.

Selective interpretation involves interpreting ambiguous information so that it becomes consistent. Utilizing selective interpretation, most people interpret close friends' attitudes as more congruent with their own than is actually true (Berscheid & Walster, 1978). People use selective interpretation to avoid potential dissonance.

Finally, **selective retention** refers to remembering and learning consistent information with much greater ability than we do inconsistent information. Cognitive Dissonance Theory predicts that if a couple were arguing about whether to spend a vacation camping or on a cruise, the partner who wished to camp would not remember the details of the cruise package and the one desiring the cruise would not remember much about the camping plans. If Juan heard a lecture once about how important conflict can be in close relationships, he may well remember that in his current situation of frequent fighting with his partner. Similarly, Ali might focus on stories she heard in the past about good works that the Alliance has done.

Attitudes seem to organize memory in this selective retention process (Lingle & Ostrom, 1981). When thinking about someone as your teacher, you will remember her ability to lecture, her command of the subject, her ability to get a discussion started, and her accessibility to help you with assignments. If, on the other hand, you were thinking about the same person as an actor, you would recall her ability to project a character and to gain your interest. Once you have formed an attitude about someone as a teacher rather than an actor, that influences your recall about that person.

selective exposure
a method for reducing dissonance by seeking information that is consonant with current beliefs and actions

selective attention
a method for reducing dissonance by paying attention to information that is consonant with current beliefs and actions

selective interpretation
a method for reducing dissonance by interpreting ambiguous information so that it becomes consistent with current beliefs and actions

selective retention
a method for reducing dissonance by remembering information that is consonant with current beliefs and actions

COGNITIVE DISSONANCE THEORY

Let's sum up the preceding sections this way: When people are confronted with cognitive inconsistency, they usually wish to achieve cognitive dissonance. And as Sohn and Lariscy (2015) note, people selectively pay attention to information that is consistent with previously held beliefs. Communicators also "weigh unequal values on different pieces of information" (p. 239). When this mental equilibrium exists, a **confirmatory bias** has taken place.

confirmatory bias
the tendency to confirm a preconception or interpretation of phenomena

minimal justification
offering the least amount of incentive necessary to obtain compliance

Minimal Justification

One of the interesting and counterintuitive assertions that Festinger advances in this theory has to do with what he calls minimal justification. **Minimal justification** refers to offering only the minimum incentive required to get someone to change. The experiment that Festinger and his colleague James Carlsmith performed that established the principle of minimal justification is the now-famous $1/$20 study. Festinger and Carlsmith (1959) recruited male students at Stanford University and assigned them to do a boring, repetitive task consisting of sorting spools into lots of 12 and giving square pegs a quarter turn to the right. At the end of an hour of this monotonous assignment, the experimenter asked the research participants to do him a favor. The researcher explained another person was needed to continue doing this task, and offered to pay the participants to recruit a woman in the waiting room by telling her how enjoyable the task was. This woman was actually a research assistant also, and she was helping the researchers examine how the men tried to persuade her. Some of the men were offered $1 to recruit the woman, whereas others were offered $20 for the same behavior. (Remember, this was 1959, and both these sums were worth a great deal more than they are now.) Festinger and Carlsmith found that the men engaged in this study differed in their attitudes at the end. Those who received $20 for recruiting the woman said that they really thought the task was boring, whereas those who received only $1 stated that they really believed the task was enjoyable.

From these results came the notion of minimal justification. Festinger and Carlsmith argued that doing something a person does not believe in for a minimal reward sets up more dissonance than doing that same thing for a larger reward. If people engage in deception for a lot of money, they will acknowledge that they did it for the money. If they engage in deception for only $1, they do not have a ready explanation that will make their attitudes and behaviors form a consonant relationship. To reduce their dissonance, they have to make some type of change to bring consistency to their cognitions. Therefore, they may change their opinion of the task to make sense of why they told the woman in the waiting room that it was fun. Now they believe they told her it was fun because, in fact, it *was* enjoyable.

Minimal justification focuses more on changing attitudes than changing behavior because the concept acknowledges that behavior could be changed by offering someone a lot of money to do something. But, imagine that your school wants to persuade the students to *want* to engage in more volunteer activities as well as to actually engage in the activities. If the goal is to believe that social activism is a value, the school might offer students a T-shirt for volunteering rather than an A in a class for participating in service learning, for example. Students receiving a T-shirt probably wouldn't say they volunteered for 10 hours a week all semester just to get the shirt, while students could say their volunteer activities were simply a result of wanting an A grade.

Cognitive Dissonance Theory and Persuasion

Much of the research following from Festinger's work focuses on persuasion, especially with regard to decision making. A large amount of research concentrates on cognitive dissonance as a post-decision phenomenon. Several studies examine **buyer's remorse,** which refers to the dissonance people often feel after deciding on a large purchase. One study examining buyer's remorse focused on automobile purchases (Donnelly & Ivancevich, 1970). In their study, they located people who were waiting for delivery of cars they had signed contracts to buy. These people were divided into two groups. One group was contacted twice to reassure them about the wisdom of their purchase. Another group was not contacted between the contract signing and the delivery of the car. About twice as many in the group that was not contacted canceled the order for the car. This finding supported the theory that dissonance may be activated after making a large purchase. Further, the study showed that providing people with information about the wisdom of their decision can reduce the dissonance. This finding speaks to the importance of the decision and to manipulating the dissonance ratio, factors we discussed earlier in the chapter.

buyer's remorse
post-decision dissonance related to a purchase

Student Voices

Nancy

I certainly have experienced buyer's remorse. And I think I probably handled it in the way Cognitive Dissonance Theory predicts. When my husband and I bought our first house, I was a nervous wreck, and the only way I calmed myself down was to think about how bad our other choices were and to spend time talking with Neil about how great this house was. We kind of talked ourselves into believing we made a fabulous choice.

Another study (Knox & Inkster, 1968) investigated this regret period after a decision in a different context. This study had experimenters approach people either shortly before or shortly after they had placed a $2 bet at a Canadian racetrack. The bettors were asked how confident they felt about their horse's chances. Their findings indicated that people were more confident that their horse would win after they had placed the bet than they were before they placed the bet. They interpreted these findings as consistent with CDT because they reasoned that after the bet has been placed, people feel dissonance. The decision to choose one particular horse is dissonant with the belief that the horse has flaws that could prevent it from winning the race. A simple coping mechanism for reducing this dissonance is to increase the beliefs about the attractiveness of the horse that you bet on, or the chosen alternative. Thus, the theory would predict, and Knox and Inkster found, bettors expressing more confidence after making their decision than before. As Robert Wicklund and Jack W. Brehm (1976) point out, when a decision is irrevocable, as in a bet placed, people have to work quickly to reduce the inevitable dissonance that results.

Another study (Brownstein, Read, & Simon, 2004) looked at cognitive dissonance at the racetrack. Participants were given information about horses and then were asked to rate each horse's chance of winning the race. The respondents rated the horses three times before placing their bets and one time afterward. Consistent with Cognitive Dissonance Theory's predictions, the researchers found that the ratings of the chosen horse increased after the choice had been made.

Vani Simmons, Monica Webb, and Thomas Brandon (2004) studied whether cognitive dissonance principles could help college students stop smoking. They tested an experimental learning intervention based on the theory. One hundred forty-four college students who smoked were asked to create educational videos about the risks of smoking or about quitting smoking. They found that intentions to quit smoking were increased by making the videos as CDT would predict.

Festinger and two colleagues examined post-decision dissonance in a pioneering case study (Festinger, Riecken, & Schachter, 1956). Festinger and his colleagues joined a doomsday cult based in Chicago in the 1950s. The group was led by a middle-aged man and woman. The woman, whom the researchers named Mrs. Keech, began to receive messages from spiritual beings who seemed to be predicting a great disaster, a flood that would end the world. Then the spiritual beings transmitted information to Mrs. Keech that the members of the cult would be saved before the flood. The group was instructed that spacemen would arrive and transport the believers to safety on another planet. The believers began to make preparations for the end of their world and their departure to another world. The appointed time for departure was midnight, and the group gathered in Mrs. Keech's living room to await the spaceship that would take them to safety. As the moments slipped by, it became apparent that no one was coming to rescue the believers, and, in fact, they did not need to be rescued because the world was not under water. At first, the cult seemed on the verge of disintegration as a result of the extreme dissonance everyone was feeling. Yet the group was so committed to their beliefs that they found ways to reconcile the dissonance.

The group reconciled their dissonance in two specific ways. First, Mrs. Keech claimed a new message came from the spiritual beings telling the group that their faith had caused God to save the world from destruction. Thus, the group used selective interpretation and allowed new information through selective attention. Second, Mrs. Keech said she had received an additional message telling the group to publicize the situation. The group became energized again, reduced their dissonance, and confirmed themselves in their decision to be members of the group.

Some researchers have observed the relationship of dissonance and communication strategies in situations other than decision making. Patrice Buzzanell and Lynn Turner (2003) examined family communication in families where the major wage earner had lost his or her job within the past 18 months. Buzzanell and Turner interviewed family members to assess the communication issues created by the job loss.

Buzzanell and Turner found that job loss did create feelings of dissonance in most family members, and the researchers argued that family members reduced their dissonance about job loss by using three interesting strategies. First, families adopted a tone of normalcy, telling the interviewers that nothing had really changed after the job loss. Second, families deliberately foregrounded positive themes and backgrounded negative ones. Finally, families maintained gendered identity construction, working to assure the man who had lost his job that he was still the man of the family.

In all of these strategies, family members worked to reduce the dissonance created by job loss.

Integration, Critique, and Closing

Although researchers have been using and revising Festinger's theory since 1957, the theory's genesis is clearly quantitative and most of the work undertaken today remains true to this experimental approach. And, while some writers contend that the theory is a great theoretical achievement in social psychology (Barrett, 2017), most of the criticisms relate to the theory's utility and usefulness.

Integration

Communication Tradition	Rhetorical | Semiotic | Phenomenological | Cybernetic | **Socio-Psychological** | Socio-Cultural | Critical
Communication Context	**Intrapersonal** | Interpersonal | Small Group | Organizational | Public/Rhetorical | Mass/Media | Cultural
Approach to Knowing	**Positivistic/Empirical** | Interpretive/Hermeneutic | Critical

Critique

Evaluation Criteria	Scope | Logical Consistency | Parsimony | **Utility** | **Testability** | Heurism | Test of Time

Utility

One concern of CDT relates to critics' complaints that the theory may not possess utility because other theoretical frameworks can explain the attitude change found in the $1/$20 experiment better than cognitive dissonance.

Irving Janis and Robert Gilmore (1965) argue that when people participate in an inconsistency, such as arguing a position they do not believe in, they become motivated to think up all the arguments in favor of the position while suppressing all the arguments against it. Janis and Gilmore call this process *biased scanning*. This biased scanning process should increase the chances of accepting the new position—for example, changing one's position from evaluating the spool-sorting task as dull to the position that it really was an interesting task.

Janis and Gilmore (1965) note that when a person is overcompensated for engaging in biased scanning, suspicion and guilt are aroused. Thus, they are able to explain why the large incentive of $20 does not cause the students in Festinger and Carlsmith's (1959) experiment to have an increased attitude change.

Other researchers (Cooper & Fazio, 1984) argue that the original theory of cognitive dissonance contains a great deal of "conceptual fuzziness." Some researchers note that the concept of dissonance is confounded by self-concept or impression management. Impression management refers to the activities people engage in to look good to themselves and others. For example, Elliot Aronson (1969) argues that people wish to appear reasonable to themselves and suggests that in Festinger and Carlsmith's (1959) experiment, if "dissonance exists, it is because the individual's behavior is inconsistent with his self-concept" (p. 27). Aronson asserts that the Stanford students' dissonance resulted from seeing themselves as upright and truthful men contrasted with their behavior of deceiving someone else because they were being paid to do so.

In the study we discussed earlier by Patrice Buzzanell and Lynn Turner (2003) concerning family communication and job loss, we could conceive of the strategies the families adopted as employing impression management rather than reducing dissonance. When fathers reported that nothing had changed in their family despite the job loss, they may have been rationalizing to continue to seem reasonable to themselves, just as Aronson suggests.

In the preceding critiques, researchers disagree about what cognitive state is at work: dissonance, biased scanning, or impression management. Daryl Bem (1967) argues that the central concept of importance is not *any* type of cognition but, rather, is behavioral. Bem states that rather than dissonance in cognitions operating to change people, self-perception is at work. Self-perception simply means that people make conclusions about their own attitudes the same way others do—by observing their behavior. Bem's alternative explanation allows more simplicity in the theory as well.

In Bem's conceptualization, it is not necessary to speculate about the degree of cognitive dissonance that a person feels. People only need to observe what they are doing to calculate what their attitudes must be. For instance, if I am not working out regularly, but I believe fitness and health are important goals, I must not really believe working out is so important to good health. In our chapter-opening story about Ali Torres, Bem would argue that the longer Ali works at the Alliance, the more likely she is to come to believe that she is doing something worthwhile. Bem's argument suggests that if Ali's friend asks her if she likes her job, she might reply, "I guess I do. I am still there."

Claude Steele's work (Steele, 1988, 2012; Steele, Spencer, & Lynch, 1993) also offers a behavioral explanation for dissonance effects: self-affirmation. However, unlike Bem, Steele and his colleagues argue that dissonance is the result of behaving in a manner that threatens one's sense of moral integrity. You can see how this explanation might work quite well in Ali Torres's situation. Her discomfort might not be because she holds two contradictory beliefs but because she doesn't respect herself for staying in a job where she is not accomplishing anything of significance.

Other scholars believe that Cognitive Dissonance Theory is basically useful and explanatory but needs some refinements. For example, Wicklund and Brehm (1976) argue that CDT is not clear enough about the conditions under which dissonance leads to change in attitudes. They believe that choice is the missing concept in the theory. Wicklund and Brehm posit that when people believe they have a choice about the dissonant relationship, they will be motivated to change that relationship. If people think they are powerless, then they will not be bothered by the dissonance, and they probably will not change. Regarding our beginning scenario about Ali Torres, Wicklund and Brehm would argue that we could predict whether she will leave her job based on how much choice she believes she has in the matter. If, for instance, she is tied to Gary, Indiana, because of family responsibilities or if she believes she would have trouble locating a new job in the city, she may not be motivated to act on her dissonant cognitions. On the other hand, if nothing really ties her to Gary, or there are plenty of other job opportunities, she will be motivated to change based on those same cognitions.

Another refinement is suggested by the work of Joel Cooper and Jeff Stone (2000). Cooper and Stone point out that in the more than 1,000 studies using CDT, only rarely has the group membership of the person experiencing dissonance been considered. Cooper and Stone believe that group membership plays an important role in how people experience and reduce dissonance. For example, they found that social identity derived from religious and political groups had an impact on how people responded to dissonance. Somewhat related to Cooper and Stone's notion is work that examines "spiritual dissonance" and examines people who volunteer for religious groups (McGuire, 2010).

Other critics note that CDT is not as useful as it should be because it does not provide a full explanation for how and when people will attempt to reduce dissonance. First, there is what has been called the "multiple mode" problem. This problem exists because, given a dissonance-producing situation, there are multiple ways to reduce the dissonance. As we discussed earlier in the chapter, there are several ways to bring about more consonance (such as changing your mind or engaging in selective exposure, attention, interpretation, or retention). The weakness in the theory is that it doesn't allow precise predictions.

This prediction problem is also apparent in the fact that the theory does not speak to the issue of individual differences. People vary in their tolerance for dissonance, and the theory fails to specify how this factors in to its explanation.

Student Voices

Amelia

This theory makes so much sense, and I can apply it to my own struggle to quit smoking. I know smoking isn't good for me, and I have tried to quit. Everyone tells me I should; and I know it's true. It makes me feel like an idiot that I continue to do something that's harmful to my health. But it's so hard to quit. I have noticed that I use some of the ways to reduce dissonance that the theory talks about. Like I've said that everyone has to die of something, so I've tried to reduce the importance of the dissonance. And I've also mentioned that I smoke low tar cigarettes, and I don't smoke as much as some of my friends—trying to add to the consonant beliefs. The only technique I haven't actually used is to quit, which would remove the dissonance completely!

Testability

Another weakness that scholars point out relates specifically to our criterion of testability. As you recall, testability refers to the theory's likelihood of ever being proven false. Theories that have a seeming escape clause against being falsified are not as strong as those that do not. Researchers have pointed out that because Cognitive Dissonance Theory asserts that dissonance will motivate people to act, when people do not act, proponents of the theory can say that the dissonance must not have been strong enough, rather than concluding that the theory is wrong. In this way it is difficult to disprove the theory.

Although Cognitive Dissonance Theory has its shortcomings, it does offer us insight into the relationship among attitudes, cognitions, affect, and behaviors, and it does suggest routes to attitude change and persuasion. Social cognition researchers as well as communication scholars continue to use many of the ideas from CDT. As Steven Littlejohn and Karen Foss (2017) observe, Festinger's theory is not only the most important consistency theory, it is one of the most significant theories in social psychology. CDT has been the framework for over a thousand research studies (Perloff, 1993), most of which have supported the theory. Additionally, numerous critiques and interpretations have refined and revised the theory. And some researchers (e.g., Harmon-Jones, 2009; Hoelzl, Pollai, & Kastner, 2011) believe that continuing to refine the theory by examining cognitions more specifically and combining it with other theoretical models will yield rich theoretical insights.

Closing

Cognitive Dissonance Theory has contributed greatly to our understanding of cognitions and their relationship to behaviors. The concept of dissonance remains a powerful one in the research literature, informing studies in psychology, cognitive psychology, communication, and other related fields.

Discussion Starters

TECH QUEST: Describe how CDT might explain what happens when people meet online and then feel differently about one another after meeting face to face.

1. Explain the relationship of selective attention, exposure, interpretation, and retention to cognitive dissonance. Provide examples where appropriate. How do you think Ali Torres might use these processes, given her situation?

2. Give an example of two attitudes you hold that have an irrelevant relationship to each other. Cite two consonant attitudes you hold. Do you have any attitudes that are dissonant with each other? If so, have you done anything about them? Explain how your actions fit with the theory.

3. What do you think about the problem of CDT's testability suggested in this chapter? Could the theory be revised to make it testable?

4. Suppose you want some friends to change their drinking and driving behaviors. How could you apply the theory in persuading your friends?

5. Do you agree with the minimal justification notion? Provide an example in which minimal justification seemed to work to persuade someone.

6. How do you think group membership affects dissonance and what role do you believe it plays in dissonance reduction?

7. Besides persuasion, what other communication applications would you suggest for CDT?

CHAPTER 7

Expectancy Violations Theory

*Based on the research of **Judee Burgoon***

One of the things that always intrigued me in communication was looking at things that are counter-intuitive; things that challenge the basic truisms that everybody holds and that we should all buy into.

—Judee Burgoon

Margie Russo

As she prepared for her interview with Ingraham Polling, Margie Russo felt confident that she would be able to handle any questions posed to her. As a 44-year-old mother of three young children, she felt that her life experiences alone would help her respond to any of the more difficult questions. She was a Girl Scout leader, served as treasurer of the Parent Teacher Organization at the middle school, and worked part time as an executive assistant. She knew these experiences would be invaluable as she answered questions in her interview.

Despite her confidence, Margie suddenly felt anxious about her interview with Alyssa Mueller, the polling company's human resources representative. When told by the office assistant that Ms. Mueller was ready to see her, Margie approached Alyssa's office, knocked on her door, and went into the room. When she was still more than 10 feet away from the big desk, Alyssa looked up and asked, "Are you Ms. Russo?" Margie responded, "I am." Alyssa replied, "Well, c'mon over here and sit down and let's chat a bit."

As Margie approached her interviewer, an uneasy feeling fell over her, a nervousness that she had never experienced before and had certainly not expected. Alyssa could sense Margie's anxiety and asked if she could get her some coffee or tea.

"No, thank you," said Margie. "Well, why don't you sit down?" asked Alyssa.

Margie really wanted this job. She had been preparing for the interview with her husband, who asked her a number of different kinds of questions the night before. She didn't want to lose her chance at getting this job.

As the two sat and discussed the job and its responsibilities, Margie's mind began to wander. Why was she so nervous? She had been around people, and she knew that she had expertise for the job. Yet Margie was very nervous, and she had butterflies in her stomach.

Alyssa focused on the duties Margie would be responsible for and to whom she would report. As she spoke, Alyssa walked around her office a bit, at times leaning on the side of her desk in front of Margie's chair. Alyssa had a number of different questions remaining but wanted Margie to speak. She asked her whether she had seen a good movie recently. "Oh, sorry, Alyssa," Margie replied. "I just don't have time for movies."

"I guess I should have figured that out," said Alyssa. "You really are a busy person. I'm very impressed by how you seem to manage so many things at one time. Your children are very lucky. How does your family do when you're so busy?"

"Oh, they're fine, thanks. I do get some free time, but I try to spend as much time as I can with my children." Margie was feeling more relaxed as she began to talk about how busy she was helping her two daughters sell Girl Scout cookies. She then talked about her ability to juggle several things at once.

Alyssa responded, "That's great! Let's talk some more about how you handle deadlines."

It was apparent that as the two talked Margie became more comfortable speaking to Alyssa. Eventually, she dismissed her nervousness and felt that she was well on her way to becoming employed with Ingraham Polling.

An important part of any discussion of communication is the role of nonverbal communication. What we do in a conversation (or how we say something) can be more important than what we actually say (Knapp, Hall, & Horgan, 2014). To understand nonverbal communication and its effects on messages in a conversation, Judee Burgoon developed Expectancy Violations Theory 1978; 2015 Since that time, Burgoon and a number of her associates have studied various messages and the influence of nonverbal communication on message production. Burgoon (1994) discusses the intersection of nonverbal communication and message production when she states that "nonverbal cues are an inherent and essential part of message creation (production) and interpretation (processing)" (p. 239). The theory was originally called the Nonverbal Expectancy Violations Theory, but Burgoon later dropped the word *nonverbal* because the theory now examines issues beyond the domain of nonverbal communication, something that we will explore a bit later in the chapter. Nonetheless, from its early beginnings in the late 1970s, Expectancy Violations Theory (EVT) has been a leading theory in identifying the influence of nonverbal communication on behavior and is a theory that addresses how people respond to unexpected communication (Guerrero, 2008).

Our chapter-opening story of Margie Russo and Alyssa Mueller represents the nature of the theory. Margie entered the conversation with her interviewer with a sense of trepidation, and once their brief interaction was under way, she began to feel uneasy about the manner in which the space between them changed. Alyssa moved closer to Margie during the interview, causing Margie to feel uncomfortable. However, once the conversation centered on Margie's children, she did not view Alyssa or her closeness as a threat to her confidence.

Expectancy Violations Theory suggests that people hold expectations about the nonverbal behavior of others. Burgoon contends that unexpected changes in conversational distance between communicators are arousing and frequently ambiguous. Interpreting the meaning behind an expectancy violation depends on how favorably the "violator" is perceived. Returning to our opening scenario, in many interviews, the interviewer is not expected to lean on a desk in front of the job candidate. When this occurred, Margie became uncomfortable. It was only after Alyssa began to talk about the movies that Margie began to feel more at ease. In other words, she started to view Alyssa in a more favorable light.

In our discussion thus far, we have been using examples from nonverbal communication, primarily distance. Burgoon's (1978) early writing on EVT integrated specific instances of nonverbal communication; namely, personal space and people's expectations of conversational distance. When the theory was first conceptualized, space was a core concept of the theory. Although the theory has expanded beyond personal space, it is important to provide you an understanding of Burgoon's original thinking before you can understand the expansion of the theory. Further, because spatial violations constitute a primary feature of the theory, it is important to understand the various spatial distances before we delve further.

Space Relations

The study of a person's use of space is called **proxemics.** Proxemics includes the way people use space in their conversations as well as perceptions of another's use of space. Many people take spatial relations between communicators for granted, yet, as we (West & Turner, 2017) conclude, people's use of space can seriously affect their ability to achieve desired goals. Spatial use can influence meaning and message, and people's spaces have intrigued researchers for some time. Burgoon began her original work on EVT by studying interpretations of space violations.

proxemics
study of a person's use of space

T*I*P

Theory-Into-Practice

Expectancy Violations Theory

Theoretical Claim: Understanding various proxemic differences helps us to manage our expectations of another's behavior.

Practical Implication: Jessie and Carla are roommates but each was born and raised in a different country (Jessie was born in Venezuela and Carla was born in Canada). Living in a small dorm room, the two found out early on that they would have a hard time finding private "space." Yet, when each goes out, the two have different experiences and expectations. Jessie generally doesn't mind when people stand close to her to talk; Carla does. Even when talking to her family, Carla wants to keep a distance that she maintains with friends or classmates. Jessie has no expectation of distance, except for those whom she first meets and especially guys she may be interested in dating.

Burgoon (1978) starts from the premise that humans have two competing needs: affiliation and personal space. **Personal space,** according to Burgoon, can be defined as "an invisible, variable volume of space surrounding an individual which defines that individual's preferred distance from others" (p. 130). Burgoon and other Expectancy Violations writers believe that people simultaneously desire to stay in close proximity to others, but also desire some distance. This is a perplexing but realistic dilemma for most of us. Few people can exist in isolation, and yet people prefer their privacy at times.

personal space
individual's variable use of space and distance

Proxemic Zones

Burgoon's Expectancy Violations Theory has been informed by the pioneering and classic work of anthropologist Edward Hall (1992, 1996). After studying North Americans (in the Northeast), Hall claimed that four proxemic zones exist—intimate, personal, social, and public—and each zone is used for different reasons. Hall includes

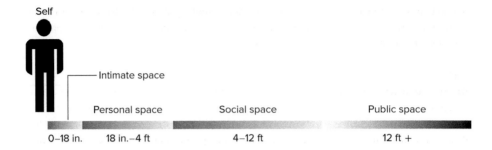

Figure 7.1
Proxemic Zones

Self

Intimate space

Personal space | Social space | Public space

0–18 in. | 18 in.–4 ft | 4–12 ft | 12 ft +

ranges of spatial distance and the behaviors that are appropriate for each zone. We have highlighted the proxemic zones in Figure 7.1.

Intimate Distance   This zone includes behaviors that exist in a range encompassing 0–18 inches. Hall (1966) notes that this includes behaviors that range from touch (for instance, making love) to being able to observe a person's facial characteristics. Whispers, for instance, carried out in this **intimate distance** range have the ability to become extremely powerful. Hall finds it interesting that when U.S. citizens find themselves in intimate surroundings but are not with intimate partners, they often attempt to create a nonintimate experience. Consider what happens in an elevator. People usually fix their eyes on the ceiling, the buttons, or the door as the elevator passes floor after floor. People keep their hands at their side or grasp some object. Hall finds it amusing that many people expend so much energy extracting themselves from intimate distances. Margie Russo in our opening story seems to be troubled by the intimate distance created by Alyssa. If she wasn't in an interview, she'd likely remove herself from the situation. It's important to point out that some invasions of personal space may be construed as sexual harassment, regardless of the intent. For this reason, we need to remain sensitive to the various perceptions of intimate distance.

Personal Distance   This zone includes those behaviors that exist in an area ranging from 18 inches to 4 feet. According to Hall (1966), **personal distance** encompasses being as close as holding another's hand to keeping someone at arm's length. You may find that most, if not all, of the intimate relationships you have are within the closest point of the personal distance zone. Personal distance is likely to be used for your family and friends. The farthest point—4 feet—is usually reserved for less personal relationships, such as sales clerks. Hall indicates that in the personal distance zone, the voice is usually moderate, body heat is detectable, and breath and body odor may be perceptible.

Social Distance   With a proxemic range spanning 4–12 feet, the **social distance** category characterizes many conversations in U.S. culture, for instance, between and among coworkers. Hall (1966) contends that the closer social distance is usually reserved for those in a casual social setting, for example, a cocktail party. Although the distance seems a bit far, Hall reminds us that we are able to perceive skin and hair texture in the close phase of this category. The far phase is associated with individuals who have to speak louder than those in the close phase. In addition, the far phase can be considered to be more formal than the close phase. The far phase of social distance allows people

intimate distance
very close spatial zone spanning 0–18 inches, usually reserved for those whom we share personal feelings

personal distance
spatial zone of 18 inches to 4 feet, reserved for family and friends

social distance
spatial zone of 4–12 feet, reserved for more formal relationships such as those with coworkers

to carry on simultaneous tasks. For instance, receptionists are able to carry on with their work while they converse with approaching strangers. It is possible, therefore, to monitor another person while completing a task.

Public Distance   The range encompassing 12 feet and beyond is considered to be **public distance.** The close phase of public distance is reserved for fairly formal discussions, for instance, in-class discussions between teachers and students. Public figures usually are at the far phase (around 25 feet or more). As you may have determined, it is difficult to read facial reactions at this point, unless media enhancements (for instance, large-screen projection) are used in the presentation. Whereas the close phase characterizes teachers in a classroom, the far phase includes teachers in a lecture hall. Also, actors use public distance in their performances. Consequently, their actions and words are exaggerated. Teachers and actors, however, are just two of the many types of people who use public distance in their lives.

public distance
spatial zone of 12 feet and beyond, reserved for very formal discussions such as between professor and students in class

Territoriality

Before we close our discussion of personal space, we explore an additional feature: **territoriality,** or a person's ownership of an area or object. Frequently, we lay claim to various spatial areas that we want to protect or defend. People decide that they want to erect fences, put on nameplates, or designate spaces as their own (e.g., Marissa's room, Mom's car, etc.). Three types of territories exist: primary, secondary, and public (Altman, 1975; Lyman, 1990). **Primary territories** signal an individual's exclusive domain. For instance, one's own workshop or computer are primary territories. In fact, many people put their names on their primary territories to further signify ownership. **Secondary territories** signal some sort of personal connection to an area or object. Secondary territories are not exclusive to an individual, but the individual feels some sort of association to the territory. For instance, many graduate students feel that a campus library is their secondary territory; they don't own the building, but they frequently occupy a space in the building. **Public territories** involve no personal affiliations and include those areas that are open to all people—for example, beaches, parks, movie theaters, and public transportation areas.

territoriality
person's ownership of an area or object

primary territories
signal a person's exclusive domain over an area or object

secondary territories
locations that signal a person's affiliation with an area or object

public territories
locations that signal open spaces for everyone, including beaches and parks

Territoriality is frequently accompanied by prevention and reaction (Knapp et al., 2014). That is, people may either try to prevent you from entering their territory or will respond once the territory is invaded. Some gangs use territorial markers in a neighborhood to prevent other gangs from invading their turf. Knapp et al. note that if prevention does not work in defending one's territory, a person may react in some way, including getting both physically and cognitively aroused. In sum, humans typically stake out their territory in four primary ways: markers (marking our spot), labels (identification symbols), offensive displays (demonstrating aggressive looks and behaviors), and tenure (being there first and staying the longest) (Knapp, 1978).

Our elaborated discussion of space has relevance to Expectancy Violations Theory not only because the theory is rooted in proxemics, but also because it has direct application to the distances previously discussed. EVT assumes that people will react to space violations. To this end, our expectations for behavior will vary from one distance to another. That is, people have a sense of where they want others to place themselves in a conversation. For instance, consider Margie and Alyssa from our

EXPECTANCY VIOLATIONS THEORY

opening story. Just as Margie has expectations for Alyssa's behavior in an interview, Alyssa, too, expects Margie to behave in a predictable way. Alyssa expects Margie to maintain a comfortable distance as well. She does not expect Margie to come into the office, put her briefcase on the desk, and pull a chair up next to Alyssa. According to EVT, if Margie's behavior is unexpected and Alyssa evaluates her behavior negatively, Alyssa may become more concerned with the expectancy violation than with Margie's credentials. The proxemic zones proposed by Hall, then, are important frameworks to consider when interpreting another's behavior.

Thus far, we have introduced you to how personal space is associated with Expectancy Violations Theory. The theory has evolved over the years, with Burgoon and other EVT proponents clarifying their original findings and concepts. Although we provide her pioneering theory in detail in this chapter, we also integrate updates and revisions of the theory where appropriate. To further explore the theory, we will first provide the basic assumptions of the theory and then examine a number of issues associated with the theory.

Theory At a Glance • *Expectancy Violations Theory*

Expectancy Violations Theory is concerned primarily with the structure of nonverbal messages. It asserts that when communicative norms are violated, the violation may be perceived either favorably or unfavorably, depending on the perception the receiver has of the violator. Violating another's expectations is a strategy that may be used rather than conforming to another's expectations.

Assumptions of Expectancy Violations Theory

Expectancy Violations Theory is rooted in how messages are presented to others and the kinds of behaviors others undertake during a conversation. According to Burgoon (2015), the theory "arose out of an effort to resolve conflicting views of proxemics in human interactions" (p. 1). In addition, three assumptions guide the theory:

- Expectancies drive human interaction.
- Expectancies for human behavior are learned.
- People make predictions about nonverbal behavior.

expectancies
thoughts and behaviors anticipated in conversations

The first assumption states that people carry expectancies in their interactions with others. In other words, expectancies drive human interaction. **Expectancies** can be defined as the cognitions and behaviors anticipated and prescribed in a conversation with another person. Expectancies, therefore, necessarily include individuals' nonverbal and verbal behavior. In her early writings of EVT, Burgoon (1978) notes that people do not view others' behaviors as random; rather, they have various expectations of how others should think and behave. Reviewing the research by Burgoon and her associates, Tim Levine and his colleagues (2000) suggest that expectancies are a result of social norms, stereotypes, hearsay, and the idiosyncrasies of communicators. Consider, for instance, our story of Margie Russo and Alyssa Mueller. If you were the interviewer, what sort of

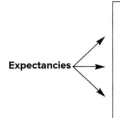

Individual communicator factors (*gender, personality, age, appearance, reputation*)

Relational factors (*prior relational history, status differences, levels of attraction and liking*)

Context factors (*formality/informality, social/task functions, environment restrictions, cultural norms*)

Figure 7.2
Influences on Expectancies

expectations would you have for the nonverbal and verbal behavior of the interviewee? Many people conducting the interview would certainly expect a specific level of confidence, manifested by a warm handshake, a give-and-take conversational flow, and active listening skills. Interviewees would also be expected to keep a reasonable distance from the interviewer during the interview process. Many people in the United States do not want people whom they do not know to stand either too close or too far away from them. Whether it is in an interview situation or even a discussion between two people who have a prior relationship, Burgoon and other EVT writers (e.g., Kalman & Rafaeli, 2012) argue that people enter interactions with a number of expectations about how a message should be delivered and how the messenger should deliver it. See Figure 7.2 for factors that influence a person's expectations.

Judee Burgoon and Jerold Hale (1988) contend that two types of expectations exist: pre-interactional and interactional. **Pre-interactional expectations** include the types of interactional knowledge and skills the communicator possesses *before* he or she enters a conversation. People do not always understand what it takes to enter and maintain a conversation. Some conversationalists may be very argumentative, for example, and others may be extremely passive. Most people do not expect such extreme behavior in their dialogues with others. **Interactional expectations** pertain to an individual's ability to carry out the interaction itself. Most people expect others to maintain appropriate conversational distance. In addition, in communicating with others, listening behaviors such as prolonged eye contact are frequently expected. These and a host of other behaviors are important to consider when examining the role of expectations before and during an interaction.

Of course, depending on the cultural background of communicators, these behaviors can vary tremendously from one person to another. In addition, whether our expectations are met will usually be influenced by the culture in which we live and by whether we have internalized cultural patterns for conversation expectations.

This leads us to our second assumption of EVT—that people learn their expectations from both the culture at large and the individuals in that culture. For instance, the U.S. culture teaches that a professor–student relationship is underscored by professional respect. Although not explicitly stated in most college classrooms, professors have more social status than students, and therefore certain expectations exist in their relationships with their students. For instance, we expect teachers to be knowledgeable about subject matter, to present it to students in a clear manner, and to be available if students are concerned or confused about a topic. We also expect professors to recognize, acknowledge, and affirm students in the classroom who offer their thoughts (Finn & Schrodt, 2012). The teacher–student relationship is just one

pre-interactional expectations
the knowledge or skills a communicator brings to an interaction

interactional expectations
an individual's ability to carry out the interaction

example of a co-culture teaching its citizens that expectations exist in a particular relationship. Most discussions between teachers and students, therefore, are laden with cultural expectations of how the two should relate to each other. A number of societal institutions (the family, the media, business and industry, and so forth) are central in prescribing what cultural patterns to follow. These at-large cultural prescriptions ultimately may be followed by individuals in conversation with each other.

Individuals within a culture are also influential in communicating expectations. Burgoon and Hale (1988) remark that differences based on our prior knowledge of others, our relational history with them, and our observations are important to consider. For instance, Alyssa Mueller's past experiences with prospective employees influence how she perceives an interaction and her expectations of job candidates in an interview (relational history). In addition, expectations result from our observations. In one family, for instance, standing very close to one another is a family norm, and yet this norm is not shared in other families. Interesting scenarios occur in conversations between individuals with different norms; expectations for conversational distance vary and may influence perceptions of the interaction or have other consequences.

Student Voices

Eddie

It seems like there are big differences in how we allow violations to occur. As a gay guy, I've made comments to girls who have a great shape and have even played with their hair to tell them that it's incredibly styled. In a lot of those situations, I hear the same thing: "If you were a straight guy, you would never be touching me." I guess it makes a difference whether or not there is perception of inappropriateness.

The third assumption pertains to the predictions people make about nonverbal communication. Later in this chapter we note that EVT theorists have applied the notion of expectancies to verbal behavior. Nonetheless, the original statement of EVT related specifically to nonverbal behavior. To this end, it's important to point out a belief inherent in the theory: People make predictions about another's nonverbal behavior.

In later writings of EVT, Judee Burgoon and Joseph Walther (1990) expanded the original understanding of EVT via personal space to other areas of nonverbal communication, including touch and posture. They suggest that the attractiveness of another influences the evaluation of expectancies. In conversations, people do not simply attend to what another is saying. As you will learn in this chapter, nonverbal behavior affects the conversation, and this behavior prompts others to make predictions.

Let's use an example to explain this assumption a bit further. Suppose someone whom you feel is attractive starts to make direct eye contact with you at a grocery store. At first, you may feel a bit odd with the prolonged stare. But because you are attracted to the person, that initial awkwardness may fade into comfort. Then you may begin to surmise that the person is interested in you because you see a decrease in physical distance between the two of you. This example illustrates the fact that you were making predictions (e.g., the person is attracted to you) based on his or her nonverbal behavior (e.g., eye contact and personal space). Before you begin to believe your own projection of attractiveness, however, keep in mind that your reaction may be either misguided or simply wrong. Despite your level of confidence, nonverbal communication is frequently ambiguous and is open to multiple interpretations (Knapp et al., 2014). We now turn our attention to additional concepts and features of EVT: arousal, threat threshold, violation valence, and communicator reward valence.

Arousal

Burgoon originally felt that deviations from expectations have consequences. These deviations, or violations, have what is called "arousal value" (Burgoon, 1978, p. 133). By this she means that when a person's expectations are violated, the person's interest or attention is aroused, and he or she uses a particular mechanism to cope with the violation. When **arousal** occurs, one's interest or attention to the deviation increases and one pays less attention to the message and more attention to the source of the arousal (Bachman & Guerrero, 2006; LaPoire & Burgoon, 1996). Burgoon and Hale (1988) later termed this "mental alertness" or an "orienting response," in which attention is diverted toward the source of the deviation.

arousal
increased interest or attention when deviations from expectations occur

A person may be both cognitively and physically aroused. **Cognitive arousal** is an alertness or an orientation to a violation. When we are cognitively aroused, our intuitive senses become heightened. **Physical arousal** includes those behaviors that a communicator employs during an interaction—such as moving out of uncomfortable speaking distances, adjusting one's stance during an interaction, and so forth. Most EVT studies have investigated cognitive arousal (via self-report inventories), yet little research has examined physiological arousal. One interesting study that examined physical arousal in conversation was undertaken by Beth LaPoire and Judee Burgoon (1996). Specifically, they asked college students to engage in a practice medical interview. During the interaction, the researchers studied heart rate, skin temperature, and pulse volume changes every 5 seconds while they assessed expectancy violations. Only heart rate and pulse volume demonstrated any statistical significance. Results indicated that after subjects registered cognitive arousal to a violation, they first experienced heart rate decreases and pulse volume increases. This was followed by pulse volume decreases. In sum, people notice when others are not adhering to interaction expectations. Arousal remains a complicated but important part of EVT. As you can see, arousal is more than simply recognizing when someone commits a violation.

cognitive arousal
mental awareness of deviations from expectations

physical arousal
bodily changes as a result of deviations from expectations

Threat Threshold

Once arousal exists, threats may occur. A second key concept associated with EVT is **threat threshold,** which Burgoon (1978) defines as the "distance at which an interactant experiences physical and physiological discomfort by the presence of another" (p. 130). In a sense, the threat threshold is a tolerance for distance violation. Burgoon maintains that "when distance is equated with threat, closer distances are perceived as more threatening and farther distances as less threatening" (p. 134). In this sense, distance is interpreted as a statement of threat from a communicator. People may either

threat threshold
tolerance for distance violations

reward or punish a threat. Burgoon arrives at this conclusion by consulting the research on liking and attraction. This research suggests that closer distances are reserved for people we like or to whom we are attracted. Some people don't mind when others stand close to them; their threat threshold, therefore, is high. Others become very uncomfortable around those who stand too close; for them, the threat threshold is low. So, for instance, if you are attracted to a person you see each morning at Starbucks, your threat threshold will likely be high as he or she talks to you and comes closer to you as your conversation progresses. During this same interaction, however, you may discover that this is not the sort of person you want to hang out with, and you may find your threat threshold getting smaller. Burgoon notes that the size of the threshold is based on how we view the initiator of the threat, which we discussed earlier as the communication reward valence. Once a violation occurs, however, we again interpret the violation. Although Burgoon later decided that the threat threshold is not necessarily associated with the other communicator, the concept remains important to consider as you try to understand the violation–communication reward valence interplay in EVT.

Violation Valence

violation valence
perceived negative or positive assessment of an unexpected behavior

Throughout this chapter, we have emphasized that when people speak to others, they have expectations. Many of these expectations are based on social norms of the other person. When expectations are violated, however, many people evaluate the violation on a valence. **Violation valence** refers to the positive or negative assessment of an unexpected behavior. Violation valence focuses on the deviation of an expectation.

Violation valence requires making sense of a violation through interpretation and evaluation (Burgoon & Hale, 1988). Quite simply, communicators try to interpret the meaning of a violation and decide whether they like it. If, for instance, a professor is speaking very close to you, you may interpret the behavior as an expression of superiority or intimidation. Consequently, the violation valence would be negative. Or you may view the violation as something positive; you might think the professor is demonstrating a sense of connection. Your violation valence, then, would be positive. Most of the research in the area of violations suggests that violations are likely to have a negative impact on close relationships (e.g., Cohen, 2007).

To better understand the violation valence, consider two situations between coworkers Noland and Rick. Standing in the break room, Noland begins to talk about his phone call to his wife this morning. As he discusses his conversation about where they decided to go for vacation, Noland begins to close this distance between him and Rick. Rick feels very uncomfortable with the distance in that his expectations for spatial distance between coworkers is violated. In other words, Rick is negatively aroused by Noland's distance behavior. A different situation, however, might prompt a different reaction. Imagine that Noland corners Rick to tell him that he heard that the company was laying off 20 percent of its workers within two months. Because Rick was recently hired by the company, he might be positively aroused and allow Noland to violate his personal space. Most likely, he will positively evaluate Noland and allow the violation to take place.

It may be perplexing to think that violations can be viewed positively. Yet there are many such examples. For instance, in a job interview, the candidate who is able

EXPECTANCY VIOLATIONS THEORY

to convince the interviewer that he or she is the most qualified is usually the person who gets the job. Most job interviews are very structured and have an agreed-on informal process. Most job candidates follow the interview script and do not violate anyone's expectations. At times, though, candidates do not follow the script; they violate expectations. Although some interviewers may think these candidates are too independent, others (say, in the dot.com industry) may see them as creative, bold, and original. These may be the qualities that ultimately get the person the job. Thus, the violation was not expected in an interview, yet resulted in a favorable impression.

Communicator Reward Valence

What happens when our expectations are not met in a conversation with another? Burgoon believes that when people depart, or *deviate,* from expectations, how that deviation is received depends on the reward potential of others. Let's explain this a bit further. Burgoon, along with Deborah Coker and Ray Coker (1986), notes that not all violations of expected behavior necessarily yield negative perceptions. Specifically, the researchers offer the following: "In cases where behaviors are ambiguous or have multiple interpretations, acts committed by a high-reward communicator may be assigned positive meanings, and the same acts committed by a low-reward communicator may be assigned negative meanings" (p. 498). Communicators can offer each other a number of rewards, including smiles, head nods, physical attractiveness, attitude similarity, socioeconomic status, credibility, and competence. In our opening story, Alyssa Mueller's demeanor in asking about Margie's children was apparently viewed as reward behavior because Margie's nervousness immediately subsided. Burgoon thinks people have the potential to either reward or punish in conversations and maintains that people bring both positive and negative characteristics to an interaction. She terms this **communicator reward valence.**

Burgoon holds that the concept of reward includes a number of characteristics that allow a person to be viewed favorably or unfavorably. Burgoon (2015) has stated that "highly regarded communicators, such as those with high status, reputed expertise, purchasing power, physical attractiveness, similarity to partner, or who give positive feedback, have more favorable meanings ascribed to their nonverbal behavior than those with lower reward valence regardless of actions" (p. 8). According to Expectancy Violations Theory, interpretations of violations depend on the communicator and his or her value. So, for instance, Margie Russo may not view Alyssa's close proximity as a positive deviation from expected behavior in an interview. Yet Alyssa's behavior was more positively received because of other characteristics; namely, her courteous manner and interest in Margie's children.

Let's apply this idea to eye behavior in a number of different contexts. A prolonged stare from a person on public transportation is probably not going to be received favorably, but it may be received favorably from one's romantic partner. If a keynote speaker at a dinner banquet looked above the listeners' heads, many people would be bewildered by this lack of eye contact. But when strangers pass on the street, lack of eye contact is expected. Or, think about your response to receiving a constant stare from your supervisor or a coworker. Finally, cultural differences influence perceptions of eye contact. A wife who avoids eye contact while telling her husband that

communicator reward valence
the sum of the positive and negative characteristics of a person and the potential for him or her to carry out rewards or punishments

she loves him may elicit a different evaluation than if she had direct eye contact, but this interpretation varies across cultural groups. Some (e.g., Irish Americans) would expect another to look directly at them when saying something very personal, such as "I love you." Others (e.g., Japanese Americans), however, do not place such value on eye contact. In each of these contexts, violations of expected eye behavior may be interpreted differently according to how we receive the communicator.

Integration, Critique, and Closing

Expectancy Violations Theory is one of the few theories specifically focusing on what people expect—and their reactions to others—in conversations. Unequivocally, the research has followed a quantitative approach since its inception in the 1970s. The assumptions and core concepts clearly demonstrate the importance of nonverbal messages and information processing. EVT also enhances our understanding of how expectations influence conversational distance. The theory uncovers what takes place in the minds of communicators and how communicators monitor nonverbal (and verbal) behavior during their conversations. Among the criteria for evaluating a theory, four seem especially relevant for discussion: scope, utility, testability, and heurism.

Integration

Communication Tradition	Rhetorical	Semiotic	Phenomenological	Cybernetic	**Socio-Psychological**	Socio-Cultural	Critical
Communication Context	**Intrapersonal**	**Interpersonal**	Small Group	Organizational	Public/Rhetorical	Mass/Media	Cultural
Approach to Knowing	**Positivistic/Empirical**	Interpretive/Hermeneutic	Critical

Critique

Evaluation Criteria	**Scope**	Logical Consistency	Parsimony	**Utility**	**Testability**	**Heurism**	Test of Time

Student Voices

Star

Talking about space differences got me thinking about how people use it. I remember a time where a vendor at a ballpark got pretty close to me as I bought some popcorn. As I gave him the money, I could tell he was standing way too close to me. As a matter of fact, he was what I would call (using Hall's category) "intimate" in his space. Really, though, I didn't mind it all that much. He was cute, I was single, and we were both kind of bored, I think!

Scope

At first glance, the scope of this theory may appear to be too broad; nonverbal communication is an expansive area. Yet Burgoon's theory has parameters in that she originally conceptualized one category of nonverbal communication as she articulated her theory: personal space. She has investigated and expanded her research to include other nonverbal behaviors such as eye gaze, yet her original work was clear in scope.

Utility

The practicality of EVT is apparent. Burgoon's theory presents advice on how to elicit favorable impressions and discusses the implications of space violations, a topic that affects countless conversations. In particular, researchers who employ EVT in their work have investigated topics that make a difference in the lives of people, whether related to relationship challenges (Wright & Roloff, 2015) or cell phone usage (Miller-Ott & Kelly, 2015). This sort of research suggests that it has fulfilled the criterion of utility.

Testability

Some scholars (e.g., Sparks & Greene, 1992) have criticized the clarity of concepts in Burgoon's theory, suggesting that testability may be problematic. Sparks and Greene comment that self-perceptions of arousal are not valid measures. They specifically note that Burgoon and her associates failed to establish valid indices of observers' ratings and believe "we should not accept the claim about the validity of any nonverbal index until that validity has been demonstrated" (p. 468). This intellectual debate may appear trivial to you, yet recall that arousal is a key component of EVT. LaPoire and Burgoon (1992) responded to this criticism by first claiming that Sparks and Greene did not fairly reflect the objectives of Burgoon's research. Additionally, LaPoire and Burgoon (1996) contend that because arousal is such a complicated and layered concept, their approach to defining arousal remains valid.

Even Burgoon (2015) suggests that the testability of the theory merits attention. In particular she states that EVT lacks testing across large, demographic groups and in non-Western cultures. Although she believes there are consistencies and applications across various groups, much more investigation is needed. Generally speaking, EVT is a testable theory. In Chapter 3, we noted that testability requires that theorists be specific in their concepts. In fact, Burgoon (1978) is one of a few theorists who clearly defines her terms; as she refined her theory, she also clarified past ambiguities. In doing so, she presents a foundation from which future researchers might continue to draw and replicate her claims.

Heurism

The scholarship related to Expectancies Violation Theory has proliferated over the decades since EVT's inception. The theory has been incorporated in a myriad of studies that span a number of diverse topic areas. For instance, EVT has been incorporated into an array of interesting and important areas, including political humor (Walther-Martin, 2015), obesity (Schyns, Roefs, Mulkens, & Jansen, 2016), and victim impact statements (Lens, van Doorn, Pemberton, Lahlah, & Bogaerts, 2016). The theory has also been incorporated into studies related to clothing and teacher credibility (Sidelinger & Bolen,

2016), human–computer interactions (Burgoon, Bonito, Lowry, Humphreys, Moody, Gaskin, & Giboney, 2015), forgiveness in dating relationships (Guerrero & Bachman, 2011), media figures/celebrities (Cohen, 2010), and marital interactions (Schoebi, Perrez, & Bradbury, 2012). An interesting and compelling study by Rory McGloin and Kristine Nowak (2011) examined the employment of avatars to determine the extent to which consumers were predisposed to purchasing particular products. The researchers successfully argued that an individual has certain impressions of an avatar's credibility and consequences exist when those expectations are violated.

Closing

Expectancy Violations Theory is an important theory because it offers a way to link behavior and cognitions. It is one of the few communication theories that offers us a better understanding of our need for both other people and personal space. For that, Burgoon's work continues to be critical and groundbreaking in the communication discipline.

Discussion Starters

TECH QUEST: Arousal is a key component of Expectancy Violations Theory. Explore how blogs might be discussed when examining the multifaceted nature of arousal. That is, can blogs be "arousing" in technological relationships? Explain why or why not.

1. In addition to distance behaviors, what other nonverbal behaviors are present in interview situations like the one between Margie and Alyssa?

2. Explain how EVT might inform research and thinking on touch behavior. For instance, does the theory help us to understand the difference between appropriate and inappropriate touch? Explain with examples.

3. Provide some nonverbal expectations that you have learned from your culture. Discuss what similarities and differences exist.

4. How do you suppose arousal manifests itself in conversations between supervisors and employees? Identify a few arousal mechanisms.

5. Suppose you want to study expectancy violation in school. How might you begin to investigate violations? Be as specific as possible, and identify some methods for studying expectations.

6. Employing at least two examples, differentiate between communicator reward valence and violation valence.

7. Discuss the application of any component of EVT to a job interview.

Relationship Development

AUTHORS OF SELF-HELP BOOKS MAKE MILLIONS OF DOLLARS promoting ways to begin, develop, and maintain our interpersonal relationships. However, the sad reality is that there are no "four-easy steps" or one specific formula associated with relationship success. As we all can testify, our various relationships with friends, family, partners, co-workers, spiritual leaders, and others are filled with dynamics that defy simple description and are not fully explained in self-help books. This becomes especially important as we think about the fact that most of these books, sought out by millions of people, pretty much ignore theory and don't have a solid research base to back up their claims.

This is precisely why the theories in this section, called "Relationship Development," are important to consider. They represent scholarship examining all types of interpersonal relationships and the numerous patterns and processes involved in relationship development. In sum, these theories address how and why relationships begin, develop, and are maintained.

Six theories are discussed in this section. Uncertainty Reduction Theory suggests that when strangers meet, their focus is on reducing levels of uncertainty about each other and about their relationship, and that relationships develop as a function of decreased uncertainty. Social Exchange Theory explains that people maintain a relationship based on their sense of the costs and benefits of being in it. Social Penetration Theory examines how a person's decision to reveal personal information to another influences the direction of their relationship. As relationships progress, the participants are likely to experience conflicting impulses ("I want to be close, but I want my independence," for example). How people deal with these tensions is the essence of Relational Dialectics Theory. Communication Privacy Management Theory states that people in relationships constantly manage boundaries between the thoughts and feelings they are willing to share and those they are not. Finally, Social Information Processing Theory deals with how people initiate and develop relationships through computer-mediated communication. The theory explains how relationships progress relying on verbal and temporal cues.

Relational life is interesting, challenging, complex, entertaining, and exhausting. The theories we present help unravel the reasons we continue to be part of other people's lives and why they stay with us. When you encounter these theories, you will also become familiar with a number of engaging topics. You will read about uncertainty, rewards, depth and breadth, tensions, privacy, and motivation. In each theory, the emphasis is on how communication moderates these topics. As you read the next six chapters, pay attention to the different ways each theory conceptualizes and explains relational life and the central role communication plays in our interpersonal relationships.

CHAPTER 8

Uncertainty Reduction Theory

Based on the research of **Charles Berger** and **Richard Calabrese**

> URT talks about the struggle, in a sense, that people have in their everyday lives in adapting to an ever-changing world.
>
> —Charles Berger

Edie Banks and Malcolm Rogers

Edie Banks and Malcolm Rogers are in the same philosophy class at Urban University but, until today, they really had not spoken together, although they had seen each other in the class every Monday, Wednesday, and Friday for the past three months. Malcolm had noticed Edie and found her attractive, but he wondered why she never spoke up in class. Edie thought Malcolm had made some good comments in the class discussions, and he was cute! Today, as Edie was leaving the classroom, she noticed Malcolm staring at her from the corner of the room where he sat with his friends. Although Edie had thought about getting to know Malcolm, she felt a little uncomfortable about having him stare so hard at her, and she hurried to get out of the classroom and away from his gaze.

Unfortunately, her friend Maggie stopped her at the doorway with a question about the assignment for next week, and so Edie and Malcolm reached the hallway at the same time. There was an awkward pause as they smiled uncertainly at each other. Malcolm cleared his throat and said, "Hi. That was a pretty interesting lecture in class today, wasn't it?" Edie shrugged, smiled back, and replied, "I'm not sure I get what's going on in there. I'm majoring in engineering, and this is just an elective for me. Sometimes I think I should have taken bowling instead." Malcolm smiled and said, "I'm a communication studies major myself, but this class relates to a lot of what we've talked about in some of my comm classes, so it's OK for me. But I guess I'd have the same reaction you're having if I got stuck in an engineering class! I probably couldn't engineer my way out of a paper bag." The two laughed for a minute. There was an awkward silence and finally Edie said, "Gotta run. Catch you later," and hurried off down the hall.

Malcolm walked to his next class wondering if they would talk again, if Edie was putting him down, if she thought he had been rude about her major, if she liked him, if he liked her, or if he cared. Edie, for her part, was kicking herself for sounding like an idiot the first time she'd talked to Malcolm. "Why in the world would I say I should have taken bowling?" she asked herself. "Malcolm probably thinks I'm totally stupid!" But then she wondered why he'd been staring so intently at her before. It was a little creepy—maybe it didn't matter whether he thought she was dumb, she might not want to get to know him after all. Edie sighed to herself. It was confusing.

Sometimes called Initial Interaction Theory, Uncertainty Reduction Theory (URT) was originated by Charles Berger and Richard Calabrese in 1975. It continues to be an important theory today, because, as Leanne Knobloch (2008) stated, "[E]veryday life is infused with uncertainty" (p. 133). Berger (2016a) is similarly clear: "Attempting to reduce uncertainty is a pervasive and vital activity across a wide range of human endeavors" (p. 1). Berger and Calabrese's goal in constructing this theory was to explain how communication is used to reduce uncertainties between strangers engaging in their first conversation together. Berger and Calabrese believe that when strangers first meet, they are primarily concerned with increasing predictability in an effort to make sense out of their communication experience. Berger (2011) commented on the theory saying that:

> [T]he main supposition underlying the theory is that when strangers meet, they are faced with myriad uncertainties about each other's attitudes, beliefs values and potential actions. In the service of predicting and, in some cases explaining, each other's beliefs and actions so that communicative choices can be made, individuals seek to reduce their uncertainties by acquiring information about each other. (p. 215)

As we discussed in Chapter 3, people act as implicit researchers and in URT, Berger and Calabrese posited that, as implicit researchers, we are motivated both to predict and to explain what goes on in initial encounters. **Prediction** can be defined as the ability to forecast the behavioral options likely to be chosen from a range of possible options available to oneself or to a relational partner. **Explanation** refers to attempts to interpret the meaning of past actions in a relationship. These two concepts—prediction and explanation—make up the two primary subprocesses of uncertainty reduction.

Our opening example of Malcolm and Edie illustrates Berger and Calabrese's basic contentions about meeting someone for the first time. Because Malcolm does not know Edie, he is not sure how to interpret her comments to him. Nor is he certain about what will happen the next time they see each other. There are so many possible explanations for what was said that Malcolm's uncertainty level is high. This is consistent with the ideas of theorists Claude E. Shannon and Warren Weaver (1949), who note in their information theory that uncertainty exists whenever the number of possible alternatives in a given situation is high and the likelihood of their occurrence is relatively equal. Conversely, they say, uncertainty is decreased when the alternatives are limited in number and/or there is an alternative that is usually chosen. Berger and Calabrese used Shannon and Weaver's work as a foundation for URT.

For example, when Teresa walks into her Spanish I classroom on the first day of class and the person sitting nearest the door smiles at her, Teresa has a few alternative explanations for this behavior. The person could be friendly, trying to get to know her, squinting in the sunlight, or mistaken in thinking she knows Teresa. Because a college classroom is often governed by a norm of friendliness and because the alternative explanations are few in number, Teresa will probably decide the smile was one of friendly welcoming, reducing her uncertainty fairly easily. But if Teresa walked into a job interview and found another candidate in the waiting room with her who glanced her way and smiled, the alternative explanations would be more numerous. They would contain all of the above possibilities and others, including that the person is sizing her up as competition, the person thinks she's weak competition, the person is trying to get her to let her guard down, and so forth. These increased alternatives will increase uncertainty, causing Teresa to attempt to reduce it. Berger and Calabrese theorize that communication is the

prediction
the ability to forecast one's own and others' behavioral choices

explanation
the ability to interpret the meaning of behavioral choices

vehicle by which people reduce their uncertainty about one another. In turn, reduced uncertainty creates conditions ripe for the development of interpersonal relationships.

After Berger and Calabrese (1975) originated their theory, it was later slightly elaborated (Berger, 1979; Berger & Bradac, 1982). The current version of the theory suggests that there are two types of uncertainty in initial encounters: cognitive and behavioral. Our cognitions refer to the beliefs and attitudes that we and others hold. **Cognitive uncertainty**, therefore, refers to the degree of uncertainty associated with those beliefs and attitudes. When Malcolm wonders whether Edie was ridiculing his major and whether he really cares, he experiences cognitive uncertainty. **Behavioral uncertainty**, on the other hand, pertains to "the extent to which behavior is predictable in a given situation" (Berger & Bradac, 1982, p. 7). Because we have cultural rituals for small talk, Edie and Malcolm probably have an idea of how to behave during their short conversation. If one of them had violated the ritual by either engaging in inappropriate **self-disclosure** (revealing private information about oneself to another) or totally ignoring the other, their behavioral uncertainty would have increased. People may be cognitively uncertain, behaviorally uncertain, or both before, during, or following an interaction.

Furthermore, Berger and Calabrese (1975) argued that uncertainty reduction has both proactive and retroactive processes. Proactive uncertainty reduction comes into play when a person thinks about communication options before actually engaging with another person. When Edie attempted to avoid Malcolm at the classroom door, she was trying to deal with her uncertainty proactively. If Malcolm preplanned what he might say to Edie, he would also be using proactive processes. Retroactive uncertainty reduction consists of attempts to explain behavior after the encounter itself. Thus, Malcolm's questions to himself about what Edie did and said and his own reactions are part of the retroactive process. The same is true of Edie's interior monologue after her encounter with Malcolm.

In addition, Berger and Calabrese (1975) and Berger (2015) theorized that uncertainty is related to other concepts rooted in communication and relational development: verbal output, nonverbal warmth (such as pleasant vocal tone and leaning forward), information seeking (asking questions), self-disclosure, reciprocity of disclosure, similarity, and liking. Each of these concepts is related to uncertainty. URT posits a dynamic movement of interpersonal relationships in their initial stages. This

cognitive uncertainty
degree of uncertainty related to cognitions

behavioral uncertainty
degree of uncertainty related to behaviors

self-disclosure
personal messages about the self disclosed to another

Theory At a Glance • *Uncertainty Reduction Theory*

When strangers meet, their primary focus is on reducing their level of uncertainty in the situation because uncertainty is uncomfortable. People can be uncertain on two different levels: behavioral and cognitive. They may be unsure of how to behave (or how the other person will behave), and they may also be unsure of what they think of the other person and what the other person thinks of them. High levels of uncertainty are related to a variety of verbal and nonverbal behaviors.

theory has been described as an example of original theorizing in the field of communication (Miller, 1981) because it employs concepts (such as information seeking, self-disclosure) that are specifically relevant to studying communication behavior. URT attempts to place communication as the cornerstone of human behavior, and to this end a number of assumptions about human behavior and communication underlie the theory.

Assumptions of Uncertainty Reduction Theory

As we have mentioned in previous chapters, theories are frequently grounded in assumptions that reflect the worldview of the theorists. Uncertainty Reduction Theory is no exception. The following assumptions frame this theory:

- People experience uncertainty in interpersonal settings and it generates cognitive stress.
- When strangers meet, their primary concern is to reduce their uncertainty and increase predictability.
- Interpersonal communication is a developmental process that occurs through stages, and it is the primary means of uncertainty reduction.
- The quantity and nature of information that people share change through time.
- It is possible to predict people's behavior in a lawlike fashion.

We will briefly address each assumption. First, in a number of interpersonal settings, people feel uncertainty. Because differing expectations exist for interpersonal occasions, it is reasonable to conclude that people are uncertain or even nervous about meeting others. Consider the case of Malcolm and Edie, for instance. Although there are a great many cues in the environment that can help Malcolm and Edie make sense out of their interaction, there are complicating factors as well. For example, Malcolm may have noticed Edie hurrying to leave the room. There may be several alternative explanations for this behavior, including another class that is a distance away, a general predisposition toward hurrying, having to go to the bathroom, feeling faint and wanting fresh air, wanting to avoid meeting Malcolm at the door, and so forth. Given all these alternatives, it is likely that Malcolm (or anyone in his situation) feels uncertain about how to interpret Edie's behavior. Further, this assumption asserts that uncertainty is an aversive state. As Berger and Calabrese (1975) state, "When persons are unable to make sense out of their environment, they usually become anxious" (p. 106). The theory assumes that it takes a great deal of emotional and psychological energy to remain uncertain, and people would prefer not to experience that.

The next assumption underlying URT advances the proposition that when strangers meet, two concerns are important: reducing uncertainty and increasing predictability. Denise Haunani Solomon (2015) underscores this by stating: "Initial interactions are fraught with unknowns about the partner's personal traits and attitudes, how the partner will behave and respond to messages, how people should conduct themselves, and what direction the interaction might go (p. 1). Uncertainty Reduction

Theory suggests that information seeking is a primary method to reduce uncertainty and attain some sort of predictability. Information seeking usually takes the form of asking questions in order to gain some predictability. Think about the last time you had an initial encounter with someone in an interpersonal setting. More than likely a great deal of time in this interaction was occupied with questions and answers (e.g., Where are you from? What is your major? Do you live on campus?, etc.) This process can be quite engaging, and many people do this unconsciously. Jessica Deyo and her colleagues (2011) found that in speed-dating contexts, participants' behaviors adhered to this assumption albeit in a speeded-up fashion. The first minute of the speed date was filled with questions and answers focused on demographic information.

The third assumption of URT suggests that interpersonal communication is a process involving developmental stages and it is the primary means people have for reducing uncertainty. According to Berger and Calabrese (1975), generally speaking, most people begin interaction in an **entry phase,** defined as the beginning stage of a communication encounter between strangers. The entry phase is guided by implicit and explicit rules and norms, such as responding in kind when someone says, "Hi! How are you doing?" Individuals then enter the second stage, called the **personal phase,** or the stage where the interactants start to communicate more spontaneously and to reveal more idiosyncratic information. The personal phase can occur during an initial encounter, but it is more likely to begin after repeated interactions. The third stage, the **exit phase,** refers to the stage during which individuals make decisions about whether they wish to continue interacting with this partner in the future. Although all people do not enter a phase in the same manner or stay in a phase for a similar amount of time, Berger and Calabrese believe that this universal framework exists that explains how interpersonal communication shapes and reflects the development of interpersonal relationships.

The fourth assumption underscores the nature of time. It also focuses on the fact that interpersonal communication is developmental. Uncertainty reduction theorists believe that initial interactions are key elements in the developmental process. To illustrate this assumption, consider the experiences of Rita, who spent a few anxious minutes by herself before entering the YWCA to attend her first meeting of Parents, Family, and Friends of Lesbians and Gays (PFLAG). She immediately felt more comfortable when Dan, another newcomer, came over to introduce himself and welcome her to the group. As the two exchanged information about their anxieties and uncertainties, they both felt more confident. As they talked, Rita and Dan reduced their uncertainties about what the other members of the support group would be like. Charles Berger and Kathy Kellerman (1994) believe that Rita and Dan are goal directed and therefore will employ a number of communication strategies to acquire social information. Reducing uncertainty is key for both Rita and Dan. A bit later in the chapter, we will discuss some of these strategies.

The final assumption indicates that people's behavior can be predicted in a lawlike fashion. Recall from Chapter 3 that theorists have some guidelines to help them in the job of theory construction. One of the guidelines we reviewed was covering law, which assumes that human behavior is regulated by generalizable principles that

entry phase
the beginning stage of an interaction between strangers

personal phase
the stage in a relationship when people begin to communicate more spontaneously and personally

exit phase
the stage in a relationship when people decide whether to continue or leave

function in a lawlike manner. Although there may be some exceptions, in general people behave in accordance with these laws. The goal of a covering law theory is to lay out the laws that will explain how we communicate. As you might imagine, covering law theories have a difficult task. Although some aspects of the natural world may operate under laws, the social world is much more variable. That is why covering laws in the social science are called "lawlike." A pattern is outlined, but the deterministic notion implied with natural laws is relaxed a bit. Still, even to approach the goal of lawlike statements is daunting. Thus, theories like URT begin with what may seem like commonsense observations in order to establish regularities that govern people's behaviors. Covering law theories are constructed to move from statements that are presumed to be true (or axioms) to statements that are derived from these truisms (or theorems).

Key Concepts of URT: The Axiom and Theorem

Embedded in Uncertainty Reduction Theory—unlike any other communication theory—are a number of different tenets or conclusions. Each has been identified as an area for research exploration by Berger (2015) and Calabrese (1975). We explore each of these below.

Axioms of Uncertainty Reduction Theory

axioms
truisms drawn from past research and common sense

Uncertainty Reduction Theory is an axiomatic theory. This means that Berger and Calabrese began with a collection of **axioms,** or truisms drawn from past research and common sense. These axioms, or what some researchers might call propositions, require no further proof than the statement itself. Berger and Calabrese extrapolated this axiomatic thinking from earlier researchers (Blalock, 1969), who concluded that causal relationships should be stated in the form of an axiom. Axioms are the heart of the theory. They have to be accepted as valid because they are the building blocks for everything else in the theory. Each axiom presents a relationship between uncertainty (the central theoretical concept) and one other concept. URT originally posited seven axioms. To understand each, we refer back to our chapter-opening example of Edie and Malcolm.

> **Axiom 1:** As the amount of verbal communication between strangers increases, the level of uncertainty for each interactant in the relationship decreases. As uncertainty is further reduced, the amount of verbal communication increases. (The verbal communication axiom.)

Regarding Malcolm and Edie's situation with reference to this axiom, the theory maintains that if they talk more to each other, they will become more certain about each other. Furthermore, as they get to know each other better, they will talk more with each other.

> **Axiom 2:** As nonverbal affiliative expressiveness increases, uncertainty levels decrease in an initial interaction situation. In addition, decreases in uncertainty

level will cause increases in nonverbal affiliative expressiveness. (The nonverbal expressiveness axiom.)

If Edie and Malcolm express themselves to each other in a warm nonverbal fashion, they will grow more certain of each other, and as they do this, they will increase their nonverbal affiliation with each other: They may be more facially animated, or they may engage in more prolonged eye contact. The two might even touch each other in a friendly fashion as they begin to feel more comfortable with each other.

Axiom 3: High levels of uncertainty cause increases in information-seeking behavior. As uncertainty levels decline, information-seeking behavior decreases. (The information-seeking axiom.)

This axiom, which we will discuss later, is one of the more provocative propositions associated with URT. It suggests that Edie will ask questions and otherwise engage in information seeking as long as she feels uncertain about Malcolm. The more certain she feels, the less information seeking she will do. The same would apply to Malcolm.

Axiom 4: High levels of uncertainty in a relationship cause decreases in the intimacy level of communication content. Low levels of uncertainty produce high levels of intimacy.

Because uncertainty is relatively high between Edie and Malcolm, they engage in small talk with no real self-disclosures. The intimacy of their communication content is low, and their uncertainty level remains high. The fourth axiom asserts that if they continue to reduce the uncertainty in their relationship, then their communication will consist of higher levels of intimacy.

Axiom 5: High levels of uncertainty produce high rates of reciprocity. Low levels of uncertainty produce low levels of reciprocity.

According to URT, as long as Edie and Malcolm remain uncertain about each other, they will tend to mirror each other's behavior. For example, after Edie shares that she is lost in the class and that she is an engineering major, Malcolm reveals his major to her and admits that he would probably have troubles in engineering classes. Immediate reciprocation of that sort (I tell you where I am from and you tell me where you are from) is a hallmark of initial encounters. The more people talk to each other and develop their relationship, the more they trust that reciprocity will be made at some point. If I don't tell you something that mirrors your communication today, I will probably do so the next time we talk or the time after that. With this in mind, strict reciprocity is replaced by an overall sense of reciprocity in our relationship.

Axiom 6: Similarities between people reduce uncertainty, whereas dissimilarities increase uncertainty.

Because Edie and Malcolm are both college students at Urban University, they may have similarities that reduce some of their uncertainties about each other immediately. Yet they are different sexes and have different majors—dissimilarities that may contribute to their uncertainty level.

Axiom 7: Increases in uncertainty level produce decreases in liking; decreases in uncertainty produce increases in liking.

As Edie and Malcolm reduce their uncertainties, they typically will increase their liking for each other. If they continue to feel highly uncertain about each other, they probably will not like each other very much. This axiom has received some indirect empirical support. In a study examining the relationship between communication satisfaction and uncertainty reduction, James Neuliep and Erica Grohskopf (2000) found that participants playing interviewers in an organizational role play were more likely to feel positively toward the participants playing the job seekers (and more likely to hire them) when their uncertainty was low. The seven axioms and their relationships are summarized in Table 8.1.

Theorems of Uncertainty Reduction Theory

theorems
theoretical statements derived from axioms, positing a relationship between two concepts

Berger and Calabrese combined all seven axioms in every possible pairwise combination to derive 21 theorems (Table 8.2). **Theorems** are theoretical statements that are derived from axioms. Theorems also suggest a relationship between two concepts. For instance, if the amount of verbal communication is negatively related to uncertainty (Axiom 1) and uncertainty is negatively related to intimacy levels of communication (Axiom 4), then verbal communication and intimacy levels are positively related (Theorem 3, see Table 8.2). You can generate the other 20 theorems by combining the axioms using the deductive formula above. You need to use the rule of multiplication for multiplying positives and negatives. For example, if two variables have a positive relationship with a third, they are expected to have a positive relationship with each other. If one variable has a positive relationship with a third, whereas the other has a negative relationship with the third, they should have a negative relationship with each other. Finally, if two variables

Table 8.1 Axioms of Uncertainty Reduction Theory

AXIOM	MAIN CONCEPT	RELATIONSHIP QUALITY	RELATED CONCEPT
1.	↑ Uncertainty	Negative	↓ Verbal Communication
2.	↑ Uncertainty	Negative	↓ Nonverbal Affiliative Expressiveness
3.	↑ Uncertainty	Positive	↑ Information Seeking
4.	↑ Uncertainty	Negative	↓ Intimacy Level of Communication
5.	↑ Uncertainty	Positive	↑ Reciprocity
6.	↓ Uncertainty	Negative	↑ Similarity
7.	↑ Uncertainty	Negative	↓ Liking

Table 8.2 Theorems of Uncertainty Reduction Theory Deduced from Axioms

AXIOM	MAIN CONCEPT	RELATIONSHIP QUALITY	RELATED CONCEPT
1.	↑ Verbal Communication	Positive	↑ Nonverbal Affiliative Expressiveness
2.	↑ Verbal Communication	Negative	↓ Information Seeking
3.	↑ Verbal Communication	Positive	↑ Intimacy Level of Communication
4.	↑ Verbal Communication	Negative	↓ Reciprocity
5.	↑ Verbal Communication	Positive	↑ Similarity
6.	↑ Verbal Communication	Positive	↑ Liking
7.	↑ Nonverbal Affiliative Expressiveness	Negative	↓ Information Seeking
8.	↑ Nonverbal Affiliative Expressiveness	Positive	↑ Intimacy Level of Communication
9.	↑ Nonverbal Affiliative Expressiveness	Negative	↓ Reciprocity
10.	↑ Nonverbal Affiliative Expressiveness	Positive	↑ Similarity
11.	↑ Nonverbal Affiliative Expressiveness	Positive	↑ Liking
12.	↑ Information Seeking	Negative	↓ Intimacy Level of Communication
13.	↑ Information Seeking	Positive	↑ Reciprocity
14.	↑ Information Seeking	Negative	↓ Similarity
15.	↑ Information Seeking	Negative	↓ Liking
16.	↑ Intimacy Level	Negative	↓ Reciprocity
17.	↑ Intimacy Level	Positive	↑ Similarity
18.	↑ Intimacy Level	Positive	↑ Liking
19.	↑ Reciprocity	Negative	↓ Similarity
20.	↑ Reciprocity	Negative	↓ Liking
21.	↑ Similarity	Positive	↑ Liking

each have a negative relationship with a third, they should have a positive relationship with each other. This process allows URT to be a comprehensive theory.

Expansions of Uncertainty Reduction Theory

Many researchers have tested URT and based their studies on the tenets of the theory. Furthermore, Berger and several colleagues continue to refine and expand the theory, taking into account research findings. URT has been expanded and modified in a few areas. These areas include antecedent conditions, strategies, developed relationships, social media, and context.

Antecedent Conditions

Berger (1979) has suggested that three antecedent (prior) conditions exist when seeking uncertainty reduction. The first condition occurs when the other person has the *potential* to reward or punish. If Edie is a very popular, charismatic figure on campus, her attention may be seen as a reward by Malcolm. Likewise, Malcolm might experience a rejection by her as punishing. If Malcolm finds out that a friend thought Edie was boring and unattractive or if he discovers she has a bad reputation on campus, he will not see her attention as rewarding or her rejection as punishing. Thus, according to Berger, Malcolm will be more motivated to reduce his uncertainty the more attractive Edie appears to him.

A second antecedent condition exists when the other person behaves contrary to expectations. In the case of Edie and Malcolm, social norms might suggest that staring is impolite. When Edie perceives Malcolm staring intently at her for an extended period of time, her expectations of his behavior are violated, and Berger predicts that her desire to reduce her uncertainty increases.

The third and final condition exists when a person expects future interactions with another. Malcolm knows that he will continue to see Edie in class for the rest of the semester. Yet, because he has discovered that she is an engineering major, he may feel that he can avoid her in the future. In the first case, Berger would expect Malcolm's desire to increase predictability to be high—he knows he'll be seeing Edie often; in the second case, Malcolm's desire level is lower because Edie has a different major, and they can avoid each other after this class ends.

Strategies

passive strategies
reducing uncertainties by unobtrusive observation

active strategies
reducing uncertainties by means other than direct contact

interactive strategies
reducing uncertainties by engaging in conversation

A third area of expansion pertains to strategies. Berger (2015) suggests that people—in attempting to reduce uncertainty—use tactics from three categories of strategies: passive, active, and interactive. At the core of each is the goal of "desired information" (p. 2) from those with whom we are communicating. First, there are **passive strategies,** whereby an individual assumes the role of unobtrusive observer of another. **Active strategies** exist when an observer engages in some type of effort other than direct contact to find out about another person. For instance, a person might ask a third party for information about the other. Finally, **interactive strategies** occur when the observer and the other person engage in direct contact or face-to-face interaction—that is, conversation that may include self-disclosures, direct questioning, and other information-seeking tactics. Although these strategies are critical to reducing uncertainty, Berger believes that certain behaviors, such as

Student Voices

Max

When I read about the strategies to reduce uncertainty, it made sense. When I first moved here to go to school I am sure I used all of these strategies. I spent a lot of time at the Union, kind of just watching what everyone was doing, and I remember asking someone I knew a little bit from high school to tell me more about someone else I'd just seen in passing, but who looked really nice. And, finally, of course, I got up the nerve to actually talk to her and we went through a lot of small talk before things got going.

asking inappropriately sensitive questions, may increase rather than decrease uncertainty, and people may need additional reduction strategies. Kami Kosenko (2011) found support for all these strategies in a study examining transgender adults' communication about safer sex. In this study all of these strategies were illustrated in the participants' responses.

To briefly illustrate these strategies, consider Malcolm and Edie. The time they spend in class covertly observing each other falls into the passive category. When Malcolm observes how Edie reacts to jokes the professor tells in lecture, he is utilizing a particular passive strategy called **reactivity searching**, or observing Edie doing something. A different passive strategy, called **disinhibition searching,** would require Malcolm to observe Edie in more informal settings outside the classroom to see how she behaves when her inhibitions are down. If either one of them engages friends to find out information about the other, he or she will be using an active strategy. When they speak after class, they use an interactive strategy to find out about each other and to reduce their uncertainties.

Tara Emmers and Dan Canary (1996) argue that in established relationships an additional strategy is employed. They call this strategy "uncertainty acceptance," and it includes responses such as simply trusting your partner. Emmers and Canary suggest that accepting or trusting your partner even when you are not completely certain about what is happening is a viable strategy for coping with uncertainty in developed relationships.

reactivity searching
a passive strategy involving watching a person doing something

disinhibition searching
a passive strategy involving watching a person's natural or uninhibited behavior in an informal environment

Developed Relationships

When Berger and Calabrese (1975) conceived their theory, they were interested in describing initial encounters between strangers. They stated a clear and narrow boundary around their theoretical insights. In the intervening years, however, the theory has been expanded to include developed relationships, as the acceptance strategy discussed previously indicates. Berger (1982, 1987) has updated his theory since its inception. First, he comments that uncertainties are ongoing in relationships, and thus the process of uncertainty reduction is relevant in *developed* relationships as well as in *initial* interactions. This conclusion broadens earlier claims by Berger and Calabrese that specifically limited URT to initial encounters.

The inclusion of the three antecedent conditions discussed previously (potential for reward or punishment, deviation from expectations, and anticipation of future interactions) points us toward an examination of uncertainty in developed relationships. Specifically, we will expect rewards from, be surprised by, and anticipate future interactions with those with whom we have ongoing relationships.

Uncertainty in developed relationships may be different than it is in initial encounters. It may function dialectically within relationships; that is, there may be a tension between reducing and increasing uncertainty in developed relationships. Berger and Calabrese (1975) observe, "While uncertainty reduction may be rewarding up to a point, the ability to completely predict another's behavior might lead to boredom. Boredom in an interpersonal relationship might well be a cost rather than a reward" (p. 101). Gerald R. Miller and Mark Steinberg (1975) mention a similar belief, noting that people have a greater desire for uncertainty when they feel secure than they do when they feel insecure. This suggests that as people begin to feel certain about their relationships and their partners, the excitement of uncertainty becomes desirable. Neuliep and Grohskopf (2000) agree, stating that the linear relationship between uncertainty and other communication variables may not hold in stages beyond initial interaction.

Let's examine this contradiction between certainty and uncertainty a bit further with an example. In our chapter-opening vignette, Malcolm and Edie met for the first time after class. If their subsequent conversations evolve into a relationship, then their relationship will involve a level of predictability—that is, both will be able to predict certain things about the other because of the time they spend together. Yet this predictability (certainty) may get tedious after a time, and they may feel their relationship is in a rut. At this point, the need for uncertainty, or novelty, will become high, and the couple might try to build some variety into their routine to satisfy this need. Yet Leanne Knobloch and her colleagues (2007) observe that uncertainty is undesirable in marriage because it leads the partners to be more negative in evaluating conversations with each other.

Uncertainty and uncertainty reduction processes operate in dating relationships in somewhat the same ways that Berger and Calabrese theorize they do in initial interactions. One study (Mongeau, Jacobsen, & Donnerstein, 2007) found that reducing uncertainty was cited as a primary goal in dating. Research conducted by Sally Planalp and her colleagues (Planalp, 1987; Planalp & Honeycutt, 1985; Planalp, Rutherford, & Honeycutt, 1988) discovered that dating couples found that at times their uncertainty increased. When this happened, the individuals were motivated to reduce it through their communication behaviors. In a study of 46 married couples, Lynn Turner (1990) reached similar conclusions. Therefore, according to these researchers, we must not assume that once relationships begin, uncertainty disappears.

Another example of how Uncertainty Reduction Theory has been extended into developed relationships is found in the research of Malcolm Parks and Mara Adelman (1983). Parks and Adelman studied the social networks (friends and family members) of an individual and indicate that these third-party networks can be quite important information sources about a romantic partner. They note that network "members may comment on the partner's past actions and behavioral tendencies. They may supply ready-made explanations for the partner's behavior or serve as sounding boards for the individual's own explanations" (p. 57). They conclude that the more partners communicate with their social networks, the less uncertainty they will experience. Furthermore, the researchers found that the less uncertainty people feel, the less likely they will be to dissolve a relationship with another.

Based on this expansion into established relationships, Berger and Gudykunst (1991) posited the eighth axiom and seven resulting new theorems, which we discussed previously. As we mentioned, the new axiom asserted that romantic partners who interact with their partner's social network experience less uncertainty about their partner than do those who do not have this interaction. The more interaction with the social network, the less uncertainty there will be.

Some researchers who were interested in how URT applied to established relationships suggested that people in this stage experienced a different type of uncertainty than did those in initial encounters. This uncertainty was labeled **relational uncertainty** and defined as lack of certainty about the future and the status of the relationship. Berger (1987) discussed this new uncertainty type and noted that it mars relational stability. Additional research (e.g., Ficara & Mongeau, 2000; Knobloch & Solomon, 2003) established that relational uncertainty is distinct from the individual uncertainty that Berger and Calabrese originally theorized about. Relational uncertainty is found to be different from individual uncertainty because it exists at a higher level of abstraction (Knobloch & Solomon, 2003). Relational uncertainty was found to be useful in predicting several other behaviors within relationships, such as how participants will handle face threats (Knobloch, Satterlee, & DiDomenico, 2010) and communicative responses to betrayal (Levine, Kim, & Ferrara, 2010).

Marianne Dainton and Brooks Aylor (2001) examined how relational uncertainty operated in three different types of relationships: long-distance relationships with no face-to-face interaction, long-distance relationships with some face-to-face interaction, and geographically close relationships. The researchers were interested to see how relational uncertainty, jealousy, maintenance, and trust interacted in these three types of relationships. This is an important investigation because, as they note, 25–40 percent of romantic relationships between college students are long distance.

They found overall, as URT would predict, that the more uncertainty existed in a relationship the more jealousy, the less trust, and the fewer maintenance behaviors also existed. Dainton and Aylor also found support for trust as "a potent means for reducing relational uncertainty" (p. 183). The researchers also found that face-to-face contact is critical to reducing relational uncertainty. The people in long-distance relationships with no face-to-face interaction suffered from significantly more relational uncertainty. However, those who were geographically close did not differ significantly from those in long-distance relationships with some face-to-face interaction, which is not exactly what URT would predict. The researchers conclude that this is a fruitful line for further research into the utility and heurism of URT.

Social Media

Another area where URT has expanded is in social media. For instance, Artemio Ramirez, Jr. and Joseph Walther (2009) and others (e.g., Flanagin, 2007; Tidwell & Walther, 2002) have noted that URT can be applied to computer-mediated communication. Some research (e.g., May & Tenzek, 2011) indicates that information seeking on the Internet is similar to how URT describes it in a pre-online environment—involving the passive, active, and interactive strategies that we've discussed previously. Cynthia Palmieri, Kristen Prestano, Rosalie Gandley, Emily Overton, and Qin Zhang (2012) found that self-disclosures on Facebook decreased uncertainty, in line with URT's predictions. And, in another study using URT principles, Jayeon Lee (2015) examined the role that social media plays in perceptions of journalists. Lee discovered that the social media activities of journalists affected audience viewpoints. In particular, Lee concluded that journalists who self-disclosed items related to their personal life were viewed positively. However, when these journalists provided feedback to commenters, they were deemed as less professional than those who did not provide feedback.

Ramirez and Walther (2009), however, observe that there are some significant differences in information seeking online versus face to face. According to these researchers, online information seeking allows communicators to "employ several approaches to information acquisition sequentially or simultaneously in order to reduce uncertainty" (p. 73). Further, the online environment means that information-seeking sources may begin to pile up without a person's consent and outside of their control. Googling (or using other online search engines to obtain information about a specific person) someone provides a great deal of information about them that they may not even be aware is in the public domain. Finally, Artemio Ramirez and his colleagues (Ramirez, Walther, Burgoon, & Sunnafrank, 2002) have noted that Googling forms a special case of active information-seeking strategy they call **extractive strategy.**

extractive strategy
an active information-seeking strategy involving online searches to obtain information about a specific person.

Other researchers (e.g., Gibbs, Ellison, & Lai, 2011) have observed that in the online dating arena, uncertainty reduction is a salient concern. Further they note that online disclosures (unlike those offline) do not need to occur in the symmetric fashion that Berger and Calabrese (1975) described (first I tell you where I am from and then you reciprocate by telling me where you grew up). Instead, online information-seeking behaviors may occur prior to hearing a person's disclosures, as well as simultaneously or after disclosures are made. For instance, Andrea can Google Mark at any time during a possible online connection and use extractive strategies. Further, Gibbs and her colleagues suggest that this asymmetric information exchange is important to online daters because the risk of deception online is so large that it contributes to concerns about personal safety. However, Gibbs and colleagues found that online daters use a great deal of interactive strategies such as direct questioning online which confirmed URT's claims as well as earlier research (Antheunis, Valkenburg, & Peter, 2010). But one-third of Gibbs's 562 respondents reported triangulating information (comparing what a person said to information about them on websites or in public records), supporting the notion that the online environment adds different information-seeking strategies.

Context

Thinking back to our discussion in Chapter 2, URT has been extensively studied in one additional context: culture. Research shows that uncertainty varies across cultures. Let's illustrate this cultural application.

The expansion and adaptation of URT to culture is credited to William Gudykunst (1993, 2005). Thus far, our examples clearly relate to the interpersonal context. Gudykunst (1995) extended Berger and Calabrese's formulation of URT into a new theory that deals specifically with culture, which he identified as Anxiety-Uncertainty Management (AUM). According to James Neuliep (2015), uncertainty is a cognitive state while anxiety pertains to an affective (emotional) state. This AUM expansive suggests that "many people, regardless of culture, experience anxiety when communicating, or when they anticipate communicating, with persons from different cultures or ethnic groups, especially during initial encounters" (Neuliep, p. 7). Neuliep (2012) also contends that uncertainty is an aversive state—a claim also identified as a basic assumption of the URT.

Gudykunst and Tsukasa Nishida (1986a) discovered differences in low- and high-context cultures. According to Edward T. Hall (1977), **low-context cultures** are those in which meaning is found in the explicit code or message. Examples of low-context cultures are the United States, Germany, and Switzerland. In these cultures, plain, direct speaking is valued. Listeners are supposed to be able to understand meaning based merely on the words a speaker uses. In **high-context cultures,** nonverbal messages play a more significant role, and most of the meaning of a message is internalized by listeners or resides in the context. Japan, Korea, and China are examples of high-context cultures. These cultures value indirectness in speech because listeners are expected to ignore much of the explicit code in favor of understood meanings cued by nonverbals and context.

With respect to research on low- and high-context cultures, Gudykunst and Nishida (1986b) found that frequency of communication predicts uncertainty reduction in low-context cultures, but not in high-context cultures. The researchers also discovered that people use direct communication (asking questions) to reduce their uncertainty in individualistic cultures. In collectivistic cultures, more indirect communication is used with individuals who are not identified as members of the cultural in-group. Based on this research, then, people from different cultures engage in different kinds of communication to reduce their uncertainty.

Gudykunst and Mitchell Hammer (1987) undertook an additional study examining URT and culture. Instead of studying cultures outside the United States, however, they focused their research on African Americans. Interestingly, they found that URT did not apply to their African American respondents. Specifically, African Americans were not more confident in their impressions of others after asking them questions, and they were not attracted to people about whom they could make predictions. Consequently, uncertainty reduction may not be applicable in all cultural communities.

A concept similar to uncertainty reduction is **uncertainty avoidance,** which is an attempt to shun or avoid ambiguous situations (Hofstede, 1991; Smith, 2015). In other words, uncertainty avoidance refers to a person's tolerance for uncertainty. Geert Hofstede believes that the perspective of people in high-uncertainty avoidance cultures is "What is different is dangerous," whereas people in low-uncertainty avoidance cultures subscribe to "What is different is curious" (1991, p. 119). Gudykunst and Yuko Matsumoto (1996) point out that a number of cultures differ in their uncertainty avoidance (Figure 8.1), and understanding that these differences exist can help us understand communication behaviors in other countries.

Although not as developed as Anxiety-Uncertainty Management, researchers have begun to cast the principles of URT into other contexts beyond the interpersonal. One such example is Michael Boyle and his colleagues' (2004) work examining people's information-seeking behaviors in the United States after the terrorist attacks of September 11, 2001. Boyle and his coresearchers argue that "although uncertainty reduction theory has primarily been used in interpersonal communication research [its] basic logic can be applied to mass communication research" (p. 157). In addition, some work has set uncertainty reduction

low-context cultures
cultures, as in the United States, where most of the meaning is in the code or message

high-context cultures
cultures, like Japan, where the meaning of a message is in the context or internalized in listeners

uncertainty avoidance
an attempt to avoid ambiguous situations

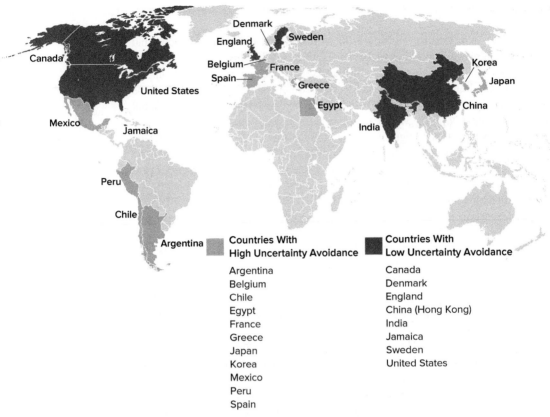

Figure 8.1 Countries and Uncertainty Avoidance

principles in the context of the workplace (Hargie, Tourish, & Wilson, 2002; Morrison, 2002).

Integration, Critique, and Closing

Uncertainty Reduction Theory has attracted scholars from a variety of disciplines. The beginnings of our relationships are usually unpredictable and URT helps us understand those challenges. Further, Berger (2016b) posits that "uncertainty is 'big business'" (p. x) in that governmental and non-governmental organizations lose billions of dollars because "managers abhor uncertainty" (p. x). Finally, the theory has enjoyed a quantitative tradition, providing an empirical lens on an often overlooked communication behavior (uncertainty).

Over a decade after the publication of the original theory, Berger (1987) admitted that Uncertainty Reduction Theory "contains some propositions of dubious validity" (p. 40). Other writers concur. Although URT has stimulated a great deal of discussion and research, it also has been criticized. As you think about how useful URT is, keep the following criteria in mind: utility and heurism.

Integration

Communication Tradition	Rhetorical	Semiotic	Phenomenological	Cybernetic	**Socio-Psychological**	Socio-Cultural	Critical
Communication Context	**Intrapersonal**	**Interpersonal**	Small Group	Organizational	Public/Rhetorical	Mass/Media	Cultural
Approach to Knowing	**Positivistic/Empirical**	Interpretive/Hermeneutic	Critical

Critique

Evaluation Criteria	Scope	Logical Consistency	Parsimony	**Utility**	Testability	**Heurism**	Test of Time

Utility

Some researchers believe that the major assumptions of the theory are flawed. Michael Sunnafrank (1986) argues that reducing uncertainty about the self and another in an initial encounter is not an individual's primary concern. Instead, Sunnafrank argues, "a more primary goal is the maximization of relational outcomes" (p. 9). Sunnafrank calls for a reformulation of URT that takes into account the importance of predicted outcomes during initial interactions. This has come to be known as predicted outcome value (POV). Drawing on our chapter's opening, Sunnafrank would contend that Malcolm will be more concerned with maximizing rewards in a potential relationship with Edie than in figuring out what she might do and why she is doing it. Actually, Sunnafrank suggests that URT might kick in after Malcolm decides what the predicted outcomes of talking with Edie will be. Jina Yoo's (2009) findings offered some empirical support for POV's claims as opposed to URT's.

Berger's (1986) response to Sunnafrank is that outcomes cannot be predicted without knowledge and reduced uncertainty about oneself, one's partner, and one's relationship. It is Berger's contention that uncertainty reduction is independent of as well as necessary to predicted outcome values. In fact, he believes that if one remains highly uncertain, there really are no predicted outcome values. Furthermore, Berger responds to Sunnafrank's critique by noting that the act of predicting an outcome serves as a means to reduce uncertainty. Thus, Berger concludes that Sunnafrank has simply expanded the scope of URT rather than offering an alternative to it.

A second problem with URT's utility has to do with its validity. Recall that even Berger (1987) has admitted some validity problems, yet he is not willing to give up on the theory. Some of his more skeptical colleagues, however, assert that given the tight logical structure of an axiomatic theory, if one building block is wrong, then much of the resulting theory is suspect. Kathy Kellermann and Rodney Reynolds (1990) point to Axiom 3, which suggests that high uncertainty causes high levels of information-seeking behavior, as problematic.

Piercarlo Valdesolo writes in *Scientific American* online that predicted outcome values and uncertainty reduction might work in concert to predict whether relationships move from initial encounters to a greater level of development. Valdesolo reflects back to a dilemma he had when he began a romantic relationship just before Valentine's Day. He recounts that he had a hard time trying to figure out how to celebrate the holiday with a relatively new romantic partner: Should he play hard to get or wear his heart on his sleeve? Valdesolo notes that he might have gotten some help from a recent study that showed women Facebook profiles of men who had supposedly viewed their Facebook profile. The women were divided into groups: One group was told that these men liked them the most of any profiles they'd viewed; one group was told the men found them to be average; and the third group was told the men either liked them the most or they thought they were average. The women responded most positively to the men they weren't sure about, not the ones they thought liked them the most. Valdesolo comments that being uncertain only works if "your target actually likes you. Indeed, the more people tend to think about the possibility of uncertain negative outcomes (what is the biopsy going to show?) the worse they come to feel about that outcome." So, uncertainty is aversive when the POV is negative, but not so much when the POV is positive. Valdesolo comments that he wishes he knew that when he first started his relationship, but he did marry her anyway!

Source: Valdesolo, P. A scientific dating insight: Create uncertainty—The aphrodisiac effect of not knowing how much they like you, scientificamerican.com/article.cfm?id=a-scientific-dating -insig&page=2

Their study of over a thousand students failed to find support for the third axiom. Instead, they found that "*wanting* knowledge rather than *lacking* knowledge is what promotes information-seeking in initial encounters with others" (p. 71 [emphasis added]). Kellermann and Reynolds point out that many times we may be uncertain about another, but because we have no interest in the other, we are not motivated to reduce our uncertainties by information-seeking behaviors. People engage in communication, therefore, not to reduce uncertainty, but because they care about the other, are interested in the other, or both. In a different vein, Dale Brashers (2001) also questions the validity of Axiom 3. He notes with reference to post–September 11 anxieties that sometimes more information results in a greater sense of uncertainty. Interestingly, however, Dell McKinney and William Donaghy (1993) found some empirical support for Axiom 3, so the debate on this issue undoubtedly will continue concerning URT's usefulness.

Heurism

Reflecting on our criteria for theory evaluation, this theory is highly heuristic. For instance, URT has been integrated into research examining small groups (Booth-Butterfield, Booth-Butterfield, & Koester, 1988) as well as research in doctor–patient communication (Perrault & Silk, 2015) and computer-mediated communication (Lundy & Drouin, 2016). It is clear from our earlier discussions that URT has been expanded into many contexts, making it highly heuristic.

Student Voices

Steve

I enjoyed the section of the chapter that talked about expanding the theory into developed relationships. I have been working for the same boss for four years, yet many times I feel a sense of uncertainty with her like the theory talks about. You'd think I'd know what to expect from Tara after working for her for several years, but she still keeps surprising me. Last week, she completely changed her attitude, and I wasn't quite sure how to take it. For several weeks she's been telling me that we had to finish a project much more quickly than the time we usually take with our work. So I have been killing myself to get it done. Then last week she said we could slow down, and she didn't explain herself at all. I immediately used active strategies and started asking a couple of other people in the office to see if I could figure out what she was thinking. So, overall, I think the theory should be expanded to developed relationships, and it should also apply to relationships in the workplace. We have a ton of uncertainty at my job!

Closing

Uncertainty Reduction Theory has made a very important contribution to the field of communication, even as it has generated a few theoretical disputes. Although this theory may be somewhat linear in nature (recall our discussion on communication models in Chapter 1), it has provoked a great deal of commentary and research, and it places communication in a central position. It marked a beginning when communication researchers began focusing on their own discipline for theoretical explanations rather than borrowing theories from other disciplines.

Discussion Starters

TECH QUEST: How does communicating via social media sites impact the utility of URT? For instance, does knowing a lot about a stranger before actually meeting him or her face to face (by reading the person's Facebook page, for instance, or by following him or her on Twitter) mean that the axioms and theorems of URT no longer hold true? Or do social media only provide different channels for collecting information about people, further supporting the claims of URT?

1. Why is examining initial interactions like that of Edie and Malcolm an important undertaking for communication theorists? Provide at least one example to support your view.

2. Uncertainty reduction is the process of using communication to increase our ability to explain and predict others' behaviors. Do you think that predicting and explaining others' behaviors are really important concerns when people interact with one another?

3. Are there times when asking questions in initial encounters with others only results in more uncertainty? Give examples. Has reducing your uncertainty about someone ever led to you liking the person less? Describe how this occurs.

4. Do you agree with Berger and Calabrese's assumption about the developmental process of interpersonal relationships? Give examples that support or contest the notion that relationships use communication to pass through entry, personal, and exit phases.

5. What additional factors or events exist—other than those presented in this chapter—when two people meet for the first time? Be sure to be specific and provide appropriate examples.

6. If you could talk with Berger or Calabrese, what would you say to either of them about the utility of their theory in your life? Apply the theory to any aspect or relationship type in your life today in answering this question.

7. How useful is URT when it comes to examining communication across cultures? What do you think of the extensions that have been made to URT to make it apply to intercultural communication?

CHAPTER 9

Social Exchange Theory

*Based on the research of **John Thibaut** and **Harold Kelley***

> *The adjustment one individual makes affects the adjustments the others must make, which in turn require readjustment.*
> —John Thibault and Harold Kelley

Meredith Daniels and LaTasha Evans

Meredith Daniels and LaTasha Evans have been best friends since they served as hall monitors together in the fourth grade. After elementary school they moved on together to Collins High School. There they suffered through homework, dating dilemmas, and other typical high school concerns. In addition, they coped with racial issues because Meredith is European American and LaTasha is African American. In their hometown of Biloxi, Mississippi, the heritage of racism formed a barrier to their friendship. Although Biloxi is now fairly progressive, Meredith's grandfather was very uncomfortable about her friendship with LaTasha. Also, LaTasha's Uncle Benjamin had participated in Freedom Marches in the 1960s and had formed some unfavorable opinions about Whites. For a short time, her uncle had been a member of a Black separatist organization. He had some difficulty with LaTasha and Meredith's friendship, too. Both of the young women had worked hard to maintain their relationship despite their family members' objections.

When LaTasha and Meredith were together, they often wondered why race was such a big deal. They seemed like sisters to each other, closer than many sisters they knew. They had the exact same sense of humor, and they could always cheer each other up with a goofy look or some silly joke about their past. They enjoyed the same movies (horror/thrillers) and the same subjects in school (English and French) and had similar taste in clothes (boho-glam) and boyfriends (intellectual guys).

But at home they often had to defend their friendship to their families. Meredith's parents said that they did not object to the friendship, but were unhappy when Meredith socialized with African American boys and went to parties where she might be one of only two or three White girls in attendance. LaTasha's parents also had no problem with Meredith; they liked her and understood the friendship. But they drew the line when it came to dating White boys. LaTasha's parents were very proud of their African American heritage, and they told all their children how important it was to maintain their traditions and way of life. For them this meant that the family must stay African American: no dating or marriage with someone of another race. LaTasha's cousin had married a Japanese woman, and the whole family was having a great deal of difficulty accepting the couple.

Now that LaTasha and Meredith were entering their senior year at high school, things had become even more difficult. LaTasha's parents were adamant that she attend a historically Black college after graduation. Meredith's family wanted her to go to a small college in southern California because both her parents had graduated from this school, and they had many relatives living near the college. Both LaTasha and Meredith, however, wanted to go to college together or at least be somewhat near each other. In addition, they resented how much time and energy all the discussions about college seemed to take up. It was almost ruining their senior year!

When they were together, they could usually forget about all the hassle and just have fun as usual, but the pressure was taking a toll on their friendship. Although they tried not to think about it, they both were concerned about the future. It was hard not to be able to tell each other everything as they always had in the past, but Meredith and LaTasha found that talking to each other about college was stressful, so they mainly avoided the subject. Privately, each wondered what was going to happen and how she would get along next year without her best friend. ∎

A Social Exchange theorist examining Meredith and LaTasha's relationship would predict that it might be heading for some trouble because the relationship currently seems to be costing the two more than it is rewarding them. Social Exchange Theory (SET) is based on the notion that people think about their relationships in economic terms. Michael Roloff (2015) put it this way: "Human survival is based on the ability to acquire needed resources [and] communication is a tool by which individuals can negotiate an exchange as well as provide resources" (p. 1). People tally up the costs of being in a relationship and compare them to the rewards that are offered by being in that relationship. **Costs** are the elements of relational life that have negative value to a person, such as the time and effort one has to put into maintaining a relationship or the negatives one has to put up with in their partner (such as the amount of time he or she likes to spend with online games). In our chapter-opening scenario, the stress and tension that LaTasha and Meredith feel about the issue of college are now costs to their relationship. Their relationship always had the cost of generating conflict in their respective families. **Rewards** are the elements of a relationship that have positive value. In Meredith and LaTasha's case, the fun they have together, the loyalty they show for each other, and the sense of understanding they share are all rewards.

George Homans is generally credited with bringing the notion of an exchange perspective to human behavior. Homans examined the idea of exchange in small groups and it was later explored in interpersonal relationships (Trevino & Tilly, 2016). Although some of what we present in this chapter can be applied to group behavior, the essence of what we delve into relates to how individuals think about and cultivate their relationships with others.

Social Exchange theorists argue that people assess their relationships in terms of costs and rewards (Roloff, 2009; Stafford, 2008). All relationships require some time and effort on the part of their participants. When friends spend time with each other, which they must do to maintain the relationship, they are unable to do other things with that time, so in that sense the time spent is a cost. Friends may need attention at inopportune times, and then the cost is magnified. For instance, if you had to finish a term paper and your best friend just broke up with her boyfriend and needed to talk to you, you can see how the friendship would cost you something in terms of time. Yet relationships provide us with rewards, or positives, too. Families, friends, and loved ones generally give us a sense of acceptance, support, and companionship. Some friends

costs
elements of relational life with negative value

rewards
elements of relational life with positive value

open doors for us or provide us with status just by being with us. Friends and families keep us from feeling lonely and isolated. Some friends teach us helpful lessons.

The Social Exchange perspective argues that people calculate the overall worth of a particular relationship by subtracting its costs from the rewards it provides (Monge & Contractor, 2003):

$$Worth = Rewards - Costs$$

Positive relationships are those whose worth is a positive number; that is, the rewards are greater than the costs. Relationships where the worth is a negative number (the costs exceed the rewards) tend to be negative for the participants. Social Exchange Theory goes even further, predicting that the worth of a relationship influences its **outcome**, or whether people will continue with a relationship or terminate it. Positive relationships are expected to endure, whereas negative relationships will probably terminate.

outcome
whether people continue in a relationship or terminate it

Although, as we will explore in this chapter, the situation is more complicated than this simple equation, it does give the essence of what exchange theorists argue. John Thibaut and Harold Kelley (1959) say, for example, that "every individual voluntarily enters and stays in any relationship only as long as it is adequately satisfactory in terms of his [sic] rewards and costs" (p. 37). As Ronald Sabatelli and Constance Shehan (1993) note, the Social Exchange approach views relationships through the metaphor of the marketplace, where each person acts out of a self-oriented goal of profit taking. However, Laura Stafford (2008) qualifies that economic exchanges and social exchanges have some differences: Social exchanges involve a connection with another person; social exchanges involve trust, not legal obligations; social exchanges are more flexible; and social exchanges rarely involve explicit bargaining. As we shall see later in the chapter, some researchers are not sure if the claims of Social Exchange work only in the marketplace or do describe interpersonal exchanges as well.

We have been talking in general about exchange theories and the perspective of Social Exchange; this is because (1) Social Exchange provides an overarching view of human beings that might be taken up by other specific theories like Social Penetration Theory that we discuss in the next chapter, and (2) there are several different theories of Social Exchange. Michael Roloff (1981, 2015) discusses five specific theories. Roloff observes that these theories are tied together by a central argument that "the guiding force of interpersonal relationships is the advancement of both parties' self-interest" (p. 14). Furthermore, Roloff notes that these theories do not assume that self-interest is a negative thing; rather, when self-interest is recognized, it will actually enhance a relationship. Yet Roloff also argues that there are significant differences among these five theories—some of which derive from the fact that they were developed by researchers in different disciplines (e.g., psychology, social psychology, and sociology). It is beyond our purposes here to differentiate among all the theories of Social Exchange. We will concentrate on explicating what may be the most popular theory, John Thibaut and Harold Kelley's (1959) Theory of Interdependence. Although Thibaut and Kelley called their theory the Theory of Interdependence, it is often referred to as Social Exchange Theory because it fits into the exchange framework (Roloff, 2015).

Assumptions of Social Exchange Theory

All Social Exchange theories are built upon several assumptions about human nature and the nature of relationships. Some of these assumptions should be clear to you after our introductory comments. Because Social Exchange Theory is based on a metaphor of economic exchange, many of these assumptions flow from the notion that people view life as a marketplace. In addition, Thibaut and Kelley base their theory on two conceptualizations: one that focuses on the nature of individuals and one that describes the relationships between two people. They look to drive reduction, an internal motivator, to understand individuals and to gaming principles to understand relationships between people. Thus, the assumptions they make also fall into these two categories.

The assumptions that Social Exchange Theory makes about *human nature* include the following:

- Humans seek rewards and avoid punishments.
- Humans are rational beings.
- The standards that humans use to evaluate costs and rewards vary over time and from person to person.

The assumptions Social Exchange Theory makes about the *nature of relationships* include the following:

- Relationships are interdependent.
- Relational life is a process.

We will look at each of these assumptions in turn.

The notion that humans seek rewards and avoid punishment is consistent with the conceptualization of drive reduction (Roloff, 1981). This approach assumes that people's behaviors are motivated by some internal drive mechanism. When people feel this drive, they are motivated to reduce it, and the process of doing so is a pleasurable one. If George feels thirsty, he is driven to reduce that feeling by getting a drink. This whole process is rewarding and, thus, "To be rewarded means that a person had undergone drive reduction or need fulfillment" (Roloff, 1981, p. 45). This assumption helps Social Exchange theorists understand why LaTasha and Meredith enjoy each other's company: They feel a need for understanding and companionship, and this need (or drive) is fulfilled (or reduced) by spending time together.

The second assumption—that humans are rational—is critical to Social Exchange Theory. The theory rests on the notion that within the limits of the information that is available to them, people will calculate the costs and rewards of a given situation and guide their behaviors accordingly. This also includes the possibility that, faced with no rewarding choice, people will choose the least costly alternative. In the case of LaTasha and Meredith, it is costly to continue their friendship in the face of all the stress and family objections they are experiencing. Yet both young women may believe that it is less costly than ending their friendship and denying themselves the support and affection that they have shared for the past nine years.

James White, David Klein, and Todd Martin (2014) point out that assuming rationality is not the same as saying that people engage in rationalization. By assuming that people are rational beings, Social Exchange Theory asserts that people use rational thinking to make choices. But when we rationalize, we "attempt to provide an apparently rational justification for [our] behavior after the behavior occurred" (p. 37). Thus, rationalizing provides a fabricated attempt to make a choice look rational after the fact. This distinction becomes important when we discuss some of the criticisms of Social Exchange Theory at the end of this chapter.

The third assumption—that the standards people use to evaluate costs and rewards vary over time and from person to person—suggests that the theory must take diversity into consideration. No one standard can be applied to everyone to determine what is a cost and what is a reward. Thus, LaTasha may grow to see the relationship as more costly than Meredith does (or vice versa) as their standards change over time. However, Social Exchange Theory is a lawlike theory, as we described in Chapter 3, because SET claims that although individuals may differ in their definition of rewards, the first assumption is still true for all people: We are motivated to maximize our profits and rewards while minimizing our losses and costs (Pascale & Primavera, 2016).

As we mentioned earlier in this chapter, Thibaut and Kelley take those three assumptions about human nature from drive reduction principles. In their approach to relationships, they developed a set of principles that they call *Game Theory*. The classic game they developed that illustrates their first assumption about relationships is called the Prisoner's Dilemma (Figure 9.1). This game supposes that two prisoners are being questioned about a crime they deny committing. They have been separated

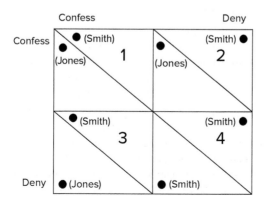

**Figure 9.1
The Prisoner's
Dilemma**

for the questioning, and they are given two choices: They can confess to the crime, or they can persist in their denials. The situation is further complicated by the fact that the outcome for them is not completely in their own hands, individually. Instead, each prisoner's outcome is a result of the combination of their two responses. The configuration of their possible choices is called a 2×2 matrix because there are two of them and they each have two choices: confess or deny.

Student Voices

Veronica

I first met my now fiancé on Match.com. We had quite a discussion about whether we wanted to get married or continue to live together. The costs of getting married were, in my eyes, pretty limited because we'd have some tax benefits. In her eyes, there were several risks like whether or not we were both prepared to say "till death do us part" or whether or not we are ready to be monogamous. We both thought about this a lot to ourselves and in the end, felt that the benefits of being married outweighed the costs of cohabiting.

If we call one of the prisoners Jones and the other Smith, we can see their choices and outcomes:

1. Jones confesses and Smith confesses = they both receive a life sentence.
2. Jones confesses and Smith denies = Jones goes free and Smith is jailed for life.
3. Jones denies and Smith confesses = Smith goes free and Jones is jailed for life.
4. Jones denies and Smith denies = they both serve a short jail term.

It is clear that the outcomes for Smith and Jones are interdependent. The outcome in each case depends on the relationship between Smith's and Jones's answers, not on one answer alone. This concept is so central to Thibaut and Kelley that they named their theory the Theory of Interdependence rather than Social Exchange or Game Theory. They did so because they wished to avoid the notion of win–lose in Game Theory, and they wished to stress that social exchange is a function of interdependence. Even though they used the Prisoner's Dilemma as a starting point, Thibaut and Kelley were interested in social relationships, which is why we can apply these concepts to relationships like LaTasha and Meredith's.

When we think of LaTasha and Meredith's situation, we can see that if Meredith decides to cut back on her friendship with LaTasha, LaTasha will inevitably be affected. Her own decisions about the costs and rewards of the relationship are contingent on Meredith's decision. Thus, whenever anyone member of a relationship acts, both the other and the relationship as a whole are influenced. In a study of family members who care for elderly relatives (Raschick & Ingersoll-Dayton, 2004), the authors found there was interdependency in the care-giving and care-receiving relationship.

The second assumption that Thibaut and Kelley make is that relational life is a process. In stating this, the researchers are acknowledging the importance of time and change in relational life. Specifically, time affects exchanges because past experiences guide judgments about rewards and costs, and these judgments impact subsequent exchanges. For example, if Kathy dislikes school and has a very low opinion of teachers and then takes a class that exceeds her expectations, and she finds that she really likes this particular teacher, their relationship and Kathy's expectations about future relationships with teachers will be shaped by the process. Further, the notion of process allows us to see that relationships constantly change and evolve.

Given these assumptions about humans and relationships, we are ready to examine two of the major parts of the theory: evaluation of a relationship and exchange patterns.

Evaluating a Relationship

As we mentioned previously, SET is more complex than the simple equation of worth that we initially presented. Social exchange includes "both a notion of a relationship, and some notion of a shared obligation in which both parties perceive responsibilities to each other" (Lavelle, Rupp, & Brockner, 2007, p. 845). When people calculate the worth of their relationships and make decisions about staying in them, a few other considerations surface. One of the most interesting parts of Thibaut and Kelley's theory is their explanation of how people evaluate their relationships with reference to whether they will stay in them or leave them. Thibaut and Kelley claim that this evaluation rests on two types of comparisons: comparison level and comparison level for alternatives. The **comparison level (CL)** is a standard representing what people feel they should receive in the way of rewards and costs from a particular relationship. Thus, Meredith has a subjective feeling about what she should give and what she should get, in return, from a friendship. Her CL has been shaped by all her past friendships, by family members' advice, and by popular culture such as TV and film representations of friendships that give her an idea of what is expected from this relationship.

Comparison levels vary among individuals because they are subjective. Individuals base their CL, in large part, on past experiences with a specific type of relationship. Because individuals have very different past experiences with similar types of relationships, they develop different comparison levels. For example, if Suzanne has had many friendships that required her to do a great deal of listening and empathizing, her CL will include this. If Andrew has not experienced friends requiring this listening behavior from him, he will not expect to encounter this cost in friendship. Because we often interact with people from our own culture, we share many relational expectations due to messages we have received from popular culture (Rawlins, 1992). Thus, we overlap somewhat in our expectations for relationships, and our CLs may not be totally different from one another's.

Thibaut and Kelley argue that our satisfaction with a current relationship derives from comparing the rewards and costs it involves to our CL. If our current relationship meets or exceeds our CL, the theory predicts we will be satisfied with the relationship. Yet people sometimes leave satisfactory relationships and stay in ones that are not so satisfying. Thibaut and Kelley explain this seeming inconsistency with their second standard of comparison, the **comparison level for alternatives (CLalt).**

comparison level (CL)
a standard for what a person thinks he or she should get in a relationship

comparison level for alternatives (CLalt)
how people evaluate a relationship based on what their alternatives to the relationship are

This refers to "the lowest level of relational rewards a person is willing to accept given available rewards from alternative relationships or being alone" (Roloff, 1981, p. 48). In other words, the CLalt provides the threshold for evaluating a relationship compared to the realistic alternatives to that relationship (Dillow, Malachowski, Brann, & Weber, 2011). For example, Michael Kramer (2005) studied community theater participation. He notes that people who live in towns where there is only one community theater are likely to stay with fewer rewards than those who have other options in their town. He observes that this emphasizes the importance of CLalt.

CLalt provides a measure of stability rather than satisfaction—that is, the CLalt suggests how likely it is that Meredith would leave her relationship with LaTasha, even though it is a satisfying one, for something she thinks would be better. If we further examine LaTasha and Meredith's relationship using CL and CLalt, we might speculate that Meredith finds her friendship with LaTasha very satisfying in general. She might give it an eight out of a 10-point ranking where one is horrible and 10 is perfect. The eight would be Meredith's outcome score for her relationship with LaTasha. If Meredith's expectations of friendship, or her CL, is only a six, then Meredith should be satisfied with her friendship with LaTasha. Furthermore, if Meredith thinks that by being alone now as she decides about college she would rate herself at a three, and she has few other friends that could even come close to her relationship with LaTasha, then her CLalt will be low. Her 8 outcome with LaTasha will exceed it, and Social Exchange Theory predicts that Meredith will want to remain friends with LaTasha.

If we calculate these numbers based on the format specified in Table 9.1, Meredith's outcome, eight, is greater than her CL (6), and her CL is greater than her CLalt, which is three. Thus, her pattern fits the first example in the table and the theory predicts that the state of her relationship is satisfying and stable.

This kind of calculation—although perhaps a little unrealistic in turning a relationship into a single number—suggests why some people remain in relationships that are abusive. If people see no alternative and fear being alone more than being in the relationship, Social Exchange Theory predicts they will stay. Some have written about women in abusive relationships, using this theoretical reasoning to explain why women stay with violent men (Walker, 1984). Other researchers

Table 9.1 How Outcome, CL, and CLalt Affect the State of a Relationship

RELATIVE VALUE OF OUTCOME, CL, CLALT	STATE OF THE RELATIONSHIP
Outcome > CL > Clalt	Satisfying and stable
Outcome > CLalt > CL	Satisfying and stable
CLalt > CL > Outcome	Unsatisfying and unstable
CLalt > Outcome > CL	Satisfying and unstable
CL > CLalt > Outcome	Unsatisfying and unstable
CL > Outcome > Clalt	Unsatisfying and stable

> means greater than; < means less than
Source: Adapted from Roloff, 1981, p. 48. Reprinted by permission of Sage Publications, Inc.

(Cox & Kramer, 1995) note that managers in organizations use these calculations to help them make decisions about dismissing employees. And Bishop, Scott, Goldsby, and Cropanzano (2005) investigate how employees use social exchange in forming commitments to their jobs. Table 9.1 summarizes six possible combinations among the outcome, the CL, and the CLalt and the resulting state of the relationship predicted by the theory.

Exchange Patterns: SET in Action

In addition to studying how people calculate their relational outcomes, Thibaut and Kelley were interested in how people adjust their behaviors in interaction with their relational partners. Thibaut and Kelley suggest that when people interact, they are goal directed. This is congruent with their assumption that human beings are rational. People, according to Thibaut and Kelley, engage in **behavioral sequences,** or a series of actions designed to achieve their goal. These sequences are the heart of what Thibaut and Kelley conceptualize as social exchange. As Thibaut and Kelley note, when people engage in these behavioral sequences they are dependent to some extent on their relational partner. For instance, if one person wishes to play gin rummy, cooperation from a partner is required. This interdependence brings up the concept of **power**—the dependence a person has on another for outcomes. If Meredith depends more on LaTasha for rewards than vice versa, then LaTasha has greater power than Meredith in their relationship. Some researchers (Darr, 2016) observe that certain exchanges, such as gift giving, bestow status and power on the giver. Other researchers (Trussell & Lavrakas, 2004) suggest there is probably an optimal amount a giver can give before status and power might begin to decline.

There are two types of power in SET: fate control and behavior control. **Fate control** is the ability to affect a partner's outcomes. For example, if Meredith withholds her friendship from LaTasha, she affects LaTasha's outcome. If LaTasha cannot replace Meredith as a friend, Meredith's behavior gives her fate control over LaTasha. This presumes that Meredith does not care about the relationship. If she does, then withholding her friendship is a punishment for her as well, which gives LaTasha a certain amount of fate control in the relationship, too.

Behavior control is the power to cause another's behavior to change by changing one's own behavior. If Meredith calls LaTasha on the phone, it is likely that LaTasha will stop whatever else she is doing and talk to Meredith. If LaTasha is with Meredith and falls silent, Meredith will probably change her behavior in response. She might stop talking too, or she might question LaTasha to find out if something is wrong.

Thibaut and Kelley state that people develop patterns of exchange to cope with power differentials and to deal with the costs associated with exercising power. These patterns describe behavioral rules or norms that indicate how people trade resources in an attempt to maximize rewards and minimize costs. Thibaut and Kelley describe three different matrices in social exchange to illustrate the patterns people develop. These matrices include the given matrix, the effective matrix, and the dispositional matrix.

The **given matrix** represents the behavioral choices and outcomes that are determined by a combination of external factors (the environment) and internal factors (the specific skills each interactant possesses). When two people engage in

behavioral sequences
a series of actions designed to achieve a goal

power
the degree of dependence a person has on another for outcomes

fate control
the ability to affect a partner's outcomes

behavior control
the power to change another's behavior

given matrix
the constraints on your choices due to the environment and/or your own skill levels

SOCIAL EXCHANGE THEORY

an exchange, the environment may make some options more difficult than others. LaTasha's and Meredith's families, for instance, are part of the environment that is making their friendship more difficult. A scarcity of money would be another aspect of the given matrix that would make some alternatives less likely for some relationships. Furthermore, the given matrix depends on the skills people bring to the social exchange. If people lack skills for ballroom dancing, for example, it is unlikely that they will spend time dancing together. To a certain degree, the given matrix represents "the hand you are dealt."

People may be restricted by the given matrix, but they are not trapped by it. They can transform it into the **effective matrix,** "which represents an expansion of alternative behaviors and/or outcomes which ultimately determines the behavioral choices in social exchange" (Roloff, 1981, p. 51). If a man does not know how to tango, he can take lessons in this dance and learn it, transforming the given matrix into the effective matrix. If Meredith and LaTasha think their families are bothering their friendship too much, they can engage in conflict with them until they change their families' minds. Or they can stop talking about each other at home and keep their friendship secret so that they can avoid their families' negative sanctions.

The final matrix, the **dispositional matrix,** represents the way two people believe that rewards ought to be exchanged between them. If Meredith and LaTasha think that friends ought to stick together no matter how much outside interference they receive from family members, that will affect their dispositional matrix. Some people view exchanges as competition, and this belief will be reflected in their dispositional matrix.

Thibaut and Kelley assert that if we know the kinds of dispositions a person has (the dispositional matrix) and the nature of the situation in which he or she is operating (the given matrix), then we will know how to predict the transformations the person will make (the effective matrix) to impact the social exchange. Thus, if we understand that LaTasha expects great loyalty from her friends, and from herself as a friend, and we know that her family's opposition to her friendship to Meredith is not too strong, we might predict that LaTasha will defend Meredith to her family and attempt to change their beliefs. If her family has a stronger opposition, we might predict that LaTasha will simply remain friends with Meredith without trying to change her family's beliefs. The dispositional matrix guides the transformations people make to their given matrix; these transformations lead to the effective matrix, which determines the social exchange.

In their theory, Thibaut and Kelley do not explicitly deal with communication behaviors, such as self-disclosure, a topic we discuss in Chapter 10 in conjunction with Social Penetration Theory. Yet some of their discussion about the three matrices implies that self-disclosure does play an important role in social exchange. As Roloff (1981) observes,

> Self-disclosure would seem to imply the communication of two things:
> (1) the dispositions one has, and (2) the transformations (strategy) one is going
> to employ in this exchange. Since dispositions affect a person's strategy, we
> might assume that knowledge of dispositions might well allow us to predict
> the transformations. (p. 77)

This self-disclosure, like all disclosures about the self, contains risks. It could provide the relational partner with information that could be used against the discloser. If people

effective matrix
the transformations you are able to make to your given matrix, by learning a new skill, for example

dispositional matrix
the beliefs you have about relationships

know how another transforms the given matrix, they have an edge in social exchanges. For example, if LaTasha knows that Meredith tries to resolve problems in a cooperative fashion, she can use Meredith's cooperative nature against her to get what she wants in an exchange. An understanding of how the matrices affect communication behavior is one reason communication researchers are interested in Social Exchange Theory.

Exchange Structures

Exchanges may take several forms within these matrices. These include direct exchange, generalized exchange, and productive exchange (Figure 9.2). In a **direct exchange,** reciprocation is confined to the two actors. For instance, when Brad washes his father's car and then his dad lets him use the car on Saturday night, the exchange is direct. One social actor provides value to another and the other reciprocates. In a longtime friendship like Meredith and LaTasha's, they consistently participate in direct exchanges. It isn't necessary to reciprocate immediately, but when LaTasha does a favor for Meredith, she knows that Meredith will eventually respond in kind.

A **generalized exchange** involves indirect reciprocity. One person gives to another and the recipient responds, but not to the first person. Generalized exchanges occur, for example, when someone moves away from the neighborhood and friends and neighbors help pack up the moving van. Because the person has moved away, he or she won't help any of those neighbors move when they are ready to relocate. The favor is reciprocated by helping someone else, in the new neighborhood. Generalized exchanges involve the community or social network rather than simply two specific people as in the examples we have discussed with LaTasha and Meredith.

Finally, exchanges may be productive, meaning that both actors have to contribute for either one of them to benefit. In a direct or generalized exchange, one person is the beneficiary of another's provision of value. One receives a reward and the other incurs a cost. In a **productive exchange,** both people incur benefits and costs simultaneously. If LaTasha and Meredith do a project together for their senior English class, they engage in productive exchange. Both of them have to do the work, and they both share equally in the grade they receive.

direct exchange
an exchange where two people reciprocate costs and rewards

generalized exchange
an exchange where reciprocation involves the social network and isn't confined to two individuals

productive exchange
an exchange where both partners incur costs and benefits simultaneously

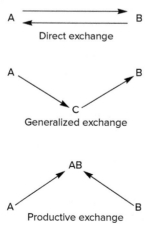

Figure 9.2
Exchange Structures

Integration, Critique, and Closing

Social Exchange Theory has generated a great deal of research and has been called "one of the major theoretical perspectives in the field of social psychology" (Cook & Rice, 2003, p. 53). SET is grounded in quantitative research, making it an empirically driven framework from which to examine interpersonal relationships. As you reflect on SET, the criteria of scope, utility, testability, and heurism are important to address.

Integration

Communication Tradition	Rhetorical	Semiotic	Phenomenological	Cybernetic	**Socio-Psychological**	Socio-Cultural	Critical
Communication Context	**Intrapersonal**	**Interpersonal**	Small Group	Organizational	Public/Rhetorical	Mass/Media	Cultural
Approach to Knowing	**Positivistic/Empirical**	Interpretive/Hermeneutic	Critical

Critique

Evaluation Criteria	Scope	Logical Consistency	Parsimony	**Utility**	**Testability**	**Heurism**	Test of Time

SOCIAL EXCHANGE THEORY

Scope

When examining SET on the basis of scope, some critics comment that it fails to explain the importance of group solidarity in its emphasis on individual need fulfillment (England, 1989). This critique combines some of the issues raised previously and argues that "the exchange framework can be viewed as valuing the separative self to the extent that rationality and self-interest are emphasized" (Sabatelli & Shehan, 1993, p. 397). By prioritizing this value, the connected self is overlooked and undervalued. In some ways, this objection has ontological considerations as well, but it also suggests that the scope of the theory is too narrow. SET only considers the individual as a unique entity without focusing on the individual as a member of a group. Because of this, SET cannot account for relationships in cultures that prioritize connection over individuality, for example.

Student Voices

Brittany

Thinking about Social Exchange Theory helped me understand my friend Lindsay's relationship with her boyfriend, Stan. I never could get what she saw in him at all until I read about CLalt. Then a light bulb went on. Even though I think Lindsay is great, she has very low self-esteem, and Stan is her first real boyfriend. She's never said so, but I bet she thinks that if she leaves Stan she won't be able to get another boyfriend. We go to a rather conservative school, and Lindsay is a liberal person. Stan is less conservative than most of the other guys we know, so I am guessing that Lindsay thinks there aren't a lot of other guys around for her—because of both her low self-esteem and her political views. Now that I understand it a little better, I might try talking to Lindsay. She could do a lot better than Stan, and I hope she will see that.

Utility

The criterion of utility suggests that if the theory doesn't present an accurate picture of people, it will be faulted as not useful. The real question is: Are humans really that calculating (Zafirovski, 2005)? SET has been criticized for the conceptualization of human beings it advances. In the theory, humans are seen as rational calculators, coming up with numerical equations to represent their relational life. Many people object to this understanding of humans, asking whether people really rationally calculate the costs and rewards to be realized when in a relationship. Social Exchange assumes a great deal of cognitive awareness and activity, which several researchers have questioned (Berger & Roloff, 1980). Researchers have not come to a definitive answer about how much people calculate their relational life, but this calculation probably ebbs and flows according to many factors. First, some contexts may make people more self-aware than others. As LaTasha and Meredith receive more pressure to decide about college, they may think about their relationship more than they did when they were younger. Second, some individual differences might affect how people process information. Some people are simply more self-aware than others (Snyder, 1979). As researchers continue to work with this theory, they must account for these and other factors relative to this calculation.

In addition, critics wonder if people are really as self-interested as Social Exchange Theory assumes. Steve Duck (1994) argues that applying a marketplace mentality to the understanding of relational life vastly misrepresents what goes on in relationships. He suggests that it is wrong to think about personal relationships in the same way that we think about business transactions, like buying a house or a car. This suggestion relates to the approaches to knowing one brings to the theory, as we discussed in Chapter 3. For some people, the analogy of the marketplace is appropriate, but for others it is not and may be highly offensive.

Testability

A common criticism of Social Exchange Theory is that it's not testable. As we discussed in Chapter 3, one important attribute of a theory is that it is testable and capable of being proven false. The difficulty with SET is that its central concepts—costs and rewards—are not clearly defined. As Sabatelli and Shehan (1993) note,

> It becomes impossible to make an operational distinction between what people value, what they perceive as rewarding, and how they behave. Rewards, values, and actions appear to be defined in terms of each other (Turner, 1978). Thus, it is impossible to find an instance when a person does not act in ways so as to obtain rewards. (p. 396)

When the theory argues that people do what they can to maximize rewards and then also argues that what people do is rewarding behavior, it is difficult to disentangle the two concepts. This issue relates to the difference between rationalization and rationality that we discussed earlier in the chapter. As long as Social Exchange Theory operates with these types of circular definitions, it will be untestable and, thus, unsatisfactory. However, Roloff (1981) observes that some work has been done to create lists of rewards in advance of simply observing what people do and labeling that as rewarding because people are doing it. Edna Foa and Uriel Foa (1974) began this work of clearly defining rewards. Roloff further argues that despite this problem, there has been a great deal of empirical work using Social Exchange theories.

Heurism

People who support SET point out that it has been heuristic. Studies in many diverse areas, from corporations (Muthusamy & White, 2005) to foster care (Timmer, Sedlar, & Urquiza, 2004) have been framed using the tenets of Social Exchange. Researchers have also examined communication in romantic relationships (Frisby, Sidelinger, & Booth-Butterfield, 2016), theater groups (Kramer, 2005), and micro-blogging (Liu, Min, Zhai, & Smyth, 2016) using SET. In addition, some researchers (e.g., DeHart, 2012) have suggested that Social Exchange Theories might offer a useful framework for examining coaching people to exhibit positive communication. Furthermore, the emphasis that Thibaut and Kelley placed on interdependence is congruent with many researchers' notions of interpersonal relationships. As a theory that examines human relationships, Social Exchange Theory has resonated with a number of scholars.

Closing

Despite being around for decades, Social Exchange Theory continues to find relevance in an ever-changing complex society. The theory emphasizes the needs for people to assess the benefits and risks of their relationship and ultimately calculate the value of the relationship. Given the unpredictability of relational life, we're likely to see this theory incorporated into research for years to come.

Discussion Starters

TECH QUEST: In this chapter we suggested that a cost in many relationships is the time spent nurturing them. Do you think that the multitasking behaviors that many people have now adopted, whereby they can conduct a face-to-face conversation at the same time they are texting or using another electronic device, will change that particular cost for people?

1. Discuss Meredith and LaTasha's given matrix, transformational matrix, and dispositional matrix.

2. Explain the problem with Social Exchange Theory regarding testability. Is there anything that Social Exchange theorists could do to make the theory more testable? Use examples in your response.

3. Choose a current relationship of yours and perform a cost-benefit analysis on it. Assess whether the relationship meets, fails to meet, or exceeds your comparison level.

4. How does Social Exchange Theory explain the unselfish things that people do that do not seem calculated to gain rewards for themselves?

5. Have you ever stayed in a relationship because you thought you did not have any other alternatives? Explain.

6. How realistic do you think gaming principles like those used to develop the Prisoner's Dilemma are? Give examples that support or contest the use of a 2 × 2 matrix to model human choices.

7. Do you believe that SET is too culture specific and can't account for communication in cultures that aren't individualistic?

Social Penetration Theory

*Based on the research of **Irwin Altman** and **Dalmas Taylor***

Communication and disclosure intimacy appear to be the sine qua non of developing satisfying interpersonal relationships.
— Irwin Altman and Dalmas A. Taylor

Jason LaSalle

About three years ago, Jason LaSalle's wife, Miranda, died in a car accident, leaving Jason a single parent of 8-year-old twins. Since his wife's death, he has struggled both financially and emotionally. He has worried about making his rent and van payments and about meeting his children's needs. For the past three years, Jason has worked odd jobs around the neighborhood to supplement his modest income as custodian for a local cinema complex. In addition, Jason has been lonely. He is shy around others, especially women. Miranda was the only woman he really felt comfortable with, and he misses her a great deal.

Jason's sister, Kayla, is always trying to get Jason out of the house. One night, she hired a baby-sitter and picked him up to go out. This evening was especially important to Kayla because she had also invited her friend Elise Porter, who was recently divorced. Kayla thought that Elise might be a good match for her brother. She was hoping that Elise's easygoing nature and her great sense of humor would appeal to Jason. Throughout the evening, Jason and Elise talked about a variety of things, including their experiences as single parents, her divorce, and the two children they were each raising. Much of their night was spent dancing or talking to each other. The evening ended with Jason and Elise promising to get together again soon.

As Jason drove home to his apartment he couldn't help, but think about Miranda. He was lonely. It had been three years since he had shared any intimacy with an adult. When he arrived home, his sadness increased as he caught sight of a family picture taken at Disney World shortly before Miranda's death. He wasn't sure if it was a good time to pursue an intimate relationship, and yet he wanted a chance to see what kind of person Elise was. He knew that future dates would inevitably require him to talk about Miranda, and he felt that such conversations would be very difficult. He would have to open up emotionally to Elise, and the thought of being placed in such a vulnerable position seemed challenging.

After he paid the babysitter and closed the door behind her, he walked into the twins' room and gave each a kiss on the forehead. Sitting drinking his tea in the living room, Jason felt that he was embarking upon something new, exciting, and a bit frightening.

When we say we're close to someone, we often act as though others understand precisely what we mean. That is not always the case, however. Saying that you are close or intimate with someone may not be universally understood.

To understand the relational closeness between two people, Irwin Altman and Dalmas Taylor (1973) conceptualized Social Penetration Theory (SPT). The two conducted extensive study in the area of social bonding among various types of couples. Their theory illustrates a pattern of relationship development, an evolution that they identified as social penetration. **Social penetration** refers to a process of relationship bonding whereby individuals move from superficial communication to more intimate communication. According to Altman and Taylor, intimacy involves more than physical intimacy; other dimensions of intimacy include intellectual and emotional, and the extent to which a couple shares activities (West & Turner, 2017). The social penetration process, therefore, necessarily includes verbal behaviors (the words we use), nonverbal behaviors (our body posture, the extent to which we smile, etc.), and environmentally oriented behaviors (the space between communicators, the physical objects present in the environment, etc.).

Altman and Taylor (1973) believe that people's relationships vary tremendously in their social penetration. From husband–wife to supervisor–employee to golf partners to physician–patient, the theorists conclude that relationships "involve different levels of intimacy of exchange or degree of social penetration" (p. 3). The authors note that relationships follow some particular **trajectory,** or pathway, to closeness. Furthermore, they contend that relationships are somewhat organized and predictable in their development. Because relationships are critical and "lie at the heart of our humanness" (Rogers & Escudero, 2004, p. 3), Social Penetration theorists attempt to unravel the simultaneous nature of relational complexity and predictability. And, although many individuals may have established online relationships, Altman and Taylor did not conceptualize this development in their writing.

The opening story of Jason LaSalle and his arranged date illustrates a central feature of Social Penetration Theory (SPT). The only way for Jason and Elise to understand each other is for them to engage in personal conversations; such discussion requires each sharing personal bits of information. As the two become closer, they will move from a nonintimate relationship to an intimate one. In addition, each person's personality will influence the direction of the relationship. So Jason and Elise's relationship will be influenced by Jason's shyness and Elise's easygoing manner. The future of Jason's relationship with Elise is based on a multiplicity of factors—factors that we will explore throughout this chapter.

Early discussions of SPT began during the 1960s and 1970s, an era when opening up and talking candidly was highly valued as an important relational strategy. Through the years, however, communication researchers and practitioners acknowledged that cultures can vary tremendously in their endorsement of openness as a relational skill, and scholars such as Barry Farber and his colleagues (2012) question the initial enthusiasm for too much relational openness in general. Therefore, as you read this chapter, keep in mind that we are discussing a theory that is rooted in a generation for which speaking freely and without boundary was a highly valued characteristic. Nevertheless, much of the theory remains relevant today as we live in a society where openness is still a valued personal characteristic. Simply look at daytime television talk shows hosted by Dr. Oz or Dr. Phil for evidence of this.

social penetration
process of bonding that moves a relationship from superficial to more intimate

trajectory
pathway to closeness

Interpersonal relationships evolve in some gradual and predictable fashion. Social Penetration theorists believe that self-disclosure is the primary way that superficial relationships progress to intimate relationships. Although self-disclosure can lead to more intimate relationships, it can also leave one or more persons vulnerable.

To begin, we outline several assumptions of Social Penetration Theory. We then identify the catalyst for the theory and provide a detailed example of the stages of the penetration process.

Assumptions of Social Penetration Theory

Social Penetration Theory (called a "stage theory" by Mongeau & Henningsen, 2008), has enjoyed widespread acceptance by a number of scholars in the communication discipline. Part of the reason for the theory's appeal is its straightforward approach to relationship development. Although we alluded to some assumptions earlier, we will explore the following assumptions that guide SPT:

- Relationships progress from nonintimate to intimate.
- Relational development is generally systematic and predictable.
- Relational development includes depenetration and dissolution.
- Self-disclosure is at the core of relationship development.

First, relational communication between people begins at a rather superficial level and moves along a continuum to a more intimate level. On their date arranged by Kayla, Jason and Elise no doubt talked about trivial issues related to being single parents. They probably shared how difficult it is to have enough time in the day to do everything, but they probably did not express how desperate they feel at 3:00 A.M. when they awake from a nightmare, for example. These initial conversations at first may appear unimportant, but as Jason discovers, such conversations allow an individual to size up the other and provide the opportunity for the early stages of relational development. There is little doubt that Jason feels awkward, but this awkwardness can pass. With time, relationships have the opportunity to become intimate.

Not all relationships fall into the extremes of nonintimate or intimate. In fact, many of our relationships are somewhere in between these two poles. Often, we may want only a moderately close relationship. For instance, we may want a relationship with a coworker to remain sufficiently distant so that we do not know what goes on in her house each night or how much money she has in the bank. Yet we need to know enough personal information to have a sense of whether she can complete her part of a team project.

The second assumption of Social Penetration Theory pertains to predictability. Specifically, Social Penetration theorists argue that relationships progress fairly systematically and predictably. Some people may have difficulty with this claim. After all, relationships—like the communication process—are dynamic and ever changing, but even dynamic relationships follow some acceptable standard and pattern of development.

To better understand this assumption, again consider Jason LaSalle. Without knowing all the specifics of his situation, we could figure out that if he pursues a relationship with Elise, he will have to work through his emotions about Miranda. In addition, he must inevitably reconcile how their families might merge if the relationship progresses into more intimacy. We could probably predict that the relationship will move slowly at first while both Jason and Elise work out their feelings and emotions.

These projections are grounded in the second assumption of the theory: Relationships generally move in an organized and predictable manner. Although we may not know precisely the direction of a relationship or be able to predict its exact future, social penetration processes are rather organized and predictable. We can be fairly sure, for instance, that Jason and Elise will not introduce each other to important people in their families before they date a few more times. We would also expect that neither would declare his or her love for the other before they exchanged more intimate information. Of course, a number of other events and variables (time, personality, and so forth) affect the way relationships progress and what we can predict along the way. As Altman and Taylor (1973) conclude, "People seem to possess very sensitive tuning mechanisms which enable them to program carefully their interpersonal relationships" (p. 8).

The third assumption of SPT pertains to the notion that relational development includes depenetration and dissolution. At first, this may sound a bit peculiar. Thus far, we have explored the coming together of a relationship. Yet relationships do fall apart, or **depenetrate**, and this depenetration can lead to relationship dissolution. Elise, for example, may be unprepared for Jason's past and may wish to depenetrate and ultimately dissolve the relationship.

depenetrate
slow deterioration of relationship

Addressing depenetration and dissolution, Altman and Taylor liken the process to a film shown in reverse. Just as communication allows a relationship to move forward toward intimacy, communication could move a relationship back toward *non-intimacy*. If the communication is conflictual, for example, and this conflict continues to be destructive and unresolved, the relationship may take a step back and become less close. And Social Penetration theorists think that depenetration—like the penetration process—is often systematic.

If a relationship depenetrates, it does not mean that it will automatically dissolve or terminate. At times, relationships experience **transgressions**, or the violation of relational rules, practices, and expectations. These transgressions may seem unworkable and, at times, they are. In fact, Sean Horan (2012) points out that transgressions can be quite influential in relational life. In Chapter 5, we discussed unwanted repetitive patterns of conflict in couples. We noted that recurring conflicts characterize a

transgression
a violation of relational rules, practices, and expectations

number of different relationship types and that couples generally learn to live with these conflicts. You may believe conflict or relational transgressions will inevitably lead to dissolution, but depenetration does not necessarily mean that the relationship is doomed.

The final assumption contends that self-disclosure is at the core of relationship development. **Self-disclosure** can be generally defined as the purposeful process of revealing information about yourself to others. Usually, the information that makes up self-disclosure is of a significant nature. For instance, revealing that you like to play the piano may not be all that important; revealing a more personal piece of information, such as that you are a practicing Catholic or that you use marijuana for medicinal reasons may significantly influence the evolution of a relationship.

self-disclosure
purposeful process of revealing information about yourself to others

According to Altman and Taylor (1973), nonintimate relationships progress to intimate relationships because of self-disclosure. This process allows people to get to know each other in a relationship. Self-disclosure helps shape the present and future relationship between two people, and "making [the] self accessible to another person is intrinsically gratifying" (p. 50). Elise will understand the challenges that lie ahead for her in a relationship with Jason by hearing Jason reveal his feelings about his wife's death and his desire to begin dating again. In turn, because social penetration requires a "gradual overlapping and exploration of their mutual selves by parties to a relationship" (p. 15), Elise, too, would have to self-disclose her thoughts and feelings.

T*I*P

Theory-Into-Practice

Social Penetration Theory

Theoretical Claim: Reciprocity with similar levels of "risk" typically leads to increased intimacy between people.

Practical Implication: Lana told her roommate, Rachel, that she did not have enough financial aid to stay in school. Rachel, in turn, disclosed that if her father had not taken out a loan on their condo, she would have to quit school (too). Rachel's reciprocity brings the two even closer together because it serves to validate Lana's experience.

Finally, we should note that self-disclosure can be strategic or nonstrategic. That is, in some relationships, we tend to plan out what we will say to another person. In other situations, our self-disclosure may be spontaneous. Spontaneous self-disclosure is widespread in our society. In fact, researchers have used the phrase "**stranger-on-the-train** (or plane or bus) phenomenon" to refer to those times when people reveal information to complete strangers in public places. To be precise, stranger-on-the-train refers to those moments of "sharing with an anonymous seat-mate intimate details [of which] not even our closest friends are aware" (Bareket-Bojmel & Shahar, 2011, pp. 732–733). Think about how many times you have been seated next to a stranger on a trip, only to have that person disclose personal information throughout the journey. Interpersonal communication researchers continue to investigate why people engage in this activity.

stranger-on-the-train
the event that occurs when strangers reveal personal information to others in public places

"Tearing Up" the Relationship: The Onion Analogy

Previously we discussed the importance of revealing information about oneself of which others are unaware. In their discussion of SPT, Altman and Taylor incorporate an onionskin structure (Figure 10.1). They believe that a person like Jason LaSalle can be compared to an onion, with the layers (concentric circles) of the onion representing various aspects of a person's personality. The outer layer is an individual's **public image,** or that which is available to the naked eye. This is the "publicly observable self" [where] "private information that is stored at deeper layers must be discovered" (Fox, 2015, p. 6). Jason's public image is an African American male in his mid-40s who is slightly balding. Elise Porter is also an African American, but is significantly taller than Jason and has very short hair. A layer of the public image is removed, however, when Jason discloses to his date his frustrations with being a single father.

public image
outer layer of a person; what is available to others

As the evening evolves for the two of them, Jason and Elise no doubt begin to reveal additional layers of their personalities. For instance, Elise may reveal that she, too, experiences single-parent anxieties. This **reciprocity,** or the process whereby one person's openness leads to the other's openness, is a primary component in SPT. In fact, researchers have shown consistently that when one person divulges personal information, the other person is likely to reciprocate similar levels of sensitive information (Acquisti, John, & Loewenstein, 2012). Reciprocity has been shown to be significant in both established and new relationships, such as Jason and Elise's. Further, in terms of online relationships, people are more inclined to self-disclose to others online (e.g., Facebook) than face to face (Palmieri, Prestano, Gandley, Overton, & Zhang, 2012). And, in an interesting study comparing U.S. American and Ghanaian University students (Lin & Sackey, 2015), those in the Ghana were more favorable toward disclosing via Facebook. The Ghanaian

reciprocity
the return of openness from one person to another

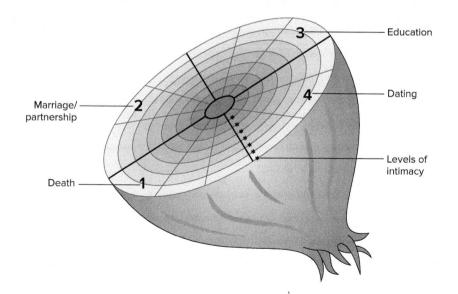

Marriage/partnership — 2

Death — 1

3 — Education

4 — Dating

Levels of intimacy

Figure 10.1
The Social Penetration Process of Jason LaSalle

SOCIAL PENETRATION THEORY

students were also more likely to chat and send disclosive messages on Facebook than their U.S. counterparts.

Before leaving the discussion of self-disclosure, we should point out that penetration can be viewed along two dimensions: breadth and depth. **Breadth** refers to the number of various topics discussed in the relationship; **breadth time** pertains to the amount of time that relational partners spend communicating with each other about these various topics. **Depth** refers to the degree of intimacy that guides topic discussions. In the initial stages, relationships can be classified as having narrow breadth and shallow depth. For Jason LaSalle, it is feasible that his first date with Elise was characterized this way. Most likely, the two did not discuss many topics, and what they did discuss probably lacked intimate overtones. As relationships move toward intimacy, we can expect a wider range of topics to be discussed (more breadth), with several of those topics marked by depth.

A few conclusions are important with respect to the breadth and depth of self-disclosure. First, shifts or changes in central layers (of the onion) have more of an impact than those in outer, or peripheral, layers. Because an individual's public image, or outer layer, represents those things that others can see, or what we can term the *superficial*, we expect that if there are changes in the outer layer, the consequence is minimal. For example, if Elise changed her hairstyle, her relationship with Jason would be less affected than if she changed her opinion about premarital sex.

Second, the greater the depth, the more opportunity for a person to feel vulnerable. Imagine that Jason reveals some inadequacy about himself to Elise—for instance, the fact that he was on welfare for two years after his wife's death. When he reveals this personal information to Elise, she can respond in several different ways. She can simply say, "Wow," and not venture further into the discussion. Or she can reply, "That must have been very hard for you," communicating compassion. A third possible response is "I don't see anything wrong with that. Millions of people need some help at some point in their lives." The latter response demonstrates even more compassion and an effort to diffuse the possible anxiety that Jason is feeling. How Elise responds influences how vulnerable Jason feels. As you can see, the first response may elicit a high degree of vulnerability, whereas the third response may invoke little vulnerability.

As you reflect on the topic of self-disclosure, keep in mind that an individual should be judicious in using self-disclosure. Although self-disclosure generally moves a relationship toward more closeness, if people disclose too much during the early stages of a relationship, they may actually end the relationship. Some partners may be ill equipped and underprepared to know another so intimately. Also note that trust is an inherent part of the disclosure and reciprocity processes. In fact, it is very difficult to disentangle the relationship between trust and self-disclosure as the two are inextricably linked (Such, Espinoza, Garcia-Fornes, & Sierra, 2012). If we desire reciprocity in disclosure, we must try to gain the trust of the other person and, similarly, feel trustful of the other person. One goal in self-disclosure, then, is to be thoughtful and appropriate. We have included other guidelines for self-disclosure in Table 10.1.

breadth
the number of topics discussed in a relationship

breadth time
amount of time spent by relational partners discussing various topics

depth
degree of intimacy guiding topic discussion

Table 10.1 Guidelines for Self-Disclosure

ASK YOURSELF	SUGGESTION
Is the other person important to you?	Reveal significant pieces of information about yourself to those people with whom you have developed a personal relationship.
Is the risk of disclosing reasonable?	Try not to reveal significant information about yourself if there is great risk associated with it. Assess the risk potential of your disclosure.
Are the amount and type of disclosure appropriate?	Discern whether you are revealing too much or too little information. Examine the timing of the disclosure.
Is the disclosure relevant to the situation at hand?	Constant disclosure is not typically useful in a relationship. Don't share everything.
Is the disclosure reciprocated?	Unequal self-disclosure creates an imbalanced relationship. Wait for reciprocity.
Will the effect be constructive?	If not employed carefully, disclosure can be used in destructive ways. Use care in disclosing information that may be perceived as damaging.
Are cultural misunderstandings possible?	Maintain cultural sensitivity as people disclose to you and you disclose to others.

A Social Exchange: Relational Costs and Rewards

Social Penetration Theory is grounded in several principles from many theories related to relationship development. Principle among these are Social Exchange Theory (Thibaut & Kelley, 1959). As we discussed in Chapter 9, this theory suggests that social exchanges "entail services that create unspecified obligations in the future and therefore exert a pervasive influence on social relations" (Blau, 1964, p. 140). Altman and Taylor based some of their work on social exchange processes; that is, an exchange of resources between individuals in a relationship. Specifically, rewards and costs relate to Social Exchange Theory.

Taylor and Altman (1987) argue that relationships can be conceptualized in terms of rewards and costs. You may recall these terms in Chapter 9. Nonetheless, let's restate their meanings. Rewards are those relational events or behaviors that stimulate satisfaction, pleasure, and contentment in a relational partner, whereas costs are those relational events or behaviors that stimulate negative feelings. Quite simply, if a relationship provides more rewards than costs, then individuals are more likely to stay in that relationship. However, if an individual believes that there are more costs to being in a relationship, then relationship dissolution is probable. For instance, Jason LaSalle will most likely regulate the closeness of his relationship with Elise by assessing a **reward–cost ratio,** which is defined as the balance between positive and negative relationship experiences. If Jason believes

reward-cost ratio
balance between positive and negative relationship experiences

he is deriving more pleasure (nurturance, supportive teasing, and so forth) than pain (frustration, insecurity, and so forth) from being in his relationship with Elise, then it is likely that he is fairly satisfied at the moment. His own expectations and experiences must also be taken into account in the reward–cost ratio. As Taylor and Altman point out, "[R]ewards and costs are consistently associated with mutual satisfaction of personal and social needs" (1987, p. 264).

To understand this a bit better, consider the following two conclusions observed by Taylor and Altman: (1) Rewards and costs have a greater impact early on in the relationship than later in the relationship, and (2) relationships with a reservoir of positive reward/cost experiences are better equipped to handle conflict effectively. We will examine each of these briefly.

The first conclusion suggests that there are relatively few interpersonal experiences in the early stages, resulting in individuals focusing more on a single reward or a single cost. So, for instance, it is probable that Jason will be impressed with Elise if she is willing to give Jason space during the early stages of their relationship; for Jason, rushing into a relationship may be a bit overwhelming, and Elise's patience may be viewed as an important relational reward. Elise, however, may view Jason's early ambivalence as an indicator of things to come. She may, therefore, decide that his uncertainty is simply too much of a cost to endure and want to dissolve the relationship sooner than Jason does.

With respect to the second conclusion regarding costs and rewards, Taylor and Altman note that some relationships are better able to manage conflict than others. As relational partners move on in a relationship, they may experience a number of disagreements. Over the years, couples become accustomed to managing conflict in various ways, creating a unique relational culture that allows them to work through future issues. There may be more trust in handling a conflict in established relationships. In addition, the relationship is not likely to be threatened by a single conflict because of the couple's stockpile of experiences in dealing with conflict.

www.CartoonStock.com

In sum, then, relationships often depend on both parties assessing the rewards and costs. If partners feel that there are more rewards than costs, chances are that the relationship will survive. If more costs are perceived than rewards, the relationship may depenetrate or dissolve. However, keep in mind that both partners may not see an issue similarly; a cost by one person may be viewed as a reward by the other.

The Social Exchange perspective relies on both parties in a relationship to calculate the extent to which individuals view the relationship as negative (cost) or positive (reward). According to Social Exchange thinking, as relationships come together, partners ultimately assess the possibilities within a relationship as well as the perceived or real alternatives to a relationship (Carpenter & Greene, 2015). These evaluations are critical as communicators decide whether the process of social penetration is desirable. In the following section, we identify the stages of the social penetration process.

Stages of the Social Penetration Process

The decision about whether a potential relationship appears satisfying is not immediate. As we mentioned earlier, Social Penetration Theory is viewed as a "stage" theory (Carpenter & Greene, 2015). Furthermore, relationship development occurs in a rather systematic manner, and decisions about whether people want to remain in a relationship are not usually made quickly. Not all relationships go through this process, and those that do are not always romantic relationships. To demonstrate how each stage functions in relationships that are *not* romantic, we provide a scenario for you to think about. We then talk about each stage and refer back to the example. Figure 10.2 outlines the four stages of the social penetration process.

Consider the relationship between Carmen and Brennan, two 21-year-olds who both decided to live off-campus for their junior year. The two did not know each other before meeting in their Psych course, but both found that they wanted to live away from campus and both wanted to pledge one of the sororities. The two come from different parts of the country: Carmen is from Los Angeles, and Brennan was raised in rural Pennsylvania. They also differ in family makeup in that Carmen is one of four siblings and Brennan is an only child. Finally, Carmen is the first in her family to attend college while Brennan is a third-generation college student. They have only met each other in class and are now about to have their first breakfast together.

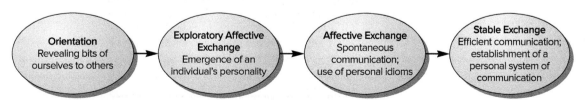

Figure 10.2 Stages of Social Penetration

Orientation: Revealing Bit by Bit

orientation stage
stage of social penetration that includes revealing small parts of ourselves

The earliest stage of interaction, called the **orientation stage,** occurs at the public level; only bits of ourselves are revealed to others. During this stage, comments are usually on the cliché level and reflect superficial aspects of individuals. People usually act in socially desirable ways and are cautious of disturbing any societal expectations. Individuals smile pleasantly and react politely in the orientation stage. Conflict is usually avoided at this stage (Carpenter & Greene, 2015).

Taylor and Altman (1987) note that people tend not to evaluate or criticize during the orientation stage. This behavior would be perceived as inappropriate by the other and might jeopardize future interactions. If evaluation does occur, the theorists believe that it will be couched in soft overtones. In addition, both parties actively avoid any conflict so that they have further opportunity to size up each other.

The orientation stage can be understood by examining the dialogue between Carmen and Brennan during their breakfast:

CARMEN: I have to admit that I am a bit weirded out about all of this. I mean I know you from class, but I am anxious. I do feel ok, though, and think this will work out.

BRENNAN: I agree. [awkward silence]

CARMEN: But, look: We both love lacrosse, and maybe we'll both make the team. We both want to rush, and I hope . . . [Brennan interrupts]

BRENNAN: I love to study near . . . Sorry. You go ahead.

CARMEN: No, you go.

BRENNAN: I was going to say that I hope that we have some chances to get away and maybe even head up to my family's lake house. I love to study near the water and if it's warm, I definitely love to swim. I haven't had time this past summer, though, because I was working too much at the Local Buzz.

CARMEN: Believe it or not, I don't know how to swim! I tried to learn, but I just don't seem to be coordinated.

BRENNAN: Hey! I'm a good swimmer. I'll teach you when we get some time.

CARMEN: Ha. If I eat any more of this stuff, I'll definitely know how to float!

As you can see, both women speak in a rather superficial and very formalized conversation, and neither one is really judging the other. In fact, Brennan has an opportunity to tell Carmen how strange it is that she doesn't know how to swim, but she chooses to stay supportive.

Exploratory Affective Exchange: The Self Emerges

In the orientation stage, interactants are cautious about revealing too much about themselves to each other. The **exploratory affective exchange stage,** however, is an expansion of the public areas of the self and occurs when aspects of an individual's personality begin to emerge. Both people begin to "explore" each other and small pieces of their private life becomes more public. The theorists note that this stage is comparable to the relationships we have with casual acquaintances and friendly neighbors. Like other stages, this stage includes both verbal and nonverbal behaviors. People might begin to use some catch phrases that are idiosyncratic to the relationship. There is a small amount of spontaneity in communication because individuals feel more relaxed with each other, and they are not as cautious about blurting out something that they may later regret. Also, more touch behavior and more affect displays (such as facial expressions) may become part of the communication repertoire with the other person. Taylor and Altman tell us that many relationships don't proceed beyond this stage.

exploratory affective exchange stage
stage of social penetration that results in the emergence of our personality to others

To gain a clearer picture of the exploratory affective exchange stage, think again about Carmen and Brennan. This time, however, consider that the two have been roommates for about eight weeks now, and each is getting a better idea about the personality of the other. Both are now pledging Delta Sigma and are sitting in their apartment talking about their pledging experience.

BRENNAN: Okay, Carmen. I don't know why we're doing this.

CARMEN: I know. At times, I think it's weird that we're doing all this just to have this "sisterhood" experience. But, we both know that the group does a lot of good and I mean the girls are just very cool and not stuck on themselves. I grew up in a family where helping each other out was important. I think this sort of thing is why I like the girls.

BRENNAN: I know, but I'm not having any fun! I am so tired, too, and I . . . .

CARMEN: Please, Brennan, will you just chill?! We both agreed to do this and if you want to back out now, do it. But, sometimes you're such a downer.

BRENNAN: I'm not whining. Just because I say I'm having second thoughts on pledging doesn't mean I'm a whiner. I'm just not sure if this is working toward conformity or . . . .

CARMEN: Whatever. I know that I wanted to pledge because I wanted a group of friends who I could trust and who would be there if I needed help. I wish you would just relax about things.

Clearly, Brennan and Carmen are starting to feel more comfortable around each other. In fact, Brennan's "chill" and "whatever" language reflects the sort of catchphrases to which Taylor and Altman refer. Furthermore, Carmen is slowly revealing more personal information about her family and her perceptions of Brennan as a whiner. Brennan, in turn, openly questions the value of the pledge process. Their exploratory affective exchange is generally one characterized by candor, engagement, and ease.

Affective Exchange: Commitment and Comfortability

affective exchange stage
stage of social penetration that is spontaneous and quite comfortable for relational partners

personal idioms
private, intimate expressions stated in a relationship

This stage is characterized by close friendships and intimate partners. The **affective exchange stage** includes those interactions that are more "freewheeling and casual" (Taylor & Altman, 1987, p. 259) in that communication is frequently spontaneous and individuals make quick decisions, often with little regard for the relationship as a whole. This stage represents further commitment to the other individual; the interactants are comfortable with each other.

The stage includes those nuances of a relationship that make it unique; a smile may substitute for the words "I understand," or a penetrating gaze may translate into "We'll talk about this later." We might also find individuals using **personal idioms** (Hopper, Knapp, & Scott, 1981), which are private ways of expressing a relationship's intimacy through words, phrases, or behaviors. Idiomatic expressions—such as "honey" or "bubbles"—carry unique meaning for two people in a relationship. David Atkins and his research team (2012) contend that personal idioms act as a couple's private communication system. These idioms are different from the catchphrases we discussed in the exploratory affective exchange in that idioms usually characterize more established relationships, whereas catchphrases may develop at any point in an initial interaction. We should add that this stage, like the exploratory affective exchange stage, may also include criticisms. As the theorists contend, these criticisms, hostilities, and disapprovals may exist "without any thought of threat to the relationship as a whole" (Altman & Taylor, 1973, p. 139). Consequently, barriers to closeness may be broken down, but many people still protect themselves from becoming too vulnerable.

Returning to our example, Carmen and Brennan have been together for a little more than 10 weeks. They have had ample opportunity to understand a number of idiosyncrasies about each other; living with someone usually does that to people. Their conversation centers around a date that Brennan had on Saturday night:

BRENNAN: I simply refuse to believe that I even spent one hour with him! I mean I have dated a lot of guys, but this one was one of the weirdest.

CARMEN: I've seen some of your dates, Bren. Ah, remember "Jack and the Beanstalk!" Hello?

BRENNAN: Hmm. I know. Hey, at least he didn't take his cat on a date!

CARMEN: I knew you would say that. But, listen, that guy was so nice . . . you never see guys act like gentlemen these days!

BRENNAN: Yeah, and it's a wonder why his four cats didn't claw you while you guys were together!

CARMEN: I know the kind of guy you like, Brennan. And, yes, we're very different from each other on guys. I just keep things to myself a lot and won't wear my heart on my sleeve like you do! I'm much more discreet shall we say?

BRENNAN: There's a reason why I call you "Carmen Chameleon!"

CARMEN: Funny girl.

As you can sense, there is noticeable comfort in the relationship right now. Altman and Taylor would argue that although it appears that the two know each other so well, they are willing to expose their relational values, their perceptions of the other's dating experiences, among other things. There is a slight tension embedded in their conversation, but nothing that seems to prompt the other to terminate the conversation. Their interpersonal "barriers" appear to be down and both are comfortable sharing very personal comments about each other. And, to be sure, affective exchanges may include both positive and negative exchanges.

Stable Exchange: Raw Honesty and Intimacy

The fourth and final stage, **stable exchange,** pertains to an open expression of thoughts, feelings, and behaviors that results in a high degree of spontaneity and relational uniqueness. During this stage, partners are highly intimate and synchronized; that is, behaviors between the two sometimes recur, and partners are able to assess and predict the behavior of the other fairly accurately. At times, the partners may tease each other about topics or people. This teasing, however, is done in a friendly manner.

Social Penetration theorists believe that there are relatively few misinterpretations in communication meaning at this stage. The reason for this is simple: Both partners have had numerous opportunities to clarify any previous ambiguities and have begun to establish their own personal system of communication. As a result, communication, according to Altman and Taylor, is efficient. At this stage, two independent people begin to emerge as "one" insofar as they have begun to peel away the levels that they have used to protect themselves (recall our onion analogy).

We return to our example of Carmen and Brennan. It is now final exam week, and obviously the two are very tense. Yet they both realize that this week must be free of conflict, and both also realize that after this week, they will not see each other for a month because of the break. The stable exchange stage is very apparent when we listen to their conversation:

> CARMEN: So, okay, this week we *have* to be careful not to blow up at each other. I have three finals and a paper due.
>
> BRENNAN: Tell me about it. Did I ever tell you that if I don't get at least a B average, my parents told me that I'm on "probation," and they won't help with my tuition?
>
> CARMEN: Seriously? I wish I even had help with my tuition; even my fees for pledging almost put me over. Next term, I'm going to have to pick up another part-time job.
>
> BRENNAN: I'm lucky, I know.
>
> CARMEN: Yep. Not everyone has mommy and daddy to help them.
>
> BRENNAN: Hey, I'm not going to apologize because my parents work hard.
>
> CARMEN: I'm not asking you to apologize. I never told you this, either, but if I don't get one of the Delta scholarships, this year may be my last here.
>
> BRENNAN: That's crazy. Don't even say that.
>
> CARMEN: I'm gonna keep studying. I can't think about anything, but right now.

The stable exchange stage includes individuals who are willing to expose intimate parts of themselves. Clearly, both Carmen and Brennan care about each other and manifest various levels of vulnerability. Although our earlier example suggested a conflicted relationship, there is now what Altman and Taylor (1973) call **dyadic uniqueness,** or distinctive relationship qualities such as humor and sarcasm.

As we mentioned earlier, this multistage approach to intimacy can get convoluted with periodic spurts and slowdowns along the way. In addition, the stages

stable exchange stage
stage of social penetration that results in complete openness and spontaneity for relational partners

dyadic uniqueness
distinctive relationship qualities

are not a complete picture of the intimacy process. There are a number of other influences, including a person's background and values and even the environment in which the relationship exists. The social penetration process is a give-and-take experience whereby both partners continue to work on balancing their individual needs with the needs of the relationship.

Finally, similar to most of the theories you will read about in this book, Altman and Taylor could never have envisioned the Internet when conceptualizing this theory. As you review it, consider the technological influences inherent in the stages (we address the interplay between relationship development and online communication in Chapter 11). For instance, as we all know, some relationships grow online and this online disclosure can influence the path of the relationship. Twitter idioms and hashtags for instance, affect the conversations taking place between people (Mayty, Gupta, Goyall, & Mukherjee, 2015). In fact, using Twitter, in particular, as a conversational platform, has been the subject of research over the past several years (e.g., Rudra, Chakraborty, Sethi, & Das, 2015). Consider how the stages might be influenced if technology was introduced into the penetration process.

Integration, Critique, and Closing

Social Penetration Theory has been appealing since its inception over 40 years ago. Altman and Taylor have proposed an intriguing model by which to view relational development. The theory's empirically derived conclusions have drawn the attention of researchers over the years. The theory had its beginnings during a time of openness in society. As you think about the theory and its value, consider the following criteria: scope and heurism.

Integration

Communication Tradition	Rhetorical	Semiotic	Phenomenological	Cybernetic	**Socio-Psychological**	Socio-Cultural	Critical Intrapersonal
Communication Context	**Interpersonal**	Small Group	Organizational	Public/Rhetorical	Mass/Media	Cultural
Approach to Knowing	**Positivistic/Empirical**	Interpretive/Hermeneutic	Critical

Critique

Evaluation Criteria	**Scope**	Logical Consistency	Parsimony	Utility	Testability	**Heurism**	Test of Time

Scope

The scope of SPT is of concern. In fact, the scope of the theory "makes it difficult to adequately test it as a whole" (Mongeau & Henningsen, 2008, p. 370). Some scholars contend, for instance, that self-disclosure—one of the key themes of the theory—may be too narrowly interpreted. For instance, Rachel Freeth (2012) believes that self-disclosure depends on a number of factors (e.g., timing, relationship intimacy, etc.), not simply the need to reveal to people over time. Further, self-disclosure is a fairly complex process, sometimes catching people off guard (Winzenburg, 2012).

Further, Mark Knapp, Anita Vangelisti, and John Coughlin (2013) reject the notion that relationship development is as linear as is suggested in SPT. They believe relationships are embedded in other relationships, and in turn, these relationships affect the communication between partners. Therefore, other people may influence the direction of a relationship. In addition, the linearity of the theory suggests that the reversal of relational engagement (recall that Altman and Taylor likened relationship disengagement to a film shown in reverse) is relational disengagement. Leslie Baxter and Erin Sahlstein (2000) assert that the concept of information openness and closedness cannot be understood in isolation; there is much more going on in a relationship than simple self-disclosure.

To be fair, Altman later revisited the social penetration processes and amended his original thinking with Taylor. Altman explained that being open and disclosive should be viewed in conjunction with being private and withdrawn (Altman, Vinsel, & Brown, 1981; Taylor & Altman, 1987). In a sense, Altman proposes what Baxter and Montgomery articulate in their theory on Relational Dialectics Theory (Chapter 11). C. Arthur VanLear (1991) underscored this thinking by concluding that there are two competing cycles of openness and closedness in both friendships and romantic relationships. Jason LaSalle and Elise Porter from our opening story will surely experience this push and pull of self-disclosure as their relationship progresses. It is likely that as both of them share pieces of information, each will also remain private about other issues.

Heurism

There can be no doubt that Social Penetration Theory and the concept of self-disclosure has yielded literally thousands of studies. Therefore, SPT is highly heuristic. Researchers have studied and written about the effects of self-disclosure, for example, on various types of relationships and across a variety of populations. Families (Turner & West, 2017), physicians (Trahan & Goodrich, 2015), alcoholics (Greenberg & Smith, 2015), and teachers (McKenna-Buchanan, Munz, & Rudnick, 2015) have all been investigated. Furthermore, the effects of culture on the

Student Voices

Sam

We talked about reciprocity in relationships. My own relationship with my boyfriend has a lot of reciprocity. He and I are constantly revealing parts of ourselves to each other, and we also talk about our emotional reactions to the other's self-disclosure. It's weird to be romantically involved with someone who's willing to return the same kind of intimacy I give. In the past, my relationships have been anything, but reciprocal. Now, I think I've found someone who can let me know his reactions to what I say and how I feel.

penetration process (e.g., Chen, 2006) have also been investigated. Scholars in the area of relationship development and its ancillary areas, including relational control (Rogers & Escudero, 2004) and relational maintenance (Dindia, 2003) owe much of their thinking to the scholarship examining social penetration. Finally, HIV status (Catona, Greene, Magsamen-Conrad, & Carpenter, 2016), blogging (Tang & Wang, 2012), and Internet dating (Gibbs, Ellison, & Lai, 2011) and their relationship to self-disclosure have also been studied.

Closing

Despite some criticism, Social Penetration Theory remains an integral theory pertaining to relationship development and has generated scholarly interest. In particular, the theory has resonated with interpersonal communication scholars and those interested in looking at how relational intimacy evolves. Relationship development can be exhausting, invigorating, and challenging at times, and SPT helps people understand those challenges.

Discussion Starters

TECH QUEST: Most Social Penetration theorists and researchers have emphasized face-to-face relationships. Yet, we know that this is a limited view of interpersonal relationships, in general, and self-disclosure, in particular. Therefore, discuss how the notion of reciprocity, in particular, is influenced by technology. How does the process vary from face to face to online?

1. If their relationship develops further, what do you think Jason and Elise will talk about as the two get to know each other better? Will there be any risk involved as they disclose to each other? Explain with examples.

2. When self-disclosing to another person, several things can go wrong. Explain the consequences of poorly planned or inappropriate self-disclosure. Provide examples along the way.

3. What similar patterns cut across escalating relationships? Discuss marital relationships, relationships between friends, and parent–child relationships as individuals move toward intimacy.

4. Some critics have charged that Social Penetration Theory focuses too much on self-disclosure. Others, however, contend that self-disclosure forms the basis of most intimate relationships. What do you think? Is there a compromise between the two views?

5. If you outlined the stages of a past romantic relationship of yours, would it follow the sequencing that Altman and Taylor suggest? What similarities are there to the social penetration process? What differences are there? Provide examples.

6. Apply SPT principles to workplace relationships you have encountered.

7. Other than an onion, what additional analogies can you think of that would apply to SPT?

CHAPTER 11

Relational Dialectics Theory

*Based on the research of **Leslie Baxter** and **Barbara Montgomery***

> *From the perspective of relational dialectics . . . a month from now, a year from now, five years from now, we will be somewhere else with these ideas.*
>
> —Leslie Baxter

Eleanor Robertson and Jeff Meadows

Eleanor Robertson and Jeff Meadows worked together to clean up the mess left from the dinner party they had just given for their friend Mary Beth's 35th birthday. They both agreed that the party had been a great success and that everyone had had a wonderful time. They were having fun talking about their friends—who was breaking up and who was getting together.

Eleanor smiled as she thought about how much she and Jeff had learned about each other and their relationship in the two years they had lived together. Eleanor used to get upset when Jeff wanted to be with friends and not spend all his time with her alone. Now she thought she understood Jeff's desire to have others in their lives. She also found that the more she was able to let go of her possessive feelings and behaviors, the more Jeff wanted to be close.

Jeff came over and hugged Eleanor. He said, "Honey, that was a great party. The food was perfect—I'm glad we decided to do Italian. Thanks for all your help to make everything go so well. Mary Beth really appreciated it, I know. And since she and I have been friends forever, it really means a lot to me."

Eleanor pulled away and laughed at Jeff. "I didn't do too much, sweetheart," she said to Jeff. "You were the one who was busy in the kitchen. But I am glad Mary Beth had fun. I really like her a lot, too."

Jeff and Eleanor finished cleaning up and started talking about what they would do tomorrow. They decided they would take a picnic to Golden Gate Park and then maybe go to a movie— they agreed they'd decide on the movie after the picnic depending on how they felt. It sounded like a fun Sunday—they had a plan, but they could change their minds and skip the movie if picnicking in the park was too inviting.

Eleanor was very happy and thought about telling Jeff how much she loved and needed him, but she decided to keep quiet about the depth of her feelings for now. Jeff probably knew how she felt, and she was a little afraid of revealing all her feelings to him right now. It had been a perfect day, and she didn't want to spoil it by saying something that might make Jeff withdraw a little. She wasn't sure she wanted to be so vulnerable to Jeff at this point in their relationship, even though when they first started going out together, she had told him she loved him repeatedly. Now she found herself being a bit more guarded and self-protective even though she loved him more now than she did then.

When researchers examine the story of Eleanor and Jeff, they might speculate that their relationship is moving through stages. Researchers who work within the framework of Social Penetration Theory (see Chapter 10), for example, would point to the fact that Jeff and Eleanor have worked through some of their earlier issues and now interact with each other at a deeper level of intimacy than they once did. These researchers might point to the fact that the relationship between Eleanor and Jeff is more coordinated and less conflictual than it once was as an indication that they have moved to a more intimate stage of relational development. Yet, other researchers would look at Jeff and Eleanor and see their story as best explained by a different theoretical position, called Relational Dialectics Theory.

Relational Dialectics Theory (RDT) maintains that relational life is characterized by ongoing tensions between contradictory impulses (Baxter & Norwood, 2016). Although that may sound confusing and messy, researchers who espouse the dialectical position believe it accurately depicts the way that life is for people. People are not always able to resolve the contradictory elements of their beliefs, and they can hold inconsistent beliefs about relationships. For example, the adage "absence makes the heart grow fonder" seems to coexist easily with its opposite, "out of sight, out of mind."

Leslie Baxter and Barbara Montgomery (1996) formulated the most complete statement of the theory in their book *Relating: Dialogues and Dialectics,* although both of them had been writing about dialectical thinking for several years prior to that book's publication. Baxter and Montgomery's work was directly influenced by Mikhail Bakhtin, a Russian philosopher who developed a theory of personal dialogue. Social life for Bakhtin was an open dialogue among many voices, and its essence was the "simultaneous differentiation from yet fusion with another" (Baxter, 2004, p. 1). According to Bakhtin, the individual self is only possible when it is in context with another. Bakhtin notes that human experience is constituted through communication with others. And, as Baxter (2011) states, the concept of a relationship for Bakhtin is only possible by maintaining two distinct voices.

From Bakhtin's thinking, Baxter and Montgomery (1996) shaped the notion of the dialectical vision. We can best explain this vision of human behavior by contrasting it to two other common approaches: the monologic and dualistic approaches. The **monologic approach** pictures contradictions as either/or relationships. For instance, monologic thinking would lead to the belief that Jeff and Eleanor's relationship was *either* close *or* distant. In other words, the two parts of a contradiction are mutually exclusive in monologic thinking, and as you move toward one extreme, you retreat from the other. See Figure 11.1 for a visual representation of this notion.

In contrast, the **dualistic approach** sees the two parts of a contradiction as two separate entities, somewhat unrelated to each other. In our example of Eleanor and Jeff, dualistic thinkers might choose to evaluate them separately, rating how close each one feels compared to the other. Furthermore, dualism allows for the idea that relationships may be evaluated differently on these scales at different times (Figure 11.1).

Alternatively, thinkers with a **dialectic approach** maintain that multiple points of view play off one another in every contradiction. Although a contradiction involves

monologic approach
an approach framing contradiction as either/or

dualistic approach
an approach framing contradiction as two separate entities

dialectic approach
an approach framing contradiction as both/and

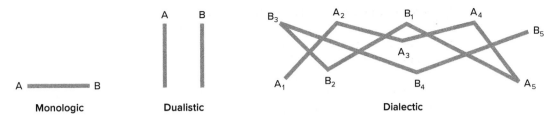

Figure 11.1 Monologic, Dualistic, and Dialectic Approaches to Relational Contradictions

two opposing poles, the resulting situation expands beyond these two poles. As Baxter and Montgomery (1996) observed, "[d]ialectical thinking is not directed toward a search for the 'happy mediums' of compromise and balance, but instead focuses on the messier, less logical, and more inconsistent unfolding practices of the moment" (p. 46). A simple way of putting it is that dialectic thinking substitutes *both/and* for *either/or*, recognizing that people want multiple (and often contradictory) goals in their relational lives. Thus, in RDT, there are often more than two different elements involved in a relational situation (Baxter & Scharp, 2015).

As Eleanor and Jeff interact, many voices contribute to their sense of their relationship: their memories of their past conflicts about Jeff's friends, their current sense of confidence in their relationship, their concerns about their future, their friendships with others, and so forth. Dialectic theory holds that it is not accurate to say that only one or two positions exist in relational contradictions. Leslie Baxter and Dawn Braithewaite (2008) give the example of a college student saying, "Well, I'm kinda like, seeing him, but we're not, ya know, serious" (p. 349) to illustrate a struggle in meaning with voices of *both* closeness *and* distance competing with each other.

We now turn our attention to the assumptions underlying RDT.

Theory At a Glance • *Relational Dialectics Theory*

Relational Dialectics Theory pictures relational life as constant process and motion. People in relationships continue to feel the push and pull of conflicting desires throughout the life of the relationship. Basically, people wish to have both/and, not either/or, when talking about opposing goals. For instance, people in relationships want to be both connected and autonomous, open and self-protective, and to have both predictability and spontaneity in their interactions. As people communicate in relationships, they attempt to reconcile these conflicting desires, but they never eliminate their need for both parts of the opposition.

Assumptions of Relational Dialectics Theory

RDT is grounded in four main assumptions that reflect its contentions about relational life:

- Relationships are not linear.
- Relational life is characterized by change.
- Contradiction is the fundamental fact of relational life.
- Communication is central to organizing and negotiating relational contradictions.

The most significant assumption that grounds this theory is the notion that relationships do not progress in a linear fashion. Rather, relationships consist of oscillation between contradictory desires. In fact, Baxter and Montgomery (1996) suggest that we should rethink our language and our metaphors about relationships. They note that the phrase *relational development* connotes some linear movement or forward progress, when, in fact, relationships do not steadily move in one direction.

The second assumption of RDT promotes the notion of process or change, although not necessarily framing this change as linear progress. Baxter and Montgomery observe that "relationship process or change . . . refers to quantitative and qualitative movement through time in the underlying contractions around which a relationship is organized" (1996, p. 52). Thus, Jeff and Eleanor are different now than they were a year ago. But that difference is not a linear move toward intimacy as much as it is a difference in the way they express their togetherness and their independence.

The contradictions or tensions between opposites never go away and never cease to provide tension, the third assumption of RDT. People manage these tensions and oppositions in different ways, but they are present continuously in relational life. The push and pull represented by dialectic tensions construct relational life, and one of our main communication tasks is managing these tensions. This approach differs from other types of relational theories in that it considers homeostasis to be un-natural: Change and transformation are the hallmarks of relational interaction in this perspective (Carr & Wang, 2012; Semlak & Pearson, 2011).

The final assumption of RDT pertains to communication. Specifically, this theory gives a central position to communication. As Baxter and Montgomery (1996) observe, "From the perspective of relational dialectics, social actors give life through their communicative practices to the contradictions that organize their relationships. The social reality of contradictions is produced and reproduced by the communicative action of social actors" (p. 59). It is through communication practices that people achieve **dialectical unity**, or the way in which people are able to make contradictions feel complete and satisfactory (Harrigan & Braithwaite, 2010).

When Jeff praises Eleanor for the party, for example, he is expressing affection and negotiating closeness. When Eleanor keeps silent instead of saying, "I love you," to Jeff, she is protecting herself and keeping a bit of distance between them. As Eleanor and Jeff plan their picnic for the next day, they are discussing how much

dialectical unity
the way people use communication to make sense of contradictions in their relationships.

predictability and how much novelty they wish to have. Planning initially provides predictability, but the couple's stated willingness to be flexible in their plan allows for spontaneity as well. Thus, Jeff and Eleanor's communication practices organize the three basic dialectics we will discuss later in the chapter: autonomy and connection, openness and protection, and novelty and predictability.

Core Concepts of Dialectics

The following elements are basic to the dialectical perspective: totality, contradiction, motion, and praxis (Rawlins, 2009). **Totality** suggests that people in a relationship are interdependent. This means that when something happens to one member of a relationship, the other member(s) will be affected as well. For example, if Jeff gets a promotion at work that entails more travel than his former position, Eleanor will have to deal with his absences. She may compensate by making more friends outside their relationship, and this will affect Jeff somewhat when he is home. He will have to meet new friends and share Eleanor's time, for example.

totality
acknowledges the interdependence of people in a relationship

In addition, totality means that the social and cultural context affects the process; communicating in relationships "involves the constant interconnection and reciprocal influence of multiple individual, interpersonal, and social factors" (Rawlins, 1992, p. 7). For instance, Eleanor and Jeff's relationship is affected by their social circle, by their location in San Francisco, and by the historical moment in which they live.

Contradiction refers to oppositions—two elements that contradict each other. As such, contradiction is the central feature of the dialectic approach. Dialectics are the result of oppositions. When Eleanor desires to tell Jeff that she loves him but also wishes to withhold that information to protect herself, she is experiencing contradiction. **Motion** refers to the processual nature of relationships and their change over time. When Eleanor reflects on how different her relationship with Jeff is now compared to what they had two years ago, she is experiencing motion. Think back to one of your own relationships. Compare how you relate now to how you did when you first met. No doubt you will see motion at work also.

contradiction
the central feature of the dialectic approach; refers to oppositions

motion
the processual nature of relationships

Student Voices

Helena

I am constantly being pushed and pulled by contradictions in my relationship with my sister. She's my best friend and my worst enemy. I'd do anything for her and she feels the same, but I can't think of anyone who can make me madder or more upset than she can. Plus, because we're twins, the notion of autonomy and connection is really up there for me. It's a pain when people say we're so alike or when they can't tell us apart, but there is a cool part to having a twin and being so bonded. Dialectics theory was made for me and my sister, Lisa.

praxis
refers to the choice-making capacity of humans

Finally, **praxis** means that humans are choice makers. Although we do not have completely free choice in all instances and are restricted by our previous choices, by the choices of others, and by cultural and social conditions, we are still conscious and active choice makers. For example, Eleanor chooses to be with Jeff, and this choice restricts other choices she might make. She must get along with Jeff's parents and siblings when they get together for the holidays. She might not ever have chosen to be with these people on her own, but because she is in love with Jeff, she must spend time with them. On a more basic level, Jeff and Eleanor did not choose the time in which they live, but the culture shapes some of their choices. If they lived in the 1950s, for instance, they would be less likely to be unmarried and living together. Praxis also refers to the practical choices people make when confronted with dialectic tensions (Sahlstein, Maguire, & Timmerman, 2009).

Basic Relational Dialectics

Many different specific dialectics have been discussed with reference to relational life. As we mentioned previously, perhaps the three most relevant to interpersonal relationships are the dialectics of autonomy and connection, openness and protection, and novelty and predictability (Baxter, 1990). Other researchers have also found that these dialectics are common to relational life. For example, in one study (Erbert, 2000) marital couples were interviewed to determine how they perceived relational dialectics with reference to conflicts. Autonomy and contradiction and openness and closedness were perceived as the most important contradictions, and the predictability and novelty dialectic was deemed important for some specific conflict types.

Autonomy and Connection

autonomy and connection
an important relational tension that shows our conflicting desires to be close and to be separate

The dialectic between **autonomy and connection** refers to our simultaneous desires to be independent of our significant others and to find intimacy with them. As our story of Eleanor and Jeff illustrates, relational life involves the conflicting desires to be both close to and separate from relational partners. Jeff appreciates Eleanor's efforts on the dinner party, which makes him feel close to her. Yet the reason for the party in some sense celebrates his separateness from Eleanor. The fact that Jeff has a long-standing friendship with Mary Beth illustrates his autonomy. Seeing both autonomy and closeness as constants in relational life is a hallmark of RDT, which makes it unique from many other theories of communication in relationships.

For example, as Baxter and Montgomery (1996) observe, other theories like Social Penetration Theory (Chapter 10) and Uncertainty Reduction Theory (Chapter 8) advance a rather static view of closeness; partners move toward closeness or away from it. From this vantage point, Eleanor and Jeff may be seen as growing closer and closer as they share more experiences and affection. Dialectic theory holds that contradictions are inherent in all relationships and that the dynamic interplay between autonomy and closeness is important to understanding a relationship. So Jeff and Eleanor are seen by RDT as moving *between* closeness and distance throughout their relationship. They are not understood as moving toward or moving away from either of these two competing needs.

©Jeff Stahler/Distributed by Universal Uclick for UFS via CartoonStock.com

Theory in Popular Press • *The Dance Between Closeness and Distance*

In their blog about family life, family therapists Don MacMannus and Debra MacMannus discuss how intimacy is affected by people's varying needs for closeness and distance. The call it the "ongoing dance of intimacy" and observe that a close relationship consists of continual movements "away" and "toward." MacMannus and MacMannus caution, in line with the thinking of RDT, that closeness and distance are neither good nor bad, and intimate relationships need both. As they put it, people need time together and time apart to keep the relational bonds from feeling too tight or too loose.

Source: MacMannus, D., & MacMannus, D. M. How's your family really doing? howsyourfamily .com/how-to-balance-closeness-and-distance-in-relationship/.

Communication researchers are interested in dialectic thinking because of the communication implications of the theory. Baxter and Montgomery (1996) discuss how couples' private communication codes illustrate the presence of both connection and autonomy in relationships. For instance, nicknames celebrate something inherently individual in that they are usually highlighting an individual trait (such as Shorty, Chief, or Sweetness). Yet they also indicate a relational closeness in that distant friends do not invoke pet names for one another. In the simple practice of calling someone by a nickname, we are coding individuation and closeness.

Openness and Protection

A second critical tension in relational life has to do with openness and protection. The **openness and protection** dialectic focuses on our conflicting desires first to be open and vulnerable, revealing personal information to our relational partners, and second to be strategic and protective in our communication. As Eleanor mulls over how much to tell Jeff about her feelings, she is wrestling with the tension between disclosure and silence, or the openness and protection dialectic.

The dialectic position features both with respect to candor and concealment. For instance, Leslie Baxter and Erin Sahlstein (2000) mention how gossiping can honor both openness and privacy as gossipers simultaneously disclose about others while keeping silent about themselves. Paige Toller and Dawn Braithwaite (2009) found that parents who had suffered the loss of a child used strategies that alternated between openness and concealment with their spouses. In one strategy, however, they seemed to combine the two poles by using an open nonverbal approach while keeping silent verbally about their feelings. Angela Hoppe-Nagao and Stella Ting-Toomey (2002) found six ways that married couples manage the tension between openness and closedness: (1) topic selection, (2) time alternation, (3) withdrawal, (4) probing, (5) antisocial strategies, and (6) deception.

Topic selection involved making some topics taboo, or off limits for discussion, thereby guarding privacy while assuring openness on all other topics. Time alternation meant blocking out specific times to talk about sensitive topics. Withdrawal and probing were either leaving the conversation or asking for more information from the partner. Yelling, crying, or pouting were examples of antisocial communication. Deception involved small distortions of the truth or omissions to keep some things private and to avoid conflict in the relationship.

Student Voices

Kellye

It's easy to see how dialectics are in my family. I have a mother who has severe arthritis and she needs help around the house. My dad can't do it alone and he wants to have someone come in to help out. She has this need to be independent, but also knows that there is no way that she and my dad can do it alone—a need to be dependent. It's one dialectic we are experiencing right now.

Novelty and Predictability

The dialectic between **novelty and predictability** refers to the conflict between the comfort of stability and the excitement of change. The dialectic position sees the interplay of certainty and uncertainty in relationships. Jeff and Eleanor's planning behavior illustrates this interplay. When they make a plan together, they are accomplishing at least two things with reference to predictability about themselves and their relationship. First, their plan defines them as in a relationship, because planning is a relational activity. It also establishes a routine so they know what they will be doing in the short-term future. Yet they leave the plan a bit open ended to allow for creativity and novelty. With their plan for Sunday, Eleanor and Jeff have dealt simultaneously with their contradictory needs for routine and spontaneity.

Contextual Dialectics

What we have just discussed are **interactional dialectics** in that they are located within the relationship itself—they are part of the partners' interaction with each other (Rawlins, 1992). Researchers have also discussed other dialectics that affect relational life. William Rawlins calls these **contextual dialectics,** which means that they derive from the place of the relationship in the culture.

interactional dialectics
tensions resulting from and constructed by communication

Contextual dialectics are formed from the tension between the public definitions of a given relationship—friendship, for example—and the private interactions within a specific friendship. Rawlins discusses two contextual dialectics—between the public and the private and between the real and the ideal. Although perhaps a little less important to us than interactional dialectics, these two do affect interpersonal communication in relationships. The **public and private dialectic** refers to the tension between the two domains: a private relationship and public life. Rawlins discusses the fact that in the public realm friendship occupies a rather marginal position. Lillian Rubin (1998) makes the same observation, noting that public expectations favor kin relationships over friendships even when individuals may value their friends more highly than their kin. Rawlins notes that friendship suffers in comparison to other relationships because there is no institution to sanction it. Eleanor and Jeff's cohabiting relationship may have the same marginal status because, unlike marriage, it is not legally sanctioned.

contextual dialectics
tensions resulting from the place of the relationship within the culture

public and private dialectic
a contextual dialectic resulting from a private relationship and public life

Rawlins (1992) argues that tension arises in a close friendship between this marginal public status and the friendship's deep private character. Rawlins states that this dialectic results in friendships (and by implication, other unsanctioned relationships) acting with what he calls *double agency*. By this he means that these relationships fulfill both public and private functions. Rawlins observes that sometimes the public functions constrain the private ones. For instance, people who form friendships in the workplace may encounter negative feedback from their significant others who see the friendships as a threat to their relationship. When Jeff and Eleanor first became serious, Eleanor felt threatened by Jeff's female friends. The public aspects of friendships and love relationships provide tension.

The dichotomy of the public and the private is obvious when we think about political figures. Politicians live a public life but have private lives as well. Dialectical thinking shows us that private, relational life is intertwined with public life. Although the two spheres can be separated to an extent, in many meaningful ways Dialectic Theory shows us that they are interwoven. Certainly, we have seen this to be the case when politicians' private misdeeds have become public as in the cases of John Edwards and Arnold Schwarzenegger, among others.

This public and private dialectic interacts with the dialectic of the real and the ideal. The tension of the **real and ideal dialectic** is featured when we think of old family sitcoms (1950s/1960s), such as *Leave It to Beaver:* We receive an idealized

real and ideal dialectic
a contextual dialectic resulting from the difference between idealized relationships and lived relationships

Table 11.1 Interactional and Contextual Dialectics

TRADITIONAL INTERACTIONAL DIALECTICS	CONTEXTUAL DIALECTICS
Autonomy-Connection: desiring a separate identity and wanting a bond between partners	**Public-Private:** contrasting the public and private aspects of a relationship
Openness-Protection: wanting to tell personal information while seeking privacy	**The Real-The Ideal:** comparing a lived relationship to a fantasy of that relationship
Novelty-Predictability: wanting change while desiring stability	

message of what family life is like in televised families and then when we look at the families we live in, we have to contend with the troublesome realities of family life. The tension between these two images forms this dialectic. If Eleanor reads a lot of romance novels emphasizing complete openness between romantic partners, she may feel a tension between that vision and her lived experience with Jeff, which involves some sharing but not complete openness.

In addition, this dialectic contrasts all the expectations one has of a relationship with its lived realities. Generally, expectations about relationships are lofty and idealized. Friendships are seen as sites of affection, loyalty, and trust. Families are pictured as havens in a troubled world. Loved ones are believed to provide unconditional affection and support. Yet we know that interpersonal relationships are not always pleasant and can have a dark side that contrasts starkly with these ideals. Dialectic Theory attempts to explain how people live with and manage this contradiction.

Finally, cultural and contextual factors influence these two dialectics. In cultures where friends are elevated to the status of family (e.g., some Middle Eastern cultures), the tension will be experienced quite differently than in Rawlins's description, if it is felt at all. In addition, social mores and expectations vary over time, and the dialectics are influenced by these changes. For example, Ernest Burgess and Harvey Locke (1953) distinguished between an institutional and a companionate marriage. Prior to the 1950s, marriage was expected to be an economic institution, critical to the survival of the human race. More recently in the United States, marriage has been viewed as a love relationship where one's partner functions as one's best friend. The tensions between the ideal and the real may shift depending on the contours of the socially prescribed ideal. The institutional marriage didn't raise the expectations for the relationship nearly as much as the current ideal. See Table 11.1 for a summary of the basic relational dialectics.

Beyond Basic Dialectics

The basic dialectic tensions we have just reviewed characterize many interpersonal relationships, but a growing body of research is uncovering additional tensions and questioning whether autonomy–connection, openness–protection, and novelty–predictability permeate relationships in all contexts (Braithwaite & Baxter, 1995).

In two studies examining RDT in an online environment, Kristen Norwood and Leslie Baxter (2011) found a different set of four dialectics that animated online letters people wrote seeking birth mothers willing to allow them to adopt their babies. Other researchers (Pederson, 2014) discovered that online narratives of forgiveness present three competing discourses: outward practice versus inward process, liberation for self versus liberation for others, and long process versus epiphany.

In studies about friendship, Marnel Goins (2011) found the tensions characterizing talk among Black women friends were completely different than the basic dialectics and included: consumerism versus savings, using "good" or "bad" English, satisfaction versus dissatisfaction with their appearance and acceptance or rejection of race-based "otherness." Rawlins (1992) found no evidence of the novelty–predictability dialectic in his study. Instead, he found a dialectic focusing on the tensions between judgment and acceptance. This dialectic emerges in the tension between judging a friend's behaviors and simply accepting them. In studying friendships in the workplace, Ted Zorn (1995) found the three main dialectics, but he also found some additional tensions that were specific to the workplace context.

Julie Apker, Kathleen Propp, and Wendy Zabava Ford (2005) note that the workplace is a relatively unexplored context for applying RDT. When they studied nurses working in health care team interactions, they found several dialectics related to how the nurses negotiated their status and identity. They called these *role dialectics* because they spoke to the tensions nurses experienced relative to being both equal to and subordinate to the physicians on the health care team.

In examining people's participation in a community theater group, Michael Kramer (2004) advanced 11 dialectic tensions ranging from commitment to group and commitment to other life activities to tolerance and judgment (of the other members). Michaela Meyer (2003) examined the relationship between two characters in the television show *Dawson's Creek* and found the dialectic of connection–autonomy as well as a new dialectic, informing–constituting identity formation. It is possible that relational context makes a difference in the dialectics; these new dialectics were discovered in online communications, friendships, the workplace, a community group, and a televised friendship. Perhaps it is also the case that ethnicity also made a difference in the types of dialectics researchers found.

Yet, other researchers (Baxter, Braithwaite, Golish, & Olson, 2002; Bryant, 2003; Toller, 2005) examined issues of illness and death in the context of the family and also uncovered additional dialectics. They found that the dialectic of presence–absence was an important consideration for families dealing with Alzheimer's patients (Baxter et al., 2002), for those experiencing the death of a parent and becoming part of a stepfamily (Bryant, 2003), or for parents losing a child (Toller, 2005). Tamara Golish and Kimberly Powell (2003) advanced a further dialectical tension, that of joy–grief. They noted that parents experiencing a premature birth experienced the contradictory emotions of joy and grief and needed to find communication strategies for managing this contradiction. A study in stepfamilies' communication (Baxter, Braithwaite, Bryant, & Wagner, 2004) found the dialectic of one parent versus two parents in authority to be important to children. The children experience a tension between wanting their biological parent to have all the authority and wanting their stepparent to share authority with their biological parent. Also in the context of stepfamilies, other researchers (Braithwaite, Toller, Daas, Durham, & Jones, 2008) found children voicing the dialectic of control and restraint. See Table 11.2 for a listing of some of these new dialectics.

Table 11.2 New Dialectics

INTERACTIONAL DIALECTIC	CONTEXT WHERE FOUND
Judgment–Acceptance	Friendship
Subordinate–Equal	Workplace
Group–Individual	Community group
Ordered activities–Emergent activities	Community group
Inclusion–Exclusion	Community group
Acceptable behavior–Unacceptable behavior	Community group
Presence–Absence	Families/Stepfamilies
Joy–Grief	Families
Informing–Constituting identity	Televised friendship
One parent–Two parent authority	Stepfamilies
Control–Restraint	Stepfamilies

Responses to Dialectics

Although the dialectic tensions are ongoing, people do make efforts to manage them. Some research (Jameson, 2004) examines politeness as a general method for managing dialectic tensions. Baxter (1988) identifies four specific strategies for this purpose: cyclic alternation, segmentation, selection, and integration (Table 11.3).

Table 11.3 Responses to Dialectic Tensions

RESPONSE	DESCRIPTION
Cyclic alternation	Choosing different poles for different times. Being close when young and more distant with age, for example.
Segmentation	Choosing different poles for different contexts. Being close at home and more distant at work, for example.
Selection	Choosing one pole and acting as though the other does not exist. Being an extremely close family, for example.
Integration	Synthesizing the oppositions in dialectic tensions; composed of three substrategies.
Neutralizing	A substrategy of integration; involves choosing a compromise between the oppositions. Being moderately close, for example.
Disqualifying	A substrategy of integration; involves exempting certain issues from the general pattern. Deciding to be open on all topics except sex, for example.
Reframing	A substrategy of integration; involves transforming the oppositions so they no longer appear to oppose one another. Deciding that closeness can only be achieved if there's a little distance too, for example.

RELATIONAL DIALECTICS THEORY

Cyclic alternation occurs when people choose one of the opposites to feature at particular times, alternating with the other. For instance, when sisters are very young, they may be inseparable, highlighting the closeness pole of the dialectic. As adolescents, they may favor autonomy in their relationship, seeking separate identities. As adults, when they are perhaps living in the same town, they may favor closeness again.

Segmentation involves isolating separate arenas for emphasizing each of the opposites. For example, a husband and wife who work together in a family business might stress predictability in their working relationship and novelty for times they are at home. The third strategy, selection, refers to making a choice between the opposites. A couple who choose to be close at all times, ignoring their needs for autonomy, use selection.

Finally, integration involves some kind of synthesis of the opposites. Integration can take three forms: neutralizing, disqualifying, or reframing the polarities. Neutralizing involves compromising between the polarities. People who choose this strategy try to find a happy medium between the opposites. Jeff and Eleanor may decide they cannot really be as open as Eleanor would like, yet they cannot be as closed as Jeff might want either. Thus, they forge a moderately open relationship. Disqualifying neutralizes the dialectics by exempting certain issues from the general pattern. A family might be very open in their communication in general yet have a few taboo topics that are not discussed at all, such as sex and finances. Reframing refers to transforming the dialectic in some way so that it no longer seems to contain an opposition. Julia Wood and her colleagues (1994) discuss how couples reframe by defining connection as including differences. Thus, the dialectic between autonomy and connection is redrawn as a unity rather than as an opposition. If Eleanor and Jeff begin to see their closeness as a function of their ability to also be separate from each other, they are reframing, or redefining, what it means to be close.

Baxter and Montgomery (1996) review these and other techniques for dealing with dialectical tensions. They argue that any techniques that people use share three characteristics: They are improvisational, they are affected by time, and they are possibly complicated by unintended consequences. Let's look at these three characteristics in turn.

Improvisational, according to Baxter and Montgomery, means that whatever people do to deal with a particular tension of relational life, they do not alter the ongoing nature of the tension. For example, Jeff and Eleanor have come to a moderately open relationship to neutralize the dialectical tension, but they have not changed the fact that openness and protectiveness continue to be an issue in their relationship.

The aspect of time refers to the notion that, when dealing with dialectics, communication choices made by relational partners are affected by the past, enacted in the present, and filled with anticipation for the future. When Jeff praises Eleanor for the party they gave for Mary Beth, he does so knowing that they have argued about his friends in the past and hoping that these arguments will not continue in the future. In speaking about applying the dialectical approach to friendship, Rawlins (1992) comments that "configurations of contradictions compose and organize friendships throughout an ongoing process of change across the life course" (p. 8). He further observes that the way friends coordinate and manage their tensions over time is a key factor in dialectical analysis. The conclusion he draws is that "dialectical inquiries are intrinsically historical investigations" (p. 8), concerned with developmental processes over time.

cyclic alternation
a coping response to dialectical tensions; refers to changes over time

segmentation
a coping response to dialectical tensions; refers to changes due to context

selection
a coping response to dialectical tensions; refers to prioritizing oppositions

integration
a coping response to dialectical tensions; refers to synthesizing the opposition; composed of three substrategies

neutralizing
a substrategy of integration; refers to compromising between the oppositions

disqualifying
a substrategy of integration; refers to exempting certain issues from the general pattern

reframing
a substrategy of integration; refers to transforming the oppositions

RELATIONAL DIALECTICS THEORY

Finally, Baxter and Montgomery point out that relational partners may enact a strategy for coping with a tension, yet it may not work out as they intended. For example, the husband and wife who work together and employ segmentation as we described earlier may feel they are coping with the novelty and predictability tension. But they may become dissatisfied because they spend a lot of time at work and so do not get enough novelty in their relationship.

Integration, Critique, and Closing

Dialectical process thinking adds a great deal to our explanatory framework for relational life. First, we can think specifically about issues around which relational partners construct meaning. Second, we can remove a static frame and put our emphasis on the interplay between change and stability. We do not have to choose between observing patterns and observing unpredictability because we recognize the presence of both within relationships. Likewise, dialectical thinking directs people to observe the interactions within a relationship, among its individual members, as well as outside a relationship, as its members interact with the larger social and cultural systems in which they are embedded. This approach helps us focus on power issues and multicultural diversity.

In general, scholars have been excited about the promise generated by Relational Dialectics Theory, and the responses to it have been generally positive. With respect to its methodological approach, Baxter and Norwood (2016) state the following: "Although the 1996 version of RDT was ecumenically receptive to both quantitative and qualitative methods, the 2011 version of the theory favors the latter." Baxter and Scharp (2015) also posit that the theory has now been effectively discussed in critical research. Therefore, all three ways of knowing are relevant to RDT. As you think about RDT, parsimony, utility, and heurism are three evaluative criteria to consider.

Integration

Communication Tradition	Rhetorical I Semiotic I Phenomenological I Cybernetic I Socio-Psychological I **Socio-Cultural** I Critical
Communication Context	Intrapersonal I **Interpersonal** I Small Group I Organizational I Public/Rhetorical I Mass/Media I Cultural
Approach to Knowing	**Positivistic/Empirical** I **Interpretive/Hermeneutic** I **Critical**

Critique

Evaluation Criteria	Scope I Logical Consistency I **Parsimony** I **Utility** I Testability I **Heurism** I Test of Time

Parsimony

With respect to parsimony, some researchers question whether the dialectics of autonomy and connection, openness and protection, and novelty and predictability are the only dialectics in all relationships. In some ways, the original conception of RDT may have been too parsimonious in only listing three basic dialectics. For instance, many of the studies we have cited have generated additional dialectics. Yet, the proliferating list of dialectic tensions that we've mentioned raises the opposite concern about how well the theory does on the criterion of parsimony. Endless lists of new dialectic tensions make the theory problematic. However, it's possible that some of these newer tensions may enable RDT to explain relational life in a more complete manner, eschewing the need for a parsimonious model.

Utility

Perhaps the most positive appeal of the theory is that it seems to explain the push and pull people experience in relationships much better than some of the other, more linear, theories of relational life. Most people experience their relationships in ebb-and-flow patterns, whether the issue is intimacy, self-disclosure, or something else. That is, relationships do not simply become more or less of something in a linear, straight-line pattern. Instead, they often seem to be both/and as we live through them. Dialectics offers a compelling explanation for this both/and feeling, making the theory fulfill the criterion of utility.

Heurism

Leslie Baxter (2006) observed, the most important criterion for a theory like RDT is heurism because the theory's goal is to shed light on the "complex and indeterminate process of meaning-making" (p. 130). As such, we might not judge it so stringently on the criterion of parsimony before looking into how well it has stimulated research. It seems to have been successful in this regard. Researchers have examined how RDT might be explained in a number of different areas and contexts, including parent–child relationships (Scharp & Thomas, 2016), romantic relationships (Faulkner & Ruby, 2015), Alcoholics Anonymous members (Thatcher, 2011), cohabiting couples (Moore, Kienzle, & Flood Grady, 2015), adult students (O'Boyle, 2014), nonvoluntary family relationships (Carr & Wang, 2012), among others. The sustained use of RDT as a theoretical framework across so many different interpersonal contexts speaks well to its performance as a heuristic theory.

Closing

Baxter and Montgomery (1996) observe that dialectics is not a traditional theory in that it offers no axioms or propositional arguments. Instead, it describes example, what coping strategies people might use to deal with the major dialectic tensions in their

Student Voices

Martin

I can believe that dialectics is a useful theory because it definitely opened my eyes about my relationship with my brother. The push–pull idea says it all. When we were younger, we couldn't stand each other. But I did notice that if he went away for a while or I just didn't see him, I'd start to miss him. When he got back, I went back to hating him again. Now that we're older, I wouldn't say we hate each other, but we still react negatively if one gets too close. Yet we can't get too far apart either, or that's bad. If we haven't talked in a couple of days, one of us will surely call the other just to check in. I always thought we had an odd relationship. It helps to see that we're struggling with what everyone else does in relationships with others—wanting connection and independence at the same time.

relationships. This lack of predictive ability may be the result of the relative youth of dialectics as a theoretical frame for relational life, but more likely, it results from differing goals: An empirical or positivistic theory seeks prediction and final statements about communication phenomena; dialectics is a more interpretative theory and it operates from an open-ended, ongoing viewpoint. Baxter and Montgomery end their 1996 book with a personal dialogue between themselves about the experience of writing about a theory that encourages conversation rather than provides axiomatic conclusions. They agree that in some ways it is difficult to shake the cultural need for consistency and closure.

Many researchers agree that the dialectic approach is an exciting way to conceive of communication in relational life. Although quite a bit of research has been undertaken using RDT, expect to see more refinements of this theory and more studies testing its premises. Leslie Baxter (2011) underscores this sentiment by noting that "growing a theory is a process akin to raising a child" (p. 1). In that vein, RDT is a theory that continues on a journey of exploration and investigation.

Discussion Starters

TECH QUEST: Suppose a new dialectic (online–offline) was being studied in communication research. How do you think that tension would be played out in a relationship, and what would it entail? Could people use current dialectic strategies (cyclic alternation, segmentation, etc.) to deal with it or would they have to develop new strategies in your opinion?

1. Can you think of other dialectic tensions that will pervade the relational life of Eleanor and Jeff besides those discussed in the chapter?

2. Do you think relationships are better explained through stage theories or dialectics? Why? Provide examples.

3. How do you think communication is used to deal with conflicting desires within a relationship? How does RDT help us understand communication behaviors?

4. A few of the articles cited in the chapter have to do with RDT applied in ethnicities other than White, European American. How do you think culture and ethnicity impact the theory? Is it universal across cultures? Or do you see its claims as culture specific?

5. Provide an example of a dialectical tension that was managed through cyclic alternation.

6. Provide an example of how you could use segmentation to resolve a dialectical tension.

7. Provide an example of how you could use reframing to resolve a dialectical tension.

CHAPTER 12

Communication Privacy Management Theory

*Based on the research of **Sandra Petronio***

To tell or not to tell is a condition that we frequently face, yet the question is complicated.

—Sandra Petronio

Lisa Sanders

Lisa Sanders knew it would be hard making it through the workday without being sidetracked by someone. She rushed around the office, keeping her eyes down, trying to avoid getting sucked into a conversation with anyone. She enjoyed her work and loved her coworkers, but the downside was that somebody always wanted to chat, and she simply had no time to waste today. She had already used too much precious work time going through her email. She had deleted about 65 pieces of junk, which was really getting to be a problem. The worst was that somehow she was on a porn list, and she kept getting solicitations for all sorts of nasty things. She just hoped that the office didn't have some type of surveillance to observe all those messages. It made her feel vaguely uneasy.

She went into the break room for a cup of coffee. That was a mistake. Yolanda and Michael were there, and they wanted to ask her opinion about a change the front office was making in how they did the billing. One thing led to another, and soon the three were talking about Yolanda's concerns about going on maternity leave next month. Lisa found herself enjoying the conversation even though she knew she had to get back to work.

After work, she went to Central U. to take a night class so that someday she could finish her B.A. She was hopeful that she'd finish within the year, and she had her eye on a management position that she expected would be vacant by then. During the break, she visited with her friend Doug Banda, who was also finishing up his degree. She confided in Doug that she didn't think she was doing very well balancing work, school, and her personal life. It was a continual challenge, and today it was getting the better of her. She almost surprised herself with how emotional she got while talking to Doug. Doug was a good friend; he just listened and offered a friendly hug of support. She felt better after talking with him.

Finally, class was over and Lisa went home and listened to her voice mail. Lisa's mother had called with the usual gossip about the family. Most of the message had to do with Lisa's sister-in-law, Margo. Lisa's mom didn't get along very well with Margo, and she often called Lisa to let off steam about something her daughter-in-law had done (or hadn't done). Today it was the fact that Ed's wife was taking the kids on a vacation and Lisa's mom wouldn't get to see them for two weeks. While she was listening, her roommate, Amanda Torelli, came home.

Lisa liked Amanda and she certainly couldn't afford the apartment without a roommate, but sometimes it felt like she didn't have a moment to herself. Amanda had an overpowering personality, and she filled the apartment to the extent that Lisa often felt crowded. Amanda always had something to say, and tonight was no exception. Amanda wanted to tell Lisa all about her most recent fight with her boyfriend, Joel. Amanda and Joel were always fighting, and Lisa privately thought Amanda should dump the guy. But then she realized that Amanda liked playing the drama queen role, so she stopped telling Amanda any of her true reactions. Lisa grabbed a glass of wine and some crackers as she settled on the couch to listen to Amanda's latest tale of woe.

As Lisa encounters the various people in her life—coworkers, classmates, family members, roommates, and so forth—she engages in a complex negotiation between privacy and disclosure. This chapter presents the theory of Communication Privacy Management (CPM), which helps us sort through and explain the complexities of this process. Sandra Petronio (2002) states that CPM is a practical theory designed to explain the "everyday" issues described in Lisa's activities. As many researchers have observed, the question of whether to tell someone something we are thinking is a complicated one, yet it's one we face frequently in our daily lives (e.g., Venetis et al., 2012). As Petronio (2016) notes, CPM is a "road map" that helps to explain "how people make judgments about managing their private information with other people" (p. 1).

Examining Lisa's day, we can see at least five instances when Lisa is occupied with questions of disclosure: (1) She worries about keeping those unwanted pornographic emails a secret from people at work, (2) she engages in conversation with coworkers without telling them that she's feeling harried, (3) she confides in a friend about feeling unbalanced in her work and personal life, (4) she listens to her mother's voice mail–recorded complaints, and (5) she hears her roommate's disclosures without telling her what she really thinks about her boyfriend.

All of these examples illustrate CPM's contention that deciding what to reveal and what to keep confidential is not a straightforward decision but rather a continual balancing act. Both disclosure and privacy have potential risks and rewards for Lisa in all of the situations she encounters.

Lisa also has to think about the risks and rewards her decisions may create for those with whom she interacts. How would Amanda feel if Lisa told her that she thought her boyfriend was a loser? The act of revealing or withholding personal information has effects on relationships as well as on individuals. What happens to the relationship between Lisa and Doug as she confides in him about her feelings? All these concerns, relational and individual, create the complicated process of balance that Petronio addresses with Communication Privacy Management Theory. As Petronio (2002) observes:

> We try to weigh the demands of the situation with our needs and those of others around us. Privacy has importance for us because it lets us feel separate from others. It gives us a sense that we are the rightful owners of information about us. There are risks that include making private disclosures to the wrong people, disclosing at a bad time, telling too much about ourselves, or compromising others. On the other hand, disclosure can give enormous benefits. . . . [We may] increase social control, validate our perspectives, and become more intimate with our relational partners when we disclose. . . . The balance of privacy and disclosure has meaning because it is vital to the way we manage our relationships. (pp. 1–2)

Thus, there was a need for a theory like CPM that attempts to do what few other theories have done: Explain the process that people use to manage the relationship between concealing and revealing private information.

Communication Privacy Management Theory is unlike most of the other theories presented in this text because it is relatively recent. For example, our discussion in Chapter 18 on Aristotle's *Rhetoric* centers on a theoretical approach to public address and persuasion that goes back thousands of years. Of course, not all of the theories in this text have the history of Aristotle's *Rhetoric,* but most have been in use for longer than CPM. This recency is notable for two reasons. First, it is exciting because it indicates the currency of thought in the communication discipline. It indicates that fresh, new thinking continues to illuminate questions of communication behavior. Having new theories illustrates the vibrancy of communication as a field. In case you were tempted to dismiss theory as something from musty tomes written by dead Greeks, Petronio's CPM Theory shows that theorizing is alive and well in our own century.

Second, and related to the excitement generated by its recency, is the fact that CPM grows specifically from a focus on communication. This also shows the maturing and growth of the field of communication. Some of the other theories in this text, you will remember, originated in other disciplines. Communication researchers found them useful for some reason and borrowed them for their own work. For example, Symbolic Interaction Theory (Chapter 4), comes from sociology. Cognitive Dissonance Theory (Chapter 6) originated in psychology. Communication researchers have found these and other theories useful for framing their studies examining communication behaviors. However, it may be even more helpful to have theories that place communication concepts centrally in the explanation process. CPM Theory does just that: allowing researchers to be more focused in their examinations of the communication process and specific communication practices.

Evolution of Communication Privacy Management Theory

Although the formal theory is relatively recent, the ideas that form the theory show a historical evolution. Over 30 years ago, Petronio and her colleagues published some studies outlining principles that would eventually become part of CPM (e.g., Petronio & Martin, 1986; Petronio, Martin, & Littlefield, 1984). In these studies, the researchers were interested in how people decided on the rules guiding their disclosure behavior. They noted that men and women have different criteria for judging when to be open and when to stay silent. These criteria lead to differing rules for men and women on the subject of disclosure. The notion of gender differences and the concept of disclosure as rule governed are now parts of CPM Theory.

In 1991, Petronio published her first attempt to codify all the principles of the theory. Her work then differed from her later (Petronio, 2002) conceptualization in two ways. First, the theory had more limited boundaries in 1991. At that time, Petronio referred to it as a **microtheory** because its boundaries were confined to privacy management within a marital dyad. Now, as we explain in this chapter, the theory is less restricted and attempts to explain privacy and disclosure in many more contexts than marriage. Petronio now refers to CPM as a **macrotheory** because its boundaries include a large variety of interpersonal relationships, including groups and organizations.

microtheory
a theory with limited boundaries

macrotheory
a theory with extensive boundaries

Theory At a Glance • *Communication Privacy Management Theory*

Disclosure in relationships requires managing private and public boundaries. These boundaries are between those feelings that one wants to reveal and those one wants to keep private. Disclosure in relationship development is more than revealing private information to another, however. Negotiation and coordination of boundaries is required. Decisions regarding disclosure require close monitoring.

The second change in the theory was a name change. In 1991, Petronio called the theory Communication Boundary Management. When she published the fuller statement of the theory (Petronio, 2002), she renamed it Communication Privacy Management Theory. Petronio explained the new name as better "reflecting the focus on private disclosures. Though the theory uses a boundary metaphor to explain the management process, the name change underscores that the main thrust of the theory is on private disclosures" (2002, p. 2). Petronio (2004, 2010, 2016) expects (and hopes) that the theory will continue to grow and evolve as it is applied to practical questions of disclosure in relationships. Her 2004 article was subtitled "Please Stand By" indicating that the theory continues to evolve and her ideas keep sharpening as empirical data allow her and others to see and correct any weaknesses in CPM's explanatory power.

Assumptions of CPM

Communication Privacy Management Theory is rooted in assumptions about how individuals think and communicate as well as assumptions about the nature of human beings. CPM adheres to aspects of both rules and systems approaches that we discussed in Chapter 3, and it makes three assumptions about human nature congruent with rules and systems:

- Humans are choice makers.
- Humans are rule makers and rule followers.
- Humans' choices and rules are based on a consideration of others as well as the self.

With respect to the first assumption, Petronio believes that CPM theory helps people better understand the choices they make and how these choices assist them in their relationships with others. Think, for instance, about how you decide to tell a colleague about a poor job performance review you received. Your decision whether or not to reveal this personal information may have (lasting) relational consequences. As Petronio and Reierson (2009) state, you have the "right to control" (p. 366) the information and if you decide to reveal it to your colleague, it becomes "co-owned" (p. 366) by your colleague.

The second and third assumption can be grouped together since both relate to rules. CPM theorists acknowledge that rules play an instrumental part in our relational lives

Table 12.1 Assumptions of CPM

CPM THEORY	ALL DIALECTIC THEORIES
Human choice	Relational life characterized by change
Human-made rules	Contradiction as the fundamental fact of relational life
Social concerns	

(refer back to Chapter 3 for a more detailed discussion of this topic). Rules tell us what to reveal and what to withhold from others based on a "mental calculus." This calculus is grounded in a number of different areas, including culture, gender, and context. A bit later in the chapter we explore the relationship of rules to CPM. For now, however, keep in mind that "since people assume the right to retain jurisdiction over their private information" (Petronio, 2015, p. 3), they will necessarily invoke rules to maintain that right.

CPM Theory is a dialectic theory because it focuses on the tensions inherent in being open to others while also maintaining privacy. Petronio (2016) comments on the intersection between her theory and RDT: "Grounding CPM theory within a dialectical framework allows more insights into privacy management by capturing the underlying logic and management of private information people actually use in their daily lives" (p. 2). That is, the principles of change and contradiction function prominently in our lives and our needs for autonomy and sociability influence our privacy decisions.

These assumptions, taken together, represent a perception of active human beings and a picture of humans as engaged in relational life to the extent that self and other are intertwined (Table 12.1). The notion of being intertwined is important to CPM. Not only are the self and the other in an engaged relationship, but disclosure is also intertwined with the concept of privacy. As Petronio has argued, privacy is only understood in a dialectical tension with disclosure. If we disclose everything, we won't have a concept of privacy. Conversely, if all information is private, the idea of disclosure won't make sense. It's only by pairing them that each concept can be defined.

Key Terms and Principles of CPM

As we have noted, CPM is concerned with explaining people's negotiation processes around disclosing private information. Our first task, then, is defining **private information.** Petronio (2000) commented that people define private information as information about things that matter deeply to them. The process of communicating private information in relationships with others becomes **private disclosures.**

The emphasis away from *self-disclosure* marks a distinction between CPM's definition of disclosure and that of traditional research on openness (e.g., Jourard, 1971) and as identified in other theories such as Social Penetration Theory, for example (Chapter 10). CPM views the definition differently in three ways. First, private disclosure puts more emphasis on the personal content of the disclosure than does traditional self-disclosure literature. In doing this, CPM gives more credence to the substance of disclosures, or what is considered private. In addition, CPM examines how people disclose through a rule-based system. In so doing, CPM focuses on rule structures created for sharing and withholding private disclosures. Finally, CPM does

private information
information about things that matter deeply to a person

private disclosures
the process of communicating private information to another

Table 12.2 Principles of CPM

Principle 1:	**Ownership**	People believe they own the information about themselves.
Principle 2:	**Control**	People develop boundaries to control their personal information.
Principle 3:	**Rules**	People share and withhold information based on a system of rules.
Principle 4:	**Co-ownership**	Others become co-owners of people's private information based on rules about linkage, permeability, and ownership.
Principle 5:	**Turbulence**	When the rules are not followed and mistakes are made, turbulence results.

not consider that disclosures are only about the self. Disclosures form a communicative process. As Petronio (2002) observes, "[T]o fully understand the depth and breadth of a disclosure, CPM does not restrict the process to only the self, but extends it to embrace multiple levels of disclosure including self and group (p. 3). She is clear in noting that "disclosure, as a concept, is defined as more dynamic than consigning it to only the self. CPM also recognizes that people can give permission to access their private information without disclosing" (Petronio, 2016, p. 5).

Communication Privacy Management Theory accomplishes this by proposing five, interrelated, principles: private information ownership, private information control, private information rules, private information co-ownership and guardianship, and private information boundary turbulence. We will explain each of these basic principles of the theory in turn. (See Table 12.2.)

Principle 1: Private Information Ownership

The first principle asserts that people believe they "own" information about themselves, and they can manage it however they want. As Sandra Petronio (2010) notes this belief in ownership is a *perception*, and as such, may not always be factual. Petronio points to research such as work she has done with Jeff Child and Judy Pearson (Child, Pearson, & Petronio, 2009), which focused on student bloggers that illustrates this discrepancy. While people claim they have privacy, or complete ownership of their private information, that claim is often contradicted online.

Principle 2: Private Information Control

The second principle of CPM builds on the first. The logic of these two principles is as follows: Because I "own" the private information about me, I can choose how I want to control that information. Thus, Lisa from our chapter-opening story makes the decision to keep her feelings about her roommate's romantic life private; she believes she owns this information and she has the power to decide when to share or withhold it. Petronio (2010) notes that the level of control may range from high to moderate to low. For example,

In an entry for Motherlode, the parenting blog, Jillian Keenan discusses how lucky it was that there was no blogging when she was a rebellious teenager, so her mother wasn't able to write publically about the things she did. When Keenan was 15, and having a heated argument with her mother, she pulled out a knife and said to her mother, "This is how much pain I'm in. What do I have to do to make you understand that?" She goes on to say that she then "dipped the tip of the knife into my skin and cut a very shallow gash on the back of my arm." Now, as an adult, she looks back at that melodramatic action and other mistakes she made growing up and reflects on how she was able to own that information about herself. She isn't so sure that is true of teens today. Keenan acknowledges that parents might need an outlet for their own frustrations and concerns about their children, but she concludes that

it is one thing to broadcast your own pain. It is quite another to broadcast your child's. In this Internet age, children deserve to struggle into adulthood with some degree of privacy. If my mother had publicized that moment when I cut my arm, it could have devastated my future in incalculable ways.

Given the Internet's ubiquity it may become difficult to own your own information.

Source: Keenan, J. (2012). Thanks, Mom, for not telling the world I pulled a knife on you, parenting.blogs.nytimes.com/2012/12/27/thanks-mom-for-not-telling-the-world-i-pulled-a-knife-on-you/?emc=eta1.

if something is a secret that very few people are allowed to hear, the control is high. If Robyn decides to tell only her husband about a diagnosis of breast cancer and withhold the information from the rest of her family and friends, she is keeping high control over the information. If she decides to tell a few more people, her control becomes moderate, and as more people are allowed access to the information, Robyn's control is low.

private boundaries
the demarcation between private information and public information

This principle introduces the concept of **private boundaries.** CPM relies on the boundary metaphor to make the point that there is a line between being public and being private. On one side of the boundary, people keep private information to themselves; on the other side, people reveal some private information to others in social relationship with them. Some research indicates that deciding to disclose private information can be a healthful choice (Joseph & Afifi, 2010); however, it is the discloser's choice. The boundaries around personal information are within people's control to set and change.

Boundaries may be set differently related to a variety of factors, however, some of which are not completely within a person's control. For instance, age may have an influence on how boundaries are established. Children in the United States maintain relatively small privacy boundaries. The boundaries increase as children grow into adolescence and adulthood and cultivate a more developed sense of privacy. As people enter old age, their boundaries begin to shrink. In addition, gender and culture may play

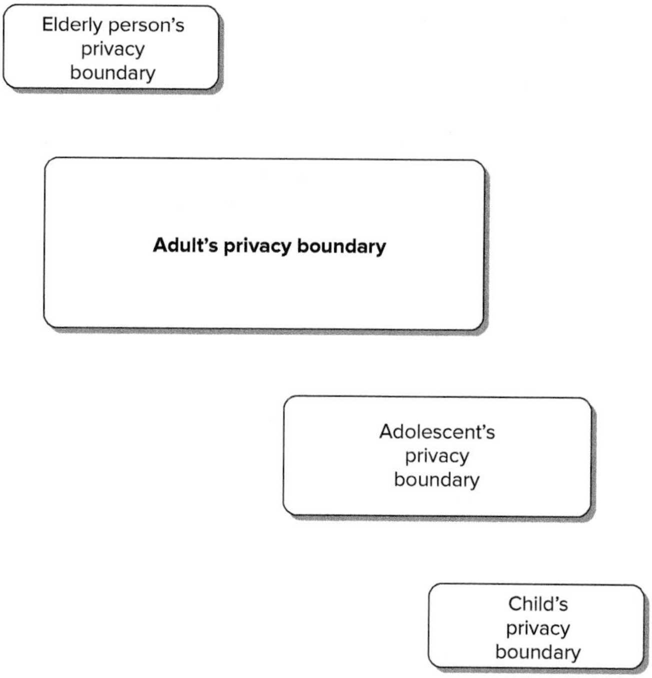

Elderly person's privacy boundary

Adult's privacy boundary

Adolescent's privacy boundary

Child's privacy boundary

Figure 12.1
Boundaries and the Life Span
Boundaries of Privacy: Dialectics of Disclosure by Sandra Petronio, the State University of New York Press, © 2002 State University of New York. All Rights Reserved.

a role in how boundaries are drawn. One study (Cho, Rivera-Sánchez, & Lim, 2009) showed that age, gender, and nationality influenced people's conceptions of privacy online. Older females from individualistic cultures were the most concerned about online privacy and did the most to establish privacy boundaries online.

Principle 3: Private Information Rules

Principle Three relates to the first two. This principle asserts that people make decisions about controlling the private information they own based on rules. Petronio (2013) believes that people are the "sole owners" (p. 9) of the information they possess. Privacy rules are foundational to CPM, so we'll discuss them at some length. First, privacy rules have two main features: development and attributes. **Rule development** is guided by people's decision criteria for revealing or concealing private information. CPM Theory (Petronio, 2013; 2015) states that two criteria are used for developing privacy rules. Two types of criteria are used to determine whether or not to allow another person access to information: core and catalyst. Petronio (2015) defines **core criteria** as those that are "more resilient and often function in the background" (p. 3) and **catalyst criteria** as opportunities when "privacy rules have to be responsive to needed change" (p. 3). Let's briefly look at each.

With respect to core criteria, CPM theorists assert that decisions to reveal or conceal can be dependent on issues such as culture. Think about how culture (e.g., gender, cultural community, sexual identity, etc.) guides an individual's expectations for privacy. Thus we might understand Amanda's desire to be transparent to Lisa in our chapter opening by noting that she is Italian American, a culture that generally values openness of expression.

rule development
one of the features of privacy rule characteristics; describes how rules come to be decided

core criteria
one criterion used to that influences the type of privacy rules people might use to regulate private information; provide guidance for privacy management

catalyst criteria
one criterion used to determine whether to allow another person access to information; account for reasons privacy rules change

Catalyst criteria relate to the reasons why privacy rules may shift or otherwise necessitate change. Petronio (2015) explains that sometimes a person may incorrectly assess the consequence of a privacy rule. She provides the example of divorcing parents. Suppose that the couple decides to reveal information about the divorce to their children, knowing that research is clear that the information may cause stress for the family. The couple—once the two discover that their disclosure is harmful—will likely reconsider any future disclosures. Petronio notes that the motivation to disclose, the risk of the disclosure, the context of the situation, and the relationships involved can all prompt the privacy rule changes that will occur.

The decision criteria help explain the process of rule development, which is one element of privacy rules. The second aspect of privacy rules concerns **privacy rule attributes,** which refer to the ways people acquire rules and the properties of the rules. Generally, the theory suggests that people learn rules through socialization processes or by negotiation with others to create new rules.

privacy rule attributes
one of the features of privacy rules; they refer to the ways people acquire rules and the properties of the rules

For example, Lisa was socialized in her company through informal networks that taught her it was important to spend time nurturing relationships with her co-workers. The organization often invoked the metaphor of a family, hosted many social events for the workers, and tried in several other ways to impress on employees that close relationships were an important part of the organizational culture. When learned rules are inadequate or need modifying, then people collaborate to forge new rules. For instance, if the company determined that its workers were disclosing to one another to the detriment of productivity, they might work to renegotiate the rules.

Principle 4: Private Information Co-ownership and Guardianship

The fourth principle refers to how private information is shared and becomes *co-owned*. When private information is shared, the boundary around it is called a **collective boundary**, and the information is not only about the self; it belongs to the relationship. When private information remains with an individual and is not disclosed, the boundary is called a **personal boundary** (Figure 12.2). When Lisa and her mother talk about Lisa's brother's wife, that information belongs to them as a dyad, and neither one of them reveals it to Margo or Lisa's brother, creating a collective boundary. When Lisa privately holds her opinion of Joel, Amanda's boyfriend, that information has a personal boundary.

An important element of this principle is **boundary coordination**, which refers to how we manage information that is co-owned. For example, when Lisa and her mother talk about Margo, Lisa's sister-in-law, it is clear that the information is to be kept from Margo and Lisa's brother. Boundary coordination is the process through which that decision is made and through which Lisa and her mother become co-owners of private information.

Petronio (2010) notes that co-ownership is regulated through boundary linkage, boundary ownership rights, and boundary permeability. **Boundary linkage** refers to the connections that form boundary alliances between people. For example, when Lisa tells private information to Doug, they are linked in a privacy boundary. Physicians form linkages with their patients because the medical profession stresses patient confidentiality. If you overhear a piece of private information that wasn't intended for you, you are technically linked; however, the linkage is weak because you know you weren't the intended recipient of the information.

collective boundary
a boundary around private information that includes more than one person

personal boundary
a boundary around private information that includes just one person

boundary coordination
one of the processes in the privacy rule management system; describes how we manage private information that is co-owned

boundary linkage
the connections forming boundary alliances between people

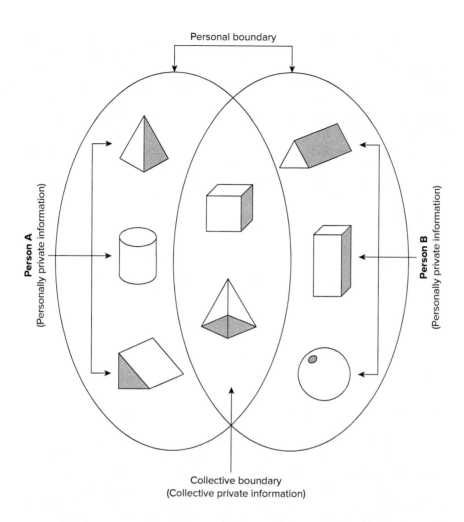

Personal boundary

Person A
(Personally private information)

Person B
(Personally private information)

Collective boundary
(Collective private information)

Figure 12.2
Boundary Types
*Boundaries of
Privacy: Dialectics of
Disclosure by Sandra
Petronio, the State
University of New
York Press, © 2002
State University of
New York. All Rights
Reserved.*

Boundary ownership refers to rights and privileges accruing to co-owners of private information. For boundary ownership to be exercised accurately, the rules need to be clear. For instance, if your friend tells you private information, are you allowed to share it with someone else (Mikucki-Enyart, 2011)? If your friend has told you explicitly not to tell anyone her secret, then the boundary is clear and unambiguous. However, if she just told you the secret without specifying whether you could tell anyone else, you might feel unsure about your co-ownership. You could suspect you aren't supposed to tell, but without instructions you feel uncertain.

Yet boundaries are dynamic and may be redrawn over time. For example, when Rachel Norton was 18, her brother had an accident with the family car. Together, she and her brother had the car repaired and paid for the repairs without telling their parents. Now that they are both adults, they have told their parents about the incident. Thus, the boundary broadened to include the whole family. It may also be the case that co-owners do not agree about boundary issues. Amanda, from our opening story, might think that her tales about Joel, her boyfriend, link Lisa into a boundary that Lisa, herself, would rather not be included in.

boundary ownership
*rights and privileges
accruing to
co-owners of
private information*

boundary permeability
the extent to which information is able to pass through a boundary

thick boundaries
closed boundaries allowing little or no information to pass through

thin boundaries
open boundaries allowing all information to pass through

boundary turbulence
conflicts about boundary expectations and regulation

Finally, boundary coordination is accomplished through **boundary permeability,** which refers to how much information is able to pass through the boundary. When access to private information is closed, boundaries are said to be **thick boundaries;** when access is open, people have **thin boundaries** in place.

Principle 5: Private Information Boundary Turbulence

The fifth principle refers to what happens when the privacy rules break down or people make mistakes in enacting them. **Boundary turbulence** exists when the rules of boundary coordination are unclear or when people's expectations for privacy management come into conflict with one another. Boundary regulation is not always a smooth operating system, and the people involved can experience clashes that Petronio labels turbulence. For example, if Lisa refused to listen to Amanda's problems one evening, they might come into conflict. If you discovered that a friend told another about some private information you had shared and meant for that friend to keep private, boundary turbulence would ensue. CPM Theory asserts that when individuals experience boundary turbulence, they will try to make adjustments so that they can reduce the turbulence and achieve coordination.

Boundary turbulence can occur for a number of different reasons. In some cases, the turbulence results from what Petronio (2010) calls "fuzzy boundaries" by which she means that the boundaries are ambiguous. One partner could claim that he or she didn't know he or she wasn't supposed to reveal information, for instance. Or, the partners could define the information differently. A romantic partner might think one is entitled to know all about the partner's past while the other person may believe that the past is private and doesn't need to be revealed. In any event, turbulence will ensue when "expectations for privacy management are unfulfilled" (Petronio, 2010, p. 182).

Integration, Critique, and Closing

Communication Privacy Management Theory has enjoyed significant attention from scholars in communication as well as from those in other disciplines. The theory appears to resonate because its boundaries and boundary rules guide all sorts of behaviors in all types of relationships. Moreover, researchers have studied the theory

COMMUNICATION PRIVACY MANAGEMENT THEORY

and its various assumptions and concepts using both a quantitative and qualitative lens. As you think about the merits of CPM, three criteria for theory evaluation are relevant: logical consistency, utility, and heurism.

Integration

Communication Tradition	Rhetorical	Semiotic	Phenomenological	Cybernetic	Socio-Psychological	**Socio-Cultural**	Critical
Communication Context	Intrapersonal	**Interpersonal**	Small Group	Organizational	Public/Rhetorical	Mass/Media	Cultural
Approach to Knowing	**Positivistic/Empirical**	**Interpretive/Hermeneutic**	Critical

Critique

Evaluation Criteria	Scope	**Logical Consistency**	Parsimony	**Utility**	Testability	**Heurism**	Test of Time

Logical Consistency

One criticism of the theory that Petronio (2002) has discussed relates to its logical consistency. Some critics have observed that CPM uses the term *dialectic* inaccurately, claiming to be dialectic in nature when it's really based on dualistic thinking. The basis for the criticism stems from Baxter and Montgomery's (1996) distinctions among monologic, dualistic, and dialectic approaches (see Chapter 11). Using these distinctions, Baxter and Montgomery have argued that CPM takes a dualistic approach, treating privacy and disclosure as independent of one another and able to coexist in tandem.

Student Voices
Cleo

One of the biggest issues that this theory made me think about was the health care system. I feel that there is a lot of boundary turbulence going on in that. Also, the whole idea of my ownership of my private information is a big issue with health care. I mean, are they really keeping it private? Also, the theory kind of helps explain why I don't like it when the school calls to tell me something on the phone about my son's health. The phone seems like the wrong way for me to hear that Nathan had a seizure. I know they have to use the phone, but I remember how lonely and impersonal it felt when the school called with that news. It was the first we knew that Nathan had a problem. Now that he's been diagnosed, I keep in contact with the school all the time. I have gotten to know the nursing staff at his school, and it doesn't feel so bad to talk to them now.

Petronio (2002) responds to this criticism by noting that perhaps the accusation of dualistic thinking comes from the use of the terms *balance* and *equilibrium* in the early versions of CPM Theory. Petronio argues that CPM is not focused on balance in the psychological sense. She states: "Instead, [CPM] argues for coordination with others that does not advocate an optimum balance between disclosure and privacy. As an alternative, the theory claims there are shifting forces with a range of privacy and disclosure that people handle by making judgments about the *degrees* of privacy and publicness they wish to experience in any given interaction" (pp. 12–13 [emphasis in original]). Thus, Petronio argues that it is legitimate to call CPM Theory dialectical in nature.

Utility

Communication Privacy Management Theory has much promise of utility. It offers an explanation for the delicate process of coordination disclosing and concealing that people perform continually in their relationships with others. Furthermore, CPM may provide insights as that process of coordination becomes even more complex. CPM is needed to explain those daily intrusions into our lives due to technological advances. As technology moves more and more of what we have considered private information into the public realm, we will need to understand the rule-based management system underlying this trend. As Petronio (2015) aptly notes, "potential applications of communication privacy management continue to grow" (p. 7).

Heurism

Communication Privacy Management Theory demonstrates heurism because it has been utilized as a framework in a variety of situations, including romantic relationships (e.g., Nichols, 2012), military families (Owlett, Richards, Wilson, DeFreese, & Roberts, 2015), academic advising (e.g., Thompson, Petronio, & Braithwaite, 2012), and health care (e.g., Romo, 2012; Petronio & Sargent, 2011).

One promising and exciting area where CPM has been investigated is with blogging and Facebook. Jeff Child (e.g., Child & Petronio, 2011; Child & Starcher, 2016; Child & Westermann, 2013; Child, Petronio, Agyeman-Budu, & Westermann, 2011) has been in the forefront of scholars who have explored notions of privacy and how it relates to online experiences. His research remains critical for those who are interested in the interface of social media platforms and CPM. The heuristic nature of the theory and its evaluation on the other criteria all argue for CPM's success as a theoretical framework for communication questions.

Closing

As we continue to understand the decision to reveal private information to others, Communication Privacy Management Theory will be an important and valuable reference. Our conversations and relationships with others are complex. To this end,

CPM provides us a useful framework as we seek to unravel the many and varied communication practices we undertake in our lives.

Discussion Starters

TECH QUEST: Can CPM Theory explain disclosures and privacy attempts encountered in online interactions? Do you think the concept of privacy and private disclosures is changed in online environments? Is it still a relevant concept when it seems as though we are willingly giving up our privacy in so many ways online? Explain your answer.

1. Apply CPM Theory to Lisa Sanders's case. How might it help Lisa to understand her situation?

2. Within the past 10 years there has been an increase in the number of studies using CPM, which seems to indicate it is standing the test of time. Do you agree that CPM will stand the test of time? Why or why not?

3. What approach to theory building does Petronio take in CPM Theory (laws, rules, systems, or some combination)? Explain your answer.

4. What topics of interest can you use CPM Theory to investigate?

5. Do you agree with Petronio's defense of CPM against the critique that it uses the concept of dialectics but really takes a dualistic approach to privacy management? Explain your reasoning.

6. Explain the concept of control with reference to communication boundaries. What contexts can you think of where control might be an issue? Explain your choices.

7. Provide an example of how boundary turbulence affects communication privacy management processes.

CHAPTER 13

Social Information Processing Theory

*Based on the research of **Joseph Walther***

There are times when less interpersonal or socioemotional communication is beneficial.

—Joseph Walther

Corrina Abrams

Corrina Abrams was bored. She was studying for her midterm in business statistics and needed a break. She felt as though she would freak out if she continued to try any more practice problems. As she got up to get a drink, she thought about going online to check any email from the "betogether.com" website. The site—a dating location—was popular among college students and was often the topic of conversation whenever Corrina and her friends got together. That evening, as Corrina checked her email, she noticed one from another college student who wrote with the subject line "Salut. Je m'ennuie." Corrina Googled the French salutation ("Hello, I'm bored") and immediately responded to him. She was happy to read the email (written in English) from Marcus, a Canadian who, like Corrina, was also a college student. She figured a five-minute break chatting with a guy who was also in college would be pretty cool.

As she sat and chatted with her Canadian email companion, she soon realized that she was discussing some pretty personal information with him. She told him about helping her roommate deal with a recent assault, how she was the first kid in her family to go to college, and how she remained close friends with both of her parents after their divorce. Marcus, in turn, revealed that he was in a technical college because his parents couldn't help him with tuition and that he was paying for school by doing some amateur modeling. For some reason, she liked where the conversation with Marcus was going. He seemed very different from any other person and he never judged her nor did he pry inappropriately.

Over the course of a month, Corrina and Marcus continued to email, instant message, and text each other. They were amazed how much they had in common. They both loved country music and had dozens of country music CDs. They both loved reading *Wired* magazine. The two also talked about each other's family and about the differences between online relationships and those that began in a bar or coffee shop. And, although Corrina was excited to talk, she didn't really want to tell Marcus about her low grades in college and the fact that she was on academic probation. It was too important for her to focus on the positive, especially since she liked the fact that she felt he was similar to her in a lot of ways. After several days of e-chats, Corrina thought that Marcus was simply too good to be true. And Marcus seemed to be quite enamored with her. He figured that because she was a business major, Corrina was smart and would graduate with a job in hand. The credentials of his new online interest impressed him. It was clear that the two had shared quite a bit of information over the week. And, they hadn't even met face to face! Yet.

Eventually, the two "Facebooked" each other, and soon, a few in their Friendship circles began to merge. They posted pictures of themselves ("He really is cute," she admitted; "Wow, she could be in a magazine," he thought). These were only pictures, but the two developed a virtual world that reflected their personalities. The social linkage that started on a whim now turned into a full-blown technological relationship of six weeks.

Still, Corrina couldn't stop wondering whether all of this was simply a fantasy or whether it could develop into something bigger. She knew there was a difference between talking online and seeing someone in person—she and Marcus talked and laughed a lot about that. And she realized she had never even seen anything other than Marcus's face on her computer screen!

After a while, Corrina was seriously thinking of meeting her newfound acquaintance. But, then again, she thought, maybe just continuing the online relationship would fulfill her needs right now—she just wasn't sure. She kept wondering whether it was too good to be true. Had she really found a soul mate nearly 400 miles away in another country? She still couldn't believe that all of this happened simply because she went online during a night of studying!

The development and maintenance of our relationships have, as you have read elsewhere in this book, fascinated researchers for decades. In fact, it's fair to say that one of the most researched areas in the communication field is the evolution of human relationships. The theories in this section of the book, in fact, underscore the complexity and excitement of theories related to relationships. Yet, very few theories have infused and focused on one development of the 21st century that remains pivotal to millions of relationships around the globe: the Internet.

When looking at how relationships developed years ago and how relationships develop today, we need to examine the role of technology. Decades ago, it was customary—even required—that relationships undergo a predictable trajectory. Although some variation existed, the relational journey went something like this: We meet someone in person, we "date" that person socially, we introduce that person to our friends and family, and we marry that person (see Chapter 10 on Social Penetration Theory for more information on predictable relational development). To some of you, this approach may still make sense to you. Yet to others of you, this may sound like a scene out of a 1950s movie! After all, you might ask, what about dating sites and other technologies that are influencing relationships?

The development of online relationships is at the heart of a theory known as Social Information Processing (SIP). The theory, introduced by Joseph Walther (1992, 1993, 2008, 2015) long before other scholars envisioned the enormous influence of the Internet, rests upon the interplay among technology, relationships, and self-presentations. For Walther and other SIP advocates, the possibility of developing and cultivating online relationships is not only probable, it occurs with high degrees of success and relationship satisfaction.

To imagine what SIP suggests, we almost have to suspend our traditional interpretation of what it means to have a "relationship." As you have read in other chapters that focused on relationship development, many interpersonal communication theorists prior to Walther argued that relational life is one that is shaped and sustained by face-to-face (FtF) communication. Walther tweaked this fundamental perspective and determined that the nonverbal cues to which we are

Individuals have the ability to establish online relationships and these relationships are equal to or greater than the intimacy achieved in face-to-face (FtF) relationships. Even without nonverbal cues, through various technologies (e.g., email, texting, etc.), online relationships have the potential to be significant in people's lives. Individuals use the computer-mediated communication environment (CMC) to get to know each other and use this information to form impressions of each other. Because messages travel via one primary channel, it takes longer for relationships to achieve the same level as those that are FtF. In some cases, online relationships may be viewed as more important than FtF relationships.

accustomed in our FtF relationships, although important, were not essential to having an interpersonal relationship. He acknowledges that while both individuals in either FtF or online relationships have the same needs for uncertainty reduction and affinity (see Chapter 8 on Uncertainty Reduction Theory), online interactants "adapt their linguistic and textual behaviors" to how others communicate with them (Walther & Anderson, 1994, p. 65). That means that unlike FtF relationship development, online relationship development, according to Social Information Processing Theory, states that relational participants will engage each other personally through both the words they use and also the frequency of those words.

So, it is not only what Corrina and Marcus reveal about each other that allows their relationship to develop and mature, but also the number of times that they communicate with each other. A difference exists, for instance, if Corrina emails Marcus once a week instead of once a day. And, after six weeks, Walther and others would suggest that this relationship has all the workings of an intimate experience.

Social Information Processing Theory has, at its core, impression management (D'Angelo & Van Der Heide, 2016; Walther, 2015). For our purposes, we define **impression management** as either a strategic or unconscious effort to influence another's perception. Much of the earlier research on impression management focused on FtF communication and the nuances with meeting someone. A person's self-image was viewed as important in relational development. Later applications of impression management were undertaken once online communication began (Ellison, Heino, & Gibbs, 2006). Ellison and her colleagues, for example, found that various self-presentational behaviors exist in online dating environments. They report on three selves: the **actual self** (attributes of an individual), the **ideal self** (attributes an individual ideally possesses), and the **ought self** (attributes an individual should possess). These selves are manifested and are of particular importance in online conversations and relationships, allowing an individual to manage his or her online persona or identity.

Identity management is directly associated with the social information process (Rosenberg & Egbert, 2011). As online participants, we necessarily forego our reliance upon nonverbal cues in our dialogues. Therefore, the linguistic cues we send

impression management
the strategic or unconscious effort to influence

actual self
the attributes a person possesses

ideal self
the attributes a person ideally possesses

ought self
the attributes a person should possess

SOCIAL INFORMATION PROCESSING THEORY

"Well, this is certainly awkward. It seems that we've *both* been a bit imaginative in creating our online profiles."

www.CartoonStock.com

to others will be undertaken with a concern for self-presentation. Walther (2011) contends that we "accrue impressions" of others in our online relationships. He further states that "communicators are motivated to develop interpersonal impressions" (p. 458). Therefore, we can see that impressions are central to SIP and that the theory relies heavily on how individuals are interpreting (the words of) each other online.

Theoretical Turbulence: The Cues Filtered Out

Many of the communication theories (e.g., Social Penetration Theory) we address in this book are rooted in other theoretical perspectives from various fields of study. Yet unlike some theories (e.g., Communication Accommodation Theory), SIP was conceptualized, in part, by addressing the shortcomings of other theories that addressed communication mediums. These theories are termed **cues filtered-out theories** (Culnan & Markus, 1987; Walther & Parks, 2007), meaning that because of a devoid of nonverbal cues, online relational development has little integrity. Walther's research critiqued past methodological and conceptual problems with theoretical thinking. He subsequently worked toward establishing an interpersonal communication theory that more accurately reflected the intersection among communication, online environments, the self, and

cues filtered-out theories
theories that address the lack of nonverbal cues as being detrimental to online relationship development

relationships. Let's briefly discuss two of those theoretical perspectives that influenced Walther's theory: Social Presence Theory and Media Richness Theory. We provide a snapshot of each theoretical lens below.

Social Presence Theory (Short, Williams, & Christie, 1976) relates to the extent that individuals are aware of each other via various communication media, that is, the awareness of individuals during an interaction—their characteristics, qualities, physicalities, and so forth. According to the theory, some mediums have a higher degree of social presence (e.g., video) and others possess lower degrees of social presence (e.g., audio and text-based). High-degree mediums are viewed as opportunistic for relational growth and lower-degree mediums are perceived as being more impersonal and unemotional in nature. Social presence is a "subjective quality," meaning that individuals may not agree on whether or not there is a high or low degree of engagement in an interaction. With respect to online environments, social presence manifests in the manner in which messages are sent and received by others in the mediated environment. To a large extent, according to the theory, a high degree of social presence results in a warmer (and more satisfying) interpersonal experience.

Media Richness Theory (Daft & Lengel, 1986) also functions in the evolution of Social Information Processing Theory. The theory, first explored in the organizational context, suggests that while communicating online, the medium is too narrow to allow for relationship development. To this end, individuals experience uncertainty and equivocality in their communication with others. In the theory, "richness" is evaluated in several ways, including the medium's capacity for immediate feedback, the number of cues and channels used, and the extent to which a message is personalized (Gu, Higa, & Moodie, 2011). Similar to Social Presence Theory, scholars studying Media Richness posit that mediums interpreted as "rich media" help to support both verbal and nonverbal cues. According to the theory, "richest" media are FtF communications, which prompt individuals to communicate faster; rich media are used for more complex conversations and tasks. The "leanest" media are telephones, memos, and letters, which frequently prompt others to avoid communicating in more complex ways.

Walther (2011) believes that while both theories have important theoretical notions, the online world is much more complex than what is inferred by Social Presence and Media Richness. For example, text-based communication between online participants—despite the absence of nonverbal cues—has relational value. To this end, both Social Presence Theory and Media Richness Theory suffer from a limited understanding of relational life online. Walther argues that if interactants communicate enough times and with sufficient breadth and depth, nonverbal communication does not remain paramount in relationship development. His premise is that email, for instance, may prove to be quite valuable to others as it can be sent rapidly with highly personalized words. Consider Corrina from our opening example. She clearly established a foundation with Marcus via email. Other platforms eventually provided more information, but the two relied upon a "lean" medium. In addition, Facebook, despite its showing of a lot of people with a lot of information about one's self, likely provides both college students "rich" personal displays, intimate pictures, and other symbols.

Social Presence Theory
a theory that posits the extent to which people are aware of each other via various communication media

Media Richness Theory
a theory that advances the notion that communication can be classified according to message complexity

Assumptions of Social Information Processing Theory

By now, we hope that you are getting an idea that online relationships have the potential to be expressive, intimate, and in many cases, long term. Social Information Processing researchers like Joseph Walther are intrigued by how identities are managed online and how relationships are able to move from one of superficiality to one of intimacy. To further delineate SIP, we offer the following three assumptions related to the model:

- Computer-Mediated Communication provides unique opportunities to connect with people.
- Online communicators are motivated to form (favorable) impressions of themselves to others.
- Online interpersonal relationships require extended time and more accumulated messages to develop equivalent levels of intimacy seen in FtF interpersonal relationships.

Our first assumption rests on the premise that computer-mediated communication is a unique opportunity to build interpersonal relationships with others. First, although we alluded to it earlier, let's define CMC. Those studying the nexus between human communication and technology embrace **computer-mediated communication**, which is a process in which people perceive, interpret, and exchange information via large networked telecommunications systems. These CMC systems are vast, almost always text based, and include, among others, Instant Messaging and email. CMC has been identified as "an organic setting" (Tong & Walther, 2013, p. 3) and it can be both synchronous and asynchronous. **Synchronous communication** occurs when both sender and receiver are online simultaneously. **Asynchronous communication** exists when time constraints influence the sending and receiving of various messages and responses. Asynchronous messages exist at various times and do not require the concurrent presence of a sender.

The relationship between CMC and relational development is underscored by Walther (2011): "[C]omputer-mediated communication (CMC) systems, in a variety of forms, have become integral to the initiation, development, and maintenance of interpersonal relationships" (p. 443). Consider the various systems to which Social Information Processing scholars subscribe: email, Twitter, Facebook, LinkedIn, texting, blogging, videoconferencing, and others. Now, consider whether or not you have had an interpersonal relationship via any of these formats. Chances are that many or most of you will say that you've built a relationship via these technological venues. You will likely agree with Walther and others who claim that CMC systems provide for relational growth.

Yet some of you may not fully embrace, for instance, this notion of relationship development over the Internet. You may subscribe to the belief that for interpersonal communication and an interpersonal relationship to exist, face-to-face communication must inevitably occur (consider our definition of "interpersonal communication" in Chapter 2). Perhaps you think that although CMC is a legitimate way to cultivate an understanding of another, to establish a relationship requires the parties

computer-mediated communication (CMC)
process in which people perceive, interpret, and exchange information via large networked telecommunications systems

synchronous communication
a process that occurs when both sender and receiver are online simultaneously

asynchronous communication
a process that occurs when both sender and receiver are online at different times, owing to time constraints

I'm sure I'm the only one who disagrees with some parts of this theory. I'm sure it has been researched a lot and I know there's a lot of validity to it. But, I'm having a hard time understanding how we can have more online intimacy than in person. I think if we start believing this stuff, then we will never know that being with someone—face-to-face—is more important than being online. I know that this contradicts the theory, but I don't ever want people to think that we can get really close online and think that's the same as getting close in person. Just doesn't make sense to me.

to actually meet. Perhaps you feel that despite an ongoing interaction, Corrina and Marcus from our chapter-opening story will never develop a "relationship."

Much of Joseph Walther's research (e.g., DeAndrea & Walther, 2011a; Walther, 2011) undercuts this latter perception. He first argues that people will communicate personal information online and in many cases, people will disclose more online than they will in person. In fact, research shows that people will reciprocate high levels of intimate information while online (Kalbfleisch, 2016), a topic we revisit later in the chapter. Further, a study by Walther and Jeong-woo Jang (2012) demonstrates that even participatory websites (e.g., YouTube, TripAdvisor.com, etc.) and their online interactants can "both facilitate and complicate social influence" (p. 2), providing additional evidence that CMC remains opportunistic for online discussions, reactions, and relationships. Think of this claim in this way: As you visit a website, many times you are there for social support, information, or simply to talk, read, and/or listen. Relational life is similar. Many times, "visitors" enter our lives and we end up keeping them around for quite some time. In essence, they become part of our relational fabric. So, consider the serendipity related to Corrina and Marcus. She was not anticipating meeting anyone. Yet CMC provided her the chance to chat with someone and based upon the levels of disclosure and the mutual exchange of personal information, the two are on their way to an interpersonal relationship.

CMC is clearly different than face-to-face communication, but it offers an unparalleled opportunity to meet someone whom you would never meet FtF. Moreover, just as in FtF encounters, relationships established via CMC systems, too, prompt emotions and feelings we find in all relationships, including social support, jealousy, and happiness (Green-Hamann, Eichhorn, & Sherblom, 2011; Utz & Beukeboom, 2011). Finally, since CMC systems are available around the globe, the uniqueness of being able to cultivate online relationships with someone who is, say, 5,000 miles away cannot be ignored.

A second assumption of Social Information Processing Theory was alluded to earlier in the chapter. Online participants are motivated to present themselves in strategic ways. Impression management is essential in online relationships (Walther, 1994) and participants undertake efforts to ensure particular impressions. Individuals like Corrina Abrams, for example, obviously wish to avoid presenting her various "selves" to others in negative ways (recall that Corrina did not want to reveal her poor academic status in college).

Researchers have found that social networking sites (SNS) like Facebook are filled with people who wish to provide a number of different self-presentations to others (Bryant, Marmo, & Ramirez, 2011). Since the more Facebook friends one has, the more attractive the individual is viewed to be (Walther, Van Der Heide, Kim, Westerman, & Tong, 2008), managing one's online impressions is of importance to many users. In terms of romantic relationships, if someone is either single or partnered, a number of options are available to communicators that would communicate their relational image to others: (1) display relationship status (e.g., single, married, divorced, etc.); (2) utilize a picture that displays a partner; (3) provide dialogue about the user's partner; (4) dialogue in chat rooms aimed at a person's relational goals (e.g., marriage, and/or cohabitation, etc.) (Utz & Beukeboom, 2011; Winter, Haferkamp, Stock, & Kramer, 2011).

How others present and manage themselves online remains important on various SNS and on numerous CMC system platforms. Because numerous sites include others monitoring a number of different verbal and nonverbal displays, people deliberately use different behaviors to project a particular online identity (Bullingham & Vasconcelas, 2013). For some, openness is a primary goal; for others, impression management is undertaken in more covert ways. Clearly, if others' opinions make a difference in relational goals, then a person will invest some time on managing and influencing those opinions (Toma & Hancock, 2011).

A third assumption of Social Information Processing Theory states that different rates of information exchange and information accrual affect relationship development. To understand this assumption, let's reflect upon Corrina Abrams and her online relational experiences with Marcus. She relies on several back-and-forth messages with Marcus and also undertook this technological exchange over the course of several weeks. In fact, she begins to really wonder about whether or not Marcus is her "soul mate," an intuition that many people in FtF relationships also consider after numerous interactions.

This third assumption reflects Walther's contention that online relationships have the same capacity to become intimate as those that are established face to face. Recall our earlier discussion of "cues filtered-out" theories, which, as you will remember, render nonverbal cues as nearly absent in CMC platforms and systems. Despite this, a great deal of research has reported that given sufficient time and an accrual of messages, intimacy can be, and usually is, achieved.

Chronemic cues, or those cues related to how people perceive, use, or respond to time, and the accrual of messages are two notions that are interrelated. Walther (2008) states that "when sufficient time elapses so that ample communicative exchanges are made, personal and relational information accrues and CMC is no less effective than face-to-face interaction at developing impressions and managing interpersonal relations" (p. 393). Walther and other Social Information Processing researchers believe that nonverbal cues we see in FtF encounters (e.g., smiling, touching, etc.) are important. Yet online relationships that rely upon text-based or email-based communication—despite the absence of nonverbal cues (except chronemic cues)—can be highly intimate. He posits that "language and writing are held to be highly interchangeable with nonverbal cues" (p. 393).

chronemic cues
cues related to how people perceive, use, or respond to time

Years ago, as we noted previously, relational life (and many interpersonal communication theories) placed a high premium on the value of nonverbal communication. And, today, we continue to do so, as evidenced by the proliferation of research in nonverbal communication (e.g., Matsumoto, Frank, & Hwang, 2013). Yet Walther is suggesting that when we discuss online relationships, we need to suspend the notion that nonverbal cues are mandatory in order for a relationship to exist. His research supports the claim that if messages are delivered over a period of time and these "verbal messages" are adapted and transferred into nonverbal codes, an online relationship can become quite intimate (Walther, 2012).

These claims may be counterintuitive to you and prior to Walther's theory, interpersonal researchers relied extensively on the value of nonverbal communication in relationship development. And, we agree that nonverbal behaviors *are* critical to interpersonal relationships. However, Social Information Processing Theory is suggesting that although the messages are verbal, communicators "adapt" to the restrictions of online medium, look for cues in the messages from others, and modify their language to the extent that the words compensate for the lack of nonverbal cues (Walther, DeAndrea, & Tong, 2010). In addition, Walther contends that although there is no precise comparison, it does generally take (at least) four times longer to exchange as much information via CMC as it does to do so face to face (even when communicating in "real time"). Further, these messages "build up" over time and provide online participants sufficient information from which to begin and develop interpersonal relationships. All of the aforementioned allows for a relationship that is of high intimate value.

With these fundamental assumptions of Social Information Processing Theory identified, we now turn our attention to a few central features and concepts related to the theory. As you reflect on this theory and read the following, keep in mind that the theory had its beginnings in the early 1990s. To some researchers at the time, Walther's theory was considered to be both provocative and pioneering because he was the first communication theorist to discover that online relationships can be just as valuable and satisfying as those established FtF. Let's dig further into the theory by discussing two areas of the theory that have gained quite a bit of attention. First, we discuss the hyperpersonal perspective and next we address a principle that Walther has termed *warranting*.

Student Voices

Joey

I love how Walther says that we focus too much on the nonverbal when we meet up with someone. Myself: I went to a dating website and he and I spent time texting, talking on the phone, and emailing a lot before we even met. We did Skype a few times and that was the point where we both liked the "authentic" face of the other person. I know years ago, people didn't have the benefit of talking without seeing the other person. No, it may help to show that physical-ness should not take priority over the words someone is saying.

Hyperpersonal Perspective: "I Like What I Read and I Want More"

As Walther conceptualized and clarified Social Information Processing Theory, he was struck by how vivid and poignant the online communication was between interactants. He conducted research that showed, among other things, that communication between online participants was viewed as more powerful than those undertaken face to face. Walther (1996, 2011) argues that the impressions we cultivate via CMC systems and those relationships we develop and maintain "exceed the desirability and intimacy that occur in parallel off-line interactions" (2011, p. 460). Individuals online can take their time thinking about responses and can choose to do it in a synchronous manner (e.g., Instant Messaging) or without the online partner around (asynchronous). Senders and receivers have the opportunity to "think before they speak." All of this, Walther advances, tends to lead to friendlier online relational environments. He terms this the **hyperpersonal perspective** (Walther has also called this the *hyperpersonal effect* (Walther, 1996) and *hyperpersonal model* (2011)).

> **hyperpersonal perspective**
> an extension of Social Information Processing Theory that suggests people are able to develop more intimate relationships than those that are FtF

Walther's approach to understanding CMC relationships was a result of consulting and researching theories from a variety of fields, a belief we discussed previously. After investigating Social Information Processing Theory and its various trajectories, Walther (1996) discovered that despite the prevailing views of some regarding the limitation of online relationships, individuals actually took advantage of CMC and strategically positioned themselves to others in very favorable ways, in ways that a FtF context cannot. Walther believes that online participant/users "exploit" the technological aspects of the medium to manage their impressions and to help their relationships. Consequently, those relationships we establish online are often more intimate than those we establish FtF.

The hyperpersonal perspective takes all of this into consideration and much more. This perspective entails a number of different areas related to CMC and interpersonal relationships, including message tone, message complexity, personal language, editing behaviors, composing time, among others (Walther, 2007). In other words, online communicators can be selective in how they present themselves and how they respond to another individual and an inordinary depth of intimacy can take place within online relationships.

The hyperpersonal perspective is more than saying that an online relationship is intimate. Walther, in a number of different scholarly venues, articulated its complexity and for our purposes here, we elucidate the four components he studied: (1) senders, (2) receivers, (3) channel, and (4) feedback. These four, you may recall, constitute many of the models of communication we explained in Chapter 1. For now, though, let's discuss each so that you can better understand this intriguing extension of Social Information Processing Theory.

Sender: Selective Self-Presentation

According to Walther (1996; Walther & Tong, 2015), senders have the ability to present themselves in highly strategic and highly positive ways. This self-presentation is controlled and it serves as a foundation for how CMC users get to know one another. The fundamental underpinning of this component of the hyperpersonal perspective is affinity seeking. That is, senders provide information online that prompts affinity in others. Walther (1996), for instance, playfully states that when we send online messages to another, we don't need to hold in our waist and we can nod, smile, or feign interest without others knowing. Senders, then, may provide personal disclosures that represent an "idealized self." They may do more than self-disclose. Walther states that a sender's word choices and expressions of affinity ("You sound so cool") as well as the extent to which a sender agrees with a receiver are all part of a hyperpersonal experience.

Think of our earlier story of Corrina Abrams. It is clear that to impress Marcus, she is presenting herself in very positive ways. Think of the different feelings she engenders: She told Marcus that she helped her roommate after an assault ("compassion"), how she is the first child in her family to attend college ("tenacity"), and that she is good friends with both of her parents following their divorce ("nonjudgmental"). As a sender, Corrina is communicating to Marcus an image that is overwhelmingly positive. She is transmitting preferable cues (Walther, 1992) to Marcus and is certainly managing her online image in a way that casts her as an other-centered and thoughtful person. Her social currency is apparently accelerated because she chose to emphasize more flattering examples about herself. In other words, she used CMC to edit her disclosive messages, making her more desirable in Marcus's eyes. In the end, she is engaging in preferential actions to elicit preferential *re*actions.

Receiver: Idealization of the Sender

At the core of this component in the hyperpersonal perspective is attribution. **Attributions** are those evaluations and judgments we make based on the actions or behaviors of others. It's a concept that is perceptual in nature; we perceive others and come up with some conclusions based upon what we perceive. Walther (2011) believes that receivers tend to "fill in the blanks" on perceptions that are either incomplete or missing altogether; we make attributions of another's behavior (e.g., the sender). Think of his claim this way: We already know that a sender is providing favorable information to a receiver online. Now, consider the fact that because a receiver is not privy to all the "typical" cues we find in FtF conversations, the receiver tends to attribute and, according to the theory, the receiver may "overattribute." A receiver, for instance, is likely to think that a sender has more similarities than differences. A receiver may tend to compare the sender to someone else he or she knows, employing some sort of "perceptual personality" framework ("You sound like my cousin Barry. He's my favorite relative"). Finally, a receiver may experience an overreliance on the minimal cues available online and forget that the relationship he or she has with a sender is based on words—the misspellings, typographical errors, use of punctuation, and so forth (Lea & Spears, 1992; Walther, 1996).

In terms of Corrina and Marcus, as a receiver, Marcus overattributed Corrina's credentials. He perceived her major in business as indicative of her intellectual prowess. We know that impression is incorrect. Further, he assumed she would have a job before graduation, a debatable point again, given that Corrina was struggling academically and may even be on academic probation. This is not to suggest that the two will not or do not have an authentic relationship. Rather, the two are engaging in hyperpersonal behaviors that may render the relationship less profound than the two of them perceive it to be.

attributions
evaluations and judgments we make based on the actions or behaviors of others

Channel Management

Earlier in the chapter, we talked about synchronous and asynchronous communication. You may recall that when both sender and receiver are online simultaneously, we have synchronous experiences. When either the sender or receiver sends a message without the presence of the other, we have *asynchronous experiences.*

CMC does not require both sender and receiver to be online at the same time. In fact, the asynchronous nature of CMC allows online participants to reflect upon, edit, and review their comments before hitting the "Send" button. Think about the times, for instance, where you were speaking with someone face to face in the earlier stages of meeting. While exchanging information with one another, you don't have a lot of time to think about what you say and at times, your anxiety may even prompt you to blurt out something inappropriate.

Now consider the previous example as one undertaken online. Upon meeting someone, you have the opportunity to think about texts or emails before sending them. Further, prior to sending messages, you can rewrite them for clarity, sense, and relevancy. With some CMC systems, you can even "retract" emails before they reach the receiver. Online asynchronous experiences allow for "optimal and desirable" communication. Senders and receivers pay little attention to the physical cues, as we learned earlier, and so the energies and "cognitive resources" (Walther, 2011, p. 461) are placed into ensuring that the messages are of high quality. Walther contends that the more relational the affection or more desirable the other communicator is, the more editing in message composition.

Feedback

The fourth component embedded in a hyperpersonal perspective is feedback. You may remember from Chapter 1 that feedback is essentially those words or behaviors that are communicated to us in an interaction. Feedback's relationship to CMC and the hyperpersonal approach is a bit more complicated. In this case, Walther interprets **feedback** as behavioral confirmation, which is a "reciprocal influence that partners exert" (Walther, 1996, p. 27). In communication theory, we refer to this as self-fulfilling prophecy, a term we introduced in our discussion of Symbolic Interactionism (Chapter 4). This prophecy essentially is a tendency for an individual's expectation of a target person to evoke a response from that person which, in turn, reaffirms the original prediction. So, if Corrina believes that based on his emails and text, Marcus is a trusting person, she will treat him as such and he, in return, will be trusting, reaffirming her original supposition.

Walther's (2011) hyperpersonal perspective acknowledges a feedback system this way: "When a receiver gets a selectively self-presented message and idealizes its source, that individual may respond in a way that reciprocates and reinforces the partially modified personae, reproducing, enhancing, and potentially exaggerating them" (p. 463). Because cues in an online environment are limited, the feedback that does occur is often exaggerated or magnified. A sender and receiver have "heightened expectations and idealized impressions" (Ramirez & Wang, 2008, p. 34).

The four components—sender, receiver, channel, and feedback—suggest that the hyperpersonal perspective is a process—that is, it's ongoing and dynamic. As you consider Walther's theoretical extension, keep in mind that online communication is a complex process. Walther (2008) concludes that SIP is a "process" theory because

feedback
the behavioral confirmation behaviors of senders and receivers

both information and interpersonal meaning is accumulated over time, providing on-line partners an opportunity to establish a relationship. The dynamics of being online, with individuals with whom we're establishing relationships, are often unpredictable. For instance, Stephanie Tom Tong and Walther (2012) discovered that perceptual *dis*confirmation can exist. And, recall that time is of importance here (Ramirez & Wang, 2008). That is, a hyperpersonal experience is not one that occurs immediately for everyone. Corrina and Marcus, for example, communicate over several weeks and their hyperpersonal relationship may be quite different from, say, another couple, which may require additional time for intimacy to be achieved. We now turn our focus to a second feature of SIP that has attracted some scholarly attention: warranting.

Warranting: Gaining Confidence Online

As we discussed the self-presentation of online participants, you may have consid-ered the fact that individuals may simply present themselves in less than truthful ways. In fact, it is possible for people to assert online identities and believe that others will simply subscribe to everything that is written or posted. What happens if the partners decide to initiate a FtF meeting? Will the self-presentations be deemed truthful? Will the impressions be accurate?

To ameliorate distorted and deceptive online presentations, Joseph Walther and his colleague Malcolm Parks (2002) articulated the need for "warranting" behavior by communicators. In the online universe, **warranting** is defined as "the perceived legitimacy and validity of information about another person that one may receive or observe online" (Walther, 2011, p. 466). Walther argues that online relationship development—like those that are FtF—can fall prey to misleading or manipulative overtures. To this end, in order for CMC users to feel more confident about online assertions, a warranting "value of information" will frequently take place that allows for more truthfulness and accuracy in presentations. Many online partners ensure that warranting exists in order to reduce uncertainty, to engender more confidence about the veracity of comments and self-presentations, and ultimately, to grow their relationship. Warranting usually takes the form of a sender connecting the receiver with the sender's off-line network. Further, warranting varies in terms of accept-ability and integrity. Personal webpages, for instance, will have less warranting value than, say, one that has been officiated by a third party. Or, a photo included by a CMC user will have less warranting value than a photo found in an official media outlet.

Walther and his research team (2009) assert that efforts at corroborating information and visual cues will enhance the online relationship efficacy between people. In a study that included mock-up Facebook postings, the researchers found that self-proclaimed physical attractiveness by a Facebook user was found to be more believable when others confirmed the claim. What this suggests is that "one's own claims of attractiveness on Facebook are suspect" (p. 248), but when others can cor-roborate those claims, this self-presentation contains more credibility.

A central point of Social Information Processing Theory pertains to the self-presentation of information. This online impression management is opportunistic for dishonesty. According to Walther, CMC users will frequently try to ensure the accuracy of their profiles, photos, images, and words they convey. Individuals like Corrina and

warranting
the perceived legitimacy and validity of information about another person that one may receive or observe online

T*I*P

Theory-Into-Practice
Social Information Processing Theory

Theoretical Claim: Warranting allows an individual to validate the legitimacy of a person's identity via online/social media.

Practical Implication: Desiree and Jazz just met online a few weeks ago. She told her new boyfriend that she is a homebody and doesn't like to go out a lot. But, Jazz "saw" an entirely different Desiree as he looked at her past pictures boozing it up on her Instagram account. Thus, Jazz's perception of Desiree's credibility is now vastly different than when they first started chatting.

Marcus may one day meet if they continue to have a satisfying online relationship. Right now, neither may be skeptical, but if they each continue to reveal more information about one another, both may want verification of that information. And, it's likely that both will desire to know what the other looks like—in person. So, If both Corrina and Marcus now take steps to provide information that has high warranting value, it's probable that this technological relational experience will one day become a real-world experience.

Integration, Critique, and Closing

Throughout this book, we have attempted to give you theories that are both rooted in other fields of study and theories that have their infancy in the communication discipline. Social Information Processing Theory is an attempt to bridge the two. While Walther clearly identified other theoretical frameworks in the conceptualization of SIP, his theory, nonetheless, centers on communication and human relationships. Further, the theory clearly has evolved from quantitative investigation, making it positivistic in nature. With his infusion of CMC, the theory is a unique and important development in communication theory. To evaluate the theory, we examine three areas: scope, utility, and testability.

Integration

Communication Tradition	Rhetorical | Semiotic | Phenomenological | Cybernetic | **Socio-Psychological** | Socio-Cultural | Critical
Communication Context	Intrapersonal | **Interpersonal** | Small Group | Organizational | Public/Rhetorical | Mass/Media | Cultural
Approach to Knowing	**Positivistic/Empirical** | Interpretive/Hermeneutic | Critical

Critique

Evaluation Criteria	**Scope** | Logical Consistency | Parsimony | **Utility** | **Testability** | Heurism | Test of Time

Scope

Any theory dealing with computer-mediated communication will inevitably be criticized for its expansiveness and lack of nuance. Yet although Walther's theory addresses relationship development, his theoretical thinking over the years has silenced many critics who argue that it suffers from a lack of refinement. Walther spent several years ensuring that the "cumbersome" area known as CMC does not result in research that is too broad. Some original research (e.g., Tidwell & Walther, 1995) began by examining CMC relationships over time. And, it became clear that since that time, Walther's theory has evolved to scholarly levels that reflect more specificity (e.g., warranting perspective) and that address different types of online communicators. Therefore, the theory does not suffer from too much breadth. Rather, SIP has moved from a generalized thinking of online relationships to more specific discussions, including those that relate to chronemics, such as physical attraction, among other areas that have captured much research attention over the years.

Student Voices

Mira

Finally, finally! Someone in the communication field researches what I experience all the time. I know I'm a nontraditional age student in this class, but that has given me more experiences than the others. One of those experiences relates to online self-disclosure. This theory is very useful for me to think about. SIP says that people like me disclose more online than in person. I agree. And, sometimes it led to way too much intimacy way too quickly. I hope that as the theory progresses, we will see research talk about moving too fast and what happens to the online relationship. But, for now, I'm just glad I read about a theory that makes a difference in my life!

Utility

As SIP was discussed above, we're confident that many of you were shaking your heads in agreement with what Walther argues. In other words, the usefulness of the theory became apparent to you. Perhaps Walther (2011) best summarizes the usefulness of his theory: "Newer theories have also arisen, some barely tested, the ultimate utility of which remains to be seen" (p. 444). Further, given that texting occupies the most common cell phone activity and on average, over six billion text messages are sent each day in the United States (https://teckst.com/19-text-messaging-stats-that-will-blow-your-mind), Walther and his colleagues (Walther, Van Der Heide, Ramirez, Burgoon, & Pena, 2015) believe that SIP's utility will continue. So, perhaps the relative newness of the SIP theory (recall that many theories we're studying in this book have been around for years) provides pause to some of you as you consider its practicality. Yet when considering the various themes, issues, and concepts related to Walther's theory (e.g., affinity, nonverbal cues, impression management, etc.), few would argue with the usefulness and pragmatic value of studying these areas within online environments.

Testability

One area of SIP that has received some criticism relates to its testability. Interestingly, Walther has been a self-reflective critic of his own theory. First, he acknowledged that SIP did not fully clarify the role of the issue of time in CMC relationships (Walther, 2011), an issue we discussed earlier in the chapter.

Later writing by Walther (2015), however, suggested that time in CMC, messages take longer to process than those conveyed face-to-face. In particular, he believes that understanding online relational messages requires an individual to gather enough information so that he or she can draw conclusions about the person. There may be even more of a need to consider time when different online users are using different online platforms. Thus, while the original incarnation of the theory did not sufficiently investigate time, the current SIP thinking shows that time does, indeed, influence CMC.

Second, in discussing the hyperpersonal perspective, Walther admits that not all of the theoretical components of his hyperpersonal approach have been researched sufficiently. He and his research colleagues (2011) relate that "despite its importance, feedback has received the least direct attention in research on the hyperpersonal model of CMC" (p. 5). Thus, although feedback has been studied since this claim, in the development of the hyperpersonal model, a major portion of the model had received intermittent attention.

In addition, some writers have looked at the receiver's behavior in the hyperpersonal perspective. Specifically, Jiang, Bazarova, and Hancock (2011) assert that the receiver's perceptions help contribute to online intimacy. Yet the researchers conclude that the "receiver component has never been isolated from the sender's effect" (p. 61). In other words, although the hyperpersonal approach states that the sender and receiver are both unique and interrelated, researchers have not tested whether there is a particular receiver behavior that leads to greater online intimacy. Although Jiang and her colleagues found that online intimacy is a result of a sender's self-disclosure *as well as* a receiver's perceptions of the disclosure, they were among the first to provide this causal link. Walther (2015) later notes that researchers have established that self-disclosure is more frequent in CMC encounters than face-to-face encounters because CMC users "must employ 'interactive' strategies' [including] asking personal questions in order to prompt a partner's self-disclosure" (p. 9). In other words, the more information that is actively solicited will result in more self-disclosure taking place. Such a conclusion provides for a testable area related to the hyperpersonal perspective.

Third, in examining the warranting hypothesis, Walther, Brandon Van Der Heide, Lauren Hamel, and Hillary Shulman (2009) accept the fact that high warranting value may exist on those matters that have strong social desirability. For instance, physical attractiveness is a highly desirable trait in the United States, making it socially desirable. So, as Walther accepts, online communicators would seek corroboration for those qualities that society deems important (or desirable). Whether or not other less socially desirable qualities are prone to warranting overtures is not fully explained. Testing these traits, then, may require alternative processes.

Social Information Processing Theory arrived in the communication discipline at the time that the rest of the research world was starting to examine the Internet for its possible influence on interpersonal communication and human relationships. As we alluded to earlier, Joseph Walther is somewhat of a scholarly prophet, forecasting the importance of looking at online relationships in the early 1990s.

SOCIAL INFORMATION PROCESSING THEORY

Closing

We're sure that as you reviewed Walther's comparisons between CMC and FtF relationships, many of you were wondering whether or not we will continue to be engaged in CMC with little chance of face-to-face meetings. This will likely never be the case. Yet we cannot ignore the fact that Walther's theory remains a pivotal framework to consider as we envision future relationship development in an uncertainty technological time.

Discussion Starters

TECH QUEST: Social media is frequently the sort of text-based communication that SIP theorists discuss. Yet there are various types of social media. Differentiate between and among at least three types and how relationship development might differ in each.

1. Corrina and Marcus have begun to establish their relationship online after just a few conversations. Do you believe that their experiences reflect what others experience when going online in the same manner as Corrina? Do any demographic issues (e.g., age, biological sex, cultural background) make a difference in online relationship development?

2. Think of other situations in which a "cues filtered-out" approach exists. Use examples in your response.

3. Compare and contrast the coming together of a relationship online and one that is FtF.

4. Envision that you are a social media expert who is embarking upon an online relationship with someone who is not tech-savvy. Discuss the similarities and differences in this online relationship development.

5. React, with examples, to the concerns and cautions expressed by Delia (in the Student Voices box). Do you believe her views are appropriate? Why or why not?

6. Walther's followers are beginning to examine what happens when online communicators meet for the first time. What experiences have you had (or have you heard about) related to meeting in this manner?

7. Provide an example for each component of the hyperpersonal perspective and determine whether or not the approach merits modification.

Groups, Teams, and Organizations

THE UNITED STATES IS A SOCIETY THAT RELIES ON groups, teams, and organizations in order to function. Small group, team, and organizational communication have a rich history a rich tradition in communication studies. A number of important theoretical developments have occurred in the field, all of which have lasting importance for individuals in the United States and around the world. One reason we have seen such attention in this area is that most of us will work for a company or corporation at some point in our lives. In addition, global, political, social, and economic changes have prompted groups and organizations to look at their missions and purposes across the globe.

Companies and organizations continue to undergo significant changes in the 21st century. These changes are a result of corporate scandals, the need to work together in more culturally diverse work environments, the increased accountability needed in business and industry, and the fact that very few jobs these days can be accomplished at work without the help of others.

The four theories we present in this section consider the influence that changing times have on groups and organizations. Each theory looks at the role of a group member or employee in various ways as well as the influence that individuals and their behaviors have on a particular organization. For instance, Groupthink views group members as capable of being so connected that they fail to question the group's goals or tasks. Structuration Theory sees individuals and teams as being both constrained and encouraged by the structure of an organization. Organizational Culture Theory is aimed at understanding how people, processes, and products function in organizational life. Finally, how employees try to reduce ambiguity in their corporate life is the primary emphasis of Organizational Information Theory.

These theories view groups and organizational members as being both active and passive. Group and organizational life is precisely like that. At times we are consumed with getting the task accomplished and may be unaware of our eagerness to get things done. We actively work toward clarity and toward becoming part of a company. At other times, though, we may simply allow others to engage. The theories in this section help us understand a number of interesting and valuable areas, including decision making, social influence, rules, corporate climate, and employee relationships.

CHAPTER 14

Groupthink

*Based on the research of **Irving Janis***

> *Groups, like individuals, have shortcomings. Groups can bring out the worst as well as the best.*
>
> —Irving Janis

Melton Publishing Board of Directors

As they sat in the seminar room at Melton Publishing, the seven men and women privately wondered when they would discover their next superstar author. Last week the board heard the bad news: Their profits were down significantly, and they needed a best seller to counter some of the company's financial loss. The company worked hard on establishing an e-book unit, but it has struggled against the megapresses. Elizabeth Hansen, the board's director, suggested that the group review at least two books they thought could reverse the company's losses. From early reviews of one of the books—*Red Warnings,* a science-fiction novel—Hansen believed that here was an opportunity to turn around the downward spiral and give the small press a promising future. She knew that employee and board morale was down and felt that something had to be done quickly.

As director for the past few years, Elizabeth knew that, in a way, her own credibility was on the line. She was chairing a board of literary people who, for the most part, had no life experience sitting on for-profit boards. And, she knew that the similarity among the members would likely result in them agreeing to a quick and reasonable solution to the company's financial circumstances. Although no clear solution was obvious at this difficult time for the

company, Elizabeth was sure something had to be done.

Instead of Skyping, the group gathered together to talk about finances. Elizabeth opened the discussion with an upbeat message: "We'll beat this downward spiral," she said. She reminded the group that the 14-year-old company had a history of surviving rough times. "This is just another bump in the road," she reported.

The discussion soon turned to the book *Red Warnings*, which had been reviewed favorably in a national book magazine. Since the review's publication, orders for the book had skyrocketed. Elizabeth thought that the best way to generate more money for the small company, thereby resulting in more publicity, was to market *Red Warnings* aggressively: through the media, on college campuses, at science-fiction conventions across the country, and, hopefully, with a national book club selection. The book could bring in hundreds of thousands of dollars in profits, but Elizabeth knew that this would require tireless marketing. Melton Publishing is small, she thought, but not too small to promote a best seller. Social media will help, she believed to "spread the message."

Randy Miles, another board member, disagreed with Elizabeth's plans. He thought that there was simply too much risk in concentrating so much time and money on one book. Randy's way to improve the financial situation of the company could be summed up in one word: cutbacks.

After looking over the company's financial records of the past few years, he had discovered that far too many people had been hired, resulting in overspending on salary, benefits, and book production. He knew that cutting back was not a popular strategy but reasoned that this wasn't the time for worrying about being popular.

Their meeting dragged on from an anticipated two hours to approaching five hours. Elizabeth and Randy continued to explain and defend their viewpoints. At times there was heated arguing; the two would frequently raise their voices to make their points. During their arguments, the remaining board members would try to be agreeable. They knew they weren't all that knowledgeable about how to turn a company around, and, for the most part, they sat silently while the two leaders squared off against each other.

Finally, as the afternoon sun began to set, Tina, a writer from the Boston area, said, "Look, we've all been very patient while the two of you decide what's best for this company. And maybe we've learned for the future that we need to get more financial expertise on this board. But, for now, I have to speak. We need to make a decision. A hard decision. Whether a decision can even be made today is iffy. I recommend that we postpone any more talk until our next meeting so that we can all think about our options."

Randy interrupted, "Look, Tina, I appreciate your honesty, but this is not about whether we should build another bathroom! This is the company's future. I recommend that we hash this out now."

Elizabeth agreed, as did the other board members. It occurred to Tina that their "lunch meeting" was turning into a "working dinner." As evening came, it was clear that Elizabeth and Randy were getting tired. "Listen, Randy, we're running low on energy and time. I think we should just get the two motions out and have the board vote." The other members agreed; it was obvious that they were all tired.

Randy reminded the group that they shouldn't rush their decision, but Tina reminded him that he was the one who hadn't wanted to postpone a decision. Although Randy tried to attack Tina's tone, the other group members began clamoring for a vote. Each member openly expressed support for Elizabeth's aggressive marketing plan. Because the group was small and he could sense the overwhelming support for Elizabeth, Randy decided to give in. He left the meeting feeling that he had been silenced by the group at the end of their discussion.

P articipating in groups is a fact of life. Whether people are at school, work, a volunteer agency, a spirituality meeting, or other venue, they frequently spend significant working hours in groups. As Cass Sunstein and Reid Hastie (2015) state, "since the beginning of human history, people have made decisions in groups" (p. 3). To understand the nature of decision making in small groups, Irving Janis, in his book *Victims of Groupthink* (1972), explains what takes place in groups where group members are highly agreeable with one another. The original work in Groupthink focused on foreign-policy decision making, although the theory has subsequently been applied to myriad other areas. Janis contends that when group members share a common fate, there is great pressure toward conformity. He labels this pressure *Groupthink*, a term cleverly patterned after vocabulary found in George Orwell's *1984* (e.g., *doublethink*). We should point out that the word *Groupthink* was coined in 1952 by business author and editor William Whyte in *Fortune* magazine. About two decades later, Janis provided the communication context of this term and group experience.

groupthink
a way of group deliberation that minimizes conflict and emphasizes the need for unanimity

Groupthink is defined as a way of deliberating that group members use when their desire for unanimity overrides their motivation to assess all available plans of action. Janis contends group members frequently engage in a style of deliberating

Highly cohesive groups frequently fail to consider alternatives to their course of action. When group members think similarly and do not entertain contrary views, they are also unlikely to share unpopular or dissimilar ideas with others. Groupthink suggests that these groups make premature decisions, some of which have lasting and tragic consequences.

in which consensus seeking (need for everyone to agree) outweighs good sense. You may have participated in groups where the desire to achieve a goal or task was more important than developing reasonable solutions to problems. Janis believes that when highly similar and agreeable groups fail to consider fully any dissenting opinions, when they suppress conflict just so they get along, or when the group members do not consider all solutions, they are prone to groupthink. He argues that when groups are "in" groupthink, they immediately engage in a mentality to "preserve group harmony" (Janis, 1989, p. 60). To this end, making peace is more important than making clear and appropriate decisions.

Our example of the board of directors at Melton Publishing exemplifies the groupthink phenomenon. The board members are a group of people who apparently get along. The members are essentially connected by their literary backgrounds, making them more predisposed to groupthink. The group is under a deadline to come up with a thoughtful and financially prudent decision about the financial future of the company, especially during an era of e-book dominance. As the chapter unfolds, we will tell you more about how this group becomes susceptible to groupthink.

Before we identify the assumptions guiding the theory, we first need to point out that Janis looked at "decisions of historical decisions made by elite groups" (Fisher, 2012, p. 70). In Janis's earlier writings, his focus on foreign policy resulted in looking at "the inner circle" of those in charge, namely the U.S. President. Using principles from small group research, Janis (1982) explains why several foreign-policy decisions are flawed.

In the development of Groupthink, Janis analyzed five matters of significant national importance: (1) the preparedness policies of the U.S. Navy at Pearl Harbor in 1941, (2) the decision to pursue the North Korean Army onto its own territory by President Eisenhower, (3) the decision by President Kennedy to invade Cuba at the Bay of Pigs shortly after Fidel Castro established a Communist government, (4) the decision to continue the Vietnam War by President Johnson, and (5) the Watergate cover-up by President Nixon. Janis argues that each of these policy decisions was made by both the president and his team of advisors and that, because each group was under some degree of stress, they made hasty and what amounted to inaccurate decisions. He interviewed a number of people who were part of these teams and concluded that each of these policy fiascoes occurred because of groupthink. It was discovered that in each of these cases, the presidential advisors did not thoroughly test information before making their decisions.

In other words, there was mutual agreement to avoid critical conversations and conflict (Carlson, 2016). According to Janis, the group members failed to consider forewarnings, and their biases and desire for harmony overshadowed critical assessments of their own decisions.

Usually, the decision-making process underscoring Groupthink is historical. Randy Hirokawa, Dennis Gouran, and Amy Martz (1988), for instance, came to the conclusion that faulty decision making characterized the disaster of the space shuttle *Challenger*. Furthermore, John Schwartz and Matthew Wald (2003) comment that Groupthink principles were at work when the *Columbia*, another shuttle, broke up. A "quick analysis" by aviation giant Boeing and their engineers showed that "smart people working collectively can be dumber than the sum of their brains" (p. 4). [We will address the application of Groupthink principles in more depth later in the chapter.] In sum, then, groupthink is often present because those in positions of authority or decision-making power surround themselves with those who are willing to "go along to get along." Dan Sanker (2012) puts it this way: "[Groupthink] is a phenomenon that is responsible for otherwise intelligent and knowledgeable people making disastrous decisions" (p. 85). And, while most of the research related to groupthink has, indeed, focused on major policy-oriented decisions, you will later understand that the theory's concepts have been applied to other types of decisions.

Assumptions of Groupthink

At its core, Groupthink is a theory associated with small group communication. In Chapter 2 we noted that small groups are a part of virtually every segment of U.S. society. Janis focuses his work on **problem-solving groups** and **task-oriented groups,** whose main purpose is to make decisions and give policy recommendations. Decision making is a necessary part of these small groups. Other activities of small groups include information sharing, socializing, relating to people and groups external to the group, educating new members, defining roles, and telling stories (Galanes & Adams, 2013; Rothwell, 2016). With that in mind, let's examine three critical assumptions that guide the theory:

- Conditions in groups promote high cohesiveness.
- Group problem solving is primarily a unified process.
- Groups and group decision making are frequently complex.

The first assumption of Groupthink pertains to a characteristic of group life: cohesiveness. Conditions exist in groups that promote high cohesiveness. Ernest Bormann (1996) observes that group members frequently have a common sentiment or emotional investment, and, as a result, they tend to maintain a group identity. This collective thinking usually guarantees that a group will be agreeable and perhaps highly cohesive.

What is cohesiveness? You probably have heard of groups sticking together or having a high *esprit de corps*. This phrase essentially means that the group is cohesive. **Cohesiveness** is defined as the extent to which group members are willing to work together. It is a group's sense of togetherness. Cohesion arises from a

problem-solving groups
sets of individuals whose main task is to make decisions and provide policy recommendations

task-oriented groups
sets of individuals whose main goal is to work toward completing jobs assigned to them

cohesiveness
a cultural value that places emphasis on the group over the individual

group's attitudes, values, and patterns of behavior; those members who are highly attracted to other members' attitudes, values, and behaviors are more likely to be called *cohesive.*

Cohesion is the glue that keeps a group intact. You may have been a member of a cohesive group, although it can be difficult to measure cohesiveness. For instance, is a group cohesive if all members attend all meetings? If all members communicate at each meeting? If everyone seems amiable and supportive? If group members usually use the word *we* instead of the word *I*? All of these? You know if you have been in a cohesive group, but you may not be able to tell others precisely why the group is cohesive.

Our second assumption examines the process of problem solving in small groups: It is usually a unified undertaking. By this, we mean that people are *not* predisposed to disrupting decision making in small groups. Members essentially strive to get along. Dennis Gouran (1998) notes that groups are susceptible to **affiliative constraints,** which means that group members hold their input rather than risk rejection. According to Gouran, when group members do participate, fearing rejection, they are likely "to attach greater importance to preservation of the group than to the issues under consideration" (p. 100). Group members, then, seem more inclined to follow the leader when decision-making time arrives. Taking these comments into consideration, the board of directors at Melton may simply be a group who recognizes the urgency associated with their financial dilemma. Listening to two board members, Elizabeth and Randy, therefore, is much easier than listening to seven. The two become leaders, and the group members allow them to set the agenda for discussion.

affiliative constraints
when members withhold their input rather than face rejection from the group

The third assumption underscores the nature of most problem-solving and task-oriented groups to which people belong: They are usually complex. In discussing this assumption, let's first look at the complexity of small groups and then at the decisions emerging from these groups. First, small group members must continue to understand the many alternatives available to them and be able to distinguish among these alternatives. In addition, members must not only understand the task at hand but also the people who provide input into the task. This contention was supported many decades ago and continues today. For instance, social psychologist Robert Zajonc (1965) studied what many people have figured out for themselves: The mere presence of others has an effect on us. He offered a very simple principle regarding groups: When others are around us, we become innately aroused, which helps or hinders the performance of tasks. Nickolas Cottrell and his research team (Cottrell, Wack, Sekerak, & Rittle, 1968) later clarified the findings of Zajonc and argued that what leads people to task accomplishment is knowing that an individual will be evaluated by other individuals. Cottrell and his colleagues believe that group members may be apprehensive or anxious about the consequences that other group members bring to the group. In our opening, for instance, the board members are eager to listen to others with ideas because they do not offer ideas themselves. If any of the five nonspeakers were to openly challenge the ideas of either Elizabeth or Randy, they would be asked for their own ideas. Accordingly, they simply yield the floor to those who have a specific plan.

Marvin Shaw (1981) and the team of Isa Engleberg and Dianna Wynn (2013) discuss additional issues pertaining to groups. They note that a wide range of influences exist in a small group—age of group members, competitive nature of group members, size of the group, intelligence of group members, gender composition of the group, and leadership styles that emerge in the group. Further, the cultural backgrounds of individual group members may influence group processes. For instance, because many cultures do not place a premium on overt and expressive communication, some group members may refrain from debate or dialogue, to the surprise of other group members. This may influence the perceptions of both participative and nonparticipative group members.

If group dynamics are both complex and challenging, why are people so frequently assigned to group work? Clearly, the answer rests in the maxim "Two heads are better than one." Katherine Adams and Gloria Galanes (2013) effectively argue this point by acknowledging that groups are better at problem solving than individuals alone because of their availability to more information. Further, the two scholars note that once a group or team participates in a decision, a higher level of commitment toward the group exists. Groups and group decisions, therefore, may be difficult and challenging, but through group work, people are able to achieve their goals more expeditiously and efficiently.

The relationship of this assumption to Groupthink should not escape you. Two issues merit attention. First, groups whose members are similar to one another are groups that are more conducive to groupthink (Myers & Anderson, 2008). We term this group similarity **homogeneity.** So, as we mentioned earlier, the board of directors at Melton is homogeneous in its backgrounds—they are all part of literary inner circles. This similarity is one characteristic that can foster groupthink.

Second, group decisions that are not thoughtfully considered by everyone may facilitate groupthink. Quality of effort and the quality of thinking are essential in group decision making. For example, in our chapter-opening story, Elizabeth and Randy clearly offer opinions on what they think is the best course of action for the company. Their charisma, their ability to communicate their vision, and their willingness to openly share their ideas with the group may be intoxicating to a board that is under pressure to resolve a financial dilemma. It's important to note that the two group leaders have clear ideas about how to proceed next, failing to identify alternative and additional ways of looking at the problem.

homogeneity
group similarity

GROUPTHINK

What Comes Before: Antecedent Conditions of Groupthink

Janis believes that three conditions promote groupthink: (1) high cohesiveness of the decision-making group, (2) specific structural characteristics of the environment in which the group functions, and (3) stressful internal and external characteristics of the situation.

Group Cohesiveness

We have already discussed cohesiveness and its effects in relation to the three assumptions that guide Groupthink. Cohesiveness is also an antecedent condition. You may be wondering how cohesiveness can lead to groupthink. One reason this may be perplexing is that cohesion differs from one group to another, and different levels of cohesion produce different results. In some groups, cohesion can lead to positive feelings about the group experience and the other group members. Highly cohesive groups also may be more enthusiastic about their tasks and feel empowered to take on additional tasks. In sum, greater satisfaction is associated with increasing cohesiveness.

Despite the apparent advantages, highly cohesive groups may also bring about a troubling occurrence: groupthink. Janis (1982) argues that highly cohesive groups exert great pressure on their members to conform to group standards. Janis believes that as groups reach high degrees of cohesiveness, this euphoria tends to stifle other opinions and alternatives. Group members may be unwilling to express any reservations about solutions. And members even censor their own comments without being provoked. High-risk decisions, therefore, may be made without thinking about consequences. The risks involved in decisions pertaining to war, for instance, are high. A decision to increase military troop presence in another country entail high risks for the soldiers, for the refugees who may flee the country, and for those who remain. However, the risks associated with the decision pertaining to where a homecoming committee should hold its meetings are minimal in comparison to the bombing decision. You can see that risk varies across settings, and assessing risk is critical to the groupthink phenomenon.

Although people may feel confident that they will recognize groupthink when they see it, often they don't. Too much cohesion may be seen as a virtue, not a shortcoming. Imagine sitting around a conference table where everyone is smiling, affirming one another, and wanting to wrap things up (consider our opening story of Melton Publishing). Would you be willing to stop the head nodding and slaps on the back and ask, "But is this the best way to approach this?" To paraphrase the words from a famous fairy tale, who wants to tell the emperor that he has no clothes? Cohesiveness, therefore, frequently leads to conformity, and conformity is a primary route to groupthink.

Before moving on, let's make sure we're clear. We are not suggesting that cohesion automatically leads to groupthink. To be sure, cohesiveness is a necessary ingredient if groups or teams are to arrive at thoughtful, inclusive, and informed decisions. Still, when the effectiveness or consequences of a group's decision remains secondary to a group's cohesion, Janis contends that the group is *prone* to groupthink.

Structural Factors

Janis notes that specific structural characteristics, or faults, promote groupthink. They include (1) insulation of the group, (2) lack of impartial leadership, (3) lack of clear procedures for decisions, and (4) homogeneity of group members' backgrounds. **Group insulation** refers to a group's ability to be unaffected by the outside world and its happenings. Further, it is very easy for insulation to occur if group members do not solicit the opinions or views of those external to the group. In fact, they may be discussing issues that have relevance in the outside world, and yet the members are insulated from its influence. People outside the group who could help with the decision may even be present in the organization but not asked to participate.

group insulation
a group's ability to remain unaffected by outside influences

A **lack of impartial leadership** means that group members are led by people who have a personal interest in the outcome. An example of this point can be found in Janis's appraisal of President Kennedy's Bay of Pigs episode. When the president presided over the meetings on the Cuban invasion, Janis observes the following:

lack of impartial leadership
groups led by individuals who put their personal agendas first

> [At] each meeting, instead of opening up the agenda to permit a full airing of the opposing considerations, he allowed the CIA representatives to dominate the entire discussion. The president permitted them to refute immediately each tentative doubt that one of the others might express, instead of asking whether anyone else had the same doubt or wanted to pursue the implications of the new worrisome issue that had been raised. (1982, p. 42)

The deference of group members to their leader can be observed in the words of Arthur Schlesinger Jr., a member of Kennedy's policy group: "I can only explain my failure to do more than raise a few timid questions by reporting that one's impulse to blow the whistle on this nonsense was simply undone by the circumstances of the discussion" (cited in Janis, 1982, p. 39). It is apparent that Kennedy considered other opinions to be detrimental to his plan, and alternative leadership was suppressed. We could probably sum up this perception with one word: *hubris*.

A final structural fault that can lead to groupthink is a **lack of decision-making procedures** and similarity of group members. First, some groups have few, if any, procedures for decision making; failing to have previously established norms for evaluation of problems can foster groupthink. Dennis Gouran and Randy Hirokawa (1996) suggest that even if groups recognize that a problem exists, they still must figure out the cause and extent of the problem. Groups, therefore, may be influenced by dominant voices and go along with those who choose to speak up. Other groups may simply follow what they have observed and experienced in previous groups. In fact, when independent analyses of the *Columbia* space shuttle disaster were undertaken after the craft's breakup, John Schwartz (2005) reports that NASA management was influential in decisions to launch on the fateful day in 2003. Schwartz quotes a former shuttle commander at the Johnson Space Center in Houston: "Managers 'ask for dissenting opinion because they know they are supposed to ask for them,' but the managers 'are either defending their own position or arguing against the dissenting opinion' without seriously trying to understand it" (p. A17). In other words, group members may try to challenge management, but their words are either muted or dismissed. Perhaps one significant change in this area comes from NASA itself. In particular, in 2015, NASA asserted that managers should be participants in "open communication" [which] "should be the standard that is embraced by the highest

lack of decision-making procedures
failure to provide norms for solving group issues

management to the line supervisor" (http://ntrs.nasa.gov/archive/nasa/casi.ntrs.nasa .gov/20150016571.pdf).

A second structural fault is the homogeneity of members' backgrounds. Janis (1982) notes that "lack of disparity in social background and ideology among the members of a cohesive group makes it easier for them to concur on whatever proposals are put forth by the leader" (p. 250). We alluded to this fault earlier in the chapter. Without diversity of background and experience, it may be difficult to debate critical issues.

Student Voices

MaryJane

During my internship I worked at a major newspaper in Washington, D.C. The paper had a political bias for sure and I saw it play out all the time. I'd be sitting in on meetings where no one would disagree with the editorial page editor and a lot of the time, I saw people around the table "silence" anyone who would. Janis could do an entire case study by examining this company!

Group Stress

The final antecedent condition of groupthink pertains to the stress on the group—that is, **stress** on the group may evoke groupthink. Stress occurs when group members are influenced by issues, resources, or events both within and external to the group. When stress is high, group members may not see any reasonable solution and therefore, rally around their leader. When decision makers are under great stress imposed by forces outside the group, faulty decision making happens. Stress, as explained in this theory, is a comprehensive concept in that it includes both internal and external stress. For instance, in a work environment, if there are deadlines of an assignment and you're unable to meet those deadlines, there is internal stress in that your supervisor established a time frame and you were unable to accommodate. However, there might also be external stress in that the reason you were unable to meet the deadline is because you have other obligations that you saw as more important (e.g., attending to a sick parent, etc.).

internal and external stress *pressure exerted on the group by issues and events both inside and outside of the group*

As you can see, groups frequently insulate themselves from outside criticism, form what ostensibly are close bonds, seek consensus, and ultimately develop groupthink. To get a clearer picture of what Groupthink looks like, Janis (1982) identifies eight symptoms that can be assigned to three categories. We turn to these symptoms next.

Symptoms of Groupthink

Preexisting conditions lead groups to concurrence seeking. **Concurrence seeking** occurs when groups try to reach consensus in their final decision. Consider the interpretation of consensus seeking from Andrea Hollingshead and her colleagues (2005): "Groupthink teams place such a high priority on supporting each other emotionally

concurrence seeking *efforts to search out group consensus*

that they choose not to challenge one another" (p. 30). When concurrence seeking goes too far, Janis contends, it produces symptoms of groupthink. Janis (1982) observes three categories of symptoms of Groupthink: overestimation of the group, closed-mindedness, and pressures toward uniformity.

To illustrate these symptoms and to give a sense of how Janis conceptualized Groupthink, we examine a policy decision that because of the ongoing post-traumatic stress that military veterans frequently experience, continues to resonate today: the Vietnam War. During the height of the war, polls showed that most people felt that the objectives for going to Vietnam were ambiguous and ill-founded. War protestors were prominent in the 1960s and early 1970s, arguing that the country had no clear reason (i.e., policy) for entering the war. The controversy associated with Vietnam parallels the controversies that surrounded U.S. involvement in Iraq and Afghanistan.

We present Janis's (1982) interpretation of what took place when President Lyndon Johnson's foreign-policy advisors examined decisions about bombing North Vietnam. Janis's comments are based on extensive discussions with individuals who were presidential advisors, and many of their comments are contained in the following analysis.

Overestimation of the Group

overestimation of the group
erroneous belief that the group is more than it is

An **overestimation of the group** includes those behaviors that suggest the group believes it is more than it is. Two specific symptoms exist in this category (Katopol, 2016): illusion of invulnerability and a belief in the inherent morality of the group.

illusion of invulnerability
belief that the group is special enough to overcome obstacles

Illusion of Invulnerability   The **illusion of invulnerability** can be defined as a group's belief that they are special enough to overcome any obstacles or setbacks. The group believes it is invincible. With respect to the Vietnam War, Janis explains that President Johnson's foreign-policy group wanted to avoid peace negotiations because they did not want to be viewed as having little bargaining power. The group,

T*I*P

Theory-Into-Practice

Groupthink

Theoretical Claim: The groupthink symptom, illusion of unanimity, is frequently unconsciously undertaken by those who are shy, inexperienced, or reticent to speak up.

Practical Implication: As the majority of the school board determined that eliminating the theater program was necessary because of state budget cuts to education, Melanie sat quietly, listening to everyone speak about the need to save money/reduce costs. When a straw vote was conducted, she agreed to the program cut because she was just recently elected to the board and had little understanding of how the budget process worked.

therefore, was willing to take a risk and believed that selecting bombing targets in North Vietnam was a wise course of action. The group members based their decision to bomb on four issues: the military advantage, the risk to American aircraft, the potential to widen the conflict to other countries, and civilian casualties. Janis asks whether the group members shared the illusion that they were invulnerable when they confined their attacks to bombing targets.

Belief in the Inherent Morality of the Group   When group members have a **belief in the inherent morality of the group,** they are said to adopt the position that "we are a good and wise group" (Janis, 1982, p. 256). Because the group perceives itself to be good, they believe that their decision making must, therefore, be good. By embracing this belief, group members purge themselves of any shame or guilt, although they ignore any ethical or moral implications of their decision. Janis found it interesting that Johnson and his advisors were not concerned with bombing villages in North Vietnam; for them, the moral consequences did not outweigh the perception that the United States might be weak or fearful. In fact, the foreign-policy council continued to encourage bombing of Hanoi (North Vietnam) even though peace initiatives were concurrently under way in Poland. A sense of moral certitude prevailed because the president and his advisors believed that North Vietnam would not negotiate a surrender.

belief in the inherent morality of the group *assumption that the group members are thoughtful and good; therefore, the decisions they make will be good*

Closed-Mindedness

When a group is **closed-minded,** it ignores outside influences on the group. The two symptoms discussed by Janis in this category are stereotypes of out-groups and collective rationalization.

closed-mindedness *a group's willingness to ignore differences in people and warnings about poor group decisions*

Out-Group Stereotypes   Groups in crisis frequently engage in **out-group stereotypes,** which are stereotyped perceptions of rivals or enemies. These stereotypes underscore the fact that any adversaries are either too weak or too stupid to counter offensive tactics. For Johnson's advisors, enemy meant Communist. It was this stereotype that kept the advisors from seeing the enemy as people. Janis (1982) reasons that because the North Vietnamese were considered to be Communist enemies, this embodiment of evil justified the "destruction of countless human lives and the burning of villages" (p. 111).

out-group stereotypes *stereotyped perceptions of group enemies or competitors*

Collective Rationalization   The fourth symptom of Groupthink, **collective rationalization,** refers to the situation in which group members ignore warnings that might prompt them to reconsider their thoughts and actions before they reach a final decision. In most circumstances, this symptom can also be interpreted to be a rationalization of "bad news." President Johnson and his staff were given a number of forewarnings—from intelligence agencies, among others—about the implications of bombing North Vietnam. Some in the intelligence community believed that bombing sites such as oil facilities would do nothing to erode Communist operations. Nonetheless, Johnson's group maintained its unified position on escalating the bombing. Janis (1982) observed that the men in Johnson's inner circle were very convinced of

collective rationalization *situation in which group members ignore warnings about their decisions*

the importance of the Vietnam War to the United States. Therefore, revisiting any strategies to exit the war was out of the question.

Pressures Toward Uniformity

The **pressure toward uniformity** can be enormous for some groups. Janis believed that some groups who go along to get along may be setting themselves up for group-think. The four symptoms in this category are self-censorship, an illusion of unanimity, the presence of self-appointed mindguards, and direct pressure on dissenters.

Self-Censorship   Earlier we discussed self-censorship. **Self-censorship** refers to group members' tendency to minimize their doubts and counterarguments. They begin to second-guess their own ideas. For those in President Johnson's foreign-policy group, self-censorship was exhibited when group members dehumanized the war experience. These advisors would not allow themselves to think of the innocent people being killed because such thinking would only personalize the war. Janis argues that silencing one's own opposing views and using in-group rhetoric further bolster the decisions of the group.

Illusion of Unanimity   The sixth symptom of Groupthink is an **illusion of unanimity,** which suggests that silence is consent. Although some advisors in Johnson's inner circle felt differently about the Vietnam intervention, they were silent. This silence prompted others around the table to believe that there was consensus in planning and execution.

Self-Appointed Mindguards   Groups in crisis may include **self-appointed mindguards**—group members who shield the group from adverse information. Mindguards believe that they act in the group's best interest. Walt Rostow, White House assistant, effectively played the role of mindguard in Johnson's group. Janis relates the following: "Rostow cleverly screened the inflow of information and used his power to keep dissident experts away from the White House. This had the intended effect of preventing the President and some of his advisers from becoming fully aware of the extent of disaffection with the war and the grounds for it" (1982, p. 119). Ironically, within the group, keeping the peace at the White House was more important than maintaining it in Vietnam.

Pressures on Dissenters   The final symptom involves pressuring any group member who expresses opinions, viewpoints, or commitments that are contrary to the majority opinion. Janis calls this **pressures on dissenters.** In his interviews with those within President Johnson's inner circle, Janis discovered that the group members formed a gentlemen's club, where mutual respect and congenial talk pervaded. Janis also later realized that these men often turned to one another for support, and they were loyal to one another. Is it any wonder, then, that group members believed that everyone agreed to the course of action? This attitude would prevail, of course, considering that those who openly disagreed frequently resigned or were replaced (Janis, 1982). Robert McNamara, Secretary of Defense under President Johnson, was a dissenter who believed that bombing North Vietnam was the wrong way to get the enemy to the negotiation table. However, he was under much pressure to avoid disagreeing with members of the gentlemen's club.

(Group) Think About It: It's All Around U.S.

Thomas Jefferson once said that "difference of opinion leads to inquiry, and inquiry to truth." His words are still relevant, especially in foreign policy. Yet, considering that Janis studied national-policy decisions, his research may leave you with the impression that groupthink cannot "hit home." As we've tried to illustrate in this chapter, however, groupthink is everywhere. In addition to the large-scale decisions we identified earlier, Groupthink decision making has been evidenced in a number of domestic and global examples, including Watergate (1972), the *Columbia* (2003) and *Challenger* (1986) tragedies, the Gulf War (1991), Hurricane Katrina (2005), the cover-up of child sexual abuse at Penn State University (2012), and ISIS (2015).

On a smaller scale, and as we alluded to previously, groupthink occurs all around us in "less-critical" small groups. Decisions such as whether you will attend college, for instance, may have been prone to groupthink. If your parents went to college, your grandparents were college graduates, and you read literature stating that a college graduate will make twice as much money in a lifetime as a high school graduate, your decision to attend college may have been made without completely examining any alternatives (e.g., school-loan debt, academic preparedness, etc.). Presumably, your group (family) is a cohesive group. Your family rationalized your attendance, and most likely, you didn't raise any objections. In other words, your small group was susceptible to groupthink.

This is but one example of the many episodes of groupthink in our daily lives. We may find conditions for groupthink with staff behind the deli counter at the grocery store; on a construction site with architects, contractors, and skilled laborers; or even at an investment club meeting where a group of people make decisions about what stocks to invest in during difficult economic times.

Think Before You Act: Ways to Prevent Groupthink

It bears repeating: Our discussion of Groupthink and the issues that accompany this theory may have given you the impression that all cohesive groups will be prone to groupthink. This is not true. Janis (1982) notes that cohesiveness is a necessary but not sufficient condition of Groupthink. Nonetheless, frequently, when groups find themselves in highly cohesive situations and when decision makers are under great stress, Groupthink may materialize.

How can group members learn to avoid groupthink, or at least work toward more healthy interactions? Janis (1989; Herek, Janis, & Huth, 1987) suggests that groups engage in vigilant decision making, which involves (1) looking at the range of objectives group members wish to achieve, (2) developing and reviewing action plans and alternatives, (3) exploring the consequences of each alternative, (4) analyzing previously rejected action plans when new information emerges, and (5) having a contingency plan for failed suggestions. Janis offers additional recommendations, but critics

GROUPTHINK

Table 14.1 Preventing Groupthink

RECOMMENDATION	ACTION
Require Oversight and Control	*Establish a parliamentary committee:* Develop resources to proactively monitor ongoing policy ventures; establish incentives to intervene; link personal fate to fate of group members.
Embrace Whistle-Blowing	*Voice doubts:* Avoid suppressing concerns about group processes; continue to disagree and debate when no satisfactory answers are given; question assumptions.
Allow for Objection	*Protect conscientious objectors:* Provide for group members' exits; do not play down the moral implications of a course of action; acknowledge private concerns about ethical issues in the group.
Balance Consensus and Majority Rule	*Alter rules governing choice:* Relieve pressure on groups in minority positions; dissuade the development of subgroups; introduce a multiple advocacy approach to decisions.

Source: Adapted from 't Hart, 1990.

such as Paul 't Hart (1998) question whether Janis's recommendations inadvertently erode collegiality and foster group factionalism.

To avoid oversimplifying the groupthink problem, 't Hart (1990) has proposed four general recommendations for groups who may be prone to Groupthink: (1) Require oversight and control, (2) embrace whistle-blowing in the group, (3) allow for objection, and (4) balance consensus and majority rule. We will look at each recommendation (Table 14.1).

First, 't Hart believes that one way to enhance group decision making is to impose some external oversight and control. He argues that groups need to hold key decision makers accountable for their actions; this should be done *before* groups begin their deliberations about issues. Accountability may take the form of a committee that serves to enforce control (vis à vis rules, governance procedures, decorum, etc.). 't Hart theorizes that such committees prompt group members to challenge collective rationalizations and inaccurate perceptions. Reflecting on our example of President Johnson and his foreign-policy group, 't Hart proposes that the inner circle of advisors was insulated from external oversight. As well, there were inadequate intragroup measures to improve the group's decisions on North Vietnam.

In addition to accountability, 't Hart proposes that **whistle-blowing** be embraced in a group's culture. That is, group members "should be encouraged to voice concerns rather than to voluntarily suppress them, to question assumptions rather than to accept them at face value, and to continue to disagree and debate

whistle-blowing
process in which individuals report unethical or illegal behaviors or practices to others

when no satisfactory answers to their concerns are given by the rest of the group" (p. 385). Anna Mulrine (2008) writes that the 2003 Iraq invasion brought about great chaos in the planning and execution of decision making by the Army. To that end, the Army has developed a "cadre of devil's advocates" (p. 30) who are charged with "questioning prevailing assumptions to avoid getting sucked into that Groupthink" (p. 30) which can happen in stressful times. Ultimately, the Military Whistleblower Protection Act was amended to expand the rights of whistle-blowers protecting disclosures in legal cases and closing loopholes. President Obama eventually signed this overhaul of the Act and it became law in 2013 (http://www.in.ng.mil/Portals/0/PageContents/SoldierResources/IG/WHISTLEBLOWER_PROTECTION_ACT.pdf). Embracing whistle-blowing in this way results in looking at a decision from alternate points of view. Further, scholars such as 't Hart and Wim Vandekerckhove (2012) advocate that groups protect these sorts of whistle-blowers because groups usually need dissenting voices when decisions have lasting and significant consequences.

A third suggestion by 't Hart is that groups allow **conscientious objectors,** or group members who refuse to participate in the decision-making process because it would violate their conscience. He reasons that groupthink causes groups to downplay the moral implications of their decisions, and if conscientious objectors know that they can exit a conversation based on moral or ethical grounds, then they may be more likely to speak up. Thus, these objectors may be able to raise doubts about the decision or even to protest it. President Johnson's decision to continue bombing Vietnam, therefore, may have been different if conscientious objectors had been allowed to introduce the moral implications of killing innocent people.

Finally, 't Hart advocates that groups not require consensus but work instead toward a majority of support. Because consensus demands that every group member agree on a decision, group members often feel pressured to consent (illusion of unanimity). 't Hart believes that groups should strive toward consensus but be prepared for majority support. If groups adopt this orientation, 't Hart believes, they will function more like teams. Janis (1982) discusses the fact that several members of President Johnson's inner circle of advisors (McNamara, Rusk, Bundy) wanted to temporarily halt the Hanoi bombings; we can only speculate how the passion for consensus affected both the United States and the Vietnamese people.

conscientious objectors
group members who refuse to participate because it would violate personal conscience

Integration, Critique, and Closing

Groupthink is a theory dedicated to understanding the decision-making process in small groups. The theory has been tested and expanded using experimental methods, making it aligned with a quantitative approach. Janis believes that groups frequently make decisions with profound consequences, and although he focused his efforts on foreign-policy groups, as we learned previously, the application of Groupthink terminology resonates in many other decision-making groups. Among the criteria for evaluating a theory, four are especially relevant for discussion: scope, testability, heurism, and test of time.

GROUPTHINK

Integration

Communication Tradition	Rhetorical | Semiotic | Phenomenological | Cybernetic | **Socio-Psychological** | **Socio-Cultural** | Critical
Communication Context	Intrapersonal | Interpersonal | **Small Group** | **Organizational** | Public/Rhetorical | Mass/Media | Cultural
Approach to Knowing	**Positivistic/Empirical** | Interpretive/Hermeneutic | Critical

Critique

Evaluation Criteria	Scope | Logical Consistency | Parsimony | Utility | **Testability** | **Heurism** | **Test of Time**

Scope

Despite the fact that many Groupthink principles can be applied to several types of groups, Janis was clear in his original conceptualization in applying Groupthink solely to decision-making groups in crisis periods; he does not readily apply his thinking to every group type. Although the theory has been applied to groups as diverse as presidential advisors and ice hockey teams, the focus has been in those groups that are *decision-making* groups. Therefore, the scope of the theory could be defined as narrow.

Student Voices

Andre

I know it's not a foreign-policy group, but my small group in my business class had all the elements of Groupthink. We knew we only had a month to put together a PowerPoint presentation, and we were all working and taking classes at the same time. At times, when we had our meetings, it was like everyone agreed just to move to the next point. We were under pressure and didn't really understand the information we were researching, but we refused to slow down. We had the illusion of unanimity that Janis talked about. I know the world didn't stop when we gave our presentation, but I did know that the C we got as a grade made me think we rushed things through too much and didn't think about the consequences.

Testability

Group scholars have pointed to some validity problems with the theory, calling into question its testability. For instance, Jeanne Longley and Dean Pruitt (1980) criticize the validity of the theory. They argue that half of the symptoms of Groupthink are not associated with concurrence seeking—a key feature of the theory. They charge that "a theory should be a logical progression of ideas, not a grab-bag of phenomena that were correlated with each other in a sample of six cases" (p. 80). Further, James Rose (2011), in an exhaustive literature review on Groupthink, found that with respect to testing the entire "model" of Groupthink, problems abound. Because many of Janis's variables are not well-defined, the theory is prone to lapses in validity and reliability.

Heurism

The theory of Groupthink is a heuristic undertaking; The theory and many of its elements have been employed in a number of studies and have enjoyed the attention of many communication and social psychology scholars. In addition to foreign-policy decisions, writers have studied Groupthink and applied its concepts and tenets to the economic and social crises in Europe (Mitchell, 2015), student killings at Kent State (Hensley & Lewis, 2010), the sexual abuse cover-up at Penn State University (Cohen & DeBenedet, 2012), Hurricane Katrina (Garnett & Kouzmin, 2009), "cohesive teamwork" interventions in health care (Kaba, Wishart, Fraser, Coderre, & McLaughlin, 2016), and even to the Major League Umpires Association strike (Koerber & Neck, 2003). The theory has also generated a number of assumptions about group behavior, and Groupthink remains an important part of the literature on group decision making.

Test of Time

The theory of Groupthink has withstood the test of time. Scholars continue to investigate many of features of the theory and the theory has gained both academic and popular attention (http://www.newyorker.com/magazine/2012/01/30/groupthink). On the 30th anniversary of Groupthink, Schwartz and Wald (2003) called Janis a "pioneer in the study of social dynamics" (p. 4).Finally, given that government-policy decisions will always exist and given that many governmental leaders surround themselves with individuals who are typically conflict-avoidant, future instances of Groupthink remain rather high.

Closing

Groupthink may be more intuitively appealing than empirically driven. The theory, however, continues to receive attention in research as well as in the popular press. In fact, Janis's thinking on Groupthink has been quite influential in several fields of study, including communication, cognitive and social psychology, anthropology, and political science. Few would debate the failure of the foreign-policy fiascoes outlined by Janis: massive violence and casualties, loss of confidence in governmental decisions, and policymaking gone wrong. For these reasons alone, Janis is credited with helping us identify and examine one type of group decision-making problem.

Discussion Starters

TECH QUEST: Online critics have noted that "social media has a Group-think problem in that dissenting opinions are silenced." Do you agree or disagree with this claim? Provide some examples to support your views.

1. What advice would you give the Melton Publishing board of directors before they meet to discuss their financial situation? Frame your advice with Group-think concepts in mind.

2. Janis and 't Hart have proposed a number of ways to prevent Groupthink. Provide at least two additional ways to avoid Groupthink.

3. Have you ever been in a small group with too much cohesiveness? If so, did Groupthink develop? If so, how did you know? If not, what prevented Groupthink from occurring?

4. In his book, *Groupthink,* Janis asks if a little knowledge of Groupthink is a dangerous thing. Why do you think Janis asks this question, and what are the consequences of knowing about Groupthink? Incorporate examples into your response.

5. How widespread is Groupthink? Do you believe society is aware of the problem?

6. Apply principles of Groupthink to recent domestic and foreign-policy decisions made by the United States.

7. Discuss the delicate balance between sufficient group cohesion and exceedingly high amounts of group cohesion. Illustrate your response with examples from your own group experiences.

CHAPTER 15

Structuration Theory

*Based on the research of **Anthony Giddens**, **M. Scott Poole**, **David R. Seibold**, and **Robert D. McPhee***

> Democracy hence implies not just the right to free and equal self-development, but also the constitutional limitation of power.
>
> —Anthony Giddens

Tim Nash and Bayside City Tire Company

Bayside City Tire Company (BCT) is a multinational company with many employees. One of the employees, Tim Nash, is a new production division manager. Jeremy has been a production floor supervisor for 25 years. He has been assigned the task of showing Tim, his new boss, around for a couple of weeks.

On the first day, Jeremy takes Tim around the production floor to introduce him to the workers on his division. When approached, all of the workers call Tim by his last name: "Good morning, Mr. Nash." "It's great having you onboard," Tim responds to the workers by saying, "Mr. Nash is my father. Please, call me Tim."

As Tim and Jeremy walk away, Tim asks, "Why is everyone so formal?"

Jeremy responds, "That's company policy. We believe that addressing one another in this way establishes a sense of respect for our supervisors at Bayside City Tire."

Tim is having none of that: "This is my division, and I would really prefer if we do things my way."

Jeremy pauses, "Well, sure, this is your division, but this is the way they have been taught to communicate with one another. After all, think of how confused they will be if they

are allowed to address you by your first name, and other managers expect to be addressed as 'Mr.' or 'Ms.'"

"Hmm. I'm not liking this, but I guess I don't want to disrupt what's already established here. Ok, let's go with it. I guess I'll have to get used to the workers calling me "MISTER Nash" until I can get this straightened out. Besides, I don't want them to think that I am going against company rules or that I want to change things," Tim answers reluctantly.

Later that day, Tim talks to Angela Griffith, the human relations coordinator for BCT, about changing the policy to allow employees and staff to address one another less formally. Angela listens to Tim's ideas and tries to tell him that in the grand scheme of the BCT, the issue is not that critical. Tim disagrees, arguing that interpersonal relationships are crucial to productivity. After some discussion, Angela agrees to call a meeting of the production division managers to discuss the potential change.

At the meeting, the six production division managers all voice their opinions about the change in policy. Janette, a 15-year veteran with BCT, points out, "Personally, I like having the workers address me more formally. It's tough enough being a woman of color in this type of work environment, and I think this encourages respect in the workplace."

Darnell, who joined BCT only three years ago after graduating with his MBA, counters by stating that he thinks the workers don't feel comfortable coming to him to discuss problems because of the formality and rules that are in place at BCT. "I think Tim's onto something here," Darnell says. "We might be able to establish a friendlier work environment if we were less formal in how we address one another. Besides, what's wrong with telling our colleagues that we're not above you?"

Wayne, who is a third-generation employee of BCT, argues, "You don't mess around with tradition. This is the way it's always been, and it's worked just fine for the past 30 years."

Angela listens to all their opinions, but the managers are split 50–50 on the policy change issue. She says, "Please, let's try to arrive at some sort of closure on this. Let's take a vote and see what you all think we should do." After voting numerous times, it is obvious that the issue will not be resolved. "Okay," says Angela, "I guess we'll keep the rule in place as it is for right now since you can't agree on this." As she thought about this issue more, Angela couldn't believe that something as simple as calling someone by a first name could elicit this much energy. Yet, she also knew that these sorts of rules, while seemingly unimportant, can affect the morale and productivity, and therefore, needed to be clarified for everyone.

Just as a contractor uses a blueprint as a guide in building a structure, members of an organization use rules to state expectations of behavior and communication within the organization. As we learned in Chapter 8 (Uncertainty Reduction Theory), many people are uncomfortable with uncertainty.

Consider the need for structure in your own life. Usually, students want to know the structure or rules so they will understand what is expected of them in class. If a professor were simply to announce, "This term we'll have a couple of tests, a few quizzes, and you'll need to do a project," students would likely be uncomfortable with such limited information. They would want more specific instructions, or rules, regarding page-length requirements of any papers, due dates, expectations for exams, and so on. Thus, the school and the instructor provide students with a course syllabus, a *blueprint* of the rules for the class, in which the structure is created and maintained. However, we can also change the structure of an institution by adapting rules or creating new ones. Feedback from student evaluations, for instance, may guide a professor to alter the syllabus or the exam criteria in the future.

Sociologist Anthony Giddens believes that social institutions are produced, reproduced, and transformed through the use of rules. David Seibold and Karen Kroman Myers (2006) contend that social institutions are "organized around members' interactional processes and practices: disseminating information, allocating resources, accomplishing tasks, making choices, managing disagreements, and the like" (p. 143). The structure of these institutions is the focus of Structuration Theory.

Recall from our discussion in Chapter 3 that rules indicate and prescribe how things are to be done; they suggest a course of action in a setting. In Structuration Theory, rules in a social institution go beyond telling employees what they can and cannot do. In interactions among people, the rules guiding these conversations allow employees to maintain or alter an organization. An instance in which this would apply would involve a company's talking about poor customer service to make changes in the customer service policy. The rules governing these conversations might pertain, for instance, to hierarchy (e.g., the extent to which an employee can share a candid opinion with superiors). We return to a more detailed examination of rules later in the chapter.

In the chapter-opening example, the employees involved in the managers' meeting could potentially influence the structure of the organization by decisions made during their debate. If they had voted to change the rule of formally addressing one another, the entire organizational structure may have had to be altered. Communication is what allows for an organization to change.

Giddens (1979, 1993) views social structures as a double-edged sword. The structures and the rules that we create restrict our behavior. However, these same rules also enable us to understand and interact with others. We need rules to guide our decisions about how we are expected to behave. These rules may be either explicitly stated (such as grievance procedures that are outlined in an employee manual) or implicitly learned (such as respecting one another by providing each member of the group an opportunity to voice his or her opinion).

Groups and organizations are coordinated around various social interactions—for example, socializing new members through new employee receptions, arriving at decisions during conference calls, conducting meetings in person or via videoconference, or teaching new skills in employee-training sessions. Giddens (1984, 2003) points out that the key to making sense of the communication that occurs in these groups and organizations is to examine the structures that serve as their foundation. He makes a distinction between the concepts of system (as we discussed in Chapter 3) and structure. The term **system,** in this sense, refers to the group or organization itself and the behaviors and practices that the group engages in to pursue its goals. Organizations may engage in many behaviors/practices, including new employee assimilation processes and performance appraisals (Seibold & Myers, 2006). The term **structure** refers to the rules and resources members use to create and sustain the system, as well as to guide individual behaviors related to such behaviors/practices.

In the opening scenario, both the BCT organization and the group meeting of the division managers can be viewed as a system. Their goal is to discuss the problem of using formal names to address one another, as well as to conduct the daily operations of the organization. To assist them in accomplishing their goals in an efficient manner, both of these systems have a formal set of rules that includes guidelines for how employees are expected to address one another at BCT as well as guidelines for allowing everyone to voice their opinion during the group meeting. These represent the structures of the group and organization. Tim Nash is frustrated by the structure that restricts his employees from communicating with him informally. The rules for interactions between supervisors and subordinates contradict what he has learned about building relationships and enhancing employee productivity. Angela employs rules for conducting open discussions about issues before any decisions about changes are made. Thus, BCT is created and guided by structures—rules that explain how to demonstrate respect for one another.

system
a group or organization and the behaviors that the group engages in to pursue its goals

structure
the rules and resources used to sustain a group or organization

Although Giddens first drew attention to organizational structures, communication scholars were instrumental in ushering in an application of structuration principles to other contexts. For example, Marshall Scott Poole (1990) and his colleagues David Seibold and Robert McPhee (McPhee, 2015; McPhee, Poole, & Iverson, 2013; Poole & DeSanctis, 1990; Poole & McPhee, 2005; Poole, Seibold, & McPhee, 1986; 1996; Seibold & Myers, 2007) have studied the application of structuration principles to the communication field. Their theoretical approach has been called *Adaptive* Structuration Theory to explain how task groups use and strategically adapt information technology, rules, and resources to accomplish organizational/group goals (Poole & McPhee, 2005). We will address this adaptive nature throughout the chapter, yet, we will continue to emphasize the original thinking of Giddens and discuss Structuration Theory as a perspective with appeal to many areas in the study of communication. As Dennis Mumby (2011) suggests, there is an embedded relationship between communication and structuration principles. He notes that communication not only reflects organizational reality, but also "creates and maintains the meanings that guide organized life and motivate particular actions" (p. 194).

To begin, it's important to define structuration. In a general sense, structuration allows people to understand their patterns of behavior—the structures of their social system. Specifically, **structuration** is described as "the process by which systems are produced and reproduced through members' use of rules and resources" (Poole, Seibold, & McPhee, 1996, p. 117). For structuration theorists, organizational structures are produced and replicated by people who interact on a daily basis, trying to accomplish personal and company goals (Modaff, Butler, & DeWine, 2017).

Structuration allows people to understand their patterns of behavior—the structures of their social system. With respect to small groups, Poole and colleagues conclude that the key to understanding groups is through an analysis of the structures that underlie them. Rules and resources for communicating and arriving at decisions are typically learned from the organization itself and from members' past experiences and personal rules. These same rules and resources are reaffirmed as a result of their application or use; the group may decide to keep them in their existing format or alter them to meet the changing needs of the group.

In arriving at a decision on whether BCT should change its rule about having employees address one another formally, Angela enacts a rule of decision making that requires the group to discuss member viewpoints before making changes. BCT may also have a rule for company meetings in which the majority vote decides the action that should be taken. If Angela fails to call a meeting of the managers to solicit their opinions, many of them might be displeased. Or, if Angela doesn't give everyone the opportunity to state an opinion on the rule while the rest of the group observes an unspoken rule to respect others' opinions (i.e., challenge ideas but do not attack people), some of the group's members will be dissatisfied with the outcome of the meeting. Janette, for one, depends on the rule to maintain her credibility and authority when interacting with her male employees. The fact that Angela follows the rule of calling a meeting to discuss the issue reaffirms the belief that this is a good guideline to follow in making decisions in the organization. However, some of the group's members may not be pleased with the decision to keep the rule in its current

structuration
the production, reproduction, and transformation of social environments through rules and resources in relationships

Organizations create structures, which can be interpreted as an organization's rules and resources. These structures, in turn, create social systems in an organization. Organizations achieve a life of their own because of the way their members use their structures. Power structures guide the decision making that takes place in these organizations.

form, and they may invoke a new rule among their own teams in which they permit subordinates to address them in a less formal manner. Thus, the rule will be altered from its original state.

Structuration provides a useful foundation for examining the impact that rules and resources have on group decisions and organizational communication. Structures produce a system and they also represent the outcomes of a system (recall our discussion of the Systems perspective in Chapter 3). In addition, it helps describe how these rules are altered or confirmed through interactions. Finally, structuration is communicative: "Talk is action. If structure is truly produced through interaction, then communication is more than just a precursor to action; it is action" (Modaff et al., 2017, p. 121).

Assumptions of Structuration Theory

Structuration Theory is rather complex because it deals with people, resources, behavior, tasks, norms, and organizational life (Wiggins & Bowers, 2014). Therefore, to assist in unraveling this complexity, we first consider some of the basic assumptions that guide the theory:

- Groups and organizations are produced and reproduced through actions and behaviors.
- Communication rules serve as both the medium for, and an outcome of, interactions.
- Power structures are present in organizations and guide the decision-making process.

Underscoring the first assumption, Giddens proposes that every action or behavior results in the production of something new—a **fresh act**. Each of the actions or behaviors in which a group or organization engages is influenced and affected by the past. This history serves as a reference for understanding what rules and resources are required to operate within the system. Consider, for instance, when a group leader decides to conduct a vote using an anonymous ballot. If past voting using the ballot has proven to be effective for group members, history is influencing the rules for operation within that system.

fresh act
something new developed from action or behavior

STRUCTURATION THEORY

It is important to remember that every time we communicate with someone, we are establishing a new beginning by (1) creating a new rule or expectation, (2) altering an existing rule, or (3) reaffirming rules that have been used in the past. In establishing these new beginnings, we still rely on past rules and expectations to guide our behaviors. Thus, we never escape our history—it continually influences our decisions for behavior in groups and organizations. It also influences changes that may take place in the system.

All of our communicative actions exist in relationship to the past. Angela may have learned in past group meetings that members are not supportive of others' thoughts and opinions. She may have decided simply to state the problem and have group members vote on a potential solution without first soliciting the advice and opinions of group members. In this instance, historical rules would have been used as a reference for altering the group's rules in future interactions.

Recall the interaction between Tim and Jeremy. According to Structuration Theory, each interaction that takes place between Tim and Jeremy is new and creates something unique in the structure of their future interactions. At the same time, Jeremy and Tim each bring to the interaction a set of rules (based on their history) and expectations that will guide and shape their communication with each other. In other words, as we observed in Chapter 1, their fields of experience become critical in their communication with one another. Jeremy addresses Tim by his last name, Mr. Nash, the first time they meet. Tim responds by saying, "Please, call me Tim." Tim creates something new in the social structure by establishing a precedent (a new norm) of asking his subordinate to call him by his first name. This precedent is influenced by the past expectations that each man brings to the interaction. In other words, the experiences that Tim and Jeremy bring to the interaction affect their expectations for the structure that will guide their future communication. Tim believes that an open and relaxed communication style works, whereas Jeremy operates under a very different set of rules for interaction—formal address works best. In this case, Jeremy's rules for conversing serve the dual function of guiding his current behavior and setting expectations for future behavior.

The second assumption of Structuration Theory is the notion that rules simultaneously provide a guideline for individual behavior as well as serve as possible constraints on individual behavior. The structure of a group includes a network of rules and resources that are used by its members in making decisions about what communication behaviors are expected. Katherine Miller (2008) writes about organizational rules: "Rules act as recipes for social life, in that they are generalizable procedures about how to get things done" (p. 215). Some rules take precedence over others, and history influences the action that is enacted. That is, if a rule worked well in the past, it's likely to be retained; if not, it's likely to be modified or abandoned. Moreover, rules "make certain kinds of conduct possible, while precluding others" (Nicolini, 2013, p. 47). The challenge lies in determining which rule will be the most efficient or productive in achieving the goals of the group or organization. We return to a discussion of rules later in the chapter.

Let's take a moment to examine this issue a little more closely. Giddens (1979) asserts that a rule can only be truly understood "in the context of the historical development" as a whole (p. 65). So, Structuration Theory assumes that to understand the rules of a social system, individuals need to know some of the background resources that led to the rule. Perhaps if Tim from our chapter-opening scenario were to investigate the origins of the rule for addressing superiors, he would have a better understanding of why this rule is currently enforced. There may have been a past incident when employees showed a blatant disregard for their supervisors by substituting nicknames for the informal first names that they were permitted to use in addressing their superiors. For example, Tim may discover that Wayne was called "Wayne the Pain" by his employees years earlier when the rule was not in existence. The company subsequently developed more formal rules to help Wayne enhance his credibility and gain the respect of his employees. However, if after conducting his research, Tim does not discover a satisfactory reason for the structure or rules that are in place, he may try to alter this particular rule. Not only may his refusal to attend meetings demonstrate a personal rule, but it may also be an attempt to exert his power in the group.

The third assumption guiding Structuration Theory posits that power is an influential force in arriving at decisions in organizations. In this theory, **power** is perceived as the ability to achieve results—it enables us to accomplish our goals. Giddens believes that power is a two-way street; any time two people are engaged in communication with each other, both sources have a certain level of power that they bring to the interaction. Even subordinates have some power over superiors. We all have power, but some have more than others. It is important to consider the role that rules play in this discussion of power. Based on the history of an organization, typically rules have been established to grant some members a particular form of power over other members. In BCT, a rule of the group is that Angela has the power to call a meeting of the members.

power
imposition of personal will on others

Tim wants his employees to call him "Tim" and not "Mr. Nash," but the structure—in this case a company norm—does not allow production floor workers to communicate informally. However, Tim's personal communication rule is that his workers should call him by his first name. His rule is based on his training, which taught him that in this situation it would be better for worker morale (and productivity) if subordinates were permitted to call him "Tim." Tim's decision to tell Jeremy to support keeping things the way they are for the time being is based not solely on one rule, but also on Tim's power as a supervisor in this organization. In convincing Angela to call a meeting of division managers to discuss the feasibility of adopting this rule at BCT, Tim is once again able to exert a sense of power that is granted to him as a member of the group and as a division manager. However, we see that all of the division managers bring power in one form or another to the group decision-making process. Darnell brings the power associated with his knowledge of managerial techniques as a result of his MBA. Wayne's extensive background and knowledge of the organization's history afford him a different type of power to bring to the discussion. Angela contributes the power associated with her position as human resources coordinator at BCT.

To summarize, when it comes to decision making, no one power structure in the web of organizational rules is more important than the other. Giddens views power as a two-way street, and the fact that an actor is even invited to participate in discussions and decision making indicates that he or she has a certain amount of power over others.

STRUCTURATION THEORY

Central Concepts of Structuration Theory

Like other communication theories, Structuration Theory is composed of a number of component parts. And, Beth Bonniwell Haslett (2015) asserts that these concepts "have profound implications for organizing and communicating" (p. 6). Let's look at the various elements that are central to understanding the complexity of rules and the influence they have on communication within systems. The concepts we will discuss include agency and reflexivity, duality of structure, and social integration.

Agency and Reflexivity

Structuration Theory is based on the notion that human activity is the source that creates and recreates the social environment in which we exist. Two key terms related to this perspective are agency and agent. **Agency** is defined as the specific behaviors or activities that humans engage in, guided by the rules and contexts in which interactions take place. Agency is normally undertaken by individuals, groups, or organizations themselves (Haslett, 2015). **Agent** refers to the person who engages in these behaviors. For example, students serve as the agents who engage in the agency of attending classes at a college or university. The context of the classroom provides a template of rules that the agents (students) are expected to follow. If the context of the class is a large lecture setting, the rules might dictate that the particular agency (behaviors) to be performed in asking a question be formal in nature (e.g., raising one's hand to ask a question).

M. Scott Poole, David Seibold, and Robert McPhee (1986, 1996) apply the notion of agency to their examination of small groups by proposing that a group's members are aware of and knowledgeable about the events and activities that take place around them. This awareness guides their decision to engage in particular behaviors (agency). According to Structuration theorists, organizations (and groups) engage in a process known as reflexivity. **Reflexivity** refers to the actors' ability to monitor their actions and behaviors. In essence, members of an organization are able to look into the future and make changes in the organization's structure if it appears as if things are not going to work according to plan. An important element in agency and reflexivity is the ability of an individual to articulate the reasons for his or her choices of behavior. When an instructor asks a student why she didn't ask the question during class time, the student may respond that the number of questions being asked was too overwhelming for her to receive personal attention at that time. Thus, the agent has a level of consciousness about his or her behavior and can explain why a particular behavior was chosen over another.

In employing agency and reflexivity, organizations reflect on the structures and systems that are in place, and members have the ability to explain the reasons for the behaviors as well as the ability to identify their goals. This awareness occurs on two levels. **Discursive consciousness** refers to the ability of a person to state his or her thoughts in a language that can be shared with other members of the organization. Put another way, this consciousness pertains to knowledge that can be expressed through words to others. **Practical consciousness** refers to those actions or feelings that cannot be put into words. Modaff and colleagues (2017) state that "some activities and/or feelings are easily explained by individuals (discursive consciousness), while

agency
behaviors or activities used in social environments

agent
a person engaging in behaviors or activities in social environments

reflexivity
a person's ability to monitor his or her actions or behaviors

discursive consciousness
a person's ability to articulate personal goals or behaviors

practical consciousness
a person's inability to articulate personal goals or behaviors

other experiences, behaviors, and feelings are not as easily put into words (practical consciousness)" (p. 118).

To understand these terms, let's look at our opening scenario. Tim may be able to explain the reasons he proposed the change in BCT's rule for supervisor–subordinate communication. He engages in reflexivity by describing his past supervisory experiences and the success that he had in relating to his former employees. Thus, he is using a level of discursive consciousness. What Tim may not be able to articulate is the practical consciousness, or the internal feelings, that he experiences in a formal work environment. Tim might find it difficult to explain the warm, familial feelings that emerge when his employees address him by first name. He also might not realize the fact that when they address him as "Mr. Nash," he feels as though they are addressing his father or grandfather—maybe he does not perceive himself as being old enough to be addressed as "Mr." The agency, Tim's decision to address the issue, is based on his ability to reflect on previous experience.

Reflexivity also enables Tim to make a prediction about how these behaviors will impact employer–employee relationships in the future. Tim's ability to articulate his reasons for his attitudes and actions provides others with an understanding of why he pursues these goals. Both personal and organizational rules are influencing the decision of how employees should address supervisors in the organization. The task Tim faces is in deciding whether to maintain the organizational rule or alter it to accommodate his personal rules.

Duality of Structure

Rules and resources fulfill dual functions in organizations. According to the principle of **duality of structure,** members of an organization depend on **rules** and resources to guide their decisions about the behaviors or actions that they will employ in their communication. When an individual chooses to either follow a rule or alter the rule, then the way that the rule is followed in future interactions changes. Following a rule makes it "valid." Sarah Tracy (2013) contends that duality of structure can be interpreted as follows: "Structure is created from the top down and from the bottom up" (p. 61).

To better understand this relationship, let's explore the distinction between rules and resources. In Structuration Theory, rather than viewing rules as strictly guidelines for *why* something must be done, it is more useful to view them as an instruction manual for *how* a goal may be accomplished. As was stated earlier in this chapter, and as referred to in Chapter 3, these rules may be explicitly stated or implicitly learned. At BCT, Tim realizes that it would not be effective simply to change the communication expectations for his team without first consulting the other managers in the organization. He employs a personal rule that states that he should respect his colleagues and their reasons for organizational protocol. He accomplishes that goal by implementing this rule; he requests a meeting with the human resources coordinator. Next, a group meeting is called to give all division managers the opportunity to express their opinions. The group's rule of giving every member equal voice in arriving at decisions is employed. Finally, a vote is taken to decide the preferred action of the majority of the group's members. Tim could initially decide simply to invoke his own rules and disregard the rules of the organization, but he decides to

duality of structure
rules and resources used to guide organizational decisions about behaviors or actions

rules
general routines that the organization or group follows in accomplishing goals

discuss the issue with his colleagues and supervisors to arrive at a decision. A vital element in understanding why some rules are enforced over others lies in understanding the power that certain agents have in the decision-making process.

Resources refer to the power that individuals bring to the group or organization. Power in this regard can be both tangible (office, supplies, etc.) and intangible (decision-making style). Power is influential because it leads an individual to take action or initiate change.

An organization can employ two types of resources: allocative and authoritative. **Allocative resources** refer to the material assistance generated by an organization to help the group in accomplishing its goal. Suppose a group of college students wants to have access to a facility where they can work out during their breaks between classes or during their "off" time. Some of the group's members decide to write a proposal to college administrators and provide them with a list of activities that they are willing to undertake to raise some of the money if matching funds are secured. Thus, a plan for providing allocative, or material, resources has been established.

Authoritative resources pertain to the interpersonal characteristics that are employed during communication interactions. Recall from Chapter 2 that interpersonal communication pertains to the dynamic between two people. In Structuration Theory, interpersonal communication is viewed as the ability to influence others. Put another way, authoritative resources allow a person to execute power in an organization. Every person possesses a degree of power and influence on the operations of an organization (Modaff et al., 2017).

One key point about power in this theory is how agents can employ power to get what they want in a social system (Poole & McPhee, 2005). To understand better what we mean by power, consider one model of social power (French & Raven, 1959; Raven, 1993) that has had lasting appeal. These bases of power can be thought of as the various authoritative resources employed in organizations. As Giddens suggests (1984), when individuals are oppressed, they still have resources (such as power) available to overcome the status quo. Each power type is explained next and in Table 15.1.

Reward Power **Reward power** is based on a person's perception that another has the ability to provide positive reinforcements. These rewards may come in the form of

Table 15.1 Power Type as a Resource in an Organization

TYPE OF POWER	DEFINITION
Reward	Chris has the ability to provide something of value to Pat.
Coercive	Chris can deliver punishment to Pat.
Referent	Chris achieves agreement or compliance because Pat respects Chris and desires to be like Chris.
Legitimate	Chris exerts control over Pat because of Chris's title or position.
Expert	Chris possesses special knowledge or expertise that Pat needs.

praise, material rewards, or simply removal of negative aspects of the system. Tim's employees may decide to accommodate his request to address him by his first name because they perceive him as having power to promote them or give them raises. If this is the case, reward power is a resource that is affecting communication in the organization.

Coercive Power   If Tim's employees fear that they will be demoted or fired as a result of failing to comply with his wishes to establish relationships on a first-name basis, coercive power may be influencing decisions and communication. **Coercive power** is based on the expectation that an individual has the ability to exact punishment. A person may comply with another's request simply to avoid negative consequences such as losing credibility in front of one's coworkers or getting a rotten work schedule.

coercive power
perception that another person has the ability to punish you

Theory in Popular Press · *Women, Power, and Organizations*

Forbes magazine, one of the country's premier sources for business news, asks one of the most provocative of all business questions: Do women fear power? This essay, underscoring the notion of power, a key Structuration principle, discusses cultural notions of power and organizational life. Writer Caroline Turner is rather direct in her essay's thesis: "Could it be that women lack the ambition and appetite for power that are required to reach the top?" Turner acknowledges that the theme of women and power has ignited a "firestorm" and provides statistics that indicate that as one moves up the corporate ladder, one sees less evidence of women in leadership and powerful roles (e.g., approximately 4 percent of women are CEOs in the Fortune 500). Turner notes that there are different cultural interpretations of power and that masculine and feminine ways of manifesting power exist at many organizations. She believes that the masculine way of power and success is really about winning and competition. The feminine definition of power is about shared cooperation and less of a focus on hierarchy. Turner accepts the fact that her perceptions are rather general and that variations exist. Yet, while each has its advantages, Turner admits that effective and successful businesses manage to integrate both masculine and feminine orientations of power. She concludes by stating that an organizational culture that facilitates "gender diversity in leadership" is more apt to be a welcoming environment for both women and men. Further, she believes that the perception that women do not aspire to be in positions of power is a myth. Rather, Turner contends that many women are "turned off" by masculine scripts of power and companies that embrace an egalitarian framework of power will end up cultivating better male and female leaders.

Source: C. Turner, Do women fear power and success? forbes.com/sites/womensmedia /2012/08/27/do-women-fear-power-and-success.

referent power
perception that another person has the ability to achieve compliance because of established personal relationships

legitimate power
perception that another person has the ability to exert influence because of title or position

expert power
perception that another person has the ability to exert influence because of special knowledge or expertise

Referent Power   Perhaps Tim's employees choose to address him by his first name primarily because he is a friendly, likable person who demonstrates a genuine interest in his workers. Then, the resource guiding communication decisions is due to **referent power,** or the ability of an individual to engage compliance based on the fact that personal relationships have been established between the two interactants.

Legitimate Power   Recall Tim's comment to Jeremy: "This is my division, and I would really prefer if we do things my way." The influence a person exerts on the basis of his or her position or title is called **legitimate power.** If division managers decide to retain the current communication rules simply because they respect Wayne and his tenure with the company, legitimate power is a resource guiding their decision. This type of power is associated with one's right to exert influence.

Expert Power   **Expert power** refers to one's ability to exert influence over others based on the knowledge or expertise that one possesses. In the opening scenario, we learned that Darnell holds an MBA and has extensive knowledge about effective managerial communication strategies in the workplace. If the division managers decide to base their decision to adopt a less-formal environment in the workplace on Darnell's knowledge, his expert power serves as a resource in the decision.

If we were to view power as a resource, as defined in Structuration Theory, duality of structure could be applied to explain how power was used in generating action in the group as well as in determining if power was altered or changed as a result of the action that was taken. For example, many students have assigned expert power to a teacher based on their previous experiences in classes with knowledgeable instructors. However, if an instructor were to enter a classroom and employ profanity or only provide examples based on supermarket tabloids, those same students might alter their personal rule that all teachers possess expert power; they might decide to employ a rule in the future that requires them to be tentative in their decision to assign power to an instructor. This is an example of duality of structure.

Student Voices

Gretchen

I want to write about how power dominates the organization. I worked for a company where no one other than the supervisor had a college degree. He loved that he was the only college graduate, and put the rest of the employees down. He'd do it in a pretty subtle way by saying things like, "I know you all haven't gone to college to know the latest. . . ." The irony about what he'd say was that his college degree did not really qualify him to oversee us (you didn't have to have a college degree to work on painting luminous decorations on alarm clocks!), but he had what we learned was reward power: He made out the schedule. If you needed to have a day off because you couldn't get a baby-sitter or if you wanted a day off to go watch the Red Sox, he was in a (powerful) position to allow (or not allow) that. The guy certainly tried to wield his power at times and it really destroyed the morale in our work unit.

Social Integration

In addition to agency and reflexivity and a duality of structure, an additional key concept functions prominently in Structuration Theory. **Social integration** refers to the reciprocity of communication behaviors among persons in interactions. This is an ongoing process whereby members of an organization become acquainted with one another and form expectations based on previous impressions or information that is learned. If members are interacting with one another for the first time, their knowledge of one another will be quite limited, and the process of social integration will be much more extensive. However, as members become acquainted with one another, the social integration process relies heavily on structures that are recalled from past interactions.

social integration
reciprocity of communication behaviors in interaction

We already know that each interactant brings his or her own background, experiences, and expectations to a communication event. However, as a member of an organization, an individual brings knowledge to the situation that is subject to change based on the influence of both internal and external sources. As we gain a sense of how we and others fit into the group, we begin to communicate and act in ways that indicate the roles we expect each member to fulfill. Expectations for patterns of behavior are established, but these expectations could potentially change as the members of the group interact and evolve.

It's important to note that organizational scholars have found that social integration may be limited. That is, it may be nearly impossible to avoid the fact that people lose self-sufficiency and control (in organizations and in life). These are termed "dividuals," meaning that their individuality has been compromised. As Nicolas Bencherki and James Snack (2016) observe: "people are not whole, coherent entities that fit in a single organization, in the same way as the Matryoshka dolls nest within each other. Rather, they each constitute societies that hold together the many 'pre-individual' elements that constitute them" (p. 284). Thus, although social integration is a profound communication process in Structuration Theory, it can be limited insofar as people may lose their full identity as an organizational member.

Recall the meeting of the division managers. Because Tim is the newest member of the group, the other division managers may be uncertain about what type of power to attribute to him as he presents his ideas. The same applies to Tim's interactions with his subordinates. As Tim and the others engage in subsequent interactions, his view of himself and others' views of Tim will evolve.

Application of Time and Space

We now examine the role of time and space in organizations. Structuration theorists believe that all social interaction in an organization is composed of temporal (time) and spatial (space) dimensions. This time–space distanciation is an important feature of the theory. The actual communication or interaction that takes place in the organization can be examined as existing in real time and as taking place in real locations (space).

We hear a message as it occurs in a context. For instance, think about a conversation that your supervisor has with you about company layoffs while the two of you are walking to your cars at the end of the workday. The supervisor's decision to talk about this topic, in this place (parking lot), and at this particular time would be of interest to Structuration theorists. However, researchers would likely need to look more deeply to determine the factors that motivated your boss to communicate this message to you. Furthermore, does your boss make reference to past experiences with company layoffs? Does she look ahead to potential consequences if such a layoff were to happen? And, especially relevant to many communication researchers, if a layoff were to be announced, how would it be communicated to employees? A mass email? Public posting? How would the conversation, as Poole and McPhee (2005) express it, "bind" (p. 180) space and time in the discussion of company layoffs?

Essentially, space is viewed as a contextual element that has meaning for the various members of a group or organization. The elements of time and space are factors that enable us to engage in communication. One's view of his or her tenure in a group spans both time and space and influences the decisions that are made. For example, in our opening scenario, it is not likely that a single event or a single location has solely influenced Tim's action to request a change in the company's policy. Rather, it is a series of experiences and references that are the result of his own managerial history—and perhaps even his own experience as an employee in an organization—that have influenced his choice of action.

Integration, Critique, and Closing

Organizations remain central to our lives. It is estimated that company employees spend almost 90 percent of their time in group or team meetings. In fact, 54 percent of employees spend up to 30 percent of their day in team settings and as much as 50 percent of their time working in a team setting (kenblanchard.com/img/pub/pdf_critical_role_teams.pdf). Structuration Theory provides an important framework for understanding these communication opportunities. The theory has been historically linked to empiricism, making it aligned with quantitative methods. Still, some organizational scholars have used case studies, resulting in research that employs qualitative methods as well. Among the criteria relevant to evaluating theory, we identify two for our discussion: scope and parsimony.

Integration

Communication Tradition	Rhetorical	Semiotic	Phenomenological	**Cybernetic**	Socio-Psychological	**Socio-Cultural**	Critical
Communication Context	Intrapersonal	Interpersonal	**Small Group**	**Organizational**	Public/Rhetorical	Mass/Media	Cultural
Approach to Knowing	**Positivistic/Empirical**	**Interpretive/Hermeneutic**	Critical

Critique

Evaluation Criteria	**Scope**	Logical Consistency	**Parsimony**	Utility	Testability	Heurism	Test of Time

Scope

Structuration Theory can be applied to numerous social settings involving teams and small groups (McPhee, et al., 2013; Poole, 2013) and scores of communication interactions. As noted previously, the areas of communication that have applied the theory with the most theoretical success are organizational communication and group/team communication. Our focus has been on the organizational environment, namely, how the structures created in organizations influence communication and decisions.

Still, some concerns related to the theory's breadth exists. At first glance, you may view the theory as too expansive, resulting in too broad a scope. With a discussion of rules, resources, power, and discourse, it would seem that the theory is trying to do too much at one time. Indeed, in his review of the theory, Rob Stones (2005) asserts that Giddens's theory should be "clearer, tighter, and more systematic than Giddens has been about Structuration theory's distinctive and defining characteristics" (p. 1). Other writers (Miles, 2014) describe the theory as "a very ambitious effort" (p. 324) that tries to collapse various schools of thought into one theory.

Parsimony

Recall that this criterion responds to the following question: Is the theory easy to understand or cumbersome? Many organizational communication and management theorists have argued the theory is laden with terminology that is challenging to understand. For example, Wafa Kort and Jamel Gharbi (2013) state that "there is a consensus toward the difficulty that the readers encounter when they try to understand Structuration theory" (p. 95). Stephen Banks and Patricia Riley (1993) agree. They point out that Structuration Theory is difficult to understand: "Structuration lacks certain characteristics that communication researchers and other social science scientists often find appealing: It is not quickly read, immediately intuitive, or parsimonious" (p. 178). Banks and Riley present many concepts as they examine the intricate process of how organizations and groups structure their communication and arrive at decisions. Their advice to those who are researching this theory in an attempt to understand organizations and groups is to "begin at the beginning" (p. 181). This requires insight and understanding of the historical rules brought into an organization by each member—and this is an extremely difficult task to accomplish. Furthermore, Banks and Riley suggest that scholars resist the temptation to apply preestablished categories in explaining how organizations (and groups) are developed and how they experience change. Perhaps Daniel Broger's (2011) comments summarize the notion of the theory's potential ambiguity. He notes that the theory "requires considerable time and effort on the part of scholars not familiar with social theory in general and structuration theory in particular to come to grips with Giddens's comprehensive theory" (p. 3).

Closing

Structuration theorists Giddens, Poole, Seibold, and McPhee provide communication scholars a theory that considers the interplay between and among people and their resources in organizations (and small groups). The theory has drawn its critics, and Giddens has not helped his own theoretical reputation since he failed to address many of the criticisms and failed to provide clarifications on the criticisms levied against him and his theory (Broger, 2011). Nonetheless, complexity and deference is not tantamount to theoretical rejection. Structuration Theory, therefore, will continue to resonate to those interested in the rules, principles, and processes in organizational life.

Discussion Starters

TECH QUEST: Structuration Theory suggests that organizational agents can utilize power in various ways. With the advent of social media, however, power seems to be much more diffused than when this theory was conceptualized. Indicate whether or not you agree with this and why.

1. Recall a time when you were involved in a group similar to the Bayside City Tire Company—a time when a decision had to be made. What were some of the rules that influenced the process of decision making? Were the rules changed as a result of the decision that was reached or the process that was followed in arriving at that decision? If so, how?

2. One of the assumptions of this theory is that power structures are present in groups and guide the decision-making process by providing us with information on how to best accomplish our goals. Discuss the potential positive and negative implications of power as an element of structuration.

3. Giddens proposes that structure (rules and resources) should not be viewed as a barrier to interaction, but as a necessary part of the creation of the interaction. Do you agree or disagree with this position? Defend your answer.

4. Identify elements of other communication theories that are evident in the Structuration approach to groups, teams, and organizations.

5. Structuration Theory proposes that structures themselves should be viewed as being nontemporal and nonspatial. Discuss the significance of this idea. Provide an example from your own experience of the influence of time and space in a group or organization.

6. How would you explain your family using any of the principles of Structuration Theory?

7. Structuration theorists state that the theory has the potential to provide real-world applications. Discuss your reaction to this claim.

CHAPTER 16

Organizational Culture Theory

Based on the research of **Clifford Geertz, Michael Pacanowsky,**
and **Nick O'Donnell-Trujillo**

> We believe that the particular potential of the organizational culture metaphor lies in its ability to liberate our thinking about both organizations and communication.
>
> —Michael Pacanowsky and Nick O'Donnell-Trujillo

Amelia Callahan

As an employee of Grace's Jewelers, Amelia Callahan knew that her job was unlike those of her friends. The company employed about 180 people throughout its 20 stores in the southeastern United States and targeted primarily teenage girls who frequented malls. Its founder, Grace Talmage, made it a point to visit employees like Amelia each month, helping them to feel good about working in such a small company.

Amelia's relationship with Grace had always been quite cordial. Why wouldn't it be? She received excellent commission rates and a reasonable health care package (including dental and vision care) and got along superbly with her supervisor. In addition, Amelia and the other employees were able to wear casual clothing to work, which made them the envy of other workers in the mall. All of this may explain why Amelia had worked for the company for almost nine years and why she had no plans to leave—until now.

After 24 years in the business, Grace decided it was time to sell the business and retire. Because of the profits that Grace has shown over the years, Jewelry Plus, a large retail jewelry store, decided to bid for the small chain. Although Grace did not want to sell to such a retail giant,

their bid was simply too good to pass up. In the end, she decided to sell her business, much to the disappointment of her employees. Amelia was especially concerned after hearing gossip about the larger company's treatment of its employees and its way of handling day-to-day operations. She privately wondered how much would change once Grace sold the stores. She needed the job, though, and decided to stay on.

Amelia's instincts were right. Once the company's transition was completed, she had to undergo a "new employee" orientation, which meant standing in front of all of the new employees and informally talking about why she had applied to the company. Among the new company policies were new dress codes and a new policy for store exchanges. Amelia could no longer wear casual clothing; instead, she had to wear a company uniform and black shoes with low heels.

With respect to store exchanges, company policy changed from "complete satisfaction or 100 percent money-back guarantee" to "product must be returned within 10 days with register receipt." Although Amelia thought that this new policy would turn many customers away, the success of Jewelry Plus was proof enough that it had worked in the past.

Finally, with the new company, her health benefits no longer included dental or vision coverage. This lack of coverage was grist for the gossip mill. The story that Amelia heard during her orientation was that an employee actually lost two back teeth because she couldn't afford the dental bills! With all the changes in store policies, dress codes, and company philosophies, Amelia and a number of her coworkers felt overwhelmed. In fact, many of Amelia's coworkers, with whom she had worked over the past nine years, quit their jobs. As a single parent, however, Amelia felt that she couldn't resign just yet.

On top of all that, her new boss was a disaster! Amelia and her coworkers nicknamed him "The Shadow" because he stood right behind them as they waited on and rang up their customers. Having her supervisor watch everything she did was annoying and seemed pointless to Amelia, especially considering the fact that most of her customers were teenagers, who were fickle in their purchasing behaviors.

Despite these concerns, Amelia went to the company's first picnic. She didn't really want to, but she thought that she should give the company a chance. As she and her old and new coworkers drank ice tea and ate hot dogs, they seemed to bond. Former employees of Grace's Jewelers told the workers of the retail giant about the way things used to be. They seemed to be genuinely interested in hearing about people like Gabby, the 70-year-old retiree who wouldn't stop talking to customers. There was a great deal of laughing about the old times.

The day ended quite differently from the way Amelia had envisioned it. She made a few friends, reminisced about the past, and felt a bit more comfortable with her future. Although she knew that her boss would be difficult to deal with, Amelia decided that she would try to make the most out of her job. At the very least, she thought, she had some people in whom to confide.

Once you graduate from college, it's likely that many of you will work for an organization. Organizational life is characterized as much by change as it is by anything else. Change is frequently marked by such feelings as excitement, anxiety, uncertainty, frustration, and disbelief. These emotions are especially acute during stressful times, for example, during a recession and during company layoffs.

Go to any bookstore on campus or at the mall and you're sure to see a number of books on organizational life. This pop culture approach to the world of corporate America is everywhere. Some authors tell us that there are *Ten Easy Ways to Get a Raise* or that there are *Eight Safe Steps to Being Promoted*. Other authors have made millions touting the importance of *Communicating with Difficult People* and *Working to Live and Living to Work*. Most of these books center on what people can do to make their lives easier in the workplace. The problem, however, is that organizational life is very complex. Further, few "easy ways" to anything exist in organizations and clearly, one difficult person one day may turn into a pleasant person the next day.

To understand organizational life beyond pop culture—including an organization's values, stories, goals, practices (including technological), and philosophies—Michael Pacanowsky and Nick O'Donnell-Trujillo (1982, 1983, 1990) conceptualized Organizational Culture Theory (OCT). Pacanowsky and O'Donnell-Trujillo believe that organizations can best be understood using a cultural lens, an idea originally proposed by anthropologist Clifford Geertz. They indicate that researchers are limited in their understanding of organizations when they follow the scientific method, a process we outline in Chapter 3. According to Pacanowsky and O'Donnell-Trujillo, the scientific method is constrained by its task of measuring, rather than discovering. Pacanowsky and O'Donnell-Trujillo (1982) argue that Organizational Culture Theory invites all researchers "to observe,

"That's our mission statement."

record, and make sense of the communicative behavior of organizational members" (p. 129). They embrace the "totality or lived experience within organizations" (Pacanowsky, 1989, p. 250). The theorists paint a broad stroke in their understanding of organizations by stating that "culture is not something an organization has; a culture is something an organization is" (Pacanowsky & O'Donnell-Trujillo, 1982, p. 146).

Culture is communicatively constructed by organizational practices, and culture is distinct to each organization. For the theorists, understanding individual organizations is more important than generalizing from a set of behaviors or values across organizations. Further, it is important to accept the notion that organizational culture "is created over a period of time," although culture is rather resilient and long-lasting (inthelibrarywiththeleadpipe.org/2012/thats-how-we-do-things-around-here). These thoughts form the backdrop of the theory.

Think about the types of organizations to which you now belong. They may vary in scope and size and may contain a number of practices that are unique to the organization. For instance, one organization that we all have in common is an academic one—a college or university. You've heard and perhaps shared stories about certain professors and classes to take or to avoid. There are various rites of passage in college, such as new-student orientation, fraternity or sorority rush, and eating cafeteria food! Practices such as advising and internships also characterize institutions of higher education. Years ago, students visited professors to get information and clarification on different subjects; today, much of that is done via email.

It is clear that the essence of organizational life is found in its culture. In this sense of the word, *culture* does not refer to the variety of races, ethnicities, and backgrounds of individuals, a perspective we discussed in Chapter 2. Rather, according to

People are like spiders who are suspended in webs that they created at work. An organization's culture is composed of shared symbols, each of which has a unique meaning. Organizational stories, rituals, values, and rites of passage are examples of the culture of an organization.

organizational culture theorists, culture is a way of living in an organization. Organizational culture includes the emotional and psychological climate or atmosphere. This may involve employee morale, attitudes, and levels of productivity, competition, autonomy, and cooperation (Moon, Quigley, & Marr, 2012). Organizational culture also includes all the symbols (actions, routines, conversations, etc.) and the meanings that people attach to these symbols. Cultural meaning and understanding are achieved through the interactions employees and management have with one another. Joann Keyton (2005) states the following about organizational culture: "Although difficult to describe, as an employee we know what it's like in our organization" (p. 1). We begin our discussion of OCT by first interpreting culture and then presenting three assumptions of the theory.

The Cultural Metaphor: Of Spider Webs and Organizations

The origin of the word *culture* is interesting. Culture originally referred to preparing the ground for tending crops and animals. It was interpreted as fostering growth. When we contextualize "culture" within an organization, we need to understand that there is more than "what meets the eye." In other words, **organizational culture** includes what is visible. Yet, organizational culture also includes what we cannot "see," including, as we alluded to earlier, convictions, priorities, among others (Bremer, 2012).

organizational culture
the essence of organizational life

Pacanowsky and O'Donnell-Trujillo (1982) believe that organizational culture "indicates what constitutes the legitimate realm of inquiry" (p. 122). In other words, organizational culture is the essence of organizational life. As we mentioned earlier, they apply anthropological principles to construct their theory. Specifically, they adopt the Symbolic-Interpretive approach articulated by Clifford Geertz (1973) in their theoretical model. Geertz remarks that people are animals "suspended in webs of significance" (p. 5). He adds that people spin webs themselves. Pacanowsky and O'Donnell-Trujillo (1982) comment on Geertz's metaphor:

> The web not only exists, it is spun. It is spun when people go about the business of construing their world as sensible—that is, when they communicate. When they talk, write a play, sing, dance, fake an illness, they are communicating, and they are constructing their culture. The web is the residue of the communication process. (p. 147)

A primary goal of researchers, then, should be to think about all possible weblike configurations (features) in organizations.

ORGANIZATIONAL CULTURE THEORY

Geertz invokes the image of a spider web deliberately. He believes that culture is like the webs spun by a spider. That is, webs are intricate designs, and each web is different from all others. Furthermore, webs "represent strength, life, and cohesion, but they are also things that need constant maintenance . . . ." (Modaff, Butler, & DeWine, 2011, p. 95). For Geertz, cultures are like this as well. Basing his conclusions on various cultures around the world, Geertz argues that cultures are all different and that their uniqueness should be celebrated. To understand a culture, Geertz believes that researchers should begin to focus on the meaning shared within it. We examine more of Geertz's beliefs later.

Pacanowsky and O'Donnell-Trujillo (1983) apply these basic principles to organizations. Employees and managers alike spin their webs. People are critical in the organization, and therefore, it is important to study their behaviors in conjunction with the overall organization. Pacanowsky and O'Donnell-Trujillo claim that members of organizations engage in a number of communication behaviors that contribute to the culture of the company. They may do this through a number of ways, including gossiping, joking, backstabbing, or becoming romantically involved with others. Further, with 88 percent of companies using some form of social media (http://www.adweek.com/socialtimes/social-media-companies/502447), we need to accept that some of this communication will take place via technology.

The organizational culture at Jewelry Plus will be inevitably revealed in a number of ways. You will recall that Amelia learned of the new owner through gossip and that the company picnic was a way for her to learn more about the new company culture. No doubt she will experience an organizational culture with her new job that is very different from what she experienced with Grace's Jewelers. The company has changed, the faces are new, and the rules reflect new ownership. Amelia also contributes to the spinning of the organizational web by both responding to company stories and passing them on to others. In sum, the web of organizational culture has been spun. This broad perspective underscores why Pacanowsky and O'Donnell-Trujillo argue that organizational culture "is not just another piece of the puzzle; it **is** the puzzle" (p. 146).

Assumptions of Organizational Cultural Theory

The study of organizations and workplace settings began earnest in the late 1960s, especially because of a 1967 NASA conference on organizational communication (Rocci & de Saussure, 2016). Since the NASA gathering, organizational culture scholars have tried to understand the various challenges, goals, behaviors, and people in the workplace. Three assumptions guide Organizational Culture Theory. As you work through these assumptions, keep in mind the diversity and complexity of organizational life. Also, understand that these assumptions emphasize the process view of organizations that Pacanowsky and O'Donnell-Trujillo advocate:

- Organizational members create and maintain a shared sense of organizational reality, resulting in a better understanding of the values of an organization.
- The use and interpretation of symbols are critical to an organization's culture.
- Cultures vary across organizations, and the interpretations of actions within these cultures are diverse.

The first assumption pertains to the importance of people in organizational life. Specifically, individuals share in creating and maintaining their reality. These individuals include employees, supervisors, and employers. At the core of this assumption are an organization's values. Values are the standards and principles within a culture that have intrinsic worth to a culture. Values inform organizational members about what is important. Pacanowsky (1989) notes that values derive from "moral knowledge" (p. 254) and that people display their moral knowledge through narratives or stories. The stories that Amelia hears and shares, for example, will result in her understanding the organization's values.

People share in the process of discovering an organization's values. Being a member of an organization requires active participation in that organization. The meanings of particular symbols—for instance, why a company continues to interview prospective employees when massive layoffs are under way—are communicated by both employees and management. The symbolic meaning of hiring new people when others are being fired will not escape savvy workers; why dedicate money to new personnel when others are losing their jobs? Pacanowsky and O'Donnell-Trujillo (1982) believe that employees contribute to the shaping of organizational culture. Their behaviors are instrumental in creating and ultimately maintaining organizational reality.

The reality (and culture) of an organization are also determined in part by the symbols, the second assumption of the theory. Earlier we noted that Pacanowsky and O'Donnell-Trujillo adopted the Symbolic-Interpretive perspective of Geertz. This perspective underscores the use of symbols in organizations, and, as we mentioned in Chapter 1, symbols are representations for meaning. Organizational members create, use, and interpret symbols every day. These symbols, therefore, are important to the company's culture. Mary Jo Hatch (2006) extends the notion of symbols in her discussion of the categories of symbolic meaning (Table 16.1).

Symbols include the verbal and nonverbal communication in an organization. Frequently, these symbols communicate an organization's values. Symbols may

Table 16.1 Symbols of an Organizational Culture

GENERAL CATEGORY	SPECIFIC TYPES/EXAMPLES
Physical Symbols	Art/design/logo buildings/decor dress/appearance material objects
Behavioral Symbols	Ceremonies/rituals traditions/customs rewards/punishments
Verbal Symbols	Anecdotes/jokes jargon/names/nicknames explanations stories/myths/history metaphors

take the form of slogans that carry meaning. For example, several companies—past and present—have slogans that symbolize their values, including State Farm Insurance ("Like a good neighbor, State Farm is there"), the *New York Times* ("All the News That's Fit to Print"), and Disneyland ("The Happiest Place on Earth"). The extent to which these symbols are effective relies not only on the media, but also on how the company's employees enact them. For example, Disneyland's belief that it is the happiest place on earth would be quite odd if its employees didn't smile or if they were rude. In fact, the corporate culture of Disney ensures that they retain the most loyal, engaged, and customer-centered employees (Lipp, 2013).

For evidence of verbal symbols in an organization, consider this story. A supervisor named Derrick communicates a great deal about values in casual conversation with his employees. Derrick frequently tells long stories about how he handled a particular issue at a previous workplace. He often launches into detailed accounts of how, for instance, he managed to get his employees a bonus at the end of the year. His stories inevitably begin with a short vignette about his upbringing in Arkansas and end with a moral. At first, employees were unsure how to handle this type of communication. As time went on, however, they soon realized that Derrick was trying to demonstrate a connection with his employees and to indicate that although problems may seem insurmountable, he knows ways to handle them. Through many of his stories, he communicates that he cares about the issues of the company and the workers; he also communicates a new view of what he thinks the organizational culture should be.

Our third assumption of OCT pertains to the variety of organizational cultures. Simply put, organizational cultures vary tremendously. The perceptions of the actions and activities within these cultures are just as diverse as the cultures themselves. Consider what it is like for Amelia as she moves from Grace's Jewelers to Jewelry Plus. We have already provided a number of examples that underscore the various cultural issues within each company. Her perceptions, however, and her participation in the culture may differ from those of others. Some people might appreciate a cultural change after working so many years for the same small company.

As an employee in a small jewelry store, Amelia knew that a store's problems could readily be resolved and that any suggestions for changes were welcomed and enacted. The culture was such that employees were empowered to make quick decisions, often without supervisor approval. Exceptions to the store return policy, for instance, were handled by all employees. The store's founder felt that employees were in the best position to deal with difficult problems needing quick resolutions. In addition, employee rewards for customer service were routine, and conflict mediation and anger management programs were available for both employees and management. These organizational practices communicate the importance of a shared sense of organizational reality among employees. Employees at Grace's Jewelers got together regularly for F.A.C.—Friday Afternoon Club—at a local restaurant. These activities communicated the esprit de corps in the company. The employees of Grace's were members of an organizational culture who "constitute and reveal their culture to themselves and to others" (Pacanowsky & O'Donnell-Trujillo, 1982, p. 131).

The organizational culture of Jewelry Plus is very different from that of Grace's, and Amelia's experiences with Jewelry Plus are very different from hers with Grace's

Jewelers. The corporate giant has no exception to its policy on store returns, and any suggestions for store improvement must be placed in the employee suggestion box or emailed to the national headquarters. A sense of community is not encouraged at Jewelry Plus because tasks clearly promote autonomy. There are some efforts to ensure that employees have time together—through breaks, lunch, or holiday gatherings—but these opportunities are too limited to foster collegiality. In addition, email is closely monitored by supervisors. Clearly, without collegiality, stories, rituals, and rites of passage are restricted. It should be obvious that significant differences exist in the organizational cultures of Grace's and Jewelry Plus.

We have presented three assumptions of Organizational Culture Theory. Each is grounded in the belief that when researchers study organizational cultures, they will uncover a complex and intricate web. Pacanowsky and O'Donnell-Trujillo believe that the Symbolic-Interpretive perspective provides a realistic picture of the culture of a company. To gain a better sense of how they went about studying organizations, we turn our attention to the primary methodology employed in their work and the work of their predecessor, Clifford Geertz: ethnography.

Ethnographic Understanding: Laying It On Thick

Communication and performance studies scholar Dwight Conquergood (1992, 1994) studied one of the most intriguing of all research topics in communication: gang communication. In an effort to understand gang communication, Conquergood moved into a run-down building in Chicago known at the time as "Big Red." He lived in the building for nearly two years, observing and participating in virtually all parts of life occupied by gang members. Through observing, participating, and taking notes, Conquergood's research offered a view of gang communication virtually ignored in the media. He uncovered many private rituals and symbols, and his work enabled the gang population to have a "voice" never written about in the communication discipline. His efforts in revealing gang-related stories to others is part of ethnography, the underlying methodology of Organizational Culture Theory.

You will recall that Pacanowsky and O'Donnell-Trujillo based much of their work on Geertz's. Because Geertz's work was ethnographic in nature, let's briefly discuss the ethnographic orientation of Geertz and explain its relationship to the theory.

Geertz (1973) argues that to understand a culture one must see it from the members' points of view. In order to do this, Geertz believes researchers should become ethnographers. Ethnography is a qualitative methodology that uncovers and interprets artifacts, stories, rituals, and practices to reveal meaning in a culture (Pachirat, 2013). Ethnographers frequently refer to their study as naturalistic research in that they believe that the manner in which they study cultures is much more natural than, say, that of quantitative researchers. In this spirit, Geertz remarked that ethnography is not an experimental science but rather a methodology that uncovers meaning. Discovering meaning, then, is paramount to ethnographers. Geertz, and later Pacanowsky and O'Donnell-Trujillo, primarily subscribe to direct observation, interviews, and participant observation in finding meaning in culture.

ORGANIZATIONAL CULTURE THEORY

Student Voices

Jackson

When we talked about ethnography, I knew I'd do my ethnographic study on where I work. It's a fast-food place, but there is so much politics in who gets what schedule, where we are assigned to work, and whether or not we get overtime. It's a place where the manager has the final say. Although she pretends to think it's an "inclusive" place where employees have input, it's anything but that. It's a top-down restaurant where punishments are great and rewards are few.

field journal
personal log to record feelings about communicating with people in a different culture from one's own

thick description
explanation of the layers of meaning in a culture

As an ethnographer, Geertz spent many years studying various cultures. His writings have addressed a number of diverse subjects, from Zen Buddhism to island life in Indonesia. During his stay in some of these places, he relied heavily on field notes and kept a **field journal**, recording his feelings and ideas about his interactions with members of a specific culture. In his writings, Geertz (1973) concludes that ethnography is a kind of **thick description**, or an explanation of the intricate layers of meaning underlying a culture. Ethnographers, therefore, strive to understand the thick description of a culture and "to ferret out the unapparent import of things" (p. 26). Interestingly, Geertz believes that any cultural analysis is incomplete because the deeper one goes, the more complex the culture becomes. Therefore, it is not possible to be completely certain of a culture and its norms or values.

Geertz (1983) points out that this qualitative methodology is not equivalent to walking a mile in the shoes of those studied. This thinking only perpetuates "the myth of the chameleon fieldworker, perfectly self-tuned to his [her] exotic surroundings, a walking miracle of empathy, tact, patience, and cosmopolitanism" (p. 56). Geertz suggests that a balance must be struck between naturally observing and recording behavior and integrating a researcher's values into the process. He states that "the trick is to figure out what the devil they think they are up to" (p. 58). This, as you might imagine, can be quite difficult for ethnographers.

Pacanowsky and O'Donnell-Trujillo were drawn to Geertz's ethnographic experiences and his articulation of the importance of observation, analysis, and interpretation. Their own research experiences with different co-cultures proved invaluable. For instance, Pacanowsky (1983) observed police in the Salt Lake [Utah] valley, and Trujillo (1983) studied a new- and used-car dealership. The diversity of their experiences in these smaller cultures in the United States prompted them to acknowledge that cultural performances, or what we call storytelling, are instrumental in communicating about an organization's culture. We return to the topic of performance a bit later in this chapter.

Organizational Culture Theory is rooted in ethnography, and organizational culture should be understood with ethnographic principles in mind. In fact, ethnographer Bruce Lunsford (2015) found the theory and its origins to be "amazing, illuminating, excellent, and useful" (pp. 2, 3). Let's explore ethnography by using our example of Amelia Callahan. If ethnographers were interested in studying the culture of her new job at Jewelry Plus, they might begin by examining several areas: For instance, what sort of new corporate rules are in place? What do new employees like Amelia think about them? What types of strategies are used to ease the transition for employees like Amelia? Are there any corporate philosophies or ideologies? Are there morale problems? How are they resolved? Has the company responded to employee complaints? If so, how? If not, why not? These and a host of other questions would begin the ethnographic process of understanding the organizational culture of Jewelry Plus.

We could never fully capture the excitement of ethnography in this limited space. Yet we hope that you have grounding in the basic processes associated with ethnography and an understanding of why Pacanowsky and O'Donnell-Trujillo embrace such a methodology in their work on organizational culture. We now wish to expand on the topic of performance, which is a key component in OCT.

The Communicative Performance

Pacanowsky and O'Donnell-Trujillo (1982) contend that organizational members act out certain communication performances, which result in a unique organizational culture. **Performance** is a metaphor that suggests a symbolic process of understanding human behavior in an organization. Organizational performances frequently mimic the theater, in that both supervisor and employees choose to take on various roles, or parts, in their organization. To some extent, the workplace can be viewed as stage and each "actor" enacts different scripted and unscripted dialogues. Let's explore their system of performances.

The theorists outline five cultural performances: ritual, passion, social, political, and enculturation. In Table 16.2, we identify these performances. As we discuss each, we will provide various examples from different contexts to communicate the diversity embedded in each performance. Although the category system is not

performance
metaphor suggesting that organizational life is like a theatrical presentation

Table 16.2 Cultural Performances in Organizations

Ritual Performances	Personal rituals—checking voicemail and email; task rituals—issuing tickets, collecting fees; social rituals—happy-hour gatherings; organizational rituals—department meetings, company picnics
Passion Performances	Storytelling, metaphors, and exaggerated speech—"this is the most unappreciative company," "follow the chain of command or it'll get wrapped around your neck"
Social Performances	Acts of civility and politeness; extensions of etiquette—customer thank-yous, water cooler chat, supporting another's "face"
Political Performances	Exercising control, power, and influence—"barking" bosses, intimidation rituals, use of informants, bargaining
Enculturation Performances	Acquired competencies over organizational career—learning/teaching roles, orientations, interviews

necessarily exclusive, you will get an idea about the extent to which organizations vary in terms of how human behavior can be understood. Further, recall back to our discussion of organizational symbols. As you read about performance, keep in mind this is one way that an organization and its people interpret their environment.

Ritual Performances

ritual performances
regular and recurring presentations in the workplace

personal rituals
routines done at the workplace each day

task rituals
routines associated with a particular job in the workplace

social rituals
routines that involve relationships with others in the workplace

Communication performances that occur on a regular and recurring basis are termed **ritual performances**. Rituals include four types: personal, task, social, and organizational. **Personal rituals** include things that you routinely do each day at the workplace. For instance, many organizational members regularly check their voice mail or email when they get to work each day. **Task rituals** are routinized behaviors associated with a person's job. Task rituals get the job done. For instance, task rituals of employees of the Department of Motor Vehicles include issuing eye and written examinations, taking pictures of prospective drivers, administering driving tests, verifying car insurance, and the stories that employees share with one another collecting fees. **Social rituals** are the verbal and nonverbal routines that normally take into consideration the interactions with others. For instance, some organizational members get together for a happy hour in bars on Fridays, celebrating the week's end.

Theory-Into-Practice

Organizational Culture Theory

Theoretical Claim: Culture is an intangible and crucial component of all organizations.
Practical Claim: As the HR guru of *BGone,* a start-up focusing on European travel, Hinto knows that the company's mission is related to (a) how employees are treated and their opportunities (e.g., monthly social events, child care, stock options, etc.) and (b) community commitments (e.g., mentoring, etc.). Taken together, these efforts comprise the organizational culture that Hinto must communicate to all employees.

organizational rituals
routines that pertain to the organization overall

With respect to your own social rituals, consider the social routines you experience in your classes. Many of you arrive early to catch up with your classmates on what has happened since the last time you spoke and continue the social ritual either during a class break or after class. Social rituals may also include nonverbal behaviors in an organization, including casual Fridays and employee-of-the-month awards. Finally, **organizational rituals** include frequently occurring company events such as division meetings, faculty meetings, and even company picnics like the one Amelia Callahan attended.

passion performances
organizational stories that employees share with one another

Passion Performances

The organizational stories that members enthusiastically relate to others are termed **passion performances**. Many times, people in organizations become fervent in their storytelling. Consider, for instance, the experience of Adam, who works at a national retail store. Adam and his coworkers hear and retell stories about their department supervisor. The story goes that the boss walks the perimeter of their department every 30 minutes to get an expanded view of the workers and customers. If the supervisor sees something that he thinks is peculiar, he calls the employee into the back room, reviews a videotape of the event, and asks the employee what he or she will do to improve any future problems. Adam relates that all of his coworkers passionately tell this story over and over to both new and seasoned employees. In fact, even after six years, Adam's passion for sharing the story is the same as when he told it for the first time.

Social Performances

Whereas passionate performances, like Adam's, appear to have little regard for the butt of the story, **social performances** are the common extensions of civility, politeness, and courtesy used to encourage cooperation among organizational members. The adage that "a little goes a long way" relates directly to this performance. Whether with a smile or a "good morning" greeting, establishing some sense of collegiality is frequently part of an organization's culture.

Performing these "niceties" may be viewed as either trivial and yet, it is often difficult to be polite. When the mood is tense, it is both trying and somewhat insincere to smile or to wish another a "good morning." Most organizations wish to maintain a professional decorum, even in difficult times, and these social performances help to accomplish this.

social performances *organizational behaviors intended to demonstrate cooperation and politeness with others*

Political Performances

When organizational cultures communicate **political performances**, they are exercising power or control. Acquiring and maintaining power and control is a hallmark of U.S. corporate life. In fact, some might argue that power and control pervade organizational life. Nonetheless, because by their nature most organizations are hierarchical, there must be someone with the power to accomplish things and with enough control to maintain the bottom line.

As organizational members engage in political performances, they essentially communicate a desire to influence others. That is not necessarily a bad thing. Let's consider an extended example here. Consider the experiences of a group of nurses, for instance, at Spring Valley Hospital. For years, the nurses were quiet regarding their second-class status relative to the hospital's physicians. Recently, however, the nurses decided to speak out about their treatment. They talked to physicians, other medical staff, and patients. In this instance, they were exercising more control over their jobs. Their cultural political performances centered on being recognized for their competency as medical professionals and for their commitment to the mission of the hospital. Their goal was to be legitimized in the hospital by the physicians, their coworkers, and the patients. Their performances, no doubt, were critical in establishing a modified organizational culture.

political performances *organizational behaviors that demonstrate power or control*

Enculturation Performances

The fifth type of performance identified by Pacanowsky and O'Donnell-Trujillo is termed **enculturation performance**. Enculturation performances refer to how

enculturation performances *organizational behaviors that assist employees in discovering what it means to be a member of an organization*

members obtain the knowledge and skills in order to become contributing members of the organization. These performances may be bold or subtle, and they demonstrate a member's competency within an organization. In the chapter-opening scenario, for example, a number of performances will be enacted to enculturate Amelia into her new position. She will watch and listen to her colleagues "perform" their thoughts and feelings on a number of issues: work hours, employee discounts, and the company newsletter, among others. In sum, Amelia will begin to know the organization's culture.

As we mentioned previously, these performances may overlap. It is possible, therefore, to have social performances considered ritual performances. Think about, for instance, greeting one coworker with "Good morning" or fetching coffee for another each day. In this example, the acts of politeness are considered to be a personal (and even task) ritual. Therefore, the performance may be both a social and a ritual performance.

Furthermore, performances may arise from a conscious decision to act out thoughts and feelings about an issue, as in our example of the nurses at Spring Valley Hospital. Or the performances may be more intuitive, as in our example of Amelia Callahan. It is clear that Pacanowsky and O'Donnell-Trujillo believe that communicative performances are critical to an organization's culture and are important symbols of communication.

Integration, Critique, and Closing

Organizational Culture Theory, as articulated by Pacanowsky and O'Donnell-Trujillo, remains an important influence on organizational communication theory and research. The majority of research conducted using OCT has been qualitative in nature since the theorists contend that honoring the organizational "voice" is essential to understanding the organization. To evaluate the effectiveness of the theory, we discuss three criteria: logical consistency, utility, and heurism.

Integration

Communication Tradition	Rhetorical	Semiotic	Phenomenological	Cybernetic	Socio-Psychological	**Socio-Cultural**	Critical
Communication Context	Intrapersonal	Interpersonal	Small Group	**Organizational**	Public/Rhetorical	Mass/Media	Cultural
Approach to Knowing	Positivistic/Empirical	**Interpretive/Hermeneutic**	Critical

Critique

Evaluation Criteria	Scope	**Logical Consistency**	Parsimony	**Utility**	Testability	**Heurism**	Test of Time

Logical Consistency

The logical consistency of the model should not go unnoticed. Recall that logical consistency refers to the notion that theories should follow a logical arrangement and remain consistent. From the outset, Pacanowsky and O'Donnell-Trujillo tried to remain true to their belief that the organization's culture is rich and diverse; they felt that listening to the communicative performances of organizational members was where we must begin in understanding "corporate culture." This is the basis from which much of the theory gained momentum.

Still, some believe consistency is lacking. Eric Eisenberg, H. L. Goodall, and Angela Tretheway (2014), for instance, observe that Organizational Culture Theory relies heavily on shared meaning among organizational members. They comment that stories, for example, are not shared similarly across employees because different organizational stories are told by different organizational narrators. That is, although the theory posits that stories are told and retold and contribute to the culture of an organization, the stories may not have shared meaning.

Student Voices

Nola

I remember working for a company that had the worst corporate culture you could imagine. I worked for a telemarketer, and even during our breaks we felt very uncomfortable. We never dared talk about other employees, share stories of our families, or even try to give ideas to the company. Without doubt, there was a lot of tension in the workplace. One time, my sister had to stop at work to get my car keys. Even she couldn't believe it. She said that no one should be forced to work in that environment. If I didn't need the money, I would have quit after one day on the job!

Utility

The theory is useful because the information is applicable to nearly every employee in an organization. The approach is useful because much of the information from the theory (e.g., symbols, stories, rituals) has direct relationship to how employees work and their identification with their work environment (Schein, 2016). Because the theorists' work is based on real organizations with real employees, the researchers have made the theory more useful and practical.

Heurism

The appeal of Organizational Culture Theory has been far and wide, resulting in a heuristic theory. Researchers have focused several of the theory's fundamental themes in research examining engineering initiatives (Templin, 2012), college campus facilities (Harris & Cullen, 2008), and nursing homes (Johnston & Womack, 2015). Organizational culture has framed research examining Muslim employees (Alkhazraji, 1997), law enforcement officers (Frewin & Tuffin, 1998), student discipline (van der Westhuizen, Oosthuizen, & Wolhuter, 2008), and nurses (Gaudine & Thorne, 2012). It has influenced scholars to consider organizational culture in how they teach their classes (Messersmith, Keyton, & Bisel, 2009). And, the notion of trust in an organization has been investigated across multiple cultures, including Russia and Poland (Morreale & Shockley-Zalabak, 2014).

Closing

Pacanowsky and O'Donnell-Trujillo were among the first communication scholars to examine organizational life by looking at both employees and their behaviors. Looking at organizational culture in this way will enable researchers to appreciate the importance of connecting with the people and their performances at work. The theory will continue to be an important one to understand as organizational life becomes more layered and more complex.

Discussion Starters

TECH QUEST: Organizational Culture Theory suggests that the culture of an organization (norms, attitudes, values, beliefs, community issues, etc.) communicates a great deal about that organization. How might a Wiki assist in defining and communicating the culture of an organization?

1. How can employees like Amelia Callahan ease into a new and different organizational culture? What advice would you give her as she begins her new job with Jewelry Plus?

2. Consider some of the organizations to which you belong. Identify the cultural performances that you have either observed or shared. How could you use these performances in your work?

3. Geertz has compared culture to a spider web. What other metaphors can you think of that could represent organizational cultures?

4. Explain how organizational culture can vary within a large organization. Use examples in your response.

5. Imagine that you're an ethnographer who has been assigned to study your school's culture. How might you go about studying it? What sort of cultural artifacts or rituals would you find?

6. Based on your job experiences, explain the frequency of the various cultural performances identified by Pacanowsky and O'Donnell-Trujillo.

7. How would you apply principles of OCT to your family?

CHAPTER 17

Organizational Information Theory

*Based on the research of **Karl Weick***

Sensemaking is tested to the extreme when people encounter an event whose occurrence is so implausible that they hesitate to report it for fear that they will not be believed.

—Karl Weick

Dominique Martin

As she read about the increasing corporate scandals, Dominique Martin knew that it would be just a matter of time. Her instincts became real when the Vice President of Compliance and Standards at BankNG emailed her to come speak to him about the new federal regulations on oversight and financial disclosure. Dominique was an expert on banking compliance and she was the go-to person at BankNG whenever new regulations emerged. With the recent bill signed into law, Dominique's instructions were clear: "Get it done," her vice president told her.

Dominique Martin could feel the stress build as the months progressed and as she considered all the avenues related to the "FedReg" project. Her expertise was sought at every moment as various BankNG units involved in regulation contacted her for assistance. In fact, she became even busier as media coverage caused many in the media to question the ability of companies to accommodate the new law, causing even more pressure for Dominique. The task was not an easy one because the law involved new procedures for auditing, corporate governance, internal operations, and financial disclosure. Special-project teams dealing with the challenge of bringing their bank and its systems up to date were immediately established.

As she approached the door of the conference room, Dominique thought about how happy and relieved she would be once the conversion was over. Should BankNG's standards be enacted efficiently and effectively, Dominique wondered whether or not she would be promoted at the bank. But, for now, she had to deal with BankNG's compliance and she needed a team that was responsive, competent, and immediate. The vice president appointed her project manager, and today she would meet for the first time with members of various teams via Skype. Several employees from the Boston, Dallas, Denver, and Seattle offices would take part. The project goal involved the conversion of all BankNG information systems so that they would be compatible for the required changes. The FedReg project team consisted of almost 80 people who would be responsible for various aspects of the conversion. Dominique was used to managing a team of 12 employees who were all located in the same city, so dealing with nearly seven times as many colleagues was a very new challenge.

As Dominique began the meeting, she asked each team leader in the various cities to introduce their team members and their assigned duties. As they went around to the various locations, Dominique became overwhelmed. Although a compliance checklist was available, BankNG was simply too large and too complex for a simple checklist to be effective. There were so many different areas to manage in this project: conducting proper homework on the law and its various components, coordinating information with the federal regulatory agencies, providing updates to and obtaining feedback from the bank board members and shareholders, establishing an audit committee, keeping the other divisions within the bank informed of changes that were being made, and how those changes would affect their departments . . . and that was only the beginning! Each of the teams needed to be kept informed about the others' progress in order to meet their deadlines.

As the meeting progressed, Dominique realized that the success of this project would depend on effective communication with all the various teams in the different states. They developed a communication strategy to help keep the teams in the different offices across the country informed of the events associated with the project. Although the home office was located in Boston, the regional offices needed to be made aware of the plans and protocols so that everyone was on board. The plan included hiring an internal communication coordinator to man-age all the messages that would be sent about compliance. Next, they decided that a company wiki would be established so that all project members could communicate about the information needed to complete the project. Also, an electronic newsletter would be distributed periodically to update all members of BankNG about the progress that was being made. Finally, they decided that they would use computer software to record the goals, resources, deadlines, and accomplishments associated with the project. In the end, despite the pressures and stressors, Dominique's leadership prevailed and compliance was achieved at BankNG with little resistance and few problems.

Although several years have passed, Dominique continues to wonder whether she facilitated the regulatory project effectively. She knew that she was a good team leader, but even today, she thinks about whether her thoughts, actions, and activities were the most appropriate at the time. She felt confident that everyone had a voice in the matter and that their conversations helped move FedReg along. Still, she couldn't rid herself of a nagging doubt about whether she managed the events to the best of her ability.

The task of managing vast amounts of information is a typical challenge for many organizations. As our options for new communication channels increase, the number of messages that we send and receive, as well as the speed at which we send them, increases as well. Not only are organizations faced with the task of decoding the messages that are received, but they are also challenged with determining which people need to receive the information to help achieve the organization's goals. New media are enabling companies to accomplish their goals in ways never before seen. Videoconferencing, teleconferencing, wikis, and webinars allow people like Dominique to provide teams with the opportunity to share and react to great amounts of information simultaneously. Each of the teams was given the opportunity to decide what information was essential to its tasks or to request additional information that would be needed in the future. Clearly, the introduction of new technologies is reshaping existing organizational functions and structures (Lovejoy & Saxton, 2012).

Sometimes the information an organization receives is ambiguous. In the case of the FedReg project, each team depended on the others to provide information so that it could complete its portion of the project. Teams needed the information to be presented in a way they could understand. The "Customer/Shareholder Services" team may have little knowledge of computer jargon, so they depend on the technicians to clarify the information and present it to them in a way that they could then communicate to their customers and shareholders. Without this exchange and management of information—particularly given the federal directive—BankNG's regulation accommodation would probably fail.

Some writers of organizational communication have used the metaphor of a "living system" to describe organizations (Triolo, 2012). Just as living systems engage in a process of activities to maintain their functioning and existence, an organization must have a procedure for dealing with all the information it needs to send and receive to accomplish its goals. Much like systems, organizations are made up of people and teams that are interrelated. Each depends on the other to accomplish their goals.

Consider the process that colleges and universities go through to recruit new students. The publications office conducts research to find out what criteria matter to potential students. Are graduation rates and job placement something high school students are looking for in deciding where to pursue their education? Is the diversity of the student body an important factor in making a decision? Does student financial aid remain paramount? Will the recent rating by *The Princeton Review* have an impact on student decisions? Or, are students attracted to a campus that has superior computer facilities? After collecting these data, the publications office will use this information to develop publicity materials that appeal to potential students. Recruitment fairs may be held in major cities to provide parents and students with the opportunity to ask admissions counselors about the school. While this process is taking place, the school collects feedback and monitors the reactions of potential students and their parents in order to make changes in their current recruitment strategies. The admissions office reduces uncertainty about what qualities are attractive to students while at the same time assisting students in making their decision by providing information about the school.

Karl Weick developed an approach to describe the process by which organizations (like a college or university) collect, manage, and use the information that they receive. Rather than focusing his attention on the structure of the organization in terms of the roles and rules that guide its members, Weick emphasizes the process of organizing. In doing so, the primary focus is on the exchange of information that takes place within the organization and how members take steps to understand this material. Weick (1995) believes that "organizations talk to themselves" (p. 281). To this end, organizational members are instrumental in the creation and maintenance of message meaning.

Weick sees the organization as a system taking in confusing or ambiguous information from its environment and making sense out of it. Therefore, organizations will evolve as they try to make sense out of themselves and their environment. Rather than focusing on Dominique's role as project manager or on the specific communication rules for sending messages between and among superiors and subordinates, Weick's Organizational Information Theory (OIT) directs our attention to the steps that are necessary to manage and use the information for the BankNG project. As it becomes more difficult to interpret the information that is received, an organization needs to solicit input from others (often multiple sources) to make sense of the information and to provide a response to the appropriate people or departments.

The main activity of organizations is the process of making sense of equivocal and ambiguous information. Organizational members accomplish this sensemaking process through enactment, selection, and retention of information. Organizations are successful to the extent that they are able to reduce equivocality through these means.

The Only Constant Is Change (in Organizations)

Weick's theory focuses on the process that organizations undergo in their attempt to make sense out of all the information that bombards them on a daily basis. Often the process results in changes in the organization and its members. In fact, Weick states that "organizations and their environments change so rapidly that it is unrealistic to show what they are like now, because that's not the way they're going to be later" (1969, p. 1). According to this approach, it would be unrealistic to try to depict what colleges or universities and their surrounding environment look like today because it is likely that they will change. The major fields of study chosen by students may change as organizations' needs for employees change. Consider, for instance, the early 1990s. To assist them in making changes in their computer systems, many companies were seeking graduates in the fields of computer technology and management information systems. Today, however, as a result of the dot-com crash during the 2011 recession, many of these same individuals are either underemployed or employed in an area outside their major field of study. As you can see, organizational demands are often influenced by cultural demands.

The focus of Organizational Information Theory is on the communication of information that is vital in determining the success of an organization. It is quite rare that one person or one department in an organization has all the information necessary to complete a project. This knowledge typically comes from a variety of sources. However, the task of information processing is not completed simply by attaining information; the difficult part is in deciphering and distributing the information that is gained. To understand this process better, we will discuss how two major perspectives influenced OIT: General Systems Theory and the Theory of Sociocultural Evolution.

General Systems Theory

To explain the influence of information from an organization's external environments and to understand the influence that an organization has on its external environments, Weick applied General Systems Theory in the development of his approach to studying how organizations manage information. As we discussed in Chapter 3, Ludwig von Bertalanffy is most frequently associated with the systems approach. von Bertalanffy believed that patterns and wholes exist across different types of phenomena. To this end, he proposed that when there is a disruption in one part of a system, it affects the entire system. In sum, systems theorists argue that there are complex patterns of interaction among the parts of a system, and understanding these interactions will help us understand the entire system.

Systems thinking is especially useful in understanding the interrelationships that exist among various organizational units. Organizations are usually made up of different departments, teams, or groups. Although these units may focus on independent tasks, the goals of the organization as a whole typically require sharing and integrating the information that each of the teams has to arrive at a solution or conclusion. Organizations depend on combined information so that they can make any necessary adjustments in order to reach their goal. They may need additional information, they may need to send information to other departments or people within the organization, or they may need outside consultants to make sense of the information. If one team fails to address the information needed to fulfill its obligation in the completion of the project, achieving the final goal will probably be delayed for the entire organization.

In the chapter-opening scenario, we learned that Dominique needed to consult with different teams from different states. Each state's team had a particular responsibility in order to complete the FedReg project. Yet, the interrelationships among the teams cannot be ignored. That is, each has a dependency on the other; one needs the other for information and cannot act without it. If such information were not received, enacting BankNG's changes would be delayed.

An important component of General Systems Theory, and one that is essential to making sense of information in an organization, is feedback, or the information received by an organization and its members. It's important to remember that this information can be either positive or negative. The organization and its members can then choose to use the information to maintain the current state of the organization or can decide to initiate some changes in accordance with the goals that the system is trying to accomplish. It is through feedback that units are able to determine if the information that is being transmitted is clear and sufficient to achieve the desired goals.

The decision of the organization to request or provide feedback reflects a selective choice made by the group in an effort to accomplish its goals. If an organization hopes to survive and accomplish its goals, it will continue to engage in cycles of feedback to obtain necessary information and reduce its uncertainty about the best way to accomplish its goals. This process reflects a Darwinian approach to how organizations manage information, as we discuss next.

Darwin's Theory of Sociocultural Evolution

A second perspective that has been used to describe the process by which organizations collect and make sense out of information is the **theory of sociocultural evolution.** You may have heard of the "survival of the fittest," which is an apt phrase to describe the theory. The eventual goal of any organization is survival, and, like humans, it works to discover the best strategies for getting by. Although

theory of sociocultural evolution
Darwin's belief that only the fittest can survive challenging surroundings

this approach is used to describe the social interactions that take place in an organization with regard to making sense out of information, its origins are in the field of biology.

The theory of evolution was originally developed to describe the adaptation processes that living organisms undergo in order to thrive in a challenging ecological environment. Charles Darwin (1948) explained these adaptations in terms of mutations that allow organisms to cope with their various surroundings. Some organisms could not adapt and died, whereas others made changes and prospered. Taking the example of Dominique Martin and the FedReg challenge, corporations that took steps to accommodate the law quickly have a greater chance to prosper and thrive. Those who did not make the attempt to adapt to the changing legal landscape will likely be faced with severe consequences including financial penalties.

Campbell (1965) extends this theory to explain the processes by which organizations and their members adapt to their social surroundings. The socio-cultural theory of evolution examines the changes people make in their social behaviors and expectations to adapt to changes in their social surroundings. Many times, these changes involve team-member efforts to be creative (Sawyer, 2012).

Consider the scenario at the beginning of this chapter. Suppose that Dominique had a team of representatives from BankNG's offices in Japan involved in this project. If she wanted to make a quick decision on how to address the FedReg changes in the Japanese offices, her first tendency would likely be to employ a communication style that U.S. employees would perceive as efficient. However, she would soon realize that the Japanese approach to business is quite different from that practiced in the United States. Instead of quickly presenting the facts and determining financial processes, Japanese bank employees prefer an approach that emphasizes the development of rapport. Only after the relationship has been developed would the issue of signing an agreement be presented. Dominique must engage in the process of sociocultural evolution to adapt to the norms and expectations of her overseas team.

Weick adapts sociocultural evolution to explain the process that organizations undergo in adjusting to various information pressures. These pressures may be the result of information overload or ambiguity. Although the evolutionary approach is useful in describing the adaptations that are necessary to process information, General Systems Theory is also an essential piece in this puzzle because it highlights the interrelatedness among organizational teams, departments, and employees in the processing of information. We now continue our discussion of OIT and identify its underlying assumptions.

Assumptions of Organizational Information Theory

Organizational Information Theory is one way of explaining how organizations make sense out of information that is confusing or ambiguous. It focuses on the process of organizing members of an organization to manage information rather than on the structure of the organization itself. A number of assumptions underlie this theory:

- Human organizations exist in an information environment.
- The information an organization receives differs in terms of equivocality.
- Human organizations engage in information processing to reduce equivocality of information.

The first assumption states that organizations depend on information in order to function effectively and accomplish their goals. Weick (1979) views the concept of information environment as distinct from the physical surroundings in which an organization is housed. He proposes that these information environments are created by the members of the organization. They establish goals that require them to obtain information from both internal and external sources. However, these inputs differ in terms of their level of understandability.

Consider the university admissions office example. A school can use numerous channels to gain information about student needs: It may develop a website to answer prospective students' questions and to solicit student feedback; it may conduct surveys at high school academic fairs to gain more information about student desires; it may host focus group interviews with current students to discover needs and concerns; or it may ask alumni to provide examples from their educational experiences to attract future students. Once it has received messages from all of these external sources, the university must decide how to communicate messages internally to establish and accomplish its goals for current and future students. The possibilities for information are endless, and the university must decide how to manage all the available potential messages.

The second assumption proposed by Weick focuses on the ambiguity that exists in information: Messages differ in terms of their understandability. An organization needs to determine which of its members are most knowledgeable or experienced in dealing with particular information that is obtained. A plan to make sense of the information needs to be established. In fact, Karl Weick (2015) argues that when things are ambiguous, people will do their best to work with it. That is, he believes that at times, employees have no choice but to deal with ambiguous messages. The key is to simply accept it and try to make sense of it, an idea we explore a bit later in the chapter.

At BankNG, each member of each team must be able to interpret and understand the messages accurately. Given the federal law requirements, however, and the complexities related to the law, many messages are not always clear because individuals often assume understanding and often communicate in ways that are less than clear. Further, each office has had little experience working with such a massive undertaking. Messages in BankNG, then, according to Weick's theory, may be frequently equivocal. **Equivocality** refers to the extent to which messages are complicated, uncertain, and unpredictable. Equivocal messages are often sent in organizations. Because these messages are not clearly understood, people need to develop a framework or plan for reducing their ambiguity about the message.

You may be tempted to think that equivocality is ineffectual in an organization. Yet, as Eric Eisenberg (2007) reminds us, equivocality is not necessarily problematic. He states that rather than viewing equivocality as difficult, "Weick turned this

equivocality
the extent to which organizational messages are uncertain, ambiguous, and/or unpredictable

idea on its head, arguing instead that equivocality is the engine that motivates people to organize" (p. 274). Eisenberg further clarifies that equivocality may "make coordinated action possible" (p. 274). When individuals in an organization reduce equivocality, they engage in a process that tries to make sense out of excessive information received by the organization. We delve further into equivocation a few more times later in the chapter.

In an attempt to reduce the ambiguity of information, the third assumption of the theory proposes that organizations engage in joint activity to make information that is received more understandable. Weick (1979) sees the process of reducing equivocality as a joint activity among members of an organization. It is not the sole responsibility of one person to reduce equivocality. Rather, this is a process that may involve several members of the organization. Consider the BankNG example. Each department needs to use information from other units, but they also need to provide information to these same units to accomplish the tasks necessary to meet the organization's federal compliance. This illustrates the extent to which departments in an organization may depend on one another to reduce their ambiguity. An ongoing cycle of communicating feedback takes place in which there is a mutual give-and-take of information.

Key Concepts and Conceptualizing Information

Weick's theory of Organizational Information contains a number of key concepts that are critical to an understanding of the theory. They include information environment, rules, and cycles. We now explore each in detail.

Information Environment: The Sum Total

Information environment is an integral part of Weick's theory. Information environment is a core concept in understanding how organizations are formed as well as how they process information. Every day, we are faced with literally thousands of stimuli that we could potentially process and interpret. However, it is unrealistic to think that an organization or its members could possibly process all the information that is available. Thus, we are faced with the tasks of selecting information that is meaningful or important and focusing our senses on processing those cues. The availability of all stimuli is considered to be the **information environment**. Organizations are composed and are sustained because of information that is vital to their formation and continues to be essential to their existence. For example, the FedReg project team was formed because new federal laws required publicly held companies to revamp their financial protocols. If the bank is to survive during a competitive era, it must comply or else face dire consequences on the horizon. So, the information environment not only comprises internal communications between and among different units and offices, but there are external stimuli (e.g., governmental mandates) that also must be considered.

Essentially, organizations have two primary tasks to perform in order to successfully manage these multiple sources of information: (1) They must interpret the external information that exists in their information environment, and (2) they must

information environment
the availability of all stimuli in an organization

coordinate that information to make it meaningful for the members of the organization and its goals. These interpretation processes require the organization to reduce the equivocality of the information to make it meaningful.

Rules: Guidelines to Analyze

Weick (1979) proposes two communication strategies that are essential if the organization hopes to reduce message equivocality. The first strategy requires that organizations determine the rules for reducing the level of equivocality of the message inputs as well as for choosing the appropriate response to the information received. In a sense, then, organizations self-govern with respect to getting things accomplished. In Organizational Information Theory, **rules** refer to the guidelines that an organization has established for analyzing the equivocality of a message as well as for guiding responses to information. For example, if any of the FedReg team leaders experience ambiguity over the information that is provided to them from the computer technicians, they are instructed to contact the technician team leader for clarification. If they were to contact Dominique first, an additional step would be added to the process of reducing equivocality because she would have to contact the technicians and then report back to the team leaders. Recall the example of the university admissions office, which conducted research in order to design materials that appeal to students. As a result, when it receives information from students inquiring about the university, the rule that it applies in dealing with the information environment is to respond to that message by sending out their informational brochure. Both organizations have rules for determining the equivocality of the information and for identifying the appropriate way in which they should respond to the messages.

Weick provides examples of rules that might cause an organization to choose one cycle of information or feedback over another for reducing the equivocality of messages. These rules include duration, personnel, success, and effort. Examples of duration and personnel rules guiding communication can be seen in our chapter-opening story. **Duration** refers to a choice made by an organization to engage in

rules
guidelines in organizations as they review responses to equivocal information

duration
organizational rule stating that decisions regarding equivocality should be made in the least amount of time

ORGANIZATIONAL INFORMATION THEORY

Key Concepts and Conceptualizing Information **295**

Part of what allows an organization to reduce organizational equivocality is the notion of self-governance. Dov Seidman, the founder and CEO of LRN, a company dedicated to advocating principled and ethical practices in culture, took the notion of self-governance seriously by first ripping up the company's organizational chart. His perspective was clear: "We would all 'report' to our company mission." Seidman decided to get 20 teams from around the globe to imagine the notion of self-governance. Self-governance, in this regard, meant abandoning top-down decision making and rather, making power and authority "highly collaborative." The rules in this sort of organization are not firm but instead take into consideration employee values and the types of relationships existing in the company. Seidman states that decisions are undertaken by elected employee councils that handle things like recruiting, performance management, and conflict resolution. Other self-governing behaviors, including an unlimited vacation policy, spending money without hierarchical approval, and publishing Seidman's performance review (conducted by any employee who wanted to review him), are part of the new "rules" of self-governance. Seidman concludes that self-governing has been "enlightening, frustrating, nerve-racking, authentic, and urgent."

Source: Letting the mission govern a company. (2012, June 24). *New York Times*, p. 7.

communication that can be completed in the least amount of time. For example, BankNG has rules that state who should be contacted to clarify technical information. These rules prevent people from asking those who are not knowledgeable about the topic. In establishing these rules, BankNG increases its efficiency by having employees go directly to the person who can provide the necessary information, thus eliminating delays that might result from having to channel questions through several different people. In doing so, BankNG is also guided by the rule of **personnel.** This rule states that people who are the most knowledgeable should emerge as key resources to reduce equivocality. Computer technicians, not human resources personnel, are consulted to reduce equivocality of technical information associated with the project.

When an organization chooses to employ a plan of communication that has been proven effective in the past at reducing equivocality of information, **success** is the influential rule that is being applied. A university knows that many of its potential students' questions and concerns can be answered via a well-researched brochure. It has proved to be a successful recruiting tool in the past, as the enrollment figures of the school have increased by 4 percent per year over the past five years. Thus, the university knows that this is a successful way of reducing information ambiguity for students.

personnel
organizational rule stating the most knowledgeable workers should resolve equivocality

success
organizational rule stating that a successful plan of the past will be used to reduce current equivocality

Effort is also a rule that influences the choice to use a brochure to promote the university. This rule guides organizations in choosing an information strategy that requires the least amount of effort to reduce equivocality. Rather than fielding numerous phone calls from potential students asking the same questions about the school, the university's decision to print a brochure that answers frequently asked questions is the most efficient means of communicating all the university has to offer. The decision made by many companies to implement automated telephone customer service is another example of how organizations reduce equivocality of information. Rather than requiring a customer to explain the reason for the call multiple times as the customer is connected to various employees, the customer chooses a number that best matches the problem or concern. This directs the customer to the appropriate department.

Cycles: Act, Respond, Adjust

If the information that is received is highly equivocal, the organization may engage in a series of communication behaviors in an attempt to decrease the level of ambiguity. Weick labels these *systems of behavior cycles*. The more equivocal the message, the more **cycles** needed to reduce equivocation (Herrmann, 2007). The cycle of communication behaviors used to reduce equivocality includes three stages: act, response, and adjustment. An **act** refers to the communication statements and behaviors used to indicate one's determination to reduce ambiguity. For example, as a team leader, Dominique may say to a member of the auditor independence team, "The financial disclosure research team wants your group's input on the ethics related to the stock transactions of the company officers." In deciding to solicit information and subsequently reduce any ambiguity, Dominique is employing the rule of personnel.

A second step in the communication cycle is response. **Response** is defined as a reaction to the act. That is, a response that seeks clarification in the equivocal message is provided as a result of the act. The auditor team leader might reply, "It is essential that all possible avenues examining conflict of interest and officer stock transactions be explored. This is absolutely of primary importance."

As a result of the response, the organization formulates a response in return as a result of any **adjustment** that has been made to the information that was originally received. If the response to the act has reduced the equivocality of the message, an adjustment is made to indicate that the information is now understood. If the information is still equivocal, the adjustment might come in the form of additional questions designed to clarify the information further. In other words, if Dominique is still uncertain, she will likely continue to ask questions, thereby reducing message equivocality.

Feedback is an essential step in the process of making sense of the information that is received. Weick uses the term double-interact loops to describe the cycles of act, response, and adjustment in information exchanges. **Double-interact loops** refer to multiple communication cycles that are used to assist the organization's members in reducing the equivocality of information. Employees may have working lunches, informal chats in the employee break room, interviews, conference calls, among other undertakings to continue to reduce information equivocality. Imagine the double interact as you imagine shoveling snow. The goal is to get the snow removed so that no accidents occur. Double interacts in companies are necessary to "clean up" the

effort
organizational rule stating that decisions regarding equivocality should be made with the least amount of work

cycles
series of communication behaviors that serve to reduce equivocality

act
communication behaviors indicating a person's ambiguity in receiving a message

response
reaction to equivocality

adjustment
organizational responses to equivocality

double-interact loops
cycles of an organization (e.g., interviews, meetings) to reduce equivocality

ORGANIZATIONAL INFORMATION THEORY

ambiguities and uncertainties. Failure to do so will not only prohibit goals from being attained, but also can have consequences. Because these cycles require members in the organization to communicate with one another to reduce the level of ambiguity, Weick suggests that the relationships among individuals in the organization are more important to the process of organizing than the talent or knowledge that any one individual brings to the team. Hence, the General Systems Theory philosophy—"the whole is greater than the sum of its parts"—is apparent.

The Principles Related to Equivocality

By now, we're sure that you are able to see that one central feature of Organizational Information Theory is equivocality. Indeed, it is a critical theme woven throughout the theory, even as the theory has been revisited and refined by scholars (Weick, 2011). In this section, we discuss equivocality by looking at three guiding principles of equivocality and also at ways to reduce this communication process in organizational life.

Organizations use several principles when dealing with equivocality. An organization must analyze the relationship among the equivocality of information, the rules the organization has for removing the equivocality, and the cycles of communication that should be used. When analyzing the relationship among these three variables, a few conclusions are possible. If a message is highly equivocal, chances are that the organization has few rules for dealing with the ambiguity. As a result, the organization has to employ a greater number of cycles of communication to reduce the level of equivocality of the information. The organization will examine the degree of equivocality of the information (inputs) it receives and determine if it has sufficient rules that will be of assistance in guiding the cycle of communication that should be employed to reduce the ambiguity.

To exemplify, a technical question is highly equivocal to those who are not trained in the field of expertise. Thus, the organization may not have a set of rules to guide communication responses and may rely solely on one rule (i.e., personnel) to guide the cycles of communication. If inputs are easily understood by many members of the organization (e.g., a customer may ask, "Is BankNG doing anything to prepare for federal regulations?"), more rules (i.e., success, effort, duration) can be employed in reducing the equivocality. The more equivocal the message, the fewer rules that are available to guide cycles of communication; the less equivocal the message, the more rules that are available to assist the organization in reducing equivocality, thus reducing the number of cycles that are needed to interpret the information.

A second principle proposed by Weick (1979) deals with the association between the number of *rules* that are needed and the number of *cycles* that can be used to reduce the equivocality. If the organization has only a few rules available to assist it in reducing equivocality, a greater number of cycles will be needed to filter out the ambiguity. In our chapter-opening example, a majority of the members in the organization view technical information related to federal regulation as highly equivocal. The only rule that many of them have for dealing with this equivocality is to communicate with a person (personnel) who is knowledgeable in the appropriate area (e.g., external auditing, financial disclosure, etc.). Thus, more cycles of information exchange will be employed between the technician and the organization's employees to reduce the ambiguity of the information.

The third principle proposed by Weick relates to a direct relationship between the number of cycles used and the amount of equivocality that remains. The more cycles that are used to obtain additional information and make adjustments, the more equivocality is removed. Weick proposes that if a larger number of cycles is used, it is more likely that equivocality can be decreased than if only a few cycles are employed.

Although BankNG has increased the potential for equivocality of information by providing its employees with multiple resources for obtaining information about the project's status (videoconferences, telephone conferences, wikis), it has also provided its employees with a larger number of potential cycles that can be employed to reduce this equivocality. Employees can engage in online dialogues in an attempt to answer their questions and concerns about the FedReg project. They can download database files that track the progress of the project and inquire if other teams will be meeting various deadlines that are crucial to their success in the project's completion. And they have the benefit of having an internal communication team to manage all the messages they receive from various sources. Thus, there is the potential for a greater number of cycles that can be used to reduce the equivocality of information.

Reducing Equivocality: Trying to Use the Information

Reducing equivocality is both necessary and complex. According to Weick (1995) and W. Timothy Coombs (2015), organizations evolve through stages in an attempt to integrate the rules and cycles so the information can be easily understood and is meaningful. The process of equivocality reduction is essentially an interpersonal process and occurs through the following three stages: enactment, selection, and retention.

Enactment: Assigning Message Importance

Enactment refers to how information will be received and interpreted by the organization. Andrew Herrmann (2007) states, "Enactment starts with the bracketing or framing of a message in the environment by an individual" (p. 18). During this stage, the organization must analyze the inputs it receives to determine the amount of equivocality that is present and to assign meaning to the information. Existing rules are reviewed in making decisions about how the organization will deal with the ambiguity. If the organization determines that it does not have a sufficient number of rules for reducing the equivocality, various cycles of communication must be analyzed to determine their effectiveness in assisting the organization in understanding the information. Weick believes that this action stage is vital to the success of an organization. If a university made no effort to interpret information from potential students, it would not be able to address their concerns and desires in choosing a college to attend effectively. Eric Eisenberg and H. L. Goodall (2013) observe that enactment may be Weick's most "revolutionary" concept (p. 109).

enactment
interpretation of the information received by the organization

Weick believes that one affiliate of enactment is **sensemaking**, or the attempt to create understanding in situations that are complex and uncertain. For Weick (1995), sensemaking includes "the placement of items into frameworks, comprehending, redressing surprise, constructing meaning, interacting in pursuit of mutual understanding, and patterning" (p. 6). Sensemaking "starts with chaos" (Weick, Sutcliffe, &

sensemaking
creating awareness and understanding in situations that are complex or uncertain

Obstfeld, 2009) and covers many forms of communication, including routines, arguments, symbols, commitments, and other actions and behaviors (Salem, 2007). Weick (2012) also believes that sensemaking involves storytelling. Although Weick finds sensemaking activities in all three stages (enactment, selection, retention), enactment is most often identified with sensemaking.

Weick (2012) contends that decisions and sensemaking are related but are not synonymous. In fact, Weick quotes a firefighter/crew chief as he "shifts" from decisions to sensemaking:

> If I make a decision it is a possession, I take pride in it, I tend to defend it and not to listen to those who question it. If I make sense, then this is more dynamic and I listen and I can change it. A decision is something you polish. Sensemaking is a direction for the next period. (cited in Weick, 2012, p. 22)

Interestingly, some researchers believe that a prospective *sensemaking* happens at times. In their study of surgical teams, Ragnar Rossness, Tor Evjemo, Torgeir Haavik, and Irene Waero (2015) contend that when surgical teams considered plausible projections of issues that might occur during the surgery and how these situations might be handled, the surgery was viewed as safer and more efficient. Therefore, some sort of decisions take place but these decisions are considered in light of the consequences and implications of the decision.

Selection: Interpreting the Inputs

Once the organization has employed various rules and cycles to interpret its information environment, it must analyze what it knows and choose the best method for obtaining additional information to further reduce equivocality. This stage is referred to as **selection.** In this stage of organizing, the group is required to make a decision about the rules and cycles that will be used. If the information is still ambiguous, the organization has to look into the resources that it has available and determine if it has any additional rules that could help in reducing the ambiguity.

selection
choosing the best method for obtaining information

For instance, imagine Kelvin is overwhelmed with a task that was assigned to him by his boss. As he considers all the inputs required of him, Kelvin becomes visibly agitated and anxious. He has one week to report back to his supervisor, and he is entering a time period at work during which he is constantly interrupted by colleagues seeking his assistance. His perception of being inundated has resulted in his dealing with a project that has a high degree of equivocality. As he oversees the project, he has to attend several meetings, which, interestingly, result in additional information and additional ambiguity. If Kelvin is to reduce his feeling of being overwhelmed, he will have to develop a plan to obtain information and disseminate it appropriately in order to finish the task. Reviewing organizational rules regarding communication channels may assist Kelvin as he manages the inputs. In this case, his selection process will be instrumental in his reduction of equivocality. As an organizational member, his expertise will also be quite important in the equivocality decline (Weick & Sutcliffe, 2015).

Retention: Remembering the Small Stuff

Once the organization has reviewed its ability to deal with ambiguity, it analyzes the effectiveness of the rules and cycles of communication and engages in retention. In the

retention stage, the organization stores information for later use. This stage requires organizations to look at what to deal with and what to ignore or leave alone. If a particular rule or cycle was beneficial in assisting the organization in reducing the equivocality of information, it's likely that it will be used to guide the organization in future decisions of a similar nature. Suppose that Dominique found the videoconferences to result in even more confusion among the team members because they were bombarded with more information than was either desired or required to complete various tasks in the project. She will remember this and likely refrain from using the technology as a means of sharing project information in the future. Instead, she may choose to use online discussions to allow team members to choose the information essential to their portion of the task and skip over information that is of little relevance to them. If strategies for dealing with equivocality are deemed to be useful, they will be retained for future use.

So, through enactment, selection, and retention, organizations can begin the process of reducing and eliminating their ambiguity. These three processes are not always going to occur at once; indeed, one may take much longer than the other. As we noted earlier, these stages are primarily interpersonal in nature and dealing with human relationships—like organizational decisions—can be unpredictable.

retention
collective memory allowing people to accomplish goals

Integration, Critique, and Closing

Karl Weick's Organizational Information Theory has been identified as a powerful theoretical framework for explaining how organizations make sense of the information they receive for their existence. The theory draws from other theoretical perspectives that explain the processes that organizations undergo to receive input from others. Further, the theory has been investigated using the experimental method, making it an empirically driven process. Weick emphasizes the importance of human interaction in information processing, thus, centralizing communication as a key focus of the "theoretical latticework" (Herrmann, 2007, p. 18) associated with OIT.

Student Voices

Kathryn

During high school, I worked as a deli clerk at a convenience store. I hated the job but needed the money to save for college. I do remember a time when equivocality was present at the workplace. The manager had a habit of coming into work and surprising employees without any notice. We couldn't stand it, and we looked at his actions as equivocal. The employees described the work environment as equivocal because there were different views of the manager's behavior. One of us thought she (the manager) was keeping us on our toes. Another thought she came into work without notice because she didn't trust us to be by ourselves. Personally I thought she would pop into work without telling anyone because she wanted to show her power. I never did find out why she surprised us with her "visits," but I'm long gone now.

Integration

Communication Tradition	Rhetorical	Semiotic	Phenomenological	**Cybernetic**	Socio-Psychological	Socio-Cultural	Critical
Communication Context	Intrapersonal	Interpersonal	Small Group	**Organizational**	Public/Rhetorical	Mass/Media	Cultural
Approach to Knowing	**Positivistic/Empirical**	Interpretive/Hermeneutic	Critical

Critique

Evaluation Criteria	Scope	**Logical Consistency**	Parsimony	**Utility**	Testability	**Heurism**	Test of Time

Logical Consistency

Recall that theories must make sense and make clear the concepts under discussion. Weick's theory seems to fail the test of logical consistency. One prevailing criticism pertains to the belief that people are guided by rules in an organization. Yet organizational scholars note that "we puzzle and mull over, fret and stew over, and generally select, manipulate, and transform meaning to come up with an interpretation of a situation" (Papa & Daniels, 2014, p. 114). In other words, some organizational members may have little interest in the communication rules in place at work. Individuals are not always so conscious or precise in their selection procedures, and their actions may have more to do with their intuition than with organizational rules. As employees become more immersed in the organizational milieu, they may be guided more by instinct if that instinct is accurate, ethical, and thoughtful.

An additional criticism underscoring the problems of logical consistency is that Organizational Information Theory views organizations as static units in society (Taylor & Van Every, 2000). These researchers challenge Weick's view by noting that "at no point are inherent contradictions in organizational structure and process even remotely evoked" (p. 275) in his research. Organizations have ongoing tensions, and these need to be identified and examined in light of Weick's claims. Furthermore, given the dynamic changes in organizations due to corporate mergers, downsizing, offshore outsourcing of employee work, and the evolution of technology, static or frozen assessments of organizations are shortsighted.

With his model of organizational organizing, Karl Weick has provided communication scholars an understanding of how decisions are made and the key processes pertaining to those decisions. As individuals encounter an organization, they need to understand the communication processes taking place. As OIT continues to be refined, centralizing communication will be instrumental. As Eric Eisenberg (2007) states, "Weick's most valuable contributions have been his insistence on the centrality of language and communication in the construction of organizational reality, and his sustained focus on communication as a site for improving our understanding of cognition, culture, and social interaction (p. 284).

Utility

The theory's utility is underscored by its focus on the communication process. Organizational Information Theory focuses on the process of communication rather than on the role of communicators themselves. This is of great benefit in understanding how members of an organization engage in collaborative efforts with both internal and external environments to understand the information they receive. Rather than attempt to understand the people in an organization—and their unpredictability—Weick decides to unravel the complexities of information processing, which makes this a rather useful theoretical undertaking.

Heurism

OIT is heuristic and has prompted considerable scholarly discussion. The theory has inspired thinking in research on a variety of topics, including environmental flooding (Ulmer, Sellnow, & Seeger, 2007), nomadic work (Bean & Eisenberg, 2006), surgical procedures (Rosness et al., 2015), organizational humor (Heiss & Carmack, 2012), leadership in high schools (Carraway & Young, 2015), and cohesion in the U.S. Army (Van Epps, 2008). The theory has also been applied to such diverse populations as zoo volunteers (Kramer & Danielson, 2016) and Ghanaians living with HIV/AIDS (Latzoo, 2015). Charles Bantz (1989) observes that in terms of Weick's influence on research overall, "[I]t is not surprising that a variety of scholars picked up the organizing concept directly from Weick or integrated it into their ongoing research" (p. 233). Weick clearly was influential in the work of organizational communication scholars.

Closing

Karl Weick has centralized the notion of organizational ambiguity and his theory resonates today. Organizational Information Theory continues to attract theorists and practitioners interested in the intersection of organizations, messages, and people. It has been called "the sensemaking model" (Abu-Shaqra & Luppicini, 2016, p. 62) and has prompted researchers from across a number of disciplines to study the vagaries of organizational life. To that end, the theory will continue to resonate in cultures where corporations have to deal with uncertain and challenging ebbs and flows.

Discussion Starters

TECH QUEST: Examine various forms of social media and rank-order their level of equivocality as they relate to organizational decision making. From Twitter to Facebook, develop some of the challenges of each as they relate to equivocality.

1. Based on your understanding of the concepts of Organizational Information Theory, what additional avenues could Dominique engage in to facilitate a solution

to the FedReg project in BankNG? Respond using at least two concepts discussed in the chapter.

2. Recall an organization in which you are or were a member. Can you remember an incident when you or the organization received ambiguous information? If so, what rules did you or the organization use in dealing with this equivocality?

3. Weick describes the process of enactment, selection, and retention to understand how organizations deal with information inputs. Provide an example of how your school has employed these strategies in making sense of information on your campus.

4. Discuss the importance of the principle of requisite variety in dealing with ambiguity. Do you think that highly equivocal information requires more complex communication processes in order to make sense of the input? Defend your answer.

5. Does your college or university solicit feedback from students regarding its promotion of the organization? Discuss the methods that your school uses.

6. Discuss how organizational rules function in OIT.

7. Apply equivocality to an organization with which you are familiar.

The Public

WHEN WE LISTEN TO A SPEECH, WATCH A PLAY, participate in a conversation, or consume media, we are members of an audience. We are the public. As audience members, we act out the transactional nature of communication discussed in Chapter 1. We simultaneously serve as both sender and receiver of messages. Both verbal and nonverbal communication, therefore, are important in audience-centered messages.

The public is at the core of the three theories we selected for this section of the book. As one of the classic works of the Western world, the Rhetoric is an attempt to show speakers that to be persuasive with their audiences, they should follow some suggestions. This advice includes looking at the speech, considering the speaker, and analyzing the audience. Dramatism pertains to the important role that the public plays in persuasion. Dramatists believe that unless the audience identifies with the speaker, persuasion is not possible. The Narrative Paradigm proposes to look at the audience as participants in a storytelling experience. Narrative theorists contend that a person's stories are effective when they appeal to a listener's values.

The public in communication theory refers to how we—as listeners, consumers, and audiences—play a role in deciding the extent to which others will affect us. Reading about the theories in this section will introduce you to several noteworthy topics related to the audience, including audience analysis, speech effectiveness, speaker integrity, credibility, and character.

CHAPTER 18

The *Rhetoric*

*Based on the writings of **Aristotle***

> *Character may almost be called the most effective means of persuasion.*
> —Aristotle

Camille Ramirez knew that she would have to take a public speaking course for her major. Although she had been active in high school—serving as treasurer for the student council and playing on the lacrosse team—she had never done any public speaking. Now that she was in her second semester, she wanted to get the required course out of the way, so she had enrolled in Public Speaking 101.

The class seemed to be going quite well. She felt fairly confident about her speaking abilities; she had received two As and one B on her speeches so far. The final speech, however, would be her most challenging. It was a persuasive speech, and she decided that she would speak on the dangers of drinking and driving. The topic was a personal one for Camille because she would talk about her Uncle Jake, a wonderful man who had died last year in an accident with a drunk driver. As she prepared for the speech, she thought that she would blend both emotion and logic into her presentation. Camille also thought that she would have to identify both sides of the drinking issue—the desire to let loose and the need to be responsible.

On the day of her speech, Camille took several deep breaths before the class started; it was a strategy that had worked before her previous speeches. As she approached the lectern, she could feel the butterflies well up in her stomach. She reminded herself about the topic and its personal meaning. So, as planned, she began with a short story about her favorite time with Uncle Jake—the time they went to Philadelphia to see the Liberty Bell. Camille then talked about the night—two weeks after her trip—that her uncle died; he was driving home from his daughter's soccer game, and a drunk driver slammed his car from behind, forcing Jake to the embankment. His car then slid into a pond where he drowned.

The room was silent as Camille finished the story. She proceeded to identify why she was speaking on the topic. She told the group that considering their classroom was filled with people under the age of 25, it was important that they understand how fragile life is. Her words resonated with the group. For the next five minutes, Camille mentioned her Uncle Jake several times as she repeated the importance of not drinking and getting behind the wheel of a car.

Camille felt relieved as she finished her speech. She thought that she had done a decent job with her assignment, and she also felt that it helped her to be able to talk about her uncle again. After class, several of Camille's classmates came up and congratulated her. Many of them posted words of sympathy on her Facebook page. They told her that it took a lot of guts to talk about such a personal subject in front of so many people. A few of them also commented that they felt her topic was perfect for the audience; in fact, one of her classmates said that he wanted Camille to give the same speech to his fraternity brothers. As Camille walked to her dorm, she couldn't help but think that she had made a difference and that the speech was both a personal and a professional success.

■

Contemporary life provides us scores of opportunities to speak in front of others. Politicians, spiritual leaders, physicians, custodial supervisors, and investment brokers are just a few of the many types of people who spend much of their time speaking to others—in both formal and informal ways. Especially as members of the academy, whether by choice or by accident, we find ourselves speaking in the classroom, in our organizations, with our professors (and students), on our dorm floors, among many other locations.

Studying public speaking and communication in general is important in U.S. society for several reasons. First, for nearly two decades, the National Association of Colleges and Employers (http://naceweb.org/s02242016/verbal-communication -important-job-candidate-skill.aspx?terms=communication%20skills) has identified "communication skills" as paramount to securing and maintaining a job. Second, public speaking, by definition, suggests that as a society we are receptive to listening to views of others, even views that may conflict with our own. Deliberation and debate in the United States are hallmarks of a democracy (West, 2012). Third, when one speaks before a group, the information resonates beyond that group of people. For instance, when a politician speaks to a small group of constituents in southwest Missouri, what she says frequently gets told and retold to others. When a minister consoles his congregation after a fatal shooting at a local middle school, the words reverberate even into the living rooms of those who were not present at the service.

Finally, effective communication is identified as paramount in communication among individuals from various parts of the globe (Williams & Remillard, 2016); it is not just a topic that resonates solely in the United States. Clearly, effective public speaking has the ability to affect individuals beyond the listening audience, and it is a critical skill for us as citizens of a democratic society.

Despite the importance of public speaking in our lives, it remains a dreaded activity. In fact, some opinion polls state that people fear public speaking more than they fear death! Comedian Jerry Seinfeld reflects on this dilemma: "According to most studies, people's number one fear is public speaking. Number two is death. Death is number two. Does that seem right? This means to the average person, if you have to go to a funeral, you're better off in the casket than doing the eulogy" (youtube.com/watch?v=kL7fTLjFzAg).

Public speaking is not so funny to people like Camille Ramirez. She must work through not only her anxiety about speaking before a group, but also her anxiety about discussing a very personal topic. For Camille, having a sense of what to speak about and what strategies to adopt are foremost in her mind. Based on her classmates' reactions, her speech remains effective. Camille may not know that the reasons for her success may lie in the writings of Aristotle, published more than 25 centuries ago.

Aristotle is generally credited with explaining the dynamics of public speaking. *The Rhetoric* consists of three books: one primarily concerned with public speakers, the second focusing on the audience, and the third attending to the

Rhetorical Theory centers on the notion of rhetoric, which Aristotle calls the available means of persuasion. That is, a speaker who is interested in persuading his or her audience should consider three rhetorical proofs: logic (logos), emotion (pathos), and ethics/credibility (ethos). Audiences are key to effective persuasiveness, and rhetorical syllogisms, requiring audiences to supply missing pieces of a speech, are used in persuasion.

speech itself. His *Rhetoric* is considered by historians, philosophers, and communication experts to be one of the most influential pieces of writing in the Western world. In addition, many still consider Aristotle's works to be the most significant writing on speech preparation and speech making. In a sense, Aristotle was the first to provide the "how to" for public speaking. Lane Cooper (1932) agrees. Nearly 90 years ago, Cooper observed that "the rhetoric of Aristotle is a practical psychology, and the most helpful book extant for writers of prose and for speakers of every sort" (p. vi). According to Cooper, people in all walks of life—attorneys, legislators, clergy, teachers, and media writers—can benefit in some way when they read Aristotle's writings. That is some accolade for a man who has been dead for over 2,500 years!

To understand the power behind Aristotle's words, it's important first to understand the nature of the *Rhetoric*. In doing so, we will be able to present the simple eloquence of Rhetorical Theory. First, in order for you to understand the historical context of the theory, we present a brief history of life in Aristotle's day followed by a discussion of his definition of rhetoric.

The Rhetorical Tradition

The son of a physician, Aristotle was encouraged to be a thinker about the world around him. He went to study with his mentor, Plato, at the age of 17. Aristotle and Plato had conflicting worldviews; therefore, their philosophies differed as well. Plato was always in search of absolute truths about the world. He didn't care much whether these truths had practical value. Plato felt that as long as people could agree on matters of importance, society would survive. Aristotle, however, was more interested in dealing with the here and now. He wasn't as interested in achieving absolute truth as he was in attaining a logical, realistic, and rational view of society. In other words, we could argue that Aristotle was much more grounded than Plato, trying to understand the various types of people in Athenian society.

Because he taught diverse groups of people in Greek society, Aristotle became known as a man committed to helping the ordinary citizen—at the time, a landowning male. During the day, common citizens (men) were asked to judge murder trials, oversee city boundaries, travel as emissaries, and defend their property against would-be land collectors (Golden, Berquist, Coleman, & Sproule, 2011). Because there were no professional attorneys at that time, many citizens hired **Sophists,** teachers of public speaking, to instruct them in basic principles of persuasion. These teachers established small schools where they taught students about the public speaking process and where they produced public speaking handbooks discussing practical ways to become more effective public speakers. Aristotle, however, believed that many of these handbooks were problematic in that they focused on the judicial system to the neglect of other contexts. Also, he thought that authors spent too much time on ways to arouse judges and juries: "It is not right to pervert the judge by moving him to anger or envy or pity—one might as well warp a carpenter's rule before using it," Aristotle observes (cited in Rhys & Bywater, 1954, p. 20). Aristotle reminds speakers not to forget the importance of logic in their presentations.

sophists
teachers of public speaking (rhetoric) in ancient Greece

The *Rhetoric* could be considered Aristotle's way of responding to the problems he saw in these handbooks. Although he challenges a number of prevailing assumptions about what constitutes an effective presentation, what remains especially important is Aristotle's definition of **rhetoric:** the available means of persuasion. For Aristotle, however, availing oneself of all means of persuasion does not translate into bribery or torture, common practices in ancient Greece, where slavery was institutionalized. What Aristotle envisions and recommends is for speakers to work beyond their first instincts when they want to persuade others. They need to consider all aspects of speech making, including their audience members. When Camille prepared for her speech by assessing both her words and her audience's needs, she was adhering to Aristotle's suggestions for successful speaking.

rhetoric
the available means of persuasion

For some of you, interpreting rhetoric in this way may be unfamiliar. After all, the word has been tossed around by so many different types of people that it may have lost Aristotle's original intent. For instance, Jasper Neel (1994) comments that "the term *rhetoric* has taken on such warm and cuddly connotations in the postmodern era" (p. 15) that we tend to forget that its meaning is very specific. For people like Neel, we must return to Aristotle's interpretation of rhetoric or we will miss the essence of his theory. Politicians often indict their opponents by stating that their "rhetoric is empty" or that they're all "rhetoric, with little action." These sorts of criticisms only trivialize the active and dynamic process of rhetoric and its role in the public speaking process. Indeed, rhetoric is an "art of using language" (Cuddon, 2013, p. 606) and therefore, simply because someone talks or chats aimlessly does not mean that person is using rhetorical discourse. Consider this important caveat as you review this chapter.

Assumptions of The *Rhetoric*

Hundreds of various interpretations of Aristotle have been cataloged over the years. We understand the difficulty in distilling this information in a chapter such as this. Nonetheless, we have found that much of The Rhetoric can be understood with two primary assumptions in mind. We examine the following two:

- Effective public speakers must consider their audience.
- Effective public speakers employ a number of proofs in their presentations.

The first assumption underscores the interpretation of communication that we presented in Chapter 1: Communication is a transactional process. Within a public speaking context, Aristotle suggests that the speaker–audience relationship must be acknowledged and even primary in the speaking process. Speakers should not construct or deliver their speeches without considering their audiences. Speakers need to be audience centered. They should think about the audience as a group of individuals with motivations, decisions, and choices and not as some undifferentiated mass of homogeneous people. The effectiveness of Camille's speech on drinking and driving derived from her ability to understand her audience. She knew that students, primarily under the age of 25, rarely think about death, and, therefore, her speech prompted them to think about something that they normally would not consider. Camille, like many other public speakers, engaged in **audience analysis,** which is the process of evaluating an audience and its background (e.g., age, sex, educational level, etc.) and tailoring one's speech so that listeners respond as the speaker hopes they will.

audience analysis
an assessment and evaluation of listeners

Aristotle believed that audiences are crucial to a speaker's ultimate effectiveness. He observes, "Of the three elements in speech-making—speaker, subject, and person addressed—it is the last one, the hearer, that determines the speech's end and object" (http://www.americanrhetoric.com/aristotleonrhetoric.htm). Each listener, however, is unique, and what works with one listener may fail with another. Expanding on this notion, Christopher Tindale (2015) observes that audiences are not always open to rational argument. Consider Camille's speech on drinking and driving. Her speech may have worked wonderfully in the public speaking classroom, but she might have different results with a group of alcohol distributors. As you can see, understanding the audience is critical before a speaker begins constructing his or her speech. Further, as James Herrick (2016) asserts: In the end, rhetoric is about gaining compliance and in order to do that, the audience must be considered.

The second assumption underlying Aristotle's theory pertains to what speakers do in their speech preparation and their speech making. Aristotle's proofs refer to the means of persuasion, and, for Aristotle, three proofs exist: ethos, pathos, and logos. **Ethos** refers to the perceived character, intelligence, and goodwill of a speaker as they become revealed through his or her speech. Eugene Ryan (1984) notes that ethos is a broad term that refers to the mutual influence that speakers and listeners have on each other. Ryan contends that Aristotle believed that the speaker can be influenced by the audience in much the same way that audiences can be influenced by the speaker. Interviewing Kenneth Andersen, a communication ethicist, Pat Arneson (2007) relates Andersen's thoughts about Aristotle and ethos. Ethos, according to Andersen, is "something you create on the occasion" (p. 131). To that end, a speaker's ethos is not simply something that is brought into a speaking experience; it is the speaking experience. Melissa Waresh (2012) contends that ethos must necessarily take into consideration the relationship between speaker and audience. She states: "Ethos is character. Character implicates trust. Trust is based on relationship. Relationship persuades" (p. 229).

ethos
the perceived character, intelligence, and goodwill of a speaker

Aristotle felt that a speech by a trustworthy individual was more persuasive than a speech by an individual whose trust was in question. Michael Hyde (2004) contends that Aristotle felt that ethos is part of the virtue of another and, therefore, "can be trained and made habitual" (p. xvi). **Logos** is the logical proof that speakers employ—their arguments and rationalizations. For Aristotle, logos involves using a

logos
logical proof; the use of arguments and evidence in a speech

number of practices, including using logical claims and clear language. To speak in poetic phrases results in a lack of clarity and naturalness. **Pathos** pertains to the emotions that are drawn out of listeners. Aristotle argues that listeners become the instruments of proof when emotion is stirred in them; listeners judge differently when they are influenced by joy, pain, hatred, or fear. Let's return to our example of Camille to illustrate these three Aristotelian proofs.

pathos
emotional proof; emotions drawn from audience members

The ethos that Camille evokes during her presentation is important. Relating a personal account of her relationship with her Uncle Jake and describing his subsequent death at the hands of a drunk driver bolster perceptions of her credibility. Undoubtedly, her audience feels that she is a credible speaker by virtue of her relationship with Jake and her knowledge of the consequences of drinking and driving. Logos is evident in Camille's speech when she decides to logically argue that although drinking is a part of recreation, mixing it with driving can be deadly. Using examples to support her claims underscores Camille's use of logical proof. The pathos inherent in the speech should be apparent from the subject matter. She chooses a topic that appeals to her college listeners. They most likely will feel for Camille and reflect on how many times they or their friends have gotten behind the wheel after having a few drinks. The proofs of Aristotelian theory, therefore, guide Camille's effectiveness.

Each of these three—ethos, logos, and pathos—is critical to speech effectiveness. But each, alone, may not be sufficient. Keep in mind Kenneth Burke's belief that according to Aristotle, "an audience's confidence in the speaker is the most convincing proof of all" (Burke, 2007, p. 335).

For Aristotle, logos is much more than offering evidence in a speech. He delineates this proof in more detail in his writings. In his discussion, he notes that speakers who consider logos must necessarily consider syllogisms. We now turn our attention to this critical Aristotelian principle.

The Syllogism: A Three-Tiered Argument

We noted that logos is one of the three proofs that, according to Aristotle, create a more effective message. Nestled in these logical proofs is something called syllogisms. The term requires clarification because there is some debate among scholars on its precise meaning.

Communication scholars have studied the *Rhetoric* and its meaning for years and have attempted to untangle some of Aristotle's words. We look here at the term syllogism, defined as a set of propositions that are related to one another and draw a conclusion from the major and minor premises. Typically, syllogisms contain two premises and a conclusion. A **syllogism** is nothing more than a deductive argument, a group of statements (premises) that lead to another group of statements (conclusions). In other words, premises are starting points or beginners used by speakers. They establish justification for a conclusion. In a syllogism, both major and minor premises exist. Symbolically, a syllogism looks like this:

syllogism
a set of propositions that are related to one another and draw a conclusion from the major and minor premises

$$A \rightarrow B$$

$$B \rightarrow C$$

$$\text{Therefore, } A \rightarrow C$$

Consider this classic example of a syllogism:

Major Premise:	All people are mortal.
Minor Premise:	Aristotle is a person.
Conclusion:	Therefore, Aristotle is mortal.

Let's use the beginning story about Camille and construct a syllogism that she might employ in her speech:

Major Premise:	Drunk driving can kill people.
Minor Premise:	College students drink and drive.
Conclusion:	Therefore, college students can kill others (by drinking and driving).

As a speaker, you might (unwittingly) incorporate syllogisms to persuade your audience. However, in an often complex and convoluted society, drawing such a clear conclusion from preliminary premises may not be appropriate. Syllogistic reasoning may undercut a point you're making. For example, it is usually difficult to draw a clear conclusion when dealing with the behaviors of close friends or family members. Personality, relational history, and timing all intersect to make drawing a simple conclusion quite difficult. Further, syllogistic reasoning is, like many issues in this book, impacted by culture. Audience members do not always share a speaker's logical progression of ideas. Therefore, speakers need to be cautious in expecting audience members to draw conclusions in similar ways.

Syllogisms are a critical part of the speaking process for Aristotle. Speakers use them to enhance effectiveness in their speeches. In addition, speakers also incorporate other techniques that are labeled *canons*.

Canons of *Rhetoric*

Aristotle was convinced that, for a persuasive speech to be effective, speakers must follow certain guidelines or principles, which he called *canons* (Campbell, Schultz-Huxman, & Burkholder, 2015). These are recommendations for making a speech more compelling. Classical rhetoricians have maintained Aristotle's observations, and to this day, most writers of public speaking texts in communication follow canons for effective speaking that early Greeks and Romans advocated.

Although his writings in the *Rhetoric* focused on persuasion, these canons have been applied in a number of speaking situations. Five prescriptions for effective oratory exist and we now discuss these canons, which are highlighted in Table 18.1.

invention
a canon of rhetoric that pertains to the construction or development of an argument related to a particular speech

Invention

The first canon is invention. This term can be confusing because invention of a speech does not mean invention in a scientific sense. **Invention** is defined as the construction or development of an argument that is relevant to the purpose of a

Table 18.1 Aristotle's Canons of *Rhetoric*

CANON	DEFINITION	DESCRIPTION
Invention	Integration of reasoning and arguments in speech	Using logic and evidence in speech makes a speech more powerful and more persuasive.
Arrangement	Organization of speech	Maintaining a speech structure—Introduction, Body, Conclusion—bolsters speaker credibility, enhances persuasiveness, and reduces listener frustration.
Style	Use of language in speech	Incorporating style ensures that a speech is memorable and that a speaker's ideas are clarified.
Delivery	Presentation of speech	Delivering an effective speech complements a speaker's words and helps to reduce speaker anxiety.
Memory	Storing information in speaker's mind	Knowing what to say and when to say it eases speaker anxiety and allows a speaker to respond to unanticipated events.

speech. Invention is discovering all the proofs a speaker plans to use. Invention is broadly interpreted as the body of information and knowledge that a speaker brings to the speaking situation. This stockpile of information can help a speaker in his or her persuasive approaches.

Suppose, for instance, you are presenting a speech on DNA testing. Invention associated with this speech would include appeals woven throughout your speech (e.g., "DNA helps living organisms pass along information to their offspring," "DNA is the fundamental blueprint for all life," or "DNA testing has proven to be instrumental in capturing rapists"). In constructing your arguments, you may draw on all these examples.

Aids to invention are identified as topics. **Topics,** in this sense, refer to the lines of argument or modes of reasoning a speaker uses in a speech. Speakers may draw on these invention aids as they decide which speaking strategy will persuade their audiences. Topics, therefore, help speakers enhance their persuasiveness.

Speakers look to what are called **civic spaces,** or the metaphorical locations where rhetoric has the opportunity to effect change, "where a speaker can look for 'available means of persuasion'" (Kennedy, 1991, p. 45). Recall, for instance, Camille's decision to talk about drinking and driving in her public speaking class. As she speaks, she defines her terms, looks at opposing arguments, and considers ideas similar to her own. That is, she identifies a "location" in her speech where she is able to adapt to an audience that may be losing attention. Camille does whatever it takes to ensure that she has the chance to persuade her audience.

topics
an aid to invention that refers to the arguments a speaker uses

civic spaces
a metaphor suggesting that speakers have "locations" where the opportunity to persuade others exists

Arrangement

arrangement
a canon of rhetoric that pertains to a speaker's ability to organize a speech

A second canon identified by Aristotle is called arrangement. **Arrangement** pertains to a speaker's ability to organize a speech. Aristotle felt that speakers should seek out organizational patterns for their speeches to enhance the speech's effectiveness. Artistic unity among different thoughts should be foremost in a speaker's mind. Simplicity should also be a priority because Aristotle believed that there are essentially two parts to a speech: stating the subject and finding the proof, or what he calls "demonstrating it" (Kennedy, 1991, p. 258). At the time, he felt that speakers were organizing their speeches haphazardly, making them less-effective speakers.

Aristotle, however, is very clear in his organizational strategy. Speeches should generally follow a threefold approach: introduction, body, and conclusion. The **introduction** should first gain the audience's attention, then suggest a connection with the audience, and finally provide an overview of the speech's purpose.

introduction
part of an organizational strategy in a speech that includes gaining the audience's attention, connecting with the audience, and providing an overview of the speaker's purpose

Introductions can be quite effective in speeches that are intended to arouse emotionally. Gaining attention by incorporating emotional wording is an effective persuasive technique. Consider Camille's introductory words. She obviously captures the audience's attention by personalizing a very difficult subject. She then suggests her relationship with the topic, followed by an overview of her speaking purpose:

> Jake McCain was killed by someone he didn't know. Jake was a wonderful man and the person who killed him never knew that. Yet, Jake's death could have been prevented. You see, he was killed by someone who was drunk. The driver may have a future, but Jake will never have a chance to see his grandchild grow up or see his sister get married. I know about Jake McCain: He's my uncle. Today, I wish to discuss the dangers of drunk driving and identify how you can avoid becoming one of the many thousands who get behind a wheel after drinking too much.

body
part of an organizational strategy in a speech that includes arguments, examples, and important details to make a point

Arrangement also includes the body and conclusion of the speech. The **body** includes all of the arguments, supporting details, and necessary examples to make a point. In addition to the entire speech being organized, the body of the speech also follows some sort of organizational structure. Aristotle states that audiences need to be led from one point to another.

conclusion
part of an organizational strategy in a speech that is aimed at summarizing a speaker's main points and arousing emotions in an audience

Finally, the **conclusion** or epilogue of a speech is aimed at summarizing the speaker's points and arousing emotions in the audience. Conclusions should be arrived at logically and should also attempt to reconnect with listeners. Camille's conclusion clearly demonstrates her desire to leave her listeners with a message:

> So I leave you today after examining the prevalence of drunk driving, the current laws associated with this behavior, and what you and I can personally do to help rid our society of this terrible and overlooked part of being a college student. The next time you go and have a drink, don't forget to give your keys to a friend. Or get a cab. I'm sure your family will thank you. Do it for me. Do it for my Uncle Jake.

We can feel Camille's passion for a topic that is both personal and personally difficult.

www.CartoonStock.com

Style

The use of language to express ideas in a certain manner is called **style.** In his discussion of style, Aristotle includes word choice, word imagery, and word appropriateness. He believes that each type of rhetoric has its own style, yet style is often overlooked. He notes that strange words or **glosses** (e.g., antiquated words and phrases, such as "gyp" or "girl Friday") should be avoided. Speaking in terms that are too simplistic will also turn off an audience. To bridge this gap between the unfamiliar and the too familiar, Aristotle introduces the notion of **metaphor,** or a figure of speech that helps to make the unclear more understandable. Metaphors are critical devices to employ in speeches, according to Aristotle, because they have the capacity to change the perceptions and the minds of listeners.

Style can be better understood through an example from Camille's speech on drunk driving. If Camille were concentrating on style, her speech would have the following passage:

> Drinking is often viewed as a means to release. After a very long day at work or at school, there may be nothing better than having a cold beer. So they say. Yet, too often, one beer turns into two, which by the end of a few hours, has turned into a six-pack. And the result can be tragic: How many times have you watched your friend or family member get into a car after a six-pack? This person can be as dangerous as a bullet, unleashed from a gun that is randomly pointed at someone. If you must drink, it's not only your business; but, it's my business, too.

Camille's words evoke some strong imagery; mentally, we can recreate the scene that she has laid out. Her word choice is unmistakable in that she uses familiar words. Finally, she uses the compelling metaphor of a bullet.

style
a canon of rhetoric that includes the use of language to express ideas in a speech

glosses
outdated words in a speech

metaphor
a figure of speech that helps to make the unclear more understandable

Memory

memory
a canon of rhetoric that refers to a speaker's effort in storing information for a speech

Storing invention, arrangement, and style in a speaker's mind is **memory.** In contrast to the previous four canons, Aristotle does not spend significant time delineating the importance of memory in speech presentation. Rather, he alludes to memory in his writings. Throughout the *Rhetoric*, for instance, Aristotle reminds us to consider a number of issues prior to the presentation (e.g., examples, signs, metaphors, delivery techniques, etc.). He further notes that to speak persuasively, a speaker has to have a basic understanding of many of these devices when constructing and presenting a speech. In other words, speakers need to have memorized a great deal before getting up to speak.

Theory-Into-Practice

Theoretical Claim: Audience analysis influences speaking effectiveness.

Practical Implication: When a politician speaks to senior citizens, she should consider talking about topics that resonate with this group (e.g., telemarketing fraud, Medicare, etc.). In doing so, it's likely her audience will be more apt to listen attentively and act accordingly.

Today, people interpret memory in speech-making differently from Aristotle. Memorizing a speech often means having a basic understanding of material and techniques. Although other rhetoricians like Quintilian made specific recommendations on memorizing, Aristotle felt that familiarizing oneself with the speech's content was understood. When Camille presents her speech on drinking and driving, for example, she has some parts of her speech committed to memory and other parts overviewed on notes.

Student Voices

Vlad

I know that I'm probably oversimplifying a great theory, but a lot of the *Rhetoric* is something that I remember from my public speaking class. I was always told to keep my speeches organized and to persuade people by getting to them emotionally. I did my persuasive speech on organ donation because my sister was waiting for a kidney. I know my delivery was pretty smooth because I believed in what I was saying. That probably also improved my ethos.

delivery
a canon of rhetoric that refers to the nonverbal presentation of a speaker's ideas

Delivery

Thus far we have concentrated on how a speech is constructed. Aristotle, however, was also interested in how a speech is delivered. In this case, **delivery** refers to the nonverbal presentation of a speaker's ideas. Delivery normally includes a host of behaviors, including eye contact, vocal cues, pronunciation, enunciation, dialect, body movement, and physical appearance. For Aristotle, delivery specifically pertains to the manipulation of the voice. He especially encouraged speakers to use appropriate levels of pitch, rhythm, volume, and emotion. He believed that the way in which something is said affects its intelligibility.

Aristotle believed that delivery could not be easily taught, yet it is crucial for a speaker to consider. He also taught that speakers should strive to be natural in their delivery. Speakers should not use any vocal techniques that may detract from the words and should strive to capture a comfortable presence in front of an audience. In other words, speakers should avoid being "gimmicky" in their presentations and strive for authenticity.

The canons of rhetoric are incorporated into a number of different persuasive speeches. Our exploration of Aristotle's Rhetorical Theory concludes with a discussion of the three types of rhetoric.

Types of Rhetoric

You will recall that during Aristotle's time citizens were asked to take part in a number of speaking activities—from judge to attorney to legislator. It was in this spirit that Aristotle identified different speaking situations for citizens to consider when conversing on trade, finance, national defense, and war. He denoted three types of rhetoric, or what he called three types of oratory: forensic, epideictic, and deliberative. **Forensic rhetoric** pertains to establishing a fact; at the core of forensic rhetoric is justice. **Epideictic rhetoric** is discourse related to praise or blame. **Deliberative rhetoric** concerns speakers who must determine a course of action—something should or should not be done. The three types refer to three different time periods: forensic to the past, epideictic to the present, and deliberative to the future. We discuss these three rhetorical types next and illustrate them in Figure 18.1.

forensic rhetoric
a type of rhetoric that pertains to speakers prompting feelings of guilt or innocence from an audience

epideictic rhetoric
a type of rhetoric that pertains to praising or blaming

deliberative rhetoric
a type of rhetoric that determines an audience's course of action

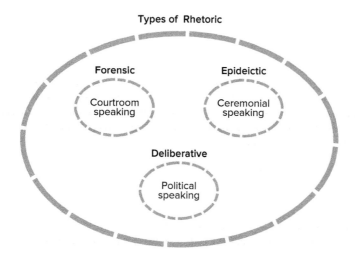

Types of Rhetoric

Forensic

Courtroom speaking

Epideictic

Ceremonial speaking

Deliberative

Political speaking

Figure 18.1
Types of Rhetoric

Forensic oratory, or judicial rhetoric, specifically refers to speaking in courtrooms. Its intent is to establish guilt or innocence; in Aristotle's day, forensic speakers directed their presentation to courtroom judges. Aristotle examined forensic rhetoric within a legal framework, and thus many of his beliefs on the law are found in the *Rhetoric*. Amelie Rorty (1996) notes that forensic speaking requires focusing on arguments that tap into judges' psyches, including their beliefs about why certain criminals act the way they do and which types of circumstances tempt people to break the law. Because past actions are frequently indicative of a person's current behavior, forensics orators rely on previous behaviors.

Aristotle recognized that a person's character is critical in forensic rhetoric. He interprets character as both status (i.e., whether a person is young or old, rich or poor, fortunate or unfortunate) and morality (i.e., whether a person is just or unjust, reasonable or unreasonable). If people act voluntarily, Aristotle argued, the choices they make have consequences. To establish guilt, the forensic speaker needs to establish motivation for doing wrong. In speaking before an audience, then, speakers will invoke what Aristotle called the "moral habits" of a person.

Examples of forensic rhetoric abound in our society. Forensic speakers have played prominent roles in U.S. courtrooms. Attorneys, in particular, have effectively and persuasively used their forensic rhetoric over the years. One of the most memorable forensic presentations in history took place in the closely watched trial of football legend O. J. Simpson. Prosecutors tried to implicate Simpson's morals by playing a tape recording of a 911 call in which Simpson could be heard yelling at his wife and by showing pictures of her beaten body to the jury. More recent forensic efforts by prosecutors include the legal proceedings of corruption charges by former Illinois governor, Rod Blagojevich, the Bernie Madoff investment scandal, and the trial of home décor guru Martha Stewart, who was found guilty of lying to government agents about stock trading. In all these cases, forensic speaking was used to undercut the moral integrity of the defendant and to establish guilt (Stewart, 2012).

The second type of rhetoric, epideictic, is also called ceremonial speaking. Speeches during Aristotle's time were given in public arenas with the goal of praising, honoring, blaming, or shaming. Epideictic rhetors include people, events, organizations, or nations in their speeches. These speeches usually focus on social issues because, according to Aristotle, people are interested in the here and now. Epideictic speaking cannot be separated from ethos, Aristotle stated. He believed that by understanding the need to praise or blame, epideictic speakers understand the importance of their own character. For instance, a speech criticizing prison conditions may not resonate deeply with an audience if the speaker is on death row for rape and murder.

At times, there are speeches that simply are generic in nature and yet, the target of blame is implied. In 2012, for instance, the Sandy Hook Elementary School killings of more than 20 school children and staff resulted in many epideictic speeches about the need for stricter gun laws and the lax oversight of semiautomatic weapons. While many speeches did not name the National Rifle Association by name, it was clear that many speakers were blaming this organization for its influence on restricting gun legislation.

Epideictic speaking is greatly informed by the study of virtues or values—a theme that Aristotle borrowed from Plato. The epideictic speaker must be able to relate the virtues of the topic to a diverse audience. Aristotle felt that courage and justice ranked above all virtues, but virtue is defined according to the law of the land.

Epideictic rhetoric is exemplified in funeral practices in our country. Eulogies, which are commonplace at many funerals, usually laud the life of the deceased. Commenting on contemporary values, the epideictic speaker at a funeral frequently compares the virtues of the dead person with those of society. For instance, after the death of his grandmother, one of your authors was asked to give the eulogy at the funeral. During his speech, he talked about his grandmother's uplifting spirit and how she rarely complained about her ailments or about her financial situation. He evoked images of contemporary society in his speech, noting how unusual it is today for someone to refrain from self-centered complaining. His speech centered on a prevailing virtue of his grandmother—her selflessness—and also commented on society as a whole.

The third type is deliberative rhetoric, also called political rhetoric, and it was the focus of much of Aristotle's comments on rhetorical discourse. As we mentioned earlier, deliberative rhetoric is associated with the future—what an audience will do or think as a result of a speaker's efforts. Deliberative speaking, then, requires the speaker to be adept at understanding how his or her thoughts are aligned with those of the audience. The deliberative speaker should be prepared to consider subjects that are relevant to the audience and to which the speaker can personally relate. Aristotle identified five subjects on which people deliberated in his day: revenue, war and peace, the defense of the country, commerce, and legislation (san.beck.org/EC22 -Aristotle.html). Today's list of deliberative topics might include health insurance, taxes, relationships, education, and civil rights. Deliberative speakers might try to raise interest in these topics, and once interest is piqued, they might find that listeners are more prone to being persuaded.

Larry Arnhart (1981) comments that the deliberative rhetorician needs to know not only the actual subject of deliberation but also the elements of human nature that influence deliberation. There are a number of topics, therefore, which are suited for deliberation and others that are not. Aristotle focused on what deliberative speakers can say to an assembly (a body of legislators, for example), and today this delib- erative oratory continues. Consider the following example. When asked to give a short presentation to her state's legislative committee on health insurance, Beverly, a 64-year-old mother of four, spoke about the health insurance of elderly people. As the caretaker of her 90-year-old mother-in-law, a patient in a local nursing home, Beverly knew precisely the kinds of persuasive strategies to use with the group of politicians. Her speech focused on the difficulties of being old and how these prob- lems are amplified by not having enough insurance. She asked the legislators to con- sider their own aging parents in their discussions. She outlined five points of action for the committee to follow. Three of the points could be undertaken immediately: establishing a task force, interviewing elderly citizens, and setting up a toll-free num- ber to solicit citizen concerns and complaints. The remaining two required funding from the legislature. At the conclusion of her brief speech, Beverly was satisfied that her suggestions would not be ignored.

Aristotle would have approved of Beverly's rhetoric. Her recommendations were doable (the committee enacted three of the five), and she made her experiences rel- evant to her audience by asking the group to think about their own parents. This approach elicited personal identification, which is an important tactic in deliberative speaking. By eliciting these feelings, Beverly knew that she would be able to get her audience to agree with her thinking.

Integration, Critique, and Closing

Aristotle's *Rhetoric* remains an influential theoretical foundation in communication studies. You can pick up any public speaking text and find discussions on delivery, organization, and style. Students of public speaking have benefited greatly from the words and values of Aristotle, and for this reason the theory will resonate deeply for years to come. With a few exceptions, his theory has drawn the attention of scholars who primarily identify as interpretive and critical, making the theory aligned with the qualitative approach. However, keep in mind that some offshoots of the theory (e.g., communication apprehension) are studied within an experimental lens. Therefore, one could say that both the quantitative and qualitative approaches are honored within this theory. The evaluative criteria for communication we wish to discuss center on three primary areas: logical consistency, heurism, and test of time.

Integration

Communication Tradition	**Rhetorical** | Semiotic | Phenomenological | Cybernetic | Socio-Psychological | Socio-Cultural | Critical
Communication Context	Intrapersonal | Interpersonal | Small Group | Organizational | **Public/Rhetorical** | Mass/Media | Cultural
Approach to Knowing	Positivistic/Empirical | **Interpretive/Hermeneutic** | **Critical**

Critique

Evaluation Criteria	Scope | **Logical Consistency** | Parsimony | Utility | Testability | **Heurism** | **Test of Time**

Logical Consistency

Critics of Aristotle's theory have taken issue with some tenets of the theory perhaps because some scholars believe that conclusions are often drawn based on Aristotle's "scattered remarks and examples" (Curzer, 2015, p. 129). For instance, Aristotle has been criticized for contradiction and incoherence. Charles Marsh (2006), for instance, reports on one critic who undercut the notion of ethos as proposed by Aristotle: "In a society so small, where everyone knew one another, how could [Aristotle] think—was he really that dumb—that a person of bad character could hoodwink the other leaders of society?" (p. 339). Lord (1994) contends that in developing his theory, Aristotle blasts his contemporaries for focusing too much on the audience's emotions. Although Aristotle encourages speakers to avoid focusing on emotions while making their points, he proceeds to do just that when he stresses the importance of presenting emotions and invoking audience passions (pathos) during a speech. This makes the theory somewhat inconsistent.

John Cooper (1996) challenges Lord's critique. He argues that Aristotle was simply responding to the Sophists' messages of the day. Because most of the speeches in ancient Greece were directed to judges and rulers, Aristotle indicated that speakers should try to elicit feelings of pity in the courtroom. To do that, Aristotle felt that speakers should try to view judges in congenial ways.

Further criticism of the logical consistency of the theory has been offered. First, as we alluded to a bit earlier, scholars agree that the *Rhetoric* is a rather unorganized undertaking; in fact, the theory is assembled from Aristotle's lecture notes. It is not surprising, then, that Aristotle seems to discuss topics in a random and arbitrary manner. At times, Aristotle introduces a topic and then drops it, only to return to it later. His terminology is especially problematic for some scholars. You may not find this too earth-shattering, but recall that researchers need clear foundations of terms before they can embark upon testing or clarifying theory. Larry Arnhart (1991) concludes that Aristotle defined his terms in less than precise ways so that audiences (readers) would have a broader understanding of his words and ideas. Arnhart believes that this conscious decision to remain unclear does not mean that Aristotle's thoughts should be discarded.

Finally, the logical consistency is further challenged by an examination of how Aristotle views the audience. Critics charge Aristotle with ignoring the critical nature of listeners. For instance, Jasper Neel (1994) states, "Aristotle makes clear that the introduction [of a speech] has nothing to do with the 'speech itself.' It exists only because of the hearer's weak-minded tendency to listen to what is beside the point" (p. 156). Eugene Ryan (1984) is more blunt: "Aristotle is thinking of listeners who have some difficulty keeping their minds on the speaker's business, are easily distracted, tend to forget what has gone on before, [and] are not absorbed with abstract ideas" (p. 47). From these writers, we get the impression that Aristotle perceived audiences to be incapable of being discriminating listeners or critical thinkers. It's important to note, though, that Aristotle was writing at a time when people were rather passive listeners; they did not watch the evening news and did not have access to information about world events. Furthermore, when one considers that the *Rhetoric* is based on lecture notes and that students back then were not accustomed to openly challenging their mentors, Aristotle's view of the audience is not so implausible.

Heurism

Few would argue that Aristotle's *Rhetoric* is one of the most heuristic theories found in communication. Scholars in political science, medicine, English composition, and philosophy have studied Rhetorical Theory and incorporated Aristotelian thinking in their research. The theory has spawned a number of subareas in the communication discipline, such as communication apprehension, and has generated research. In fact, much of the writing in public speaking is based on the writings of Aristotle. Some interesting research has discussed the deliberative rhetoric of an African American activist (McClish, 2007). Much of the discussion related to preaching in churches can be directly attributed to Aristotle's thinking (Broadus, 2012). Aristotelian proofs have been employed to student umbilical cord blood banking (White, 2006), and in the analyses of environmental reports (Higgins & Walker, 2012). In addition, Aristotle has been invoked in a wide range of studies examining such diverse topics as military digital games (Sparrow, Harrison, Oakley, & Keogh, 2015), the Scottish vote on independence (Mackay, 2015), and hip-hop music (Sciullo, 2014). Aristotle's theory will continue to resonate with scholars across disciplines and in a variety of contexts.

Test of Time

No other theory in the communication discipline has withstood the test of time as well as Aristotle's *Rhetoric*. With centuries behind it and public speaking textbooks, teachers, and researchers communicating Aristotelian principles, it's hard to believe that any other theory in the field of communication will ever achieve such longevity!

Closing

As the 21st century continues, we are in an informed position to reflect on some of the greatest written works of all time. The *Rhetoric* is clearly such a work. Aristotle's words continue to resonate in a society that is far different from his day. Some people may reject his thoughts as outdated in an age in which multiple ways of knowing are embraced. Yet, some scholars are more direct in their acclaims of this thinker: "The rationale, scientific, and technological culture that pervades much of the Western world owes more to him than anyone else" (Woodfin & Groves, 2012, p. 3). Clearly, a theory focusing on how speakers use and engender emotions, logic, and trustworthiness cannot be ignored.

Discussion Starters

TECH QUEST: Aristotle never could envision social media as he was discussing public speaking. Considering the vast availability of various social media platforms such as LinkedIn and Instagram, discuss how public speeches can be both enhanced and undermined by social media.

1. In the chapter-opening scene, Camille Ramirez relied on Aristotle's view of public speaking. Do you believe that she could have been more effective? In what way? Use examples in your response.

2. Aristotle's critics have focused on the fact that his theory is simply a collection of lecture notes that are contradictory, vague, and often narrow. Do you agree or disagree, based on the information in this chapter? What examples can you point to for support?

3. Employ syllogistic reasoning for and against each of the following topics: physician-assisted suicide, same-sex marriage, and medicinal marijuana use.

4. Discuss what canon of rhetoric is most important when politicians speak to their constituents. Use examples to defend your view.

5. If Aristotle were alive today and you were his student, what additional suggestions would you offer him for a new edition of the *Rhetoric*? Why do you believe your suggestions are important to address in public speaking? Incorporate examples in your response.

6. Aristotle spent a great deal of time discussing the role of the audience. If you were giving a speech on safety to a group of convenience store employees, what sort of audience analysis would you undertake?

7. Explain how principles from the *Rhetoric* relate to job interviews.

CHAPTER 19

Dramatism

*Based on the research of **Kenneth Burke***

Stories are equipment for living.
—Kenneth Burke

Karl Nelson

Karl Nelson really looked forward to this part of his morning routine. He settled down with his first cup of coffee and the morning paper. Although he loved his tablet and smart phone, he loved the feel of a newspaper in his hands, something that he knew was fast becoming a lost practice. Karl allowed himself an hour to read all the news of the day and to savor his caffeine fix. In many ways this was his favorite part of the day, and he got up extra early to make sure he would have enough time for it after his workout and before he left for the office. But, today he was not happy. He looked at the headlines with disgust. He was so sick of reading about politicians who had no common sense. Today he was reading about Alan Spector, the mayor of Grenada, New Mexico, where Karl lived. The article was about the fact that Spector had campaigned on a "clean" platform, claiming that he would make government respectable again, and now he was apologizing to his wife for having had an affair with their nanny. Undoubtedly he would never have confessed, but the tabloids had just revealed that he'd had a child, who was now 10, with this woman!

Karl looked up from his paper just as his partner, Max, came into the breakfast room. Karl asked, "Max, have you read about Spector? That man is such an incredible low-life hypocrite. How could he pretend to be Mr. Clean during his campaign, talking all about family values, when he's cheating on his wife with their nanny?"

Max just shrugged and laughed. He was used to seeing Karl getting worked up over current events. It didn't seem all that important to him, but Karl certainly cared about this stuff. Max grabbed a cup of coffee and left to go to work. Karl went back to reading the paper.

The article described how Spector admitted the affair and had apologized profusely to his family and to his constituents. The nanny hadn't made a public statement. Karl thought the story in the paper made Spector look pretty bad, and he wondered if he should be impeached. He hoped Spector wouldn't be able to escape punishment because he really felt let down and deceived.

Karl noticed that it was getting late, so he put the rest of the newspaper in his briefcase and left for work. When he got to the office, a couple of people were talking about the Spector scandal. His colleague Diane agreed with him, saying that Spector was a hypocrite. But another colleague, Randy, disagreed, saying that we are always forgiving people for mistakes, and that the United States was a country of second chances. Randy said that this was really between Spector and his wife anyway.

As Karl drove home from work that night, he listened to the local news on the radio. A commentator said that people in the United States loved to build up public figures, but then they loved even more to see them fall. The commentator agreed with Karl's coworker, Randy. She said that we are a nation that loves a comeback, and maybe Spector would be back in political life someday. Karl disagreed. He thought Spector deserved disapproval because he'd done the wrong thing and because he'd been so judgmental about other people who made mistakes in the past. This Spector case was disgusting, Karl thought, and he hoped the guy never got into public office again.

∎

Some rhetoricians might analyze Alan Spector's problems and Karl's responses to them using Dramatism, a theoretical position seeking to understand the actions of human life as drama. Kenneth Burke is known as the originator of Dramatism, although he did not initially use that term himself. Burke, who died in 1993 at the age of 96, was a fascinating person, and he was unlike many of the other theorists we cover in this book. Burke never earned an undergraduate degree, much less a Ph.D. He was self-taught in the areas of literary criticism, philosophy, communication, sociology, economics, theology, and linguistics. He taught for almost 20 years at several universities, including Harvard, Princeton, and the University of Chicago. His breadth of interests and perhaps his lack of formal training in any one discipline made him one of the most interdisciplinary theorists we will study. His ideas have been applied widely in various areas including literature, theater, communication, history, and sociology. No doubt one reason Burke is so widely read and applied has to do with his focus on symbol systems. Dramatism provides researchers with the flexibility to scrutinize an object of study from a variety of angles. It's likely, therefore, that regardless of your major, you will find something useful in Burke's theory.

Dramatism, as its name implies, conceptualizes life as a drama, placing a critical focus on the acts performed by various players. Just as in a play, the acts in life are central to revealing human motives. Dramatism provides us with a method that is well suited to address the act of communication between a text (e.g., the newspaper story about Alan Spector), and the audience for that text (e.g., Karl), as well as the inner action of the text (e.g., Spector's motives and choices). When Karl reads about Spector's case, it is as if he sees him as an actor. In Burke's terms, Karl understands Spector as an actor in a scene, trying to accomplish purposes because of certain motives. Thus, he comments on his motives as he evaluates his act of cheating on his wife with their nanny. Burke's theory of Dramatism allows us to analyze both Spector's rhetorical choices in this situation (how he framed his case) and Karl's responses to his choices.

Drama is a useful metaphor for Burke's ideas for three reasons: First, drama indicates a grand sweep, and Burke does not make limited claims; his goal is to theorize about the whole range of human experience. The dramatic metaphor is particularly useful in describing human relationships because it is grounded in interaction or dialogue. In its dialogue, drama both models relationships and illuminates relationships (Daas, 2011). Secondly, drama tends to follow recognizable types or genres: comedy, musical, melodrama, and so forth. Burke feels that the very way we structure and use language may be related to the way these human dramas are played out. Thirdly, drama is always addressed to an audience. In this sense, drama is rhetorical. Burke views literature as "equipment for living," which means that literature or texts speak to people's lived experiences and problems and provide people with responses for dealing with these experiences (Winslow, 2010).

Burke's theory compares life to a play and states that, as in a theatrical piece, life requires an actor, a scene, an action, some means for the action to take place, and a purpose. The theory allows a rhetorical critic to analyze a speaker's motives by identifying and examining these elements. Furthermore, Burke believes, guilt is the ultimate motive for speakers, and Dramatism suggests that rhetors are most successful when they provide their audiences with a means for purging their guilt.

In this way, Dramatism studies the ways in which language and its usage relate to audiences (French & Brown, 2011).

Assumptions of Dramatism

Similar to a few other theorists in this book, Kenneth Burke's thinking is so complex that it is difficult to reduce it to one set of assumptions or to a specific ontology, a term we introduced to you in Chapter 3. Some of the assumptions that follow illustrate the difficulty of labeling Burke's ontology. Researchers such as Brummett (1993) have called Burke's assumptions a symbolic ontology because of his emphasis on language. Yet, as Brummett cautions, "The best one can do, in searching for the heart of Burke's thought, is to find a partial ontology, a grounding-for-the-most-part. For Burke, people *mainly* do what they do, and the world is *largely* the way it is, because of the nature of *symbol systems themselves*" (p. xii; emphasis in original). Brummett's comment prefigures the following three assumptions of Burke's Dramatism Theory:

- Humans are animals who use symbols.
- Language and symbols form a critically important system for humans.
- Humans are choice makers.

The first assumption speaks to Burke's realization that some of what we do is motivated by our animal nature and some of what we do is motivated by symbols. Recall the semiotic tradition we discussed in Chapter 2 to understand this notion. For example, when Karl drinks his morning coffee, he is satisfying his thirst, an animal need. When he reads the morning paper and thinks about the ideas he encounters there, he is being influenced by symbols. The idea that humans are animals who use symbols represents a tension in Burke's thought. As Brummett (1993) observes, this assumption "teeters between the realizations that some of what we do is motivated by animality and some of it by symbolicity" (p. xii). Of all the symbols that humans use, language is the most important for Burke. To further understand the role of symbols in human interaction, recall the discussion we undertook in Chapter 4 on Symbolic Interaction Theory.

In the second assumption (the critical importance of language), Burke's position is somewhat similar to the concept of linguistic relativity known as the Sapir–Whorf hypothesis (Sapir, 1921; Whorf, 1956). Edward Sapir and Benjamin Whorf noted that it is difficult to think about concepts or objects without words for them. Thus, people are restricted (to an extent) in what they can conceive by the limits of their language. For Burke, as well as for Sapir and Whorf, when people use their language, they are used by it as well. When Karl tells Max that Spector is a hypocrite, he is choosing the symbols he wishes to use, but at the same time his opinions and thoughts are shaped by hearing himself use these symbols. Furthermore, when a culture's language does not have symbols for a given motive, then speakers of that language are unlikely to have that motive. Thus, because English does not afford many symbols that express much nuance of opinion about Spector's behavior and motivations, our discussions are often polarized. When Karl talks with his colleagues Diane and Randy, the discussion is focused on whether Spector was right or wrong. There is not much choice in between, and Burke would argue that this is a direct result of our symbol system. Think back to other controversies you have talked about (e.g., the moral implications of cloning, stem cell research, contrasts between presidential candidates, invading Iraq, etc.). You may remember the discussions as either/or propositions—positions were cast as either right or wrong. Burke's response is that symbols shape our either/or approach to these complex issues.

Burke asserts that words, thoughts, and actions have extremely close connections with one another. Burke's expression for this is that words act as "terministic screens" leading to "trained incapacities," meaning that people cannot see beyond what their words lead them to believe (Burke, 1965). For example, despite educational efforts, U.S. public health officials still have difficulty persuading people to think of the misuse of alcohol and tranquilizers when they hear the words *drug abuse*. Most people in the United States respond to "drug abuse" as the misuse of illegal drugs, such as heroin and cocaine (Brummett, 1993). The words *drug abuse* are "terministic screens," screening out some meanings and including others. For Burke, language has a life of its own, and "anything we can see or feel is already *in* language, given to us *by* language, and even produced *as us* by language" (Nelson, 1989, p. 169; emphasis in original). This explanation is somewhat at odds with the final assumption of Dramatism.

The second assumption suggests that language exerts a determining influence over people, but the final assumption states that human beings are choice makers. Burke persistently suggests that behaviorism has to be rejected because it conflicts with human choice. Thus, as Karl reads about Alan Spector, he forms his opinions about his behavior through his own free will. Much of what we discuss in the rest of the chapter rests on the conceptualization of agency, or the ability of a social actor to act out of choice.

As Charles Conrad and Elizabeth Macom (1995) observe, "The essence of agency is choice" (p. 11). Yet, as Conrad and Macom go on to discuss, Burke grappled with the concept of agency throughout his career, largely because of the difficult task of negotiating a space between complete free will and complete determinism. Despite this, Burke kept agency in the forefront of his theorizing. More recently (French & Brown, 2011) researchers continue to struggle with how agency affects people's symbolic actions and allocations of blame.

To understand Burke's scope in this theory, we need to discuss how he framed his thinking relative to Aristotelian rhetoric.

Dramatism as New Rhetoric

In his book *A Rhetoric of Motives* (1950), Burke is concerned with persuasion, and he provides an ample discussion of the traditional principles of rhetoric articulated by Aristotle (see Chapter 18). Burke maintains that the definition of rhetoric is, in essence, persuasion, and his writings explore the ways in which persuasion takes place. In so doing, Burke proposes a new rhetoric (Nichols, 1952) that focuses on several key issues, chief among them being the notion of identification. In 1952, Marie Nichols said the following about the difference between Burke's approach and Aristotle's: "The difference between the 'old' rhetoric and the 'new' rhetoric may be summed up in this manner: whereas the key term for the 'old' rhetoric was persuasion and its stress was upon deliberate design, the key term for the 'new' rhetoric is identification and this may include partially 'unconscious' factors in its appeal" (p. 323; emphasis in original). Yet, Burke's purpose was not to displace Aristotle's conceptualizations, but rather to supplement the traditional approach.

Identification and Substance

substance
the general nature of something

Burke asserts that all things have **substance,** which he defines as the general nature of something. Substance can be described in a person by listing demographic characteristics as well as background information and facts about the present situation, such as talents and occupation. Thus, from our opening scenario, we may understand Karl's substance by noting he is a 38-year-old Polish American male, high school math teacher, collector of rare coins, tennis player, and crossword puzzle enthusiast. In addition, Karl has been in a relationship with Max for seven years and lives in Grenada, New Mexico. Of course, many other pieces of information make up Karl's substance as well, but these facts give us a starting point.

identification
when two people have overlap in their substances

division
when two people fail to have overlap in their substances

Burke argues that when there is overlap between two people in terms of their substance, they have **identification.** The more overlap that exists, the greater the identification. The opposite is also true, so the less overlap between individuals, the greater the **division** that exists between them. For instance, the fact that Alan Spector is a wealthy, Jewish, married man who is the mayor of Grenada, New Mexico, and appears in the media frequently provides little in terms of identification between him and Karl. They are both white, male professionals who live in the United States, but they overlap on little else.

However, it is also the case that two people can never completely overlap with each other. Burke recognizes this and notes that the "ambiguities of substance" dictate that identification always rests on both unity and division. As Shane Borrowman and Marcia Kmetz (2011) note, identification and division are inevitably paired, and it is difficult to talk about one without the other. Burke observed that individuals will unite on certain matters of substance, but at the same time remain unique, being "both joined and separated" (Burke, 1950, pp. 20–21). Furthermore, Burke indicates that rhetoric is needed to bridge divisions and establish unity. Rukhsana Ahmed (2009) demonstrated in a rhetorical analysis of a political speech made by Begum Zia in Bangladesh, that the Burkean concept of identification has applications in non-Western discourse. In Ahmed's analysis Zia was able to make rhetorical appeals convincing her audience that the divisions between them could be bridged. Theodore Sheckels (2009) used Burke's concept of identification to make a similar argument about Thabo Mbeki's 1996 speech in South Africa. Burke refers to this process as **consubstantiation,** or increasing their identification with each other. Finally, as Debora Antunes stated in 2016, we should note that symbols are "carriers of identification" (http://kbjournal.org/antunes), underscoring one of our assumptions of the theory that we discussed earlier in the chapter.

> **consubstantiation**
> *when appeals are made to increase overlap between people*

The Process of Guilt and Redemption

Consubstantiality, or issues of identification and substance, are related to the guilt/redemption cycle because guilt can be assuaged as a result of identification and divisions. For Burke, the process of guilt and redemption undergirds the entire concept of symbolizing. **Guilt** is the central motive for all symbolic activities, and Burke defines guilt broadly to include any type of tension, embarrassment, shame, disgust, or other unpleasant feeling. Central to Burke's theory is the notion that guilt is intrinsic to the human condition. Because we are continuously feeling guilt, we are also continuously engaging in attempts to purge ourselves of guilt's discomfort. This process of feeling guilt and attempting to reduce it finds its expression in Burke's cycle, which follows a predictable pattern: order (or hierarchy), the negative, victimage (scapegoat or mortification), and redemption.

> **guilt**
> *tension, embarrassment, shame, disgust, or other unpleasant feeling*

Order or Hierarchy   Burke suggests that society exists in the form of an **order,** or **hierarchy,** which is created through our ability to use language. Language enables us to create categories like richer and more powerful—the haves and the have-nots. These categories form social hierarchies. Often we feel guilt as a result of our place in the hierarchy. If we are privileged, we may feel we have power at the expense of those with less wealth and power. This feeling prompts guilt.

> **order or hierarchy**
> *a ranking that exists in society primarily because of our ability to use language*

DRAMATISM

The Negative **The negative** comes into play when people see their place in the social order and seek to reject it. Saying no to the existing order is both a function of our language abilities and evidence of humans as choice makers. When Burke penned his often-quoted definition of Man, he emphasized the negative:

> Man is
> the symbol-using inventor of the negative
> separated from his natural condition by instruments
> of his own making goaded by the spirit of hierarchy
> and rotten with perfection. (1966, p. 16)

When Burke coined the phrase "rotten with perfection," he meant that because our symbols allow us to imagine perfection, we always feel guilty about the difference between the real state of affairs and the perfection that we can imagine. Further, "rotten with perfection" also means that our ability with symbols allows us to get stuck in symbolic "ruts" and fail to see the fact that we are merely constructing our perspectives. This leads us to believe in the "rightness" of our perspectives so strongly that we become closed minded, which is detrimental to ourselves and others (Steiner, 2009).

Victimage **Victimage** is the way in which we attempt to purge the guilt that we feel as part of the human condition. There are two basic types of victimage, or two methods to purge our guilt. Burke calls the type of victimage that we turn in on ourselves **mortification.** When we apologize for wrongdoing and blame ourselves, we engage in mortification. When Alan Spector said he did the wrong thing and apologized, he was engaging in mortification. Let's use an unfortunate historical example to demonstrate this point. In 1998, Republican leaders said they would have felt more sympathetic about President Clinton's affair if he had admitted he was wrong and had not perjured himself. Clinton refused to engage in mortification. Instead he turned to another purging technique called *scapegoating.*

In **scapegoating,** blame is placed on some sacrificial vessel. By sacrificing the scapegoat, the actor is purged of sin. Clinton attempted to scapegoat the Republicans and others (Ole-Acevedo, 2012) as deserving the real blame for the country's problems after confessing to an inappropriate relationship with Monica Lewinsky. When the news first broke in 1998, before Clinton admitted his relationship with Lewinsky, Hillary Rodham Clinton appeared on television suggesting that the rumors about her husband were the result of a complex "right-wing conspiracy" that was out to get her and her husband. This type of rhetoric illustrates Burke's concept of scapegoating. Interestingly, in 2014—over 15 years later—Monica Lewinsky felt that she was the scapegoat (http://www.foxnews.com/politics/2014/05/06/monica-lewinsky-speaks-out-says-was-made-scapegoat.html), suggesting two very different interpretations of the term.

Redemption The final step in the process is **redemption,** which involves a rejection of the unclean and a return to a new order after guilt has been temporarily purged. Inherent in the term *redemption* is the notion of a redeemer. The redeemer in the Judeo-Christian tradition is the Savior (Christ) or God. When politicians blame problems on the media or on the opposing party, they offer themselves as potential redeemers—those who can lead the people out of their troubles. A key in the redemption phase is the fact that guilt is only temporarily relieved, through the redeemer or any other method. As any order or hierarchy becomes reestablished, guilt returns to plague the human condition.

The Pentad

In addition to devising the theory of Dramatism, Burke (1945) created a method for applying his theory toward an understanding of symbolic activities. He called his method the **pentad** because it consists of five points for analyzing a symbolic text like a speech or a series of articles about a particular topic, for instance. The pentad may help determine why a speaker selects a particular rhetorical strategy for identifying with an audience. The five points that make up the pentad include the act, the scene, the agent, agency, and purpose. Almost 20 years after creating this research tool, Burke (1968) added a sixth point, attitude, to the pentad, making it a hexad, although most people still refer to it as the pentad (Figure 19.1). We will examine each of the points in turn.

pentad
Burke's method for applying Dramatism

The Act   Burke considered the **act** to be what is done by a person. In the case of Alan Spector, the act would be getting caught having an affair that resulted in a child while he was married.

act
one prong of the pentad; that which is done by a person

The Scene   The **scene** provides the context surrounding the act. In Spector's case, the scene would include a time period in which American politicians are under fire for corruption and hypocrisy. We don't have much information about the way Alan Spector would contextualize the scene because he has provided very limited information publicly about any contributing factors to the act.

scene
one prong of the pentad; the context surrounding the act

The Agent   The **agent** is the person or persons performing the act. In the case of Alan Spector, he is the agent. However, if a researcher wished to analyze Karl's act of deciding he did not support Spector, then Karl would be the agent.

agent
one prong of the pentad; the person performing the act

Agency   **Agency** refers to the means used by the agent to accomplish the act. Possible forms of agency include message strategies, storytelling, apologies, speech making,

agency
one prong of the pentad; the means used to perform the act

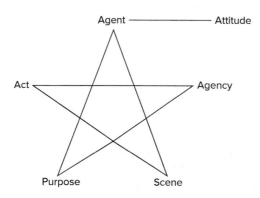

Figure 19.1
Burke's Pentad

and so forth. In Spector's case, the agency included the justifications and apologies he made publicly.

Purpose   The **purpose** refers to the goal that the agent had in mind for the act—that is, why the act was done. In Spector's case, the purpose was unclear. He provided no reasons. Karl believed he did it because he was weak.

Attitude   **Attitude** refers to the manner in which an actor positions himself or herself relative to others. Again, in Spector's case, this is a contested point. Karl might say that he acted from an attitude of superiority. Many of the articles he read commented that Spector believed himself to be above the law.

The pentad has been used as a guide for those of us who use symbols in our conversations with others (Rountree & Rountree, 2015). When using the pentad to analyze a symbolic interaction, the analyst first determines all the elements of the pentad and identifies what occurred in a particular act. After labeling the points of the pentad and fully explicating each, the analyst then examines the **pentadic** or **dramatistic ratios,** or the proportions of one element relative to another. By isolating any two parts of the pentad and examining their relationship to each other, we determine a ratio. An agent–act ratio, for instance, is at issue when we attempt to understand how a good person might do a bad thing. In analyzing the ratios in this manner, the researcher is able to discover a dominant element. Is the agent emphasized more than the situation or vice versa? An examination of the dramatistic ratio suggests something about point of view and rhetorical strategies. Steven Hunt (2003) calls these ratios the "interaction effects of two or more elements" (p. 379) and argues that observing these interactions is one criterion by which to judge the worth of a piece of rhetorical criticism. And, according to Floyd Anderson and Matthew Althouse in 2016, a minimum of 24 different ratios exist (http://kbjournal .org/anderson).

purpose
one prong of the pentad; the goal the agent had for the act

attitude
a later addition to the pentad; the manner in which the agent positions himself or herself relative to others

pentadic or dramatistic ratios
the proportions of one element of the pentad relative to another element

---

Theory in Popular Press • *Burke's Ideas in Political Persuasion*

Writing about one of the most historical races in political history between Massachusetts incumbent U.S. Senator, Scott Brown and challenger Elizabeth Warren, David Cantanese explains the importance of identification and division to the campaign rhetoric. He notes that Warren was able to stage a big comeback in the polls because of her ability to convince women voters that Brown was not consubstantial with them while she was. Cantanese states that Warren was persuasive to Massachusetts' independent women voters by shifting the focus from Brown's message of working together across differences to her message of identifying with women's issues.

Source: Catanese, D. (2012). "How Elizabeth Warren Staged Her Comeback," Politico.com, November 3, politico.com/news/stories/1112/83253.html.

Integration, Critique, and Closing

There is no question that Kenneth Burke has made an immeasurable contribution to the field of communication with his theory of Dramatism. Various researchers have praised Burke in the following terms: "He has become the most profound student of rhetoric now writing in America" (Nichols, 1952, p. 331); "Kenneth Burke is more than a single intellectual worker; he is the ore for a scholarly industry" (Brummett, 1993, p. xi); and in 1981, the *New York Times* recognized Burke as a leading American critic, saying he was "the strongest living representative of the American critical tradition, and perhaps the largest single source of that tradition since its founder, Ralph Waldo Emerson" (cited in Chesebro, 1993, p. xi). Burke's work is widely praised and frequently cited. In fact, the National Communication Association, one of the main organizations for communication teachers, researchers, and professionals, has an entire division devoted to Burkean criticism and there is an entire journal devoted to him (kbjournal.org). And, to be sure, the research surrounding Dramatism has almost exclusively been qualitative, honoring the notion of "voice" that Burke felt was important.

As we analyze Dramatism, four criteria become relevant: scope, parsimony, utility, and heurism.

Integration

Communication Tradition	**Rhetorical** ǀ **Semiotic** ǀ Phenomenological ǀ Cybernetic ǀ Socio-Psychological ǀ Socio-Cultural ǀ **Critical**
Communication Context	Intrapersonal ǀ Interpersonal ǀ Small Group ǀ Organizational ǀ **Public/Rhetorical** ǀ Mass/Media ǀ Cultural
Approach to Knowing	Positivistic/Empirical ǀ **Interpretive/Hermeneutic** ǀ Critical

Critique

Evaluation Criteria	**Scope** ǀ Logical Consistency ǀ **Parsimony** ǀ **Utility** ǀ Testability ǀ **Heurism** ǀ Test of Time

Scope

Dramatism has been criticized for being too wide in scope. Burke's goal is no less than to explain the whole of human experience with symbolic interaction. This is an extremely broad and ambitious goal, and some critics believe it renders the theory too broad to be meaningful. When you contrast Dramatism with a theory like Uncertainty Reduction Theory, which we discussed in Chapter 8, you can see the two extremes of theoretical scope. URT seeks to explain the first few minutes of an initial encounter between strangers. Dramatism encompasses all human symbolic interaction. Some critics might suggest that when a theory attempts such a lofty goal it is doomed to be overly complex and obtuse. Whether or not you see the range of Dramatism's goal as a weakness is somewhat subjective. Interestingly, for Burke and many who followed him, the wide scope of Dramatism is part of its appeal.

Parsimony

Some critics complain that Burke's theory is too unclear and obtuse to be useful. Herbert Simons (2004) states that Burke was more "convolutionist than revolutionist" (p. 152). Dramatism is seen by some as overly complex and confusing (Foss, Foss, & Trapp, 1991). Even proponents of Burke acknowledge that he is difficult to read. Marie Hochmuth Nichols concluded her pioneering 1952 essay on Burke by saying,

> Burke is difficult and often confusing. He cannot be understood by casual reading of his various volumes. In part the difficulty arises from the numerous vocabularies he employs. His words in isolation are usually simple enough, but he often uses them in new contexts. To read one of his volumes independently, without regard to the chronology of publication, makes the problem of comprehension even more difficult because of the specialized meaning attached to various words and phrases. (p. 330)

However, Nichols also provides a rebuttal to some of these criticisms by concluding that some of the difficulty arises from "the compactness of his writing, the uniqueness of his organizational patterns, the penetration of his thought, and the breadth of his endeavor" (p. 330). In other words, Burke is a genius and worth the effort it requires to understand his original thinking. When a student is diligent, Burke's theory repays the hard work with many rewards.

Utility

Some researchers (Condit, 1992; Murray, 2003) observe that Dramatism falls short on the criterion of utility. This critique is lodged mainly because of what Burke leaves out of the theory. For example, Celeste Condit (1992) argues that the theory would be more useful if it addressed gender and culture more expansively. Condit observes that although Burke was supportive of feminism, his support came mainly in the form of including women under the sign of "man." She notes that given the historical context in which Burke wrote, his support for women was not inconsequential. Many writers in Burke's generation completely ignored women, so Burke was making a contribution by including women at all. Condit maintains, however, that now the scene has altered, and it is inappropriate to subsume women under the word man. Here Condit is talking both about the use of the generic man to represent all people and about our ability as a society to begin to think in new ways about sex and gender.

As Condit notes, "We must extend our language beyond duality to a broad 'humanity' and to 'human beings,' discovering ways to speak that emphasize human plurality" (p. 351). Condit says the definition of man that Burke provides, which we discussed earlier in the chapter, is not adequate to include women. She recasts the definition from the perspective of a radical feminist who would see the following as descriptive of man's woman:

> Woman is
> the symbol-receiving (hearing, passive) animal
> inventor of nothing (moralized by priests and saints)
> submerged in her natural conditions by instruments of man's making
> goaded at the bottom of hierarchy (moved to a sense of orderliness)
> and rotted by perfection. (p. 351)

Then she recasts the definition to move beyond an essentialism defining men and women as opposite to each other and essentially the same as others of the same sex:

> People are
> players with symbols
> inventors of the negative and the possibility of morality
> grown from their natural condition by tools of their collective making
> trapped between hierarchy and equality (moved constantly to reorder)
> neither rotten nor perfect, but now and again lunging down both paths.
> (p. 352)

Condit's argument is that Burke's approach needs to be broadened both to include women and to move past a focus on one sex or the other to be truly inclusive of both. But, she asserts that merely broadening the language of "man/his" to include "people/their" will not in itself be sufficient to challenge the hold that language exerts as a terministic screen against women in the United States. We need to change both our language and our thinking about women, men, gender, and inclusivity for significant progress to occur.

Condit also suggests that Burke emphasizes universality among cultures at the expense of particularity. For Condit, this is especially the case in the matter of Burke's contention that victimage is a transcultural experience—a method for purging guilt in all cultures. She argues that cultures other than Western Christian ones (from which Burke draws almost exclusively) might not see victimage as the dominant motive for human conduct. For example, Buddhism might provide different motives than Christianity does. Furthermore, if we examine trickster tales from Native American or African American cultures, we might see victimage characterized in a strikingly different fashion from what Burke describes. The trickster is in a low-power position relative to the rest of the society, but is able to triumph through wits and cleverness. The trickster is not a victim in the Christian sense that we see in Dramatism; rather, the trickster emerges victorious by turning the rules of the system against those in power.

In sum, Condit's critique does not deny the enormous contribution made by Burke's theory. Instead, she simply suggests some extensions and modifications for improving the theory. Jeffery Murray (2003) agrees with Condit, asserting that although Burke's theory continues to be widely used, it is necessary to expand it to include the voices of those who have been marginalized. Murray uses what he calls an "Other-Burkean" frame to analyze Nazi propaganda and a speech former U,S. Senator Ted Kennedy made after the death of Mary Jo Kopechne, a passenger in his car who died when he drove off a bridge in Massachusetts. In both cases, Murray argues that paying attention to what was omitted in the rhetoric and to "Others" whose concerns are not highlighted by the pentad (such as the Jews in relationship to the Nazis, and Mary Jo Kopechne) provides a rich analysis.

Heurism

With regard to heurism, most critics agree that Dramatism is very successful. For instance, Dramatism was originally used in rhetorical analyses of speeches, but now the focus has widened to other discourse in the public sphere including "editorials, pamphlets and monographs, books, docudramas, radio and television news, movies, music, and even the Internet" (Hunt, 2003, p. 378). The manner in which Dramatistic principles and concepts has been applied is vast. For example, Burke's thinking has been applied to the Syrian Civil War and President Assad (Bakke & Kuypers, 2016). Facebook has been analyzed using the pentad (Castelen, Mottart, & Rutten, 2009). Amanda Nell Edgar (2014) employed the Dramatistic lens to understand the R & B culture and Chris Brown's assault on Rihanna. The medical profession (e.g., Bareiss, 2015) utilized Dramatism to understand non-suicidal self-injuries. Finally, Luke Rowland's (2016) assessment of Japanese multilingual signage used Burkean principles in its research. Clearly, Burke has influenced scholars from across a swath of disciplines.

Student Voices

Amber

I can see applying Dramatism for real. When I look at President Bush's speeches about invading Iraq, I see how he's the agent and the U.S. public is the audience. The act would be invading Iraq itself—although there are a lot of subacts involved, like going after (and capturing) Saddam Hussein. I am pretty sure Bush had a lot of purposes going on there too. For one thing, there are the purposes he stated in his speeches. First he said that Iraq harbored terrorists and so had something to do with 9/11, and that they were hiding weapons of mass destruction. Now he's changed the purpose to how bad Hussein was and how cruel he was to the people of Iraq. Then there are all the reasons that other people say are going on. Like, maybe he wanted to do it for oil or to get revenge for his father's problems with Saddam. This whole situation is pretty confusing, but I think using Dramatism to sort it out might really help clarify it. I guess we'll never really know why public figures like the president do what they do, but a rhetorician can really go to town trying to figure it out.

Closing

There is general consensus that Burke's theory provides us with imaginative and innovative insights into human motives and interaction. Dramatism provides us with a theory that models the big picture. It allows an analysis of human motivations and behavior, and its focus on language as the critical symbol system makes it especially attractive to communication researchers.

DRAMATISM

Discussion Starters

TECH QUEST: The notion that language usage is related to an audience is one fundamental argument of Dramatism. Explore the limitations of using texting and email to convey your emotions in a message.

1. How could Karl talk about Alan Spector's situation in a less polarized fashion? What are the linguistic barriers to such a discussion? Does a feminist critique of Burke's theory enable you to think of less polarized language? Explain your answer.

2. Use the pentad to analyze a public figure and the discourse surrounding some current controversy involving this figure.

3. How do you understand the use of the pentad as a method relative to Dramatism as a theory? Do all theories have specific methods that are used only with them? Why or why not?

4. Do you agree with Burke that guilt is the primary human motive? If not, what do you think is the primary human motive?

5. Burke believes that symbols, and language, in particular, are critical in life. When he says that symbolic action is more than mere physical or material reality, what do you think he means?

6. Do you agree with Condit that Burke's theory is culture specific rather than universal? Explain your answer.

7. Apply any element of Dramatism to your life.

CHAPTER 20

The Narrative Paradigm

*Based on the research of **Walter Fisher***

> *The narrative paradigm does not deny reason and rationality; it reconstitutes them, making them amenable to all forms of human communication.*
> —Walter Fisher

Miles Campbell

Miles Campbell rolled over in bed and turned off his screaming alarm. He burrowed under the covers for a minute before he realized he'd better get up or he would miss his chem lab. He was tempted to sleep in, but a vision of his mother's face flashed before him, and he thought about how hard she had worked to help him get to college. He didn't want to disappoint her by not doing his very best now that he was here. So Miles sighed and shrugged off the covers. He slipped out of bed and splashed cold water on his face. By the time he was dressed and headed for the kitchen, he felt better about his day and about life in general.

In the kitchen he heard his housemates, Robert and Carlos, arguing about something. Seems like a normal morning, Miles thought. Those two can never get along. "What has got you guys up and yelling so early in the morning?" Miles asked as he began making his breakfast. Both Robert and Carlos looked up and grinned at Miles. "You won't think it's a big deal, Miles," Carlos said, "but we are discussing the candidates who are running for president of the Student Multicultural Association." "Yeah, you're right, Carlos," Miles laughed. "That doesn't seem like something worth arguing about to me!"

Robert handed Miles a copy of two campaign flyers. "Well, you might not think it's all that big a deal, but look at the difference between these two and tell me that Laura Huyge doesn't make more sense than Jorge Vega." Miles glanced at the two flyers that Robert had given him. Huyge was an Asian American graduate student, and she had presented a list of 10 points that represented her platform. She stated her interest in promoting cultural sensitivity and appreciation for diversity within the student body. Her flyer also listed a few ways that she planned to accomplish her goals. Her first big initiative, if she were elected, would be to sponsor a workshop with outside speakers and several hands-on activities to get students of different ethnicities talking to one another about difference and respect.

Miles looked up at Robert and Carlos and said, "Well, Laura sounds reasonable enough." Robert clapped Miles on the back, smiling broadly. Carlos interrupted, saying, "Hey, man, you haven't even looked at what Jorge has to say. Keep reading, man."

Miles put Laura's flyer aside and took up Jorge's. Jorge had chosen a completely different presentation style for his campaign flyer. Instead of laying out a specific platform point by point as Laura had, Jorge's flyer told a series of short stories. In the first one, Jorge related an incident in class when an African American woman could not get the professor's attention for anything she had to say. Every time she tried to contribute in class, the professor ignored her and asked a European American's opinion. Because she was the only Black person in the class, this woman believed the professor was prejudiced, but she wasn't sure what she could do about it. Another story in the flyer described a classroom situation in which the only two Latino students believed that they were called on to give the "Latin perspective" on every issue the professor raised. They were both really tired of being tokens. A third story talked about how certain bars on campus were considered "Black" and others were "Latino" and others were "White." This story told of two African American students who went to a White bar and felt really isolated.

As Miles read these stories, he thought that Jorge had it down cold. His description of life at the university was totally accurate. He himself had been ignored in classes and wondered if it had been because of his race. He'd also experienced being asked for the "Black" opinion, and he really resented that. Also, his social life rarely included people outside his own race, except for Carlos and a couple of Carlos's friends who were also Latinos. He never socialized with the Whites on campus. Jorge had given Miles a lot to think about, and he decided he would vote for Jorge.

Throughout this book we have begun each chapter with a story about a person or several people who experience something through which we can illustrate the chapter's theory. The reason we have made this choice may be found within the theory of narration that Walter Fisher calls the Narrative Paradigm. The Narrative Paradigm promotes the belief that humans are storytellers and that values, emotions, and aesthetic considerations ground our beliefs and behaviors. In other words, we are more persuaded by a good story than by a good argument. Thus, Fisher would explain Miles's decision to vote for Jorge on the basis of the stories Jorge presented in his campaign flyer. Fisher asserts that the essence of human nature is storytelling.[1]

Fisher is not alone in this belief. Some researchers acknowledge the legacy of narrative. Robin Clair, Stephanie Carlo, Chervin Lam, Jon Nussman, Canek Phillips, Virginia Sanchez, Elaine Schnabel, and Liliya Yakova (2014) succinctly note: "The history of narrative might be traced to the origin of language, to the first symbolic sound or gesture" (p. 2). Other researchers (e.g., Ramsey, Venette, & Rabalais, 2011) have examined what they call "narrative malleability" of constructs observing that people's minds can be changed about something based on good stories told by a credible storyteller. Jody Koenig Kellas and Haley Kranstuber Horstman (2015) contend that stories have the potential to make sense of the complex, help socialize people into groups (e.g., the family), and can create, reinforce, or challenge an individual's identity. And, Koenig Kellas (2015) tells us that stories and storytelling have been adopted by many different disciplines including sociolinguisitics, English, sociology, and psychology. For many years, Communication Studies has also been influenced by the interest in narration. John Lucaites and Celeste Condit (1985) assert "the growing belief that narrative represents a universal medium of human consciousness" (p. 90). Kirsten Theye (2008) agrees, arguing that "narratives are crucial in human communication as a way of explaining the world" (p. 163). In addition, scholars (e.g., Koenig Kellas, 2013) assert that stories do more than explain the world, they shape our world. Finally, Art Bochner (2014) sums up narrative this way: "Narrative can be a dense, cerebral, and complicated topic" (p. 13).

---

[1]Although some scholars differentiate between stories and narrative, for purposes of illustration, we will use the terms interchangeably as argued by Koenig Kellas (2015).

It is notable that Fisher calls his approach a paradigm rather than a theory. Fisher uses that term to signal the breadth of his vision because a paradigm is considered broader than a theory. Fisher states that "there is no genre, including technical communication, that is not an episode in the story of life" (1985, p. 347). Thus, Fisher has constructed an approach to theoretical thinking that is more encompassing than any one specific theory. Fisher states that his use of the term *paradigm* refers to an effort to formalize and direct our understanding of the experience of all human communication (Koenig Kellas, 2008).

Furthermore, the use of the term *paradigm* indicates that Fisher's thinking represents a major shift from the thinking that had supported most previous theories of communication. Fisher believes he is capturing the fundamental nature of human beings with the insight that we are storytellers and that we experience our lives in narrative form. He contrasts his approach with what he calls the rational paradigm, which characterized previous Western thinking. In this way, Fisher presents what can be called a **paradigm shift,** or a significant change in the way people think about the world and its meanings.

Fisher (1987) explains the paradigm shift by recounting a brief history of paradigms that have guided Western thinking. He notes that originally *logos* meant a combination of concepts including story, rationale, discourse, and thought. Fisher explains that this meaning held until the time of Plato and Aristotle, who distinguished between logos as reason and mythos as story and emotion. In this division, mythos, representing poetical discourse, was assigned a negative status relative to logos, or reason. The concept of rhetoric fell somewhere between the elevated logic of logos and the inferior status of poetics or mythos. Ranking mythos, logos, and rhetoric in this way reinforced the concept that not all discourse is equal. In fact, according to Aristotle (see Chapter 18), some discourse is superior to others by virtue of its relationship to true knowledge. Only logos, Aristotle asserted, leads to true knowledge because it provides a system of logic that can be proven valid. Logos was found in the discourse of philosophy. Other forms of discourse lead to knowledge, but the knowledge they produce is probabilistic, not true in an absolute, invariable sense.

This Aristotelian distinction did not prevent Aristotle himself from valuing all the different forms of communication equally, but it did provide a rationale for later theorists' preference for logic and reason over mythos, or story, and rhetoric. Much subsequent scholarship has focused on a struggle over these forms of discourse. Beginning at the end of the Renaissance period in Europe, the scientific revolution changed people's way of thinking about the world. It dethroned philosophy as the source of logic, placing logic instead within science and technology. But Fisher contends that this change was not a far-reaching one because both philosophy and science privilege a formal system of logic that continues to leave poetics or rhetoric in a devalued position. The mind-set, employed by many scholars, that regards logical thinking as primary is what Fisher calls the **rational world paradigm.**

Struggles among these different branches of knowledge continue today, but Fisher asserts that the Narrative Paradigm finds a way to transcend these struggles. Fisher argues that "acceptance of the narrative paradigm shifts the controversy from a focus on who 'owns' logos to a focus on what specific instances of discourse, regardless of form, provide the most trustworthy, reliable, and desirable guides to

belief and to behavior, and under what conditions" (1987, p. 6). Thus, the Narrative Paradigm represents a different way of thinking about the world than that posited by the rational world paradigm. With narrative, Fisher suggests, we move away from an either/or dualism toward a more unified sense that embodies science, philosophy, story, myth, and logic. The Narrative Paradigm presents an alternative to the rational world paradigm without negating traditional rationality.

Fisher argues that the Narrative Paradigm accomplishes this shift through recognizing that "some discourse is more veracious, reliable, and trustworthy in respect to knowledge, truth, and reality than some other discourse, but no *form* or *genre* has final claim to these virtues" (1987, p. 19; emphasis in original). In asserting this, Fisher lays the groundwork for reclaiming the importance of the narrative, or story, without denigrating logic and reason, and he establishes a new way of conceptualizing rhetoric. Furthermore, Fisher asserts that story, or mythos, is imbued in all human communication endeavors (even those involving logic) because all arguments include "ideas that cannot be verified or proved in any absolute way. Such ideas arise in metaphor, values, gestures, and so on" (1987, p. 19). Fisher thus attempts to bridge the divide between logos (rational argument) and mythos (story or narrative).

Theory At a Glance • The Narrative Paradigm

This approach is founded on the principle that humans are storytelling animals. Furthermore, narrative logic is preferred over the traditional logic used in argument. Narrative logic, or the logic of good reasons, suggests that people judge the credibility of speakers by whether their stories hang together (have coherence) and ring true (have fidelity). The Narrative Paradigm allows a democratic judgment of speakers because no one has to be specially trained in persuasion to be able to draw conclusions based on the concepts of coherence and fidelity.

Assumptions of the Narrative Paradigm

Despite Fisher's attempt to show the Narrative Paradigm as a fusion of logic and aesthetic, he does point out that narrative logic is different from traditional logic and reasoning. We will discuss how these two differ throughout the chapter because this is an important distinction for Fisher and one that he continually refined as his thinking about the Narrative Paradigm evolved. An important aspect of the assumptions of the Narrative Paradigm is that they contrast with those of the rational world paradigm, just as the two logics differ. Fisher (1987) stipulated five assumptions:

- Humans are naturally storytellers.
- Decisions about a story's worth are based on "good reasons."
- Good reasons are determined by history, biography, culture, and character.

Table 20.1 Contrast Between Narrative and Rational World Paradigms

NARRATIVE PARADIGM	RATIONAL WORLD PARADIGM
1. Humans are storytellers.	1. Humans are rational beings.
2. Decision making and communication are based on "good reasons."	2. Decision making is based on arguments.
3. Good reasons are determined by matters of history, biography, culture, and character.	3. Arguments adhere to specific criteria for soundness and logic.
4. Rationality is based in people's awareness of how internally consistent and truthful to lived experience stories appear.	4. Rationality is based in the quality of knowledge and formal reasoning processes.
5. The world is experienced by people as a set of stories from which to choose among. As we choose, we live life in a process of continual recreation.	5. The world can be reduced to a series of logical relationships that are uncovered through reasoning.

- Rationality is based on people's judgments of a story's consistency and truthfulness.
- We experience the world as filled with stories, and we must choose among them.

We can see how these clearly contrast to the parallel assumptions Fisher highlights in the rational world paradigm. This contrast is revealed in Table 20.1. We will briefly discuss each of the assumptions of the Narrative Paradigm, comparing them with their opposites in the rational world paradigm.

First, the Narrative Paradigm assumes that the essential nature of humans is rooted in story and storytelling. As our opening example of Miles illustrates, stories persuade us, move us, and form the basis for our beliefs and actions. Miles had not heard much about the election for the president of the Multicultural Student Association on campus. In fact, Miles was rather apathetic about the election and had no real interest in, or opinions about, either candidate. Yet, after reading the compelling stories that Jorge included in his campaign literature, Miles decided to vote for Jorge. Miles found Laura's campaign material interesting but not nearly as involving as Jorge's. If the assumption of the rational world paradigm held true, we would expect the more rational argument to hold sway over Miles, and he should have decided to vote for Laura. The Narrative Paradigm explains his preference for Jorge.

Fisher also believes in this first assumption because he observes that narrative is universal—found in all cultures and time periods. Fisher asserts, "Any ethic, whether social, political, legal, or otherwise, involves narrative" (1984, p. 3). This universality of narrative prompts Fisher to suggest the term *Homo narrans* as the overarching metaphor for defining humanity. Fisher was influenced in his approach by reading moral theory espoused by Alasdair MacIntyre (1981). MacIntyre observes that "man [sic] is in his actions and practice, as well as in his fictions, essentially a story-telling animal" (p. 201).

Fisher used MacIntyre's ideas as the foundation for the Narrative Paradigm. James Elkins (2001) agrees with Fisher's assumption about the centrality of stories for humans. Elkins observes that people "turn to stories to both survive and to imagine, as well as for a host of instrumental purposes, for pleasure, and because we must. Stories are part of our human inheritance" (p. 1). Other researchers (e.g., Bute & Jensen, 2011) concur noting stories provide humans the means to account for their own experiences and behaviors.

The second assumption of the Narrative Paradigm asserts that people make decisions about which stories to accept and which to reject on the basis of what makes sense to them, or good reasons. We will discuss what Fisher means by good reasons later in the chapter, but he does not mean strict logic or argument. This assumption recognizes that not all stories are equally effective; instead, the deciding factor in choosing among stories is personal rather than an abstract code of argument, or what we traditionally call reason. From Fisher's point of view, in our chapter-opening vignette, Laura has told a story in her campaign flyer, too. Miles simply chooses to reject her story and accept Jorge's because it is more personally involving to him. Events such as a presidential election to a war in the Middle East to protesters in front of the U.S. Supreme Court show us the reality of competing stories.

As people listen to these conflicting stories, they choose among them. Their choices do not stem from traditional logic but from narrative logic. When people shift from traditional logic to narrative logic, Fisher believes their lives will be improved because narrative logic is more democratic than formal logic. As Fisher (1984) asserts, "All persons have the capacity to be rational in the narrative paradigm" (p. 10). Whereas formal logic calls for an elite trained in the complexities of the logical system, the Narrative Paradigm calls on the practical wisdom that everyone possesses.

The theory's third assumption deals with what specifically influences people's choices and provides good reasons for them. The rational world paradigm assumes that argument is ruled by the dictates of soundness (Toulmin, 1958). For Stephen Toulmin, the anatomy of an argument is the movement from data to a conclusion. This movement needs to be judged by soundness, or an examination of the formal logic that guides the conclusion. In contrast, the Narrative Paradigm suggests that soundness is not the only way to evaluate good reasons. In fact, soundness may not even be an accurate way of describing how people make this judgment. The Narrative Paradigm assumes that narrative rationality is affected by history, biography, culture, and character. Thus, Fisher also introduces the notion of *context* into the Narrative Paradigm. People are influenced by the context in which they are embedded. Therefore, the material that appears persuasive to Miles is the material that is specifically relevant to him personally. It is not material that adheres to a code of formal logic and persuasion.

The fourth assumption forms a core issue of the narrative approach. It asserts that people believe stories insofar as the stories seem internally consistent and truthful. We will discuss this further in the next section when we describe the concept of narrative rationality.

Finally, Fisher's perspective is based on the assumption that the world is a set of stories, and as we choose among them, we experience life differently, allowing us to recreate our lives. Miles's choice to support Jorge may cause him to cast his own life story differently. He may no longer see himself as a loner. He may change his sense of political action based on his choice of Jorge's story. You can see how the Narrative Paradigm contrasts with the rational world paradigm, which tends to see the world as less transient and shifting and which discovers truth through rational analysis, not through narrative logic's emotional responses to compelling stories.

A study illustrating these assumptions in a courtroom context examined the Narrative Paradigm's utility for professional communication. Consider one of the most watched trials in U.S. history. Christine Kelly and Michele Zak (1999) assert that former football player O. J. Simpson's acquittal was due to the triumph of narrative argument over rational argument. The defense was victorious because it framed Simpson's story in a manner that resonated with the jury whereas the prosecution relied on the rational world paradigm, directed more toward the judge and the opposing lawyers. Kelly and Zak note that the prosecutors "drew on the language of technical expertise and took responsibility for presenting a careful case in a court of law without reference to the lives of the jury" (p. 301). Other research examines how narratives exert influence in health care settings (e.g., Gray, 2009; Wamucii, 2011), with reference to tabloid news (e.g., McCartha & Strauman, 2009), and political campaigns (e.g., Falk, 2009; Underation, 2009).

Key Concepts in the Narrative Approach

Tracing the assumptions of the Narrative Paradigm leads us to a consideration of some of the key concepts that form the core of the theoretical framework: narration, narrative rationality (which includes coherence and fidelity). Coherence is made up of three types: structural, material, and characterological; and fidelity leads to the logic of good reasons.

Narration

narration
an account to which listeners assign meaning

Narration is often thought of simply as a story, but for Fisher, narration is much more than a plotted story with a beginning, middle, and end. In Fisher's perspective, narration includes any verbal or nonverbal account with a sequence of events to which listeners assign a meaning. Specifically, Fisher states, "When I use the term 'narration,' I do not mean a fictive composition whose propositions may be true or false and have no necessary relationship to the message of that composition. By 'narration,' I mean symbolic actions—words and/or deeds—that have sequence and meaning for those who live, create, or interpret them" (1987, p. 58). This definition implies the need for a storyteller and a listener. Jody Koenig Kellas (2015) articulates this narration process: "Most stories also include a description of characters, a dramatic tension that moves toward explanation or resolution, temporal sequencing, and a moral or story point" (p. 2).

Fisher's definition is extremely broad and parallels what many people think of as communication itself. This, of course, is Fisher's point: All communication is narrative. He argues that narrative is not a specific genre (stories as opposed to poems, for example), but rather, it is a mode of social influence. Furthermore, it is his contention that all life is composed of narratives. When you listen to a class lecture, when you give an excuse to a professor for not turning in a paper on time, and when you read the newspaper, send a Tweet, talk to your friends, you are hearing and shaping narratives.

Narrative Rationality

Given that our lives are experienced in narratives, we need a method for judging which ones to believe and which to disregard. This standard can be found in **narrative rationality,** which provides us with a means for judging narratives that is quite different from the traditional methods found in the rational world paradigm. As we mentioned previously, traditional tests of rationality include whether claims correspond to actual facts, whether all relevant facts have been considered, whether arguments are internally consistent, and whether the reasoning used conforms to standards of formal and informal logic (Fisher, 1978). Narrative rationality, in contrast to traditional logic, operates on the basis of two different principles: coherence and fidelity.

Coherence   The principle of coherence is an important standard for assessing narrative rationality, which will ultimately determine whether or not a person accepts a particular narrative or rejects it. **Coherence** refers to the internal consistency of a narrative. When judging a story's coherence, the listener would ask whether the narrative seemed to hang together in a consistent manner. Narratives possess coherence when all the pieces of the story are present; we do not feel that the storyteller has left out important details or contradicted elements of the story in any way. Coherence is the standard of sensemaking applied to a given narrative and "sensemaking is at the heart of all narrative" (Koenig Kellas, 2015, p. 4). This sensemaking is usually obtained when the characters in a story behave in relatively consistent ways.

When Miles read the narratives contained in Jorge's campaign literature, he saw a consistent thread running through them: His university has racial problems. If Jorge had presented some problems based on race and then shaped the narrative to conclude that all was well with race relations at the university, Miles would have rejected the story for being inconsistent.

Coherence is often measured by the organizational and structural elements of a narrative. Art Bochner (2014) notes that "coherence is an achievement, not a given" (p. 287). When a storyteller skips around and leaves out important information, interrupts the flow of the story to add elements forgotten earlier, and generally is not smooth in structuring the narrative, the listener may reject the narrative for not possessing coherence. Coherence is based on three specific types of consistency: structural coherence, material coherence, and characterological coherence.

STRUCTURAL COHERENCE   The type of consistency Fisher calls **structural coherence** rests on the degree to which the elements of the story flow smoothly. When stories are confusing, when one part does not seem to lead to the next, or when the plot is unclear, then they lack structural coherence. If a friend tells you a story about breaking up with her boyfriend on email, but she fails to explain any of the

narrative rationality
a standard for judging which stories to believe and which to disregard

coherence
a principle of narrative rationality related to the internal consistency of a story

structural coherence
a type of coherence referring to the flow of the story

events leading up to the breakup or why she chose to send an email, and then skips back to telling you how she and her boyfriend first met, you would think her story lacked structural coherence.

material coherence
a type of coherence referring to the congruence between one story and other related stories

MATERIAL COHERENCE   **Material coherence** refers to the degree of congruence between one story and other stories that seem related to it. For example, you may have heard several stories about why two friends of yours have stopped speaking to each other. If all the stories but one attribute the problem to one friend having misled the other, causing an embarrassing situation, you are unlikely to believe the one unique story. You would believe that the different story lacked material coherence.

characterological coherence
a type of coherence referring to the believability of the characters in the story

CHARACTEROLOGICAL COHERENCE   **Characterological coherence** refers to the believability of the characters in the story. For instance, let's imagine that you have a professor whom you dislike a great deal. This professor ridicules you and other students in the class whenever anyone contributes to class discussions. In addition, the professor makes racist, homophobic, and sexist jokes in class. Your impression is that this professor is a thoroughly objectionable person. Given this background, you would be unlikely to accept a story in which this professor was shown in an admirable or even heroic light. You would reject the story for not possessing characterological coherence.

fidelity
a principle of narrative rationality judging the credibility of a story

Fidelity   The other critical standard for assessing narrative rationality is **fidelity,** or the truthfulness or reliability of the story. Stories with fidelity ring true to a listener. When Miles reads the stories that Jorge has in his campaign literature, he thinks to himself that those events have happened to him at the university. Miles wonders if Jorge has been following him around campus, watching what goes on in his life. This makes the stories powerful to Miles. They possess a great deal of fidelity for him. Fisher (1987) notes that when the elements of a story "represent accurate assertions about social reality" (p. 105), they have fidelity.

Student Voices

Justin

I understand Fisher's point about coherence and how hard it is to accept a story about someone you really dislike doing something great. But I'm wondering how the theory explains a story that makes you change your mind about someone. If I didn't like a professor but then found out that he was doing some great things for the planet like starting some big recycling center or something, I might change my mind and start liking him a little bit more. I know in the past, learning more information about someone has made me like them more (if it was good information). When I first met my girlfriend, I didn't like her right off the bat, but the more I learned about her, the better I liked her. I don't see that idea explained in the theory.

The Logic of Good Reasons

Related to Fisher's notion of fidelity is the primary method that he proposes for assessing narrative fidelity: the logic of **good reasons** (Koenig Kellas, 2015). Fisher asserts that when narratives possess fidelity, they constitute good reasons for a person to hold a particular belief or take an action. For example, Miles sees Jorge's stories as possessing fidelity, which makes the stories persuasive; the stories form good reasons for Miles to vote for Jorge.

Fisher (1987) explains his concept of logic by saying that it means "a systematic set of procedures that will aid in the analysis and assessment of elements of reasoning in rhetorical interactions" (p. 106). Thus, logic for the narrative paradigm enables a person to judge the worth of stories. The logic of good reasons presents a listener with a set of values that appeal to her or him and form warrants for accepting or rejecting the advice advanced by any form of narrative. This does not mean that any good reason is equal to any other; it simply means that whatever prompts a person to believe a narrative is bound to a value or a conception of what is good.

As Fisher describes it, this logic is a process consisting of two series of five questions that the listener asks about the narrative. The first five questions are the following:

1. Are the statements that claim to be factual in the narrative really factual?
2. Have any relevant facts been omitted from the narrative or distorted in its telling?
3. What are the patterns of reasoning that exist in the narrative?
4. How relevant are the arguments in the story to any decision the listener may make?
5. How well does the narrative address the important and significant issues of this case?

These questions constitute a logic of reasons. To transform this into a logic of good reasons, there are five more questions that introduce the concept of values into the process of assessing practical knowledge. These questions are as follows:

1. What are the implicit and explicit values contained in the narrative?
2. Are the values appropriate to the decision that is relevant to the narrative?
3. What would be the effects of adhering to the values embedded in the narrative?
4. Are the values confirmed or validated in lived experience?
5. Are the values of the narrative the basis for ideal human conduct?

Fisher illustrates the logic of good reasons with a book written by Jonathan Schell (1982). *The Fate of the Earth,* which was a very popular book in the 1980s, argues that the nuclear weapons race must cease. Fisher asserts that even though experts found the book inaccurate on technical grounds, the narrative it espoused was extremely popular with the general public. Fisher argues that this was because the book tells a story that meets the criteria of coherence and fidelity. It focuses on a set of values that many people found relevant at that point in history. As the Narrative Paradigm predicts, the well-told story—consisting of narrative rationality—was more compelling to readers than the expert testimony that refuted the factual accuracy of the narrative. The relationship among the elements making up narrative rationality is illustrated by Figure 20.1.

good reasons
a set of values for accepting a story as true and worthy of acceptance; provides a method for assessing fidelity

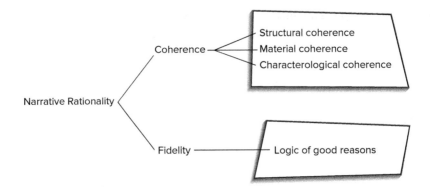

Figure 20.1
Elements of Narrative Rationality

Integration, Critique, and Closing

Fisher's Narrative Paradigm offers new insights into communication behavior and directs our attention to democratic processes in the area of rhetorical criticism. Fisher contributes the idea that people's lived experiences make them capable of analyzing rhetoric. Furthermore, the Narrative Paradigm helps us to see the nature of multiple logics at work in our communication encounters. Thus, the Narrative Paradigm has made a substantial contribution to our understanding of human communication and human nature in general. And, clearly, the theory has been studied almost exclusively using a qualitative lens.

As you think about the Narrative Paradigm, consider the criteria of scope, logical consistency, utility, and heurism.

Integration

Communication Tradition	**Rhetorical** | Semiotic | Phenomenological | Cybernetic | Socio-Psychological | Socio-Cultural | Critical
Communication Context	Intrapersonal | Interpersonal | Small Group | Organizational | **Public/Rhetorical** | Mass/Media | Cultural
Approach to Knowing	Positivistic/Empirical | **Interpretive/Hermeneutic** | Critical

Critique

Evaluation Criteria	**Scope** | **Logical Consistency** | Parsimony | **Utility** | Testability | **Heurism** | Test of Time

Scope

The critique that the Narrative Paradigm is too broad mainly focuses on Fisher's claim that all communication is narrative. Researchers object to that claim for two reasons: First, some have questioned the utility of a definition that includes everything. How meaningful is the definition of narrative if it means all communication behavior? Critics have directed us to consider the question: Is there value in treating a ritual greeting ("Hi, how was your day?") and an involved narrative explaining one's desire for a divorce in the same way? Second, some researchers, notably Robert Rowland (1987, 1989), suggest that some forms of communication are not narrative in the way that Fisher maintains. According to Rowland, science fiction and fantasy do not conform to most people's values. Rather, these genres often challenge existing values. Rowland also questions the utility of considering a novel (such as Arthur Koestler's *Darkness at Noon*) and a political pamphlet (such as one produced by the Committee on the Present Danger) both as narratives as Fisher does. Although both tell stories about the repressive character of the former Soviet system, they do so in such different ways that Rowland believes it does a disservice to both writings to place them in the same category. Furthermore, it complicates our understanding of the definition of narrative when two such disparate examples can both be labeled as narrative.

Logical Consistency

The Narrative Paradigm has been faulted for failing to be consistent with some of the claims that Fisher makes about it. For instance, Rowland (1987) finds that the narrative approach does not actually provide a more democratic structure compared with the hierarchical system espoused by the rational world paradigm, nor does it completely offer an alternative to that paradigm. Rowland says that Fisher overstates the problem of domination of the public by the elite, or by the expert, in the rational world paradigm. In addition, Rowland argues that "there is nothing inherent in storytelling that guarantees that the elites will not control a society" (p. 272).

Student Voices

Colin

I understand exactly what Fisher meant with the terms *coherence* and *fidelity*. I have a friend named Marco who constantly tells crazy stories, and I spend a lot of time trying to figure out whether to believe him or not. And I do use coherence and fidelity to decide if he's being truthful or just trying to get me to fall for a bunch of bull. When he told me about how he got trapped in his car the other day in a parking ramp—I guess the locks froze and he couldn't open the doors—I first thought about the stories he's told me before (which I believed) to see if this one fit with those. Then I considered him as a character and whether this was something likely to happen to him. I also tried to judge how well the story hung together—I asked him a bunch of questions to see if he'd contradict himself or anything. Finally, I decided to believe him. It was a pretty funny story.

Utility

The Narrative Paradigm has elicited both criticism and praise with respect to its usefulness. K. McClure (2009) argues that the Narrative Paradigm is an overly conservative theory because its focus on fidelity actually weds it to normative conceptions of rationality rather than freeing us from them as Fisher proposes he will do. William Kirkwood (1992) observes that Fisher's logic of good reasons focuses on prevailing values and fails to account for the ways in which stories can promote social change. In some ways, both Kirkwood and Fisher agree that this observation is more of an extension to the theory than a punishing critique.

Kirsten Theye (2008) argues that her analysis of Vice President Dick Cheney's apologies, after shooting his friend in a hunting accident in 2006, shows that Fisher's distinction between narrative coherence and narrative fidelity is not useful. She states that it's impossible to separate the two. Her suggestion is to forget the two components as separate concepts and instead focus on the basic question underlying narrative rationality: "whether a story rings true to the audience based on their experiences" (p. 174).

Interestingly, narrative theorists other than Fisher have embraced the utility of the theory. Clair et al. (2014), for instance, has concluded that "narrative [theory] has found its permanent spot in health communication literature" (p. 7), literature that includes important topics such as medical decision making, aging, and health care organizations. Clearly, while some may consider limited usefulness with the theory, others contend that its value and utility are expansive.

Heurism

Despite criticisms, which primarily urge refinements of the theory, not its abandonment, Fisher's Narrative Paradigm has contributed a great deal to the study of human communication. For one thing, the idea of people as storytellers has proved captivating and heuristic. Storytelling seems an apt metaphor for understanding how humans use communication to make sense of the world (Johnson, 2016; Suter, Koenig Kellas, Webb, & Allen, 2016; Thompson & Schrodt, 2015). Fisher has provided a new paradigm for understanding human nature, squarely located in the symbolic realm of communication. Further, some research shows that stories can improve the healing process, particularly with marginalized and vulnerable populations (Lee, Fawcett, & DeMarco, 2016). Finally, further demonstrating the value of storytelling outside of the academy, Jennifer Gray (2015) found that there were differences in stories between women who continued their pregnancies and those who chose not to continue. Both populations, however, strived to make sense of their experiences.

Closing

Future scholarship will extend the framework of the Narrative Paradigm to remediate its shortcomings and capitalize on its strengths. In constructing the Narrative Paradigm, Fisher has provided a rich framework for such scholarship to take place. Since both Eastern and Western societies rely upon stories for meaning, we will see this theory utilized across the globe by scholars.

Discussion Starters

TECH QUEST: With Twitter and other forms of social media, many people are becoming involved quickly in stories for which they may not have firsthand knowledge. What do you think this might mean for the Narrative Paradigm? If many storytellers elaborate and change a story, does that make it more or less likely to have coherence and fidelity? Or do you think these two elements might be less important in an age of social media?

1. Can you think of any other explanations besides the Narrative Paradigm for Miles's preference for Jorge's candidacy after he read the campaign flyers?

2. Do you agree with Fisher that humans are storytellers? What does that mean to you in a practical sense?

3. When you listen to others' stories, do you evaluate them based on coherence and fidelity? Can you think of any other criteria that you use to evaluate the stories that you hear?

4. What support does Fisher have for his contention that all communication is narration? Can you think of some communication that is not narrative in nature? If all communication is narration, do you think the theory is too broad in scope?

5. The Narrative Paradigm suggests that when an expert argument is compared to a good story, the expert argument will fail because it will lack the coherence and the fidelity that a narrative possesses. Do you agree or disagree with this claim? Give an example where expert testimony failed to persuade you. Give an example of a good story that failed to persuade you.

6. Choose a story that has been in the news recently and analyze it for narrative rationality.

7. If Fisher discards the rational world paradigm, why does he advocate narrative rationality? How are they different?

The Media

ARGUABLY, VERY FEW INSTITUTIONS IN OUR LIVES affect us more than media. Mediated messages and images surround us, and provide us with information and entertainment, as well as ways to connect with others. Television, film, Netflix, cell phones, the Internet, and social media are more than a small part of our lives, and it's apparent we'll never be able to reverse this fact, even if we would want to. Imagine trying to spend a week (or even a day) without your computer, your phone, or your TV. For most of us, that would be impossible!

It is in this spirit that we offer the six theories in this section called "The Media." Each theory places media, in some format, as central to our lives, and the media theorists represented here believe that we respond in different ways to the barrage of electronic technology. Agenda Setting suggests that media sources, like television and radio, act as gatekeepers in putting an agenda out to the public. Then members of the public determine what they think about that agenda on their own—so, media don't tell us what to think, they just tell us what to think *about*. The central feature of the Spiral of Silence Theory pertains to the influence of media on whether or not people will speak out about an issue. Uses and Gratifications Theory suggests that the viewer/listener is active in their media consumption. The theory concerns itself with what people do with particular media. Cultivation Theory focuses on the role of television in our lives. This theory is concerned with the effects of heavy television viewing on people's perceptions of the world, especially with reference to how much violence takes place in reality. In "exposing" the media for their role in maintaining power relationships in society, Cultural Studies highlights the influence that mediated structures have on culture. Cultural theorists aim to unravel the power relationships in society in order to provide marginalized populations more voice. Examining how technology has ruled our lives, Media Ecology Theory argues that the primary media of the age (currently the Internet, for instance) usually take precedence over the content of the message.

We will continue to be affected by media throughout our lives. Technology continues to develop, and even as we write these words, new ways of bringing messages to people are being conceptualized. While learning about the theories in this section, you will encounter a number of timely topics pertaining to the media: dominance, patriarchy, personal needs and values, and the ethics associated with media reporting.

CHAPTER 21

Agenda Setting Theory

*Based on the research of **Maxwell McCombs** and **Donald Shaw***

> *In some instances, established traditions are used to inform agenda-setting research. In other instances, agenda setting informs older traditions.*
>
> —Maxwell E. McCombs and Donald Shaw

Sally D'Amato

Sally was fixing dinner for her extended family and she had the TV playing in the background. She was only half listening, but she stopped peeling carrots when the news came on and she heard the story of Isaiah Shepherd. Sally couldn't remember having heard of him before, but she paused in her dinner preparations to listen. Shepherd was a star football player at Northwestern University who came from Washington, D.C. The newscaster spoke of how Shepherd had told people that his grandmother and girlfriend, both living in D.C., had died on the same day. His grandmother had been ill, and his girlfriend had been in a car accident and then contracted leukemia. This story was especially remarkable because on the day they died, Northwestern had a game and Shepherd went on to play well despite his sorrow. Now it was being revealed that the girlfriend had never existed, and all of Shepherd's interactions with her had taken place online. Either Shepherd had been the victim of a cruel hoax or he, himself, had participated in fooling the public about this. Sally thought that was a very weird story. All during dinner, she talked to her family about how such a thing could happen. They debated back and forth as to whether Shepherd had been a part of the hoax or if he'd been fooled along with others. Sally was pretty sure Isaiah had to be in on it.

A few weeks later, Sally was at the nursing home where she worked as an aide. She was in the break room and the radio was on; she stopped to listen as she sipped her coffee. As the news anchor was talking about presidential inaugurations over the years, she mentioned President Obama's in particular. Although much could be said of the 2008 historical inauguration, instead, the focus was on whether Beyonce had lip-synched the national anthem. Just then, Sally's friend and colleague, Nathan, came into the break room and Sally asked him what he thought about Beyonce's performance at the inauguration. Interestingly, despite all that they could talk about, the two couldn't get the lip-synching out of their minds, even talking about other famous lip-synching singers like Eminem, Ashlee Simpson, and Kanye West.

The following week, Sally was at her computer at home working on a paper for her class in Contemporary Problems at the local college. Sally was trying to finish the BA she had started 15 years ago so she could go on to become a registered nurse. This class satisfied a social-cultural core requirement, and she was actually enjoying it even though it didn't seem to have anything to do with nursing. The professor had asked the class to write about what they thought had been one of the most compelling social problems of the past 10 years. Sally typed in "social problems in the

U.S." for a Google search and she was amazed at the results. She stopped counting the various problems after she got to 100. Sally realized there were a lot of issues in the world that she hadn't thought about much, and wondered a bit about why that was the case. She thought back over the past few weeks and considered some of the issues she had been thinking and talking about. Upon reflection, she had to admit some of them weren't too significant. Sally doubted that Isiah Shepherd's fake girlfriend or Beyonce's lip-synching the national anthem would even make the list for the top 200 social issues! And yet these things had been given a lot of coverage in the media. Sally got to work on her paper. She knew she had a lot of work ahead of her.

∎

Sally's interactions with the media and her subsequent conversations with friends and family about various topics can be explained by the theory we profile in this chapter: Agenda Setting. Agenda Setting Theory explains that media set the agenda for the public; they tell people what is important by the number of times a story is reported and, by implication, if they do not report on a story (or bury it on the back pages of the newspaper), they indicate what stories are unimportant. Media sources also tell the public what is important by what features of a story they emphasize and which they do not. For example, the story about Isaiah Shepherd focused on whether he was in on the hoax or not, and this question structured the conversations that Sally had with others about the story. Newscasters could have emphasized other issues such as online relationships in general, the media spotlight that is on student athletes, or the culture of Washington, D.C. but because they didn't, Sally didn't spend too much time talking about those aspects of the story. Agenda Setting Theory argues that the media exert an influence over their consumers in these ways. However, the theory also suggests that the influence isn't all one way, and Sally (and other members of the public) also have an impact on the media.

Over time scholars have had various ideas about how influential the media are in people's lives. In the early days of mass media, people were seen as helpless victims of the powerful mass media. This notion was eventually discredited and replaced by what is called a limited effects model of the mass media which acknowledge that media influence people, but they also assert that media's influence is minimized or limited by certain aspects of individual audience members' personal and social lives. In addition, researchers argue, audience members, themselves, play a role in the mass communication process (see our more complete discussion of this history of media effects in our chapter on Uses and Gratifications Theory, Chapter 23). Agenda Setting research began with a belief in the powerful effects of the media, but later refinements put it into the camp of limited effects (McCombs, 2004; McCombs & Bell, 1996; McCombs & Shaw, 1993; Min & McCombs, 2016).

History of Agenda Setting Research

Before delving into the assumptions of the theory, let's provide some relevant background. The history of agenda setting research can be conceptualized in two stages: (1) pretheoretical conceptualization, and (2) the establishment of the theory. We will discuss each of these two historical stages briefly.

Pretheoretical Conceptualizing

Most researchers (e.g., Dearing & Rogers, 1996) talk about the first stage of agenda setting research as consisting of the conceptualizations of several scholars in different fields beginning to think and write about the relationships among the media, the audience, and the policymakers in the United States. The first person to contribute to this line of thought according to James Dearing and Everett Rogers was Robert E. Park. Park was a sociologist at the University of Chicago (1915–1935), and he is thought to be the first scholar of mass communication. He devised the notion of media gatekeeping and began to discuss some of the issues that are now incorporated into Agenda Setting Theory. Park noted that editors are gatekeepers because they have the power to "kill" stories and to promote other stories that are submitted to them by correspondents, reporters, and news agencies. This statement related to the later developments in Agenda Setting Theory because Park distinguished between issues that become public and those that do not come to the public's attention.

After Park's contributions, Walter Lippmann was a pioneer of the pretheoretical stage. Walter Lippmann was a scholar of propaganda and public opinion as well as an influential newspaper columnist and presidential adviser. In 1922, he wrote a book called *Public Opinion,* and he titled the first chapter "The World Outside and the Pictures in Our Heads." He made the argument that the mass media connect the two. According to Lippmann, the events that happen in the world are brought to people by the mass media and the way these events are reported shape how people structure the images of these events in their minds (Fahmy, Bock, & Wanta, 2014). Lippmann did not use the term *agenda setting*, but his writing was very influential in later development of the theory.

In 1948, Harold D. Lasswell, a political scientist at the University of Chicago, contributed an important chapter to an anthology about communication that had far-reaching implications for Agenda Setting Theory. In this chapter, Lasswell talked about two important functions of mass media: surveillance and correlation. **Surveillance** is the process of newspeople scanning the information that is in the environment and deciding which of the many events that are occurring deserve attention in their news outlets. In discussing this function, Lasswell was echoing Park's notion of gatekeeping. Lasswell argued that news reporters, editors, and so forth decide which of the multitude of possible stories will be the ones to reach the public via their papers or other outlets. Obviously in this process the media do exert powerful effects—they are in charge of what the public gets information about and how that information is presented. People often complain that the news is all bad and that the good things that happen don't get reported (the old adage "if it bleeds, it leads" refers to the likelihood that bad news will be featured in the media). This speaks to the surveillance process that is controlled by newspeople.

Lasswell (1948) describes the function of **correlation** as the way that media direct our attention to certain issues through communicating them to the public and policymakers. In this function, media synchronize the various groups in society to pay attention to the same things at the same time. Lasswell spoke of the "correlation of the parts of society in responding to the environment" (p. 38). The result of the media orchestration of our attention was "a correlation of attention on certain issues at the same time by the media, the public, and policymakers" (Dearing & Rogers, 1996,

surveillance
the process of newspeople scanning the information that is in the environment and deciding which of the many events that are occurring deserve attention in their news outlets

correlation
the way that media direct our attention to certain issues through communicating them to the public and to policymakers

pp. 11–12). This function is illustrated when there is a national/international event (like a presidential inauguration, the Super Bowl, or the Olympics) or a national catastrophe (like the Boston Marathon bombing or Hurricane Sandy). The media correlate our attention to these things in real time, so that it's likely we will hear about storm damage at the same time we hear or read about a dress of the First Lady.

Establishing the Theory of Agenda Setting

All of these ideas by earlier researchers came together in the second stage of agenda setting research. This stage is marked by the study that Maxwell McCombs and Donald Shaw (1972) published which took these early concepts and put them to an empirical test. This landmark study examined the public and the media's agendas during the 1968 presidential election. Agenda Setting Theory was focused on issues of political import in its beginnings. McCombs and Shaw were interested to test the hypothesis, derived from the ideas of scholars like Lasswell, Park, and Lippmann, that the mass media create an agenda through their selection of what to include in the news, and this agenda influences public perception of what is important. In this first study, McCombs and Shaw hypothesized a causal relationship between the media and the public agendas, which stated that the media agenda would, over time, become the agenda for the public.

To test their hypothesis, they interviewed 100 undecided voters during the three weeks just prior to the presidential election in November of 1968. Although elements of their hypotheses changed in subsequent studies, one of the enduring contributions of this early work was the way they measured the two variables of interest: the public agenda and the media agenda. The public agenda for these undecided voters was measured by their responses to a survey question: "What are you *most* concerned about these days? That is, regardless of what politicians say, what are the two or three *main* things that you think the government *should* concentrate on doing something about?" (McCombs & Shaw, 1972, p. 178). They ranked the issues based on the frequency with which they were mentioned and found five main issues— foreign policy, law and order, fiscal policy, public welfare, and civil rights, which were mentioned most frequently by the respondents. These five issues formed the public agenda.

They measured the media agenda by counting the number of news articles, editorials, and broadcast stories in the nine main mass-media outlets that served the area where the undecided voters lived. These mass-media sources included television, newspapers, and news magazines. McCombs and Shaw found an almost perfect correlation (1967) between the rank order of the five issues on the media agenda as measured by their content analysis of the media coverage of the election campaign, and the five issues on the public agenda as determined by their survey of the 100 undecided voters.

At this point in the history, the ideas articulated by Lippmann and others now had a name: "McCombs and Shaw named this transfer of salience from the media agenda to the public agenda the agenda setting influence of mass communication" (McCombs & Bell, 1996, p. 96). The theory was launched and hundreds of articles, books, and monographs have followed. Since its inception, over 400 studies have utilized Agenda Setting Theory (Zhou, Kim, & Kim, 2015) in some form. Even a

In choosing and displaying news, editors, newsroom staff, webcasters, and anchors play an important part in shaping social and political reality. When readers and viewers consume news, they not only learn about a given issue, but they also learn how much importance to attach to that issue by the amount and position it's given by the press. In thinking about what candidates are saying during a campaign, the mass media may well determine the important issues—that is, the media may set the "agenda" of the campaign. How influential the media are in this agenda setting function depends on several factors including media credibility, the extent of conflicting evidence, shared values, and the audience's need for guidance.

Google search of the theory yields millions and millions of results. Clearly, the theory has resonated with both scholars and laypeople with many modifications undertaken over the years. We now examine a few of the theory's assumptions and key terminology.

Assumptions of Agenda Setting Theory

Agenda Setting Theory rests on three basic assumptions:

- The media establish an agenda and in so doing are not simply reflecting reality, but are shaping and filtering reality for the public.
- The media's concentration on the issues that comprise their agenda influence the public's agenda, and these together influence the policymakers' agenda.
- The public and policymakers have the possibility to influence the media's agenda as well.

These three assumptions are woven into Agenda Setting Theory and suggest the interaction that the theorists specified among the media, the public, and policymakers. First, the media both shape and filter the reality in which we live. We may not be aware of it, but media are constantly providing us a lens both to understand and to reflect our social reality. Along the way, the media also establish an agenda for us to consider. Imagine, for instance, all of the information around us. Now, imagine the various media (e.g., radio, television, the Internet, social media, etc.). Somehow all of this information has to be packaged in some way and the media ensures the way that we receive information and the extent to which the information reaches us. In other words, media shape what we hear, read, or attend to and we are usually unwittingly compliant in that process. Consider, for instance, our opening story. Nate and Sally focused on lip-synching rather than on the groundbreaking presidential inauguration. It's likely that the media influenced the conversation by filtering out other (more important) information related to the 2008 celebration.

A second assumption of Agenda Setting Theory relates to the gatekeeping function of the media. In particular, the media's focus on the issues that comprise an agenda and in turn, influence the public's agenda and subsequently the agenda of decision makers. Let's think about this a bit further with an example. Over the past several years, there has been a concerted effort to deal with bullying episodes taking place in schools. Although the number of kids being bullied is high, it was the media's sustained attention to the topic that inevitably prompted parents to talk to school boards to demand local policy change and ultimately prompted state legislatures to enact anti-bullying laws. This one topic of bullying, then, allowed the media to become gatekeepers of the bullying topic in that it highlighted the kids who were bullied, their stories of survival, and the ways in which schools could/should reduce bullying.

One final assumption of the theory assumes that the policymakers and the public can affect the media's agenda. Because an interrelationship exists among the three elements (the media, the public, and those in prominent decision-making roles), it's possible that the media will initiate an agenda because of the influence (or pressure) brought about by the other two elements. For example, consider the increase in attention pertaining to bathroom use of transgendered individuals. Lawmakers either voted to narrow the laws on bathroom use or in a few cases, expanded them to accommodate preferential bathroom usage. Few would argue against the fact that legal changes were undertaken because of trans activism. Clearly, although some media outlets were reporting on this topic for a few years prior to any national dialogue, it was the policymakers and the public who prompted the issue to come to the forefront of the media's agenda.

Two Levels of Agenda Setting

agenda
a list of the most important issues of the day as decided by an entity, such as the media

Agenda Setting Theory proposes that the agenda setting function has three levels (Rogerson & Roselle, 2016). The original conception of the theory identified only the first level of agenda setting. This level focuses on the list of important issues that comprises the **agenda** as decided by some entity such as the media. A second level, sometimes called *attribute agenda setting*, was added to the theory that focuses on which parts (or attributes) of those issues are most important. The third level is rather recent and acknowledges the interplay between news and reality. In particular, Lei Guo (2016) suggests "network agenda setting" as a third level. In particular, Guo notes: "The news tells us not only what to think and how to think, but also determines how we associate different messages to conceptualize social reality" (p. 3).

The first level speaks to the broad media agenda, and the second level refers to the process known as **media framing** or the way media depictions of events (that have made it onto the media agenda) influence and constrain how consumers can interpret them. The third level presupposes the first and second level, in that the media still set the agenda, but do so in much more "complicated ways" (Guo, 2016, pp. 3–4).

Framing was first discussed by Todd Gitlin (1980) in his examination of how CBS television coverage of the 1960s student movement made it seem less important than it actually was. Researchers noted that framing could be accomplished in many ways. In newspapers, things like the size of headlines, photographs included with the story, a story's overall length and placement allow the editors to frame its importance and highlight the aspects of it that are deemed most important. On television, the visuals accompanying the story add to the ability of newspeople to frame a story. Some research (e.g., Miller & Roberts, 2010) has examined what they call visual agenda setting, which is concerned exclusively with visuals. This study asked 466 Louisiana State University students to respond to imagery about Hurricane Katrina six weeks after the storm. They found that most people chose the compelling, repetitious imagery shown in the dominant media. So they concluded that the principles of visual agenda setting were supported. However, they also found that the result was qualified by how close the respondent was to the news event. Students who were more personally affected by Katrina chose more personal images and abandoned the images that the media selected.

Other researchers expanded the notion of framing to include affect, for instance (e.g., Coleman & Wu, 2010; Entman, 1993), and also talked about a related process: **priming** (Clausen & Oxley, 2017), a cognitive process whereby what the media present temporarily, at least, influences what people think about afterwards in processing additional information. For example, if you watch or hear news reports about the ongoing nuclear tests conducted by North Korea, you might be primed to have more anxiety about that country's ability to bomb the United States than if you had not paid attention to those news reports.

Three-Part Process of Agenda Setting

The agenda setting process consists of three parts: setting the media agenda, setting the public agenda, and setting the policy agenda. The **media agenda** refers to the priority of issues to be discussed in mediated sources. The **public agenda** is the result of the media agenda interacting with what the public thinks. And, finally, the public agenda interacts with what is considered important by policymakers to create the **policy agenda**. In a simple format, the theory states that the media agenda affects the

media framing
how media depictions of events influence and constrain the way consumers can interpret the events

priming
a cognitive process whereby what the media present temporarily, at least, influences what people think about afterwards in processing additional information

media agenda
the priority placed on issues discussed in mediated sources

public agenda
the result of the media agenda interacting with what the public thinks

policy agenda
the result of the public agenda interacting with what policy makers think

AGENDA SETTING THEORY

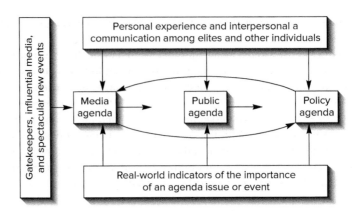

Figure 21.1
The Impact of Public and Media Agenda on Policy Agenda
Source: Rogers and Dearing (1988).

Personal experience and interpersonal a communication among elites and other individuals

Gatekeepers, influential media, and spectacular new events

Media agenda

Public agenda

Policy agenda

Real-world indicators of the importance of an agenda issue or event

public agenda, which in turn, impacts the policy agenda, a process we suggested in one of the assumptions of the model. (See Figure 21.1).

In addition, this simple formulation is complicated by a few other factors. First, agenda setting is concerned with **salience**, or the degree to which an agenda issue is perceived as important relative to the other issues on the agenda (McCombs, 2014). Agenda setting researchers are more interested in salience than in the usual concerns of public opinion researchers such as positive and negative attitudes toward an issue. Salience allows agenda setting researchers to capture what the media agenda is and what the media are telling the public to think about. Thus, how salient or important an issue is perceived to be by the audience will have an effect on the degree of influence felt. Although you might disagree with Sally and Nate talking about lip-synching rather than presidential inaugurations in our opening, the Westernized "celebrity culture" focus seems to be one reason for their attention to the topic. Further, Agenda Setting became a limited effects model in part because of the later recognition that the power of the media agenda is dependent on a variety of factors including: media credibility, the extent of conflicting evidence available to the consumer, the extent to which people share the values of the media, and the public's need for guidance or orientation (Sevenans & Walgrave, 2016; Walgrave & Van Aelst, 2006).

If an audience member does not believe a media source is credible, he or she will likely dismiss the agenda promoted on that source. If Mandy is a liberal, she would be unlikely to believe much of what she might hear from a source like Glenn Beck on the radio, for example. And, if Samuel is conservative, he will probably dismiss most of the agenda promoted on *Full Frontal with Samantha Bee* or on any political podcast perceived as liberal or progressive. Thus, the public agenda will be swayed only by the media sources they find credible. Conflicting information also complicates the tenets of Agenda Setting and provides a contingency that the theory has to incorporate. If Tina listens to several news programs and they all tell her something slightly different about the economy, for instance, the Agenda Setting function is complicated. Further, if Randy listens to talk shows that promote the value of the sanctity of marriage, he will likely be convinced by their agenda because he shares that value. However, if Marianne believes that

salience
the degree to which an agenda issue is perceived as important relative to the other issues on the agenda

marriage is an oppressive institution, she will probably not accept the agenda on those shows.

The contingency condition that Agenda Setting researchers have discussed the most is the need for guidance or orientation (McCombs, 2004). This factor explains why people sometimes do not adopt the media agenda by discussing two key variables: relevance and uncertainty. **Relevance** is defined as a motivation to seek orientation on an issue from the media due to the perception of personal importance that the issue holds for someone. If people believe they are not at all involved in an issue such as greenhouse gases, for instance, they will not look to the media for guidance on the issue and thus will not be affected by the media agenda. **Uncertainty** refers to how much information people think they have about an issue. If they believe they have a great deal of information about the two candidates in a presidential election, their uncertainty is low, and thus they will not have a need for guidance from the media. If, however, they are unsure if they have enough information, they need more

relevance
a factor explaining why people seek guidance from the media agenda. It refers to how personally affected they feel by an issue

uncertainty
a factor explaining why people seek guidance from the media agenda. It refers to how much information a person believes they already possess about an issue

---

Theory in Popular Press · Combatting the Media Agenda

Priscilla Gilman writes about how the media agenda posed a problem for her in the aftermath of the Sandy Hook Elementary/Newtown, Connecticut, killings in 2012. Gilman, the mother of an autistic child, notes that the media seemed to be trying to explain the killer's horrific behaviors by labeling him as suffering from autism. She writes, "It began as insinuation, but quickly flowered into outright declaration. Words used to describe the killer, Adam Lanza, began with "odd," "aloof," and "a loner," shaded into "lacked empathy," and finally slipped into "on the autism spectrum" and suffering from "a mental illness like Asperger's." By Sunday, it had snowballed into a veritable storm of accusation and stigmatization." Gilman is using her column to try to counteract the framing that occupied many media stories about the tragedy in Newtown. She points out that there are factual errors in this framing: first, she argues that autism is not a mental illness, it is a neurodevelopmental disability or disorder. Further, those who are on the autism spectrum, according to Gilman, do not necessarily lack empathy. They can be very empathic although they may express their empathy and concern for others in unconventional ways.

Gilman concludes by stating that countless studies have shown that people with autism are no more likely than those without it to engage in violence, and to the contrary, are more likely to be the victims of violence (i.e., bullying behaviors) than the perpetrators. It remains to be seen if the media agenda, the public agenda, and the policy agenda will converge in policies that respect the value of each child as Gilman urges, or will take up the frame that Gilman disputes here.

Source: Gilman, P. (2012, December 17). Don't blame autism for Newtown. *New York Times* online, nytimes.com/2012/12/18/opinion/dont-blame-autism-for-newtown.html.

guidance from the agenda the media present. These two variables work together to explain deviations from the general principles of Agenda Setting Theory. If relevance and uncertainty are both high, then Agenda Setting should be predictive. If relevance and uncertainty are both low, then these are contingency conditions that allow the theory to be more flexible. What sort of relevance and uncertainty did Sally possess in the opening vignette?

Expansions and Refinements to Agenda Setting Theory

The original study that McCombs and Shaw published in 1972, was predicated on a powerful effects model of the media. McCombs and Shaw's hypothesis, that the media agenda impacts the public's agenda, was founded on the image of a rather passive audience. The second phase of research on the theory moderated that stance. This phase merged Agenda Setting with some of the ideas of Uses and Gratifications Theory (see Chapter 23). In the Uses and Gratifications approach, the audience is pictured as a group of active seekers, employing media for specific uses, and to satisfy particular gratifications. This next phase of Agenda Setting incorporated that notion and began to ask about why some voters expose themselves to certain messages more than other voters do.

Further research (Weaver, Graber, McCombs, & Eyal, 1981) expanded Agenda Setting Theory beyond the public issues that McCombs and Shaw had begun exploring in 1972. Other key political elements were added to the agenda like candidate image and voter interest in campaigns. More recent research added the question: Who sets the media agenda? This is a complicated question and research has suggested a variety of answers. Steven Littlejohn and Karen Foss (2011) suggest that there are four types of power relations between the media and other sources that might provide an answer: (1) high-power source and high-power media; (2) high-power source and low-power media; (3) lower-power source and high-power media; and (4) both media and source are low power.

In the first case, a popular president could be a source to a well-funded media outlet with a decent reputation like CNN. In this situation, the two would be equals in setting the agenda, which will work well for them if they see things similarly; but this will result in struggles if they are not on the same side of the important issues of the day. In the second scenario, the source (an influential politician) has more power than the media (a local paper), and so then the source will be able to set the agenda for the media. In the third relationship, the media are able to set their own agenda because the source is not considered to have much of a voice. In this case, the media may marginalize the source and the source will have trouble getting access to the public to discuss their issues. A welfare group who wants to have their agenda broadcast on national television may be in this situation. Finally, in the last relationship Littlejohn and Foss suggest that events will probably set the public agenda because neither the source nor the media have much power (a local official and a small town website).

In addition, researchers have examined what they call intermedia influence on the agenda setting process and have noted that news organizations affect one another's agendas. For example, some research (Lim, 2011) has investigated the influence major news websites have on each other's agendas. This study, which was set in South Korea, found that the major news websites there did influence the agendas of online newspapers as well as, to a certain extent, each other. Other studies (e.g., Johnson, 2011; Maier, 2010; Meraz, 2011; Ragas & Kiousis, 2010) found some support for the influence that various media have on one another. In addition, Maxwell McCombs and Tamara Bell (1996) observed that the intermedia effect can come from individual newsworkers as well as news organizations. As they note, journalists live in "an ambiguous social world" so they often rely on one another for confirmation and as a source of ideas. McCombs and Bell mention several studies of cases where journalists followed one another in reporting about specific issues. They refer to this agenda influence as **pack journalism**. To some extent, pack journalism is similar to groupthink, a theoretical model we discussed in Chapter 14. McCombs and colleagues (e.g., McCombs & Funk, 2011) have suggested that intermedia influence is the wave of the future for agenda setting research. With this backdrop, we now turn our attention to several key assumptions and terms related to the theory.

pack journalism
the phenomenon of journalists having their agendas influenced by other journalists

Integration, Critique, and Closing

Agenda Setting Theory is a venerable theory of mass communication; it has a history spanning back to the beginning of the twentieth century, and it is still being employed today in studies of media and public communication. It is clearly a theory that has been understood using an empirical approach, making it aligned with quantitative methods. Although it has its detractors, and some of its central concepts may need adaptation in an era of new media and fragmented publics, it still has many adherents and it fares well as measured against the traditional criteria for evaluating theories, especially empirical theories.

Student Voices

Christian

I like parts of this theory. It makes sense to me that what I talk about with my friends and family is influenced by what I hear and see in media. If that weren't the case, I'd just be talking about stuff that actually happens in front of me here at school. So, that part of the theory seems right to me. But, I just can't see how there can be a public agenda anymore. We all read and listen to such different sources, how can there be topics that occupy everyone at the same time? If I'm reading a blog about aviation and my sister is reading *Motherlode* (because she has a new baby), I can't see us having the same agenda. I think this theory was right when it was first developed in the 1970s, but it has to be changed to keep up with the times.

Integration

Communication Tradition	Rhetorical	Semiotic	Phenomenological	Cybernetic	**Socio-Psychological**	Socio-Cultural	Critical

Communication Context	Intrapersonal	Interpersonal	Small Group	Organizational	Public/Rhetorical	**Mass/Media**	Cultural

Approach to Knowing	**Positivistic/Empirical**	Interpretive/Hermeneutic	Critical

Critique

Evaluation Criteria	**Scope**	Logical Consistency	Parsimony	**Utility**	Testability	**Heurism**	Test of Time

Scope

Some researchers have critiqued the scope of Agenda Setting Theory. Occasionally, the complaint is that the scope is too large and sometimes the opposite is discussed. Some of the problems around this issue have to do with the concept of framing. First, some research (e.g., Takeshita, 2006) asserts that framing is a separate theory from Agenda Setting, and could supersede it altogether. This is labeled an identity problem with Agenda Setting. Toshio Takeshita comments that some researchers believe Agenda Setting Theory, in adding the second level of attribute agenda setting (or framing), is actually colonizing other theories and overreaching the appropriate scope for the theory. Takeshita concludes that the two theories can coexist and more empirical work will determine which one provides the better explanation for media's influence on the public. Further, Takeshita notes that Agenda Setting Theory has the advantage over framing theory in methodological terms because scholars have developed clear operational definitions of the media and the public agendas which work well in quantitative studies.

Utility

With regard to utility, some questions have been raised about whether the theory remains useful given the new media environment. When people have so much freedom in their quests for information and the media sources are multiple and fragmented, perhaps the tenets of Agenda Setting Theory will not be supported. Some studies have been conducted to test this question and the results have been somewhat mixed, although on the whole, they suggest that Agenda Setting Theory can still be applied in a media environment that is anything but monolithic. In a study exploring age-related differences in agenda setting (Coleman & McCombs, 2007), the researchers found that even though media use differentiated the generations (the youngest generation used newspapers and television significantly less than the older two generations and used the Internet significantly more), the agenda setting effect was still apparent regardless of which type of media was used.

Jennifer Brubaker (2008), however, found that television viewers and Internet users ranked a series of issues differently than the general media did. Brubaker concluded that Agenda Setting is not useful as a theoretical framework when people have so much more freedom in their media choices. Still other research (e.g., Ragas & Kiousis, 2010) did find evidence of first- and second-level agenda setting relationships. This study examined the agenda setting effects among explicitly partisan news media coverage, political activist groups, citizen activists, and official campaign advertisements on YouTube, all in support of the same candidate, Barack Obama, in 2008. The authors concluded that Agenda Setting Theory is applicable across a variety of new media.

Sharon Meraz (2011) found a slightly more complicated result in that her study revealed that traditional media were unable to set the agenda for political blogs. Yet, she also found that ideologically diverse political blog networks were able to have an impact on traditional media's online news agenda, and, to a lesser extent, their newsroom blog agenda. She concluded that there was a reduction of traditional media's agenda setting influence. But, she also argued that Agenda Setting Theory could work to explain the greater interdependence between traditional media and political blogs, and in fact, noted that some blogs like the Huffington Post were operating like the traditional media and may exert an agenda setting function of their own. Other studies (e.g., Johnson, 2011; Maier, 2010) concurred noting that although traditional news media have less of an ability to set the public agenda than in the past, they still perform an agenda setting function, and what is found on news websites and in citizen-journalists' postings often correlates strongly with what appears on mainstream media's agenda.

Finally, a study in 2010 (Weeks & Southwell) used a novel approach to test the agenda setting effects of the traditional media (television and newspapers) on the use of newer media (Google searches). This study examined the relationship of television and newspaper coverage of the rumor circulating during the 2008 presidential campaign that Barack Obama was actually a Muslim. The results showed, as Agenda Setting Theory would predict, that the more this rumor was covered in traditional media the more Google searches there were on the topic.

Heurism

With respect to heurism, Agenda Setting Theory certainly has been successful. It has supported hundreds of studies since 1972, and these studies have been situated in a wide variety of fields and topics. Although many Agenda Setting studies focus on politics, they are not confined to that topic, and they are not confined to political issues in the United States as evidenced by studies that have examined and situated the theory in Iraq, Taiwan, Mainland China, and Poland (Guo, Chen, Vu, Wang, Aksamit, Guzek, Jachimowski, & McCombs, 2015), for example. Further, the theory's application to such important topics as human trafficking (Papdouka, Evangelopoulos, & Ignatow, 2016) and physician time management and patient satisfaction (Robinson, Tate, & Heritage, 2016) further suggests a heuristic and valuable line of scholarship. As we have discussed throughout the chapter, Agenda Setting research examining new media, traditional media, political issues, and responses to visual stimuli among other issues, attest to the robust, heuristic quality of this theory.

Closing

Agenda Setting is a theoretical model that despite having its roots many decades ago, continues to be relevant today. All around the globe we have seen media transform and evolve and there can be no doubt that media resonate with millions of people. We have seen the agenda-setting function of the media front and center in a number of different areas. Moreover, media consumers are often unaware of the influence that the mediated agenda has upon them. As we move further into new forms of media and ways for the media to communicate a message, we are likely to see Agenda Setting Theory take on more prominence than ever.

Discussion Starters

TECH QUEST: Agenda Setting Theory was created in a time when there were only three television channels, relatively few radio stations, and a limited number of big city newspapers. Now, of course, the media landscape is totally different. How could you design a study that you think would contribute to answering whether online news media operate in the manner that Agenda Setting Theory predicts?

1. Does Sally's situation ring true for you? Are the topics that she hears about through media actually charting an agenda for her to think about? Have you ever had the experience that Sally has of realizing that there are a lot of issues in the world that you haven't thought about before? Do you think that is the case because the media haven't directed you to these issues or is it due to some other reasons? If there are other reasons, what are they?

2. (Why) do you think it's important to know the history of Agenda Setting Theory? (How) does it help you to understand and/or apply the theory to know about its evolution over time?

3. Pick a recent news event and discuss how the second level of agenda setting might have been at work during the reporting of it. For instance, how did the media cover the 2012 Presidential election? What were the issues that emerged as important and what elements of media framing were used to establish their importance?

4. Do you agree that framing is a part of Agenda Setting Theory or do you think that it is a competing theory that suggests Agenda Setting is no longer useful?

5. Discuss a news event that has gone through the three-stage process suggested by Agenda Setting Theory: first it is placed on the media agenda, then the public's agenda, and finally it reaches the policymakers' agenda where actual policy is made that relates to the news event.

6. Do you agree that Agenda Setting is a limited effects model? As the chapter notes the theory's originator, Maxwell McCombs has alternated in how he has framed the type of effects claimed by Agenda Setting. What do you think? Explain your answer.

7. Who do you think sets the agenda for the media? Do you agree with the material in the chapter about how the media agenda gets established? Explain your answer.

CHAPTER 22

Spiral of Silence Theory

*Based on the research of **Elisabeth Noelle-Neumann***

Journalism can be improved by harnessing the new efficiency of social research. It can be made more realistic, quicker, and more discriminating in reporting and interpreting.

—Elisabeth Noelle-Neumann

Carol Johansen

Each morning, Carol Johansen eats at the "Eldergarten" breakfast at the local senior center. She certainly can afford to go out to a restaurant, but she likes the center because she enjoys the company since her husband died. Carol encounters a rambunctious cast of characters each breakfast, including Earl, a World War II veteran who sings Broadway songs; Nancy, a former nurse who tells lively stories about former patients; and Nick, a tech-savvy New England lobsterman who is an avid newspaper reader and blogger. This morning's breakfast was especially interesting because the conversation quickly turned to an article on spanking children that Nick read online.

After reading the brief article to the group, Nick offered his opinion on the topic: "I agree with this writer. I don't see anything wrong with spanking a kid. Look at this survey in the paper. Over 60 percent of the state believes it's okay to spank, but only 40 percent of the country does. Nowadays, you can't lay a hand on a kid. They're ready to sue you, or you'll get some state worker to come into your own house and take your kid away. It's not right."

"I agree," said Nancy. "I can tell you that my neighbor's daughter is almost 8 and a holy terror. But, noooo, her mother won't touch her! I don't get it. If that was my child, I wouldn't mind putting her over my knee and giving her a good wallop! The

girl's mom and dad don't want to send 'the wrong message' to her so she gets away with a lot."

Earl became more interested in the subject as Nancy spoke. Like the others, Earl had a strong opinion on the subject: "Look. How many people at this table were spanked when they were little?" All raised their hands. "And how many of you think that you're violent people?" None showed any response. "There. That's my point. Today, they tell you that if you spank your own kid, then that kid is going to end up violent. But look at us. We aren't violent. We don't hurt anyone. There's just too much of this political correctness out there, and too many parents simply have no rights anymore."

Carol continued glancing at one of the center's flyers on the table. She, like the others, had an opinion on the subject. But her thoughts differed from those of the others. She did not believe in spanking a child at all. She had been spanked like the rest of her friends, but her dad didn't know when to stop. Carol had often been physically abused. She thought about the number of parents who are not able to stop at just one slap on the behind. She also thought about what hitting accomplished. Children can be taught right and wrong, she thought, without being hit.

"Hey, Carol," Nick interrupted, "you're pretty quiet. What's your take on all this?"

Carol thought for a quick moment. Should she disagree with the rest of them? What about

369

all the people in her community who also agree with spanking? Carol recalled seeing a news program on the topic about a month ago, and the reporter had interviewed several adult children who had been abused. She wondered how many of them were spanked when they were young and yet, all of them stated that they spank their children and they don't feel it's abuse in any way.

Carol knew that she disagreed with her breakfast colleagues, but how could she begin to explain all of her thoughts? They wouldn't understand. It's probably better simply to go with the flow, she surmised.

"Oh, I don't know. I can see how some kids need special attention. But sometimes, parents get too angry."

"C'mon Carol," Nancy interrupted. "There are a lot of . . ."

"Well, I guess I agree with it. I hope that it's not done that often, though." As the volunteer arrived at the table to pour more coffee, the conversation quickly turned to other news. Privately, Carol thought about why she had deferred to the group's will. She didn't want to be alone in her viewpoint, nor did she want to explain the personal and sordid details of her past. As Nick began to talk about last night's city council meeting, Carol wondered whether she would ever speak up on the subject again.

Our opinions of events, people, and topics change periodically in our lives. Consider, for example, your opinions about dating when you were a 15-year-old and your opinions about dating now. Or consider the opinions you held of your family members during your adolescence and those you hold today. Your opinions on various topics—including cohabiting sex and raising children—have likely evolved over the years. Opinions are not static and frequently change over the years.

One important influence on our opinions is the media. As this section of the text emphasizes, media help to shape who we are today. Often, this influence is subtle; at other times it is more direct. The media's influence on public opinion is what Elisabeth Noelle-Neumann studied, dating back to the 1930s and 1940s. It was in the early 1970s, however, that she conceptualized the Spiral of Silence Theory. And, yet, as we will learn later, today scholars continue to discuss this theory in many ways.

Originally, the theory focused on traditional types of media such as newspapers and television. Yet, as the theory attracted new attention over the years, the application of its concepts to new media emerged (Eilders & Porten-Chee, 2015). Later in the chapter, we will include a brief discussion of the newer research integrating online communication and the Spiral of Silence Theory.

Noelle-Neumann's Spiral of Silence Theory is important to address for several reasons. The theory "directly relates to speech freedom, which is the cornerstone of our democracy" (Liu, 2006). Further it is a theory that weaves communication and public opinion, two critical areas in virtually any democracy around the globe (Donsbach, Salmon, & Tsfati, 2013). Third, it has intellectual roots in six fields (Donsbach, Tsfati, & Salmon, 2014). Finally, Spiral of Silence scholars have made efforts to make their theory culturally relevant in societies where media remain important and influential (Neill, 2009). To this end, while the theory resonates with those interested in public opinion, it also has relevancy for those interested in the effect that media has upon us.

Noelle-Neumann focuses on what happens when people provide their opinions on a variety of issues that the media have defined for the public (for more information on how the media influence public discourse, look at Chapter 21). The Spiral of

Silence Theory suggests that people who believe that they hold a minority viewpoint on a public issue will remain in the background where their communication will be restrained; those who believe that they hold a majority viewpoint will be more encouraged to speak. Noelle-Neumann (1983) contends that the media will focus more on the majority views, underestimating the minority views. Those in the minority will be less assertive in communicating their opinions, thereby leading to a downward spiral of communication. Interestingly, those in the majority will overestimate their influence and may become emboldened in their communication. Subsequently, the media will report on their opinions and activities. This theory, then, adheres to the belief that we alluded to in Chapter 2: Groups are highly influential in our lives.

Theory At a Glance • *Spiral of Silence Theory*

Because of their enormous power, media have a lasting and profound effect on public opinion. Mass media work simultaneously with majority opinion to silence minority beliefs on cultural and social issues in particular. A fear of isolation prompts those with minority views to examine the beliefs of others. Individuals who fear being socially isolated are prone to conform to what they perceive to be the majority view. Every so often, however, the silent majority raises its voice in activist ways.

The minority views of Carol Johansen and the behavior of her breakfast friends underscore the gist of the Spiral of Silence Theory. Listening to her colleagues' opinions on spanking, Carol feels that she is alone in thinking that spanking is wrong. The theory suggests that Carol is influenced by media reports of over 60 percent of the state supporting spanking for discipline and also by her own recollection of a television news show featuring abused children who as grownups spanked their own children and who did not believe it was abusive. Carol perceives her opinion to be a minority view, and consequently she speaks less. Conversely, those in our sample who agree with spanking as discipline (Nick, Nancy, and Earl) are no doubt inspired by the state survey responses; this prompts even more assertive communication on their part.

The difference between this majority and minority view at the senior center is further clarified by Noelle-Neumann (1991). She believes that those in the majority have the confidence to speak out. They may even display their convictions by wearing buttons, brandishing bumper stickers, and emblazoning their opinions on the clothes they wear. (Today, these individuals will likely be blogging about their convictions.) Holders of minority views, however, are usually cautious and silent, which reinforces the public's perceptions of their weakness. Nick, Nancy, and Earl are clearly confident in their opinions, whereas Carol fosters a sense of nonassertiveness by her lack of assertiveness in expressing her opinion.

The Spiral of Silence Theory uniquely intersects public opinion and media. To understand this interface better, we first unravel the notion of public opinion, a key component of the theory. We then examine three assumptions of the theory.

The Court of Public Opinion

As a researcher, Noelle-Neumann was interested in clarifying terms that may have multiple meanings. At the core of the Spiral of Silence Theory is a term that is commonly accepted but one that she felt was misconstrued: public opinion. As a founder and director of the Allensbach Institute, a polling agency in Germany, Noelle-Neumann contended that interpretations of public opinion have been misguided. In fact, although she identified more than 50 definitions of the term since the theory's inception, none satisfied her and she further lamented that most researchers erroneously link public opinion with government, resulting in a limited understanding of the term (Noelle-Neumann, 2014).

Although many years have passed since the theory's original expression, the concept of public opinion "is particularly encumbered by the thicket of confusion, misunderstandings, and communication problems" (Noelle-Neumann & Petersen, 2004, pp. 339–340). Further, writers continue to state that public opinion is more important than ever (Claussen & Oxley, 2016). Attempting to provide some understanding of this key term in the theory, Noelle-Neumann (1984, 1993) has provided some clarity. She appropriately separates public opinion into two discrete terms: public and opinion.

She notes that there are three meanings of *public*. First, there is a legal association with the term. **Public** suggests that it is open to everyone, as in "public lands" or "public place." Second, public pertains to the concerns or issues of people, as in "the public responsibility of journalists." Finally, public represents the social-psychological side of people. That is, people not only think inwardly but also think about their relationships to others. The phrase "public eye" is relevant here. Noelle-Neumann concludes that individuals know whether they are exposed to or sheltered from public view, and they adjust themselves accordingly. She claims that the social-psychological side of public has been neglected in previous interpretations of public opinion, and yet, "this is the meaning felt by people in their sensitive social skin" (1993, p. 62).

An **opinion** is an expression of an attitude. Opinions may vary in both intensity and stability. Invoking the early French and English interpretation of opinions, Noelle-Neumann notes that opinion is a level of agreement of a particular population. In the spiral of silence process, opinion is synonymous with something regarded as acceptable.

Putting all of this together, Noelle-Neumann defines **public opinion** as the "attitudes or behaviors one must express in public if one is not to isolate oneself; in areas of controversy or change, public opinions are those attitudes one can express without running the danger of isolating oneself" (p. 178). So, for Carol Johansen, her opinion on spanking would not be regarded as acceptable by her breakfast club. Because she fears being isolated from her particular early-morning community, she silences her opinions.

Noelle-Neumann and Petersen (2004) argue that public opinion is a dynamic process and limited by time and place. To that end, they note that "a spiral of silence only holds sway over a society for a limited period of time" (p. 350). So, there are both short- and long-term components to public opinion. For instance, the public's opinion on legalizing marijuana has changed dramatically over the years. Suppose, in 1969, we were asked to answer the question: Should marijuana use be legalized? At that time, per the Gallup poll, only about 12 percent of respondents would have answered affirmingly. Today, that Gallup poll shows that almost 60 percent of respondents support legalizing marijuana use (http://www.gallup.com/poll/186260

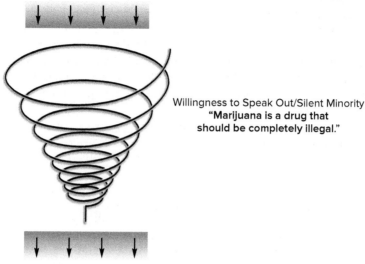

Majority View [as reported by the media]
"People should be able to smoke pot for medicinal reasons."

Willingness to Speak Out/Silent Minority
**"Marijuana is a drug that
should be completely illegal."**

[but because of a fear of isolation...many remain silent]
**"I don't want to be perceived as without
compassion for the sick and suffering."**

**Figure 22.1
The Spiral of
Silence: Medicinal
Marijuana**

/back-legal-marijuana.aspx). Think about the dynamics related to the changes in response to the question. Two reasons for changing public opinion seem reasonable. First, an increase in support is likely due to the belief that medical marijuana use can have lasting benefits for sick patients. Second, this upward trend in support may also be due to the fact that crime rates are down considerably since the 1960s, prompting some people to think that criminalizing usage is a waste of time. These and other reasons help to explain the dynamism surrounding public opinion (look at Figure 22.1 for an illustration of this topic as it relates to the theory).

Essentially, **public opinion** refers to the collective sentiments of a population on a particular subject. Most often, the media determine what subjects will be of interest to people, and the media often make a subject controversial. For example, the drug Viagra, used to treat impotence, was considered a medical marvel until the media discovered that many health plans covered this drug but did not cover female contraceptives. Many media outlets subsequently reported that this was an overtly sexist practice.

Noelle-Neumann (1991) notes that public opinion may be influenced by who approves or disapproves of our views. In 2011, for instance, President Obama instructed the Department of Justice not to defend the Defense of Marriage Act, a law, at the time, that prohibited same-sex partners to marry. Your opinion on whether you support this congressional action will likely be shaped by spokespeople on both sides of the issue as well as by friends and family members. A spiral of silence is the response to the shifting opinions of others.

SPIRAL OF SILENCE THEORY

Assumptions of Spiral of Silence Theory

With public opinion as our backdrop to the theory, we now explore three assumptions of the Spiral of Silence Theory. Noelle-Neumann (1991, 1993) has previously addressed these assertions:

- Society threatens deviant individuals with isolation; fear of isolation is pervasive.
- This fear of isolation causes individuals to try to assess the climate of opinion at all times.
- Public behavior is affected by public opinion assessment.

The first assumption asserts that society holds power over those who do not conform through threat of isolation. Noelle-Neumann believes that the very essence of our society depends on people commonly recognizing and endorsing a set of values. And it's public opinion that determines whether these values have equal conviction across the populations. When people agree on a common set of values, then their fear of isolation decreases. When there is a difference in values, fear of isolation sets in.

Like many theorists, Noelle-Neumann is concerned with the testability of this assumption. After all, she notes, are members of a society really threatened with isolation? How could this be? She believes that simple polling could not tap this area (e.g., How much do you fear isolation?). Questions such as these ask respondents to think too abstractly, because it's likely that few respondents have ever thought about isolation.

Noelle-Neumann employs the research values of Solomon Asch (1951), a social psychologist in the 1950s. Asch conducted the following laboratory experiment more than 50 times with 8–10 research subjects:

Which of the following lines on the right is equal to the line on the left?

_____   1. _____

                     2. _____

                     3. _____

You are probably quick to say that line 3 is equal to the line provided in the question. The group of research subjects, however, disagreed. After going around the room, the experimenter's assistants (who were in on the experiment) all named line 1 as the one that was equal to the line on the left. The unsuspecting subjects began to name line 1 as the correct response. In fact, Asch discovered that several times around, the unsuspecting subjects named the incorrect response. Asch believed that individuals frequently feel great pressure to agree with others, even though the others are incorrect. Borrowing from the theory, there is a very real fear of isolation.

Elizabeth Blakeslee (2005) of the *New York Times* notes that Asch's research conclusions on social conformity still exist today. She reports on the implications of following a group in many areas of society, including jury decisions and elections. She notes that "the unpleasantness of standing alone can make a majority opinion seem more appealing than sticking to one's own beliefs" (p. D3). Others agree that particularly in the United States, there may be more conformity than people either perceive or believe (Fischer, 2010).

Responding to primary criticisms of the Asch studies—that people did not have a real fear of isolation but rather a lack of confidence in their own judgment—Noelle-Neumann engaged in a more realistic threat-of-isolation test. She believed that requiring subjects to assess a moral or aesthetic conviction was more realistic than any laboratory experiments conducted by Asch. In fact, Noelle-Neumann felt that there had to be "topical controversy" on a "morally charged" topic that prompted people to be involved (Eilders & Porten-Chee, 2015) in order for a spiral of silence to be present. Indeed, these moral issues should be contemporary (in the public spotlight) and issues on which the public is divided. Think about same-sex marriage, abortion rights, human cloning, and other topics on which divergent points of view exist.

For Noelle-Neumann, freedom to smoke was (and continues to be) an issue "in the spotlight." During interviews with smokers, she showed them a picture with a person angrily saying, "It seems to me that smokers are terribly inconsiderate. They force others to inhale their health-endangering smoke." Respondents were asked to phrase responses to the statement. The results indicated that in the presence of non-smokers, many smokers were less willing to support smokers' rights overtly.

The second assumption of the theory identifies people as constant assessors of the climate of public opinion. Noelle-Neumann contends that individuals receive information about public opinion from two sources: personal observation and the media. First, let's discuss how people are able to personally observe public opinion and then examine the role of the media.

Noelle-Neumann (1991) states that people engage in a quasi-statistical ability to appraise public opinion. A **quasi-statistical sense** means that people are able to estimate the strength of opposing sides in a public debate. They are able to do this by listening to the views of others and incorporating that knowledge into their own viewpoints. For instance, Carol Johansen's quasi-statistical sense makes her believe that she is the only person at her breakfast table who opposes spanking. She can see that she is vastly outnumbered on the topic and therefore is able to assess the local public opinion on the subject. Noelle-Neumann calls this a quasi-statistical frequency "organ" in that she believes that people like Carol are able to numerically estimate where others fall on the topic. The theorist states that this organ is on "high alert" during periods of instability. So our quasi-statistical sense works overtime

quasi-statistical sense
personal estimation of the strength of opposing sides on a public issue

when we see that our opinions on a subject are different from those of the majority around us. This sense is, as a rule, an unconscious process.

Personal observations of public opinion can often be distorted and inaccurate. Noelle-Neumann (1993) calls the mistaken observations about how most people feel **pluralistic ignorance**. She notes that people "mix their own direct perceptions and the perceptions filtered through the eyes of the media into an indivisible whole that seems to derive from their own thoughts and experiences" (p. 169). Consider Carol's assessment of the opinions on spanking. With the vast majority of people around her supporting this type of discipline, she may believe that she is clearly in the minority. One or both sides in the debate, however, can overestimate their ability to estimate opinion. Especially with such lopsided support on a topic (as with the group at the senior center), Noelle-Neumann believes that people can become disillusioned.

People not only employ their personal observations of public opinion, but as we've argued earlier in this chapter and in others, but also rely on the media. Yet, Noelle-Neumann insists that the media's effects are frequently indirect. Because people are inherently social in nature, they talk about their observations to others. And, people seek out the media to confirm or disconfirm their observations and then interpret their own observations through the media. This can be illustrated through Carol's future behaviors. First, if she returns home from the senior center and reveals her beliefs on spanking to others, she may encounter several neighbors who share her opinion. Next, if she watches the evening news and learns that the majority of the country oppose spanking, this will likely resonate deeply with her. She will also be affected by any media reports that disproportionately publicize opposition to spanking. Finally, later discussions that Carol might have on the subject may invoke the media. She may tell others that even the blogs she read online tend to support her point of view.

The final assumption of the theory is that the public's behavior is influenced by evaluations of public opinion. Noelle-Neumann (1991) proposes that public behavior takes the form of either speaking out on a subject or keeping silent. If individuals sense support for a topic, then they are likely to communicate about it; if they feel that others do not support a topic, then they maintain silence. She continues, "The strength of one camp's signals, or the weakness of the other's, is the driving force setting the spiral in motion" (p. 271). In sum, people seem to act according to how other people feel.

Noelle-Neumann believes that human beings have an aversion to discussing topics that do not have the support of the majority. To test this assumption, consider interviewing people on your campus about a controversial issue such as physician-assisted suicide. If straw polls in your campus newspaper show that almost 70 percent of the campus opposes this, then according to the theory, students, faculty, and staff may be less inclined to speak out in favor of the practice. A willingness to speak out may have more to do with one's convictions and an assessment of overall trends in society. That is, if there is a liberal climate on your campus, there may be more willingness to speak out; if a conservative climate exists, people may feel less inclined to offer their opposition.

These three assumptions are important to consider as we further delineate Noelle-Neumann's theory. In Figure 22.1, we illustrate several concepts and themes emerging from the theory's assumptions.

pluralistic ignorance
mistaken observation of how most people feel

Personal opinions, a fear of being alone in those opinions, and public sentiment lay the groundwork for discussing the remainder of the theory. Each of these areas is influenced by a powerful part of U.S. society: the media. Let's now overview the powerful influence of the media in the Spiral of Silence Theory.

The Media's Influence

As we have discussed, the Spiral of Silence Theory rests on public opinion. Noelle-Neumann (1993) cautions, however, that "much of the population adjusts its attitudes to the tenor of the media" (p. 272). Nancy Eckstein and Paul Turman (2002) agree. They claim that "the media may provide the force behind the spiral of silence because it is considered a one-sided conversation, an indirect public form of communication where people feel helpless to respond" (p. 173). Further, as Francis Delisay (2012) concludes, "[M]edia can influence the public's perceptions of opinion climates" (p. 485). Finally, some authors boldly state that "media essentially tell the public which key policy issues to think about and to some degree how they should form opinions about those issues" (Spencer, Croucher, & McKee, 2011, p. 28).

A willingness to speak out depends greatly on the media. Without support from others for divergent views, people will remain consonant with the views offered in the media. In fact, Noelle-Neumann (1993) believes that the media even provide sometimes biased words and phrases so people can confidently speak about a subject. And, if certain words or phrases are favored by the media, then many people will fall silent (Consider the difference, for instance, if the media used "abuse" rather than the word "spanking.") The extent to which Carol Johansen in our chapter-opening scenario will offer her views about spanking, then, will likely rest on what position the various media have taken on the subject. And, although many of us rely on the Internet, George Gerbner (Cultivation Analysis, Chapter 24) reminds us that television is the most influential of all media forms.

In explaining why the media have such influence, Noelle-Neumann believes that the public is not offered a broad and balanced interpretation of news events. Consequently, the public is given a limited view of reality. This restrictive approach to covering cultural events and activities narrows an individual's perception. Certainly, many audiences are active and critical and not all will be so passive in believing everything the media say. Yet, as W. James Potter (2016) acknowledges, most people in the United States seek out media that are aligned with their values and practices. Inevitably, Potter concludes, many suffer from media and information literacy.

Consider the theorist's three characteristics of the news media: ubiquity, cumulativeness, and consonance. **Ubiquity** refers to the fact that the media are pervasive sources of information. Because media are everywhere, they are relied on when people seek out information. The morning television news, the Internet, the office gossip, and so forth, all point to the media's ubiquity. Nick, a member of Carol Johansen's morning group, is quick to talk about the recent surveys done in the state about perceptions of spanking. He has the source immediately at hand. Even Carol recalls a television program as she thinks about spanking.

The **cumulativeness** of the media refers to the process of the media repeating themselves across programs and across time. Frequently, you will read a story in the

ubiquity
the belief that media are everywhere

cumulativeness
the belief that media repeat themselves

morning newspaper, listen to the same story on the radio as you drive to work, and then watch the story on the evening news. You may also pull up a website during the day and find the story there. Noelle-Neumann calls this a "reciprocal influence in building up frames of reference" (1993, p. 71). It can become problematic when the original source is left unquestioned, and yet, four media (newspaper, radio, television, and the Internet) rely on that source. The theory suggests that conformity of voice influences what information gets released to the public to help them develop an opinion.

consonance
the belief that all media are similar in attitudes, beliefs, and values

Finally, **consonance** pertains to the similarities of beliefs, attitudes, and values held by the media. In fact, events or news items are frequently shared by multiple news agencies (e.g., the Associated Press, etc.). Noelle-Neumann states that consonance is produced from a tendency for newspeople to confirm their own thoughts and opinions, making it look as if those opinions were emanating from the public.

Each of these three qualities—ubiquity, cumulativeness, consonance—allows for majority opinions to be heard. Those wishing to avoid isolation will usually remain silent.

It is not surprising that the media are influential in public opinion. Many surveys have demonstrated that people consider the media to have too much power in U.S. society. In fact, 66 percent of the U.S. population believes that the media have too much influence and political clout (http://www.rasmussenreports.com/public_content /politics/general_politics/february_2016/voters_say_money_media_have_too_much _political_clout). Consider also that information is frequently filtered through news reporters and their agencies. As a result, what is presented—or in the case of this theory, what is perceived—may not be an accurate picture of reality. Imagine, for

---

Theory in Popular Press • Russian Internet Usage and the Spiral of Silence

A bill in the Russian parliament passed in 2012 that effectively shut down popular websites in the country. Author David Herszenhorn of the *International Herald Tribune*, writes that because of the government's steps to shut down popular Internet sites like Wikipedia, there will be unexpected repercussions from across the globe. Herszenhorn identifies a journalism professor at Moscow State University who stated, "[T]he Internet is the only thing that stands between Russia and the Spiral of Silence." The author argues that the efforts to shut down various web content is an effort to repress free speech and protest, thereby making it difficult for those "at the end of the spiral" to speak up. Fearing isolation, Herszenhorn notes, people will likely silence their own (political) views. While some protection was needed to protect children from unsavory Internet content, Herszenhorn quotes the professor who believes that the Internet "has given life to political discourse in a very free and independent way."

Source: Herszenhorn, D. (2012, July 12). In Russia, critics decry law to limit web content. *International Herald Tribune*, p. 13.

instance, the frustration of many unemployed disabled individuals as they read or listen to reports about the success of the Americans with Disabilities Act. Or, maybe you have watched stories about the many people who have been forced off of welfare, but you probably haven't seen many stories describing the dire circumstances of many families as a result of funding cuts. And, although there have been news reports on employers hiring military veterans, this is hardly helpful to the many vets still looking for long-term employment. If the media report these "success" stories often enough, Noelle-Neumann says they are identifying what should be noticed, deciding what questions should be asked, and determining whether various social policies and programs are effective, a point we noted earlier. In other words, people experience the climate of public opinion through the mass media.

As you can see, then, when people look to media for a glimpse into the perceptions and beliefs of the population, they are likely to receive anything but an impartial representation. **Dual climates of opinion** often exist—that is, a climate that the population perceives directly and the climate the media report. For instance, Carol Johansen may compare her personal perceptions of spanking with those surveyed perceptions published in the newspaper. What is remarkable is that despite the differences in opinion, many people decide to remain silent. To understand what motivates people to speak out, Noelle-Neumann developed the train test.

dual climates of opinion
difference between the population's perception of a public issue and the way the media report on the issue

The Train Test

For Spiral of Silence theorists, examining whether or not people will speak out requires a methodology that is clear, testable, representative, and replicable. To support her claims, Noelle-Neumann conceptualized the train test (or plane or bus as well). The **train test** is an assessment of the extent to which people will speak out with their own opinion. According to the Spiral of Silence Theory, people on two different sides of an issue will vary in their willingness to express views in public. To study this, the researchers gave respondents sketches showing two people in conversation. The researcher asked a respondent, "Which of the two would you agree with, Person A or Person B?" This question would then be followed up with a more pivotal question; for example, one that might test opinions pertaining to food safety. Essentially, the train test asks people a question such as the following:

train test
an experiment used to assess the extent to which people will speak out

> Suppose that you have a five-hour train ride ahead of you and a person sits next to you and starts to discuss the problems of food safety. Would you talk or not talk about the topic to the person?

This question was repeated several times with various subjects. It focused on a number of topics, ranging from nuclear power plants to abortion to racial segregation. The test revealed a number of factors that help determine whether a person will voice an opinion. They include the following:

- Supporters of a dominant opinion are more willing to voice an opinion than those in the minority opinion.
- Because of a fear of isolation, people tend to refrain from publicly stating their position if they perceive that this perception will attract laughter, mockery, or similar threats of isolation.

- There are various ways of speaking out—for example, hanging posters, displaying bumper stickers, and distributing flyers.
- Men (ages 45–59) from large cities are more likely to speak out.
- People are more likely to voice an opinion if it agrees with their own convictions as well as fits within current trends and the spirit of the era.
- People will voice an opinion if it aligns with societal views.
- People tend to share their opinions with those who agree with them more than with those who disagree.
- People draw the strength of their convictions from a variety of sources, including family, friends, and acquaintances.

last-minute swing
jumping on the bandwagon of popular opinion after opinions have been expressed

- People may engage in **last-minute swing**, or jumping on the bandwagon of the popular opinion during the final moments of conversation.

The train test proved to be an interesting approach to studying public opinion. The method simulates public behavior when two schools of thought exist on a subject. For those who are willing to speak out, there are opportunities to sway others. And there are times when the minority opinion speaks out loudly. We now examine this group.

The Hard Core

hard core
group(s) at the end of the spiral willing to speak out at any cost

Every now and then, the silent minority rises up. This group, called the **hard core,** "remains at the end of a spiral of silence process in defiance of the threats of isolation" (Noelle-Neumann, 1993, p. 170). The hard core represents a group of individuals who know that there is a price to pay for their assertiveness. They try to buck the dominant way of thinking and are prepared to directly confront anyone who gets in their way or who refuses to allow their voices to be heard (Figure 22.2).

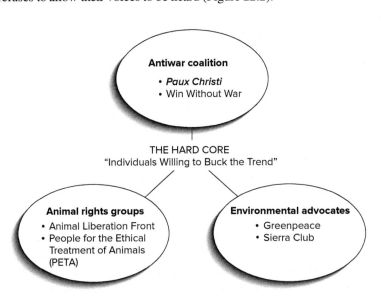

Figure 22.2
Examples of the "Hard Core" in the United States

Noelle-Neumann invokes the work of social psychologist Gary Shulman in attempting to understand the hard core better. Shulman argues that if the majority opinion becomes large enough, the majority voice becomes less powerful because no alternative opinions exist. Several years ago, for example, when AIDS first appeared in the United States, it was common for many to believe that those diagnosed with the disease should be quarantined (majority opinion). It didn't take long, however, for people's opinions to reject this narrow-minded view, primarily as a result of the hard core's efforts to educate the public. In fact, ironically, the media were pressed into educating the public about AIDS. It was not long before this silent hard core discovered that others had adopted their view. In this situation, the hard core was instrumental in changing public opinion, although it is true that the hard core frequently engaged in both rational and irrational acts to make its point.

For further evidence of the hard core, let's discuss an example pertaining to religion and religious opinion. Although we realize that not all people believe in God, God pervades our intellectual, political, and popular culture (people say "God Bless you" when others sneeze, we have "In God We Trust" on our dollar bills, politicians end their speeches with "God Bless America," and etc.).

Despite pervasive references to God, many people do not believe in God. Some of these individuals contend that the country's Constitution requires a separation between church and state, and therefore any religious references in tax-supported venues should be eliminated. However, this opinion may not be shared by the majority because over half of the country affiliates with an organized religion (Lindner, 2012). Whether the media report on visits by the Pope, present video clips of politicians leaving religious services each week, or solicit quotes for news stories from the clergy, they continue to imply that religion is an integral part of people's lives.

The minority—civil libertarians who advocate extracting religion from public-supported activities—have been vocal regarding their opinions; these hard-core dissenters have not blended into the background. For instance, over the past several years, atheist families, in particular, have sued in courts either to remove "under God" or to allow young children to abstain from the recitation. Although courts have almost always dismissed such cases, they have brought this issue to the forefront of cultural discourse. The hard core might also claim victory as they witness cities removing religious icons (nativity sets, crucifixes, etc.) from city parks during holidays. And, interestingly, with media outlets covering such legal victories, the hard core may be reconfiguring majority opinion.

If we think about more contemporary examples of the hard core, three groups seem particularly relevant: the Tea Party, Occupy Wall Street, and Black Lives Matter—all movements that were influential at some point from 2011 to 2017. These groups decided to defy expectations and cast themselves in unique, innovative, and controversial ways. The Tea Party—an offshoot of the Republican Party—worked aggressively to ensure that politicians they supported were aligned with their conservative values and practices. Occupy Wall Street, a protest movement that addressed social and economic inequality, greed, and corruption, advocated on behalf of the "99 percent," or the people they claimed were paying for the errors of those in power—the 1 percent. And Black Lives Matter, a social activist group fighting for equality, peace, and justice for all Blacks and a group dedicated to promoting the dignity and integrity of Black people everywhere. All three groups—despite having very diverse missions—clearly championed their goals and causes in the media and, despite not representing the majority of the population, the three received great media attention and continued to do so in various ways.

The Spiral of Silence and Social Media

As we alluded to earlier in the chapter, the Spiral of Silence Theory had its infancy during a time when social media did not exist. Yet, over the years, a number of researchers have employed the theory into their studies on social media. We present three of the many findings to demonstrate the new ways of thinking about the theory.

A study looking at online social capital was undertaken by Kim. She investigated social capital, or the sum of an individual's network of social connections, resources, and support, and the willingness of social network participants to speak out on an issue.

Bartel Sheehan (2015; http://uncommonculture.org/ojs/index.php/fm/article /view/5414/4468) examined three different "hot topics": immigration, a national gas tax, and an invasion of North Korea by the South. She found that online social capital did influence a willingness to speak up. In particular, it was discovered that on sites such as Facebook and Twitter, speaking up was related to "bridging" social capital. That is, people were most comfortable speaking up on these topics when they felt a connection with others who held similar views and values.

In addition to Bartel Sheehan's research, others have examined the theory within a cultural context. For example, Ali Dashti, Hamed Al-Abdullah, and Hasan Johar (2015) explored online political participation of Kuwaiti women. Up until 2006, Kuwaiti women were the only female population in the Arab states who were not afforded full political rights, including the right to run for office and vote. Technology—particularly Twitter—was instrumental as women (and others) began to express their views and talk about their political activities. This study was motivated out of this backdrop.

Dashti et al. (2015) hypothesized that while women may not be willing to share their views face to face, social networks such as Twitter facilitated these sorts of views. Their study was conducted with 323 female students in media and political science courses. The researchers discovered that gender and who a woman/participant knows influenced the willingness to talk about an issue. With men that women do not know, the women/participants acted according to the basic premises of the theory (e.g., silent when dominant voices were present). However, when these women/participants interacted with women they did not know, the women/participants had little problem challenging the majority. When discussing matters related to local political issues, there were no differences in those speaking face to face or via Twitter. The research team concluded that Twitter is one way to ease the obstacles that women often experience while discussing politics because the fear of isolation is reduced.

A third study is quite pioneering in nature and reflects a more modern approach to Noelle-Neumann's "train test" we discussed earlier in the chapter. Looking at the Edward Snowden's 2013 "revelations of widespread government surveillance of Americans' phone and email records, a team of writers" (Hampton, Rainie, Lu, Dwyer, Shin, & Purcell, 2014) at the Pew Research Center, surveyed over 1,800 adults about several issues related to the National Security Agency (NSA). They specifically were interested in their opinions about the leaks, their willingness to speak out both in face to face and online settings, and their perceptions of the different opinions of the topic.

Like Noelle-Neumann, several conclusions were drawn from this "test." Overall, the Pew Research team concluded, if people felt that their social media friends and followers disagreed with their opinions, they were less likely to state their views in public gatherings (e.g., restaurant, etc.). In addition, five additional conclusions were made from the survey:

1. People were less likely to discuss the Snowden/NSA story via social media than in person.

2. Social media did not provide an alternative discussion platform for those who were not willing to discuss the Snowden/NSA story.

3. In both personal settings and online settings, people were more willing to share their views if they thought their audience agreed with them.

4. Previous theoretical findings as to people's willingness to speak up in various settings also applies to social media users.

5. Facebook and Twitter users were less likely to share their opinions in many face-to-face settings.

Contributing to the theory's evolution, Hampton et al. (2014) identified three influential factors related to speaking out: a confidence in how much they knew, an intensity of their opinions, and the extent of their interest.

The previous three studies are just a handful of the current surplus of new research using the Spiral of Silence Theory. As more social media platforms come and go, the theory will have ongoing modifications.

Integration, Critique, and Closing

The Spiral of Silence Theory is one of the few theories in communication that focuses on public opinion. Indeed, the theory has been identified as an important foundation for examining the human condition (Csikszentmihalyi, 1991) and it has deep roots in quantitative methods. Noelle-Neumann, as a scholar, is credited for introducing survey research in Germany and co-founded the *International Journal of Public Opinion Research* (Petersen, 2012). To evaluate the theory, we draw attention to two areas: logical consistency and heurism.

Integration

Communication Tradition	Rhetorical	Semiotic	Phenomenological	**Cybernetic**	**Socio-Psychological**	Socio-Cultural	Critical

Communication Context	Intrapersonal	Interpersonal	Small Group	Organizational	Public/Rhetorical	**Mass/Media**	Cultural

Approach to Knowing	**Positivistic/Empirical**	Interpretive/Hermeneutic	Critical

Critique

Evaluation Criteria	Scope	**Logical Consistency**	Parsimony	Utility	Testability	**Heurism**	Test of Time

Logical Consistency

Noelle-Neumann's theory has not avoided substantial criticism. And much of that criticism pertains to the lack of logical consistency in several of the terms and concepts. Charles Salmon and F. Gerald Kline (1985) state that the Spiral of Silence fails to acknowledge a person's ego involvement in an issue. At times, people may be willing to speak because their ego is involved in the topic (e.g., if a promotion at work depends on assertiveness). Carroll Glynn, Andrew Hayes, and James Shanahan (1997) raise the issue of various selectivity processes, such as cognitive dissonance, which we explored in Chapter 6. Individuals will avoid a topic that conflicts with their own views.

Carroll Glynn and Jack McLeod (1985) note two additional shortcomings pertaining to the logical consistency of the theory. First, they believe that the fear of isolation may not motivate people to express their opinions. They claim that Noelle-Neumann did not empirically test her belief that fear of isolation prompts people to speak out. Yet, some scholars have found a direct relationship between fear of isolation and an examination of opinion climates and opinion expression (Kim, 2012). Second, Glynn and McLeod were troubled by how the theory was developed, and relied extensively upon, West Germany media. They doubt whether the characteristics of the media then and there (ubiquitous, cumulative, and consonant) apply to the media in the United States today.

Noelle-Neumann has responded to several of her critics, notably in defending her emphasis on the media. She remains convinced that the media is instrumental in public opinion. She writes that "by using words and arguments taken from the media to discuss a topic, people cause the point of view to be heard in public and give it visibility, thus creating a situation in which the danger of isolation is reduced" (Noelle-Neumann, 1985, p. 80). She continues by noting that not once did the spiral of silence process contradict the media's position on a topic (Noelle-Neumann, 1993). In terms of application across cultures, Noelle-Neumann agrees that any theory of public opinion must have cross-cultural applicability. However, she posits, it is important to note that most U.S. researchers desire a rational explanation for human behavior, but not all behavior can be explained sensibly.

Still, she does accept that the train test may be limited in cross-cultural adaptation. As a result, Noelle-Neumann updated the version to read:

> Assume you are on a five-hour bus trip, and the bus makes a rest stop and everyone gets out for a long break. In a group of passengers, someone starts talking about whether we should support [insert topic] or not. Would you like to talk to this person, to get to know his or her point of view better, or would you prefer not to? (p. 217)

Of course, you may doubt whether simply changing a train test to a bus test broadens the cross-cultural application of the theory.

Student Voices

Marco

I can think of myself sometimes as that person at the "end of the spiral." I was one of the students on campus that had a sit-in at my congressperson's office because he supported the Afghanistan war. I was told I wasn't a patriot and was told that I should "get a job" and not spend time wasting the time of others. I still decided to make my voice heard and I know it wasn't popular because we are "supposed" to support our troops. Well, I DID support the troops: I wanted them to come home so they could live and be with their families.

Heurism

The theory has attracted writers and scholars who have discussed its merits in a variety of ways. First, some writers (Simpson, 1996) have attempted to discredit the theory because of its lack of application beyond one culture; other scholars, however, have supported the cross-cultural application of the theory (Kim, 2012). This sort of scholarly dialogue enhances the heuristic appeal of the theory. Perhaps Donald Shaw (2014), while reviewing the corpus of research using the Spiral of Silence Theory, said it most succinctly: "her theories have taken hold worldwide" (p. 841).

Researchers have employed the theory and many of its central concepts in their studies, including the following topics: a declaration to make English the official language of the United States (Lin & Salwen, 1997), religion in the classroom (Eckstein & Turman, 2002), Twitter usage and speaking out (Miyata, Yamamoto, & Ogawa, 2015), college student sexual values (Chia & Lee, 2008), online surveillance and willingness to voice opinions (Stoycheff, 2016), and the theory's influence upon Facebook views of immigration, same-sex marriage, and abortion (Gearhart & Zhang, 2015). Further, a compendium of essays that examine Spiral of Silence Theory—over 50 years after its inception—has been published (Donsbach, 2013), suggesting further heuristic opportunities. Clearly, in the eyes of many, this theory is worth studying.

Closing

The Spiral of Silence will continue to generate discussion among media scholars. The theory has sustained considerable criticism, and with a central emphasis on political discussion, researchers will continue to assess the theory's vitality. Still, "but there is certainly accordance, even among the most ferocious critics of this theory, that it has been one of the most influential of all theories developed in communication research and political communication over the last half century" (Donsbach, Tsfati, & Salmon, 2014, p. 1).

Whether people openly express majority or minority viewpoints on an issue may not be directly proportional to the media's involvement on the issue, but it is clear that the public has come to rely on the media in global society. The theory, therefore, will likely have lasting effects that have not yet been imagined.

Discussion Starters

TECH QUEST: The Spiral of Silence Theory contends that people will frequently remain silent on controversial issues. Think about Throwback Thursday on Facebook. What would you say (if anything) if you saw pictures from a friend which were offensive, but which were taken more than 15 years ago?

1. Carol Johansen feels embarrassed about offering her opinions to a group that does not share her beliefs. Consider a similar time in your life. Did you speak out, or did you decide to remain quiet? What motivated your decision?

2. Discuss the times that you have been part of the hard-core minority. How did you behave? How did your confidence and self-esteem influence your behavior?

3. Does it make a difference to you to learn that Noelle-Neumann was once a newspaper journalist for Nazi publications? Why or why not?

4. Do you believe that given all the different mediated sources available today, the U.S. media are ubiquitous, consonant, or cumulative? Exemplify your responses.

5. Noelle-Neumann believes that the media help to influence minority views. Based on your observations of the media over the past several years, do you agree or disagree with this claim? What examples can you provide to defend your position?

6. Comment on the influence of the Internet on public opinion.

7. What do you suppose influences the "last-minute swings" of people?

CHAPTER 23

Uses and Gratifications Theory

*Based on the research of **Elihu Katz, Jay G. Blumler,** and **Michael Gurevitch***

> *Books and cinema have been found to cater to needs concerned with self-fulfillment and self-gratification: they help to connect individuals to themselves. Newspapers, radio, and television all seem to connect individuals to society.*
>
> —Elihu Katz, Jay G. Blumler, and Michael Gurevitch

Ryan Grant

It was a dreary Friday night and 20-year-old Ryan Grant was trying to figure out what he wanted to do. He worked for his father part time in his hardware store, and without question, this had been a rough week. He had to put in a lot of extra hours because they were doing inventory and his dad needed him to help catalog the merchandise. This morning he took an exam in his communication class at the university. Because he hadn't studied last week, Ryan crammed until 2 A.M. Now it was Friday, and time to escape both work and school.

Ryan felt exhausted and burned out. He wanted to be with others, but he knew he wouldn't be the best company. He considered two choices: He could stay home and watch television, either with friends or alone, or he could try to get a group of friends together to go to the movies. It could be good to go out with people who would help him loosen up. But, he could also see being at home, and not exerting so much energy.

Ryan was faced with two opposing arguments. Here was the argument for watching television: First, he wouldn't have to spend anything. He could dress and look how he wanted, and he could watch what he wanted when he wanted. There were a couple of shows on Fridays that Ryan liked.

At home, he could also command the best seat in the house. If he wanted to, he could invite over friends, making the night more social.

But, the argument for going out to the movies seemed just as strong. He could see that new action/adventure movie he'd been waiting to see. Also, because Ryan was a "techie" who appreciated all technology, the movie theater's excellent THX system and huge screen was far better than what he had at home. Finally, he could easily have fun going out. Although he had never really thought about it too seriously, he enjoyed sitting with his friends in the dark, sharing the same experience, and he loved movie popcorn!

Still, he was torn, so Ryan weighed the positives and negatives of each medium. If he chose television, he would have to deal with watching on a small screen. Also, if he did have friends over, he might have to endure fighting over what to watch. On the other hand, he could turn off the television if nothing good was on and simply hang out with his friends. The arguments for and against going to the movies seemed equivalent. On the plus side, he knew that watching a movie was a great escape from his real life, and he would be able to talk about the movie on Monday with his friends. But, it was also true that he'd have to drive to the multiplex and try to find a parking space. He also might have to stand in a long line, which he hated. To top it off, he would have to pay close to $15 for the movie ticket and popcorn. Ryan's decision about what to do came down to a simple question: What does a movie offer versus what television offers? As Ryan considered this question, a third alternative occurred to him: going to bed early.

■

R yan is doing what we all do when dealing with the mass media: he is thinking about different media and making choices. Consider how many times you have found yourself in a situation similar to Ryan's. You may have decided that you needed some relaxation and thought about all the options before making up your mind. The process may not have taken very long, but it was a process that required thinking about what was available.

In the early days of mass media (the era of the penny newspaper, radio, and silent movies), **Mass Society Theory**—the idea that average people are helpless victims of powerful mass media—defined the relationship between audiences and the media they consumed (see our discussion of the Spiral of Silence Theory in Chapter 22). This notion was eventually discredited, in large part because social science—and simple observation—could not confirm the notion of all-powerful media and media messages. Not only were most people not directly affected by media messages, but when they were influenced, they were not all influenced in exactly the same way.

In time, Mass Society Theory was replaced by what we now call the **limited effects** theories (recall that we introduced this notion of limited effects in Chapter 21). Limited effects theories conceptualize media influence as limited or minimized by some aspects of individual audience members' personal or social lives. Two approaches to the limited effects orientation have been identified. First, the **Individual Differences Perspective** sees media's power as shaped by personal factors such as intelligence and self-esteem. For example, smart people and more secure people are better able to resist unwanted media impact. A second limited effects approach, the **Social Categories Model,** views media's power as limited by audience members' associations and group affiliations. For example, Republicans tend to spend time with other Republicans, who help them interpret media messages in a consistent, Republican-friendly manner. This effectively limits any influence media messages alone might have.

You may have noticed that neither of these views affords audience members much credibility. The first (Mass Society) suggests that people simply are not smart or strong enough to protect themselves against unwanted media effects. The second (limited effects) suggests that most people have relatively little personal choice in interpreting the meaning of the messages they consume and in determining the level of impact those messages will have on them. Eventually, in response to these unflattering views of typical audience members, theorists Elihu Katz, Jay G. Blumler, and Michael Gurevitch (1974) presented a systematic and comprehensive articulation of audience members' role in the mass communication process. Their thinking was formalized as Uses and Gratifications Theory (UGT). While it is still a limited effects model, researchers working in Uses and Gratifications believe its value lies in its ability to clarify how effects can and do happen. Further, Marianne Dainton and

Mass Society Theory
the idea that average people are the victims of the powerful forces of mass media

limited effects
the perspective replacing Mass Society Theory; holds that media effects are limited by aspects of the audience's personal and social lives

Individual Differences Perspective
a specific approach to the idea of limited effects; concentrates on the limits posed by personal characteristics

Social Categories Model
a specific approach to the idea of limited effects; concentrates on the limits posed by group membership

USES AND GRATIFICATIONS THEORY

Alexandra Stokes (2015) note that although the theory was initially proposed to study one-way media (think about the linear model we explained in Chapter 1), it is now being investigated with newer forms of media.

Further, while granting the media some effects, the theory gives the audience more credibility and holds that people actively seek out specific media and specific content to generate specific gratifications (or results). Theorists in Uses and Gratifications view people as active because they are able to examine and evaluate various types of media to accomplish communication goals. As we saw in our opening, Ryan not only identified the specific media that he was willing to consider, but was also able to determine for himself the uses he could and would make of each, and the personal values of those uses. Researchers in Uses and Gratifications Theory ask the following question: What do consumers do with the media?

Assumptions of Uses and Gratifications Theory

Uses and Gratifications Theory provides a framework for understanding when and how individual media consumers become more or less active and the consequences of that increased or decreased involvement. Many of the assumptions of UGT were clearly articulated by the founders of the approach (Katz et al., 1974). They contend that there are five basic assumptions of Uses and Gratifications Theory:

- The audience is active and its media use is goal oriented.
- The initiative in linking need gratification to a specific medium choice rests with the audience member.
- The media compete with other sources for need satisfaction.
- People have enough self-awareness of their media use, interests, and motives to be able to provide researchers with an accurate picture of that use.
- Value judgments of media content can only be assessed by the audience.

The theory's first assumption, about an active audience and goal-oriented media use, is fairly straightforward. Individual audience members can bring different levels of activity to their use of media. Audience members are also driven to accomplish goals via the media. What is not so straightforward, however, is that the term, audience, can resonate in different ways. Sonia Livingston (2015), for instance, notes: "although the notion of audience remains the most commonly accepted collective term for people's relations (now pluralized) to the media in all their forms, this does not bring consensus" (p. 132). That is, an authentic interpretation of the audience may be fraught with challenges because an audience member may be a reader, viewer, watcher, or listener, each with various responsibilities and engagement levels.

Denis McQuail and his colleagues (1972) identify several ways of classifying audience needs and gratifications. They include **diversion,** which is defined as escaping from routines or daily problems; **personal relationships,** which occurs when people substitute the media for companionship; **personal identity**, or ways to reinforce an individual's values; and **surveillance,** or information about how media will help an

diversion
a category of gratifications coming from media use; involves escaping from routines and problems

personal relationships
a category of gratifications coming from media use; involves substituting media for companionship

personal identity
a category of gratifications coming from media use; involves ways to reinforce individual values

surveillance
a category of gratifications coming from media use; involves collecting needed information

USES AND GRATIFICATIONS THEORY

Table 23.1 Needs Gratified by the Media

NEED TYPE	DESCRIPTION	MEDIA EXAMPLES
Cognitive	Acquiring information, knowledge, comprehension	Television (news), video ("How to Install Ceramic Tile"), movies (documentaries or films based on history, e.g., *Stonewall Uprising*)
Affective	Emotional, pleasant, or aesthetic experience	Movies, television (sitcoms)
Personal integrative	Enhancing credibility, confidence, and status	Video ("Speaking With Conviction")
Social integrative	Enhancing connections with family, friends, and so forth	Internet (email, Facebook, Instagram, Listservs)
Tension release	Escape and diversion	Television, movies, video, radio, Internet

Source: Adapted from Katz, Gurevitch, & Haas (1973). On the use of the mass media for important things. *American Sociological Review, 38,* 164–181.

individual accomplish something. In Table 23.1 we present additional categories of needs that are fulfilled by the media.

In our chapter opening, we saw Ryan choosing between two competing media: television and film. All of us have our favorite content within a given medium, and we all have reasons for selecting a particular medium. At the movies, for instance, many of us like love stories rather than historical war films; some of us prefer to be entertained at the end of a long day rather than be educated about a historical event (diversion). Although it's getting more difficult to do because of state laws, some drivers prefer to talk on their cell phones over long trips; it not only passes the time but also allows people to stay connected with their family and friends (personal relationships). Truck drivers, for example, may prefer to listen to call-in radio talk shows rather than spend their long nights driving in silence (personal identity). Finally, there are people who enjoy watching home improvement shows on cable so that they can learn how to do projects around the house (surveillance). Audience members choose among various media, then, for different gratifications.

Uses and Gratifications' second assumption links need gratification to a specific medium choice that rests with the audience member. Because people are active agents, they take initiative. We may choose shows like Ellen when we want to laugh and National Public Radio's programming when we want to be informed, but no one decides for us what we want from a given medium or piece of content. We may well choose NPR because we want to be entertained by the anchors. The implication here is that audience members have a great deal of autonomy in the mass communication process.

The third assumption—that media compete with other sources for need satisfaction—means that the media and their audiences do not exist in a vacuum. Both are part of the larger society, and the relationship between media and audiences is influenced by that society. On a first date, for example, going out to the movies is a more likely use of media than is renting a video and watching it at home. Someone who is an infrequent consumer of media—who, for example, finds more gratification in conversations with friends and family—may turn to the media with greater frequency when seeking information during a national political election.

The fourth assumption of UGT relates to a methodological issue that has to do with researchers' ability to collect reliable and accurate information from media consumers. To argue that people are aware enough of their own media use, interests, and motives to be able to provide researchers with an accurate picture of that use reaffirms the belief in an active audience; it also implies that people are cognizant of that activity. In fact, the early research in Uses and Gratifications included questioning respondents about why they consumed particular media. This qualitative approach, which we explained in Chapter 3, included interviewing respondents and directly observing their reactions during conversations about media. The thinking surrounding this data collection technique was that people are in the best position to explain what they do and why they do it. Interestingly, as the theory evolved, the methodology also changed. Researchers began to abandon their qualitative analysis in favor of more quantitative procedures. Yet, the questionnaires employed in these procedures emanated from many of the interviews and observations collected in the qualitative period.

The fifth assumption is also less about the audience than it is about those who study it. It asserts that researchers should suspend value judgments linking the audience's needs to specific media or content. Uses and Gratifications theorists argue that because it is individual audience members who decide to use certain content for certain ends, the value of media content can be assessed only by the audience. Even tacky and offensive content found in reality shows like "Duck Dynasty" may be functional if it provides gratification for the audience.

Some contemporary mass communication researchers (such as Turow, 2013) lament what they see as the negative, debasing influence of consumer product advertising on U.S. culture. The United States has become a nation of consumers: Love has been reduced to giving someone flowers; freedom now means the ability to buy a Slurpee rather than a canned soda at 7-Eleven; a "good" mother is one who packs Lunchables in her child's lunchbox. In the absence of hard evidence of the large-scale effect some critics fear, it's easier to assume that watching ads for these products—and the subsequent purchase of flowers, a Slurpee, and Lunchables—is not only an individual choice, but a harmless one. (See our discussion of the intersection of media, culture, and individuals in Chapter 25 on Cultural Studies.)

As you can see, UGT underscores an active media consumer. Considering that this overarching principle contradicts the views offered by other media theorists and other theoretical perspectives, it is important to trace the theory's development, which we do in the next section.

People are active in choosing and using particular media to satisfy specific needs. Emphasizing a limited effects position, this theory views the media as having a limited effect because users are able to exercise choice and control. People are self-aware, and they are able to understand and articulate the reasons they use media. They see media use as one way to gratify the needs they have. Uses and Gratifications Theory is primarily concerned with the following question: What do people do with media?

Stages of Uses and Gratifications Research

Unlike many of the theories we explore in this text, Uses and Gratifications theorists have investigated the use/gratification perspective in stages. The first stage of UG research (prior to the formulation of the theory itself), consisted of acknowledging that people can and do actively participate in the mass communication process. The pioneering work of Herta Herzog (1944) was instrumental in establishing this perspective. Herzog sought to classify the reasons people engage in different forms of media behavior, such as newspaper reading and radio listening. Wanting to understand why so many women were attracted to radio soap operas, Herzog interviewed dozens of soap opera fans and identified three major types of gratification. First, some people enjoyed the dramas because of the emotional release they found in listening to the problems of others. Second, listeners seemed to engage in wishful thinking—that is, they gained a vicarious satisfaction from listening to the experiences of others. Finally, some people felt that they could learn from these programs because "if you listen to these programs and something turns up in your life, you would know what to do about it" (p. 25). Herzog's work was critical to developing UGT because she was the first published researcher to provide an in-depth examination of media gratifications. She is sometimes credited with having originated UGT (although its label was to come much later).

Ten years later Wilbur Schramm (1954) developed a means of determining "which offerings of mass communication will be selected by a given individual" (p. 19). His **fraction of selection** visually represents precisely the process that Ryan goes through when he makes his choice of a movie or a television show:

fraction of selection
Schramm's idea of how media choices are made: the expectation of reward divided by the effort required

$$\frac{\text{Expectation of reward}}{\text{Effort required}}$$

Schramm sought to make clear that audience members judge the level of reward (gratification) they expect from a given medium or message against how much effort they must make to secure that reward—an important component of what would later become known as the Uses and Gratifications perspective.

The second stage of Uses and Gratifications research began when researchers created typologies representing all the reasons people had for media use. For example, Alan Rubin (1981) found that motivations for television use clustered into the following categories: to pass time, for companionship, excitement, escape, enjoyment, social interaction, relaxation, information, and to learn about a specific content. Other researchers (McQuail, Blumler, & Brown, 1972) asserted that media use could be categorized with only four basic divisions: diversion, personal relationships, personal identity, and surveillance.

Jay Blumler and another colleague, Denis McQuail (1969), began untangling reasons that people watch political programs. They found a number of motives for watching political broadcasts. This work formed an important foundation for researchers in Uses and Gratifications. Later work would begin to point out specifically how people see mass media. These teams of researchers found that there was a need either to connect with or to disconnect from others. Researchers found categories of needs associated with acquiring information or knowledge, pleasure, status, strengthening relationships, and relax. As you will recall, Ryan Grant was trying to work through two simultaneous needs: the need for strengthening friendships and the need to relax.

In the third stage, Uses and Gratifications researchers have been interested in linking specific reasons for media use with variables such as needs, goals, benefits, the consequences of media use, and individual factors. In this effort, researchers are working to make the theory more explanatory and predictive. Alan Rubin and Mary Step (2000) conducted a study that exemplifies this stage of UG research. Rubin and Step examined the relationship of motivation, interpersonal attraction, and **parasocial interaction** (the relationship we feel we have with people we know only through the media) to listening to public affairs talk radio. They found that motivations for exciting entertainment and information acquisition interacted with perceptions of the parasocial relationship to explain why listeners tuned in to talk radio and why they found a host credible.

Currently, researchers using UGT are interested in how the theory operates with respect to newer media, and we will discuss this research a bit later in the chapter. In addition, contemporary research using UGT continues to explore how and why audiences consume traditional media for their own gratifications. For example, Darrin Brown, Sharon Lauricella, Aziz Douai, and Arshida Zaidi (2012) were interested in the motivations people had for watching crime dramas on TV. They found some support for the idea that people satisfied their curiosity through watching these shows.

parasocial interaction
the relationship we feel we have with people we know only through the media

Media Effects

The history of UGT has much to do with how researchers shifted and changed their positions on the media effects. As we explained previously, researchers moved from a position where they saw the media as very powerful to one where media effects were seen as more limited. Uses and Gratifications Theory moved even further to the position of the active audience and less powerful media. However, there was controversy about how in control audience members might be under the theory. Jay Blumler (1979), one of the originators of UGT, believed that some scholars had gone too far in describing the active audience. He argued that the theory meant to assert that even when audience members are active—even when they determine for themselves the uses they wish to make of mass media and the gratifications they seek from those uses—effects can and do occur. The failure of researchers in traditional Uses and Gratifications to consider the possibility of important media effects led the authors of the original work to chastise their colleagues 11 years later by noting that a "vulgar gratificationism" (Blumler, 1985, p. 259) should be purged from the theory. Blumler asserted that it was not the theorists' intention to imply that audience members are always totally free in either the uses they make of media or the gratifications they seek from them; the world in which media consumers live shapes them just as surely as they shape it, and content does have intended meaning.

Student Voices

Andre

It's funny what some people think demands their attention—all the "infotainment" and reality shows on TV seem to be showing that people just really want to know about people partying on the Jersey shore or Kim and Kanye. The book talks about how people are hungry for information about a current event such as the presidential election or the shootings in Connecticut, but it seems like people care more about the latest movie star mental breakdown than they do about real news. I'm not sure what the theory would say about this, but people's motivations for watching TV seem only to be escapism now, and I don't know if that's our choice or just what media offers us.

Blumler and his colleagues point to a second set of premises that make clear their belief that people's use of media and the gratifications they seek from it are inextricably intertwined with the world in which they live. Elihu Katz, Jay G. Blumler, and Michael Gurevitch (1974) originally wrote in developing UGT that "social situations" in which people find themselves can be "involved in the generation of media-related needs" (p. 27) in five ways. First, social situations can produce tensions and conflicts, leading to pressure for their easement through the consumption of media. That is, we live in the world, and events in it can compel us to seek specific media and content. For a time in 2012 nearly everyone was talking about Super Storm Sandy. It was a sizeable catastrophe in U.S. history, and all media provided a great deal of information about the natural disaster and the human problems that resulted. This was a social situation wrought with tension and conflict. Where did you go to ease the pressure? Did you seek out more information through TV, radio, or the Internet? Did you use social media sites (SNSs) to find out if your East Coast friends were safe?

Second, social situations can create an awareness of problems that demand attention, information about which may be sought in the media. Simply stated, the world in which we live contains information that makes us aware of things that are of interest to us, and we can find out more about those interests through the media. Everyone everywhere—work, school, virtually every social situation you entered—was talking about the storm and the rescue efforts. This problem demanded your attention. You probably turned to the media—for information, perspective, and analysis.

Third, social situations can impoverish real-life opportunities to satisfy certain needs, and the media can serve as substitutes or supplements. In other words, sometimes the situations in which you find yourself make the media the best, if not the only, source possible. Your social situation as a college student made it difficult, if not impossible, for you to go to New Jersey to see for yourself how the rescue was proceeding. You weren't able to ask the U.S. President or other officials about available supplies and money, or whether political considerations held up important resources for the rebuilding efforts, as Governor Christie suggested. You needed to know what was going on in this disaster, but the reality of your position in society meant that you had little choice but to rely on the media to meet that need.

Fourth, social situations often elicit specific values, and their affirmation and reinforcement can be facilitated by the consumption of related media materials. Again, you are a college student. You are an educated person. The media offer an appropriate location for the affirmation and reinforcement of the knowledge and awareness that you value.

Finally, social situations demand familiarity with media; these demands must be met to sustain membership in specific social groups. As a college student, you are viewed as the future of our country. Not only should you have had an opinion about the government's response to Sandy, but you should have had something to say about the media's performance throughout that crisis. Lacking those opinions, you may have been regarded as out of it or uninformed.

In rejecting "vulgar gratificationism," Katz and his colleagues (1974) note that we should ask three things. First, are the mass media instrumental in creating this social situation? What role did various media outlets play? Based on what information did we form our opinions? Second, are the mass media instrumental in making the satisfaction of this situation's related needs so crucial? Why, for instance, was it important to have an opinion at all? Who put this issue on the public's agenda? Who determined that it was more important than any of the myriad events that were happening in the world?

Uses and Gratifications Theory and its assumptions gained acceptance for a number of reasons. First, the limited effects researchers began to run out of things to study. Once all the variables that limited media influence were chronicled, what was left to say about the process of mass communication? Second, the limited effects perspective failed to explain why advertisers spend billions of dollars a year to place their ads in the media or why so many people spend so much time consuming the media. Third, some observers speculate that people often decide whether specific media effects are desirable and intentionally set out to achieve those effects. If this is so, researchers ask, what does this say about limited effects? Finally, while many negative effects were documented by limited effects researchers such as the relationship between viewing mediated violence and subsequent aggressive behavior, positive uses of media were left unexamined.

These factors produced a subtle shift in the focus of those researchers working within the limited effects paradigm. Their attention moved from the things media do to people to the things people do with media. If effects occur at all, either positive or negative, it is because audience members want them to happen, or at least let them happen.

Key Concepts: The Audience as Active

By now, you know that Uses and Gratifications Theory is a model that takes into consideration the importance of audience. And it is this word—audience—that comprises the foundation for a discussion of the key terms related to the theory. We briefly expand our discussion of the theory by identifying the various types of audience embedded in the theory. A theory that is based on the assumption that media consumers are active must delineate what it means by **"the active audience."** The interpretation of an "active audience" is an important part of consumer/consumption activity (Grob, Heusinkveld, & Clark, 2015). For our purposes, however, we draw upon the words of Mark Levy and Sven Windahl (1985) who deal with the topic this way:

> As commonly understood by gratifications researchers, the term "audience activity" postulates a voluntaristic and selective orientation by audiences toward the communication process. In brief, it suggests that media use is motivated by needs and goals that are defined by audience members themselves, and that active participation in the communication process may facilitate, limit, or otherwise influence the gratifications and effects associated with exposure. Current thinking also suggests that audience activity is best conceptualized as a variable construct, with audiences exhibiting varying kinds and degrees of activity. (p. 110)

Jay G. Blumler (1979) offers several suggestions as to the kinds of audience activity in which media consumers could engage. They include utility, intentionality, selectivity, and imperviousness to influence. and these form the essence of the important terms for UGT.

First, the media have uses for people, and people can put media to those uses. This is termed **utility.** People listen to the car radio or check an app (e.g., Waze) on their cell phones to find out about traffic. They go online to download Spotify. They read Consumer Reports to find out about the latest ratings on new car options. **Intentionality** occurs when people's prior motivations determine their consumption of media content. When people want to be entertained, they usually tune in to comedy. When they want greater detail about a news story, they usually tune into news-centered networks such as CNN or MSNBC. A third type of audience activity is termed **selectivity,** which means that audience members' use of media may reflect their existing interests and preferences. If you like jazz, you might listen to the jazz program on the local radio station. If you're interested in tech trends, you are a likely reader of *Wired*. If you're interested in local politics, you probably subscribe to Politico or read political blogs. Finally, an **imperviousness to influence** suggests that audience members construct their own meaning from content and that meaning influences what they think and do. They often actively avoid certain types of media influence. For example, some people buy products on the basis of quality and value rather than in response to advertising campaigns. Or they exhibit no

the active audience
a variable concept focused on an audience engaging with the media on a voluntary basis, motivated by their needs and goals

utility
using the media to accomplish specific tasks

intentionality
a cognitive behavior that occurs when people's prior motives determine use of media

selectivity
audience members' use of media reflects their existing interests

imperviousness to influence
refers to audience members constructing their own meaning from media content

aggression against others, no matter how much they enjoy action/adventure films and television shows.

In addition to audience activity as a central concept of UGT, activity and activeness, too, remain central. UGT also distinguishes between activity and activeness to understand better the degrees of audience activity. Although the terms are related, **activity** refers more to what the media consumer does (e.g., she chooses to go online for news rather than read it in the newspaper). **Activeness** is closer to what really interests researchers in Uses and Gratifications: the audience's freedom and autonomy in the mass communication situation.

Activeness is relative. Some people are active participants in the mass communication process; others are more passive. We all know people who live their lives through TV or who follow every fad and fashion presented in the mass media. Terms like *couch potato* and *sofa spud* developed from the idea that many folks simply sit back and take in whatever is presented on the TV set in front of them. On the other hand, we also know people who are quite adroit at consuming media. Your friend may listen to rap because of the beat. You may listen to rap not only for its rhythms, but also for its social commentary. For you, watching a documentary on climate change may prompt you to think about the amazing photography. For your sister, however, the movie may have been interpreted as a social commentary about the lack of U.S. action on global warming.

Activeness is also individually variable. A person can be inactive at times ("I'll just turn on the television for background noise") and then become quite active ("The news is on! I'd better watch"). Our level of activeness often varies by time of day and type of content. We can be active users of the Internet by day and passive consumers of Jimmy Fallon on television.

activity
refers to what the media consumer does

activeness
refers to how much freedom the audience really has in the face of mass media

Uses and Gratifications and the Internet, Social Media, and Cell Phones

Throughout this book, we have tried to provide you the most recent research related to a particular theory that may have its origins during an earlier time in the field's history. Uses and Gratifications Theory, as you know, is one such theory. To this end, we wish to provide you an overview, however, of how the emergence of computer-mediated communication has revived the integrity of the theory. Let's examine a few areas that will illustrate the theory's durability. We maintain our focus on the user in this discussion. In 1994, George Gilder predicted the way a hybrid of the television and the computer would affect our culture:

> Rather than exalting mass culture, the teleputer will enhance individualism. Rather than cultivating passivity, the teleputer will promote creativity. Instead of a master-slave architecture, the teleputer will have an interactive architecture in which every receiver can function as a processor and transmitter of video images and other information. The teleputer will usher in a culture compatible with the immense powers of today's ascendant technology. Perhaps most important, the teleputer will enrich and strengthen democracy and capitalism around the world. (p. 46)

In the years since Gilder's predictions, some of what he suggests has come to pass. Television viewing has changed and can now be individually customized to a larger degree. It now must compete with multiple media, but much of what Gilder spoke of remains unrealized.

Although Gilder's predictions are not (yet) reality, almost everyone expects that new media will continue to change our future. And, many researchers believe that UGT will be able to explain the ways that people use the Internet, SMS, as well as cell phone technology, and other media. As James Shanahan and Michael Morgan (1999) observed, there is an "underlying consistency of the content of the messages we consume and the nature of the symbolic environment in which we live" (p. 199) even if the delivery technology changes. They assert that new technologies have always developed by adopting the message content from the technology that was previously dominant. They argue, for example, that films took their content from serialized literature, radio did the same, and television simply repackaged radio programming. Marshall McLuhan (see Chapter 26) noted that new media merely provide new bottles for old wine. The question for Uses and Gratifications researchers is whether the motivations people brought to their use of "old" media will apply to "new" media. Theorists are interested in finding out whether new media so alters the message and the experience that Uses and Gratifications Theory no longer applies or has to be radically modified. Access to new technologies has changed and extended our abilities for entertainment and information gathering, and media researchers require greater understanding of the personal and social reasons people have for using new media.

Theory in Popular Press • Using Social Media

Boonsri Dickinson reported on the *Business Insider* blog in 2012 that companies are getting smarter about how they use social media, and indeed, are able to target specific media for specific needs. Dickinson notes that a company called Grip has worked with other companies to satisfy the following specific gratifications:

- Using social media to help hedge funds analyze consumer sentiment about certain kinds of investments.
- Tracking tweets and Flickr shots to help firefighting professionals fight forest fires.
- Using Twitter in Mexico to help the government see crime reports and patterns.
- Using Twitter and Facebook to help agencies predict election results.
- Using Twitter to aid the CDC in predicting flu outbreaks among other things.

Source: Dickinson, B. (2012, March 19). Nine unusual ways social media is being used to predict the future. *Business Insider,* businessinsider.com/9-ways-social-media-data-is-being-used-2012-3?op=1.

Researchers using UGT thinking have found it to be a valuable theoretical framework to understand cell phone usage (Lauricella, Cingel, Blackwell, Wartella, & Conway, 2014; Leung & Wei, 2000), social media use and privacy concerns and privacy strategies (Quinn, 2016), digital game playing (De Shutter & Malliet, 2014; Lucas & Sherry, 2004), and social networking websites such as Facebook (Dainton & Stokes, 2015) and its Chinese equivalent, Renren (Lanming & Hanasono, 2016). However, some research (e.g., Anderson, 2011; Zeng, 2011) suggests that while the basic logic of UGT holds in studies of a variety of media, the exact list of gratifications will change based on the specific medium. For instance, Isolde Anderson (2011) found that people utilizing CaringBridge, an online resource offering personalized websites for those in need of care (e.g., those undergoing a serious illness, military deployment, adoption, etc.), reported at least two different kinds of gratifications from CaringBridge than for traditional media. These include spiritual support from a higher power and social presence, or feeling tied to the greater community.

Robert LaRose and Matthew Eastin (2004) suggest that Uses and Gratifications Theory can also be enhanced by the addition of some new variables such as expected activity outcomes and social outcomes. Expected activity outcomes concern what people think they will obtain from the medium. LaRose and Eastin found that people expect that using the Internet will improve their lot in life. Social outcomes involve social status and identity. LaRose and Eastin speculate that people may enhance their social status by finding like-minded others through the Internet and expressing their ideas to them. They also suggest that "perhaps the Internet is a means of constantly exploring and trying out new, improved versions of our selves" (p. 373).

A few studies have examined how new media satisfy users' gratifications compared to traditional media (e.g., Ha & Fang, 2012; Min & Kim, 2012). These studies found that media such as email and websites are perceived as superior to traditional media and provide more gratifications for both getting news and mobilizing people to action than do traditional media. This finding held true across cultures in that the usage and adoption of social networking sites, in particular, were influenced by cultural background (Ifinedo, 2016).

Integration, Critique, and Closing

Uses and Gratifications, as a recognizable, discrete theory, had its greatest influence in the 1970s and 1980s although the relevance of the theory today is clear. As Elizabeth Perse (2014) notes, UGT is "one of the most widely used theoretical underpinnings in communication research." The limited effects paradigm held sway at the time, and media theorists needed a framework within which they could discuss the obvious presence of media effects without straying too far from disciplinary orthodoxy. As you might surmise, the theory has been investigated largely using quantitative approaches, although limited research has been qualitative in nature (De Shutter & Malliet, 2014).

Uses and Gratifications is quite straightforward when discussing how people use newspapers (newspapers are made up of discrete sections, each aimed at a specific type of reader seeking specific types of information) or magazines (publications

Student Voices

Mason

I thought the chapter-opening story about Ryan was so funny because I had the same internal debate last weekend. I was completely wiped, and I couldn't decide if I just wanted to veg out in front of the TV or hang out with my friends. I knew I would miss seeing my friends if I stayed home, but the idea of letting mindless TV wash over me was really appealing because I'd had such a hectic week. Frankly, I was kind of sick of talking to people, so sitting and watching something amusing sounded good. I definitely was looking for "tension release." But then my friends stopped by and convinced me to go to a movie with them. I guess I decided those "social integrative" needs were more important at that moment.

with very specific, demographically targeted readers) to come to some specific decision or judgment. As you read earlier, the most recent research integrating the theory relates to the online communities. Thus, the theory is experiencing a bit of a resurgence as researchers work to test its premises with new media. As you think about this theory, consider the following criteria: logical consistency, utility, and heurism.

Integration

Communication Tradition	Rhetorical	Semiotic	Phenomenological	Cybernetic	Socio-Psychological	**Socio-Cultural**	Critical
Communication Context	Intrapersonal	Interpersonal	Small Group	Organizational	Public/Rhetorical	**Mass/Media**	Cultural
Approach to Knowing	**Positivistic/Empirical**	Interpretive/Hermeneutic	Critical

Critique

Evaluation Criteria	Scope	**Logical Consistency**	Parsimony	**Utility**	Testability	**Heurism**	Test of Time

Logical Consistency

Denis McQuail (1984) believes that the theory suffers from a lack of theoretical coherence. He thinks that some of the theory's terminology needs to be further defined. He notes that the theory relies too heavily on the functional use of media, because there are times when the media can be reckless. For example, there have been instances of sloppy, inaccurate, or unethical journalism. In addition, new media allow for citizen journalism where anyone with a smart phone can publish ideas, allegations, and photos without the checks and balances or the training that accompanies professional journalism.

Utility

The theory has been criticized because some of its central tenets may be questionable. If the key concepts of the theory are shaky, then the theory may not have full utility. In other words, it may be limited in how it explains. Yet, it should be noted that some UGT scholars believe that because most of the research employed self-report instruments, it renders the audience member as less dynamic than if personal observations were used (Roggiero, 2000). Further more nuanced views of the theory have accepted the fact that audiences have indeed become more engaged and active since the original writings of the theory (e.g., Perse, 2014).

Still, some researchers (Kubey & Csikszentmihalyi, 2014) note that people report that their television watching in particular is passive and requires little concentration. Furthermore, the theory seems to highlight a reasoning media consumer, one who does not accept everything the media present. The theory does not take into consideration the fact that individuals may not have considered all available choices in media consumption. For instance, Ryan Grant has considered two choices: stay at home or go out to the movies. What other options could he consider? Uses and Gratifications does not pay too much attention to the myriad unconscious decisions made by individuals.

Heurism

We can see that the heuristic nature of the theory is without question. The research has spanned several decades, and the theory has framed a number of research studies. In addition to the early pioneers Katz, Blumler, Gurevitch, and their colleagues, others have employed the theory and its thinking in their research on gay and bisexual men (Miller, 2015), information sources related to college students (Parker & Plank, 2015), texting and public health emergency messaging (Karasz, Li-Vollmer, Bogan, & Offenbecher, 2014), and digital photo sharing on Facebook (Malik, Dhir, & Nieminen, 2016.

Closing

The value of Uses and Gratifications Theory today is in its ability to provide a framework for the consideration of the audience and individual media consumers in contemporary mass communication research and theory. Uses and Gratifications may not be the defining theory in the field of mass communication, but it serves the discipline well as we seek to understand the intersection between media choice and consumer use.

Discussion Starters

TECH QUEST: Today's "new media" was not considered in the earlier discussions of Uses and Gratifications Theory. Yet, we can all agree that we use various media in different ways. Explain how social network users might use online sites to gratify their relational needs, such as meeting new people, maintaining office relationships, and so forth.

1. Are there choices other than those identified for Ryan Grant to consider in his decision to do something on Friday night? How do these alternatives relate to Uses and Gratifications Theory? Use examples in your response.

2. How active a media consumer are you? Are you always thoughtful in your choice of media content? Do you bring different levels of activeness to different media—newspapers versus radio, for example?

3. UGT has been criticized for being too apologetic of the media industries and overly supportive of the status quo. Can you explain why this is so? Do you agree with these criticisms? Does such criticism have any place in scientific theory?

4. Uses and Gratifications Theory assumes that media present content and consumers consume it. How does the Internet threaten to disrupt this model? How might UGT adapt to allow for this transformation of traditional media consumers into online media users?

5. Discuss the relevance of UGT in the early 21st century. Incorporate examples into your response.

6. What difference would it make, according to the theory, if Ryan's movie choice was an action/adventure film and the main choices on TV were romantic comedies? How does Uses and Gratifications Theory account for media content?

7. Are there other uses and gratifications that people may get from media that the chapter doesn't discuss? Explain your answer.

CHAPTER 24

Cultivation Theory

*Based on the research of **George Gerbner***

Unlike other media use, viewing is a ritual; people watch by the clock and not by the program.

—George Gerbner

Joyce Jensen

Joyce Jensen was preparing to vote for the very first time. She had been looking forward to this privilege since she was 12 years old. She considered herself a news junkie, and she was always reading news blogs such as *The Huffington Post* and *The Drudge Report*—she tried to get all sides of an issue. She continued to devour the morning newspaper and watch both local TV news and CNN. She made it a point to watch C-SPAN, a cable station dedicated to the world of politics. She knew that she was one of only a handful in her class who could identify all of the U.S. Supreme Court justices. She was ready to take some flak for being a news nerd because the world fascinated her. She wanted to be prepared for the right and responsibility of voting.

Now she was about to vote in her first local election. She was choosing between two candidates for her state's governor. She had read a lot about the candidates and watched all the debates. Although she was still undecided, she was leaning toward Roberta Johndrew, the tough-on-crime candidate. Johndrew favored greater use of the death penalty, limits on appeals by people convicted of crimes, and putting more police on the street. Yet, Joyce thought that Frank Milnes, the education candidate, had some good ideas as well. Crime—in Joyce's state and in the country as a whole—was down for the eighth consecutive year. And Milnes argued that, despite high-profile crimes like the tragic killings at Sandy Hook Elementary School in Connecticut, according to FBI statistics all types of violent crime had actually been in decline for several years. Milnes argued that money being spent for more police, more prisons, and more executions would be better spent on improving schools. After all, Milnes asserted, more dollars in their state were being spent on incarceration than on educating young people. Better schools, he argued, would mean even less crime in the future. "What kind of state do we live in," he demanded in his campaign literature, "when we refuse to give raises to our teachers and pay our prison guards more than our teachers?"

Those were powerful arguments, thought Joyce. She regretted that teachers were not getting paid commensurate with their expertise and responsibilities. She knew that she wanted to have children eventually, and she wanted them to get the best education possible. She could see how paying teachers more might help achieve that.

But as a young, single woman, these arguments were secondary to safety considerations. There seemed to be so much crime in the city. Every night when she watched the news on television, there seemed to be more crimes reported. She was often uncomfortable when she was out at night. At times, she even felt uneasy being at

403

home alone. Maybe it is an irrational fear, she thought to herself, but it was there and it felt real.

As Joyce pondered how she would cast her vote in the booth, so much was going through her mind. She considered her present situation as a single woman as well as her desire for future children. She reflected on both Roberta Johndrew and Frank Milnes and their comments from the past several months. As she contemplated her options for another moment or two, she felt she would be able to make a good decision. So much depended on citizens making informed choices. Joyce was thrilled to exercise her right as a U.S. citizen.

■

As Walter Lippmann (1922) noted almost a century ago, people's opinions transcend their lived experiences. George Gerbner (1999) agreed with this and observed, "[M]ost of what we know, or think we know, we have never personally experienced" (p. ix). This is possible, in large part, because of the impact of media and the stories told through the media that bring events and ideas to media consumers that are beyond their own realities (Northrup, 2010). We "know" many things from the stories we see and hear in the media (Buffington & Fraley, 2008).

One of the most popular media sources providing us with this information is television. Regardless of the influence and pervasiveness of social media, television still holds a central place in our experience: Although the upswing in computer usage cannot be denied, it's also interesting to note that there has actually been an uptick in television usage, as well. For instance, in 2012, there were approximately 114 million TV households in the United States. In 2016, that number rose to 116 million (http://www.statista.com/statistics/243789/number-of-tv-households-in-the-us/). Children (kids who are just turning nine and older) in the United States spend, on average, 35 hours per week watching television (http://entertainment.time.com/2013/11/20/fyi-parents-your-kids-watch-a-full-time-jobs-worth-of-tv-each-week), which is 2.2 hours more than in 2009. Adults (15 years and older) spend approximately 2.8 hours per day, accounting nearly half of their daily leisure activities (http://www.bls.gov/news.release/atus.nr0.htm). Clearly, television remains pervasive and potentially influential in an average U.S. home. In addition, the television set regularly ushers in "mass-mediated storytelling," providing for the "dominant entertainment medium" (Romer, Jamieson, Bleakley, & Jamieson, 2016, p. 115).

The theory profiled in this chapter, Cultivation Theory began as a way to test the impact that all this television viewing had on viewers, particularly with regard to violence. It is true that television has changed a great deal since it became widely available to U.S. viewers in 1948. Yet, despite dramatic transformations in technology and social systems, the model of cultivation developed by George Gerbner in the 1960s remains healthy and thriving (Morgan & Shanahan, 2010).

causal argument
an assertion of cause and effect, including the direction of the causality

Gerbner began the Cultural Indicators Project in 1967 and its existence continues today (http://web.asc.upenn.edu/gerbner/archive.aspx?sectionID=19), conducting regular, periodic examinations of television programming and the "conceptions of social reality that viewing cultivates in child and adult audiences" (Gerbner & Gross, 1972, p. 174). In initiating what would become known as Cultivation Theory, Gerbner and his colleagues were making a **causal argument**

Calvin and Hobbes

by Bill Watterson

(television cultivates—causes—conceptions of social reality in people's minds). Cultivation Theory is a theory that predicts and explains the long-term formation and shaping of perceptions, understandings, and beliefs about the world as a result of consumption of media messages. Gerbner's line of thinking in Cultivation Theory suggests that mass communication, particularly television, cultivates certain beliefs about reality that are held in common by mass communication consumers.

Cultivation researchers can easily explain Joyce Jensen's voting quandary. Official statistics that indicate that violent crime is in steady decline are certainly real enough. But so, too, is Joyce's feeling of unease and insecurity when she is alone. Cultivation Theory would refer to these feelings of insecurity as her social reality. Moreover, that reality is as real as any other for Joyce, and it is media fueled, if not media created and maintained.

Iver Peterson (2002) made a similar observation about the anthrax scares in the United States post–September 11, 2001. He notes that although the media-fueled fears about anthrax are very pervasive and real, the actual cases of anthrax contamination are rare. Peterson quotes Clifton R. Lacy, commissioner of the NJ Department of Health and Senior Services, as saying that the risks to the citizens of New Jersey by anthrax spores are "vanishingly small" (p. A21). In the 1970s, Gerbner's view that media messages alter traditional notions of time, space, and social groupings was a direct challenge to the prevailing thought that media had little, if any, effect on individuals and on the culture. Like Uses and Gratifications Theory, which we discussed in Chapter 23, Cultivation Theory was developed in response to the beliefs about the media's limited effects that were dominant at the time. More important, however, it reflects media theory's slow transformation from reliance on the transmissional perspective to greater acceptance of the ritual perspective of mass communication.

The **transmissional perspective** sees media as senders of messages—discrete bits of information—across space (Baran & Davis, 2016). This perspective and limited effects theories are comfortable partners. If all media do is transmit bits of information, people can choose to use or not use that information as they wish. In the **ritual perspective,** however, media are conceptualized not as a means of transmitting

transmissional perspective
a position depicting the media as senders of messages across space

ritual perspective
a position depicting the media as representers of shared beliefs

"messages in space," but as central to "the maintenance of society in time" (Carey, 1975, p. 6). Mass communication is "not the act of imparting information, but the representation of shared beliefs" (p. 6).

Developing Cultivation Theory

Gerbner first used the term *cultivation* in 1969; however, Cultivation Theory, as a discrete and powerful theory, did not emerge for a number of years. It evolved over time through a series of methodological and theoretical steps by Gerbner and his colleagues and, as such, reflects that development. The method that Gerbner and others use to investigate questions of mass media cultivation is called Cultivation Analysis, and sometimes people use the terms *Cultivation Analysis* and *Cultivation Theory* interchangeably.

During the 1960s, interest in media effects, particularly effects of television, ran very high. The federal government was concerned about media's influence on society, especially media's possible contribution to rising levels of violence among young people. In 1967, President Lyndon Johnson ordered the creation of the National Commission on the Causes and Prevention of Violence. It was followed in 1972, by the surgeon general's Scientific Advisory Committee on Television and Social Behavior. Both groups examined media (especially television) and their impact (especially the effects of aggression and violence). Gerbner, a respected social scientist, was involved in both efforts.

Violence Index
a yearly content analysis of prime-time network programming to assess the amount of violence represented

Gerbner's task was to produce an annual **Violence Index**, a yearly content analysis of a sample week of network television prime-time content that would show, from season to season, how much violence was actually present on television. Its value to those interested in the media violence issue was obvious: If the link between television fare and subsequent viewer aggression was to be made, the presence of violence on television needed to be demonstrated. Moreover, observers would be able to correlate annual increases in the amount of violent television content with annual increases in the amount of real-world violent crime. But, the index was immediately challenged by both media industry and limited-effects researchers. How was violence defined? Was verbal aggression violence? Was obviously fake violence on a comedy counted the same as more realistically portrayed violence on a drama? Why examine only prime-time network television, because children's heaviest viewing occurs at other times of the day? Why focus on violence? Why not examine other social ills, such as racism and sexism?

Gerbner and his associates continuously refined the Index to meet the complaints of its critics, and what their annual counting demonstrated was that violence appeared on prime-time television at levels unmatched in the real world. The 1982 Index, for example, showed that "crime in prime time is at least 10 times as rampant as in the real world (and) an average of five to six acts of overt physical violence per hour involves over half of all major characters" (Gerbner, Gross, Morgan, & Signorielli, 1982, p. 106).

CULTIVATION THEORY

Assumptions of Cultivation Theory

In advancing the position that "the more time people spend 'living' in the television world, the more likely they are to believe social reality is congruent with television's reality" (Riddle, 2010, p. 156), Cultivation Theory makes a number of assumptions. Because it was and still remains primarily a television-based theory, these three assumptions speak to the relationship between that medium and the culture:

- Television is essentially and fundamentally different from other forms of mass media.
- Television shapes our society's way of thinking and relating.
- The influence of television is limited.

The first assumption of Cultivation Theory underscores the uniqueness of television. First, it requires no literacy, as do print media. Unlike the movies, it can be free (beyond the initial cost of the set and the cost of advertising added to the products we buy). Unlike radio, it combines pictures and sound. It requires no mobility, as do church attendance and going to the movies or the theater. Television is the only medium ever invented that is ageless—that is, people can use it at the earliest and latest years of life, as well as all those years in between.

Because it is accessible and available to everyone, television is the "central cultural arm" of our society (Gerbner, Gross, Jackson-Beeck, Jeffries-Fox, & Signorielli, 1978, p. 178). Television draws together dissimilar groups and can make them forget their differences for a time by providing them with a common experience. For example, in 2012, four billion people around the globe watched the Olympics in London. Regardless of their nationality, ethnicity, gender, politics, or other potentially divisive identities, these people had a common experience. In other words, television is the culture's primary storyteller and has the ability to gather together different groups. In addition, no one can doubt the role that television has played in the United States working through the tragedies of 9–11, Super Storm Sandy, the shootings at the movie theatre in Colorado, among others.

CULTIVATION THEORY

The second assumption pertains to the influence of television. Gerbner and Gross (1972) comment that "the substance of the consciousness cultivated by TV is not so much specific attitudes and opinions as more basic assumptions about the 'facts' of life and standards of judgment on which conclusions are based" (p. 175). That is, television doesn't so much persuade us (it didn't try to convince Joyce Jensen that the streets are unsafe) as paint a more or less convincing picture of what the world is like (Riddle, Potter, Metzger, Nabi, & Linz, 2011). Gerbner agrees with Walter Fisher, whom we discussed in Chapter 20, that people live in stories. Gerbner, however, asserts that most of the stories in current society now come from television. In an interview with Gerbner posted on YouTube (youtube.com /watch?v=toc5KHWZx4A) he states that we get a stable vision of life from the stories on TV and this vision teaches us much about our fates. And, in many cases, our fates are scary and include victimization.

Television's major cultural function is to stabilize social patterns, to cultivate resistance to change. Television is a medium of socialization and enculturation. Gerbner and his cohorts eloquently state the following:

> [T]he repetitive pattern of television's mass-produced messages and images forms the mainstream of the common symbolic environment that cultivates the most widely shared conceptions of reality. We live in terms of the stories we tell—stories about what things exist, stories about how things work, and stories about what to do—and television tells them all through news, drama, and advertising to almost everybody most of the time. (Gerbner et al., 1978, p. 178)

Where did Joyce Jensen's—and other voters'—shared conceptions of reality about crime and personal safety come from? Cultivation researchers would immediately point to television, where, despite a nationwide 20 percent drop in the homicide rate between 1993 and 1996, for example, the number of murder stories on the network evening news soared 721 percent (Kurtz, 1998). This distortion has continued in ways that the theory would predict. Barbara Wilson and her colleagues (Wilson, Martins, & Marske, 2005) found that parents who paid a great deal of attention to television news thought their children were more at risk for kidnapping than those parents who watched less TV. Yet, the Bureau of Justice Statistics rate of violent crimes among 12- to 17-year-olds since 1994 does not support this belief. The findings indicate that from 1994 to 2010 the rate of violent crimes against children ages 12–17 decreased for youth in married households by 86 percent and for those in unmarried households by 65 percent (White & Lauritsen, 2012). Further, kidnapping makes up less than 2 percent of all violent crimes against youth (Finklehor & Ormrod, 2000).

Based on this assumption, Cultivation Theory supplies an alternative way of thinking about TV violence. Some theories, like Social Learning Theory (Bandura, 1977), assume that we become more violent after being exposed to violence. Other approaches, like the notion of catharsis, would suggest that watching violence purges us of our own violent impulses and we actually become less violent. Cultivation Theory does not speak to what we will do based on watching violent television; instead, it assumes that watching violent TV makes us feel afraid because it cultivates within us the image of a mean and dangerous world.

The third assumption of Cultivation Theory states that television's effects are limited. This may sound peculiar, given the fact that television is so pervasive. Yet, the observable, measurable, and independent contributions of television to the culture are relatively small. This may sound like a restatement of minimal effects thinking, but Gerbner uses an ice age analogy to distance Cultivation Theory from limited effects. The **ice age analogy** states that "just as an average temperature shift of a few degrees can lead to an ice age or the outcomes of elections can be determined by slight margins, so too can a relatively small but pervasive influence make a crucial difference. The 'size' of an 'effect' is far less critical than the direction of its steady contribution" (Gerbner, Gross, Morgan, & Signorielli, 1980, p. 14). The argument is not that television's impact is inconsequential. Rather, although television's measurable, observable, and independent effect on the culture at any point in time might be small, that impact is nonetheless present and significant. Further, Gerbner and his associates argue that it is not the case that watching a specific television program causes a specific behavior (e.g., that watching *NCIS* will cause someone to kill a naval officer) but rather that watching television in general has a cumulative and pervasive impact on our vision of the world.

ice age analogy
a position stating that television doesn't have to have a single major impact, but influences viewers through steady limited effects

Student Voices

Milly

I'm one of those few 19-year-olds who watches TV almost constantly. I have Hulu and that means I can watch TV shows online. And, that means it doesn't matter where or when (except in class and at my job). So, according to Gerbner (and I know I'm simplifying the theory here), because I watch TV a lot, I'm getting exposed to a world that I believe is more violent than it really is. But, I love Law & Order and even some of the horror shows on FX. But, I'm not afraid to go out at night. And, I don't think the police are any more corrupt than any other profession, even though the media portray law enforcement as pathetic and prone to violence.

Processes and Products of Cultivation Theory

Cultivation Theory has been applied to a wide variety of effects issues, as well as to different situations in which television viewers find themselves. In doing so, researchers have developed specific processes and products related to the theory.

The Four-Step Process

To empirically demonstrate their belief that television has an important causal effect on the culture, cultivation researchers developed a four-step process. The first step, message system analysis, consists of detailed content analyses of television programming in order to demonstrate its most recurring and consistent presentations of images, themes, values, and portrayals. For example, it is possible to conduct a message system analysis of the number of episodes of bodily harm on such shows as *Criminal Minds*.

The second step, formulation of questions about viewers' social realities, involves developing questions about people's understandings of their everyday lives. For example, a typical Cultivation Theory question is, "In any given week, what are the chances that you will be involved in some kind of violence? About 1 in 10 or about 1 in 100?" Another is, "Of all the crime that occurs in the United States in any year, what proportion is violent crime like rape, murder, assault, and robbery?" The third step, surveying the audience, requires that the questions from step two be posed to audience members and that researchers ask these viewers about their levels of television consumption.

Finally, step four entails comparing the social realities of light and heavy viewers. For Gerbner, a "cultivation differential" exists between light and heavy viewers and perceptions of violence. A **cultivation differential** can be defined as the percentage of difference in response between light and heavy television viewers. Gerbner (1998) explains that "amount of viewing" is used in relative terms. Thus, heavy viewers are those who watch the most in any sample of people that are measured, whereas light viewers are those who watch the least.

cultivation differential
the percentage of difference in response between light and heavy television viewers

Mainstreaming and Resonance

How does television contribute to viewers' conceptions of social reality? The process of cultivation occurs in two ways. One is mainstreaming. **Mainstreaming** occurs when, especially for heavier viewers, television's symbols dominate other sources of information and ideas about the world. As a result of heavy viewing, people's constructed social realities move toward the mainstream—not a mainstream in any political sense, but a culturally dominant reality that is more similar to television's reality than to any measurable, objective external reality. Heavy viewers tend to believe the mainstreamed realities that the world is a more dangerous place than it really is, that all politicians are corrupt, that teen crime is at record high levels, that all poor families are all on welfare, that illegitimate births are skyrocketing, and so forth. Jennifer Good (2009) found that a mainstreaming effect occurred when people who were concerned about the natural environment were also heavy TV consumers. The mainstreaming effect had the result of decreasing these viewers' concerns about the environment.

mainstreaming
the tendency for heavy viewers to perceive a similar culturally dominant reality to that pictured on the media although this differs from actual reality

Mainstreaming means that heavy television viewers of different co-cultures are more similar in their beliefs about the world than their varying group membership might suggest. Thus, African Americans and European Americans who are heavy television viewers would perceive the world more similarly than might be expected (although we are very cautious as we relate this conclusion as we consider, for example, the 2014 Ferguson, Missouri shooting of Michael Brown, an 18-year-old African American man by a white police officer, as well as many other similar episodes). As Gerbner (1998) states, "Differences that usually are associated with the varied cultural, social, and political characteristics of these groups are diminished in the responses of heavy viewers in these same groups" (p. 183). Jerel Calzo and

Monique Ward (2009) found support for mainstreaming effects in their study of television viewing and attitudes toward homosexuality. They found that more exposure to media representation of gay characters tended to promote more acceptance of homosexuality.

The second way cultivation operates is through **resonance.** Resonance occurs when things on television are, in fact, congruent with viewers' actual everyday realities. In other words, people's objective external reality resonates with that of television. Some urban dwellers, for example, may see the violent world of television resonated in their deteriorating neighborhoods. As Gerbner (1998) notes, this provides "a 'double dose' of messages that 'resonate' and amplify cultivation" (p. 182). The social reality that is cultivated for these viewers may in fact match their objective reality, but its possible effect is to preclude the formation of a more optimistic social reality; it denies them hope that they can build a better life. See Figure 24.1 for a representation of the effects of mainstreaming and resonance.

resonance
a behavior that occurs when a viewer's lived reality coincides with the reality pictured in the media

Theory in Popular Press · Effects of Resonance

Monica Davey reported in the *New York Times* online that overall crime in the city of Chicago dropped by 9 percent in 2012, but the homicide rate actually increased by 16 percent in 2012. Furthermore, the increase in homicides and the drop in overall crimes was not distributed evenly across the city. Davey states "More than 80 percent of the city's homicides took place last year in only about half of Chicago's 23 police districts, largely on the city's South and West Sides. The police district that includes parts of the business district downtown reported no killings at all." Davey's article focuses on the resonance between people's experiences on the South and West Sides of Chicago and televised violence. As CT would predict, the article indicates that the people living through a mediated and a social reality of violence have little hope for a better future. Davey notes that "mothers spoke of keeping their children inside from the moment school ended, and businessmen of decisions to lock the front doors of their shops during business hours."

Source: Davey, M. (2013, January 2). A soaring homicide rate, a divide in Chicago. *New York Times* online, nytimes.com/2013/01/03/us/a-soaring-homicide-rate-a-divide-in-chicago.html.

first order effects
a method for cultivation to occur; refers to learning facts from the media

second order effects
a method for cultivation to occur; refers to learning values and assumptions from the media

Cultivation, either as mainstreaming or as resonance, produces effects on two levels. **First order effects** refer to the learning of facts such as how many employed males are involved in law enforcement or what proportion of marriages end in divorce. For example, Joyce Jensen knew from candidate Milnes's television spots that the amount of crime in her state was in decline. **Second order effects** involve "hypotheses about more general issues and assumptions" that people make about

CULTIVATION THEORY

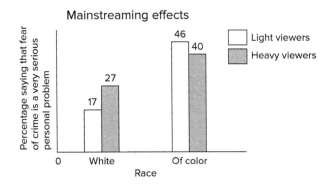

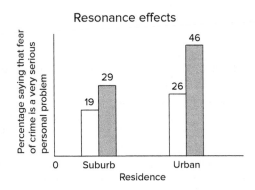

Figure 24.1
Effects of Mainstreaming and Resonance
Source: Adapted from Gerber et al., "The mainstreaming of America: Violence profile no. 11" Journal of Communication, vol. 7 (1980), p. 16, Figure 2. Reprinted by permission of John Wiley & Sons, Ltd.

their environments (Gerbner, Gross, Morgan, & Signorielli, 1986, p. 28). Questions like, "Do you think people are basically honest?" and "Do you think police should be allowed to use greater force to subdue criminals?" are aimed at these second order effects.

The Mean World Index

A product of Cultivation Theory is the Mean World Index (Gerbner et al., 1980; Morgan, Shanahan, & Signorielli, 2016), which consists of a series of three statements:

1. Most people are just looking out for themselves.
2. You can't be too careful in dealing with people.
3. Most people would take advantage of you if they got the chance.

Cultivation Theory predicts that agreement with these statements from heavy and light viewers will differ, with heavy viewers seeing the world as a meaner place than light viewers. It also predicts that the amount of television viewing is the best predictor of people's answers, overwhelming other kinds of distinctions among different people—for example, income and education.

Gerbner and his colleagues (1980) demonstrated their confidence in the Mean World Index in a study that showed heavy viewers were much more likely to see the world as a mean place than were light viewers. Better-educated, financially better-off viewers in general saw the world as less mean than did those with less education and income. But in testing the power of television, the researchers demonstrated that heavy viewers from the better-educated, better-off groups saw the world as being as dangerous as did low-income and less-educated people. In other words, heavy viewers held a mainstreamed perception of the world as a mean place, regardless of factors such as education and income. Cultivation researchers see this as evidence that television content is a factor in the construction of social realities for heavy viewers, regardless of individual or social differences.

Gerbner and his associates identify a number of other areas where the two types of viewers might differ. They include their beliefs about the likelihood of involvement with a violent crime, their fear of walking at night, and their perceptions of law enforcement. The findings are intriguing. First, they found that people with light viewing habits believed that about 1 in 100 will be a victim of violence; heavy viewers of television predicted that about 1 in 10 will be involved in violence. Second, they found that more women than men were fearful of walking alone at night and that heavy viewers overestimated the amount of violent crime. Third, heavy viewers felt that 5 percent of the culture is involved in law enforcement, whereas light viewers felt that 1 percent is involved. Important to the logic of Cultivation Theory is that the responses of the heavy viewers mirror quite accurately the results of content analyses of television, where violence is usually recorded in heavy doses: Because violence is so common on television, heavy viewers are more likely to be fearful or mistrustful of the real world. Given what we've presented here, Joyce Jensen's viewing habits may be influencing her thinking about her choice between Milnes and Johndrew.

One more final point is germane to our discussion. The relevancy of the Mean World Index to politics is especially important to consider. Although most people in the United States find politics to be of a combustible nature, when heavy viewers and politics mix, the perception of "meanness" is unequivocal. Morgan et al. (2016, p. 257) summed up this notion by stating an "in your face" political environment where "talk radio, cable news channels, Internet blogs, discussion boards, partisan websites, online videos, and pervasive social media" have cultivated a sense of "political incivility" that ultimately affects our political perceptions and voting patterns.

Cultivation Theory as Critical Theory

Cultivation Theory has made an important contribution to contemporary thinking about mass communication. Horace Newcomb (1978), an early commentator about Cultivation Theory, wrote of Gerbner and his colleagues: "Their foresight to collect data on a systematic, long-term basis, to move out of the laboratory and away from the closed experimental model, will enable other researchers to avoid costly mistakes. Their material holds a wealth of information" (p. 281).

But just what is the role of television in our culture uncovered by Cultivation Theory researchers? Cultivation theorists would argue that Joyce Jensen's apprehension—and the vote for the tough-on-crime candidate it might produce—is based on a view of the world that is cultivated by television. Learning from television produces not only perceptions of a mean world (which researchers in Cultivation Theory argue become a self-fulfilling prophecy as people's distrust of others breeds an atmosphere of further distrust) but also a warping of political, social, and cultural discourse. How many political candidates, they ask, have the courage to argue against the building of more prisons or against the death penalty? The issue is not the validity of these positions but the absence of meaningful, objective debate on them. The argument here is similar to that offered in Chapter 22, when we explained the Spiral of Silence Theory: People may be less willing to speak out about alternative approaches to crime and crime prevention because the media, especially television, cultivate a dominant social reality that renders these conversations out of step with the voters.

How can television be so powerful a force if its influence occurs as slowly as the coming of the ice age? Gerbner answers this question with his three Bs of television. Television, he wrote, *blurs* traditional distinctions of people's views of their world, *blends* people's realities into television's cultural mainstream, and *bends* that mainstream to the institutional interests of television and its sponsors (Table 24.1). Television's power rests in its utilization by powerful industries and elites to meet their own, rather than the culture's, interests. Cultivation Theory is a critical theory, as we described it in Chapter 3, because it is concerned with the way that communication perpetuates the dominance of one group over another (Littlejohn & Foss, 2011). As James Shanahan and Victoria Jones (1999) argue,

> Cultivation is sometimes taken as a return to a strong "powerful effects" view of mass media. This view isn't completely incorrect, but it misses the point that cultivation was originally conceived as a critical theory, which happens to address media issues precisely and only because the mass media (especially television) serve the function of storytelling. (p. 32)

Cultivation Theory, as a critical theory, examines an important social institution (television) in terms of how it uses its storytelling function (a theme we introduced earlier in the chapter) to serve ends other than the benefit of the larger society. In 1996, Gerbner helped found the worldwide Cultural Environment Movement to assist people in their struggle against powerful media industries. Its Viewers' Declaration of Independence reads, in part,

> Let the world hear the reasons that compel us to assert our rights and take an active role in the shaping of our common cultural environment. . . . Humans

Table 24.1 The Three Bs of Television

TERM	DEFINITION	EXAMPLE
Blurring	Traditional distinctions are blurred.	Educated people see the world similarly to those who have less education.
Blending	"Reality" is blended into a cultural mainstream.	We agree on what's real.
Bending	The mainstream reality benefits the elite.	We all want to buy more products.

T*I*P

Theory-Into-Practice

Cultivation Theory

Theoretical Claim: People who watch a lot of television are influenced by the way the world is framed by television programs.

Practical Implication: As an elderly disabled man, Clarence watches a great deal of television programming because he has little opportunity to venture out of his apartment alone. He sees newscasts that focus on manhunts, refugee deaths, world starvation, handgun violence, stock market slides, abuse, and other unfavorable reports. Clarence doesn't second-guess his television sources and thus, has conceptualized a "world view" that is distorted.

live and learn by stories. Today they are no longer hand-crafted, home-made, community-inspired. They are no longer told by families, schools, or churches but are the products of a complex mass-production and marketing process. (http://web.asc.upenn.edu/gerbner/Asset.aspx?assetID=542)

Gerbner was deeply concerned with the effects created by stories told by agencies that do not aim to teach but rather aim to sell.

In addition, Cultivation Theory shares another characteristic with other critical theories: It is political; that is, in accepting its assumptions, its proponents must commit to doing something about the situation. George Gerbner has taken to heart the critical researcher's call to action. In the mid-1990s, he developed the PROD (Proportional Representation of Diversity) index. The goal of the index was to examine the distortion in representation of various co-cultures "across the demography of the media landscape" (Shanahan & Morgan, 1999, p. 223). The index determined how well or poorly groups were represented on television relative to their numbers in the population. The first index Gerbner produced surveyed broadcast network programming and major Hollywood films for 1995–1996. Almost every group (women, African Americans, Latinos, Asian Americans, Native Americans, under age 18, over age 65, gay men and lesbians, disabled, and the poor or lower class) listed in the diversity index was grossly underrepresented in the media. The only group that was not was Native Americans, and this is probably explained by their relatively low population proportionally.

Gerbner took his critical role seriously and stated in a press release associated with the presentation of the index,

> Far from being "quotas" to be imposed on creative people, the Index reflects the limitations on creative freedom in the television and motion picture industries. This is a "report card" of industry performance. We look forward to steady improvement in the diversity and equity of the cultural environment into which our children are born and in which they come to define themselves and others. (Gerbner, 1997, cited in Shanahan & Morgan, 1999, p. 223)

Gerbner believed it is important to highlight how the media industries reflect the needs and perspectives of dominant groups.

Integration, Critique, and Closing

Gerbner and his colleagues have been influential in identifying television as a shaping force in society. Cultivation Theory helps explain the implications of viewing habits, and it has been a very popular theory in mass communication research. In a study conducted by Jennings Bryant and Dorina Miron (2004) surveying almost 2,000 articles published in the three top mass communication journals since 1956, the theory was the third most frequently utilized theory. In addition, since 2013, more than 600 studies have been published and authored by researchers unrelated to Gerbner and his team (Morgan et al., 2016). The methods employed while understanding cultivation have been primarily experimental in nature, although, as we mentioned earlier, the theory has been studied using a critical lens as well. As you think about Cultivation Theory, the following criteria for evaluation are addressed: logical consistency, utility, heurism, and test of time.

Integration

Communication Tradition	Rhetorical | Semiotic | Phenomenological | Cybernetic | Socio-Psychological | **Socio-Cultural** | **Critical**
Communication Context	Intrapersonal | Interpersonal | Small Group | Organizational | Public/Rhetorical | **Mass/Media** | Cultural
Approach to Knowing	**Positivistic/Empirical** | Interpretive/Hermeneutic | **Critical**

Critique

Evaluation Criteria	Scope | **Logical Consistency** | Parsimony | **Utility** | Testability | **Heurism** | **Test of Time**

Logical Consistency

Critics who fault the logical consistency of CT note that the methods employed by Cultivation Theory researchers do not match the conceptual reach of the theory. They note that the research supporting Cultivation Theory employs social scientific methods typically identified with the limited effects findings. Yet, Cultivation Theory examines larger cultural questions most often raised by humanists. Horace Newcomb (1978) writes, "More than any other research effort in the area of television studies the work of Gerbner and Gross and their associates sits squarely at the juncture of the social sciences and the humanities" (p. 265). In some ways, Cultivation Theory offends many humanists, who feel that their turf has been improperly appropriated and misinterpreted. In addition, the theory's logical consistency has been called into question when examining the perception of the viewer. In particular, Elizabeth Skewes (2016) advances the belief that viewing is really a function of "available time for most people" (p. 26). So, the theory may be suspect in that—as Skewes posits—viewing is "ritualistic" (p. 26) and therefore, the amount of content is more relevant to cultivation than what is being viewed at the time.

Utility

Cultivation Theory is also criticized because its claims are not always useful in explaining the phenomenon of interest: how people see the world (Mutz & Nir, 2010). Newcomb (1978) argues that violence is not presented as uniformly on television as the theory assumes, so television cannot be reliably responsible for cultivating the same sense of reality for all viewers. In addition, Cultivation Theory is criticized for ignoring other issues such as the perceived realism of the televised content, which might be critical in explaining people's understanding of reality (Minnebo & Van Acker, 2004). Furthermore, other researchers (Wilson et al., 2005) found that attention to television might be more important to cultivating perceptions than simply the amount of TV viewing. The fact that the theory seems to ignore cognitive processes such as attention or rational thinking style renders it less useful than is desired according to some researchers (Berger, 2005). Further, because in the earlier versions of the theory, Gerbner failed to establish a clear interpretation of what constitutes "violence," some writers (e.g., Hanson, 2016) contend that it can become problematic (and subsequently, less useful). For example, as Ralph Hanson points out: There is a difference between "a fantasy violence of a *Road Runner* cartoon and the more graphic gore of a *Saw* or *Hostel* movie" (p. 42). Gerbner later (http://web.asc.upenn.edu/gerbner/archive.aspx?sectionID=19) explained that violence can vary quite a bit by stating "there is blood in fairy tales, gore in mythology, murder in Shakespeare. Not all violence is alike." In the end, the utility of Cultivation Theory may be not so profound given that individuals could have a hard time effectively determining some basic foundations (e.g., definition of violence) of the theory.

Heurism

When we examine Cultivation Theory against our criteria from Chapter 3, we find that it measures up quite well with regard to heurism. Indeed, the research that has employed the theory has been prolific by any measure (Morgan et al., 2016). For example, the theory has been applied to prime time dramas (Jamieson & Romer, 2014), cultural relations in the United States (Ortiz & Behm-Morowitz, 2016), adolescent's cooperation tactics with law enforcement (Dirikx & Van den Bulck, 2014), video gaming (Breuer, Kowert, Festl, & Thorsten, 2015), and perceptions of immigrants (Seate & Mastro, 2015). The diversity of topics, as evidenced above, continue as this theory attracts scholars from around the globe.

Test of Time

As we've noted, Cultivation Theory is heuristic and long lasting, but two issues may be working against it almost 50 years after its inception. First, some studies based on its tenets are failing to find results consistent with the theory's predictions. Leo Jeffres, David Atkin, and Kimberly Neuendorf (2001), for instance, found that heavy television viewing seemed to be cultivating more diversity of opinion about public issues rather than mainstreaming people's perceptions as Cultivation Theory predicts. In other words, the three Bs that Gerbner and his colleagues discussed were not found in Jeffres, Atkin, and Neuendorf's study. Jeffres and his colleagues called the effect they found "scatter-streaming" and noted that it provided weak support for Cultivation Theory. Consistent with the Mean World Hypothesis, they did find that heavier users of TV expressed a greater need for gun control than did lighter users.

Second, as James Shanahan and Michael Morgan (1999) observe, times and media use are changing: "As more and more people grow up with TV, it is possible that it will become increasingly difficult to discern differences between light and heavy viewers" (p. 161). In addition, as TiVo, DVDs, digital cable, and other technologies alter our manner of TV viewing, it is likely that some of the theory's contentions will no longer hold true. For instance, if viewers can organize programming for themselves, it is unlikely that heavy viewing will mean the same thing for all viewers. Heavy viewing of cooking shows such as Chopped, for example, would be expected to cultivate a different reality from heavy viewing of crime shows such as Law & Order or NCIS. Kathleen Beullens, Keith Roe, and Jan Van den Buick (2011) concur, finding that *what* people watch on television is more important to the cultivation effect than simply the *amount* they watch. Their research showed that teens who watched more TV news programs appeared to take fewer risks as drivers, but teens who watched more action shows exhibited more risk-taking behaviors while driving.

Cultivation offers responses to these criticisms. First, although there may be many more channels and people may have greater control over selectivity than they once had, television's dramatic and aesthetic conventions produce remarkably uniform content within as well as across genres. Second, because most television watching is ritual—that is, selected more by time of day than by specific program or the availability of multiple channels—heavy viewers will be exposed overall to more of television's dominant images. Further, most viewers, even with dozens of channels available to them, primarily select from only five or six, evidencing a very limited range of selection.

Student Voices

Bree

I know that the criticisms of Cultivation Theory make sense. Gerbner came up with his ideas so long ago, and TV is completely different now than it was in the 1960s. Still, I have to think that some of what the theory says is true. I was so surprised to hear that violent crime was falling in the United States. I could have sworn it was on the rise. And I am thinking I get that idea because I do watch a ton of TV. And I watch a lot of crime shows: NCIS, Law & Order: SVU, and Person of Interest are some of my favorites.

Closing

Cultivation Theory has been and remains one of the most influential mass communication theories of the last several decades. It is the foundation of much contemporary research and, as we've seen, has even become an international social movement. Another source of its influence is that it can be applied by anyone. It asks people to assess their own media use alongside the socially constructed reality of the world they inhabit. Imagine yourself as Joyce Jensen preparing to cast an important vote. You may well undergo the same mental debate as she. Yet, think of how even a passing understanding of Cultivation Theory might help you arrive at your decision and understand your motivations.

Discussion Starters

TECH QUEST: Originally, Gerbner and his colleagues constructed Cultivation Theory about television and later discussed other forms of media such as films. How do you think the theory operates with regard to social media? For instance, people post a lot of drinking party pictures on Facebook. Do you think that people who spend a lot of time visiting these Facebook pages would cultivate a view of reality that overemphasizes drinking behavior as CT would predict?

1. Are you like Joyce Jensen in that you do not feel safe walking in your neighborhood at night? How much television do you watch? Do you fit the profile offered by Cultivation Theory? Why or why not?

2. Cultivation Theory is a critical theory and demands action from its adherents. Do you believe researchers and theorists should become politically active in the fields they study? Why or why not?

3. Do you agree with the hypothesis concerning the Mean World Index? Why or why not?

4. How do you define violence on television? Do you think it is possible to calculate violent acts as Gerbner and his colleagues have done? Explain your answer.

5. Do you believe that the world is a mean place? What real-world evidence do you have that it is? What television evidence do you have that it is?

6. How do you respond to the criticism that more television channels and more divisions among viewers mean that the assumptions of Cultivation Theory are no longer valid?

7. What other variables might affect people's perception of the world in addition to their amount of television viewing?

CHAPTER 25

Cultural Studies

*Based on the research of **Stuart Hall***

There is no understanding Englishness without understanding its imperial and colonial dimensions.

—Stuart Hall

Luisa and John Petrillo

Luisa and John Petrillo have lived in the same trailer park for four years with their two young children.

They realize that the wages they earn as migrant workers will make it difficult for the two to own their own home. They appreciate that Mr. DeMoss, the owner of the egg farm where they work, has provided housing for them, but they wish that they could have more privacy so that their neighbors would not be able to hear every word they say in the evening. The Petrillos do not have any desire to leave their tiny town because they realize that jobs are not that plentiful in northern New England. So they get by in the trailer park, and still dream about a big backyard where their two kids and their dog, Scooter, can play.

The Petrillos' dream often unfolds on the television shows they watch at night. Even though cable TV is expensive and not a necessity, they both love to watch shows that help them escape their daily routines. Watching TV, Luisa and John are bombarded with messages about interest rates being at an all-time low accompanied by relatively low home selling prices. Whether watching network or cable TV, they keep seeing the same commercials over and over again promoting home ownership as the "American Dream." They watch

infomercials that promote "Five Ways to Get Your American Dream." They look at each other, wondering why they continue to live the way they do—two children, two bedrooms, and a common bathing area in the migrant camp. They both know that they don't have the money to purchase a home, but they also know that they aren't happy with the way things are.

Recently, DeMoss's farm was investigated by the government for unsanitary living and working conditions. DeMoss was told to clean up the place and was threatened with daily stiff fines unless he improved the situation. Immediately, he had authorized spending a lot of money for individual lavatory facilities and began talking to the local grocery chain to work on establishing discounts to employees at the egg farm. As a gesture that will likely increase employee productivity and deter media attacks, DeMoss was also prepared to increase each worker's paycheck by 15 percent by the end of the month. He also promised to help relocate families with children to more suitable accommodations.

The Petrillos were ecstatic. They dreaded the "communal" bathing area and welcomed more privacy for their children and themselves. They were very excited about the opportunity to save money on food, and, of course, they were thrilled that their paychecks would increase almost immediately. This, they thought, was the beginning of saving for their Dream. They knew that they made just enough money to pay all of their bills, and now with the raise, the extra money would go into a rainy day fund that could eventually be used to purchase a home. For now, though, Luisa was excited about the chance to move to what DeMoss called "suitable" housing. "It has to be better than this," she thought.

■

We cannot overstate how much the U.S. culture relies on the media. Each day, for instance, millions of homes tune in to dozens of different "news" programs on television. And, although newspapers remain the top source for information on cultural events, most adults under the age of 40 rely upon a blend of sources (e.g., the Internet, social media, etc.) for their news (http://www.niemanlab .org/2015/07/new-pew-data-more-americans-are-getting-news-on-facebook-and -twitter/).

Although the media have become the primary sources for how individuals learn about events around the globe (Baran & Davis, 2016), it is the manner in which the media report events that vary significantly. Some journalists depend on fact finding. Others rely on personal testimony or stories. Still others seek out experts to comment on events and topics as they unfold, whether they pertain to celebrity trials, natural disasters, refugees' plight, war, terrorist attacks, or school shootings. In fact, a common template for following a school shooting, for instance, resulted from the coverage of the 2012 Newtown, Connecticut, the deadliest mass shooting in a school in U.S. history in which 26 students and teachers were killed. It is now predictable: First, the tragedy is usually reported in "real time," that is, as it happens, via social media such as Twitter. Next, reporters interview witnesses to get first hand accounts of the shootings. Finally, journalists gather experts on both sides of the gun control issue to assess whether gun control laws are sufficiently tough. This last effort involving experts seems to beg other questions about the media's role in such events: Are they trying to convey a larger message about society in general? Is the reporting of images and stories done thoughtfully and conscientiously or is sensationalism a primary goal?

Reporting events with hidden or disingenuous ambitions has several implications. When the media fail to report all aspects of a story, someone or some group is inevitably affected. Nowhere is this more apparent than in the early coverage of AIDS, which was first diagnosed in the gay community. Edward Alwood (1997) notes that because most news editors did not consider gay deaths to be newsworthy, major news outlets (including the esteemed *New York Times*) failed to provide coverage of the disease. In fact, the disease was killing far more people than the 34 who died from Legionnaires' disease in 1976 and the 84 women who died of toxic shock syndrome in 1980. Yet, it wasn't until the death of actor Rock Hudson in 1985 that major news stories were devoted to the subject of AIDS. By that time, however, more than 6,000 people had died from the disease. This perception has been reiterated more recently, and writers have further argued that the *New York Times* executive editor assigned news stories that aimed to "demonize homosexuality" (huffingtonpost.com/2012/11/28 /new-york-times-gays-lesbians-aids-homophobia_n_2200684.html). The media's message related to the reporting of AIDS was implied but significant: Gay men are aberrant and their deaths are not newsworthy.

Theorist Stuart Hall questioned the role of the media and their frequently sensational, false, and misleading images. Unlike other communication theorists, however, Hall focused on the role of the media and their ability to shape public opinions of marginalized populations, including people of color, the poor, and others who do not reflect a White, male, heterosexual (and wealthy) point of view.

For Hall, the personal is the political. A former high school teacher who taught English, math, and geography, Hall's background likely influenced his conceptualization of cultural studies. He spoke of doing graduate work and, as a Jamaican, tried to understand his Jamaican culture and how it influenced his thinking and behavior (MacCabe, 2008). Hall was very much concerned with how "cultural forces" influenced the culture at large (Horowitz, 2012). And, many scholars who embraced Hall's thinking simultaneously embraced the scholar himself. Ann Courthoys and John Docker (2016) offered that Hall was a "public intellectual, academic leader, writer, editor, teacher, political activist, family man and friend" (p. 302). This sort of posturing and orientation resonates throughout Cultural Studies.

Cultural Studies is a theoretical perspective that focuses on how culture is influenced by powerful, dominant groups. Cultural Studies is rooted in politics, but not the sort of electoral politics that characterize much of your understanding of politics. Rather, the theory is aligned with the politics of identity, namely the interplay between and among culture and race, ethnicity, gender, sexuality, and other markers of one's identity. Unlike several other theoretical traditions in this book, Cultural Studies does not refer to a single doctrine of human behavior. In fact, Stuart Hall (1992) persuasively argues that "Cultural Studies has multiple discourses; it has a number of different histories. It is a whole set of formations; it has its own different conjunctures and moments in the past. . . . I want to insist on that!" (p. 278).

Cultural Studies has its background and its beginnings in Britain, although scholars in the United States have also advanced our understanding of Stuart Hall's theory. As a cultural theorist and the former director of the Center for Contemporary Cultural Studies (CCCS) at the University of Birmingham in England, Hall (1981, 1989) contends that the media are powerful tools of the elite. Media serve to communicate dominant ways of thinking, regardless of the efficacy of such thinking. Cultural Studies emphasizes that the media keep the powerful people in control while the less powerful absorb what is presented to them. Luisa and John Petrillo, for

Theory At a Glance • Cultural Studies

The media represent ideologies of the dominant class in a society. Because media are controlled by corporations (the elite), the information presented to the public is consequently influenced and targeted with profit in mind. The media's influence and the role of power must be taken into consideration when interpreting a culture.

instance, exemplify a marginalized group (the poor) who have been enamored by the "American Dream" of owning a home. Of course, Cultural Studies theorists would argue that the media—in this case, the infomercial sponsors—are taking advantage of a couple who will probably never have enough money to own a home. Yet, the message from the popular media is that it is possible. All that is needed, according to the message, is "good sense and good money."

Cultural Studies is a tradition rooted in the writings of German philosopher Karl Marx. Because Marxist principles form the foundation of the theory, let's look further into this backdrop. We then examine two assumptions of Cultural Studies.

The Marxist Legacy: Power to the People

Philosopher Karl Marx (1818–1883) is generally credited with identifying how the powerful (the elite) exploit the powerless (the working class). He believed that being powerless could lead to **alienation,** or the psychological condition whereby people begin to feel that they have little control over their future. For Marx, though, alienation is most destructive under capitalism. Specifically, when people lose control over their own means of production (as happens in capitalism) and must sell their time to some employer, they become alienated. Capitalism results in a profit-driven society, and workers in a capitalistic society are measured by their labor potential.

alienation
perception that one has little control over his or her future

Marx believed that the class system—a monolithic system that pervades all society—must be unearthed by the collective working class, or proletariat. He felt that laborers were often subjected to poor working and living conditions because the elite were unwilling to yield their control. As with Luisa and John Petrillo, laborers across society are constantly relegated to secondary status. The elite, or ruling, class's interests become socially ingrained, and therefore people become enslaved in society. One of Marx's principal concerns was ensuring that some revolutionary action of the proletariat be undertaken to break the chains of slavery and ultimately to subvert alienation under a capitalistic society. The capitalistic society, according to Marxist tradition, shapes society and the individuals within it (Weedon, 2016).

Student Voices

Wil

The 2012 election was fascinating to watch while I was studying Hall's theory. It was interesting to read about how surprised some in the media were because President Obama was an "articulate" person in the debates. He loved his family, as if that was something that needed to be mentioned by the media. The ads attacking the President focused on welfare and food stamps. Some other commercials talked about Obama being "lazy." In the end, I think those in power—the white men—(still) had a problem with a black man being President and they did everything they could to cut into his credibility.

CULTURAL STUDIES

Frankfurt School theorists
a group of scholars who believed that the media were more concerned with making money than with presenting news

Marxist thinkers who believed the working class was oppressed because of corporate-owned media have been called the **Frankfurt School theorists.** These thinkers and writers believed that the media's messages were constructed and delivered with one goal in mind: capitalism. That is, although the media might claim that they are delivering information for the "common good," the bottom line (money) frames each message. Those affiliated with the Frankfurt School felt that the media could be considered an "authoritarian personality," which meant that they were opposed to the male-centered/male-owned media. In fact, Herbert Marcuse, a Frankfurt thinker, was the leader of a group of social revolutionaries whose goal was to break down this patriarchal system.

neo-Marxist
limited embracement of Marxism

The application of Marxist principles to Cultural Studies is more subtle than direct. This has prompted some scholars to consider the theory to be more **neo-Marxist,** which means the theory diverges from classical Marxism to some extent. First, unlike Marx, those in Cultural Studies have integrated a variety of perspectives into their thinking, including those from the arts, the humanities, and the social sciences. Second, theorists in Cultural Studies expand the subordinate group to include additional powerless and marginalized people, not just laborers. These groups include gay men and lesbians, racial/ethnic minorities, women, and even children. Third, everyday life for Marx was centered on work and the family. Writers in Cultural Studies have also studied recreational activities, hobbies, and sporting events in seeking to understand how individuals function in society. In sum, Marx's original thinking may have been appropriate for post–World War II populations, but his ideas now require clarification, elaboration, and application to a diverse society. Cultural Studies moves beyond a strict, limited interpretation of society toward a broader conception of culture. In short, as Janice Radway (2016) has acknowledged, the work of Stuart Hall has been both "extraordinary" and "consequential" (p. 312).

Now that you have a brief understanding of how Hall and other theorists in Cultural Studies were influenced by the writings of Marx, we examine two primary assumptions of Cultural Studies.

Assumptions of Cultural Studies

Cultural Studies is essentially concerned with how elite groups such as the media exercise their power over subordinate groups. The theory is rooted in a few fundamental claims about culture and power:

- Culture pervades and invades all facets of human behavior.
- People are part of a hierarchical structure of power.

ideology
framework used to make sense of our existence

The first assumption pertains to the notion of culture, a concept we addressed in Chapter 2. To review, we identified culture as a community of meaning. In Cultural Studies, we need a slightly modified interpretation of the word, one that underscores the nature of the theory. The various norms, ideas, values, and forms of understanding in a society that help people interpret their reality are part of a culture's **ideology.** According to Hall (1981), ideology refers to "those images, concepts and premises which provide the frameworks through which we represent, interpret, understand, and 'make sense' of some aspect of social existence" (p. 31). Hall believes that ideologies include the languages, the concepts, and the categories that different social groups collect in order to make sense of their environments.

To a great extent, cultural practices and institutions permeate our ideologies. We cannot escape the cultural reality that, as a global community, actions are not performed in a vacuum. Graham Murdock (1989) emphasizes the pervasiveness of culture by noting that "all groups are constantly engaged in creating and remaking meaning systems and embodying these meanings in expressive forms, social practices, and institutions" (p. 436). Interestingly, however, Murdock notes, being part of a diverse cultural community often results in struggles over meaning, interpretation, identity, and control. These struggles, or **culture wars,** suggest that there are frequently deep divisions in the perception of the significance of a cultural issue or event. Individuals often compete to help shape a nation's identity. For example, during the peak of the arguments related to same-sex marriage in 2015, both nonsupporters and supporters of same-sex marriage wanted to interpret what "marriage" is. One wanted to define marriage in traditional (man–woman) ways and the other defined it in less tangible (love) ways. Both groups strove to make their meanings dominant. Although ultimately, in 2015, the nine members of the U.S. Supreme Court ruled in favor of same-sex couples to marry, the struggle occurred both in the legal courts as well as in the "court" of public opinion.

culture wars
cultural struggles over meaning, identity, and influence

Dreama Moon (2008) notes that culture includes a number of diverse activities of a population. In the United States, there are many behaviors, some done daily and others less frequently. For instance, it is common for men to ask women out on a date, for families to visit one another during holidays, and for people to attend religious services at least once a week. There are also more mundane behaviors, such as getting your driver's license renewed, running on the treadmill, pulling weeds from your garden, or listening to the radio while driving home from work. For those interested in Cultural Studies, it is crucial to examine these activities to understand how the ideology of a population is maintained. Paul du Gay, Stuart Hall, Linda Janes, Hugh Mackay, and Keith Negus (1997) explain that these practices intersect to help us understand the production and dissemination of meaning in a culture. At the same time, the meaning of a culture is reflected by such practices. Culture, then, cannot be separated from meaning in society.

Meaning in our culture is profoundly sculpted by the media. The media could simply be considered the technological carrier of culture, but as this chapter will point out, the media are so much more. Consider the words of Michael Real (1996) regarding the media's role in U.S. culture: "Media invade our living space, shape the taste of those around us, inform and persuade us on products and policies, intrude into our private dreams and public fears, and in turn, invite us to inhabit them" (pp. xiii–xiv). No doubt, for example, that the media contain both intentional and unintentional messages that entice the Petrillos to accept mediated interpretations of what constitutes the dream of home ownership.

A second assumption of cultural theory pertains to people as an important part of a powerful social hierarchy. Power operates at all levels in society. However, power in this sense is not role-based. Rather, Hall is interested in the power held by social groups or the power between groups. (Goggin, 2016). Meaning and power are intricately related, for as Hall (1989) contends, "meaning cannot be conceptualized outside the field of play of power relations" (p. 48). In keeping with the Marxist

CULTURAL STUDIES

tradition, power is something that subordinate groups desire but cannot achieve. Often there is a struggle for power, and the victor is usually the person at the top of the social hierarchy. An example of what we are discussing here can be observed in the U.S. culture's preoccupation with beauty. Theorists in Cultural Studies would contend that because beauty is often defined as thin and good looking, anyone not matching these qualities would be considered unattractive. Hall may believe that the attractive people—those usually at the top of the social hierarchy—are able to wield more power than those at the bottom (the unattractive).

It appears that the ultimate source of power in our society is the media. Hall (1989) maintains that the media are simply too powerful. He is not shy in his indictment of the media's character by calling the media dishonest and "fundamentally dirty" (p. 48). In a diverse culture, Hall argues, no institution should have the power to decide what the public hears. Gary Woodward (1997) draws a similar conclusion when he states that there is a tradition whereby journalists serve as guardians of the nation's cultural activities: If the media deem something to have importance, then something has importance; an otherwise unimportant event suddenly carries importance. Today, the Society of Professional Journalists (www.spj.org) asserts that bloggers have now emerged as society's cultural guardians.

Let's revisit our story of Luisa and John Petrillo. Cultural Studies advocates would argue that as members of a minority population, the Petrillos have been inherently relegated to a subordinate position in society. Their work environment—as migrant workers on a large egg farm—is the product of a capitalistic society, one in which laborers work under difficult conditions. Although they will inevitably have difficulty owning their own home because of their low wages, writers in Cultural Studies would point to the media's barrage of images and stories touting the "American Dream." Although the message may convey hope for the Petrillos, their dream of owning their own home might better be called a fantasy because the elite power structure (the media) does not honestly convey the reality of their circumstances. Likely unknown to the Petrillos is the fact that the media are a tool of the dominant class. The future of Luisa and John Petrillo, then, will overtly and covertly be influenced by the ruling class.

Hegemony: The Influence on the Masses

The concept of hegemony is an important feature of Cultural Studies, and much of the theory rests on an understanding of this term. Scott Lash (2007) contends that "from the beginnings of cultural studies in the 1970s, 'hegemony' has been perhaps the pivotal concept" (p. 55). **Hegemony** can be generally defined as the influence, power, or dominance of one social group over another. Embedded in hegemony is a *master-narrative*, which is a "grand story told by the dominant groups to legitimate and justify their actions and policies" (Campbell & Kean, 2016, p. 18). The idea is a complex one that can be traced back to the work of Antonio Gramsci, one of the founders of the Italian Communist Party who was later imprisoned by the Italian fascists. Writers in Cultural Studies have called Gramsci a "second progenitor Marxist" (Inglis, 1993, p. 74) because he openly questioned why the masses never revolted against the privileged class:

> The study of hegemony was for him [Gramsci], and is for us, the study of the question why so many people assent to and vote for political arrangements

hegemony
the domination of one group over another, usually weaker, group

which palpably work against their own happiness and sense of justice. What on earth is it, in schools or on the telly [television], which makes rational people accept unemployment, killing queues [wards] in hospitals, ludicrous waste on needless weaponry, and all the other awful details of life under modern capitalism? (Inglis, 1993, p. 76)

Gramsci's notion of hegemony was based on Marx's idea of **false consciousness,** a state in which individuals are unaware of the domination in their lives. Gramsci contended that audiences can be exploited by the same social system they support (financially). From popular culture to religion, Gramsci felt the dominant groups in society manage to direct people into complacency. Consent is a principal component of hegemony. Consent is given by populations if they are given enough "stuff" (e.g., freedoms, material goods, etc.). Ultimately, people will prefer to live in a society with these "rights" and consent to the dominant culture's ideologies.

false consciousness
Gramsci's belief that people are unaware of the domination in their lives

The application of Gramsci's thinking on hegemony is quite applicable to today's society. Under a hegemonic culture, some profit (literally) while others lose out. What happens in hegemonic societies is that people become susceptible to a subtle imbalance in power. That is, people are likely to support tacitly the dominant ideology of a culture. The complexity of the concept is further discussed by Hall (1989). He notes that hegemony can be multifaceted in that the dominant, or ruling, class is frequently divided in its ideologies. That means that during the subtle course of being influenced, the public may find itself pushed and pulled in several directions. Unraveling such complexity is one goal of researchers in Cultural Studies. Think about, for instance, the water crisis that happened in Flint, Michigan in 2016. During that time, state officials were blaming the EPA for the contamination found in the city's drinking water. The EPA, however, pointed fingers at the state officials. In the meantime, nearly 12,000 children who were overwhelmingly African American were exposed to very high levels of lead in their water and may have long-term problems as a result. This "water democracy" would be of particular interest to Hall and his associates. Although the "audience" was given vastly different interpretations to the problem, in the end, the dominant (political) culture was trying to influence the discourse and the public's opinion of the crisis. As Ann Ryder (2016) observed: The contamination debacle was "covered up and informing the public was drastically delayed" (p. 23).

Hegemony can be further understood by looking at today's corporate culture, where—using Marx's thinking—ruling ideas are ideas of the ruling class. In most corporate cultures, decision making is predominantly made by White, heterosexual males, a fact made even more compelling when examining the fact that less than 96 percent of Fortune 500 companies have male CEOs (http://fortune.com/2014/06/03/number-of-fortune-500-women-ceos-reaches-historic-high/). Hall challenges this dominant way of thinking and relating and argues that a homogenous leadership may simply lead to a subordination of the people (workers). How is consciousness raised and how is new consciousness presented? Perhaps it is the language used in an organization, for as Hall (1997) states, "Language in its widest sense is the vehicle of practical reasoning, calculation, and consciousness, because of the ways by which certain meanings and references have been historically secured" (p. 40). People must share the same way of interpreting language; however, Hall notes that meanings change from one culture or era to another. So what exists in one organizational setting may not exist in another.

CULTURAL STUDIES

What all this means is that there are multiple ideologies in a society as complex as the United States. This translates into what Hall calls a **theatre of struggle,** which means that various ideologies in society compete and are in temporary states of conflict. Thus, as attitudes and values on different topics shift in society, so do the various ideologies associated with these topics. For example, think about what it meant to be a woman before 1920 and what it means to be a woman today. Before 1920, women were unable to vote and were generally regarded as subordinate and subservient to men. Then in August 1920, the amendment giving women the right to vote was ratified. Today, of course, women not only vote but also hold high political

Theory in Popular Press • *Tobacco Companies and Child Labor*

One of the globe's largest and most profitable industries is tobacco. In an essay from *The Guardian*, a leading U.K. newspaper, Kristin Palitza underscores one of the leading notions related to Cultural Studies: the exploitation of laborers by large corporate behemoths. Palitza features a five-year-old who works every day with his parents in Malawi's "tobacco district." The young boy doesn't attend school and his 12-year-old sister rarely attends school because of coughing, chest pains, and ongoing headaches. The author posits that there are 80,000 child tobacco workers in Malawi who suffer from nicotine poisoning. Farm owners deny knowing about the dangers and more importantly, tobacco corporate giants Philip Morris and British American Tobacco claim that they do not employ children in their operations. Nonetheless, Palitza reports, the "intermediaries" who purchase tobacco "make it difficult to trace the country from which they buy the [tobacco leaf]." In fact, "the tobacco giants, who all have anti-child labor policies in place, insist they abide by the rules." In other words, no one is taking responsibility for the growing nicotine poisoning in Malawi youth, children who often work 12-hour days and who may receive an average of $0.25 for a day's work.

In spite of both the financial (70 percent of exports earnings come from tobacco) and health (40 percent of Malawians live below the poverty line of $1.25 a day) consequences, Palitza reports that the Malawi government remains complicit; most violators receive a $34.00 fine. Most Cultural Studies theorists would agree with a researcher at the University of California tobacco control research and education center: "If major tobacco companies were genuinely committed to improving the socio-economic conditions of child workers, they should rectify harmful business practices by enforcing a policy that they will not purchase any tobacco grown using child labor."

Source: Palitza, K. (2011, September 14). Child labour: The tobacco industry's smoking gun. *The Guardian online*, guardian.co.uk/global-development/2011/sep/14/malawi-child-labour -tobacco-industry.

office. Although U.S. society still does not provide entirely equal opportunity for women, and women continue to be targets of discrimination, the culture and ideology pertaining to women's rights have changed with the times.

Hegemony is but one component of the intellectual currents associated with Cultural Studies. Although people (audiences) are frequently influenced by dominant societal forces, at times hegemonic tendencies will emerge in the population. We explore this notion further.

Counter-Hegemony: The Masses Start to Influence the Dominant Forces

We have noted that hegemony is one of the core concepts associated with Cultural Studies. Yet, audiences are not always duped into accepting and believing everything presented by the dominant forces. At times, audiences will use the same resources and strategies of dominant social groups. To some extent, individuals will use the same practices of hegemonic domination to challenge that domination. This is what Gramsci called **counter-hegemony.**

Counter-hegemony becomes a critical part of Cultural Studies thinking because it suggests that audiences are not necessarily willing and compliant. In other words, we—as audience members—are always the dumb and submissive people some have us made out to be! Danny Lesh of the Counter Hegemony Project, writes in *Counter Heg* (a blog dedicated to the counter-hegemonic movement, available at: http://counterheg.blogspot.com) that part of the goal of counter-hegemony "is to understand history from other lenses, particularly from women's, workers', and racial minorities' perspectives." That is, in counter-hegemony, researchers try to raise the volume on voices that have been voiceless. Think of counter-hegemony as a point where individuals recognize their consent and try to do something about it. In Chapter 29 on Muted Group Theory, you will be reintroduced to how silenced voices deal with dominant groups.

Counter-hegemonic messages, interestingly enough, occur quite a bit in television, affecting viewers in subtle ways. Over the years, television has been a major vehicle for counter-hegemonic messages. For instance, in the 1990s, The Cosby Show, the number 1 show at the time, showed a well-to-do African American couple living in an upscale neighborhood in New York City, raising their children with values of honesty, respect, and responsibility (Gray, 1989). Another example can be found in the show, *American Horror Story*. In a few episodes, Chad and his partner, Chad, are house stagers, going into homes to make them more attractive to potential buyers. Brian Klingenfus (http://blogs.longwood.edu/klingenfus/2013/04/19/counter-hegemony-in-american-horror-story/) observes that although Chad would be considered to be "stereotypically gay" (e.g., fashion-centered, "sassy," etc.), Patrick would be considered to be "straight from the eye of the typical viewer." The blogger contends that this relational dynamic is counter-hegemonic since the show's producers and director decided to portray Patrick as counter to the dominant view of gay men in Western society. A third example of counter-hegemony can be found in many daytime television talk shows. Since many of the shows (e.g., The Talk, The View, etc.) are comprised of solely women, viewers find topics that have been normally relegated to men (e.g., sex, politics, power, etc.).

counter-hegemony
when, at times, people use hegemonic behaviors to challenge the domination in their lives

CULTURAL STUDIES

Further, as Karin Wetchanow (http://www.iwm.at/wp-content/uploads/jc-08-101.pdf) points out, this genre embraces audience-centeredness as well as topics that relate to everyday people. This approach counters many dominant Westernized views and Wetchanow contends that such shows (starting with Oprah many years ago) "challenge authority and expertise" in ways that were unseen prior to this new female-only genre. While these shows may appear to be nothing but entertainment exemplars, they in their own ways, demonstrate how television content challenges the priorities established by the dominant forces, and subsequently, influence viewer attitudes and behaviors.

Before leaving this discussion, let's address one more point related to counter-hegemony and use one of the most popular television shows in history. The Simpsons, the longest-running comedy on television, also contains satiric counter-hegemonic messages aimed at showing that individuals who are dominated use the same symbolic resources to challenge that domination. The relevance of *The Simpsons* to the lives of people has been persuasively argued. Tim Delaney (2008) succinctly notes that the show reveals so much about us because so much of the show intersects with the social institutions (family, school, jobs, houses of worship, etc.) to which we belong. The show has included references to such diverse topics as talk shows, Kafka, the Beatles, Tennessee Williams, same-sex marriage, the invention of television, and hormone therapy! The core cast of characters—Marge (mother), Homer (father), Bart (son), Lisa (daughter), and Maggie (infant daughter)—all present different counter-hegemonic messages. For Marge, although cultural representations of a homemaker/housewife suggest a doting and supportive wife and mother, she is argu-ably the most independent of all the characters. She has tried a number of other profes-sions, from police officer to protester against handgun violence. Homer, an employee at a local nuclear power plant, shows that despite what the government may tell us about the safety of these facilities, people like Homer continue to stay employed. Lisa, con-testing societal expectations that a child should be seen and not heard, shows that she is intellectually curious, artistically savvy, and environmentally aware.

One of the more central characters of the show is Bart Simpson. Interestingly, although society tends to shut down boys of Bart's age (and girls to some extent), Bart manages to shut down the same society that tries to subdue him. His pranks range from harassing a local bar with sophomoric phone calls to disrespecting his grade school principal to calling his father by his first name. In the end, however, despite the 20 minutes of chaos, the family members show that they have high regard for one another in personal ways. As Carl Matheson (2001) notes, the show advocates "a moral position of caring at the level of the individual, one which favors the family over the institution" (p. 4).

A closer look at the television series illustrates other counter-hegemonic tones. Brian Ott (2003), for example, calls *The Simpsons* the "anti-show show" (p. 58). He states that "*The Simpsons* has always represented a sort of anti-show, spoofing, challenging, and collapsing the traditional codes, structures, and formulas of network television" (p. 59). Ott contends that the characters of Bart, Homer, and Lisa help viewers understand "lessons about selfhood" (p. 61) and that the show is watched by a number of different cultural communities, including Whites, African Americans, and Hispanics. Ott and other scholars contend that the show has managed to tran-scend traditional images of the family that demonstrated and embraced patriarchal control. Indeed, a close examination of the series shows that children are frequently viewed as subverting or overthrowing parental control and asserting dominance in their family. *The Simpsons* continues to challenge prevailing religious, political, and cultural notions that the family is weakening.

Audience Decoding

No hegemonic or counter-hegemonic message can exist without an audience's ability to receive the message and compare it with meanings already stored in their minds (O' Donnell, 2017). This is called **decoding,** the final topic of Cultural Studies we wish to address. When we receive messages from others, we decode them according to our perceptions, thoughts, and past experiences. So, for instance, when Luisa Petrillo, from our chapter-opening story, interprets information on purchasing a home, she is relying on several mental behaviors. These include her desire to have a home, her conversations with people who have already purchased a home, her library visits, and the fact that she and her family have never owned a home. Luisa will store the information she receives pertaining to a new home and retrieve it when someone engages her in a conversation on the topic. All of this is done instantaneously; that is, she will make immediate decisions about how to interpret a message once she receives it.

decoding
receiving and comparing messages

Decoding is central to Cultural Studies. But, before we delve further into this, let's review the gist of Cultural Studies up to this point. You will recall that the public receives a great deal of information from the elite and that people unconsciously consent to what dominant ideologies suggest. Theorists reason that the public should be envisioned as part of a larger cultural context, one in which those struggling for a voice are oppressed (Barker & Jane, 2016). As we discussed previously, hierarchical social relations (between the elite bosses and the subordinate

Student Voices

Alexandra

Of the different ideas related to Cultural Studies, the one that sticks out the most for me is that there is a perpetuation of power by those in power. I saw it in my town newspaper when I was home for break. On the front page, there was a huge story on the high school football team losing in the playoffs. The article talked about their wins and losses through the year and even they had a picture of the coach and his family. That same weekend, though, the speech and debate team won state finals and there was a small boxed article on page 8. There were no pictures and the coach of the team certainly didn't have her family pictured. I think this goes to show that football and sports perpetuates a dominant patriarchal script (complete with boys and a male coach) and that things like the speech and debate team (with a female coach and mostly female debaters) gets shortchanged. Oh: The editor of the paper is a father of the son who's on the football team.

workers, for example) exist in an uneven society. This results in subordinate cultures decoding the messages of the ruling class. Usually, according to Hall, the media connote the ruling class in Western society. Hall (1980a) elaborates on how decoding works in the media. He recognizes that an audience decodes a message from three vantage points, or positions: dominant, negotiated, and oppositional. We explore each of these next.

Hall claims that individuals operate within a code that dominates and exercises more power than other codes. He terms this the **dominant position.** The professional code of television broadcasters, for instance, will always operate within the hegemony of the dominant code. Hall relates that professional codes reproduce hegemonic interpretations of reality. This is done with subtle persuasion. Consider John and Luisa Petrillo from our, opener. The television images of owning a home prompt the Petrillos to believe that owning a home is within their reach. The selection of words, the presentation of pictures, and the choice of spokespeople in infomercials are all part of the staging in the professional code. Audiences, like the Petrillos, are prone to either misunderstanding a message or selectively perceiving only certain parts of a message. Why? Hall writes, "The viewer does not know the terms employed, cannot follow the complex logic of argument or exposition, is unfamiliar with the language, finds the concepts too alien or difficult or is foxed by the expository narrative" (1980a, p. 135). Television producers are worried that people like the Petrillos will not accept the intended and preferred media message of owning a home. They (the media) therefore place their professional code placed in the larger, dominant cultural code of meaning. This ensures that John and Luisa Petrillo will work toward buying a home.

The second position is a **negotiated position**; audience members are able to accept dominant ideologies, but will operate with some exceptions to the cultural rule. Hall holds that audience members always reserve the right to apply local conditions to large-scale events. This happens frequently when the media report on laws that are enacted at the national level and interpreted at the state or community level. For example, Hall might argue that although audiences may accept the elite's interpretation of a welfare reform bill in Washington, D.C. ("All people should work if they are able to"), they may have to negotiate when it does not coincide with a local or personal principle ("Children need parents at home"). Hall notes that due to the difficulty of negotiations, people are prone to communication failures.

The final way in which audiences decode messages is by engaging in an oppositional position. An **oppositional position** occurs when audience members substitute an alternative code for the code supplied by the media. Critical consumers reject the media's intended and preferred meaning of the message and instead replace it with their own way of thinking about a subject. Consider, for instance, the manner in which the media communicate feminine images of beauty. To many, the media present feminine beauty as a way to serve the sexual desire of men (Reimer & Ahmed, 2012). Some consumers, however, reject this capitalistic message and substitute more realistic portrayals.

Hall accepts the fact that the media frame messages with the covert intent to persuade. Audience members have the capacity to avoid being swallowed up in the dominant ideology, yet, as with the Petrillo family, the messages the audience receives are often part of a more subtle campaign. Theorists in Cultural Studies do

dominant position
operating within a code that allows one person to have control over another

negotiated position
accepting dominant ideologies, but allowing for cultural exceptions

oppositional position
substituting alternative messages presented by the media

CULTURAL STUDIES

not suggest that people are gullible, but rather that they often unknowingly become a part of the agenda of others (Hall, 1980b).

Integration, Critique, and Closing

Although Cultural Studies began at the CCCS in England, its influence in the United States has been vast. The theory has attracted the attention of critical theorists in particular because it is founded on the principles of criticism. Its Marxist influence has also drawn scholars from philosophy, economics, and social psychology, and its emphasis on underrepresented groups in society has enticed writers in sociology and women's studies to take notice (Steiner, 2017). In addition, Cultural Studies theorists would/could never consider using experimental methods, making this theory reliant upon qualitative investigation. For additional criticism, we discuss three criteria for evaluating a theory: logical consistency, utility, and heurism.

Integration

Communication Tradition	Rhetorical | Semiotic | Phenomenological | Cybernetic | Socio-Psychological | Socio-Cultural | **Critical**
Communication Context	Intrapersonal | Interpersonal | Small Group | Organizational | Public/Rhetorical | **Mass/Media** | Cultural
Approach to Knowing	Positivistic/Empirical | **Interpretive/Hermeneutic** | **Critical**

Critique

Evaluation Criteria	Scope | **Logical Consistency** | Parsimony | **Utility** | Testability | **Heurism** | Test of Time

Logical Consistency

Despite some glowing endorsements, the logical consistency of the theory has been challenged. This criticism relates to the audience. Even though some audiences resist the role of dupe, are they able to become interpretive and active resisters? In other words, to what extent can audiences be counter-hegemonic? Mike Budd, Robert Entman, and Clay Steinman (1990) suggest that some cultural and critical theorists overestimate the ability of oppressed and marginalized populations to escape their culture. Particularly those communities that lack the skills, insights, and networks, escaping is very difficult. In fact, as we consider the television-viewing habits of people like the Petrillos from our chapter opening, counter-hegemony may not even be considered. That is, the family may simply be repackaging and reframing the information they receive about home ownership and critically applying relevant information to their lives. This dialogue is not likely to go away because "debates over the audience were once, and continue to be, a major field of contestation in cultural studies" (Kellner & Hammer, 2004, p. 79).

Utility

Cultural Studies "makes up a vehicle that can alter our self-image" (Carey, 1989, p. 94). Therefore, it's possible to translate some of the theory into daily life, making it useful to some extent. Its utility can also be found in its dedication to studying the cultural struggles of the underprivileged. According to Hall, these populations have remained subordinate for too long. By concentrating on these marginalized social groups, a number of subfields have emerged, namely, ethnic studies and gay, lesbian, bisexual, transgender studies (Surber, 1998). Hall's theory has been called "empirically elegant" (Carey, 1989, p. 31), and its usefulness beyond the written page has been widely articulated (e.g., Grossberg, 2010). Writers have also noted that "It has experienced a period of rapid growth in the academy, appearing at many universities in a variety of forms and locations" (http://science.jrank.org/pages/7610/Cultural-Studies.html).

Student Voices

Mirri

When someone said that Stuart Hall was concerned with oppression, I couldn't help but think of my own background in Haiti. The country is very poor, and we don't have a lot of resources like the United States. We rely on other countries a lot, which makes the dominance of the elites over ordinary people pretty common. The government acts like the people's voice is important, but everyone knows that simply is not the case. Media there are controlled by the government in a lot of ways and tells people both truthful and deceitful things. It's a perfect example of the dominance over the masses.

Heurism

Many of the principles and features of Cultural Studies have been investigated. Ideology has been examined (Lewis & Morgan, 2001; Soar, 2000), and the concept of hegemony has been applied to episodes of television shows, including *The Mary Tyler Moore Show* (Dow, 1990), *Saturday Night Live* (Davis, 2012), and *Sex in the City* (Brasfield, 2007). Hegemony has even been applied to the singing of the national anthem at sporting events (Molnar & Kelly, 2012) as well as used in a study to understand educational reform in Brazil (Gandin, 2015). Research by Janice Radway (1984, 1986) focused on romance novels and the women who read them. She discovered that many women read these books silently to protest male domination in society. Feminists have embraced Cultural Studies and the efforts by Stuart Hall as he helped shape an understanding of voices that usually go unnoticed (e.g., Driscoll, 2016). In addition, focusing on the multicultural underpinning of the theory, Chris Weedon (2016) has looked at the appeal of Islamism to Western Muslims and the decision by many women to either join a jihad or marry jihadist fighters.

One final piece of heuristic evidence of Cultural Studies can be found in the expansive undertakings by scholars who have honored the tradition and the concepts of Cultural Studies. For instance, it is common to see entire issues of journals dedicated to Stuart Hall (e.g., *International Journal of Cultural Studies*) as well as written pieces showering praise and admiration on his work (e.g., Jordan, 2016). It is remarkably clear that thinkers, writers, researchers, and essayists continue to laud a theorist who had a profound effect on research and society.

Closing

Cultural Studies remains one of the few theoretical traditions that has attracted the attention of scholars from a variety of disciplines outside communication. For that reason alone, it is uniquely both interdisciplinary and multidisciplinary. Researchers interested in understanding the thinking, experiences, and activities of historically oppressed populations usually endorse Cultural Studies as a model. Although some critics have faulted the theory for a number of reasons, Stuart Hall is credited with criticizing the elite and for drawing attention to oppressed voices in society.

Discussion Starters

TECH QUEST: Much of the research surrounding Cultural Studies is political in nature; affecting cultural change remains a goal. In particular, hegemony is identified as a process that keeps the haves in power over the have-nots. Relate this thinking to the retweeting process.

1. Is the Petrillo family responsible for not trying to leave their current situation? If they are not able to achieve the "American Dream" of owning a home, should the media be blamed? Include examples when expressing your opinion.

2. Discuss how hegemony functions in world events. Now apply the concept to your campus. Identify any similarities and differences between the two applications. Use examples in your response.

3. What other cultural artifacts exist in our society that could be studied within a Cultural Studies framework?

4. British Cultural Studies is strongly focused on class differences. What do you think about applying the thinking of British Cultural Studies to Cultural Studies in North America? Do you believe that the concepts and principles are relevant to all countries? Why or why not?

5. Do you agree or disagree with the belief that oppressed populations have little voice in the United States? How does this view relate to how you feel about the theory?

6. How might Cultural Studies theorists view poverty in the United States?

7. Apply counter-hegemony to a contemporary television show.

CHAPTER 26

Media Ecology Theory

*Based on the research of **Marshall McLuhan***

> *Our conventional response to all media, namely that it is how they are used that counts, is the numb stance of the technological idiot.*
> —Marshall McLuhan

Professor Margaret Randall

As an expert on social media, Professor Margaret Randall was used to traveling around the country. She is an accomplished author, with her most recent book examining the isolation caused by people's reliance upon technology. Professor Randall's research has been celebrated by both scholars and practitioners, and she has received numerous awards and recognitions for her work on the influence of media upon our social lives. Margaret's most recent invitation was to present the keynote speech to an international group of social media professors in Costa Rica. She was both anxious and excited to go.

A week before the trip, Professor Randall was under pressure to get her speech written. She had written a few paragraphs, but she had much more homework to do. She couldn't rely on her "stump" speech with this group, given their expertise. In fact, as she sat in her office on her computer finding new research in the area, she felt that it was important to include cultural examples of her points to make her speech more compelling. Some materials she wanted required her to visit the library. So, she went across campus to (literally) check out a few materials on Costa Rica's history. When Margaret returned to her office, she continued her research on the library's databases, finding some news stories on Central and South American youth and social media usage.

As Professor Randall sat reading the information, she visited chat rooms with younger people from around the globe. She thought she'd ask them about their social media use when the chance arose. And, it occurred to her that perhaps her former colleague, Bella, who was teaching in Central America, could provide some "local perspective" on the topic. It wasn't long before Margaret and her friend were Skyping. After some back-and-forth repartee, the conversation evolved into a conversation about their families, their research, and even their reactions to the U.S. presidential debates, which Bella had watched from her Costa Rica home. After a few minutes, the two finally got to the reason for their connection and soon Professor Randall had some firsthand examples to splice into her speech.

Later that evening, as she watched television, Margaret Randall was thinking a lot about her upcoming speech. She knew that the speech was going to be taped and that it would inevitably appear on YouTube. She also knew that she couldn't afford any flubs. Her anxiety was palpable. She still had several days to refine the speech and yet, she always became nervous when she stopped to consider that her presentation was not only mediated, but also that it was her first speech given outside of the United States. And, the use of Prezi software always made her quite nervous about using a virtual canvas in her speeches.

Margaret knew that there was only one person who could calm her down: her 21-year-old daughter, Emma. She texted Emma to ask if she had a few minutes to talk on the phone. Emma is credited with getting her mom to Skype and text. Before Emma's insistence that her mother—a college professor—use other media to communicate, Professor Randall simply called her daughter or sent her email. Now, given that her daughter is several hundred miles away in college, Margaret relies on technology to ensure that she and her daughter remain connected. And, it is this connection that the two of them forge today as Emma dials her cell phone.

Communication theorists often accounted for technology in their theories, but until recently, rarely embraced it as a fundamental feature in their theories. In Chapter 13, we underscored one theory—Social Information Processing Theory—that addressed the complex intersection between technology and human relationships. We argued that theorists such as Joseph Walther focus on the coming together of people and how individuals get to know one another online. All of this is done without the benefit of nonverbal cues.

Unlike Social Information Processing Theory, theorists interested in media environment look at the entire "mediated picture"—from its history to how it affects our perceptions or feelings, among other areas. When an interplay between media and their environments occurs, the foundation of Media Ecology Theory (MET) has been established.

Professor Randall's experiences in our chapter opening would be of interest to Media Ecology theorists. Her embrace of technology and its effect upon both her professional and personal lives are of interest to scholars in media ecology. In addition, the fact that Margaret used to rely only on email, but later used other technologies to communicate with her daughter says a great deal about how technology has influenced their relationship values.

One theorist who could understand and interpret Professor Randall's relational and technological circumstances is Marshall McLuhan. In his groundbreaking book, *Understanding Media* (1964), McLuhan wrote about the influence of technologies, including clocks, televisions, radios, movies, telephones, and even roads and games. Although today we would not classify some of these as technologies, at the time, McLuhan was interested in the social impact of these primal mediated forms of communication. He was interested in, among other areas, answering the following question: What is the relationship between technology and members of a culture?

It's fair to say that McLuhan himself was part of the culture's media. He appeared regularly on television talk shows, spoke to policymakers, had a cameo role in the Woody Allen film *Annie Hall*, and even was interviewed by *Playboy* magazine. He was so enigmatic and ubiquitous that one writer called him the "high priest of popcult and metaphysician of media" (nextnature.net/2009/12/the-playboy-interview-marshall-mcluhan/).

McLuhan was a Canadian scholar of literary criticism who used poetry, fiction, politics, musical theater, and history to suggest that mediated technology shapes people's feelings, thoughts, and actions. He suggests that we have a symbiotic relationship with mediated technology; we create technology, and technology in turn recreates who we are.

MEDIA ECOLOGY THEORY

Electronic media have revolutionized society, according to McLuhan. In essence, McLuhan feels that societies are highly dependent on mediated technology and that a society's social order is based on its ability to deal with that technology. Recall that this theory was conceptualized over 50 years ago and, especially today, McLuhan's assertion about technology rings true. Indeed, "since the public's growing consciousness of the Internet . . . starting in the mid-1990s, McLuhan's reputation has experienced an astounding upsurge" (Morrison, 2006, p. 170). As Megan Garber (2011) writes, McLuhan is still a "Media Guru of the first order."

Media, in general, act directly to mold and organize a culture. This is McLuhan's theory. Because the theory centralizes the many types of media and views media as an environment unto itself, scholars aptly term McLuhan's work Media Ecology. The word **ecology,** in this sense, is simply the study of how environments influence individuals. For our purposes, we define **media ecology** as the study of how media and communication processes influence human perception, feeling, understanding, and value (media-ecology.org/media_ecology/index.html#An%20Overview%20of%20Media%20Ecology%20(Lance%20Strate). Carlos Scolari (2012–2013) writes that the notion of media ecology was borne out of conversations McLuhan had with his colleagues. Given that McLuhan's writing spans a number of different academic disciplines, given that it focuses on a variety of technologies (e.g., radio, television, etc.), and given that it pertains to the intersection of technology and human relationships and how media affect human perception and understanding (Postman, 1971), the ecological view of media is appropriate and sensible (Note: It should be pointed out that it was Postman, not McLuhan, who formally introduced the phrase "media ecology"). Paul Levinson (2000) describes the relationship of Media Ecology to communication this way: "McLuhan's work was startlingly distinct from the others [scholars] in that he put communications at center stage. Indeed, in McLuhan's schema, there was nothing else on the stage (p. 18)." Media Ecology Theory, then, is the communication field's attempt to understand the pervasive influence of media upon cultures (across the globe). Finally, discussing the interrelationship between media and technology, Niall Stephens (2014) concludes that "the media ecology

ecology
the study of environments and their influence upon people

media ecology
the study of how media and communication processes affect human perception, feeling, emotion, and value

MEDIA ECOLOGY THEORY

tradition tends to view all technologies as media, so that 'technology' and 'media' are usually synonymous" (p. 2034).

McLuhan (1964) based much of his thinking on his mentor, Canadian political economist Harold Adams Innis (1951). Innis believed that major empires in history (Rome, Greece, and Egypt) were built by those in control of the written word. Innis argued that Canadian elites used a number of communication technologies to build their "empires." Those in power were given more power because of the development of technology. Innis referred to the shaping power of technology on a society as the **bias of communication**. For Innis, people use media to gain political and economic power and, therefore, change the social order of a society. Innis claimed that communication media have a built-in bias to control the flow of ideas in a society.

McLuhan extended the work of Innis. Philip Marchand (1989) observes that "not long after Innis's death, McLuhan found an opportunity to explore the new intellectual landscape opened up by his [Innis's] work" (p. 115). McLuhan, like Innis, felt that it's nearly impossible to find a society that is unaffected by electronic media. In fact, Susan Greener (2016) posits that the range of media (e.g., screenshots, video, conversations, etc.) allows for a society of learned individuals. Our perceptions of the media and how we interpret those perceptions are the core issues associated with MET. We now discuss these themes in the three main assumptions of the theory.

bias of communication *Harold Innis's contention that technology has the power to shape society*

Assumptions of Media Ecology Theory

We have noted that the influence of media technology on society is the main idea behind Media Ecology Theory. Let's examine this notion a bit further in the three assumptions framing the theory:

- Media infuse nearly every act and action in society.
- Media fix our perceptions and organize our experiences.
- Media tie the world together.

Our first assumption underscores the notion that we cannot escape media in our lives. As we alluded above, media permeate our very existence. We cannot avoid nor evade media, particularly if we subscribe to McLuhan's broad interpretation of what constitutes media. Think about Professor Randall from our chapter-opening story. She clearly has found herself employing media in multiple ways. In fact, we could easily argue that her livelihood is contingent upon her ability to navigate multiple media environments and platforms.

Many Media Ecology theorists interpret media in expansive ways. Today, for instance, although McLuhan did not foresee the various (digital) media available for consumption (e.g., TiVo, etc.), scholars (e.g., Coupland, 2010) acknowledge that McLuhan's thinking would have relevance to these digital forms. Still, in addition to looking at traditional forms of media (e.g., radios, movies, and television), McLuhan also looks at the influence that numbers, games, and even money can have on society.

We explore these three in more detail in order for you to understand the breadth and historical thinking of McLuhan's interpretation of media.

McLuhan (1964) views numbers as mediated. He explains: "In the theater, at a ball game, in church, every individual enjoys all those others present. The pleasure of being among the masses is the sense of the joy in the multiplication of numbers, which has long been suspect among the literate members of Western society" (p. 107). McLuhan felt that in numbers a "mass mind" (p. 107) was constructed by the elites in society to establish a "profile of the crowd" (p. 106). Therefore, it may be possible to create a homogenized population, capable of being influenced.

In addition to numbers, McLuhan looks at games in society as mediated. He observes that "games are popular art, collective, social reactions to the main drive or action of any culture" (p. 235). Games are ways to cope with everyday stresses and, McLuhan notes, they are models of our psychological lives. He further argues that "all games are media of interpersonal communication" (p. 237), which are extensions of our social selves. Games become mass media because they allow for people to simultaneously participate in an activity that is generally fun and games that represent an individual's identity. Today, as you consider the various online and video games available to you (e.g., Xbox), it is not surprising that McLuhan's insights still retain relevancy since these games elicit a variety of emotions, including anger, ridicule, joy, among others.

An additional mediated form is money. McLuhan concludes that "like any other medium, it is a staple, a natural resource" (p. 133). The theorist also calls money a "corporate image" that relies on society for its status and sustenance. Money has some sort of magical power that allows people access. Money allows people to travel the globe, serving as transmitters of knowledge, information, and culture. McLuhan notes that money is really a language that communicates to a diverse group, including farmers, engineers, plumbers, and physicians.

McLuhan, then, contends that media—interpreted in the broadest sense—are ever present in our lives. These media transform our society, whether through the games we play, the radios we listen to, or the televisions we watch. At the same time, media depend on society for "interplay and evolution" (p. 49).

A second assumption of Media Ecology Theory relates to our previous discussion: We are directly influenced by media. Although we alluded to this influence previously, let's be more specific about how McLuhan views the influence of media in our lives.

Media Ecology theorists believe that media help to alter perceptions and organize our lives. McLuhan suggests here that media are quite powerful in our views of the world. Consider, for instance, what occurs when we watch television. If television news reports that the United States is experiencing a "moral meltdown," we may be watching stories on child abductions, illegal drug use, or teen pregnancies. In our private conversations, we may begin to talk about the lack of morals in society. In fact, we may begin to live our lives according to the types of stories we watch (we address this notion in detail in Chapter 23). We may be more suspicious of even friendly strangers, fearing they may try to kidnap our child. We may be unwilling to support laws legalizing medicinal marijuana, regardless of their merits, because we are concerned about possible increases in drug activity. We may also aggressively advocate an "abstinence-only" sex education program in schools, fearing that any other model would cause more unwanted pregnancies.

What occurs with each of these examples is what McLuhan asserts happens all the time: We become (sometimes unwittingly) manipulated by television. Our attitudes and experiences are directly influenced by what we watch on television, and our belief systems apparently can be negatively affected by television. Some writers (e.g., Bugeja, 2005) contend that McLuhan perceived television as instrumental to the erosion of family values.

A third assumption of Media Ecology Theory has elicited quite a bit of popular conversation: Media connect the world. McLuhan used the phrase **global village** to describe how media tie the world into one great political, economic, social, and cultural system. Recall that although the phrase is almost a cliché these days, (there are hundreds of millions of results on a Google search, for instance), it was McLuhan who argued that the media can organize societies socially. Electronic media, in particular, have the ability to bridge cultures that would not have communicated prior to this connection.

> **global village**
> the notion that humans can no longer live in isolation, but rather will always be connected by continuous and instantaneous electronic media

The effect of this global village, according to McLuhan (1964), is the ability to receive information instantaneously (an issue we return to later in the chapter). As a result, we should be concerned with global events, rather than remaining focused on our own communities. He observes that "the globe is no more than a village" (p. 5) and that we should feel responsible for others. Others "are now involved in our lives, as we in theirs, thanks to the electric media" (p. 5).

Let's revisit our chapter-opening example of Professor Randall to illustrate this assumption further. It is clear that a presentation to a group of international scholars requires an understanding of various global issues. Further, given that her presentation is in Costa Rica, Randall felt that it was important to get some understanding of how local citizens utilize social media. She consulted both the Internet and her colleague in Central America. Further, consider the fact that both Bella and Margaret watched the U.S. presidential debates, shrinking the distance between the two countries and the events that take place in those countries. All of these efforts would not have been possible if technology (telephone and computers) was not available.

The global village of Marshall McLuhan follows the General Systems perspective we outlined in Chapter 3. You will recall that Systems theorists believe that one part of a system will affect the entire system. Media Ecology theorists believe that the action of one society will necessarily affect the entire global village. Therefore, such things as wars in Africa and economic strife in Europe affect the United States, Australia, and China. According to McLuhan, we can no longer live in isolation because of "electronic interdependence" (McLuhan & Fiore, 1996).

You have now been introduced to the primary assumptions of MET. McLuhan's theory relies heavily on a historical understanding of media. He asserts that the media of a particular time period were instrumental in organizing societies. He identifies four distinct time periods, or **epochs**, in history (Table 26.1). We address them next.

> **epoch**
> era or historical age

Table 26.1 McLuhan's Media History

HISTORICAL EPOCH	PROMINENT TECHNOLOGY/ DOMINANT SENSE	McLUHAN'S COMMENTS
Tribal Era	Face-to-Face Contact/Hearing	"An oral or tribal society has the means of stability far beyond anything possible to a visual or civilized and fragmented world" (McLuhan & Fiore, 1968, p. 23).
Literate Era	Phonetic Alphabet/Seeing	"Western man [woman] has done little to study or to understand the effects of the phonetic alphabet in creating many of his [her] basic patterns of culture" (McLuhan, 1964, p. 82).
Print Era	Printing Press/Seeing	"Perhaps the most significant of the gifts of typography to man [woman] is that of detachment and noninvolvement—the power to act without reacting" (McLuhan, 1964, p. 173).
Electronic Era	Computer/Seeing, Hearing, Touching	"The computer is by all odds the most extraordinary of all the technological clothing ever devised . . . since it is the extension of our central nervous system" (McLuhan & Fiore, 1968, p. 35).

Making Media History and Making "Sense"

McLuhan (1962, 1964) and Quentin Fiore (McLuhan & Fiore, 1967, 1996) claim that the media of an era define the essence of a society. They present four eras, or epochs, in media history, each of which corresponds to the dominant mode of communication of the time (Sparks, 2016). In one of the more provocative claims, McLuhan contends that media act as extensions of the human senses in each era, and communication (technology) is the primary cause of social change (gingkopress .com/02-mcl/z_mcluhan-and-the-senses.html).

The Tribal Era

According to McLuhan, during the **tribal era**, hearing, smell, and taste were the dominant senses. During this time, McLuhan argues, cultures were "ear-centered" in that people heard with no real ability to censor messages. This era was characterized by the oral tradition of storytelling whereby people revealed their traditions, rituals, and values through the spoken word. In this era, the ear became the sensory "tribal chief" and for people, hearing was believing.

The Literate Era

This epoch, emphasized by the visual sense, was marked by the introduction of the alphabet. The eye became the dominant sensory organ. McLuhan and Fiore (1996) state that the alphabet caused people to look at their environment in visual and spatial terms. McLuhan (1964) also maintains that the alphabet made knowledge more accessible and "shattered the bonds of tribal man" (p. 173). Whereas the tribal era was characterized by people speaking, the **literate era** was a time when written communication flourished. People's messages became centered on linear and rational thinking. Out was storytelling; in were mathematics and other forms of analytic logic. This "scribal world" had the unintended consequence of forcing communities to become more individualistic rather than collectivistic (McLuhan & Fiore, 1967). People were able to get their information without help from their communities. This was the beginning of people communicating without the need to be face to face.

literate era
age when written communication flourished and the eye became the dominant sense organ

The Print Era

The invention of the printing press heralded the **print era** in civilization and the beginning of the Industrial Revolution. Although it was possible to do a great deal of printing by woodcut prior to this era, the printing press made it possible to make copies of essays, books, and announcements. This provided for even more permanency of record than in the literate age. The printing press also allowed people other than the elite to gain access to information. Today, think about self-publishing and its implications as you think about this era. Then, as today, with printing, people didn't have to rely on their memories for information as they had to do in the past. Publication made it possible for permanency of record to be achieved.

print era
the age when gaining information through the printed word was customary, and seeing continued as the dominant sense

McLuhan (1964) observes that the book was "the first teaching machine" (p. 174). Consider his words today. Very few courses in college exist without a textbook. Even with technological teaching approaches such as distance learning or interactive television, the large majority of courses still require textbooks. Books remain indispensable in the teaching–learning process.

Exemplifying the print era more specifically, McLuhan writes:

> Margaret Mead has reported that when she brought several copies of the same book to a Pacific island there was great excitement. The natives had seen books, but only one copy of each, which they had assumed to be unique. Their astonishment at the identical character of several books was a natural response to what is after all the most magical and potent aspect of print and mass production. It involves a principle of extension by homogenization that is the key to understanding Western power. (p. 174)

What McLuhan notes here is that mass production produces citizens who are similar to each other. The same content is delivered over and over again by the same means. This visual-dependent era, however, produced a fragmented population because people could remain in isolation reading their mass-produced media.

The Electronic Era

The age we live in now is electronic. Interestingly, McLuhan (1964) and his colleague (McLuhan & Fiore, 1967) note that this epoch, characterized by the telegraph, telephone, typewriter, radio, and television, has brought us back to tribalization and the art of oral communication. Instead of books being the central repository of information, electronic media decentralized information to the extent that individuals are now one of several primary sources of information. This era has returned us to a primitive-like reliance on talking to one another although as we know, some would argue that the art of conversation has really been lost (Turkle, 2015). Today, though, we define *talking* differently than the way it occurred in the tribal era. We talk through television, radio, books on tape, voice mail, cell phones, blogs, and email. The **electronic era** allows different communities in different parts of the world to remain connected, a concept we discussed previously as the global village.

McLuhan (1964) relates a description of various technologies in the electronic age:

> The telephone: speech without walls.
>
> The phonograph: music hall without walls.
>
> The photograph: museum without walls.
>
> The electric light: space without walls.
>
> The movie, radio, and TV: classroom without walls. (p. 283)

The electronic era presents unique opportunities to reevaluate how media influence the people they serve. This age allows for ear and eye and voice to work together.

This historical presentation of media by McLuhan suggests that the primary media of an age prompts a certain sensory reaction in people. McLuhan and Fiore (1968) theorize that a **ratio of the senses** is required by people, which is a conversation of sorts between and among the senses. That is, a balance of the senses is required, regardless of the time in history. For instance, with the Internet, we reconcile a variety of senses, including visual stimulation of website pictures and the auditory arousal of downloaded music. When we develop online relationships, we already know that our nonverbal communication is severely limited (for more on this information, see Chapter 13 on Social Information Processing Theory).

The Medium Is the Message

Media Ecology Theory is perhaps best known for the catchphrase "*the medium is the message*" (McLuhan, 1964), a "humble and fascinating" phrase (Hodge, 2003, p. 342). Although followers of McLuhan continue to debate the precise meaning of this equation, it appears to represent McLuhan's scholarly values: The content of a mediated message is secondary to the medium (or communication channel). The medium has the ability to change how we think about others, ourselves, and the world around us. So, for instance, in our opening example of Professor Randall, what she and Marcus communicated is less important than that they communicated via a computer, the Internet, and email.

McLuhan does not dismiss the importance of content altogether. Rather, as Paul Levinson (2001) points out, McLuhan argues that content gets our attention more than the medium does. McLuhan thinks that although a message affects our

---

electronic era
age in which electronic media pervades our senses, allowing for people across the world to be connected

ratio of the senses
phrase referring to the way people adapt to their environment

the medium is the message
phrase referring to the power and influence of the medium—not the content—on a society

conscious state, it is the medium that largely affects our unconscious state. So, for example, we often unconsciously embrace television as a medium while receiving a message broadcast around the world. Consider the fact that the 2001 terrorist attacks in New York City, Hurricane Katrina's devastating effects in 2005, the 2013 Boston Marathon bombings, and the 2016 flow of Syrian immigrants to Europe were reported not only immediately after the events but, in some cases, during the events. Many of us went to TV immediately and were captivated by the horror and the images as they occurred. We were pretty much unconscious of the medium, but rather consumed with the message. Nonetheless, we turned to television and our laptops again and again for updates as the days and months progressed, rather unaware of its importance in our lives. This represents McLuhan's hypothesis that the medium shapes the message and it is, ironically enough, our unawareness of the medium that makes a message all the more important.

McLuhan and Fiore (1967) claim that in addition to the medium being the message, the medium is the "massage." By changing one letter, they creatively present readers with another view of media. It's not clear whether the authors were making a pun on the "mass-age" or whether they were reinforcing McLuhan's earlier writings on the power of the media. McLuhan and Fiore argue that not only are we influenced by the media, but we can become seduced by it. As a population, we are entranced with new technologies. For instance, it is now customary for national media such as the *New York Times* and *USA Today* to feature special sections on technology and culture. New gadgets, gizmos, and technological inventions (and their prices) are featured for those desiring the latest. Indeed, the medium massages the masses, is part of the "mess-age" (McLuhan & Parker, 1969), and can be understood in a "mass-age" (McLuhan & Nevitt, 1972). James Morrison (2006) sums it up by stating that "'the medium is the message' because the contents of a medium vary and may even be contradictory, but the medium's effects remain the same, no matter what the content" (p. 178).

We have presented several key assumptions and issues associated with MET. We have also discussed media in very broad terms. McLuhan says that some unifying and systematic way of differentiating media is necessary. The result is an interesting analysis of hot and cool media.

Gauging the Temperature: Hot and Cool Media

To understand the "large structural changes in human outlook" (McLuhan, 1964, p. vi) of the 1960s, McLuhan set out to classify media. He explains that media can be classified as either hot or cool, language he borrowed from jazz slang. This classification system remains confounding to many scholars, and yet it is pivotal to the theory. We distinguish between the two media next and provide examples of each in Figure 26.1.

Hot media are described as media that demand little from a listener, reader, or viewer. Hot media are high-definition communications that have relatively complete sensory data; very little is left to the audience's imagination. Hot media, therefore, are low in audience participation. Meaning is essentially provided. An example of a hot medium is a movie, because it requires very little of us. We sit down, watch the film, react, maybe eat some popcorn, and then watch the credits. Hot media provide

hot media
high-definition communication that demands little involvement from a viewer, listener, or reader

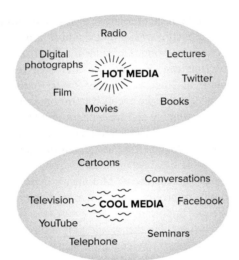

**Figure 26.1
Examples of
McLuhan's Hot
and Cool Media**

the audience what they need—in this case, entertainment. Today, one could state that tweeting a 140-character does not require high sensory involvement.

McLuhan believes that radio is a hot medium. He acknowledges that radio can serve as background sound, as noise-level control, or for listening pleasure. Little involvement is needed with radio. However, McLuhan wrote before the proliferation of radio talk shows such as Rush Limbaugh, a bombastic radio host. Given the audience engagement today in much of talk radio, we need to think about McLuhan's era rather than our contemporary day.

Unlike hot media, **cool media** require a high degree of participation; they are low definition. Little is provided by the medium, so much has to be filled in by the listener, reader, or viewer. Cool media require audiences to create meaning through high sensory and imaginative involvement. Consider, for instance, cartoons. Generally, we get a few frames of illustrations and perhaps some brief phrases. Cartoons are low definition and provide very little visual information. We need to determine the meaning of the words and the pictures, and even supply missing words or ideas that are not provided in the cartoon.

Let's make one more point about cool media. Interestingly, McLuhan (1964) contends that television can be considered a cool medium. He argues that TV is a medium that requires viewers to be actively involved. In fact, he notes that television "engages you. You have to be with it" (p. 312). Yet with the digital age upon us, television has taken on new meaning that perhaps even McLuhan could never have imagined. Would he still consider television a cool medium today? As we think about current forms of hot media, Facebook, with its uploading of images and pictures, "friending" of others, iChatting, and "liking" requires more sensory involvement, thereby exemplifying a modern-day example of cool media.

Let's provide you two different examples of hot and cool media. First, McLuhan believed that a marked difference exists between a lecture and seminar. A lecture is determined to be hot because generally, it encompasses a person standing before a

cool media
*low-definition
communication that
demands active
involvement from a
viewer, listener, or
reader*

large group talking. It requires little except to listen to the information. A seminar, however, is cool, smaller in nature with the discussion leader facilitating questions and participants sharing ideas and life experiences.

McLuhan also differentiated between hot and cool media using the 1960 presidential debates between John F. Kennedy and Richard Nixon. McLuhan discovered that for those who watched the debate on television, Kennedy had won because he exuded an objective, cool persona, perfect for the cool medium. For those who listened to the debates on the radio (a hot medium), Nixon was the winner. He was considered hot (which, in fact, his sweating showed he was!). So, the medium influences others' perceptions.

Arthur Asa Berger (2007) notes that McLuhan's thinking pertaining to hot and cool media is prompting more research interest as communication theorists try to understand the passion that people have for their cell phones. As the 21st century continues, we need to be cautious in interpreting hot and cool media in straightforward ways. For instance, multitasking (tweeting and watching television at the same time) makes a distinction between hot and cool media more difficult. Moreover, as we try to categorize various forms of (social) media as either hot or cool, we need to remind ourselves of David Bobbit: "McLuhan was not concerned with providing consistent, linear meanings of the terms 'hot' versus 'cool' media. For him, it was the *effect* the medium had that he was trying to get at" (http://enculturation.net/teaching-mcluhan).

The Circle Is Complete: The Tetrad

We continue our discussion of Media Ecology Theory by examining the most recent expansion of McLuhan's thinking about the media. With his son, Eric (McLuhan & McLuhan, 1988), and to respond to those who believed that there was no scientific grounding in his work, McLuhan developed a way to look further into the effects of technology on society. His expansion of the theory included a thorough discussion of the **laws of media**.

Although McLuhan's earlier work identified in this chapter does not fully take into account the advent of the computer, his posthumous work with his son takes into consideration the influence of the Internet. Their work was an effort to bring the theory full circle: Technology affects communication through new technology, the impact of the new technology affects society, and the changes in society cause further changes in technology. McLuhan and McLuhan offer the **tetrad** as an organizing concept that allows scholars to understand the past, present, and current effects of media.

To give us a new way of looking at the role of technology in our culture, McLuhan and McLuhan offer four laws, phrased as questions, to understand technology: (1) What do media enhance? (2) What do media make obsolete? (3) What do media retrieve? (4) What do media reverse? Each of these is aligned with the Media Effects research that we articulated in Chapter 23 (Uses and Gratifications). Let's examine and identify examples of their roles in culture (Table 26.2). We pay particular attention to the role of the Internet in our discussion.

laws of media
further expansion of Media Ecology Theory with focus on the impact of technology on society

tetrad
organizing concept to understand the laws of media

Table 26.2 Laws of Media

LAWS OF MEDIA	DESCRIPTION
Enhancement	What does the medium enhance or amplify?
Obsolescence	What does the medium push aside or make obsolete?
Retrieval	What does the medium retrieve from the past?
Reversal	When pushed to its limits, what does the medium reverse or flip into?

Enhancement

enhancement
law that states media amplify or strengthen society

The first law of media is **enhancement**; that is, media enhance or amplify society. The telephone enhanced the spoken word found in face-to-face conversations. Radio, of course, amplified the voice across distance. Television amplified the word and the visual across continents.

The Internet has enhanced society in different ways. First, it has the potential to enhance a number of senses, including sight and sound. Second, the existence of the Internet has enhanced the accessibility of information. For instance, we can now obtain birth records, credit card balances, and missing person information over the Internet. Third, the Internet can enhance class division. The "haves and the have-nots" exist along this information superhighway. Finally, decentralization of authority is enhanced by the Internet. People have access to information and events that years ago, were completely out of reach. Further, no longer do our political, scientific, or corporate leaders solely possess information; that information becomes available online.

Obsolescence

obsolescence
law that states media eventually render something obsolete or out of date

McLuhan and McLuhan (1988) note that the second law of media is that media eventually render something obsolete or out of date. Television made radio obsolete, although many of us continue to turn to radio each day while we drive. Levinson (2001) notes that radio rendered motion pictures obsolete, which in turn resulted in fewer movies to watch. DVRs may have also attempted to make movies obsolete, but we know that their efforts have been only somewhat successful.

The Internet, too, has brought about **obsolescence**. For example, as we learned earlier, the global village now exists, thanks to the Internet. The geographical splits are pretty hard to find; even the remote villages of Africa are becoming accessible by the Internet. Second, the Internet is slowly targeting micromedia (specific audiences) rather than macromedia (large masses), thereby making traditional media outlets such as CBS, NBC, and ABC change their news reporting. Finally, face-to-face dialogues are becoming outdated with the Internet. Former "tribal" conversations are now electronically derived.

retrieval
law that states media restore something that was once lost

Retrieval

The third law is **retrieval**, meaning that media recover or restore something that was once lost. What older, previously obsolesced media is brought back? Television, for

instance, restored the importance of the visual that radio did not achieve, but that was once in face-to-face conversations. Radio retrieved the town crier, the prominent voice of newsworthy events nearly 200 years ago in the United States. Print retrieved the tribe's universality of knowledge. And the Internet recovers a community that was once lost to other media. For instance, chat rooms visited by people like Professor Randall from our chapter-opening vignette have electronically rekindled conversations that flourished before radio and television.

Reversal

When "pushed to the limit of its potential" (McLuhan & McLuhan, 1988, p. 99), what do media produce or become? What do media reverse into? When too many constraints exist on a medium, it will "overheat" and become ineffective. **Reversal** contains characteristics of the system from which it arose. For instance, the public's desire to have access to entertainment in a relatively cheap medium led to the creation of radio dramas and comedy programs. The need to "see" what was heard led to the creation of these programs on television. Yet we can DVR television programs and what was once seen by millions of people at the same time is reversed into private "performances." Television, then, reversed into the early days of the print era when people could consume media privately.

reversal
law that states media will—when pushed to their limit—produce or become something else

Student Voices

Olga

When I read about the "global village," considering that McLuhan wrote about this in the 1960s, I thought it was amazing! Here's this pretty zany guy who over 50 years ago was writing about how we are connected with the rest of the world. And he was right! As someone who has lived in four countries, I have turned on the TV, gone to a website, or blogged about what is happening around the world. We are all connected more than ever, and McLuhan knew this before anyone else did.

MEDIA ECOLOGY THEORY

The Internet—as a medium pushed to its potential—reverses society into a new and unique place. The Internet has the potential to bring tribal people together when they discuss websites or chat room conversations with one another. Looking at the number of people who "surf the net" each day alone, the Internet can isolate people just as television can. Also, with the ability to download music, television shows, and films, the Internet—specifically iTunes and Hulu—has reversed itself into a medium with significant visual and auditory appeal. Finally, the Internet is a medium that "flips" on its user. That is, although it can serve to erode power, it can also perpetuate power differences among people. As a result, the Internet provides opportunities for both those in power and those who seek power or who are powerless.

Finally, to exemplify a tetrad using a 2014 CBS News report on driverless automobiles, Eric McLuhan (Zhuang & McLuhan, 2016) identified a tetrad that may help you better understand it. Specifically, he stated:

Enhances: AUTOnomy.

Obsolesces: control(ler).

Retrieves: car as robot.

Reversal: driver becomes passenger (p. 223). Clearly, as you think about cultural issues, you most likely can also develop a tetrad in much the same way McLuhan did.

Carrying the McLuhan Banner: Postman and Meyrowitz

The former president of the Media Ecology Association believes that thinking about McLuhan is like taking part in a "moveable feast" in that "if you are lucky enough to have encountered McLuhan's legacy, wherever you go for the rest of your life, his legacy stays with you" (Sternberg, 2011, p. 111). Although score of scholars identify and accept the tenets of Media Ecology Theory, two influential scholars are of particular note. Neil Postman and Joshua Meyrowitz were dedicated scholarly followers of McLuhan. Although each retained much of the values related to McLuhan's writings, each scholar adapted an individual lens as they talked about technology. We close our discussion with an overview of these two "McLuhanites."

Neil Postman's biography is an interesting one and is available elsewhere (http://neilpostman.org). Still, let's give you a glimpse into his credentials.

As Thomas Gencarelli (2006) observes, "Postman is first and foremost an educator" (p. 239). Indeed, most of his books pertain to public education in the United States and in many cases, his writing is quite satirical. In some cases, he encourages changes to the educational system by stating that it needs to be revitalized. Nowhere can that revitalization occur other than with an infusion of technology, according to Postman. The media environment, he believes, helps shape children's lives. Television, in particular, is ripe for allowing young people to be exposed to all sorts of information that was originally intended for adults. This conflation of the child and adult worlds is an ongoing concern for Postman.

Postman is clearly a man who practices what he preaches. Jim Benning (2003) relates a relevant anecdote. Postman is deeply concerned about technology's imprint in society. He states, "The tendency of American culture [is] to turn over to technology sovereignty, command, control over all our social institutions" (http://www.c-span.org/video/?7-1/life-career-neil-postman122756). In shopping for a new car, Postman has been quoted as saying, "Why do I need electric windows? My arm and hand work. If I were paralyzed I could use an electric window." His colleague and friend note that "Neil would always take what he would call an ecological perspective, a balanced view."

Postman has written more than 200 articles for the public and over 20 popular and scholarly books. Postman's research is underscored by a central theme: "All technologies are human impositions into the natural order of things and, as a result, change that order" (Gencarelli, 2006, p. 244). Among the most influential of his published works is *Technopoly: The Surrender of Culture to Technology*. In the book, Postman (1992) hypothesizes that technology negatively changes the fabric of society. Specifically, he believes that culture is subservient to the invisible (e.g., I.Q. scores) and visible (e.g., computers).

Postman coined the term ***technopoly***, which means that we live in a culture in which technology dominates our thinking and behaviors. In a technopoly, Postman argues, technological tools serve to take over the culture in which they thrive. We live in a society where being technologically driven may result in being driven mad! We trust that our technology will bring us safety and salvation, and seem to lose any sense of humility, discipline, and rationality regarding our reliance on and trust in current media. As a result, Postman laments that "tradition, social mores, myth, politics, ritual, and religion have to fight for their lives" (p. 28). Postman, like McLuhan, asks whether we want to live in a culture with such unwavering dependence on technology and such a conclusion has led scholars to call him a "pillar of media ecology" (Strate, 2004, p. 3).

technopoly
a term coined by Postman that means we live in a society dominated by technology

In addition to Postman, Joshua Meyrowitz's (1985) research interconnects with McLuhan's work. Meyrowitz's *No Sense of Place* ushered in a unique way of thinking related to space. First, he argues that space is more than physical (Dresner, 2006). That is, social situations such as contesting a parking ticket at city hall include more than the physical surroundings of the building and courtroom. Meyrowitz contends that the influence that communication has on the situation also needs to be considered.

As a communication scholar, Meyrowitz is interested in uncovering the effects of communication technology, primarily television, on a social situation. Consider, for instance, a private discussion between a husband and wife on marital infidelity. The discussion is likely to be free-wheeling, underscoring the intimacy that the couple shares. Now, put that discussion in front of a live *Dr. Phil* television audience. A new pattern of communication will likely begin, with different information flow and new rules of conduct. It is this new communication medium that Meyrowitz is interested in and one that has cultural consequences.

Meyrowitz agrees with McLuhan that electronic media have social consequences. Meyrowitz expands the notion that power relations and social class can be traced to electronic media. He draws on sociology research to conclude that media have brought about a blurring of formerly distinct roles or places. He states that "many Americans may no longer seem to 'know their place' because the traditionally interlocking components of 'place' have been split apart by electronic media. Wherever one is now—at home, at work, or in the car—one may be in touch and tuned in" (p. 308).

As noted earlier, Meyrowitz points to television for evidence of the "blurring." For instance, examine talk shows and you can get a sense of how the blurring of place occurs. What was once private (e.g., discussing your mother's alcoholism) is now public on *Maury Povich*. Even television programming has blurred gender lines; shows like RuPaul's *Drag Race* presents gendered images that do not fit neatly into preconceived notions of masculinity and femininity.

The writings of both Postman and Meyrowitz remain effective examples of Marshall McLuhan's legacy. The two carry the banner that boldly proclaims that electronic media have shaken Western society's foundation and many of its core values. Clearly, the two scholars prompt us to consider McLuhan's work in more contemporary ways. Even after more than a century after his birth, McLuhan remains relevant (siliconvalleywatcher.com/mt/archives/2011/07/the_importance_2.php).

Integration, Critique, and Closing

You probably have already figured out that Marshall McLuhan has caused quite a reaction in both academic and public circles. His ideas are provocative, and at times, have been both unilaterally dismissed and embraced. In fact, if you reviewed his original work, you may be challenged by his frequently eccentric writing style. Some have labeled his thinking "McLuhanacy" (Gordon, 1982), while others feel his writing is equivalent to "genre bending" (Carey, 1998). Without doubt, however, the research undertaken by Media Ecology theorists has been qualitative and rarely, if ever, has a study been undertaken experimentally using the theory as a foundation.

McLuhan's work and reputation, however, have been invoked with considerable regard. Let's provide you a snapshot of the kudos celebrating McLuhan. *Wired* magazine named him their "patron saint," and *Life* magazine called him the "Oracle of the Electronic Age." A concentration in McLuhan studies exists at the University of Toronto. In addition, there is a McLuhan newsletter, the *International Journal of McLuhan Studies*, symposia on McLuhan's research, a McLuhan festival, a McLuhan reading club, and even a secondary high school in Canada named the Marshall McLuhan Catholic Secondary School. Finally, the *San Francisco Chronicle* once called him "the hottest academic property around." It's hard to escape his influence both in research and in societies around the world. The theory, despite its popularity, has been evaluated by scholars and writers. We examine these critiques using the criteria of testability and heurism.

Integration

Communication Tradition	Rhetorical | Semiotic | Phenomenological | Cybernetic | Socio-Psychological | **Socio-Cultural** | **Critical**
Communication Context	Intrapersonal | Interpersonal | Small Group | Organizational | Public/Rhetorical | **Mass/Media** | Cultural
Approach to Knowing	Positivistic/Empirical | Interpretive/Hermeneutic | **Critical**

Critique

Evaluation Criteria	Scope | Logical Consistency | Parsimony | Utility | **Testability** | **Heurism** | Test of Time

Testability

MET has been criticized because many of its concepts are difficult to understand, thereby making testability of the theory challenging and, indeed, nearly impossible (Gordon & Willmarth, 2012). The question becomes apparent: How does one test something one has trouble understanding?

Criticism pertaining to the testability of the theory is represented in comments that have been offered by media scholars over the years. For instance, critics have blasted MET as "overly optimistic" about the role of technology in society (Baran & Davis, 2016). They believe that McLuhan put too much emphasis on how much technology influences society, making the very foundation of the theory rather shaky. George Gordon (1982) is more direct: "Not one bit of sustained and replicated scientific evidence, inductive or deductive, has to date justified any one of McLuhan's most famous slogans, metaphors, or dicta" (p. 42). Dwight Macdonald (1967) also attacked McLuhan's writing, noting that "he has looted all culture from cave painting to *Mad* magazine for fragments to shore up his system against ruin" (p. 203).

A great deal of criticism has been directed at McLuhan's use of words and his clarity. To some, his ideas make little sense. Some writers believe that McLuhan failed to define his words carefully and used too much exaggeration. Yet some believe that his exaggerations were simply "ploys" to get the attention of his readers and students (Logan, 2011, p. 28). It is true that McLuhan tended to write in a zigzag fashion, weaving in one point after another with no apparent topic sentence or sustained idea. One website author believed that his writing was "overgrown with arcane literary and historic allusions" (nextnature.net/ 2009/12/the-playboy-interview -marshall-mcluhan). Yet, another believed that McLuhan simply dismissed any criticism since he felt that "clear prose indicates the absence of thought" (http://www .thenewatlantis.com/publications/why-bother-with-marshall-mcluhan).

Although it's clear that some writers indict his thinking and theorizing, McLuhan (1967) offers no apology: "I don't explain—I explore" (p. i). Or, perhaps McLuhan's one line in *Annie Hall* may offer his ultimate response to critics: "You know nothing of my work!"

Heurism

Media Ecology Theory and McLuhan's thinking have been met with considerable enthusiasm. Because McLuhan was a key figure in popular culture, it's important to keep in mind that his writing prompted all sorts of responses. One indicator of the heuristic value of MET is the fact that there is now a Media Ecology Association (media-ecology.org). This organization is dedicated to promoting the theory in both practical and theoretical ways, thereby ensuring the theory's visibility. The association publishes a journal (*EME: Explorations in Media Ecology*) dedicated to the theory, a testimony to the fact that media communication scholars continue to integrate the theory into their research. There is even an "official estate" of McLuhan "to ensure the integrity of his name and legacy" (http://www.marshallmcluhan.com). The site is quite interesting with an entire section devoted to "McLuhanisms" (e.g., "All advertising advertises advertising," etc.).

Researchers have discussed McLuhan and his contributions in a variety of ways. Scholars have provided a comprehensive understanding of the theory and have discussed the theory's influential pioneers (Lum, 2006) and some have "taken up McLuhan's cause" (Anton, Logan, & Strate, 2016). Additional writers over the years have applied several of McLuhan's premises in their research (Strate & Wachtel, 2005). Furthermore, many of the theory's concepts have been incorporated into research on such diverse topics as school shootings (O'Dea, 2015), online racism (August & Liu, 2015), and YouTube as "cool" media (Trier, 2007).

Finally, in what could be considered to be a 21st century response to McLuhan's 20th century theory, the thinking and research of Sherri Turkle (2015) sustains much of what Media Ecologists advance. In her book *Reclaiming Conversation: The Power of Talk in the Digital Age,* Turkle contends that technology has allowed us to make connections, but we are rarely communicating. She espouses one of the fundamental tenets of media ecologists: "The forms and biases of our media technologies impact our everyday lives" (Zimmer, 2005, p. 5). Turkle, for example, contends that social media such as Facebook has resulted in so much "friending" and yet, surveys show that most people report having fewer friends than ever. She is clear in stating that while "mobile technology . . . is here to stay," it's time that we also understand that "it is time for us to consider how it may get in the way of other things that we hold dear" (e.g., intimacy, community, etc.) (p. 7). In sum, one cannot ignore Turkle's belief that new technologies are preventing authentic human connections. Further, she believes that "technological promiscuity," or the belief that technology can be introduced into any setting or environment, is already part of corporate life in the United States.

Closing

Marshall McLuhan and Media Ecology Theory will continue to resonate for years to come. Perhaps one day we will revisit McLuhan's original thinking on historical epochs in media history! New media will continue to evolve in our society and so will the application of McLuhan's thinking. Was McLuhan an absurd reactionary? Or was McLuhan a cultural prophet? On his gravestone are the words "The Truth Will Set You Free." Did McLuhan think he discovered Truth? Or, even in his death, does he continue to play with our imaginations? Perhaps one of McLuhan's biographers, Philip Marchand (1989), best illustrates McLuhan's contribution to the study of media: "McLuhan's comments had at least one virtue: They seemed to suggest that the world was more interesting than any of us had previously thought it to be" (p. xiii).

Discussion Starters

TECH QUEST: The medium we use to communicate was of paramount importance to McLuhan as he developed Media Ecology Theory. If McLuhan and Mark Zuckerberg (founder of Facebook) had lunch today, what do you think the two would talk about today?

1. Discuss whether you believe that Professor Randall should rely less on technology in preparing her speech and more on her life experiences. Is there too much reliance, for instance, with her consultation of the Internet databases, chat rooms, Skype, and email?

2. Describe how Media Ecology theorists might react to the current news on television today? What would be his major criticisms and his major objections? What would he be particularly interested in?

3. Do you agree or disagree with McLuhan regarding television being a cool medium? Use examples to defend your view.

4. Interpret and comment on the following statement: "Technology is the end of our beginning." Use examples to defend your view.

5. Discuss your response to theorists who choose to be part of the popular culture, including participating on talk shows and appearing in films.

6. Apply any principle of MET to (a) YouTube, (b) Google, (c) Facebook, (d) LinkedIn.

7. Why do you think little quantitative research has been undertaken with Media Ecology Theory?

Culture and Diversity

WE ALL BELONG TO SOME SORT OF A CULTURAL COMMUNITY. Some of us are members of a culture with a long history in the United States. Others of us belong to cultures that have recently found prominence in this country. As you learned in Chapter 1, the term *culture* is a complex term that carries many interpretations. The theories presented in this section underscore the various viewpoints and issues related to culture and highlight the importance of looking at culture and human behavior.

We have selected four communication theories that fall under "Culture and Diversity": Face-Negotiation Theory, Communication Accommodation Theory, Muted Group Theory, and Feminist Standpoint Theory. We chose these theories because they represent a cross section of what it means to be a member of a cultural community and because each theory, in some way, provides you some evidence of the expansiveness of culture.

Each of these theories takes into consideration what happens when we communicate with people who come from different cultural backgrounds and with different cultural expectations. For example, Face-Negotiation Theory points to the cultural effects of conflict. The theory answers the question "How do members from different cultures manage their interpersonal conflict?" Focusing on the role of both verbal and nonverbal communication in conversations, Communication Accommodation Theory rests on the belief that people from various cultural communities will adjust and adapt their communication to accommodate others. In Muted Group Theory, women are viewed as less powerful and less effective than men because their words have been provided by men to suit men's experiences. Finally, Feminist Standpoint Theory states that people view the world according to their positions in life. So the theory considers socioeconomic class and its application to a variety of marginalized (and often vulnerable) populations, including women, the poor, gay men and lesbians, and many racial and ethnic communities.

The theories in this section center on the role that society plays in communication between and among cultural groups. Reading and learning about the theories will expose you to a variety of important themes: dominance, control, oppression, power, cultural identity, conflict, and politeness. In societies that are becoming increasingly diverse and electronically connected, understanding the information in this section remains critical.

CHAPTER 27

Face-Negotiation Theory

*Based on the research of **Stella Ting-Toomey***

The manner in which individuals conceive of their self-images should have a profound influence on how they construct meanings, interpret speech codes, form relationships, and infer underlying speech rules and premises from their unique identity lens.

—Stella Ting-Toomey

Professor Jie Yang and Kevin Bruner

The first 10 weeks of her academic term in the United States had gone quite well. As a faculty member from China, Jie Yang felt that the communication courses she taught were well attended by students who were eager to participate. Students frequently asked her questions about what Chinese life was like, often concentrating on college life in particular. Jie was more than willing to answer their questions. She, too, had asked students about life in the United States and about what students thought of Chinese–U.S. relations. Although there were a few intercultural difficulties in translation, overall Yang felt that excellent relationships had been cultivated in such a short period of time. She had every reason to think that things would continue to unfold comfortably.

Yang's instincts, however, proved incorrect. As her intercultural communication class began to prepare for their individual presentations, class members were showing signs of tension. In addition to a written final project on a research topic of their choice, the professor had asked that each student provide a brief oral presentation of what they had studied. Throughout the term, she had listened to student complaints about the library staff,

about how certain journal articles were not available online, and a lot of concerns about the time crunch. Still, she felt that her assignments were important and despite the complaining, didn't back down.

One evening after class, Kevin Bruner, a graduating senior, challenged Professor Yang directly. He stated that there simply wasn't going to be enough time to complete his final presentation. He believed that the professor was asking too much of him, considering that he had missed two weeks of class early in the term because of pneumonia. "It's completely unfair," Kevin lamented. "This is way too much for me right now."

Professor Yang was sympathetic to Kevin's concerns. She agreed that he was under some pressure and reassured him that he was capable of finishing his project despite his past attendance record. "Look, you're an excellent student, Kevin," the professor related. "And obviously I can tell that you're very upset. But, you're a hard worker and I know you want to do your best. You surely don't want me to treat you any differently than the others. Everyone is under pressure here."

Kevin wouldn't hear of it. "I don't want to be disrespectful, but this is too much! I refuse to believe that you won't let a good student have some extra time. It's not like I'm not going to do

459

it." Kevin continued by outlining his plan. If she would give him an "incomplete," then he would turn in the final paper two weeks after the class ended. "I'll try to give my presentation on what I've written," he continued, "but I'm not sure it's going to be that good."

Professor Yang grew weary with the discussion. "Kevin, you underestimate yourself. You have a few weeks left. I trust you'll be able to finish it thoroughly."

The tone of the conversation quickly changed. "Well, let me see," Kevin interrupted, "I don't think you know the American system yet. I'm being up front and honest about the fact that I won't be able to finish the project. You keep telling me that I will. I know that you've only been in the States a short time and I don't think you know how our system works. You've got to give students a chance. Right now, I feel like I'm talking to a brick wall." His voice now matched the passion of his words.

Professor Yang maintained her composure, despite the offending words: "Kevin, in this class, we all have time constraints and outside responsibilities. I, like everyone else, have a lot to finish before the end of the term. But we can't simply abandon our responsibilities. I know you're a reasonable student and I don't want to give you a special accommodation that I don't give to other students. But, I know that you were out sick, so how about this: Turn in a detailed outline of your paper by Monday. You have the weekend to get it into good shape. I will look it over on Monday and then you take my comments and rework the outline into a paper. Instead of the 8–10 page requirement, you can have a 5–7 page requirement.

Kevin followed her lead. "I can't promise you that my paper is gonna be the best. But, definitely, if you'll look it over before I turn it in, that'll help a lot."

"I may be from China, but I can say that almost anywhere, professors simply want their students to do their best and have high standards," Professor Yang replied, wondering if she made the right decision. "And you should know that I do expect you to do your best. I'm sure you will get everything done on time." As Kevin walked away from his conversation, he couldn't help but think about a different approach to his conflict. He knew that he had work to do and that the boundaries had been clearly set for him by Professor Yang.

■

Working out conflicts like Kevin's is not easy. In the United States particularly, individuals try to manage their conflicts in a solution-oriented manner, frequently disregarding the other's cultural values or norms. Although people from a number of different cultures share Kevin's approach, some cultures would not endorse his strategies for conflict resolution.

Kevin finds himself in a situation common to many students. Yet, unlike many students, Kevin overtly confronts Professor Yang about her expectations. Although he was given the assignment in the early part of the term, he knows that the remaining time will not be sufficient to complete the task. He then tries to negotiate a different result with his professor. His dominating approach does little to rattle Professor Yang; she calmly works toward closure on this conflict.

Kevin's conflict with Professor Yang underscores much of the thinking behind Face-Negotiation Theory (FNT) by Stella Ting-Toomey. The theory is multifaceted, incorporating research from intercultural communication, conflict, politeness, and "facework," a topic we explore later in the chapter. Face-Negotiation Theory has cross-cultural appeal and application because Ting-Toomey has focused on a number of different cultural populations, including those in Japan, South Korea, Taiwan, China, and the United States. As Ting-Toomey (1988) comments: "Culture provides the larger interpretive frame in which 'face' and 'conflict style' can be meaningfully expressed and maintained" (p. 213). Ting-Toomey asserts that members from different cultural backgrounds have various concerns for the "face" of others. This concern leads them to handle conflict in different ways. These comments form the backdrop to Face-Negotiation Theory (FNT).

Our chapter-opening example of Kevin Bruner and Professor Yang represents the heart of FNT. Representing two different cultural backgrounds, Kevin and his professor seem to have two different interpretations of how to manage the difficulty that Kevin is having with his final project. Kevin clearly desires to turn his work in late, whereas Professor Yang wants him to turn it in with the rest of the class. She tries to ease the conflict between the two by highlighting Kevin's qualities, and clearly she does not want to embarrass Kevin. Rather, she encourages him to work out this conflict by focusing on his ability to get things done, not the remaining time left in the term.

Professor Yang and Kevin Bruner engage in behavior that researchers have termed *face*. Because face is an extension of one's self-concept, it has become the focus of much research in a number of fields of study, including management, international diplomacy, anthropology, sociology, linguistics, among others. In fact, because Face-Negotiation Theory rests primarily on this concept, let's first interpret the meaning behind the term and then examine some central assumptions of the theory.

About Face

Ting-Toomey bases much of her theory on face and facework. **Face** is clearly an important feature of life, a metaphor for self-image that pervades all aspects of social life. The concept of face has evolved in interpretation over the years. It originates with the Chinese who have two conceptualizations of face: *lien* and *mien-tzu*, two terms describing identity and ego (Ho, 1944).

face
a metaphor for the public image people display

Erving Goffman (1967) is generally credited with situating face in contemporary Western research. He noted that face is the image of the self that people display in their conversations with others. Ting-Toomey and her colleagues (Oetzel, Ting-Toomey, Yokochi, Masumoto, & Takai, 2000) observe that face pertains to a favorable self-worth and/or projected other worth in interpersonal situations. People do not "see" another's face; rather, face is a metaphor for the boundaries that people have in their relationships with others. In essence, then, face is the desirable self-image that a person wishes to convey to another based upon society's interpretation of what is "appropriate and successful" (Samp, 2015, p. 1).

Goffman (1967) described face as something that is maintained, lost, or strengthened. At the time of his writing, Goffman did not envision that the term would be applied to close relationships. As a sociologist, he believed that face and all that it entailed was more applicable to the study of social groups. Over time, however, the study of face has been applied to a number of contexts, including close relationships and small groups.

Ting-Toomey incorporates thinking from research on politeness that concludes that the desire for face is a universal concern (Brown & Levinson, 1978).

Hongyan Lan (2016) asserts: "Face and facework are regarded as universal phenomena and people of every culture are always negotiating face" (p. 41). Ting-Toomey (1988, 1991, 2004) expands on Goffman's thinking and argues that face is a projected image of one's self and the claim of self-respect in a relationship. She believes that face "entails the presentation of a civilized front to another individual" (Ting-Toomey, 1994a, p. 1) and that face is an identity that two people conjointly define in a relational episode. Further, face is a "socially approved self-image and other-image consideration issues" (Ting-Toomey & Chung, 2005, p. 268). Ting-Toomey and her colleague Beth Ann Cocroft (1994) identify face as a "pancultural phenomenon" (p. 310), meaning that individuals in all cultures share and manage face; face cuts across all cultures.

Regarding our opening, Ting-Toomey and other Face-Negotiation theorists would likely be interested in knowing that Professor Yang is from China and Kevin Bruner was born in the United States. Their cultural backgrounds influence the way that they relate to each other and the way face is enacted. That is, Ting-Toomey believes that although face is a universal concept, there are various representations of it in various cultures. Face needs exist in all cultures, but all cultures do not manage the needs similarly. Ting-Toomey contends that face can be interpreted in two primary ways: face concern and face need. **Face concern** may relate to either one's own face or the face of another. In other words, there is a self-concern and an other-concern. Face concern answers the question, "Do I want attention drawn toward myself or toward another?" **Face need** refers to an inclusion– autonomy dichotomy. That is, "Do I want to be associated with others (inclusion) or do I want dissociation (autonomy)?"

Face and Politeness Theory

As we noted earlier, Ting-Toomey was influenced by research on politeness. In a general sense, politeness is concerned with appropriateness of behavior and procedures as they relate to establishing and maintaining harmony in relationships (Kerbrat-Orecchioni, 2012). In particular, politeness theorists (Brown & Levinson, 1978, 1987) contend that people will use a politeness strategy based on the perception of face threat. Politeness theory suggests that a single message can provoke more than one face threat and can both support and threaten face needs simultaneously, and that politeness and face threats influence subsequent messages. Drawing on over a dozen different cultures around the world, and based on field work of at least three languages (Feng, 2015), politeness researchers discovered that two types of universal needs exist: positive face needs and negative face needs. **Positive face** is the desire to be liked and admired by significant others in our lives; **negative face** refers to the desire to be autonomous and unconstrained. Karen Tracy and Sheryl Baratz (1994) note that these "face wants" are necessarily a part of relationships. They support their claim as follows:

> Recognition of existing face wants explains why a college student who wanted to borrow a classmate's notes typically would not ask for them boldly ("Lend me your notes, would you?"), but more frequently would ask in a manner that paid attention to a person's negative face wants ("Would it be at all possible for me to borrow your notes for just an hour? I'll Xerox them and get them back to you right away"). (p. 288)

face concern
interest in maintaining one's face or the face of others

face need
desire to be associated or disassociated with others

positive face
desire to be liked and admired by others

negative face
desire to be autonomous and free from others

Brown and Levinson's research illustrates a dilemma for individuals who try to meet both types of face needs in a conversation. Trying to satisfy one face need usually affects the other face need. For instance, our opening example shows that Professor Yang wants Kevin to work at achieving his full potential. Her positive face needs, however, are met with the challenges of putting in more time with Kevin, thereby costing her negative face needs.

Facework

When communicators' positive or negative face is threatened, they tend to seek some recourse or way to restore their or their partner's face. Ting-Toomey (1994a), following Brown and Levinson, defines this as facework, or the "actions taken to deal with the face wants of one and/or the other" (p. 8). Ting-Toomey and Leeva Chung (2005) also comment that facework is "about the verbal and nonverbal strategies that we use to maintain, defend, or upgrade our own social self-image and attack or defend (or 'save') the social image of others" (p. 268). In other words, **facework** pertains to how people make whatever they're doing consistent with their face. Ting-Toomey equates facework with a "communication dance that tiptoes" between respect for one's face and the face of another. Catherine Kerbrat-Orecchioni (2012) interprets facework as a way to "smooth over" the actions that may damage or threaten conversations and relationships (we return to this issue a bit later in the chapter).

> **facework**
> *actions used to deal with face needs/ wants of self and others*

Tae-Seop Lim and his co-authors (Lim & Bowers, 1991; Lim & Ahn, 2015) extend the discussion by identifying three types of facework: tact, solidarity, and approbation. First, **tact facework** refers to the extent that one respects another's autonomy. This allows a person freedom to act as he or she pleases while minimizing any impositions that may restrict this freedom. For instance, Professor Yang engages in tact facework with Kevin while he relates his problems with the course assignments. She could, of course, respond to him by stating that he should just keep quiet and work, but instead she uses tact facework strategies—she asks him for suggestions while avoiding directives.

> **tact facework**
> *extent to which a person respects another's autonomy*

The second type of facework, **solidarity facework,** pertains to a person accepting the other as a member of an in-group. Solidarity enhances the connection between two speakers. That is, differences are minimized and commonalities are highlighted through informal language and shared experiences. For instance, Professor

> **solidarity facework**
> *accepting another as a member of an in-group*

Yang notes that, like Kevin, she has responsibilities, and people cannot simply go back on their duties because of a time crunch. Her conversational style reflects an approachable professor, not one who uses language reflecting a status difference.

The final type of facework is **approbation facework**, which involves minimizing blame and maximizing praise of another. Approbation facework exists when an individual focuses less on the negative aspects of another and more on the positive aspects. It is clear that despite her real feelings about Kevin's experiences, Professor Yang employs approbation facework by noting that he is a hard worker and an excellent student. She also explains that he has the ability to get everything accomplished. In other words, she recognizes Kevin's positive attributes while avoiding blame.

Our introductory comments on face and facework form an important backdrop to the understanding of Face-Negotiation Theory. The theory proposed by Ting-Toomey also rests on a number of other issues needing attention and clarification. We begin to unravel the theory in more detail by presenting three key assumptions of FNT.

Assumptions of Face-Negotiation Theory

Several assumptions of Face-Negotiation Theory take into consideration the key components of the theory: face, conflict, and culture. With that in mind, the following guide the thinking of Ting-Toomey's theory:

- Self-identity is important in interpersonal interactions, with individuals negotiating their identities differently across cultures.
- The management of conflict is mediated by face and culture.
- Certain acts threaten one's projected self-image (face).

The first assumption highlights self-identity, or the personal features or character attributes of an individual. In their discussion of face, William Cupach and Sandra Metts (1994) observe that when people meet, they present an image of who they are in the interaction. This image is "an identity that he or she wants to assume and wants others to accept" (p. 3). **Self-identity** includes a person's collective experiences, thoughts, ideas, memories, and plans. People's self-identities do not remain stagnant, but rather are negotiated in their interactions with others. People have a concern with both their own identity or face (self-face) and the identity or face of another (other-face) (West & Turner, 2016).

Just as culture and ethnicity influence self-identity, the manner in which individuals project their self-identities varies across cultures. Mary Jane Collier (1998) relates that cultural identity is enacted and "contested in particular historical, political, economic, and social contexts" (p. 132). Delores Tanno and Alberto Gonzalez (1998) note that there are "sites of identity," which they define as "the physical, intellectual, social, and political locations where identity develops its dimensions" (p. 4). Self-identity, therefore, is influenced by time and experience. Consider, for example, the self-identity of a politician as she begins her new term in office. She most likely will be overwhelmed and perhaps frustrated by her new position and the responsibilities that go along with it. Yet, over time and with experience, that frustration will be replaced with confidence and a new perspective on her identity as a representative of others.

approbation facework
focusing less on the negative aspects and more on the positive aspects of another

self-identity
personal attributes of an individual

Inherent in this first assumption is the belief that individuals in all cultures hold a number of different self-images and that they negotiate these images continuously. Ting-Toomey (1993) states that a person's sense of self is both conscious and unconscious. That is, in scores of different cultures, people carry images that they habitually or strategically present to others. Ting-Toomey believes that how we perceive our sense of self and how we wish others to perceive us are paramount to our communication experiences.

The second assumption of Face-Negotiation Theory relates to conflict, which is a central component of the theory. Conflict in this theory, however, works in tandem with face and culture. For Ting-Toomey (1994b), conflict can damage the social face of individuals and can serve to reduce the relational closeness between two people. As she relates, conflict is a "forum" for face loss and face humiliation. Conflict threatens both partners' faces, and when there is an incompatible negotiation over how to resolve the conflict (such as insulting the other, imposing one's will, etc.), the conflict can exacerbate the situation. Ting-Toomey states that the way humans are socialized into their culture influences how they will manage conflict. That is, some cultures, like the United States, value the open airing of differences between two people; other cultures believe conflict should be handled discreetly. We return to these cultural orientations a bit later in the chapter.

This confluence of conflict, face, and culture can be exemplified in our story of Professor Yang and Kevin Bruner. It is apparent that Kevin's conflict with Professor Yang centers on his desire to receive an "incomplete" and her determination to have him complete the project. Because Professor Yang does not acquiesce to his wishes, Kevin tries to maintain his face by agreeing to his professor's compromise. In other words, he expresses a need to preserve his face with his professor.

A third assumption of Face-Negotiation Theory pertains to the effects that various acts have on one's face. Incorporating politeness research, Ting-Toomey (1988) asserts that face-threatening acts (FTAs) threaten either the positive or the negative face of the interactants. FTAs can be either direct or indirect and occur when people's desired identity is challenged (Tracy, 1990). Direct FTAs are more threatening to the face of others, whereas indirect FTAs are less so.

Ting-Toomey and Mark Cole (1990) note that two actions make up the face-threatening process: face-saving and face restoration. **Face-saving** involves efforts to prevent events that either elicit vulnerability or impair one's image. Face-saving

face-saving
efforts to avoid embarrassment or vulnerability

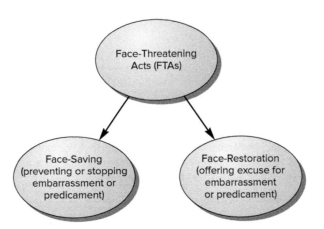

Figure 27.1
Face-Maintenance Framework Source
Source: Adapted from Ting-Toomey & Cole, 1990.

often prevents embarrassment. For instance, French is the primary language of the friend of one of your authors. Although he does speak fluent English, he periodically splices French phrases into his conversations with others. Because others are usually not prepared for this, your author introduces him as someone whose primary language is French. In this example, your author is using a face-saving technique.

face restoration
strategy used to preserve autonomy and avoid loss of face

Face restoration occurs after the loss of face has happened. Ting-Toomey and Cole (1990) observe that people attempt to restore face in response to the events. For instance, people's excuses are face-restoration techniques when embarrassing events occur (Cupach & Metts, 1994). Excuses ("I thought it was her job") and justifications ("I'm not a morning person") are commonplace in face restoration. These face-maintenance strategies and their relationship to each other are represented in Figure 27.1.

So far, we have detailed face and facework as well as three primary assumptions of Face-Negotiation Theory. We now turn our attention to a discussion of additional areas of the theory. First, we explore individualism and collectivism, and then we examine how conflict functions in the theory.

Individualistic and Collectivistic Cultures

Culture is not a static variable. It is interpreted along many dimensions. To this end, Ting-Toomey examines culture and how it interrelates with face and conflict by employing thinking derived from both Harry Triandis (1972, 1988) and Geert Hofstede (1980, 2001). Both were instrumental in identifying the cultural variability used to explain cultural differences in behavior. In FNT, culture can be organized around two ends of a continuum: individualism and collectivism (Ting-Toomey, 2010). At one end is a culture that places a premium on the value of individual identity; at the other end is a culture that values group identity. Individualistic cultures are "independent self" cultures, and collectivistic cultures are "interdependent self" cultures. Cultures across the world vary in individualism and collectivism (Table 27.1). These two dimensions play a prominent role in the way that facework and conflict are managed but Hofstede reminds us that cultural comparisons can change over

FACE-NEGOTIATION THEORY

Table 27.1 Rankings of Individualism and Collectivism Around the World*

RANK	COUNTRY	RANK	COUNTRY
1	United States	28	Turkey
2	Australia	29	Uruguay
3	Great Britain	30	Greece
4/5	Canada/Netherlands	31	Philippines
4/5	Netherlands	32	Mexico
6	New Zealand	33/35	Yugoslavia
7	Italy	33/35	Portugal
8	Belgium	33/35	East Africa
9	Denmark	36	Malaysia
10/11	Sweden	37	Hong Kong
10/11	France	38	Chile
12	Ireland	39/41	Singapore
13	Norway	39/41	Thailand
14	Switzerland	39/41	West Africa
15	Germany	42	Salvador
16	South Africa	43	South Korea
17	Finland	44	Taiwan
18	Austria	45	Peru
19	Israel	46	Costa Rica
20	Spain	47/48	Pakistan
21	India	47/48	Indonesia
22/23	Japan	49	Colombia
22/23	Argentina	50	Venezuela
24	Iran	51	Panama
25	Jamaica	52	Ecuador
26/27	Brazil	53	Guatemala
26/27	Arab countries		

*The lower the number, the more individualistic the country is rated; the higher the number, the more collectivistic the country is rated.

Although there are some surveys that show the United States, Australia, and Great Britain varying in ranking, demographers agree that these three countries are clearly the most individualistic in the world.

Source: Hofstede (2001).

time, as changes in population demographics and health opportunities, for instance, continue to influence a particular society (https://geert-hofstede.com/national -culture.html).

Ting-Toomey (2010) and her colleagues Ge Gao, Paula Trubisky, Shizhong Yang, Hak Soo Kim, Sung-Ling Lin, and Tsukasa Nishida (1991) clarify that individualism and collectivism apply not only to national cultures, but also to co-cultures within national cultures. That is, different racial and ethnic groups within the United States may vary in their individualism and collectivism. For example, Ting-Toomey and her research team observe that whereas many European Americans in the United States identify with individualistic values and beliefs, when first-generation immigrant groups from Mexico or Japan arrive, they tend to retain their collectivistic orientation. Let's explore the concepts of individualism and collectivism a bit further.

In Chapter 5, we briefly discussed the terms individualism and collectivism. But as you may recall, although a theorist may use the same word as another theorist, there may be slight variations in meaning. Thus, we briefly address these two within an FNT framework. In a general sense, when people emphasize the individual over the group, they are articulating an individualistic perspective. **Individualism** refers to the tendency of people to highlight individual identity over group identity, individual rights over group rights, and individual needs over group needs (Ting-Toomey, 1994b). Individualism is the "I" identity (I want, I need, etc.). Larry Samovar, Richard Porter, Edwin McDaniel, and Carolyn Roy (2016) believe that individualism was likely the first value that developed in the early formation of the United States. Samovar and Porter (1995) believe that "[i]ndividualism emphasizes individual initiative ('Pull yourself up by your own boot straps'), independence ('Do your own thing'), individual expression ('The squeaky wheel gets the grease'), and privacy

individualism
a cultural value that places emphasis on the individual over the group

---

Theory in Popular Press • *The United States—A Collectivist Nation?*

Boston Globe author Claude Fischer is one of the first journalists in the country to publicly question whether the United States is *really* an individualistic society. Drawing on the research that states people in the United States value and practice individualism, Fischer contends that the notion of "personal liberty"—a prized value in the States—is really not as pervasive as one may think. The author compares the United States with Europe, a continent often identified as collectivistic. The intrigue becomes clear. Fischer claims that "Americans are much more likely than Europeans to say that employees should follow a boss's orders even if the boss is wrong; to say that children 'must' love their parents; and to believe that parents have a duty to sacrifice themselves for their children. We are more likely to defer to church leaders and to insist on abiding by the law."

In his essay, Fischer seems to believe that because of the complexity related to individualism, people living in the United States often have issues "where individual rights conflict with group interests." This, then, contradicts the perception (and some of the research of Face-Negotiation theorists) that "American" citizens are highly "I-centered." In fact, Fischer boldly advances that those in the United States "seem much more willing to submerge personal liberty to the group than Europeans are." Fischer's provocative thinking is underscored in many ways, including providing evidence of surveys that show among all nationalities, Americans "turned out to be the most likely to embrace the statement: 'People should support their country even if the country is in the wrong.'"

Source: Fisher, C. (2010). Sweet land of . . . conformity? Americans aren't the rugged individuals we think we are. *Boston Globe* online, boston.com/bostonglobe/ideas/articles/2010/06/06/sweet_land_of_conformity/.

('A man's [woman's] home is his [her] castle')" (p. 85). Values that are individualistic highlight freedom, honesty, comfort, and personal equality, among others (Ting-Toomey & Chung, 2005).

As you see, individualism involves self-motivation, autonomy, and independent thinking. Individualism suggests direct communication with another. Think about Kevin Bruner's comments expressing his desire to complete his project on his own time. He is projecting individualism to Professor Yang.

According to intercultural communication scholars, individualism is esteemed in the United States (Jandt, 2015). In addition to the United States, a number of other cultures are viewed as individualistic. Australia, Great Britain, Canada, the Netherlands, and New Zealand are examples of individualistic cultures. Italy, Belgium, and Denmark are also considered individualistic. These cultures stress individual achievement and value independence.

Whereas individualism focuses on one's personal identity, collectivism looks outside the self. Ting-Toomey (1994b) comments that collectivism is the emphasis of group goals over individual goals, group obligations over individual rights, and in-group needs over individual wants. **Collectivism** is the "we" identity (*"we can do this," "we are a team,"* etc.). People in a collectivistic culture value working together and viewing themselves as part of a larger group. Collectivistic societies, consequently, value inclusion. Collectivistic values emphasize harmony, respecting parents' wishes, and fulfillment of another's needs, among others. Examples of collectivistic cultures include Indonesia, Venezuela, Panama, Mexico, Ecuador, and Guatemala.

collectivism
a cultural value that places emphasis on the group over the individual

Face Management and Culture

So, how do individualism and collectivism relate to Ting-Toomey's theory? Ting-Toomey and Chung (2005) argue that "members [of cultures] who subscribe to individualistic values tend to be more self-face-oriented and members who subscribe to group-oriented values tend to be more other- or mutual-face oriented in conflict" (p. 274). If you are a citizen of an individualistic society, you are more likely to be concerned with controlling your own autonomy and boundaries for behavior. You would also want choices to satisfy self-face needs. Dissatisfied with the assignment and its deadline, Kevin Bruner is seeking autonomy and wants another choice from his professor. Ting-Toomey believes that in individualistic cultures, **face management** is overt in that it involves protecting one's face, even if it comes to bargaining. Kevin Bruner engages in face negotiation that promotes confrontation, and as Ting-Toomey notes, members of individualistic cultures like Kevin will tend to use more autonomy-preserving face strategies in managing their conflict than will members of collectivistic societies.

face management
the protection of one's face

Collectivistic cultures "are concerned with the adaptability of self-presentation image" (Ting-Toomey, 1988, p. 224). Adaptability, then, allows for interdependent bonds with others (positive face). What this means is that members of collectivistic communities consider their relationship to others when discussing matters and feel that a conversation requires ongoing maintenance by both communicators. For instance, Professor Yang makes efforts to demonstrate her connection to Kevin by empathizing with his conflict. She also demonstrates a collectivistic orientation by asking whether it would be fair to grant Kevin an extension and not offer the same alternative to other students. Professor Yang, then, as a member of a collectivistic culture, seeks both self-face and other-face needs.

Ting-Toomey believes that conflict is opportunistic when members from two different cultures—individualistic and collectivistic—come together with a disregard for how the other handles conflictual situations. In fact, "interpersonal conflict, when managed competently, can bring about positive changes in an interpersonal relationship" (Ting-Toomey & Oetzel, 2016, p. 1). To this end, Face-Negotiation Theory takes into consideration the influence culture has on the way conflict is handled within relationships across the globe.

Managing Conflict Across Cultures

The individualistic–collectivistic cultural dimension influences the selection of conflict styles. These styles refer to patterned responses, or typical ways of handling conflict across a variety of communication encounters (Ting-Toomey & Chung, 2005; Ting-Toomey & Oetzel, 2001). The styles include avoiding (AV), obliging (OB), compromising (CO), dominating (DO), and integrating (IN). In **avoiding**, people will try to stay away from disagreements and dodge unpleasant exchanges with others ("I'm busy" or "I don't want to talk about that"). The **obliging** style includes a passive accommodation that tries to satisfy the needs of others or goes along with the suggestions of others ("Whatever you want to do is fine"). In **compromising**, individuals try to find a middle road to resolve impasses and use give-and-take so that a compromise can be reached ("Why don't I just give up one week of my vacation and you give up a week of yours?").

The **dominating** style includes those behaviors that involve using influence, authority, or expertise to get ideas across or to make decisions ("I'm in the best position to talk about this issue"). Finally, the **integrating** style is used by people to find a solution to a problem ("I think we need to work this out together"). As opposed to compromising, integrating requires a high degree of concern for yourself and for others. In compromising, a moderate degree exists.

Ting-Toomey believes that the decision to use one or more of these styles will depend on the cultural variability of communicators. Yet, conflict management necessarily takes into consideration the concern for self-face and other-face. We illustrate this relationship in Figure 27.2. From our chapter-opening story, Kevin Bruner, using a dominating style of conflict management, apparently has little concern for the face of his professor (self-face). Professor Yang, however, is more compromising in the way that she handles the conflict with her student (other-face).

Let's continue to clarify Ting-Toomey's discussion of conflict management by identifying the relationship of conflict style to facework. Ting-Toomey notes several relationships between conflict styles and face concern/face need. First, both AV and OB styles of conflict management reflect a passive approach to handling conflicts. A CO style represents a mutual-face need by finding middle-ground solutions to a conflict. Finally, a DO style reflects a high self-face need and a need for control of the conflict, whereas the IN conflict style indicates a high self-face/other-face need for conflict resolution.

avoiding
staying away from disagreements

obliging
satisfying the needs of others

compromising
a behavior that employs give-and-take to achieve a middle-road resolution

dominating
using influence or authority to make decisions

integrating
collaborating with others to find solutions

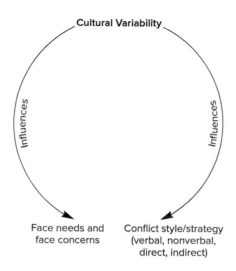

Cultural Variability

Influences

Influences

Face needs and
face concerns

Conflict style/strategy
(verbal, nonverbal,
direct, indirect)

**Figure 27.2
Cultural Variability,
Face, and Conflict**

With respect to comparisons across five cultures (Japan, China, South Korea, Taiwan, and the United States), Ting-Toomey and her research colleagues (1991) discovered the following:

- Members of U.S. cultures use significantly more dominating styles of conflict management (than Japanese and Koreans).
- The Taiwanese report using significantly more integrating styles of conflict management.
- The Chinese and Taiwanese use significantly more obliging conflict styles (than Americans).
- The Chinese use higher degrees of avoidance as a conflict style than other cultural groups.
- The Chinese use a higher degree of compromising than other cultures.

Additional research also showed that collectivistic cultures (China, Korea, and Taiwan) had a higher degree of other-face concern. Other research has found that Arab participants preferred more integrating and avoiding styles while U.S. participants identified more with a dominating style (Khakimova, Zhang, & Hall, 2013). Further, in a study examining Ecuador and the United States, James Neuliep and Morgan Johnson (2016) discovered that Ecuadorians preferred avoiding and compromising much more than U.S. respondents. Finally, one additional study (Croucher, et al., 2011) employing Ting-Toomey's intercultural conflict styles concluded that among Indians, Hindus prefer integrating and dominating styles, with little use of avoiding and obliging styles. Muslims prefer integrating and compromising styles, with little preference toward dominating and avoiding styles.

It is clear from the research on face and conflict that cultural variability influences the way conflict is managed. Let's revisit our opening discussion of Kevin Bruner and Professor Yang. According to Face-Negotiation Theory, because Professor Yang is a member of the Chinese culture—defined as a collectivistic society—she is likely to compromise with Kevin in their conflict. As you saw in our opening, she does try to compromise by asking him to write up a detailed outline and then alters the page parameters of the assignment. She also has a high degree of other-face concern. Kevin, on the other hand, is very dominating in his conflict style and possesses a great deal of self-face concern.

Finally, a word about culture and negotiation, two primary themes in Face-Negotiation Theory. While you may be tempted to ask about the differences between and among cultures with respect to negotiation skills, keep in mind that just as conflict styles are culturally based, so are negotiation styles. And, to be sure, negotiation is a "Westernized" concept that is not easily translatable to other cultures, namely Eastern societies (LeBaron, 2003). What all of this means is that we all need to be cautious and sensible when applying terminology across the globe.

Integration, Critique, and Closing

Face-Negotiation Theory assumes that people of various cultures are concerned with the presentation of their face. It is a theory that artfully infuses conflict into its framework, explaining why members of two different cultures, for instance, manage conflict differently. Ting-Toomey asserts that different cultural values exist in dealing with conflict, and these conflictual episodes, in turn, are influenced by the face concerns and face needs of communicators. FNT has a rich history, and a research agenda that has been nearly all quantitative in nature. We now discuss two criteria to discuss the theory's effectiveness: heurism and logical consistency.

Integration

Communication Tradition	Rhetorical | Semiotic | Phenomenological | Cybernetic | **Socio-Psychological** | Socio-Cultural | Critical
Communication Context	Intrapersonal | Interpersonal | Small Group | Organizational | Public/Rhetorical | Mass/Media | **Cultural**
Approach to Knowing	**Positivistic/Empirical** | Interpretive/Hermeneutic | Critical

Critique

Evaluation Criteria	Scope | **Logical Consistency** | Parsimony | Utility | Testability | **Heurism** | Test of Time

Logical Consistency

Interestingly, Face-Negotiation Theory has received some clarification from Ting-Toomey herself, prompting refinement of the theory. Recall that the theory rests on the differing experiences and perceptions of individualistic and collectivist cultures. Ting-Toomey uses this foundation to lay out the essence of her theory. At times, however, this cultural dimension may not fully explain cultural differences. In her own research, Ting-Toomey and colleagues (1991) discovered some discrepancies. She found that Japanese respondents showed more concern for self-face than U.S. respondents. In addition, although Ting-Toomey proposes that individualistic cultures are not usually compromising in their conflict styles, the highly individualistic U.S. respondents used a significantly higher degree of compromising when faced with a conflict. In this study, then, the "I" identity of the U.S. respondents was displaced.

Ting-Toomey and Cocroft (1994) respond to these differences in expectations by noting that looking at facework from the individualistic and collectivistic orientation "is a necessary starting point for facework behavior research" (p. 314). The researchers also state that many of the facework category systems in research reflect individualism–collectivism thinking, and therefore, Face-Negotiation Theory must necessarily begin from this vantage point.

Additional issues surrounding the logical consistency of Face-Negotiation Theory remain. As we have mentioned, Ting-Toomey (1988) has positioned the theory within the politeness perspective of Brown and Levinson (1987). She incorporates a number of the components of their thinking, including positive face and negative face. Ting-Toomey seems to be aligning herself with the notion that people use politeness strategies to reduce face threats (Feng, 2015). Yet, Tracy and Baratz (1994) believe that such labeling in Brown and Levinson's framework "may be too general to capture the face-concern most central to an interactant" (p. 290). That is, other issues pertaining to face concerns exist that are not identified by the researchers. Still, Susan Shimanoff (2009) states that politeness is, indeed, a practice people use to redress face-threatening acts. Ting-Toomey and Cocroft (1994) agree with the fact that Brown and Levinson have presented an original template from which to draw, but report data that demonstrates several problems with their research.

Heurism

Ting-Toomey's Face-Negotiation Theory continues to spark interest among intercultural communication researchers, making it highly heuristic. Several of the key concepts and features of the theory have been studied. For instance, conflict management examined within the framework of "face" has been investigated with juvenile delinquents and youth-at-risk (Lim, Vadrevu, Chan, & Basnyat, 2012). In addition, face has been investigated across cultures, including Malaysia, China, Japan, Germany, Mexico, and the United States (Oetzel et al., 2003; Quinn, Oetzel, Ting-Toomey, & Zhang, 2015; Rose, Suppiah, Uli, & Othman, 2008). The theory has been woven into research looking at family problems in Japan (Child, Pearson, & Nagao, 2006) and family secrets (Cho & Sillars, 2015) and it has been expanded beyond intercultural issues and has been applied to forgiveness (Zhang, Ting-Toomey, & Oetzel, 2014) and to crisis communication in Nigeria (George, 2016). In addition, on a more practical note, the theory has been incorporated into research on intercultural training and development pertaining to conflict (Ting-Toomey, 2007).

Closing

Face-Negotiation Theory will continue to intrigue communication researchers most importantly, because culture continues to be a critical issue in many societies. Particularly at a time when culture pervades all aspects of life and the global village is becoming smaller, the theory will have lasting appeal. When people from various cultures have a conflict, understanding how they maintain and negotiate face will have implications beyond the encounter. Ting-Toomey has given us an opportunity to think about how we can mediate the potential difficulties in communication among cultures, and she elegantly presents important information on a world dependent on communication.

Discussion Starters

TECH QUEST: When contextualized in Face-Negotiation Theory, face refers to how we present ourselves to others. Outline how this identity can be influenced when this image is presented on such social networks as Pinterest.

1. If he had to do it over again, what communication strategies would you recommend for Kevin Bruner in his conflict with Professor Yang? How might he save his own face and the face of his professor?

2. Have you been to one of the countries categorized here as collectivistic? If so, what communication differences did you notice between that culture and U.S. culture?

3. Do you believe that Face-Negotiation Theory relies on people being reasonable agents who are capable of handling conflict? Can conflict become unreasonable? Explain with examples.

4. Interpret the following statement by Ting-Toomey through description and example: "Collectivists need to work on their ethnocentric biases as much as the individualists need to work out their sense of egocentric superiority." Do you agree or disagree with her view?

5. What evidence do you have that face maintenance is a critical part of U.S. society? Use examples in your response.

6. Look at the *Popular Press* insert and comment on whether or not you agree with what the author is saying.

7. Apply any concept or feature of FNT to a job interview.

FACE-NEGOTIATION THEORY

CHAPTER 28

Communication Accommodation Theory

*Based on the research of **Howard Giles***

> *As an evolving and adaptive specie's, we naturally have to adjust to our surroundings; this means accommodating as well as non-accommodating each other.*
>
> —Howard Giles

Luke Merrill and Roberto Hernandez

As an upcoming spring graduate, 22-year-old Luke Merrill was already preparing for the on-slaught of interviews he would face graduating with a 3.86 grade point average. Luke knew that his grades were excellent, and as a double major (Spanish and Communication), he felt that his chances of landing a good job were pretty good.

Luke's chance to show what he's got finally came. He got an interview with a large accounting firm looking to hire someone in their client relations department. The position preferred a candidate with proficiency in two languages so he was even more excited. Luke flew to Denver for his first face-to-face interview with Roberto Hernandez, the department's director. The interview would be one that both men would remember for quite some time.

"Good morning, Luke. It's great to meet you," Roberto, said,

"Good morn . . . I mean, *buenos días* to you, Mr. Hernandez," Luke replied, realizing that he already interrupted his soon-to-be boss. And yet, the initial tension seemed to ease.

Roberto continued, "Please, have a seat. I hope your flight last night was fine. I know that this time of the year can get a little bumpy, especially over the Rockies."

"Oh, it was great. I like to fly, Mr. Hernandez. This time, I got a chance to watch a movie that I hadn't seen yet. Personally, I love movies while I fly. It distracts me from the other noise and loud talking," Luke responded.

Their conversation continued. Luke was certainly a bit on edge, but noticed that his nervous accelerated speech rate slowed to match that of his interviewer. Yet, Luke still felt awkward because he did not know exactly when Mr. Hernandez would change the subject from flying to the job.

Roberto began to talk further about his two sons, both of whom love to fly. "Like you, I love to fly," Roberto related. "My wife, though, is a different story. I wish she had the same attitude as you."

Luke replied, "Hey, maybe it's simply *machismo*, but I'm never afraid to fly."

Roberto was struck by Luke's use of the term *machismo*. Was he adjusting his speech to Spanish simply because Roberto was Mexican? As an interviewer, he knew that job candidates get nervous, and maybe this was simply a nervous habit of his. Of course, it didn't escape Roberto's notice that Luke was speaking Spanish to a Mexican American man who happened to have a strong accent. And, Roberto knew that Spanish was one of his majors in college. Yet, he didn't want to make anything out of it. "I trust you've come here with a lot of questions, Luke.

Let me begin by answering one that we haven't really addressed over the phone—the job's travel schedule."

"I'm cool with pretty much anything, Mr. Hernandez. You might say that I'm comfortable with nearly any assignment you'd give to me. We are definitely *simpatico* on that one."

Roberto was now getting visibly agitated by Luke's frequent insertion of Spanish words into the conversation. He could handle the initial greeting; after all, he had initiated it. But Luke's continuing in this manner only made Roberto more uneasy. He didn't know whether to ask Luke to leave or simply to say how confused he was over Luke's persistent behavior. Of course, he could choose to remain silent and simply send Luke a rejection letter. Roberto decided to confront the young college student instead.

"Luke, I have to admit that I think it's a bit weird that you're including Spanish here. Ok, I realize that you're interviewing with someone who is from Mexico and yes, I began our conversation with a friendly Spanish welcome. But, frankly, it's a bit much, don't you think? Maybe I'm reaching here, but it's . . . ." Roberto stared at the young job candidate.

"Mr. Hernandez," Luke explained, wishing he could start the entire interview over, "I'm sorry if I've offended you. I realize that I broke into Spanish, and to be honest with you, yeah, I guess it was inappropriate. I should know better. I was using Spanish to show you some respect, to ah . . . to show that I can weave Spanish into our conversation. . . . I'm really sorry if I was out of place. I blew this, right?"

Luke was extremely nervous. He wasn't sure what Mr. Hernandez would say next. He was mad at himself for sounding like an idiot and assumed that he had lost the job. Maybe he had tried too hard to adapt to his interviewer. Maybe an interview was the worst place for him to demonstrate his fluency in Spanish. Maybe he had misread the situation.

"Listen, Luke," Roberto advised. "I've been around this firm for almost 15 years. I've seen people come and go. I. . . ."

". . . and I think," Luke interrupted, "that I should keep my mouth shut and not pretend I'm some expert in a foreign language! Really, I'm sorry about this."

Roberto smile, albeit awkwardly. "Now, let's get on with the rest of this interview."

When two people speak, they sometimes mimic each other's speech and behavior. We may talk to another who uses the same language we do, gestures similarly, and even speaks at a similar rate. We, in turn, may respond in kind to the other communicator. Think of this as "conversational echo," where someone repeats—both verbally and nonverbally—what has been presented earlier in the conversation sequence.

Imagine, for instance, situations where you speak to someone who has gone to college. You both are probably going to use phrases and jargon that are unique to college life, including "prereqs," "electives," "independent study," "gen ed," etc. If we are speaking to someone who has not gone to college, we may make efforts to clarify our speech or use examples that the other person will understand.

Although we all have these types of experiences at the interpersonal level, sometimes there are group- or culture-based differences, such as perceived differences in age group, in accent or ethnicity, or in the pace and rate of speech. Whether in an interpersonal relationship, in a small group, or across cultures, people tend to adjust their communication to others. This adaptation is at the core of Communication Accommodation Theory (CAT), developed by Howard Giles. Formerly known as Speech Accommodation Theory (but later conceptualized more broadly to include nonverbal behaviors and speaking patterns), Communication Accommodation

Theory rests on the premise that when speakers interact, they modify their speech, their vocal patterns, and their gestures to accommodate others. Giles and his colleagues believe that speakers have various reasons for being accommodative to others. Some people wish to (1) evoke a listener's approval, (2) achieve communication efficiency, (3) assert a dominant position, and (4) maintain a positive social identity (Giles, Mulac, Bradac, & Johnson, 1987; Hogg & Giles, 2012). As you can see in our chapter-opening story, however, we do not always achieve what we aim for.

Communication Accommodation Theory had its beginnings in 1973, almost in tandem with the "accent mobility" model (Giles, 1973), which is based on various accents heard in interview situations (similar to the situation with Luke and Roberto). As the mobility model was being researched, Giles clarified and conceptualized CAT. Much of the subsequent theory and research since then has remained sensitive to the various communication accommodations undertaken in conversations among diverse cultural groups, including senior citizens, people of color, immigrants, and the visually impaired. For Giles and other accommodation theorists, *culture* is an expansive term and includes much more than, say, race and gender. Adding to the importance of discussing this theory within a cultural context, Jordan Soliz and Howard Giles (2016) observe that the theory has appealed to those who are "cross disciplinary." Further, the researchers argue that CAT has not only attracted international scholars, but that a body of this research has been published in multiple languages, making this theory truly global in nature. We discuss this theory with this cultural variability in mind.

To get a sense of the central characteristic of CAT, we first delineate what is meant by the word *accommodation*. For our purposes, **accommodation** is defined as the ability to adjust, modify, or regulate one's behavior in response to another. Accommodation, to a large extent, requires multiple levels of communication (Gallois & Giles, 2015) in that it also includes the motivations behind accommodation and the consequences related to the adjustment (Soliz & Giles, 2016). Further, since accommodation effectively requires adjustment, it's important to understand that inappropriate or insufficient adjustment can result in conversational misunderstandings (Gasiorek & Giles, 2012).

Accommodation also usually is done unconsciously. We tend to have internal cognitive scripts that we draw on when we find ourselves in conversations with others. In a conversation with a 15-year-old girl, you might find yourself using teen vocabulary (e.g., "whatever") and while referencing with an 85-year-old, you might slow your speech. This is all done without much thought and can occur overtly or covertly.

Like several other theories in this book, Communication Accommodation Theory has its infancy in another field and in this case, in social psychology. To this end, it's important to address the theoretical vehicle that launched Giles's thinking: Social Identity Theory.

accommodation
adjusting, modifying, or regulating behavior in response to others

Social Psychology and Social Identity

Much of the research and theory in the field of social psychology pertain directly to how people search for meaning in the behaviors of others and how this meaning influences future interactions with others. One of the key concepts discussed

This theory considers the underlying motivations and consequences of what happens when two speakers, usually with different cultural backgrounds, shift their communication styles. During communication encounters, people will try to accommodate or adjust their style of speaking to others. This is primarily done in two ways: divergence and convergence. Groups with strong cultural pride often use divergence to highlight group identity. Convergence occurs when there is a strong need for social approval, frequently from powerless individuals.

in the research of social psychology is identity. According to Jessica Abrams, Joan O'Connor, and Howard Giles (2003), "[A]ccommodation is fundamental to identity construction" (p. 221). Recognizing the importance of the self and its relationship to group identity, Henri Tajfel and John Turner (1986) developed **Social Identity Theory.** This theory suggests that a person's self-concept comprises personal identity (e.g., body characteristics, psychological behaviors) as well as a social identity (e.g., affiliation with a group) (Ellemers & Haslam, 2012). Researchers and theorists in Social Identity suggest that people are "motivated to join the most attractive groups and/or give an advantage to the groups to which one belongs (in-group)" (Worchel, Rothgerber, Day, Hart, & Butemeyer, 1998, p. 390). When people are given an opportunity, Worchel and colleagues contend, they will provide more resources to their own groups, rather than to out-groups. And when in-groups are identified, an individual decides the extent to which the group is central to his or her identity. Social identity, then, is primarily based on the comparisons that people make between **in-groups** (groups to which a person feels he or she belongs) and **out-groups** (groups to which a person feels he or she does not belong).

People strive to acquire or maintain positive social identity (Hughes, Kiecolt, Keith, & Demo, 2015; Tajfel & Turner, 1986), and when social identity is perceived as unsatisfactory, they will either join a group they feel more at home in or make the existing group a more positive experience. Summing up the Social Identity perspective, Tajfel and Turner observe that in-group/out-group comparisons lead social groups to differentiate themselves from one another. They note that communication exists on a continuum from "interindividual" to "intergroup." So, according to the theory, the more that Luke perceives Roberto to be either a "Mexican" or a "boss" rather than simply "Mr. Hernandez," the more Luke will rely on stereotypes or group-level impressions to understand Roberto's behavior.

Giles drew from some of the thinking related to Social Identity Theory (Giles, 2017). He felt that we accommodate not only to specific others, but also to those we perceive as members of other groups. Thus, intergroup variables and goals influence the communication process. Giles, like many social psychologists, believes that people are influenced by a number of behaviors. Specifically, he argues that an individual's speech style (accent, pitch, rate, interruption patterns) can affect the impressions that

Social Identity Theory
a theory that proposes a person's identity is shaped by both personal and social characteristics

in-groups
groups in which a person feels he or she belongs

out-groups
groups in which a person feels he or she does not belong

COMMUNICATION ACCOMMODATION THEORY

others have of the individual. Giles and Smith (1979) also comment that the nature of the setting, the conversation topic, and the type of person with whom one communicates will all intersect to determine the speech manner one adopts in a given situation. In its simplest form, if an individual is viewed favorably, communicator A will shift his or her speech style to become more like that of communicator B; that is, communicator A has accommodated communicator B. Giles and Smith maintain that people adjust their speech style to accommodate how they believe others in the conversation will best receive it. In our opening, you can see how Luke shifts his speech to accommodate what he believes (incorrectly) Mr. Hernandez will appreciate.

Giles (2012) was influenced by the belief that when members of different groups come together, they compare themselves. If their comparisons are favorable, a positive social identity will result. Jake Harwood (2006) sums up the importance of social identity and group membership: "Even our closest interpersonal relationships are imbued with group identifications that both join us to those within our groups and separate us from those not in our groups" (p. 89).

With this theoretical footing in place, we now turn our attention to the assumptions guiding the development of Communication Accommodation Theory. As we discuss these, you will be able to sense the influence of social psychology, and Social Identity Theory in particular.

Assumptions of Communication Accommodation Theory

Accommodation Theory proponents would be interested in the accommodation taking place between Luke Merrill and Roberto Hernandez. Their conversation exemplifies a number of issues that underlie the basic assumptions of the theory. Recalling that accommodation is influenced by a number of personal, situational, and cultural circumstances, we identify several assumptions below:

- Speech and behavioral similarities and dissimilarities exist in all conversations.
- The manner in which we perceive the speech and behaviors of another will determine how we evaluate a conversation.
- Language and behaviors impart information about social status and group belonging.
- Accommodation varies in its degree of appropriateness, and norms guide the accommodation process.

Many principles of CAT rest on the first assumption that there are similarities and dissimilarities between communicators in a conversation. Past experiences, you may recall, form a person's field of experience, a concept we discussed in Chapter 1. Whether in speech or behaviors, people bring their various fields of experiences into a conversation (West & Turner, 2016). These varied experiences and backgrounds will determine the extent to which one person will accommodate another. The more similar our attitudes and beliefs are to those of others, the more we will be attracted to and accommodate those others.

Let's look at a few examples to illustrate this assumption. Consider our opening scenario with Luke and Roberto. They are clearly from different professional backgrounds with different levels of work experience. Presumably, they are products of different family backgrounds with different beliefs and values. The two are clearly dissimilar in some ways, yet, they are similar in others—for example, they both like to fly and they both have an interest in working at the accounting firm.

To illustrate this assumption further, consider the following dialogue between a grandparent and a teenage granddaughter as the two talk about the girl's prom dress:

GRANDMOTHER: I don't know why you're wearing all black. You'll have people talking. You look like you're at your own funeral!

GRANDDAUGHTER: Whatever. People talked about your generation wearing weird stuff too. It's the style now.

GRANDMOTHER: But, we only wore black during very solemn times.

GRANDDAUGHTER: Oh yeah, Nana. Sure. Your generation never had any fun at all! When you look at all the old photographs, no one is ever smiling!

GRANDMOTHER: You would be surprised how much fun we had. It was different from what you think now. We did a lot when I was younger, but you just wouldn't understand.

In this conversation, the granddaughter draws conclusions about the grandparent using group-based expectations: Older people can't understand teenagers. This expectation influences the teenager's communication with her grandmother.

The second assumption rests on both perception and evaluation. Communication Accommodation is a theory concerned with how people both perceive and evaluate what takes place in a conversation (Dragojevich, Gasiorek, & Giles, 2016). **Perception** is the process of attending to and interpreting a message, whereas **evaluation** is the process of judging a conversation. People first perceive what takes place in a conversation (e.g., the other person's speaking abilities) before they decide how to behave in a conversation. Consider, for example, Luke's response to Roberto. The interviewer's informality at the beginning of the interview is perceived by Luke as a good way to break the ice and eliminate some of his tension. Luke's subsequent behavior reflects a relaxed style (too relaxed we might conclude). Luke is like most people in an interview: He gets a sense of the interview atmosphere (perception) and then reacts accordingly (evaluation).

Motivation is a key part of the perception and evaluation process in Communication Accommodation Theory (Dragojevich et al., 2016). That is, we may perceive another person's speech and behaviors, but we may not always choose to evaluate them. This often happens, for instance, when we greet another person, engage in small talk, and simply walk on. We normally don't take the time to evaluate such a conversational encounter.

Yet, there are times when perceiving the words and behaviors of another leads to our evaluation of the other person. We may greet someone, for instance, and engage in small talk, but then be surprised when we hear that the other person recently got divorced. According to Giles and colleagues (1987), it is then that we decide our evaluative and communicative responses. We may express our happiness, our sorrow, or our support. We do this by engaging in an accommodating communication style.

The third assumption of Communication Accommodation Theory pertains to the effects that language has on others. Specifically, language has the ability to communicate

perception
process of attending to and interpreting a message

evaluation
process of judging a conversation

status and group belonging between communicators in a conversation. Consider what occurs when two people who speak different languages try to communicate with each other. Giles and John Wiemann (1987) discuss this situation:

> In bilingual, or even bidialectal, situations, where ethnic majority and minority peoples coexist, second language learning is dramatically unidirectional: that is, it is very common for the dominant group to acquire the linguistic habits of the subordinate collectivity. . . . Indeed, it is no accident that cross-culturally what is "standard," "correct," and "cultivated" language behavior is that of the aristocracy, the upper or ruling classes and their institutions. (p. 361)

The language used in a conversation, then, will likely reflect the individual with the higher social status. In addition, inferred in this quotation is a desire to be part of the "dominant" group. And, dominant groups, especially when dealing with language use and policies, determine how things are going to be said and whether or not any "minority" views will be entertained (Bourhis, Sioufi, & Sachdev, 2012).

To understand this assumption better, let's return to our opening story. In the interview situation with Mr. Hernandez, Luke's language and behaviors are guided by the interviewer. This is what normally occurs in interviews: The individual with the higher social status sets the tone through his or her language and behaviors. Although Roberto is a member of a co-culture that has been historically oppressed, he nonetheless has the power to establish the interview's direction. Those wishing to identify with or to become part of another's group—for example, Luke wishing to be offered a job by Mr. Hernandez—will usually accommodate.

The fourth and final assumption focuses on norms and issues of social appropriateness. We note that accommodation can vary in social appropriateness and that accommodation is rooted in norm usage. Norms have been shown to play a pivotal role in Giles's theory (Gallois & Giles, 2015; Hogg & Giles, 2012). **Norms** are expectations of behaviors that individuals feel should or should not occur in a conversation. The varied backgrounds of communicators like Luke and Roberto, for instance, or those of a grandparent and grandchild will influence what they expect in their conversations. The relationship between norms and accommodation is made clear by Cynthia Gallois and Victor Callan (1991): "Norms put constraints of varying degree . . . on the accommodative moves that are perceived as

norms
expectations of behavior in conversations

Student Voices

Cassie

I'm originally from Botswana so I don't have the best English. So, it's always apparent to me when I visit doctors' offices here in the states. The doctors are so much worse than in Africa because it's almost like they enjoy "talking down" to me. They use words that are just full of different meanings and it's as if they are consciously trying to diverge in their communication style. It's not only annoying, it's also very serious if I ever have a serious thing to discuss.

desirable in an interaction" (p. 253). Therefore, the general norm that a younger person is obedient to an older person or that an interviewee is deferential to an employer suggests that Luke will be more accommodative in his communication to Mr. Hernandez.

It's important to understand that while normative behavior may suggest one accommodate, accommodation may not always be worthwhile and beneficial. For instance, Melanie Booth-Butterfield and Felicia Jordan (1989) found that people from marginalized cultures are usually expected to adapt (accommodate) to others and at times, these cultures lose their identity (Bourhis et al., 2012).

These four assumptions form the foundation for the remainder of our discussion of the theory. We now examine the ways that people adapt in conversations.

Ways to Adapt

Communication Accommodation Theory suggests that in conversations people have options. It's important to acknowledge that accommodation is an optional process in which two communicators decide to accommodate, one does, or neither does. That is, we may either accommodate strategically (conscious) or we may be doing it instinctively (unconscious). Further, conversants may be accommodating, but it does not mean that they necessarily agree with things. We may disagree with someone in a conversation but for the sake of argument (e.g., to make a point), we may accommodate the other.

Individuals may create a conversational community that includes using the same or similar language or nonverbal system, they may distinguish themselves from others, or they may try too hard to adapt. These choices are labeled (a) convergence, (b) divergence, and (c) overaccommodation (Gallois & Giles, 2015). We examine each next and identify them in Figure 28.1.

Convergence: Merging Thoughts Ahead

The first process associated with CAT is termed *convergence*. Giles, Nikolas Coupland, and Justine Coupland (1991) define convergence as "a strategy whereby individuals adapt to each other's communicative behaviors" (p. 7). People may adapt to speech rate, pause, smiling, eye gaze, and other verbal and nonverbal behaviors. Convergence is a selective process; as we noted earlier, we may perceive but choose not to act with people. When people do converge, they rely on their perceptions of the other person's speech or behaviors. What this means is that Luke Merrill's decision to use Spanish in his interview is partially based on his knowledge that Mr. Hernandez began the interview with a greeting in Spanish; Luke attempts to converge with the opening tone set by his interviewer.

In addition to the perception of the other's communication, convergence is also based on attraction (Gasiorek, Giles, & Soliz, 2015; Giles, 2008). Usually, when communicators are attracted to others, they will converge in their conversations. *Attraction* is a broad term that encompasses a number of other characteristics, such as liking, charisma, and credibility. Giles and Smith (1979) believe that a number of factors affect our attraction for others—for example, the possibility of future

convergence
strategy used to adapt to another's behavior

Figure 28.1
Ways to Adapt or Accommodate in Conversation

interactions with the listener, the speaker's ability to communicate, and the status differential between communicators. Having similar beliefs, having a similar personality, or behaving in similar ways causes people to be attracted to each other and is likely to prompt convergence. Remember, however, that uncovering similarities occurs over time. People may not instantly know whether they are attracted to each other and whether this will lead to identifying their similarities. And the relational history between communicators may be a critical issue in convergence. For instance, Richard Street's (1991) research indicates that physicians differ in their convergence patterns with first-time patients and with repeat patients. He cautions, however, that differences in convergence may be explained by looking at the traditional roles of doctor and patient as well as the time lag between visits.

At first view, convergence may be seen as a favorable way to accommodate another person, and it usually is. Our discussion so far implies that the other person is viewed as similar to the individual or that at least one is attracted to the other in a conversation. We already learned that attraction is a necessary precursor to convergence. Yet, as we explained previously, convergence may be based on stereotypical perceptions. As Giles and colleagues (1987) conclude, "Convergence is often cognitively mediated by our stereotypes of how socially categorized others will speak" (p. 18). What this means is that people may converge toward stereotypes rather than toward real speech and behaviors.

Writer John Kass underscores the potential negative implications of convergence in this story he wrote for the *Chicago Tribune*. Kass believes that during the 2012 presidential campaign, Vice President Joe Biden, in an effort to connect with African American voters, used both verbal and nonverbal communication to demonstrate what accommodation theorists would likely claim to be "stereotypical convergence": "Biden began waving his right hand, palm up, and he adopted what he must have thought was the accent of a black minister." Discussing President Obama's 2012 challenger (Governor Romney), Vice President Biden stated that Romney's policies would allow the banks to write the economic policies of the United States. Then the vice president said the following: "Unchain Wall Street . . . . They're going to put y'all back in chains."

Kass, comparing the vice president to a "Black preacher" who "raised his hands to the heavens," believes that not only the hand waving, but also the use of the phrases "y'all" and "back in chains" were examples of "nonsensical babbling." Kass describes the vice president's language as an example of "verpes." In a not-so-veiled critique of the vice president's proclivity to using inappropriate language with various groups, Kass states that *verpes* is the process of "repeatedly taking your shoe with your foot still inside it and shoving it all the way into your mouth so that it smacks that little punching bag thing back there called a uvula." Perhaps the vice president was relying on stereotypes in his language or perhaps he was simply passionate about his thoughts and invoked language that caused a stir. Regardless, Kass contends that "the race card" was played in a presidential election and that it was a strategic overture to a key demographic.

Source: Kass, J. (2012). Biden gets in mud pit, plays the race card. *Chicago Tribune* online, articles.chicagotribune.com/2012-08-15/news/ct-met-kass-0815-20120815_1_slight-indian -accent-vice-president-joe-biden-race-card.

There are obvious implications of stereotypical convergence. For example, many gay fathers and lesbian mothers report that too many people—including educators—rely on outdated stereotypes of gay men and lesbians when they communicate with them. Examining the cultural experiences of African Americans, Mark Orbe (1998) notes that African Americans are often identified in stereotypical ways. He points out that **indirect stereotyping** exists; that is, stereotyping when European Americans talk to their African American friends about what they believe to be African American "subjects" (sports, music, etc.). Some African Americans report that if they speak nonstandard dialect, they are especially prone to stereotypical reactions. Marsha Houston (2015) agrees. She notes that when describing themselves, White women

indirect stereotyping *imposing outdated and rigid assumptions of a cultural group upon that group*

COMMUNICATION ACCOMMODATION THEORY

in particular identify their speech as appropriate and standard and describe African American female speech as nonstandard, incorrect, or deviant.

Other cultural groups have also been the target of stereotyping. Edwin Vaughan (1998), for example, contends that blind people are repeatedly addressed as if they are deaf. Brenda Allen (2015) believes that many biracial lesbian relationships heavily rely upon outdated and narrow views of relational intimacy. Shobha Pais (1997) maintains that Asian Indian women in the United States are often perceived as strange because of their sari (fabric draped over the shoulder and head) or *salwar kameez* (pantsuit). And Charmaine Shutiva (2015) bemoans the fact that the Native American culture is erroneously viewed as stoic and unemotional, when in reality, it involves a great deal of humor and joy. These examples demonstrate that a number of cultural groups continue to be stereotyped. Stereotyped perceptions, then, may influence the extent to which an individual will converge.

Before we leave our discussion of convergence, let's briefly discuss the evaluation of convergence. Specifically, what occurs when people attempt to converge in their conversations? How do people respond? We have already illustrated a number of examples that demonstrate both positive and negative consequences of convergence. But how do we know how our convergence will be met?

First, we need to consider that an evaluation of convergence usually depends on whether the convergence is done thoughtfully. When convergence is perceived as good, it can enhance the dialogue; when it is perceived as bad, it can break down the communication process. If a communicator speaks or behaves in a style similar to a listener's, the convergence will probably be favorably perceived. But converging to ridicule, tease, or patronize will most likely be perceived negatively. There is a fine line between whether or not convergence will be perceived in the intended way. Consider, for instance, what happens when a nurse speaks to a patient in a nursing home about eating lunch (Ryan, Maclean, & Orange, 1994):

NURSE: It's time for lunch, Mrs. James.

RESIDENT: But I'm not hungry. And I don't particularly like this kind of soup.

NURSE: Everyone has to eat now, Mary. We have to get on with our day's work. Besides that, we can't suit everyone's tastes all of the time. We don't make the soup just for you, you know.

RESIDENT: I'd really rather just rest in my room and have a cup of tea later.

NURSE: Look, dearie, if you don't eat now, you won't get anything later. Let's stop being so fussy, all right?

RESIDENT: Fine.

In this conversation, you can see how convergence by the nurse might be construed as condescending by the patient. In fact, Ryan and colleagues found that this style of communicating was rated as less respectful, less nurturing, and more frustrating for the resident. There are other standards of evaluating convergence, including the norms of the situation (Did the speaker converge in an offensive way?), the ability to pull it off effectively (How does a 50-year-old use the "cool" talk of a high school student?), and the value of a language to a community (Should European Americans employ Black English vernacular in their interactions with African Americans?).

Divergence: Vive la Différence

Giles (1980) believes speakers sometimes accentuate the verbal and nonverbal differences between themselves and others. He terms this *divergence* or *nonaccommodation*. **Divergence** differs greatly from convergence in that it is a dissociation process. Instead of showing how two speakers are alike in speech rate, gestures, or posture, divergence is when there are no attempts to demonstrate similarities between speakers. In other words, two people speak to each other with no concern about accommodating each other. No effort is made to "reduce social distance or to make communication smoother" (Giles et al., 2007, p. 144). Divergence has not received as much research attention as convergence, and so our knowledge about the process is limited to a few claims about its function in Communication Accommodation Theory.

> **divergence**
> *strategy used to accentuate the verbal and nonverbal differences between communicators*

First, divergence should not be misconstrued as an effort to disagree or to not respond to another communicator. Divergence is not the same as inattentiveness. When people diverge, they have simply chosen to dissociate themselves from the communicator and the conversation. The reasons for divergence vary, including asserting "one's own identity, making a statement or fulfill[ing] personal preferences" (Yoneoka, 2011). And, yet, according to Giles (2008), not all divergences are negatively perceived.

Divergence is a way for members of various cultural communities to maintain social identity. Giles and his colleagues (1987) observe that there are occasions when people—namely, racial and ethnic groups—"deliberately use their language or speech style as a symbolic tactic for maintaining their identity, cultural pride, and distinctiveness" (p. 28). Individuals may not wish to converge in order to preserve their cultural heritage. Let's give a classic example that many of you may understand: Imagine that you are traveling in France; everywhere you go the French people you encounter encourage you to speak French. You are surprised at that until you realize that you, as a visitor, should not expect the French to converge to your language.

We've already learned that some cultural groups are immediately stereotyped and that people communicate with this categorization in mind. It's no wonder, then, that some cultural groups remain committed to divergence in their conversations with others. To illustrate this point, consider the conclusions of Richard Bourhis and Giles (1977). In this classic study, the research team studied Welsh people who were very proud of their ethnic identity, but who did not know the Welsh language. As they learned the language, the researchers asked several questions in a standard English format. During the question-and-answer period, the researchers asked the group why they wanted to learn Welsh since it is "a dying language with a dismal future." The Welsh sample rebutted with not only a strong Welsh dialect, but also Welsh words and phrases. Remarkably, the group could link together difficult Welsh words! The group, then, began to diverge from the English that was spoken to them, ostensibly out of ethnic pride.

A second reason people diverge pertains to power and role differences in conversations. In this case, think of the cultural issue of socio-economic class. Divergence frequently occurs in conversations when there is a power difference between the communicators and when there are distinct role differences in the conversation (e.g., physician–patient) (Street, 1991; Street & Giles, 1982). Street (1991), for instance, comments that "interactants having greater status may speak for longer periods, initiate most of the conversational topics, speak more slowly, and maintain a more relaxed body posture than does the less powerful"(p. 135).

Finally, although not as often as for the reasons cited previously, divergence is likely to occur because the other in the conversation is viewed to be a "member of undesirable groups, considered to hold noxious attitudes, or display a deplorable appearance" (Street & Giles, 1982, p. 195). To this end, Giles and his colleagues (1987) contend that divergence is used to contrast self-images in a conversation. To understand this point, consider the number of so-called undesirable groups in society today. Whitney Herrington (2012), for instance, notes that homeless people are historically part of what society labels as unappealing or hapless. Employing the accommodation principle of divergence, then, a homeless man asking for money outside a movie theater may find himself in a conversation with a communicator (we'll call this person Pat) who wishes to diverge to demonstrate differences between the two. Pat's divergence may take the form of an increased rate of speech or a more clipped manner. Pat may also use vocabulary and pronunciation that clearly mark him as a member of the upper-middle class and may even state that the homeless man should get a job. In each case, the divergence is carried out by the individual who wishes to imply a status difference between the two.

Student Voices

Angel

My dad is almost 75 and he is in great physical shape. He swims almost every day and he doesn't smoke or drink. One of the things that bother him the most about getting old is how a lot of people treat him. When he's getting coffee at McDonald's, the worker shouts at him as if he is hard of hearing. My sister constantly reminds him to take his thyroid medicine, even though he has a cell phone reminder each morning. He doesn't mind when people open the door for him at the aquatic center, but he tells me that barely a week goes by without someone saying "You look really great for your age" or "You must be very proud of yourself" after his laps at the pool. Giles would probably say that people are overaccommodating because of his age. Knowing my dad, he would say people are irritating and annoying because of what they say!

Overaccommodation: Miscommunicating with a Purpose

overaccommodation
attempt to overdo efforts in regulating, modifying, or responding to others

Jane Zuengler (1991) observes that **overaccommodation** is a term attributed to the behavior of people who, although acting from good intentions, are perceived, instead, as patronizing or demeaning. Overaccommodation has the effect of making the target feel worse and is also viewed as a non-accommodation technique (Speer, Giles, & Denes, 2013) . Consider, for example, the overaccommodation taking place in Luke Merrill's interview. Luke's efforts in speaking Spanish are undermined by Roberto's perception that Luke is patronizing him. In this case, and as some researchers (Coupland, Coupland, Giles, & Henwood, 1988) believe, much overaccommodation yields poor communication. Luke is not trying to patronize Roberto Hernandez. Although the speaker apparently has the intention of showing respect, the listener perceives it as distracting and disrespectful.

Overaccommodation can be done instinctively (as we noted earlier), but much of it is strategic. Further, it can exist in three forms: sensory overaccommodation, dependency overaccommodation, and intergroup overaccommodation (Zuengler, 1991). Let's define these and present an example of each.

Sensory overaccommodation occurs when a speaker overly adapts to another who is perceived as limited in some way. There is an assumption that a person has a physical or sensory limitation/handicap, such as a hearing impairment. Limitation, in this sense, refers to either a linguistic or a physical limitation. That is, a speaker may believe that he or she is sensitive to another's language disability or physical disability, but overdoes the accommodation. For example, in her study on patients with Alzheimer's disease, Heidi Hamilton (1991) felt that she had underestimated the level of competence of an Alzheimer's patient and found herself overaccommodating. Because Hamilton believed that Alzheimer's patients typically respond better to questions about the here and now rather than about past times or places, she kept this in mind as she framed her conversations with patients.

It turned out, however, that she underestimated the mental capabilities of her interviewees. Hamilton believed that she spent much more interview time on the environment surrounding the Alzheimer's patient than was necessary. This resulted in making patients seem more incompetent than they actually were.

The second type of overaccommodation is **dependency overaccommodation**, which occurs when a speaker places the listener in a lower-status role, and the listener is made to appear dependent on the speaker. In dependency overaccommodation, the listener also believes that the speaker controls the conversation to demonstrate higher status. This can be seen by examining the treatment of a number of immigrant populations in the United States.

Many cultural groups are marginalized in the United States, and dependency overaccommodation, it appears, may be one reason for this ostracizing. For instance, during assimilation into their new communities, many refugees are made to feel subordinate when conversing with others. Although government workers may believe that during their conversations with refugees they are doing what is right (helping refugees understand various procedures and rules associated with documentation), refugees may feel quite dependent on the speaker (immigration official). Given that many newly arrived strangers do not know the English language, do not have a basic understanding of cultural values or norms, and do not have a clear sense of their job skills, their perceptions of dependency are warranted.

In addition to sensory and dependency overaccommodation, there is a third type of overaccommodation called **intergroup overaccommodation**. This involves speakers lumping listeners into a particular group, failing to treat each person as an individual. At the heart of this overaccommodation is stereotyping, and there can be far-reaching consequences to this perceptual bias—ranging from discrimination to matters of life and death (Dragojevich, Giles, & Watson, 2012). Although maintaining racial and ethnic identity is critical, individual identity is equally important.

sensory over-accommodation
overly adapting to others who are perceived as limited in their abilities (physical, linguistic, or other)

dependency over-accommodation
a behavior that occurs when speakers place listeners in a lower-status role

intergroup over-accommodation
a behavior that occurs when speakers place listeners in cultural groups without acknowledging individual uniqueness

COMMUNICATION ACCOMMODATION THEORY

Consider when a speaker uses language that assigns a listener to a particular cultural group. The speaker may feel comfortable suggesting, for instance, that Mexican Americans have never been given a chance to succeed in the United States because they have been busy raising their families. To a Mexican American, this generalization may be perceived negatively. Communicating with this perception in mind may cause some Mexican Americans to accommodate negatively.

Overaccommodation usually results in listeners perceiving that they are less than equal. There are serious implications to overaccommodation, including losing motivation for further language acquisition, avoiding conversations, and forming negative attitudes toward speakers and society (Zuengler, 1991). Since one primary goal of communication is achieving intended meaning, overaccommodation is a significant roadblock to that goal.

Integration, Critique, and Closing

Communication Accommodation Theory focuses on the role of conversations in our lives and how people's communication influences those dialogues. The cultural backgrounds and expectations of the communicators remain important sources as we try to unpack the theory. Further, over the several decades of investigation, the research has consistently followed a quantitative approach. We now turn our attention to three criteria as we evaluate this communication theory: scope, logical consistency, and heurism.

Integration

Communication Tradition	Rhetorical	Semiotic	Phenomenological	Cybernetic	**Socio-Psychological**	Socio-Cultural	Critical
Communication Context	Intrapersonal	Interpersonal	Small Group	Organizational	Public/Rhetorical	Mass/Media	**Cultural**
Approach to Knowing	**Positivistic/Empirical**	Interpretive/Hermeneutic	Critical

Critique

Evaluation Criteria	Scope	**Logical Consistency**	Parsimony	Utility	Testability	**Heurism**	Test of Time

Scope

The boundaries of the theory are rather expansive. You may recall that the theory originally examined speech; it was later expanded to include the nonverbal arena. Giles (2008) underscores the broad scope of Communication Accommodation Theory by stating that over the years, it "began to take propositional forms that became increasingly more complex and, arguably, more demanding on readers" (p. 166). Its scope, however, does not necessarily undermine the theory's integrity. The cross-disciplinary interest in the theory suggests that efforts to delimit it may not be the best course of action (Giles, 2017). The changing nature of culture in Western society suggests that a theory of this nature may need to be extensive in order to understand multiple populations, particularly those who have recently migrated to the United States.

Logical Consistency

The strengths of the theory may be quite significant because the theory has elicited little scholarly criticism. Still, a few concerns pertaining to the logical consistency of the concepts have been identified. In short, some scholars contend that a few of the central features of the theory warrant further examination. Judee Burgoon, Leesa Dillman, and Lesa Stern (1993), for example, question the convergence–divergence frame advanced by Giles. They believe that conversations are too complex to be reduced simply to these processes. They also challenge the notion that people's accommodation can be explained by just these two practices. For instance, what occurs if people both converge and diverge in conversations? Are there consequences for the speaker? The listener? Giles and his colleagues (Dragojevic et al., 2016) have responded to some of these issues. They assert that there are "complex accommodative dilemmas" (p. 5) which are often unpredictable, thus accepting the complexity of conversations that often take place between people.

One might also question whether the theory relies too heavily on a rational way of communicating. That is, although the theory acknowledges conflict between communicators, it also rests on a reasonable standard of conflict. Perhaps you have been in conflicts that are downright nasty and with people who have no sense of reason. It appears that the theory ignores this possible negative side of communication (Cupach & Spitzberg, 2011; Gilchrist-Petty & Long, 2016). Further, we know from conflict research, too, that conflicts are often handled and managed differently across cultures, prompting some questions into the notion of what to do when convergence and divergence "collide." Still, Giles (Gallois, Ogay, & Giles, 2005) does not ignore this perception and believes a great deal of work is still to be done before the process of accommodation can be fully understood.

Student Voices

Michael

I work in a nursing home that specializes in Alzheimer's disease. We have more than a hundred residents with the disease, all of whom are at various stages of the disease. I have heard the "baby talk" from staff to residents before, and I've heard it a lot. We're trained and told not to talk this way and to treat every resident with dignity—that includes talking like an adult. But, I've seen my coworkers talk down to the residents, and the residents, in turn, talk that way. It's pathetic. If anything, I wish the staff would accommodate with speech that is less demeaning and more considerate.

Heurism

Without doubt, Giles and his colleagues have conceptualized a theory rich in heuristic value. The theory has been incorporated in a number of different studies. For instance, accommodation has been studied with populations that until this theory, were rarely researched, including law enforcement (Giles, Linz, Bonilla, & Gomez, 2012), patient–providers (Farzadnia & Giles, 2014), native and nonnative speakers (Rogerson-Revell, 2010), immigrant women (Marlow & Giles, 2013), gay men (Hajek, 2016), and the elderly (Harwood, 2002; Hehl & McDonald, 2012). It addition, it has been studied with advertising (Moon & Nelson, 2008), in conjunction with Twitter (Tamburrini, Cinnirella, Jansen, & Bryden, 2015), in business meetings (Robinson-Nevell, 2010), in families (Guntzviller, 2015) and even with messages left on telephone answering machines (Buzzanell, Burrell, Stafford, & Berkowitz, 1996). There is no doubt that the theory is heuristic and has lasting scholarly value in the communication field.

Closing

In his earlier writings on the theory, Giles challenged researchers to apply Communication Accommodation Theory across the life span and in different cultural settings. For the most part, his suggestions have been heeded. His research has broadened our understanding of why conversations are so complex, especially with individuals from different cultural backgrounds. Through convergence, Giles sheds light on why people adapt to others in their interactions. Through divergence, we can understand why people choose to ignore adapting strategies. He has championed a theory that has helped us better understand the culture around us and the influences of accommodation on the diverse relationships within society.

Discussion Starters

TECH QUEST: Two key issues of Communication Accommodation Theory are convergence and divergence. How might these two principles be applied to email conversations between a supervisor and an employee?

1. Rewrite the opening example of Luke Merrill and Roberto Hernandez. This time, place the two individuals in the context of teacher and student.

2. Explain how convergence might function in the following relationships: police officer–driver, therapist–client, and supervisor–subordinate. In your response, choose a conversational topic that might be unique to the relationship and integrate convergence accordingly.

3. We have noted that overaccommodation results in miscommunication. Some research in Communication Accommodation Theory has also examined underaccommodation, or the process of not adapting sufficiently to another communicator. What do you believe are some examples of underaccommodation?

4. Giles contends that self-perception can influence the accommodation process. How does a person's self-perception affect accommodation? Provide examples to illustrate your thoughts.

5. CAT has been framed in the intercultural communication context. Based on your understanding of the theory, under what additional context(s) can the theory be understood?

6. How might divergence be explained using social identity? Explain using examples from your life.

7. Discuss a situation in which accommodation might backfire on an individual.

CHAPTER 29

Muted Group Theory

*Based on the research of **Cheris Kramarae***

What if we think of ourselves as collectively having those thousand arms to work together, aided by a feminist history of connecting to ask and answer questions that are of concern to many?

—Cheris Kramarae

Patricia Fitzpatrick

Patricia Fitzpatrick sat in the back row in her political science classroom; she closed her eyes, letting the professor's words wash over her. She was wondering what in the world had possessed her to go back to college at the age of 40. It seemed like a good idea when she first thought about finishing the BA she had begun over 20 years ago, but now she thought she must have been out of her mind to try this. She felt like she didn't understand a word her professors said, and she was having an extremely difficult time keeping up with all her assignments. Most of the other students were much younger than she and seemed to have a lot more disposable income, too. She really hadn't spoken to many of them beyond a quick hello. All in all, this college idea was turning into a big hassle.

It wasn't supposed to be this way. Initially, Patricia thought finishing her degree would improve her self-esteem. She also hoped it would get her out of the dead-end job she currently had with Hudson's Department Store. She worked nights as a shipping clerk for the store, sending out orders for their mail-order business. She has worked for Hudson's for the past seven years, and it does not seem as if she will advance there. It is a pretty boring job with low pay, and Patricia was hopeful that a degree might give her more opportunities. As a single mom with three kids, she really needs a better job.

But Patricia is starting to despair about her prospects. One of the most disturbing things so far has been how tongue tied she feels in class. She has so much trouble articulating what she wants to say about the material that she ends up not saying anything in most of her classes. Patricia worries that this will count against her, especially in her smaller classes, where the professors really seem to encourage class participation. She had expected that she would have a lot to say as she learned new things, but she is finding it difficult to express her opinions. So, instead of increasing her self-esteem, college is making her feel worse about herself.

This isn't the first time that Patricia has felt inarticulate. She admits to herself that she has had a hard time speaking up long before she returned to college. At work, she is the only woman on her shift, and the men don't seem to pay attention to her when she speaks. Once she had tried to compare an experience at work to teaching her son to read, and her coworkers had looked at her like she was nuts. Then they all started laughing and calling her

"Mom." Another time she had been the chair of a committee at her daughter's school. The committee was supposed to research ways the school could raise money for more computer equipment. Patricia had to get up in front of representatives from the parents' group, teachers, and administrators and report on the committee's findings. Although the report had been okay, Patricia thought she had paused too much while she spoke. Even though she had spent a great deal of time preparing for the speech, she had still found herself occasionally groping for words.

She hoped that college would help her become more articulate. It would be wonderful to be able to speak up and say what is on her mind. Patricia isn't ready to give up, but things certainly aren't going as planned.

Some researchers analyzing Patricia's situation might be tempted to examine her individual traits, noting that she might have problems with shyness or a fear of communicating. However, the theory that we discuss in this chapter offers a different approach to explaining Patricia's situation. Muted Group Theory (MGT) asserts that, as a female, as a single mom, and as a person of low income, Patricia is a member of several groups whose power base does not allow her to express her voice, or even to always hear her own voice in her head. The groups to which Patricia belongs have experiences that are not well expressed in their language system—a language system that was devised primarily by well-to-do men to represent their own experiences. According to MGT, Patricia and others are muted because their native language often does not provide a good fit with their life experiences.

MGT focuses on the power to name experiences and explains that women trying to use man-made language to describe their experiences is somewhat like native English speakers learning to converse in Spanish. To do so, they have to go through an internal translation process, scanning the foreign vocabulary for the best word to express themselves. This process makes them hesitant and often inarticulate as they are unable to use the language fluently for their purposes. In the process, muted groups metaphorically lose their voice (Wood, 2017). As Cheris Kramarae (1981), the researcher who adapted MGT for the field of communication, observes:

> The language of a particular culture does not serve all its speakers equally, for not all speakers contribute in an equal fashion to its formulation. Women (and members of other subordinate groups) are not as free or as able as men are to say what they wish, when and where they wish, because the words and the norms for their use have been formulated by the dominant group, men. (p. 1)

Yet, it isn't the case that all women are silenced and all men have voice. MGT allows us to understand any group that is silenced by the inadequacies of their language. For instance, Kami Kosenko (2010) notes that MGT offers a heuristic explanation for how the transgender individuals in her study were "rendered mute by a biomedical discourse that fails to represent the transgender body or sexual experience" (p. 140). Furthermore, muting may take place as a result of the unpopularity of the views that a person is trying to express. Muted Group theorists criticize dominant groups and argue that hegemonic ideas often silence other ideas. Anita Taylor and M. J. Hardman (2000) comment that some feminist groups can become dominant within the feminist movement and then mute the voices of other women who question

Language serves its creators (and those who belong to the same groups as its creators) better than those in other groups who have to learn to use the language as best they can. This is the case because the experiences of the creators are named clearly in language, whereas the experiences of other groups are not. Due to their problems adapting to a language they did not create, people from other groups appear less articulate than those from groups like the creators. Sometimes these muted groups create their own language to compensate for their problems with the dominant group's language.

their ideology. Taylor and Hardman advance the example of Matilde Joslyn Gage, a nineteenth-century feminist, who argued views that made her unpopular with the other feminists of the day such as Elizabeth Cady Stanton. As a result of advancing ideas that were considered too radical, "she became a persona non grata among the women of the movement" (pp. 2–3) who had more power; consequently, Gage's voice was muted and lost to future generations.

As you can probably guess from our discussion thus far, MGT points out problems with the status quo and suggests ways to remediate these problems. Later in this chapter, we describe some of the action steps advocated by Muted Group proponents. Further, MGT is a theory that examines power issues (Nangabo, 2015). As Cheris Kramarae (2005) observes, "people attached or assigned to subordinate groups may have a lot to say, but they tend to have relatively little power to say it" (p. 55). Or if they do venture to speak, those in a greater power position may ignore, ridicule, or disrespect their contribution in a variety of ways. As Cheris Kramarae (2009) notes, muted groups "get in trouble" when they speak out in their own voices.

Origins of Muted Group Theory

Muted Group Theory originated with the work of Edwin and Shirley Ardener, social anthropologists who were concerned with social structure and hierarchy. In 1975, Edwin Ardener noted that groups making up the top end of the social hierarchy determine the communication system for the culture. Lower-power groups in the society, such as women, the poor, and people of color, have to learn to work within the communication system that the dominant group has established. Turning this generalization to the specific case of women in a culture, Edwin Ardener observes that social anthropologists studied women's experiences by talking almost exclusively to men. Thus, not only do women have to contend with the difficulties of a language that does not completely give voice to their thoughts, but their experiences are represented through a male perspective (Ardener, 2005).

In 1975, Edwin Ardener commented on why researchers (who at the time were mainly men) tended to speak and listen to men in the cultures they studied.

Ardener believes that these scholars "have a bias towards the kinds of model that men are ready to provide (or to concur in) rather than towards any that women might provide. If the men appear 'articulate' compared with the women, it is a case of like speaking like" (p. 2). Further, Shirley Ardener (1978) observes that women's mutedness is the counterpart to men's deafness. She explains that women (or members of any subordinate group) do speak, but their words fall on deaf ears, and when this happens over time, they tend to stop trying to articulate their thoughts, and they may even stop thinking them. In Ardener's view, "Words which continually fall upon deaf ears may, of course, in the end become unspoken, or even unthought" (p. 20).

The Ardeners might argue that Patricia Fitzpatrick is twice muted: once by the failure of her language to act as an accurate tool for her use and once by anyone who labels her negatively rather than acknowledging she is poorly served by her language. For Edwin Ardener, muted groups are rendered inarticulate by the dominant group's language system, which grows directly out of their worldview and experience. For the muted group, what they say first has to shift out of their own worldview and be compared to the experiences of the dominant group. Thus, articulations for the muted group are indirect and broken (Figure 29.1).

In 1981, Kramarae published an influential book called *Women and Men Speaking: Frameworks for Analysis*. In this book, Kramarae profiles several theories that come from other disciplines like MGT and suggests how these theoretical frameworks can help explain questions of communication. In her discussion of MGT, Kramarae states that her aims are somewhat more limited than those of the Ardeners, who were concerned with applying Muted Group Theory across many cultures. Kramarae's interest is in the "questions the theory raises and [the] explanations it . . . provide[s] for the communication patterns among and between women and men in Great Britain and the United States" (1981, p. 4). Kramarae asserts that MGT's assertions are especially true for the English language because English was developed and formalized by male clerics and academics. Because women were not instrumental in formalizing the English language and were in a lower power position in the culture that created it, Kramarae asserts that women would be a muted group.

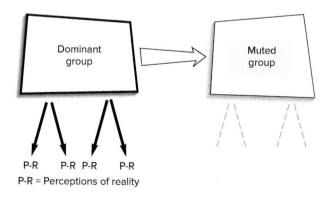

Figure 29.1
Muted Group Theory
Source: Adapted from Ardener, 1975.

P-R = Perceptions of reality

Kramarae's work on Muted Group Theory led to insights about how the English language affects women's communication behaviors. Speaking about MGT, Anita Taylor and M. J. Hardman (2000) observe that:

> English does not name concepts important to women, but to men (e.g., one can have a "seminal" idea; but was one ever described as "ovular"?). English also devalues concepts important to women, but not to men (again, the "seminal" idea is an example; if one nurtured or incubated an idea it would have quite a different feeling, as would ovulating it). English uses male referents and terms (e.g., the "generic" he and the conclusion that number is more important than gender for the third-person indefinite pronoun). (p. 8)

In a similar vein, Dennis Nangabo (2015) states more succinctly notes that it is quite challenging to communicate in a language that the majority or dominant group has created for those who are in the minority.

Makeup of Muted Groups

Much of the theorizing and application of Muted Group Theory has focused on women as a muted group. Yet, as researchers such as Mark Orbe (1998, 2005), Michael Hechter (2004), and Liliana Heradova (2009) note, the theory can be validly applied to any nondominant group. Orbe suggests that in the United States and several other cultures, society privileges specific characteristics and perspectives: male, European American, heterosexual, able-bodied, youthful, middle and upper class, and Christian. People with these characteristics form the dominant group or the group that holds the power in the culture. Other groups that coexist with the **dominant group** are generally subordinate to it in that they do not have access to as much power as do members of the dominant group. Thus, non-European groups like African Americans or Asian Americans, gays and lesbians, the elderly, the lower class, disabled people, and non-Christians, all can be members of muted groups, in the same way that women are. Orbe (1998, 2012) developed Co-Cultural Theory, based on Muted Group Theory, to capture these ideas.

dominant group
the group that holds the power in a given culture

Some researchers have suggested that men might be part of a muted group as well. Radhika Chopra (2001) examines the issue of muting for nurturing fathers. Chopra argues that the discourse of mothering represented by some feminists reduced the father to a "depersonalized cipher" whose presence is "posited as an absence, in contrast with the hands-on vital involvement of the mother" (p. 447). Chopra notes that this discourse not only silences the father but also fails to account for fathering in other societies or periods of history where the distant, silent father did not exist. Chopra points to fathers in the early American colonial period who were very involved in teaching their children both reading and writing skills as well as moral and religious lessons.

Although some Muted Group theorists might disagree that fathers (or any men) are ever in a low-power position, Chopra concludes that giving voice to "father-care" is a critical process that will remove the category of caregiving from female ownership and in so doing transform the concept of gender identity completely. Yet, because most of the research in the area of Muted Group Theory has focused on men as the dominant group and women as the muted group, we pay most attention to that relationship in this chapter.

Differentiating Between Sex and Gender

In training our focus on men and women, we need to clarify two terms: sex and gender. Generally, researchers use the term **sex** to mean biological categories, male and female, determined by the presence of XX chromosomes for females and XY chromosomes for males. In contrast, **gender** is defined as the learned behaviors that constitute femininity and masculinity in a given culture. Thus, gender is changeable and reflects whatever the culture accepts at a given time for these roles. Currently, it is within the definition of masculinity to have pierced ears, and it is within the definition of femininity to have tattoos. At an earlier time, these attributes would not have been deemed appropriate. However, it is also the case that the terms *sex* and *gender* are often blurred because women are socialized to be feminine and men are encouraged to be masculine. Therefore, we will use the terms interchangeably in this chapter.

sex
biological category divided into male and female

gender
social category consisting of the learned behaviors that constitute masculinity and femininity for a given culture

Assumptions of Muted Group Theory

Cheris Kramarae (1981) isolated three assumptions she believes are central to Muted Group Theory. We review each of her tenets in turn:

- Women perceive the world differently than men because of women's and men's different experiences and activities rooted in the division of labor.
- Because of their political dominance, men's system of perception is dominant, impeding the free expression of women's alternative models of the world.
- In order to participate in society, women must transform their own models in terms of the received male system of expression. (p. 3)

This first assumption begins with the premise that the world is a different place for women and men and that their experiences differ. Furthermore, the assumption posits an explanation for these differences. The explanation lies in the division of labor that allocates work on the basis of sex, such that women are responsible for tasks in the home and men are responsible for work outside the home. The division of labor began in Western countries in the eighteenth and nineteenth centuries as a result of social transformations, in large part related to the Industrial Revolution (Coontz, 1988). The Industrial Revolution took work out of the home and made it a paid activity. Prior to that, work had been intertwined with home life because all members of the family contributed to the family's survival, usually on subsistence farms. No one was literally paid for their specific labor; the money the family realized came from selling their produce or livestock, the result of collective work by the entire family.

The separation of the workplace from the home led to a recognition of the two as separate spheres; the conceptualization of public and private came about, and the family was classed as private life (Butler & Modaff, 2015). The result of this division was to cast women's role in the home, or private life, and men's role in the workplace, or public life. This had the effect of clearly delineating women's tasks in the home and sharply dividing what women's responsibilities were in contrast to men's. Stephanie Coontz (1988) notes that this trend occurred in all classes and ethnic groups in the United States except African Americans.

You can see the logic of blaming the division of labor for men's and women's differing worldviews. When people's occupations differ greatly, they tend to see the world in different ways. If your day is spent caring for children and the home, your experiences will vary a great deal from those of someone whose day is spent selling merchandise to others. Sandra Bem (1993) argues that this division also created what she labels a **gender polarization lens** that causes people to see women and men as very different from each other. In 1909, Clara E. Hasse, a student at Milwaukee Downer Women's College, wrote a senior essay that illustrates the lens of gender polarization. She wrote about the topic of single-sex schooling, saying, "It were far better not to class girls with boys while receiving their education, the most important reason being that they are so entirely different and therefore should be taught diversely" (p. 10). When people believe that women and men are radically different from each other, we might expect that they get treated differently. Different treatment certainly results in different experiences.

gender polarization lens
viewing men and women as polar opposites

As we have written elsewhere with Judy Pearson (Pearson, West, & Turner, 1995), "From birth it is clear that male and female babies are treated differently. . . . Male [infants] are more likely than female infants to be described as 'strong,' 'solid,' or 'independent.' Female infants, on the other hand, are often described as 'loving,' 'cute,' and 'sweet'" (p. 49). Males and females are treated differently and expected to do different activities. Even when women work outside the home, they are often still expected to take primary responsibility for the home and care for children or elderly parents as the need arises (Wood, 2017). Arlie Hochschild's research (Blair-Loy, Hochschild, Pugh, Williams, & Hartman, 2015; Hochschild, 1989) talks about the phenomenon of the **second shift,** where working mothers put in eight hours at their paid job and then come home to do a second shift there.

second shift
the phenomenon of working women putting in eight hours on the job and another day's work at home

Sometimes the differing experiences of men and women are subtle. One study (Turner, 1992) asked respondents to describe situations that they believe are uniquely experienced by their own sex and for which, currently, no word exists and then to give those experiences a name. This was patterned after an activity Judy Pearson (1985) calls creating "genlets" or "sexlets." The results were not completely supportive of Muted Group Theory because men generated essentially the same number of "genlets" as women, indicating that language fails men as well as women.

However, the types of words created did differ between men and women. Men coined words concerned with drinking and competition, whereas women created words focusing on relationships and personal issues such as appearance. Women also noted experiences where they felt fearful or uncertain, and this concern was not included in the men's words. For instance, women coined the word *herdastudaphobia*, which meant feeling fear when passing a group of strange men on the street, and they created the word *piglabelphobia*, to designate a woman's tendency to limit what she eats in front of a date for fear of being labeled a pig. Men created words such as *scarfaholic*, an eating contest among men and *gearheaditis*, an obsession with fixing up one's car to make it the best on the road. Interestingly, when men focused on issues of eating and bodybuilding, their concern was competitive. When women addressed these same issues, their concern was for their own insecurities and their desire to please others. Thus, the first assumption of MGT, that men and women have different experiences, was supported by these results.

The second assumption of Muted Group Theory goes beyond simply noting that women and men have different experiences. This assumption states that men are the dominant group, and their experiences are given preference over women's. Specifically, men are in charge of naming and labeling social life, and women's experiences are often unnamed as a result. Women then have difficulties talking about their experiences. For example, Kramarae (1981) tells the following story about a woman who attended a workshop on the topic of women as a muted group and spoke about a common problem she experienced with her husband:

> She and her husband, both working full-time outside the home, usually arrive home at about the same time. She would like him to share the dinner-making responsibilities, but the job always falls upon her. Occasionally, he says, "I would be glad to make dinner. But you do it so much better than I." She was pleased to receive this compliment, but as she found herself in the kitchen each time she realized that he was using a verbal strategy for which she had no word and thus had more difficulty identifying and bringing [it] to his awareness. She told the people at the seminar, "I had to tell you the whole story to explain to you how he was using flattery to keep me in my female place." She said she needed a word to define the strategy, or a word to define the person who uses the strategy, a word which would be commonly understood by both women and men. (p. 7)

In this example, the woman had difficulty naming her experience although she knew something was occurring that she wished to talk about. In a similar fashion, Patricia Fitzpatrick from our chapter-opening vignette is experiencing problems speaking out in class, talking to the other students, speaking to her coworkers, and generally articulating her ideas. She is uncomfortable about her difficulties, and she is blaming herself because things are not working out as she planned. Muted Group Theory takes a different perspective, however, noting that these problems are not the result of women's inadequacies, but rather are caused by the unresponsiveness of the language women have to express themselves. MGT argues that any speaker would be inarticulate if there were no words in their language to describe their thoughts.

Muted Group Theory asserts that men's political dominance allows their perceptions to be dominant. This forces alternative perceptions—those that women hold as a result of their different experiences—into a subordinate position. Women's communication is constrained because of this subordinate position. Ann Burnett and her colleagues (2009) used MGT and Co-cultural Theory to investigate men's dominance on college campuses. They found that the way rape was talked about on campus tended to mute female students, potentially contributing to the creation and perpetuation of a campus rape culture.

Cindy Reuther and Gail Fairhurst (2000) discuss the "glass ceiling" for women in organizational hierarchies and comment on how (White) men's experiences dominate the world of work. They observe that patriarchal values tend to reproduce themselves in organizations to men's advantage. They note:

> The practices leading to the replication of white males in senior levels are based in ideology. In often subtle and unconscious ways (e.g., in language, dress, and work rituals), white women and men and women of color are

pressured to commit to patriarchal and white interests and value systems. The upshot is that replication promotes conformity rather than a pluralistic system in which individuals can interact and work according to personal principles. (p. 242)

T*I*P

Theory-Into-Practice

Theoretical Claim: Men have created and controlled language that has rendered them as superior and women as subordinate.

Practical Implication: It didn't take long for Alicia to see the "man's world" in tech. During breaks with her coworkers, she heard the guys telling her to "man up." Even some of the "everyday" terms like "hard drive" or "joy stick" or "RAM" Alicia found very offensive and yet, she was rather disempowered because she was a new employee in a male-dominant company. It wasn't long, though, before a female VP was hired and one of her first directives was related to throwing out any perceived or real sexist language in policies and procedures as well as establishing a statement discouraging and prohibiting its usage.

Source: Bassett, L. (2012, August 20). *Huffington Post online,* huffingtonpost.com/2012/08/20 /todd-akin-missouri_n_1811232.html.

Overall, then, MGT assumes that men's, especially White men's, experiences are dominant and women and people of color need to subordinate their own experiences to the extent that they can in order to partake in social and organizational success.

The final assumption of Muted Group Theory speaks to the process of translation that women must go through in order to participate in social life. Women's task is to conceptualize a thought and then scan the vocabulary, which is really better suited to men's thinking, for the best words for encoding that thought. You can see how this renders women less fluent speakers than men. Tillie Olsen (1978), the author of *Silences*, says that although men are supposed to tell it straight, women have to "tell it slant" (p. 23).

The pauses that worry Patricia Fitzpatrick in our chapter-opening scenario are attributable, according to MGT, to this cumbersome process of translation that women have to engage in when speaking. Some researchers (e.g., Hayden, 1994) suggest that women's groups engage in a great deal of overlaps and simultaneous speaking because they are helping one another cope with a language system that is not well suited to their tasks. Thus, when women speak with one another, they collaborate on storytelling—not so much because women are collaborative by nature, but rather because they need to help one another find the right words to encode their thoughts.

Some of the problems inherent in the translation process are highlighted by examining instances when women's words for experiences do become part of the general vocabulary. Before the 1970s, the term *sexual harassment* did not exist but it, nonetheless, existed. Monica Hesse (2016), for example, writes in the Washington Post that it was common in the nineteenth century. She writes: "The issue had been addressed in the 19th century, when an 1887 report on 'women wage-workers' declared that household service 'has become synonymous with the worst degradation that comes to a woman,' because male employers so commonly assaulted their maids" (https://www.washingtonpost.com/lifestyle/style/anita-hills-testimony -compelled-america-to-look-closely-at-sexual-harassment/2016/04/13/36999612 -ea2e-11e5-bc08-3e03a5b41910_story.html). Ultimately, in the 1970s, activists at Cornell University coined the term (http://now.org/blog/a-brief-history-of-sexual -harassment-in-the-united-states/). Women who experienced what we now call sexual harassment had nothing to use for labeling their experiences. As Gloria Steinem has said, before the term was accepted into the vocabulary, women simply accepted harassment as part of life. For instance, Angie had a job in a library years ago, and her boss was a man who liked to comment on her figure and compare it to his wife's. At the time, Angie could only say that she had a bad job with a horrible boss. Without a label, the experience seems individual and the inappropriateness of that behavior is minimized. Labeling it sexual harassment places it in a category, suggests some coping strategies, and points to its seriousness. Furthermore, giving the experience a term, *sexual harassment,* allows us to see that it exists broadly and is supported at many levels of society. Social change is possible when we recognize the phenomenon with a label. Similarly, the terms *domestic violence, date rape, marital rape,* and *stalking* all name crimes that without the labels might simply be seen as individual problems and not recognized as serious offenses. Without these words, women faced silence when they wanted to talk about their experiences, and they were at a loss for instituting social change.

Marsha Houston and Cheris Kramarae (1991) point out that women participate in silencing as well, which is illustrated by examining some talk between African American and European American women. Houston and Kramarae observe that silencing occurs not only through preventing talk, but also by shaping and controlling the talk of others. When White women criticize African American women's talk as "confrontational," "the message to black women is, 'Talk like me, or I won't listen'" (p. 389). If subordinate group members hear this message and try to conform to it, their talk is slowed and disempowered. When Patricia Fitzpatrick, from our opening story, thinks about how her contributions sound and attempts to speak like the other students, she is hampered in her fluency.

The Process of Silencing

The central premise of Muted Group Theory is that members of marginalized groups are silenced and rendered inarticulate as speakers. This silencing does not rely on explicit enforcement or coercion. As Robin Sheriff (2000) observes, silencing of muted groups is a socially shared phenomenon. According to Sheriff, "unlike the activity of speech, which does not require more than a single actor, silence demands collaboration and the tacit communal understandings that such collaboration presupposes. Although it is contractual in nature, a critical feature of this type of silence is that it is both a consequence and an index of an unequal distribution of power" (p. 114). Thus, silence is accomplished through a social understanding of who holds the power and who does not (Gendrin, 2000). In this section we will briefly review a few of the methods used to accomplish this power distribution and resulting silencing. These methods include: ridicule, ritual, control, and harassment. This is not an exhaustive list of methods of silencing. Perhaps you can think of other ways you have experienced or observed.

Ridicule

Houston and Kramarae (1991) point out that women's speech is trivialized. "Men label women's talk chattering, gossiping, nagging, whining, bitching (Cut the cackle!)" (p. 390). Men often say that women talk about meaningless things and claim that they cannot understand how women spend so much time talking to their girlfriends. Women themselves often refer to their own talk as gabbing or gossiping. Women are also told that they have no sense of humor, and this is an opportunity for ridicule. Also, women's concerns are often trivialized by men as not being important enough to listen to, yet women are expected to be supportive listeners for men. Even in the medical context, women report that their doctors may ridicule or trivialize their concerns (Brann & Mattson, 2004).

Ritual

Some people have pointed out that many social rituals have the effect of silencing women or advocating that women are subordinate to men. One such ritual is the wedding ceremony. There are a number of aspects in a traditional ceremony that silence the bride. First, the groom stands at the front while the bride is "delivered" to him on the arm of her father. The father then "gives her away" to the groom. Furthermore, the groom stands at the right hand of the minister (or whoever officiates), and this is traditionally a place of higher status than the bride's position, to the left. The groom says the vows first. The bride wears a veil and a white gown to indicate that she has been "preserved" for the groom. The groom is told at the end that he may kiss the bride. The couple is pronounced "man" and "wife," and traditionally, the bride changes her name to the groom's. In many services, the couple is introduced immediately after the vows as Mr. and Mrs. John Smith. In her (1981) book, Kramarae talks about the process she went through concerning her name changes. When she married, her husband's name was Kramer and her name upon marriage became Cheris Rae Kramer. At the time of her marriage, it was not legal for a wife to keep her own name. Later the laws changed, and Kramarae combined her husband's last name with her middle name and created her own name. This change was accomplished with a great deal of discussion and controversy, and many people questioned her judgment. Kramarae points out that no one questioned her husband throughout the entire process, and his name remained unchanged. Although many couples work to individualize the ceremony and have changed some of these aspects, the traditional ritual implies subordination of the bride.

Control

Researchers have noted that men control many decisions, such as what goes into history books, leaving women's history untapped (Wood, 2017). In addition, the media are controlled by men; women's talk and contributions get less coverage in mainstream media. Furthermore, many communication practices place men as central and women as eclipsed. For instance, men talk more than women in mixed-sex interactions despite conventional wisdom to the contrary. In an analysis of 66 previous studies examining U.S. men's and women's talk in a variety of contexts, men's talk time exceeded women's in 61 of the cases (James & Drackich, 1993).

A communication behavior that keeps men in control is interruptions. When men interrupt women, the women often switch to talk about whatever topic the men raise. When women interrupt men, this is usually not the case. Men frequently go back to what they originally were talking about (DeFrancisco, 1991). In addition, Victoria DeFrancisco has concluded that men often fail to attend to their partners' talk; they refuse to consider what the women are speaking about and shift the conversation to a topic of their preference.

Harassment

Holly Kearl (2015) writes about street harassment, noting that women do not have free access to public streets. Men dominate public spaces in that women walking there may receive verbal threats (sometimes couched as compliments). Sexual harassment in the workplace is another method of telling women that they do not belong out of the domestic sphere. Mary Strine (1992) shows how some talk in universities naturalizes harassment, making it seem like an acceptable practice. When women who have experienced sexual harassment are labeled as hysterical, overly sensitive, or troublemakers, their concerns are generally dismissed and defined as unimportant.

Student Voices

Ethan

When I started reading about Muted Group Theory, it really seemed wrong to me. I mean there are a lot of times I am not sure exactly how to put my thoughts into words and I'm a white, heterosexual guy, so I don't qualify for any of the muted groups that the book talks about. But, when I read that sexual harassment didn't have a name for a long time, it did make me think that maybe the theory had a point. I guess it would be pretty hard to talk about something if there were literally no words to describe it. And I can see how you'd think it was something that just happened to you and not some big thing that was going on with a lot of people if there were no words for it.

Strategies of Resistance

As we mentioned at the beginning of this chapter, Muted Group Theory is a critical theory; as such, it goes beyond explaining a phenomenon—such as women's muting—to advocating change in the status quo. Houston and Kramarae (1991) offer several strategies for this purpose. One strategy of resistance consists of *naming the strategies of silencing* we have just reviewed. Through this process, the silencing is made accessible and a topic for discussion. A second approach advocated by Houston and Kramarae is to *reclaim, elevate, and celebrate women's discourse.* Houston and Kramarae mention that women are beginning to celebrate and study oral histories, diaries and journals, and the so-called alternative means of expression like sewing, weaving, and other handwork that is often done by women. Through examining these forums for expression, women are recognizing the "effectiveness, impact, and eloquence of women's communicative experiences as well as men's" (Foss & Foss, 1991, p. 21). Other researchers (Hoover, Hastings, & Musambira, 2009) have examined communication venues where women's voices are celebrated and their particular outlook is valorized, such as websites for the bereaved. While still others have investigated how women's music might provide a way to give women voice literally and figuratively (Huber, 2010; Moody, 2011).

Women also are creating a *new and more representative language* to capture their experiences. Although changing the language is an ambitious task, language is malleable, and as new concepts enter our culture, new words are created to describe them. Although much of our computer jargon has rather sexist roots (e.g., joystick, floppy, hard drive, etc.), there are newer tech words that are gender neutral (e.g., firewall, screenshot, etc.). Think of all the words we now have to talk about computers and computer-mediated communication (itself a new term!). Suzette Elgin (1988) invented a whole language, which she calls Laadan, focusing on women's experiences. Kramarae and Paula Treichler (1992) compiled a feminist dictionary to give woman-centered definitions to words of importance in women's experiences.

In addition to Houston and Kramarae's (1991) suggestions, Ezster Hargittai and Aaron Shaw (2015) note that new media offer opportunities to give voice to previously muted groups. Yet, they caution that even communication conducted via the Internet does not take place in a vacuum, and when using new media people have to be mindful of structural inequities that can keep some groups muted even online. They note that there are "profound gender inequalities" (p. 424) that exist which must be reduced and ultimately eliminated.

Through a variety of resistance strategies including naming strategies of silencing, reclaiming, elevating, and celebrating women's discourse, creating new words for uniquely gendered experiences, and using new media, muting can be resisted. In short, there are many approaches to changing the situation that MGT delineates and explains.

Integration, Critique, and Closing

Muted Group Theory has many adherents, but as you would expect with such a politically charged theory, it also prompted some concerns by others. The theory, as you likely know by now, is immersed in qualitative thinking, honoring voices and life experiences. Let's consider the criteria of utility and test of time in particular as we evaluate MGT.

Integration

Communication Tradition	Rhetorical	**Semiotic**	Phenomenological	Cybernetic	Socio-Psychological	Socio-Cultural	**Critical**
Communication Context	Intrapersonal	Interpersonal	Small Group	Organizational	Public/Rhetorical	Mass/Media	**Cultural**
Approach(es) to Knowing	Positivistic/Empirical	Interpretive/Hermeneutic	**Critical**

Critique

| Evaluation Criteria | Scope | Logical Consistency | Parsimony | **Utility** | Testability | Heurism | **Test of Time** |

Utility

First, Muted Group Theory has sometimes been criticized for not being useful because it engages in essentialism, or the belief that all men are essentially the same and all women are essentially the same and the two differ from each other. These critics note that there is great difference within groups; sometimes the difference within a group (such as women) can be greater than the difference between groups (women and men). Some theorists note other influences on communication besides gender, including socioeconomic status, age, ethnicity, or upbringing. Others disavow the notion of influences altogether, claiming that both individuals and groups are constantly changing through communication. Therefore, any attempt to state unequivocally what women or men are like falsely "freezes" those groups in time, as if they have a natural, unchangeable essence. (Ivy, 2012)

Student Voices
Vanessa

When we talked about this theory in class, all the guys in the room were quiet. It was interesting that the girls talked about when they were silenced or muted at their jobs, in class, or other places. But, not one guy said that they had been silenced. Also, I think it was sad that no guy "stood up" for the girls by saying that they were sad about it or that they would do something about it. I'm trying not to be radical here, but I wanted to just grab the guy next to me and say: You don't get it, do you?!

MUTED GROUP THEORY

Supporters of MGT agree there are many groups besides women that are muted in U.S. society. However, being female is to be part of a central group in our culture, and thus, even though MGT acknowledges that women are not all alike and there is no essential womanness that all women possess, women in the United States are often treated alike. This treatment forms a common set of experiences that allows MGT to make generalizations about men and women.

Furthermore, some critics fault the usefulness of MGT because they note that women do speak out in public forums, and they point to women such as Hillary Rodham Clinton and Sheryl Sandberg as examples of women who are not muted at all. Muted Group theorists would agree that some women have gained a public forum, but they would also point out that they may have done so by becoming extremely adept at translation. Women who bring a uniquely female perspective to the table have not fared as well, according to these theorists. Proponents of MGT argue that until we are able to hear from a wide diversity of voices rather than forcing all who wish to speak out to conform to a narrow range of options de fined by the dominant group, we will still need the critical commentary of Muted Group Theory.

Test of Time

Some critics of MGT assert that the theory has not been utilized much in communication research and occasionally when it has been employed, its tenets have not been supported. Elspeth Tilley (2010), for instance, found that men were not more likely than women to speak out in public when confronted with an employee who had breached ethical standards. Related to this notion is the fact that the theory was derived many decades ago, and the theory's assumptions have not been updated. However, Heather Kissack (2010) tested some of MGT's assumptions and found that they still hold true in the context of organizational emails. Further, with contemporary topics such as athlete's concussions (Sanderson, Weathers, Snedaker, & Gramlich, 2016) and cervical cancer (Kutto & Mulwo, 2015), it is difficult to argue against the theory's contemporariness and longevity.

Closing

Certainly Muted Group Theory is provocative and causes us to think about biases in language. It also shines a light on what we accept and what we reject from speakers. MGT also explains some problems women experience in speaking out in many settings. It is up to us to decide if these issues form a systematic bias against subordinate groups and in favor of the dominant group, as Muted Group Theory asserts.

Discussion Starters

TECH QUEST: Muted Group Theory focuses on the man-made language that is used in society and its consequences, primarily as words relate to women. Identify how cyberbullying relates to the principles of the theory and your impression of how men and women might react similarly and differently to this digital behavior.

1. Do you think Muted Group Theory provides a good explanation for the difficulties faced by Patricia Fitzpatrick from our chapter opening story? Why or why not? What other explanations might you offer to understand her situation?

2. Have you had the experience of fumbling for words to describe something that you were feeling or something that happened to you? Do you think Muted Group Theory explains that experience for you? Why or why not?

3. Can you coin terms for experiences that women have and men do not? What about the reverse? Do you agree with MGT that the English language fits the male experience of the world better than the female experience? Explain your answer.

4. We mentioned that one criticism of MGT is that it overstates the problem that women have with language. Do you agree or disagree with this criticism?

5. Have any of the reforms that are suggested by MGT taken hold in our language? Give examples of changes in the language that have made it more responsive to women's experiences.

6. What other social groups might be muted in the United States? Does MGT provide a good explanation for groups, other than women, who are silenced? Why or why not?

7. If MGT is a critical theory, what actions has it stimulated? How has it advocated for change?

CHAPTER **30**

Feminist Standpoint Theory

*Based on the research of **Nancy C. M. Hartsock** and **Julia T. Wood***

I never set out to be a feminist theorist.
—Nancy Hartsock

Angela Coburn and Latria Harris

Angela Coburn banged her books together and left class with a frown. Usually she enjoys her linguistics class and she likes Professor Townsend. But today she is upset and offended. Professor Townsend had explained the concepts of denotation and connotation by discussing a case that was in the news about 10 years ago. The case concerned a European American aide to the mayor of Washington, DC, who had lost his job for using the word *niggardly* to mean "sparingly" in a meeting with two others, one European American and one African American. Angela gasped out loud listening to the lecture. As an African American, the sound of that word is extremely offensive to her. It doesn't matter what the aide had said it meant; she knew a racial slur when she heard one. She is older than most of the students at Mead University, and she remembers the civil rights struggles of the 1960s even though she'd only been a little girl at the time. Further, she knows that there is a lot of racism in the United States, even today. So Angela couldn't believe it when Professor Townsend told that story to illustrate the lesson. There are racist students at Mead—even in class with her—and Angela feels that using that example sent the wrong message.

She was still fuming later that evening when she met Latria Harris at the coffee shop for their study group. Latria is also in Professor Townsend's linguistics class, and she and Angela study together every Wednesday. Angela enjoys their meetings; they help her keep on top of the assignments for a challenging class, and it is nice to socialize with another African American woman at the university. Angela and Latria got along well despite the difference in their ages and circumstances. Angela was a 58-year-old mother of three grown children; her husband left her many years ago, and she had raised the kids alone. She has always struggled financially and has been on welfare, but now things are looking up. She began her studies toward a BA six years ago, and she is hoping to finish this year. Latria is a 21-year-old single woman who had come to college straight from a college-prep high school, and her parents are quite wealthy.

As soon as Angela sat down, she burst out with her displeasure at Professor Townsend and the linguistics class. She spoke for some time about how upset she was until she noticed a blank look on Latria's face. "Don't you agree with me, Latria?" Angela asked. "Well," Latria responded, "I saw how upset it made you, but I can't say that I feel the same. My family doesn't use that word, but it doesn't really bother me to hear it. I know a lot of people who use it, and rappers seem to have made it mainstream. Also, I understood Townsend's point. The words sound alike but are defined completely differently. I guess Townsend was trying to say that people's connotations about the meaning of the one word may poison their responses to the other word."

Angela looked at Latria in silence for a while. Finally, she spoke: "Latria, I understand the point, too. I just think a different example should have been used. Those words sound too much alike for me. And that's all some of the racists around here need to hear—a professor speaking a word like that. They will start to think it's okay to say such a thing. And it is not okay. No way. People have died because of that word."

Latria looked at Angela in some disbelief. "I know you're upset, but I think you're carrying this too far. I want to stand by you, but I just can't see it as a big deal."

Angela and Latria fell silent, each pursuing her own thoughts. Finally, Angela said, "Girl, I guess we aren't going to agree about this. Maybe we should just get to studying this week's assignments." Angela smiled as she spoke and looked warmly at her friend, so Latria opened her book with relief. The last thing she wants to do is to offend or disrespect Angela. Latria gives Angela a lot of credit for everything she has gone through and for how hard she works at all her classes. Really, Angela is an inspiration to Latria. She grinned back at Angela as they began their work.

Feminist Standpoint Theory (FST) provides an entry point for understanding some of the dynamics illustrated above. FST offers a framework for understanding women's positions relative to the systems of power. This framework is built on knowledge generated from the everyday lives of people—acknowledging that individuals are active consumers of their own reality and that individuals' own perspectives are the most important sources of information about their experiences (Johnston, Friedman, & Peach, 2011; Wood & Fixmer-Oraiz, 2017). FST gives authority to women's own voices.

The theory claims that women's (and all people's) experiences, knowledge, and communication behaviors are shaped in large part by the social groups to which they belong. Thus, insofar as Angela and Latria share membership in social groups, they may share similar experiences. The fact that they are both African American women students gives them common ground, but standpoints are derived from multiple social locations (Jaggar, 2016), and Angela and Latria's economic differences and ages make a difference in their positions of power (Cox & Ebbers, 2010). And the key to developing a standpoint rests with the concept of power or, as Sandra Harding (2016) contends, the "power of the weak" (p. 336).

Everyday people, not the elite, provide the framework for Feminist Standpoint Theory because of the belief that they possess knowledge different from that of those in power. This knowledge forges standpoints in opposition to those in power. Standpoints come from resisting those in power and refusing to accept the way society defines their group (Wood, 2004). FST advocates criticizing the status quo because the status quo represents a power structure of dominance and oppression. Alison Jaggar (2016) advances that "from the point of view of the capitalist [for instance] society appears very differently from the working class" (p. 304). She goes on to say that while capitalists try to forge perceptions of "freedom, human rights and material abundance" (p. 303), members of the working class view capitalism as "coercion, violence, and material scarcity" (p. 303). To this end, "envisioning more just social practices" (Hartsock, 1997, p. 373) is crucial. Thus, Feminist Standpoint Theory points to problems in the social order and suggests new ways of organizing social life so that it will be more equitable and just. Some research (e.g., Blackwell, 2010; Elmore, 2009) focuses specifically on how women forge strategies of resistance to the inequities in the social system. In this regard, the theory belongs to the class of theories we call critical theories (see Chapters 2 and 3).

Historical Foundations of Feminist Standpoint Theory

Although communication researchers have only recently begun to apply Feminist Standpoint Theory to studies of communication behavior (see, e.g., Wood, 2008), it is a theoretical framework with a long history. Feminist Standpoint Theory is derived from Standpoint Theory, which originated in 1807, when the German philosopher Georg Wilhelm Friedrich Hegel discussed how the master–slave relationship engendered different standpoints in its participants. Hegel wrote that although slaves and masters live in a common society, their knowledge of that society is vastly different. These differences stem from the very different positions they occupy within the society. Hegel argued that there can be no single vision concerning social life. Each social group perceives a partial view of society. Karl Marx also claimed that the position of the worker (vis-à-vis class) shapes the worker's access to knowledge.

Nancy Hartsock drew on Hegel's ideas and Marxist theory to begin to adapt Standpoint Theory for use in examining relations between women and men, thus creating Feminist Standpoint Theory. Hartsock published "The Feminist Standpoint: Developing the Ground for a Specifically Feminist Historical Materialism" in 1983, beginning the adaptation of ST into FST. Hartsock was concerned with the debates regarding **feminism** and Marxism that occurred in the 1970s and early 1980s, focusing on the absence of women's issues in Marxist theory. Hartsock's interest was to "make women present" in Marx's theory and, in so doing, to forge a feminist-Marxist theory (Hartsock, 1997).

feminism
an ideology and a movement focusing on women's social position and desiring to end oppression based on gender and sex

Hartsock was interested in expanding Marx's account to include all human activity rather than simply focusing on what was primarily male activity within capitalism. She used Marx's claim that "a correct vision of class society is available from *only one* of the two major class positions in capitalist society" (Hartsock, 1983, p. 106, emphasis added). On the basis of this idea, Hartsock observed that Marx developed a powerful critique of class structure. Hartsock suggested that it is Marx's critique of class relationships rather than his critique of capitalism that is most helpful to feminists.

Hartsock applied Hegel's concepts about masters and slaves and Marx's notions of class and capitalism to issues of sex (the biological categories of male and female) and gender (the behavioral categories of masculinity and femininity). In some ways this complicates matters because there is no consensus on the exact meaning of "feminist." Many authors have noted that there are different kinds of feminism (Barker & Jane, 2016). For our purposes, we need to acknowledge this diversity, yet stipulate that the defining characteristic that unites all types of feminism is a focus on women's particular social position and a desire to end any suppression based on sex or gender.

In the early 1990s, Julia Wood (e.g., 1992) brought the tenets of FST to the field of communication studies. Wood shows how it isn't women's essential nature that affects their communication behaviors as much as it is their shared standpoints. Communication researchers became interested in how one's social location relative to the power structure impacts women's interactions. Wood and her colleague (Dennis & Wood, 2012) for instance, explored how Black mothers' reluctance to discuss sex with their daughters could be a result of their knowledge of how Black women were exploited sexually.

The Critique of Theory and Research by Feminist Theorists

This historical overview points out an interesting difference between FST and many others in this book. As we've mentioned, FST is a critical theory, but in many ways, it also expresses and embodies a critique of other mainstream theories and approaches to research. The critique lodged by Feminist Standpoint theorists begins with the observation that most research in the past has flowed from one common perspective: that of the White, middle-class male. Some feminist researchers argue that traditional approaches to research inquiry are male defined and block women's unique perspectives. Thus, the critique continues, this White, middle-class male perspective has served to silence any other perspective as a valued contributor to scientific knowledge (Chaftez, 1997).

Deanna Blackwell (2010) notes that even within avowed antiracist classrooms, White sensibilities may prevail. Blackwell talks about how even when classrooms try to foster antiracism, this is done with White students in mind (i.e., with the goal of raising the White students' awareness about race) and in so doing, students of color are rendered less visible or seen only as mentors to their White peers. Blackwell turns to a variant of FST—Black Feminist Theory—to explain and protest this phenomenon (Collins, 2000; Kovolova, 2016).

Feminist Standpoint Theory, unlike many other theories, begins by highlighting the relationship between power and knowledge. In doing so, FST

> tries to hold together two tensions: the search for better knowledge and the commitment to the idea that knowledge is always intertwined with issues of power and politics. As a consequence, the foundational tenet of feminist standpoint theory is that knowledge always arises in social locations and is structured by power relations. (O'Brien Hallstein, 2000, p. 3)

In other words, FST began with an imperfect epistemology, one devised by men in power, and seeks to develop a better epistemology, while recognizing that knowledge is not separable from politics.

FEMINIST STANDPOINT THEORY

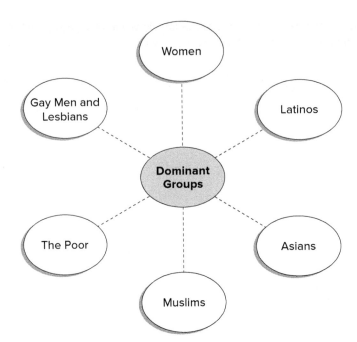

**Figure 30.1
Relationship of
Multiple Groups in
U.S. Society**
*Source: Adapted
from Wood (2004).*

It is important to keep in mind that although the feminist version of Standpoint Theory is the one that is commonly conceptualized, Standpoint Theory can be used to analyze a variety of standpoints, such as, for example, those that Angela brings to her conversation with Latria, based on race, class, and economic status. In this chapter, we explain the theory as Nancy Hartsock originally detailed it, applying its principles to women's particular standpoint. Yet, it's wise to remember that a variety of standpoints, such as those provided by status, race, and so on, can be explained by the theory, which also lends itself well to application in other co-cultural groups: "Standpoint focuses on perspectives of women, but could also take the perspectives of African American women, poor White women/men, nonwhite women and men and individuals belonging to minority ethnic and religious groups outside modern Western society" (Wallace & Wolf, 1995, p. 270). Other theorists, such as Mark Orbe (e.g., Orbe & Harris, 2015), use Standpoint Theory to examine race and culture.

The social hierarchy is not fixed. There are continual struggles in society to determine which group is dominant and who has the right to speak for them and for others (Figure 30.1). For instance, the ongoing global debate over undocumented immigrants reflects this struggle. Who has the right to "speak" on behalf of this population? And, what does their standpoint allow them to see and voice that others cannot?

Assumptions of Feminist Standpoint Theory

Feminist Standpoint Theory rests first on a few general beliefs that Janet Saltzman Chafetz (1997) says characterize any feminist theory: (1) Sex or gender is a central focus for the theory; (2) sex or gender relations are viewed as problematic, and the theory seeks to understand how sex or gender is related to inequities and contradictions; (3) sex or gender relations are viewed as changeable; and (4) feminist theory can be used to challenge the status quo when the status quo debases or devalues women.

In addition, FST, as Hartsock conceptualizes it, rests on five specific assumptions about the nature of social life:

- Material life (or class position) structures and limits understandings of social relations.

- When material life is structured in two opposing ways for two different groups, the understanding of each will be an inversion of the other. When there is a dominant and a subordinate group, the understanding of the dominant group will be both partial and harmful.

- The vision of the ruling group structures the material relations in which all groups are forced to participate.

- The vision available to an oppressed group represents struggle and an achievement.

- The potential understanding of the oppressed (the standpoint) makes visible the inhumanity of the existing relations among groups and moves us toward a better and more just world.

We will discuss each of these assumptions briefly. They are framed in the modified Marxist perspective that Hartsock favors.

The first assumption sets forth the notion that individuals' location in the class structure shapes and limits their understandings of social relations. Our chapter opening story of Angela and Latria illustrates the power of one's location in society for shaping understanding. Because of Angela's standpoint, based on her difficult circumstances raising her children alone, her struggles to finish her degree, and her age, her response to the class discussion differs sharply from Latria's perspective, whose class background and age have somewhat shielded her from Angela's position.

Second, Feminist Standpoint Theory assumes that all standpoints are partial, but those of the ruling class (or the ones in power) can actually harm those of the subordinate group. This point leads naturally to the third assumption, which asserts that the ruling group structures life in such a way as to remove some choices from the

Student Voices

Connie

The idea that a rich person's idea of poverty is limited makes sense. I know when I started at the university, I made friends with a lot of girls who came from much wealthier families than I do. It was pretty hard to make them understand that I really had to work part time and I couldn't afford to go out for pizza every other night. They kind of looked at me funny and I knew they thought I was just making excuses for not hanging out with them. I definitely felt like they did not understand where I was coming from at all. But, I did see what their lives were like—or at least I thought I did.

subordinate group. Hartsock comments that in the United States people have very little choice about participating in a market economy, which is the preferred mode for the ruling class. As Hartsock (1997) comments, the vision of the rulers structures social life and forces all parties to participate in this structure. She states: "Truth is, to a large extent, what the dominant groups can make true; history is always written by the winners" (p. 96). Furthermore, the ruling class promotes propaganda that describes the market as beneficial and virtuous. Some of the controversies in the 2016 presidential campaign illustrate these assumptions. When Donald Trump talked about his business experience, some people questioned whether his experience of dismantling companies that weren't succeeding economically or buying up foreclosed homes helped him to understand the experience of those that he put out of work in the process.

The fourth assumption asserts that the subordinate group has to struggle for their vision of social life. This leads to the final assumption, which claims that this struggle results in a clearer, more accurate vision for the subordinate group than that possessed by the ruling class. With this clear vision, the subordinate group can see the inherent inhumanity in the social order and can thus attempt to change the world for the better. This set of assumptions leads to the conclusion that although all standpoints are partial, the standpoint of an oppressed group is formed through careful attention to the dominant group. This isn't true in reverse. Thus, members of oppressed groups have a more complete standpoint than do members of dominant groups.

Added to these assumptions that characterize Hartsock's Marxist view of Feminist Standpoint Theory, most conceptions of the theory also embody a set of four beliefs about knowledge and knowledge gathering (ontology and epistemology).

1. All knowledge is a product of social activity, and thus no knowledge can be truly objective.

2. Cultural conditions "typically surrounding women's lives produce experiences and understandings that routinely differ from those produced by the conditions framing men's lives" (Wood, 1992, p. 14). These different understandings often produce distinct communication patterns.

3. It is a worthwhile endeavor to understand the distinctive features of women's experience.

4. We can only know women's experience by attending to women's interpretations of this experience.

The first belief states that knowledge is not an objective concept, but rather is shaped subjectively by knowers. Knowledge evolves from experience and this experience is a subjective one. This suggests an approach to knowing that is much different from that suggested by a belief in objective truth.

The second conclusion points to the different social locations that men and women inhabit in the United States even when they work, and live in what seem to be similar situations. In a study examining sexual harassment in the workplace, Debbie Dougherty (2001) begins with a notion grounded in this assumption: while sexual harassment may be dysfunctional for women, it may serve some functions for men. She found that men interpreted sexual harassment as a form of coping behavior for work-related stressors, a mode of therapy, and a means for demonstrating camaraderie. Women saw none of these functions in sexual harassment. Dougherty concludes that her findings indicate how different social locations have shaped men's and women's reactions. Other researchers (e.g., Richardson & Taylor, 2009) point out that this is true among women as well as between women and men. They note that sexual harassment is a different experience for Black and Hispanic women than for White women.

The third belief deals with ontology, or what is worth knowing. This notion places marginalized people (women) at the starting place for theorizing and research. Thus, Feminist Standpoint Theory is revolutionary as it replaces the dominant standpoint with standpoints outside the cultural mainstream. Sandra Harding (1991) comments on this by saying, "What 'grounds' feminist standpoint theory is not women's experiences, but the view from women's lives . . . we start our thought from the perspective of lives at the margins" (p. 269). Anne Johnston and her colleagues (2011) agreed and found that women bloggers, contrary to the dominant opinion, blog a great deal about politics, but they do so in quite different ways from their male counterparts.

Theory in Popular Press • Women's and Men's Different Social Locations

Much has been written in the popular press about difference between women and men in the United States and worldwide. Writing in the *New York Times* online, Michael Trimble notes that women cry more than men. Women cry both more intensely and more often than do men, and Trimble suggests that while there is a biological explanation for this, it may also have something to do with the differing social locations (and resulting access to power) occupied by women and men. As Trimble asserts: "Like crying, depression is, around the world, more prevalent in women than in men. One explanation might be that women, who despite decades of social advances still suffer from economic inequality, discrimination and even violence, might have more to cry about."

Source: Trimble, M. (2012, November 10). I cry, therefore I am. *New York Times Sunday Review* online, nytimes.com/2012/11/11/opinion/sunday/i-cry-therefore-i-am.html.

Finally, Feminist Standpoint Theory operates from the belief that the only way to achieve Harding's sentiment is by having women talk about their experiences and interpret them. The research participant is an active partner in the endeavor. It is a continuing goal for Feminist Standpoint theorists to develop new methodologies that give voice to those who have been silenced previously.

Through these assumptions and beliefs we get a picture of Feminist Standpoint Theory as an evolving framework, grounded in Marxism, but rejecting some of the central tenets of that perspective in favor of a feminist approach. FST seeks to understand the influence that a particular location exerts on people's views of the world and on their communication. In this quest, researchers in Feminist Standpoint Theory wish to begin with the marginalized and focus on their stories and interpretations.

As Feminist Standpoint theorists work with research participants, they recognize the limited view of their own vision and they acknowledge the subjective nature of truth(s).

Feminist Standpoint Theory and the Communication Field

After Julia Wood introduced the theory to the communication field, Feminist Standpoint Theory became popular with communication researchers. This occurred because FST advances a reciprocal relationship between communication behavior and standpoints. Communication is responsible for shaping our standpoints to the extent that we learn our place in society through interaction with others. Thus, we can imagine that when Angela's mother told her stories about her African American heritage and about her ancestors who were slaves, Angela learned much about her standpoint. Every time a teacher told Angela that she probably could not go to college and receive a BA degree, communication shaped her standpoint. Latria's situation was different, and she probably did not hear stories of slavery. She may have been encouraged to go to college by her teachers. Thus, the communication Latria engaged in didn't encourage the struggle that Angela experienced. This results in two African American women who view the world from different locations.

Similarly, one of the assumptions of the theory is that those who share a standpoint will also share certain communication styles and practices. Thus, for example, we expect that women who take care of children will communicate in a maternal fashion, whereas men who are not responsible for such caregiving will not develop the same communication behaviors (Ruddick, 1989). Marsha Houston (1992) has cited the example of communication behaviors among African American women—like loud talking and interrupting—that are shaped by their standpoints and misunderstood by those outside the group. Houston points out that some European American researchers interpret these communication behaviors differently (and usually more negatively) than do members of the group themselves.

In addition, Roseann Mandziuk (2003) points out how communication, in the form of commemorative campaigns, may try to establish standpoints in public consciousness. Mandziuk analyzes three recent campaigns that sought to commemorate Sojourner Truth and observes how they competed for the right to establish her persona in public memory. As Mandziuk notes, each of the three campaigns set forth differing standpoints for Truth, and "the questions of location, character, and ownership variously occupied the center of the debates" (p. 287).

Feminist Standpoint Theory, therefore, illustrates the centrality of communication in both shaping and transmitting standpoints. The theory points to the use of communication as a tool for changing the status quo and producing change. By giving voice to those whose standpoints are infrequently heard (Zaytseva, 2012), the methods associated with the theory focus on communication practices (Jaggar, 2016). As Julia Wood (1992) notes, "Whether women's own voices are granted legitimacy seems especially pertinent to communication scholars' assessments of the value of alternative theoretical positions" (p. 13). The concepts of voice, speaking out, and speaking for others are important to Feminist Standpoint Theory and Standpoint epistemology, and they are all concepts rooted in communication.

"All of those in favor of looking at pictures of grandchildren before we discuss *Feminist Theory* say aye."

www.CartoonStock.com

Key Concepts of Standpoint Theory

Feminist Standpoint Theory rests on several key concepts: *voice, standpoint, situated knowledges,* and *sexual division of labor*. We will discuss each concept in the next section.

Voice

Many scholars have observed that voice means something about our identity. When we find our voice or use our voice, that means that we project to others who we are and what we are all about. Voice may be best defined by its opposition to silence. Jason Stanley (2011) wrote that the service of silencing others, politicians misappropriate words and twist meanings. He calls this "linguistic strategies for stealing the voices of others" (http://opinionator.blogs.nytimes.com/2011/06/25/the-ways-of-silencing/?_r=0).

Stanley notes that silencing is robbing others of the ability to engage in speech acts, such as assertion. He goes on to observe that "there is another kind of silencing familiar in the political domain" (n.p.) as well. "It is possible to silence people by denying them access to the vocabulary to express their claims" (n.p.). This comment points to a key aspect for understanding voice, it is a relational concept; we have it to the extent that others listen to us, and do not actively work to rob us of our ability to express ourselves.

Standpoint

The central concept of the theory, **standpoint** is a location, shared by a group experiencing outsider status, within the social structure, that lends a particular kind of sense making to a person's lived experience. Furthermore, from Hartsock's perspective, "A standpoint is not simply an interested position (interpreted as bias) but is interested in the sense of being engaged" (1998, p. 107). The concept of

standpoint
an achieved position based on a social location that lends an interpretative aspect to a person's life

engagement is amplified by researchers who distinguish between a standpoint and a perspective (Hirschmann, 1997; O'Brien Hallstein, 2000). It's easy to confuse the two, but there is a critical difference. A perspective is shaped by experiences that are structured by a person's place in the social hierarchy. A perspective may lead to the achievement of a standpoint but only through effort. As O'Brien Hallstein argues, standpoints are only achieved after thought, interaction, and struggle. Standpoints must be actively sought; they are not possessed by all people who have experienced oppression. Standpoints are achieved through experiences of oppression added to active engagement, reflection, and recognition of the political implications of these experiences. Thus, we might say that Latria has a perspective while Angela has a standpoint.

Furthermore, standpoints are not free of their social and political contexts. As Sandra Harding (1991) notes, "[S]tandpoints are socially mediated" (p. 276). Because standpoints are defined by specific social locations, they are by necessity **partial,** or incomplete. The location allows only a portion of social life to be viewed by any particular group. In addition, the political aspect of standpoints stresses that individuals go through a developmental process in acquiring them. Julia Wood and Natalie Fixmer-Oraiz (2017) conclude that a standpoint is "earned" (p. 51). As Welton (1997) states, developing a standpoint requires "active, political resistance to work against the material embodiment of the perspective and experience of the dominant group. It is the act of having to push against the experience-made-reality of the hegemonic group, that makes it a political standpoint and potentially liberating" (p. 11). Moreover, as O'Brien Hallstein (1999, 2000) argues, standpoints are political because they are achieved in collaboration and dialogue with others rather than in isolation.

A specific type of standpoint is described by Patricia Hill Collins (1986, 1989, 1991) when she describes herself as an African American woman academic. This social position places her as an **outsider within,** or a person who normally would be marginalized, but has somehow gained access to the inside. In the case of outsiders moving into a social location that historically excluded them, Collins suggests that a particular clarity of vision occurs. Yang Zhao (2016) remarks that, as an immigrant, she was situated as an outsider within as she investigated the notion of transnational adoptions. Ruth Frankenberg (1993) concurs, saying that "the oppressed can see with the greatest clarity, not only their own position but . . . indeed the shape of social systems as a whole" (p. 8). This clarity of vision suggests, as Feminist Standpoint Theory argues, that the lower positions on the hierarchy possess the greatest accuracy in their standpoints, where **accuracy** refers to the ability to transcend the limits of partial vision and see beyond one's own specific social location.

Situated Knowledges

Donna Haraway (1988) contributes the term **situated knowledges,** meaning that any person's knowledge is grounded in context and circumstances. Haraway's concept suggests that knowledges are multiple and are situated in experience. For example, what one person learns from her position as a caregiver for her ailing parents is different from the knowledge that another person develops from her position as an electrical engineer. The notion of situated knowledges reminds us that what we know and do is not innate, but rather is the result of learning from our experiences. So if the engineer cared for elderly

---

partial
a recognition that no one has a complete view of the social hierarchy

outsider within
a person in a normally marginalized social position who has gained access to a more privileged location

accuracy
the ability to see more than what's available to one's own specific social location

situated knowledges
what anyone knows is grounded in context and circumstance

family members, she also would learn the caregiving knowledge. A similar point is made in discussions of Black feminist standpoints (Reynolds, 2002). Different local communities may define the standpoint somewhat differently depending on their experiences. In addition, some research (e.g., Hine, 2011) suggests that aging women share a standpoint, but also diverge from one another based on other variables such as social, health, and lifestyle factors that affect them individually at any given point in time.

Sexual Division of Labor

Hartsock's Marxist-inspired Feminist Standpoint Theory rests on the notion that men and women engage in different occupations based on their sex, which results in a **sexual division of labor.** Not only does this division simply assign people to different tasks based on sex, but it also exploits women by demanding work without providing wages. In addition, Julia Wood (2005) states that "patriarchy naturalizes male and female divisions, making it seem natural, right, unremarkable that women are subordinate to men" (p. 61). Furthermore, the inequities that women suffer in the workplace when involved in labor for wages are linked to their responsibility for unwaged domestic work. In addition, as Nancy Hirschmann (1997) points out, a feminist standpoint "enables women to identify the activities they perform in the home as 'work' and 'labor,' productive of 'value,' rather than simply the necessary and essential byproducts of 'nature' or the function of biology which women 'passively' experience" (p. 81). Thus, Feminist Standpoint Theory highlights the exploitation and distortion that result when labor is divided by sex.

sexual division of labor
allocation of work on the basis of sex

Integration, Critique, and Closing

Feminist Standpoint Theory has generated a great deal of research, interest, and spirited controversy. This theory has a rich history employing critical methods, making it primarily qualitative in nature. As you examine the value of this theory, keep in mind one of the most critical of all evaluation criteria and one that has prompted quite a bit of scholarly discussion: utility.

Integration

Communication Tradition	Rhetorical | Semiotic | Phenomenological | Cybernetic | Socio-Psychological | Socio-Cultural | **Critical**
Communication Context	Intrapersonal | Interpersonal | Small Group | Organizational | Public/Rhetorical | Mass/Media | **Cultural**
Approach to Knowing	Positivistic/Empirical | Interpretive/Hermeneutic | **Critical**

Critique

Evaluation Criteria	Scope | Logical Consistency | Parsimony | **Utility** | Testability | Heurism | Test of Time

Utility

The complaint most commonly leveled against Feminist Standpoint Theory revolves around essentialism, and a great deal has been written on this topic. As Sandra Harding (2004) has commented, the theory has caused "political, philosophic, and scientific debate" (p. 1). As we discussed in Chapter 29 with reference to Muted Group Theory, **essentialism** refers to the practice of generalizing about all women (or any group) as though they were essentially the same. Essentialism obscures the diversity that exists among women. Our chapter-opening story of Angela and Latria illustrates the mistake we make if we engage in essentialism. Although they are both African American wo men attending the same university, the differences between them cause them to interpret the classroom discussion differently. Because Feminist Standpoint Theory focuses on the location of social groups, many researchers have argued that it is essentialist. For example, Catherine O'Leary (1997) argues that although FST has been helpful in reclaiming women's experiences as suitable research topics, it contains a problematic emphasis on the universality of this experience at the expense of differences among women's experiences. Sharlene Hesse-Biber (2014) agrees with this thinking by noting that essentializing "neglects the diversity of women's lives, for example, race, class, and sexual orientation" (p. 6).

Implicit (and often explicit) in this critique are the ways that many White women researchers have excluded the standpoints and voices of women of color, women who are disabled, lesbians, poor women, and women from developing nations (Blackwell, 2010). Yet, this criticism may be unfair to Hartsock's conceptualization of the theory. Hartsock (1981) has stated that although there are many differences among women, she is pointing to specific aspects of women's experience that are shared by many: unpaid household labor and provision of caregiving and nurturance. Kristen Intemann (2016), too, believes that more contemporary views of Standpoint Theory do not "essentialize women" (p. 263). Hirschmann (1997) argues that Feminist Standpoint Theory really does accommodate difference by allowing for a multiplicity of feminist standpoints. Hirschmann suggests that standpoints can be developed from Hartsock's framework that will bring a useful approach to the tension between shared identity and difference. Wood (1992) concurs with this rebuttal, and she suggests that Feminist Standpoint Theory is different from essentialist views of women in one important way. The theory does not suggest that men and women are fundamentally different (or have different essences); rather, FST begins with the assumption that social and cultural conditions that typically surround women's lives produce different experiences and understandings from the social and cultural conditions typically surrounding men's lives. Wood concludes, "There is nothing in the logic of standpoint epistemology that precludes analysis of the intersections among conditions that structure race, class, and gender relations in any given culture" (p. 14).

More current studies conducted using a Standpoint framework have made the tension between difference and commonality central to their approach (Andrews, 2002; Houle, 2009). For example, Katrina Bell, Mark Orbe, Darlene Drummond, and Sakile Camara (2000) used Black Feminist Standpoint Theory to examine African American women's communication practices. Bell and her colleagues purposely

essentialism
the belief that all women are essentially the same, all men are essentially the same, and the two differ from each other

collected information from very diverse women in an effort to capture different lived experiences. This resulted in a sample of women who shared a racial identity, but differed in terms of many of their other social locations including age, religion, sexual identity, and so forth.

The researchers found that despite their diversity, the participants in their study did share a multiple consciousness of oppression as a result of racism, sexism, classism, and heterosexism. Yet, the participants also voiced ways in which the issue of diversity existed among African American women. Throughout their data, the participants described other aspects of their identity that became salient in their interactions with others and in many instances impeded their sense of connection with African American women. As such, the researchers saw multiple consciousness as a "dynamic process of constant negotiation" (p. 50). Thus, the researchers conclude that Black Feminist Standpoint Theory allows for the assumption of commonality of oppression while acknowledging various expressions of this common experience.

In a study of academic women, Debbie Dougherty and Kathleen Krone (2000) also sought to apply Feminist Standpoint Theory to a group of diverse women to capitalize on the creative tensions between similarity and difference. They interviewed four women in the same department in an academic institution and from the interviews they created a narrative that, although fictional, attempted to capture the standpoints voiced in the interviews. Then they had the participants comment on the narrative and identify areas for change and develop action plans. In this process, the researchers found both commonality and difference among the standpoints of the participants.

The women agreed that their standpoints were shaped by a sense of isolation, a strong desire for community, and the feeling of invisibility. Yet, they differed in their consciousness of their own oppression. The women used these differences to strengthen their relationship. The researchers note that the critique focused on essentialism may miss the point. Dougherty and Krone observe that "differences and similarities create and recreate each other, becoming so intertwined that they are difficult to separate" (p. 26).

Student Voices

Jennie

I thought Feminist Standpoint Theory was interesting, but I noticed that none of the examples referred to my specific social location. I am a Cherokee Indian, and I am very proud of my heritage. But it's certainly true that we Native Peoples are on the very bottom rungs of the social hierarchy. If anyone should have an accurate picture of the whole social structure by being on the bottom looking up, it'd be us. I guess there's always another "out" group to study. I also was thinking about the tensions between commonality and difference mentioned in the chapter. I know I get annoyed when White students assume that all Indians are the same and think that I know everything about the Crow or the Blackfeet, even though I am Cherokee and we have very different cultures.

dualisms
organizing things around pairs of opposites

A second area of criticism related to utility concerns the notion of **dualisms,** or dualistic thinking. Feminists (Cirksena & Cuklanz, 1992) note that much of Western thought is organized around a set of oppositions, or dualisms. Reason and emotion, public and private, and nature and culture are just a few of the pairs of opposites that are common organizing principles in Western thinking. Feminists have been concerned with these dualisms for two related reasons: First, dualisms usually imply a hierarchical relationship between the terms, elevating one and devaluing the other. When we suggest that decisions should be made rationally, not emotionally, for example, we are showing that reason holds a higher value in our culture than does emotion. Related to this issue is the concern that these dualisms often become gendered in our culture. In this process, men are associated with one extreme and women with the other. In the case of reason and emotion, women are identified with emotion. Because our culture values emotion less than reason, women suffer from this association. Feminist critics are usually concerned with the fact that dualisms force false dichotomies onto women and men, failing to see that life is less either/or than both/and, as Relational Dialectics Theory (Chapter 11) holds.

O'Leary (1997) argues that Feminist Standpoint Theory does not present us with a sufficiently complex understanding of experience, and as a result, it still rests on a dualism between subjective experience and objective truth. O'Leary suggests that Hartsock's framework cannot accommodate the complexities of multiple knowledges. Yet, Hartsock specifically allows for this within her original theory, arguing for clusters of standpoints. As Hartsock (1997) notes, the controversies engendered by FST indicate a "fertile terrain" for debate opening possibilities for expanding and refining the theory so that it is more responsive to diversity and clearer about the distinctions between subjectivity and objectivity.

Closing

Feminist Standpoint Theory presents us with another way of viewing the relative positions, experiences, and communication of various social groups. It has a clear political, critical bent, and it locates the place of power in social life. It has generated some controversy as people find it either offensive or compatible with their own views of social life. The theory may be compatible with other theories, enabling us to combine them to get more useful explanations for human communication behaviors. Feminist Standpoint Theory holds much promise for illuminating differences in the communication behaviors of different social groups, and suggesting tools for remediating the inequities caused by the power structure in which these groups function.

Discussion Starters

TECH QUEST: Some researchers that we cite have examined how new communication channels like blogs have given women a voice they may not have had previously. Yet, even in these venues, harassment may exist. One blogger even called the Internet a "sexist's paradise." How do you think social

FEMINIST STANDPOINT THEORY

media may or may not change some of the assumptions and tenets of Feminist Standpoint Theory?

1. Do you accept the argument of Feminist Standpoint Theory that all standpoints are partial? Explain your answer. How does the case of Angela and Latria, from the beginning of the chapter, illustrate this claim?

2. Give an example of situated knowledges in a specific context.

3. The chapter identifies this theory as a feminist theory. Discuss how a theory can be identified with a political ideology. Explain your answer.

4. If all truths are understood as coming from some subjective standpoint, how is it possible for people to communicate? If there is no objective truth, how do we reach agreement among people with different standpoints?

5. What are the limits of difference that ground a standpoint? Might we eventually end up with standpoints that are so particular that only relatively few people share them? How would this help us to understand communication between and among people?

6. How well do you think more recent scholarship has done in incorporating the tension between sharing a common standpoint and recognizing differences? Give some examples.

7. Take a position on the essentialist argument relative to Feminist Standpoint Theory, and defend your position.

Afterword←*ConnectingQuests*

A primary goal of this book is to introduce you to the richness and comprehensiveness of dozens of theories in communication. As you read throughout the book, each theory has approached communication and its numerous functions and trajectories in exciting ways. We have provided you a cross section of a number of theories that have addressed a number of various issues and themes. Whether, for example, a theorist emphasized technology, culture, or gender and applied it within an interpersonal, organizational, or mediated environment, there can be no mistake that this area known as "communication theory" has something for everyone. We have all shared this journey, and yet, we still have much more to learn and think about.

We hope that our efforts in elucidating a theory's background, assumptions, and key concepts and features of a particular theory have given you an understandable and workable framework from which to understand communication theory. All too often, textbook writers neglect to recall what it's like to absorb challenging subject matter. We're hopeful, and yes, confident that the template we followed in each chapter presented material in a way that allowed you to manage information effectively and to retrieve it successfully.

We wish to close our book by presenting one additional way to make communication theory more compelling and useful: connecting and integrating various theories. Communication theory is not created in a vacuum. Indeed, as you've read, theorists rely upon—and are influenced by—other theories to conceptualize and develop their own unique thinking. Further, many theories utilize terminology in different ways; being able to differentiate between each theory's use of a term will be of high value. To illustrate theory connections, we return to each chapter of the text and offer questions to demonstrate the interrelationship between and among various theories of communication. We hope that not only will the questions show a theory connection that you otherwise would not have considered, but also that the questions prompt further reflection. Making connections in this way will likely prompt you to recall different theories, and ideally, you will return to a particular theory to think about it in a different light. Finally, such an effort will result in a better appreciation for the contexts, traditions, and approaches that are embedded in each theory.

We offer this unique feature by asking questions for each chapter; we term this *ConnectingQuests*. Respond to each question privately and then compare your responses with others in the class. And, because you likely have not reviewed each theory in the book, to test your own knowledge, you might also develop your own *ConnectingQuests* for those chapters that you did review and now understand. Closing our book in this way is a beginning in illustrating the belief that theory building is an expansive enterprise.

So, below, find each theory in the book with accompanying connections and questions. These ConnectingQuests provide you one final effort at application and understanding:

Chapter 4: Symbolic Interaction Theory

How does Mead's concept of the *self* relate to the understanding of the role of the self in Communication Accommodation Theory?

Chapter 5: Coordinated Management of Meaning

Culture is a universal theme in many theories. Discuss the relationship between how culture functions in CMM and in Face-Negotiation Theory.

Chapter 6: Cognitive Dissonance Theory

Compare the scope of Cognitive Dissonance Theory to that of Symbolic Interaction Theory. Can you justify calling explanatory systems with such differences "theories"?

Chapter 7: Expectancy Violations Theory

Expectancy Violations Theory is primarily concerned with our expectations for other people's behavior, whereas Cognitive Dissonance Theory is concerned with our desire for consistency in attitudes and behavior. Show the relationship between the two theories using expectations, attitudes, and behavior as your overarching principles.

Chapter 8: Uncertainty Reduction Theory

How does Uncertainty Reduction Theory's view of uncertainty (and the world) relate to, or differ from, the viewpoint taken in Organizational Information Theory? Do they operate with similar or dissimilar assumptions about human behavior?

Chapter 9: Social Exchange Theory

Compare how individuals assess their relationships from both a Social Exchange perspective and from Social Penetration Theory. Explain how (or if) you see them having separate theoretical domains.

Chapter 10: Social Penetration Theory

Discuss how the principles of Social Penetration Theory and Social Information Processing Theory overlap. We already know that one rests on technology, namely texting and emailing. How is SPT be influenced by technology?

Chapter 11: Relational Dialectics Theory

Do you think that the concepts of Dialectics Theory intersect with the concepts of Uncertainty Reduction Theory as Berger suggested? Do you think the metatheoretical assumptions of the two theories are compatible? Explain your answer.

Chapter 12: Communication Privacy Management Theory

Discuss the (possible) interpretation and the role of silence in Communication Privacy Management Theory and in Relational Dialectics Theory.

Chapter 13: Social Information Processing Theory

Discuss the differences and similarities in self-presentation in both Social Information Processing Theory and Muted Group Theory. Although one theory relies on technology and another on FtF communication, what similarities can you glean?

Chapter 14: Groupthink

Determine how the role of expectations of individuals exists in both Groupthink and Expectancy Violations Theory. What sort of conversation would Janis and Burgoon have regarding expectations of behavior?

Chapter 15: Structuration Theory

Decision making is an essential component in both Structuration Theory and Groupthink. Differentiate between the two theories as to how they use the decision-making process, how the theorists interpret the term, and what parameters should be used when discussing the decision-making process.

Chapter 16: Organizational Culture Theory

According to Organizational Culture Theory, stories are considered an important element in the culture of an organization. The Coordinated Management of Meaning centers on how meaning is achieved. Compare the two theories in regard to using stories and achieving meaning.

Chapter 17: Organizational Information Theory

Organizational Information Theory and Structuration Theory each deal with the role of communication activities in an organization. Differentiate between the two theories by discussing how communication functions in both theories.

In particular, interpret what is meant by communication activities in each theory and how the theorists might interpret the information and relationships inherent in an organization.

Chapter 18: The Rhetoric

How does "the audience" function in the *Rhetoric* and in Cultural Studies? Further, discuss how technology would be influential on both theoretical models.

Chapter 19: Dramatism

Compare Burke's concept of the dramatic structure of life with Fisher's Narrative Paradigm. Would it be possible for a researcher to work comfortably with both theories without having ideational conflicts?

Chapter 20: The Narrative Paradigm

Compare the process of persuasion as it is explained through the Narrative Paradigm and how it functions in Agenda Setting Theory?

Chapter 21: Agenda Setting Theory

A fundamental issue underscoring Agenda Setting Theory is the influence of the others on the "agenda" of the media. Social Exchange Theory has its roots in economics, sociology, and psychology. To this end, explore and explain how economic, sociological, and psychological principles are at play in Agenda Setting Theory.

Chapter 22: Spiral of Silence Theory

Compare and contrast the role of the media in Spiral of Silence Theory and Cultural Studies. Drawing on each theorist's interpretation of the media, be sure to address how media content and structure influence the communication process. Use terms from each theory in your analysis.

Chapter 23: Uses and Gratifications Theory

Theories such as Uses and Gratifications highlight the use of media such as television in people's lives. In Cultivation Theory, television is seen as an instrumental tool as well. Delineate the role of television in communicating a "social reality" in both theories.

Chapter 24: Cultivation Theory

Cultivation Theory concentrates on media effects that also involve an investigation of media messages (primarily messages representing violence). How does this compare with the focus in McLuhan's Media Ecology Theory about the media in general? Can these two theories inform one another?

Chapter 25: Cultural Studies

Examine the role of culture in Cultural Studies and compare it to the role of culture in Organizational Culture Theory. What parameters exist on the interpretation of culture? What would Hall and Pacanowsky and O'Donnell-Trujillo agree about? What would they disagree about?

Chapter 26: Media Ecology Theory

Compare McLuhan's view of the audience in Media Ecology Theory with Katz, Blumler, and Gurevitch's view of the audience in Uses and Gratifications Theory. What conclusions can you draw regarding how active or passive the audience is in each theory?

Chapter 27: Face-Negotiation Theory

Ting-Toomey's theory addresses a concern for individual identity. Dramatism, too, focuses on identity, but the concept is situated very differently than the way it's proposed in FNT. Differentiate between the theories and each theorist's perspective on the use of identity.

Chapter 28: Communication Accommodation Theory

Communication Accommodation Theory emphasizes, among other things, the importance of perception in diverse communities. Feminist Standpoint Theory, too, emphasizes perception in a different, but equally important way. Differentiate between the two theories employing the concept of perception.

Chapter 29: Muted Group Theory

How would the assumptions of a researcher using Muted Group Theory compare to those of a researcher using Cognitive Dissonance Theory? Do you think that one researcher would be comfortable using both theories? Why or why not?

Chapter 30: Feminist Standpoint Theory

When discussing the Feminist Standpoint Theory, power becomes an essential concept to consider. In Communication Privacy Management Theory, power may be a driving force in the decision to self-disclose. What role do you believe power plays in a discussion of both theories of communication?

Glossary

The following is a list of terms we identified throughout this text. As you review the list, keep in mind that there may be more than one way to define a particular term. This is a result of theorists interpreting a concept differently based on the context of a particular theory. When this occurs, we have listed the term twice and included the chapter number to which each definition refers (in parentheses).

abstract symbol symbol representing an idea or thought (p. 7)

accommodation adjusting, modifying, or regulating behavior in response to others (p. 478)

accuracy the ability to see more than what's available to one's own specific social location (p. 520)

act communication behaviors indicating a person's ambiguity in receiving a message (Ch. 17) (p. 297)

act one prong of the pentad; that which is done by a person (Ch. 19) (p. 331)

actions activities based on intentional choice responses (p. 52)

the active audience, a variable concept focused on an audience engaging with the media on a voluntary basis, motivated by their needs and goals (p. 396)

active strategies reducing uncertainties by means other than direct contact (p. 144)

activeness refers to how much freedom the audience really has in the face of mass media (p. 397)

activity refers to what the media consumer does (p. 397)

actual self the attributes a person possesses (p. 220)

adjustment organizational responses to equivocality (p. 297)

affective exchange stage stage of social penetration that is spontaneous and quite comfortable for relational partners (p. 182)

affiliative constraints when members withhold their input rather than face rejection from the group (p. 241)

agency behaviors or activities used in social environments (Ch. 15) (p. 262)

agency one prong of the pentad; the means used to perform the act (Ch. 19) (p. 331)

agenda a list of the most important issues of the day as decided by an entity, such as the media (p. 360)

agent a person engaging in behaviors or activities in social environments (Ch. 15) (p. 262)

agent one prong of the pentad; the person performing the act (Ch. 19) (p. 331)

alienation perception that one has little control over his or her future (p. 423)

allocative resources material assistance used to help groups accomplish their goals (p. 264)

applied research research to solve a problem or create a policy (p. 59)

approbation facework focusing less on the negative aspects and more on the positive aspects of another (p. 464)

arousal increased interest or attention when deviations from expectations occur (p. 127)

arrangement a canon of rhetoric that pertains to a speaker's ability to organize a speech (p. 314)

asynchronous communication a process that occurs when both sender and receiver are online at different times, owing to time constraints (p. 223)

attitude a later addition to the pentad; the manner in which the agent positions himself or herself relative to others (p. 332)

audience analysis an assessment and evaluation of listeners (p. 310)

authoritative resources interpersonal assistance used to help groups accomplish their goals (p. 264)

autonomy and connection an important relational tension that shows our conflicting desires to be close and to be separate (p. 192)

attributions evaluations and judgments we make based on the actions or behaviors of others (p. 228)

avoiding staying away from disagreements (p. 470)

axiology the study of what it means to be human, which shapes the background understanding for theorizing about human communication (p. 48)

axioms truisms drawn from past research and common sense (p. 140)

behavior control the power to change another's behavior (p. 163)

behavioral sequences a series of actions designed to achieve a goal (p. 163)

behavioral uncertainty degree of uncertainty related to behaviors (p. 137)

belief in the inherent morality of the group assumption that the group members are thoughtful and good; therefore the decisions they make will be good (p. 247)

bias of communication Harold Innis's contention that technology has the power to shape society (p. 439)

body part of an organizational strategy in a speech that includes arguments, examples, and important details to make a point (p. 314)

boundaries a property of systems theory stating that systems construct structures specifying their outer limits (p. 54)

boundary coordination one of the processes in the privacy rule management system; describes how we manage private information that is co-owned (p. 212)

boundary linkage the connections forming boundary alliances between people (p. 212)

boundary ownership rights and privileges accruing to co-owners of private information (p. 213)

boundary permeability the extent to which information is able to pass through a boundary (p. 214)

boundary turbulence conflicts about boundary expectations and regulation (p. 214)

breadth the number of topics discussed in a relationship (p. 176)

breadth time amount of time spent by relational partners discussing various topics (p. 176)

buyer's remorse post-decision dissonance related to a purchase (p. 113)

calibration a property of systems theory stating that systems periodically check the scale of allowable behaviors and reset the system (p. 55)

catalyst criteria one of the criteria related to the reasons why privacy rules may shift (p. 211)

causal argument an assertion of cause and effect, including the direction of the causality (p. 404)

cause an antecedent condition that determines an effect (p. 51)

channel pathway to communication (p. 9)

characterological coherence a type of coherence referring to the believability of the characters in the story (p. 346)

charmed loop rules of meaning are consistent throughout the loop (p. 93)

chronemic cues cues related to how people perceive, use, or respond to time (p. 225)

civic spaces a metaphor suggesting that speakers have "locations" where the opportunity to persuade others exists (p. 313)

closed-mindedness a group's willingness to ignore differences in people and warnings about poor group decisions (p. 247)

co-cultures groups of individuals who are part of the same larger culture, but who can be classified around various identities (e.g., race, sex, age, etc.) (p. 39)

code converting raw data to a category system (p. 59)

coercive power perception that another person has the ability to punish you (p. 265)

cognitions ways of knowing, beliefs, judgments, and thoughts (p. 105)

cognitive arousal mental awareness of deviations from expectations (p. 127)

cognitive dissonance feeling of discomfort resulting from inconsistent attitudes, thoughts, and behaviors (p. 105)

cognitive uncertainty degree of uncertainty related to cognitions (p. 137)

coherence a principle of narrative rationality related to the internal consistency of a story (p. 345)

cohesiveness a cultural value that places emphasis on the group over the individual (Ch. 14) (p. 240)

cohesiveness the degree of togetherness between and among communicators (Ch. 2) (p. 33)

collective boundary a boundary around private information that includes more than one person (p. 212)

collective rationalization situation in which group members ignore warnings about their decisions (p. 247)

collectivism a cultural value that prioritizes group needs or values over the needs or values of an individual (we-identity) (Ch. 5) (p. 92)

collectivism a cultural value that places emphasis on the group over the individual (Ch. 27) (p. 469)

communication a social process in which individuals employ symbols to establish and interpret meaning in their environment (p. 5)

communication apprehension a generalized fear or anxiety regarding communicating in front of others (p. 37)

communicator reward valence the sum of the positive and negative characteristics of a person and the potential for him or her to carry out rewards or punishments (p. 129)

comparison level (CL) a standard for what a person thinks he or she should get in a relationship (p. 161)

comparison level for alternatives (CLalt) how people evaluate a relationship based on what their alternatives to the relationship are (p. 161)

compromising a behavior that employs give-and-take to achieve a middle-road resolution (p. 470)

computer-mediated communication (CMC) process in which people perceive, interpret, and exchange information via large networked telecommunications systems (p. 223)

concepts labels for the most important elements in a theory (p. 45)

conclusion part of an organizational strategy in a speech that is aimed at summarizing a speaker's main points and arousing emotions in an audience (p. 314)

concrete symbol symbol representing an object (p. 7)

concurrence seeking efforts to search out group consensus (p. 245)

confirmatory bias occurs when people selectively pay attention to information that is consistent with previously held beliefs (p. 112)

conscientious objectors group members who refuse to participate because it would violate personal conscience (p. 251)

consonance the belief that all media are similar in attitudes, beliefs, and values (p. 378)

consonant relationship two elements in equilibrium with each other (p. 106)

constitutive rules rules that organize behavior and help us to understand how meaning should be interpreted (p. 97)

consubstantiation when appeals are made to increase overlap between people (p. 329)

content the conversion of raw data into meaning (p. 89)

contexts environments in which communication takes place (p. 30)

contextual dialectics tensions resulting from the place of the relationship within the culture (p. 195)

contradiction a central feature of the dialectic approach; refers to oppositions (p. 191)

control direction over the important concepts in a theory (p. 47)

convergence strategy used to adapt to another's behavior (p. 483)

cool media low-definition communication that demands active involvement from a viewer, listener, or reader (p. 446)

coordination trying to make sense of message sequencing (p. 95)

core criteria one of the criteria used for developing privacy rules that are more resilient and often function in the background (p. 211)

correlation the way that media direct our attention to certain issues through communicating them to the public and to policymakers (p. 357)

costs elements of relational life with negative value (p. 156)

counter-hegemony when, at times, people use hegemonic behaviors to challenge the domination in their lives (p. 429)

covering law approach a guideline for creating theory suggesting that theories conform to a general law that is universal and invariant (p. 51)

critical approach an approach stressing the researcher's responsibility to change the inequities in the status quo (p. 47)

cues filtered-out theories theories that address the lack of nonverbal cues as being detrimental to online relationship development (p. 221)

cultivation differential the percentage of difference in response between light and heavy television viewers (p. 410)

cultural communication communication between and among individuals whose cultural backgrounds vary (p. 38)

cultural patterns images of the world and a person's relationship to it (p. 92)

culture a community of meaning with, among other things, a shared body of knowledge (p. 38)

culture wars cultural struggles over meaning, identity, and influence (p. 425)

cumulativeness the belief that media repeat themselves (p. 377)

cycles series of communication behaviors that serve to reduce equivocality (p. 297)

cyclic alternation a coping response to dialectical tensions; refers to changes over time (p. 199)

data the raw materials collected by the researcher to answer the questions posed in the research or to test a hypothesis (p. 59)

decoding receiving and comparing messages (p. 431)

deductive logic moving from the general (the theory) to the specific (the observations) (p. 59)

deliberative rhetoric a type of rhetoric that determines an audience's course of action (p. 317)

delivery a canon of rhetoric that refers to the nonverbal presentation of a speaker's ideas (p. 316)

dependency overaccommodation a behavior that occurs when speakers place listeners in a lower-status role (p. 489)

depenetrate slow deterioration of relationship (p. 173)

depth degree of intimacy guiding topic discussion (p. 176)

dialectic approach an approach framing contradiction as both/and (p. 188)

dialectical unity the way people use communication to make sense of contradictions in their relationships (p. 190)

direct exchange an exchange where two people reciprocate costs and rewards (p. 165)

discursive consciousness a person's ability to articulate personal goals or behaviors (p. 262)

disinhibition searching a passive strategy involving watching a person's natural or uninhibited behavior in an informal environment (p. 145)

dispositional matrix the beliefs you have about relationships (p. 164)

disqualifying a substrategy of integration; refers to exempting certain issues from the general pattern (p. 199)

dissonance ratio a factor in determining magnitude of dissonance; the amount of consonant cognitions relative to the dissonant ones (p. 110)

dissonant relationship two elements in disequilibrium with each other (p. 106)

divergence strategy used to accentuate the verbal and nonverbal differences between communicators (p. 487)

diversion a category of gratifications coming from media use; involves escaping from routines and problems (p. 389)

division when two people fail to have overlap in their substances (p. 328)

dominant group the group that holds the power in a given culture (p. 498)

dominant-hegemonic position operating within a code that allows one person to have control over another (p. 432)

dominating using influence or authority to make decisions (p. 470)

double-interact loops cycles of an organization (e.g., interviews, meetings) to reduce equivocality (p. 297)

dual climates of opinion difference between the population's perception of a public issue and the way the media report on the issue (p. 379)

dualisms organizing things around pairs of opposites (p. 524)

dualistic approach an approach framing contradiction as two separate entities (p. 188)

duality of structure rules and resources used to guide organizational decisions about behaviors or actions (p. 263)

duration organizational rule stating that decisions regarding equivocality should be made in the least amount of time (p. 295)

dyadic uniqueness distinctive relationship qualities (p. 183)

ecology the study of environments and their influence upon people (p. 438)

effect a condition that inevitably follows a causative condition (p. 51)

effective matrix the transformations you are able to make to your given matrix, by learning a new skill, for example (p. 164)

effort organizational rule stating that decisions regarding equivocality should be made with the least amount of work (p. 297)

electronic era age in which electronic media pervades our senses, allowing for people across the world to be connected (p. 444)

enactment interpretation of the information received by the organization (p. 299)

enculturation performances organizational behaviors that assist employees in discovering what it means to be a member of an organization (p. 283)

enhancement law that states media amplify or strengthen society (p. 448)

enmeshment the extent to which partners identify themselves as part of a system (p. 91)

entry phase the beginning stage of an interaction between strangers (p. 139)

environment situation or context in which communication occurs (p. 8)

epideictic rhetoric a type of rhetoric that pertains to praising or blaming (p. 317)

episodes communication routines that have recognized beginnings, middles, and endings (p. 90)

epistemology the nature, scope, and limits of human knowledge (p. 48)

epoch era or historical age (p. 441)

equifinality a property of systems theory stating that systems can achieve the same goals through different means (p. 55)

equivocality the extent to which organizational messages are uncertain, ambiguous, and/or unpredictable (p. 293)

essentialism the belief that all women are essentially the same, all men are essentially the same, and the two differ from each other (p. 522)

ethics perceived rightness or wrongness of an action or behavior (p. 14)

ethos the perceived character, intelligence, and goodwill of a speaker (p. 310)

evaluation process of judging a conversation (p. 481)

exit phase the stage in a relationship when people decide whether to continue or leave (p. 139)

expectancies thoughts and behaviors anticipated in conversations (p. 124)

expert power perception that another person has the ability to exert influence because of special knowledge or expertise (p. 266)

explanation the ability to interpret the meaning of behavioral choices (p. 136)

exploratory affective exchange stage stage of social penetration that results in the emergence of our personality to others (p. 181)

extractive strategy an active information-seeking strategy involving online searches to obtain information about a specific person (p. 148)

face a metaphor for the public image people display (p. 461)

face concern interest in maintaining one's face or the face of others (p. 462)

face management the protection of one's face (p. 469)

face need desire to be associated or disassociated with others (p. 462)

face restoration strategy used to preserve autonomy and avoid loss of face (p. 466)

face-saving efforts to avoid embarrassment or vulnerability (p. 465)

facework actions used to deal with face needs/wants of self and others (p. 463)

false consciousness Gramsci's belief that people are unaware of the domination in their lives (p. 427)

fate control the ability to affect a partner's outcomes (p. 163)

feedback a subprocess of calibration; information allowing for change in the system (Ch. 3) (p. 55)

feedback communication given to the source by the receiver to indicate understanding (Ch. 1) (p. 11)

feedback the behavioral confirmation behaviors of senders and receivers (Ch. 13) (p. 229)

feminism an ideology and a movement focusing on women's social position and desiring to end oppression based on gender and sex (p. 512)

fidelity a principle of narrative rationality judging the credibility of a story (p. 346)

field journal personal log to record feelings about communicating with people in a different culture from one's own (p. 280)

field of experience overlap of sender's and receiver's culture, experiences, and heredity in communication (p. 11)

first order effects a method for cultivation to occur; refers to learning facts from the media (p. 411)

forensic rhetoric a type of rhetoric that pertains to speakers prompting feelings of guilt or innocence from an audience (p. 317)

fraction of selection Schramm's idea of how media choices are made; the expectation of reward divided by the effort required (p. 392)

Frankfurt School theorists a group of scholars who believed that the media were more concerned with making money than with presenting news (p. 424)

fresh act something new developed from action or behavior (p. 259)

gender social category consisting of the learned behaviors that constitute masculinity and femininity for a given culture (p. 499)

gender polarization lens viewing men and women as polar opposites (p. 500)

generalized exchange an exchange where reciprocation involves the social network and isn't confined to two individuals (p. 165)

generalized other the attitude of the whole community (p. 79)

given matrix the constraints on your choices due to the environment and/or your own skill levels (p. 163)

global village the notion that humans can no longer live in isolation, but rather will always be connected by continuous and instantaneous electronic media (p. 441)

glosses outdated words in a speech (p. 315)

good reasons a set of values for accepting a story as true and worthy of acceptance; provides a method for assessing fidelity (p. 347)

group insulation a group's ability to remain unaffected by outside influences (p. 244)

groupthink a way of group deliberation that minimizes conflict and emphasizes the need for unanimity (p. 238)

guilt tension, embarrassment, shame, disgust, or other unpleasant feelings (p. 329)

habitual rules nonnegotiable rules that are usually created by an authority figure (p. 53)

hard core group(s) at the end of the spiral willing to speak out at any cost (p. 380)

Hawthorne experiments a set of investigations that ushered in a human relations approach to organizations (p. 35)

hegemony the domination of one group over another, usually weaker, group (p. 426)

heurism a criterion for evaluating theories; refers to the amount of research and new thinking stimulated by the theory (p. 57)

hierarchy a property of systems theory stating that systems consist of multiple levels (Ch. 3) (p. 54)

hierarchy an organizing principle whereby things or people are ranked one above the other (Ch. 2) (p. 35)

high-context cultures cultures, like Japan, where the meaning of a message is in the context or internalized in listeners (p. 149)

homeostatic a term for a stable system that isn't changing (p. 55)

homogeneity group similarity (p. 242)

hot media high-definition communication that demands little involvement from a viewer, listener, or reader (p. 445)

hyperpersonal perspective an extension of Social Information Processing theory that suggests people are able to develop more intimate relationships than those that are FtF (p. 227)

hypotheses testable predictions of relationships between concepts that follow the general predictions made by a theory (p. 52)

I the spontaneous, impulsive, creative self (p. 78)

ice age analogy a position stating that television doesn't have to have a single major impact, but influences viewers through steady limited effects (p. 409)

ideal self the attributes a person ideally possesses (p. 220)

identification when two people have overlap in their substances (p. 328)

ideology framework used to make sense of our existence (p. 424)

illusion of invulnerability belief that the group is special enough to overcome obstacles (p. 246)

illusion of unanimity belief that silence equals agreement (p. 248)

imperviousness to influence refers to audience members constructing their own meaning from media content (p. 396)

importance a factor in determining magnitude of dissonance; refers to how significant the issue is (p. 109)

impression management the strategic or unconscious effort to influence (p. 220)

in-groups groups in which a person feels he or she belongs (p. 479)

indirect stereotyping imposing outdated and rigid assumptions of a cultural group upon that group (p. 485)

Individual Differences Perspective a specific approach to the idea of limited effects; concentrates on the limits posed by personal characteristics (p. 388)

individualism prioritizing personal needs or values over the needs or values of a group (I-identity) (Ch. 5) (p. 92)

individualism a cultural value that places emphasis on the individual over the group (Ch. 27) (p. 468)

inductive logic moving from the specific (the observations) to the general (the theory) (p. 59)

information environment the availability of all stimuli in an organization (p. 294)

integrating collaborating with others to find solutions (p. 470)

integration a coping response to dialectical tensions; refers to synthesizing the opposition; composed of three substrategies (p. 199)

intentionality a cognitive behavior that occurs when people's prior motives determine use of media (p. 396)

interactional dialectics tensions resulting from and constructed by communication (p. 195)

interactional expectations an individual's ability to carry out the interaction (p. 125)

interactional model of communication view of communication as the sharing of meaning with feedback that links source and receiver (p. 10)

interactive strategies reducing uncertainties by engaging in conversation (p. 144)

interdependence a property of systems theory stating that the elements of a system affect one another (p. 54)

intergroup overaccommodation a behavior that occurs when speakers place listeners in cultural groups without acknowledging individual uniqueness (p. 489)

internal and external stress pressure exerted on the group by issues and events both inside and outside of the group (p. 245)

interpersonal communication face-to-face communication between people (p. 32)

interpersonal meaning the result when two people agree on each other's interpretations of an interaction (p. 88)

interpretive approach an approach viewing truth as subjective and stressing the participation of the researcher in the research process (p. 47)

intimate distance very close spatial zone spanning 0–18 inches, usually reserved for those whom we share personal feelings (p. 122)

intrapersonal communication communication with oneself (p. 30)

introduction part of an organizational strategy in a speech that includes gaining the audience's attention, connecting with the audience, and providing an overview of the speaker's purpose (p. 314)

invention a canon of rhetoric that pertains to the construction or development of an argument related to a particular speech (p. 312)

irrelevant relationship two elements that have no meaningful relation to each other (p. 106)

lack of decision-making procedures failure to provide norms for solving group issues (p. 244)

lack of impartial leadership groups led by individuals who put their personal agendas first (p. 244)

language a shared system of verbal and nonverbal symbols (p. 76)

last-minute swing jumping on the bandwagon of popular opinion after opinions have been expressed (p. 380)

laws of media further expansion of Media Ecology Theory with focus on the impact of technology on society (p. 447)

legitimate power perception that another person has the ability to exert influence because of title or position (p. 266)

life scripts clusters of past or present episodes that create a system of manageable meanings with others (p. 91)

limited effects the perspective replacing Mass Society Theory; holds that media effects are limited by aspects of the audience's personal and social lives (p. 388)

linear model of communication one-way view of communication that assumes a message is sent by a source to a receiver through a channel (p. 9)

literate era age when written communication flourished and the eye became the dominant sense organ (p. 443)

logical consistency a criterion for evaluating theories; refers to the internal logic in the theoretical statements (p. 56)

logos logical proof; the use of arguments and evidence in a speech (p. 310)

looking-glass self our ability to see ourselves as another sees us (p. 77)

loop the reflexiveness of levels in the hierarchy of meaning (p. 93)

low-context cultures cultures, as in the United States, where most of the meaning is in the code or message (p. 149)

macrotheory a theory with extensive boundaries (p. 206)

magnitude of dissonance the quantitative amount of discomfort felt (p. 109)

mainstreaming the tendency for heavy viewers to perceive a similar culturally dominant reality to that pictured on the media although this differs from actual reality (p. 410)

mass communication communication to a large audience via various channels (e.g., radio, Internet, television, etc.) (p. 37)

mass media channels or delivery modes for mass messages (p. 37)

Mass Society Theory the idea that average people are the victims of the powerful forces of mass media (p. 388)

material coherence a type of coherence referring to the congruence between one story and other related stories (p. 346)

me the reflective, socially aware self (p. 79)

meaning what people extract from a message (p. 7)

media agenda the priority placed on issues discussed in mediated sources (p. 361)

media ecology the study of how media and communication processes affect human perception, feeling, emotion, and value (p. 438)

media framing how media depictions of events influence and constrain the way consumers can interpret the events (p. 361)

Media Richness Theory a theory that advances the notion that communication can be classified according to message complexity (p. 222)

the medium is the message phrase referring to the power and influence of the medium—not the content—on a society (p. 444)

memory a canon of rhetoric that refers to a speaker's effort in storing information for a speech (p. 316)

message words, sounds, actions, or gestures in an interaction (p. 9)

metaphor a figure of speech that helps to make the unclear more understandable (p. 315)

microtheory a theory with limited boundaries (p. 206)

mind the ability to use symbols with common social meanings (p. 76)

minimal justification offering the least amount of incentive necessary to obtain compliance (p. 112)

models simplified representations of the communication process (p. 8)

monologic approach an approach framing contradiction as either/or (p. 188)

morphogenic a process that occurs when a system recalibrates (or changes) (p. 55)

mortification one method of purging guilt, by blaming ourselves (p. 330)

motion the processual nature of relationships (p. 191)

movements activities based on stimulus-response (p. 52)

narration an account to which listeners assign meaning (p. 344)

narrative rationality a standard for judging which stories to believe and which to disregard (p. 345)

negative face desire to be autonomous and free from others (p. 462)

negotiated position accepting dominant ideologies, but allowing for cultural exceptions (p. 432)

neo-Marxist limited embracement of Marxism (p. 424)

networks communication patterns through which information flows (p. 34)

neutralizing a substrategy of integration; refers to compromising between the oppositions (p. 199)

new media computer-related technology (p. 37)

noise distortion in channel not intended by the source (p. 9)

nominal concepts concepts that are not directly observable (p. 45)

norms expectations of behavior in conversations (p. 482)

novelty and predictability an important relational tension that shows our conflicting desires to have both stability and change (p. 194)

obliging satisfying the needs of others (p. 470)

observations focused examination within a context of interest; may be guided by hypotheses or research questions (p. 59)

obsolescence law that states media eventually render something obsolete or out of date (p. 448)

ontology the study of what it means to be human, which shapes the background understanding for theorizing about human communication (p. 48)

openness the acknowledgment that within all human systems the boundaries are permeable (p. 54)

openness and protection an important relational tension that shows our conflicting desires to tell our secrets and to keep them hidden (p. 194)

operationalize making an abstract idea measurable and observable (p. 59)

opinion expression of attitude (p. 372)

oppositional position substituting alternative messages presented by the media (p. 432)

order or hierarchy a ranking that exists in society primarily because of our ability to use language (p. 329)

organizational communication communication within and among large, extended environments (p. 34)

organizational culture the essence of organizational life (p. 275)

organizational rituals routines that pertain to the organization overall (p. 282)

orientation stage stage of social penetration that includes revealing small parts of ourselves (p. 180)

ought self the attributes a person should possess (p. 220)

out-group stereotypes stereotyped perceptions of group enemies or competitors (p. 247)

out-groups groups in which a person feels he or she does not belong (p. 479)

outcome whether people continue in a relationship or terminate it (p. 157)

outsider within a person in a normally marginalized social position who has gained access to a more privileged location (p. 520)

overaccommodation attempt to overdo efforts in regulating, modifying, or responding to others (p. 488)

overestimation of the group erroneous belief that the group is more than it is (p. 246)

pack journalism the phenomenon of journalists having their agendas influenced by other journalists (p. 365)

paradigm shift a significant change in the way most people see the world and its meanings (p. 340)

parametric rules rules that are set by an authority figure but are subject to some negotiation (p. 53)

parasocial interaction the relationship we feel we have with people we know only through the media (p. 393)

parsimony a criterion for evaluating theories; refers to the simplicity of the explanation provided by the theory (p. 56)

partial recognition that no one has a complete view of the social hierarchy (p. 520)

particular others individuals who are significant to us (p. 79)

passion performances organizational stories that employees share with one another (p. 282)

passive strategies reducing uncertainties by unobtrusive observation (p. 144)

pathos emotional proof; emotions drawn from audience members (p. 311)

pentad Burke's method for applying Dramatism (p. 331)

pentadic (or dramatisic) ratios the proportions of one element of the pentad relative to another element (p. 332)

perception process of attending to and interpreting a message (p. 481)

performance metaphor suggesting that organizational life is like a theatrical presentation (p. 281)

personal boundary a boundary around private information that includes just one person (p. 212)

personal distance spatial zone of 18 inches to 4 feet, reserved for family and friends (p. 122)

personal identity a category of gratifications coming from media use; involves ways to reinforce individual values (p. 389)

personal idioms private, intimate expressions stated in a relationship (p. 182)

personal meaning the meaning achieved when a person brings his or her unique experiences to an interaction (p. 87)

personal phase the stage in a relationship when people begin to communicate more spontaneously and personally (p. 139)

personal relationships a category of gratifications coming from media use; involves substituting media for companionship (p. 389)

personal rituals routines done at the workplace each day (p. 282)

personal space individual's variable use of space and distance (p. 121)

personnel organizational rule stating the most knowledgeable workers should resolve equivocality (p. 296)

phenomenology a personal interpretation of everyday life and activities (p. 27)

physical arousal bodily changes as a result of deviations from expectations (p. 127)

physical (external) noise bodily influences on reception of message (p. 10)

physiological noise biological influences on reception of message (p. 10)

pluralistic ignorance mistaken observation of how most people feel (p. 376)

policy agenda the result of the public agenda interacting with what policy makers think (p. 361)

political performances organizational behaviors that demonstrate power or control (p. 283)

positive face desire to be liked and admired by others (p. 462)

positivistic/empirical approach an approach assuming the existence of objective reality and value-neutral research (p. 47)

power imposition of personal will on others (Ch. 15) (p. 261)

power the degree of dependence a person has on another for outcomes (Ch. 9) (p. 163)

practical consciousness a person's inability to articulate personal goals or behaviors (p. 262)

praxis refers to the choice-making capacity of humans (p. 192)

prediction the ability to forecast one's own and others' behavioral choices (p. 136)

pre-interactional expectations the knowledge or skills a communicator brings to an interaction (p. 125)

pressure toward uniformity occurs when group members go along to get along (p. 248)

pressures on dissenters direct influence on group members who provide thoughts contrary to the group's (p. 248)

primary territories signal a person's exclusive domain over an area or object (p. 123)

priming a cognitive process whereby what the media present temporarily, at least, influences what people think about afterwards in processing additional information (p. 361)

print era the age when gaining information through the printed word was customary, and seeing continued as the dominant sense (p. 443)

privacy rule attributes one of the features of privacy rules; they refer to the ways people acquire rules and the properties of the rules (p. 212)

private boundaries the demarcation between private information and public information (p. 210)

private disclosures the process of communicating private information to another (p. 208)

private information information about things that matter deeply to a person (p. 208)

problem-solving groups sets of individuals whose main task is to make decisions and provide policy recommendations (p. 240)

process ongoing, dynamic, and unending occurrence (p. 5)

productive exchange an exchange where both partners incur costs and benefits simultaneously (p. 165)

proxemics study of a person's use of space (p. 121)

psychological noise cognitive influences on reception of message (p. 10)

public legal, social, and social-psychological concerns of people (p. 372)

public agenda the result of the media agenda interacting with what the public thinks (p. 361)

public and private dialectic a contextual dialectic resulting from a private relationship and public life (p. 195)

public communication the dissemination of information from one person to many others (audience) (p. 36)

public distance spatial zone of 12 feet and beyond, reserved for very formal discussions such as between professor and students in class (p. 123)

public image outer layer of a person; what is available to others (p. 175)

public opinion attitudes and behaviors expressed in public in order to avoid isolation (p. 372)

public territories locations that signal open spaces for everyone, including beaches and parks (p. 123)

punctuation process of identifying when an episode begins or ends (p. 90)

pure research research to generate knowledge (p. 59)

purpose one prong of the pentad; the goal the agent had for the act (p. 332)

Pygmalion effect living up to or down to another's expectations of us (p. 78)

quasi-statistical sense personal estimation of the strength of opposing sides on a public issue (p. 375)

ratio of the senses phrase referring to the way people adapt to their environment (p. 444)

rational world paradigm a system of logic employed by many researchers and professionals (p. 340)

rationale a factor in determining magnitude of dissonance; refers to the reasoning employed to explain the inconsistency (p. 110)

reactivity searching a passive strategy involving watching a person doing something (p. 145)

real and ideal dialectic a contextual dialectic resulting from the difference between idealized relationships and lived relationships (p. 195)

real concepts concepts that are directly observable (p. 45)

receiver recipient of a message (p. 9)

reciprocity the return of openness from one person to another (Ch. 10) (p. 175)

redemption a rejection of the unclean and a return to a new order after guilt has been temporarily purged (p. 330)

referent power perception that another person has the ability to achieve compliance because of established personal relationships (p. 266)

reflexivity a person's ability to monitor his or her actions or behaviors (p. 262)

reframing a substrategy of integration; refers to transforming the oppositions (p. 199)

regulative rules guidelines for people's behavior (p. 98)

relational uncertainty a lack of certainty about the future and status of a relationship (p. 147)

relationship agreement and understanding between two people (p. 91)

relationships the ways in which the concepts of a theory relate to one another (p. 45)

relevance a factor explaining why people seek guidance from the media agenda. It refers to how personally affected they feel by an issue (p. 363)

reliability the stability and predictability of an observation (p. 62)

resonance a behavior that occurs when a viewer's lived reality coincides with the reality pictured in the media (p. 411)

resources attributes or material goods that can be used to exert power in an organization (Ch. 15) (p. 264)

resources stories, symbols, and images that people use to make sense of their world (Ch. 5) (p. 96)

response reaction to equivocality (p. 297)

retention collective memory allowing people to accomplish goals (p. 301)

retrieval law that states media restore something that was once lost (p. 448)

reversal law that states media will—when pushed to their limit—produce or become something else (p. 449)

reward power perception that another person has the ability to provide positive outcomes (p. 264)

reward-cost ratio balance between positive and negative relationship experiences (p. 177)

rewards elements of relational life with positive value (p. 156)

rhetoric a speaker's available means of persuasion (p. 36)

ritual performances regular and recurring presentations in the workplace (p. 282)

ritual perspective a position depicting the media as representers of shared beliefs (p. 405)

role taking the ability to put oneself in another's place (p. 77)

roles positions of group members and their relationship to the group (p. 34)

rule development one of the features of privacy rule characteristics; describes how rules come to be decided (p. 211)

rules approach a guideline for creating theory that builds human choice into explanations (p. 51)

rules general routines that the organization or group follows in accomplishing goals (Ch. 15) (p. 263)

rules guidelines in organizations as they review responses to equivocal information (Ch. 17) (p. 295)

salience the degree to which an agenda issue is perceived as important relative to the other issues on the agenda (p. 362)

scapegoating one method of purging guilt, by blaming others (p. 330)

scene one prong of the pentad; the context surrounding the act (p. 331)

scientific method the traditional method for doing research involving controlled observations and analysis to test the principles of a theory (p. 59)

scope a criterion for evaluating theories; refers to the breadth of communication behaviors covered in the theory (p. 56)

second order effects a method for cultivation to occur; refers to learning values and assumptions from the media (p. 411)

second shift the phenomenon of working women putting in eight hours on the job and another day's work at home (p. 500)

secondary territories locations that signal a person's affiliation with an area or object (p. 123)

segmentation a coping response to dialectical tensions; refers to changes due to context (p. 199)

selection a coping response to dialectical tensions; refers to prioritizing oppositions (Ch. 11) (p. 199)

selection choosing the best method for obtaining information (Ch. 17) (p. 300)

selective attention a method for reducing dissonance by paying attention to information that is consonant with current beliefs and actions (p. 111)

selective exposure a method for reducing dissonance by seeking information that is consonant with current beliefs and actions (p. 111)

selective interpretation a method for reducing dissonance by interpreting ambiguous information so that it becomes consistent with current beliefs and actions (p. 111)

selective retention a method for reducing dissonance by remembering information that is consonant with current beliefs and actions (p. 111)

selectivity audience members' use of media reflects their existing interests (p. 396)

self imagining how we look to another person (p. 77)

self-appointed mindguards individuals who protect the group from adverse information (p. 248)

self-censorship group members minimize personal doubts and counterarguments (p. 248)

self-concept a relatively stable set of perceptions people hold about themselves (p. 73)

self-disclosure personal messages about the self disclosed to another (p. 137)

self-esteem the degree of positive orientation people have about themselves (p. 32)

self-fulfilling prophecy a prediction about yourself causing you to behave in such a way that it comes true (p. 74)

self-identity personal attributes of an individual (p. 464)

semantic noise linguistic influences on reception of message (p. 9)

semiotics the study of signs (p. 27)

sensemaking creating awareness and understanding in situations that are complex or uncertain (p. 299)

sensory overaccommodation overly adapting to others who are perceived as limited in their abilities (physical, linguistic, or other) (p. 489)

sex biological category divided into male and female (p. 499)

sexual division of labor allocation of work on the basis of sex (p. 521)

significant symbols symbols whose meaning is generally agreed upon by many people (p. 76)

situated knowledges what anyone knows is grounded in context and circumstance (p. 520)

situational contexts environments that are limited by such factors as the number of people present, the feedback, the space between communicators, among others (p. 30)

small group communication communication among at least three individuals (p. 33)

social the notion that people and interactions are part of the communication process (p. 5)

Social Categories Model a specific approach to the idea of limited effects; concentrates on the limits posed by group membership (p. 388)

social constructionism belief that people co-construct their social reality in conversations (p. 86)

social distance spatial zone of 4–12 feet, reserved for more formal relationships such as those with coworkers (p. 122)

Social Identity Theory a theory that proposes a person's identity is shaped by both personal and social characteristics (p. 479)

social integration reciprocity of communication behaviors in interaction (p. 267)

social penetration process of bonding that moves a relationship from superficial to more intimate (p. 171)

social performances organizational behaviors intended to demonstrate cooperation and politeness with others (p. 283)

Social Presence Theory a theory that posits the extent to which people are aware of each other via various communication media (p. 222)

social reality a person's beliefs about how meaning and action fit within an interpersonal interaction (p. 87)

social rituals routines that involve relationships with others in the workplace (p. 282)

society the web of social relationships humans create and respond to (p. 79)

solidarity facework accepting another as a member of an in-group (p. 463)

Sophists teachers of public speaking (rhetoric) in ancient Greece (p. 309)

source originator of a message (p. 9)

speech act action we perform by speaking (e.g., questioning, complimenting, or threatening) (p. 90)

stable exchange stage stage of social penetration that results in complete openness and spontaneity for relational partners (p. 183)

standpoint an achieved position based on a social location that lends an interpretative aspect to a person's life (p. 519)

strange loop rules of meaning change within the loop (p. 94)

stranger-on-the-train the event that occurs when strangers reveal personal information to others in public places (p. 174)

structural coherence a type of coherence referring to the flow of the story (p. 345)

structuration the production, reproduction, and transformation of social environments through rules and resources in relationships (p. 258)

structure the rules and resources used to sustain a group or organization (p. 257)

style a canon of rhetoric that includes the use of language to express ideas in a speech (p. 315)

substance the general nature of something (p. 328)

subsystems smaller systems that are embedded in larger ones (p. 54)

success organizational rule stating that a successful plan of the past will be used to reduce current equivocality (p. 296)

suprasystems larger systems that hold smaller ones within them (p. 54)

surveillance the process of newspeople scanning the information that is in the environment and deciding which of the many events that are occurring deserve attention in their news outlets (Ch. 21) (p. 357)

surveillance a category of gratifications coming from media use; involves collecting needed information (Ch. 23) (p. 389)

syllogism a set of propositions that are related to one another and draw a conclusion from the major and minor premises (p. 311)

symbol arbitrary label given to a phenomenon (p. 7)

synchronous communication a process that occurs when both sender and receiver are online simultaneously (p. 223)

synergy the intersection of multiple perspectives in a small group (p. 34)

system a group or organization and the behaviors that the group engages in to pursue its goals (p. 257)

systems approach a guideline for creating theory that acknowledges human choice and the constraints of the systems involved (p. 51)

tact facework extent to which a person respects another's autonomy (p. 463)

tactical rules unstated rules used to achieve a personal or interpersonal goal (p. 53)

task rituals routines associated with a particular job in the workplace (p. 282)

task-oriented groups sets of individuals whose main goal is to work toward completing jobs assigned to them (p. 240)

technopoly a term coined by Postman that means we live in a society dominated by technology (p. 451)

territoriality person's ownership of an area or object (p. 123)

test of time a criterion for evaluating theories; refers to the theory's durability over time (p. 57)

testability a criterion for evaluating theories; refers to our ability to test the accuracy of a theory's claims (p. 57)

tetrad organizing concept to understand the laws of media (p. 447)

the negative rejecting one's place in the social order; exhibiting resistance (p. 330)

theater of struggle competition of various cultural ideologies (p. 428)

theorems theoretical statements derived from axioms, positing a relationship between two concepts (p. 142)

theory an abstract system of concepts and their relationships that help us to understand a phenomenon (p. 44)

theory of sociocultural evolution Darwin's belief that only the fittest can survive challenging surroundings (p. 291)

thick boundaries closed boundaries allowing little or no information to pass through (p. 214)

thick description explanation of the layers of meaning in a culture (p. 280)

thin boundaries open boundaries allowing all information to pass through (p. 214)

thought an inner conversation (p. 77)

threat threshold tolerance for distance violations (p. 127)

topics an aid to invention that refers to the arguments a speaker uses (p. 313)

totality acknowledges the interdependence of people in a relationship (p. 191)

train test an experiment used to assess the extent to which people will speak out (p. 379)

trajectory pathway to closeness (p. 171)

transactional model of communication view of communication as the simultaneous sending and receiving of messages (p. 12)

transgression a violation of relational rules, practices, and expectations (p. 173)

transmissional perspective a position depicting the media as senders of messages across space (p. 405)

tribal era age when oral tradition was embraced and hearing was the paramount sense (p. 442)

ubiquity the belief that media are everywhere (p. 377)

uncertainty a factor explaining why people seek guidance from the media agenda. It refers to how much information a person believes they already possess about an issue (p. 363)

uncertainty avoidance an attempt to avoid ambiguous situations (p. 149)

unwanted repetitive patterns (URPs) recurring, undesirable conflicts in a relationship (p. 98)

utility a criterion for evaluating theories; refers to the theory's usefulness or practical value (Ch. 3) (p. 56)

utility using the media to accomplish specific tasks (Ch. 23) (p. 396)

validity the truth value of an observation (p. 63)

victimage the way we attempt to purge the guilt we feel as part of being human (p. 330)

violation valence perceived negative or positive assessment of an unexpected behavior (p. 128)

violence index a yearly content analysis of prime-time network programming to assess the amount of violence represented (p. 406)

warranting the perceived legitimacy and validity of information about another person that one may receive or observe online (p. 230)

whistle-blowing process in which individuals report unethical or illegal behaviors or practices to others (p. 250)

wholeness a fundamental property of systems theory stating that systems are more than the sum of their individual parts (p. 54)

References

Abrams, J., O'Connor, J., & Giles, H. (2003). Identity and intergroup communication. In W. B. Gudykunst (Ed.), *Cross-cultural and intercultural communication* (pp. 209–224). Thousand Oaks, CA: Sage.

Acquisti, A., John, L. K., & Lowenstein, G. (2012). The impact of relative standards on the propensity to disclose. *Journal of Marketing Research, 49*, 160–174.

Afifi, W. A., & Burgoon, J. K. (2000). The impact of violations on uncertainty and the consequences for attractiveness. *Human Communication Research, 26*, 203–233.

Ahmed, R. (2009). Interface of political opportunism and Islamic extremism in Bangladesh: Rhetorical identification in government response. *Communication Studies, 60*(1), 82–96.

Alkhazraji, K. M. (1997). The acculturation of immigrants to U.S. organizations: The case of Muslim employees. *Management Communication Quarterly, 11*, 217–265.

Allen, B. J. (2007). Theorizing communication and race. *Communication Monographs, 74*, 259–264.

Altman, I. (1975). *The environment and social behavior.* Monterey, CA: Brooks/Cole.

Altman, I., & Taylor, D. A. (1973). *Social penetration: The development of interpersonal relationships.* New York, NY: Holt, Rinehart & Winston.

Altman, I., Vinsel, A., & Brown, B. (1981). Dialectic conceptions in social psychology: An application to social penetration and privacy regulation. In L. Berkowitz (Ed.), *Advances in experimental social psychology* (pp. 130–145). New York, NY: Academic Press.

Alwood, E. (1997, October 14). The power of persuasion: The media's role in addressing homosexual issues in the future. *The Advocate,* p. 54.

An overview of media ecology. Retrieved from http://www.media-ecology.org/media_ecology/index.html#An%20Overview%20of%20Media%20Ecology%20(Lance%20Strate)

Andersen, K. E. (2003). *Recovering the civic culture: The imperative of ethical communication.* Boston, MA: Pearson/Allyn & Bacon.

Anderson, I. K. (2011). The uses and gratifications of online care pages: A study of CaringBridge. *Health Communication, 26*(6), 546–559.

Anderson, K., & Cantor, M. (2011). Inventing a gay agenda: Students' perceptions of lesbian and gay professors. *Journal of Applied Social Psychology, 41*, 1538–1564.

Anderson, R., & Ross, V. (2002). *Questions of communication: A practical introduction to theory,* 2nd ed. New York, NY: St. Martin's Press.

Anderson, T. L., & Emmers-Sommer, T. M. (2006). Predictors of relationship satisfaction in online romantic relationships. *Communication Studies, 57*, 153–172.

Andrews, M. (2002). Feminist research with non-feminist and anti-feminist women: Meeting the challenge. *Feminism & Psychology, 12*, 55–77.

Anguiano, C., Milstein, T., De Larkin, I., Chen, Y., & Sandoval, J. (2012). Connecting community voices: Using a Latino/a critical race theory lens on environmental justice advocacy. *Journal of International and Intercultural Communication, 5*(2), 124–143.

Antheunis, M. L., Valkenburg, P. M., & Peter, J. (2010). Getting acquainted through social network sites: Testing a model of online uncertainty reduction and social attraction. *Computers in Human Behavior, 26*(1), 100–109.

Apker, J., Propp, K. M., & Ford, W. S. Z. (2005). Negotiating status and identity tensions in health-care team interactions: An exploration of nurse role dialectics. *Journal of Applied Communication Research, 33*, 93–115.

Appel, E. C. (2003). Rush to judgment: Burlesque, tragedy, and hierarchical alchemy in the rhetoric of America's foremost political talkshow host. *Southern Communication Journal, 68*, 217–230.

Ardener, E. (1975). The "problem" revisited. In S. Ardener (Ed.), *Perceiving women* (pp. 19–27). London: Malaby Press.

Ardener, S. (1978). Introduction: The nature of women in society. In S. Ardener (Ed.), *Defining females* (pp. 9–48). New York, NY: Wiley.

Ardener, S. (2005). Muted group theory excerpts. *Women and Language, 28*, 50–72.

Argo, J. J., & Shiv, B. (2012). Are white lies as innocuous as we think? *Journal of Consumer Research, 38*(6), 1093–1102.

Arneson, P. (2007). A conversation about communication ethics with Kenneth A. Andersen. In P. Arneson (Ed.), *Exploring communication ethics* (pp. 131–142). New York, NY: Peter Lang.

Arnhart, L. (1981). *Aristotle on political reasoning: A commentary on rhetoric.* DeKalb, IL: Northern Illinois University Press.

Aron, A., & Aron, E. N. (1989). *The heart of social psychology: A backstage view of a passionate science,* 2nd ed. Lexington, MA: Lexington Books.

Aronson, E. (1969). The theory of cognitive dissonance: A current perspective. In L. Berkowitz (Ed.), *Advances in experimental social psychology* (pp. 1–34). New York, NY: Academic Press.

Asante, M. K. (1987). *The Afrocentric idea*: Philadelphia, PA: Temple University.

Asch, S. E. (1951). Effects of group pressure upon the modification and distortion of judgments. In J. Guetzkow (Ed.), *Groups, leadership, and men: Research in human relations* (pp. 177–190). New York, NY: Russell & Russell.

Atkins, D. C., Rubin, T. N., Steyvers, M., Doeden, M. A., Baucom, B. R., & Christensen, A. (2012). Topic models: A novel method for modeling couple and family text data. *Journal of Family Psychology, 5*, 816–827.

Aubrey, J. S., Olson, L., Fine, M., Hauser, T., Rhea, D., Kaylor, B., & Yang, A. (2012). Investigating personality and viewing-motivation correlates of reality television exposure. *Communication Quarterly, 60*(1), 80–102.

Austin, J. L. (1975). *How to do things with words.* Cambridge, MA: Harvard University Press.

Ayyad, K. (2011). Internet usage vs. traditional media usage among university students in the United Arab Emirates. *Journal of Arab & Muslim Media Research, 4*(1), 41–61.

Bachman, G. F., & Guerrero, L. K. (2006). Forgiveness, apology, and communicative responses to hurtful events. *Communication Reports, 19*, 45–56.

Bachman, G. F., & Guerrero, L. K. (2008). Relational quality and relationships: An expectancy violations analysis. *Journal of Social and Personal Relationships, 23*, 943–963.

Ballard-Reisch, D. (2010). Muted groups in health communication policy and practice: The case of older adults in rural and frontier areas. *Women & Language, 33*(2), 87–93.

Bandura, A. (1977). *Social learning theory.* Englewood Cliffs, NJ: Prentice Hall.

Banks, S. P., & Riley, P. (1993). Structuration theory as ontology for communication research. In S. A. Deetz (Ed.), *Communication yearbook 16* (pp. 167–196). Newbury Park, CA: Sage.

Bantz, C. R. (1989). Organizing and the social psychology of organizing. *Communication Studies, 40*, 231–240.

Baran, J. S. (2012). *Introduction to mass communication: Media literacy and culture.* New York, NY: McGraw-Hill.

Baran, S. J., & Davis, D. K. (2009). *Mass communication theory: Foundations, ferment, and future,* 5th ed. Belmont, CA: Wadsworth.

Baran, S. J., & Davis, D. K. (2012). *Mass communication theory: Foundations, ferment and future,* 6th ed. Belmont, CA: Wadsworth.

Bareket-Bojmel, L., & Sharar, G. (2011a). Emotional and interpersonal consequences of self-disclosure in a lived online interaction. *Journal of Clinical and Social Psychology, 30*, 225–250.

Bareket-Bojmel, L., & Shahar, G. (2011b). Emotional and interpersonal consequences of self-disclosure in a lived, online interaction. *Journal of Social and Clinical Psychology, 30*, 732–759.

Barge, J. K., & Pearce, W. B. (2004). A reconnaissance of CMM research. *Human Systems, 13*, 13–32.

Barker, R. T., Rimler, G. W., Moreno, E., & Kaplan, T. E. (2004). Family business members' narrative perceptions: Values, succession, and commitment. *Journal of Technical Writing and Communication, 34*, 291–320.

Barnlund, D. C. (1970). A transactional model of communication. In K. K. Sereno & C. D. Mortensen (Eds.), *Foundations of communication theory* (pp. 83–102). New York, NY: Harper.

Basic McLuhan: Marshall McLuhan and the senses. Retrieved from http://ns.gingkopress.net/02-mcl/z_mcluhan-and-the-senses.html

Baym N., Campbell, S. W., Horst, H., Kalyanaraman, S., Oliver, M. B., Rothenbuhler, E., … Miller, K. (2012). Communication theory and research in the age of new media: A conversation from the CM café. *Communication Monographs, 79*(2), 256–267.

Baxter, L. A. (1988). A dialectical perspective on communication strategies in relationship development. In S. Duck (Ed.), *Handbook of personal relationships* (pp. 257–273). New York, NY: Wiley.

Baxter, L. A. (1990). Dialectical contradictions in relationship development. *Journal of Social and Personal Relationships, 7*, 69–88.

Baxter, L. A. (2006). Relational dialectics theory: Multivocal dialogues of family communication. In D. O. Braithwaite & L. A. Baxter (Eds.), *Engaging theories in family communication: Multiple perspectives* (pp. 130–145). Thousand Oaks, CA: Sage.

Baxter, L. A. (2011). *Voicing relationships.* Thousand Oaks, CA: Sage.

Baxter, L. A., & Babbie, E. R. (2004). *The basics of communication research.* Belmont, CA: Wadsworth.

Baxter, L. A., & Braithwaite, D. O. (2008). Relational dialectics theory. In L. A. Baxter & D. O. Braithwaite (Eds.), *Engaging theories in interpersonal communication: Multiple perspectives* (pp. 349– 361). Thousand Oaks, CA: Sage.

Baxter, L. A., & Braithwaite, D. O. (2010). Relational dialectics theory, applied. In S. W. Smith & S. R. Wilson (Eds.), *New directions in interpersonal communication* (pp. 48–66). Thousand Oaks, CA. Sage.

Baxter, L. A., Braithwaite, D. O., Bryant, L., & Wagner, A. (2004). Stepchildren's perceptions of the contradictions in communication with step-parents. *Journal of Social and Personal Relationships, 21*, 447–467.

Baxter, L. A., Braithwaite, D. O., Golish, T. D., & Olson, L. N. (2002). Contradictions of interaction for wives of elderly husbands with adult dementia. *Journal of Applied Communication Research, 30*, 1–26.

Baxter, L. A., & Montgomery, B. M. (1996). *Relating: Dialogues and dialectics.* New York, NY: Guilford Press.

Baxter, L. A., & Sahlstein, E. M. (2000). Some possible directions for future research. In S. Petronio (Ed.), *Balancing the secrets of private disclosures* (pp. 289–300). Mahwah, NJ: Erlbaum.

Bean, C. J., & Eisenberg, E. (2006). Employee sensemaking in the transition to nomadic work. *Journal of Organizational Change Management, 19*, 210–222.

Beaver, D. G. (2011). *Teacher fashion, classroom homophily, and the impact on student evaluations.* Unpublished Masters thesis. Texas Tech University, Lubbock, TX.

Beavin-Bevelas, J. (1990). *Equivocal communication.* Newbury Park, CA: Sage.

Bell, K. E., Orbe, M. P., Drummond, D. K., & Camara, S. K. (2000). Accepting the challenge of centralizing without essentializing: Black feminist thought and African American women's communicative experiences. *Women's Studies in Communication, 23*, 41–62.

Bellamy, R. V., & Walker, J. R. (1996). *Television and the remote control: Grazing on a vast wasteland.* New York, NY: Guilford Press.

Bem, D. J. (1967). Self-perception: An alternative interpretation of cognitive dissonance phenomena. *Psychological Review, 74*, 183–200.

Bem, S. (1993). *The lenses of gender: Transforming the debate on sexual inequality.* New Haven, CT: Yale University Press.

Benning, J. (2003). Remembering Neil Postman. Retrieved from www.alternet.org

Bentley, J. M. (2012). A uses and gratifications study of contemporary Christian radio websites. *Journal of Radio & Audio Media, 19*(1), 2–16.

Berbary, L. A. (2012). "Don't be a whore, that's not ladylike": Discursive discipline and sorority women's gendered subjectivity. *Qualitative Inquiry, 18*, 606–625.

Berger, A. A. (2007). *Media & society: A critical perspective.* Lanham, MD: Rowman & Littlefield.

Berger, C. R. (1977). The covering law perspective as a theoretical basis for the study of human communication. *Communication Quarterly, 25*, 7–18.

Berger, C. R. (1979). Beyond initial interaction: Uncertainty, understanding, and the development of interpersonal relationships. In H. Giles & R. St. Clair (Eds.), *Language and social psychology* (pp. 122–144). Oxford: Blackwell.

Berger, C. R. (1982). *Social cognition and the development of interpersonal relationships: The quest for social knowledge.* Paper presented at the First International Conference on Personal Relationships, Madison, WI.

Berger, C. R. (1986). Uncertain outcome values in predicted relationships: Uncertainty reduction theory then and now. *Human Communication Research, 13*, 34–38.

Berger, C. R. (1987). Communicating under uncertainty. In M. E. Roloff & G. R. Miller (Eds.), *Interpersonal processes: New directions in communication research* (pp. 39–62). Newbury Park, CA: Sage.

Berger, C. R. (1995). Inscrutable goals, uncertain plans, and the production of communicative action. In C. R. Berger & M. Burgoon (Eds.), *Communication and social processes* (pp. 1–28). East Lansing, MI: Michigan State University Press.

Berger, C. R. (2005). Slippery slopes to apprehension: Rationality and graphical depictions of increasingly threatening trends. *Communication Research, 32*, 3–28.

Berger, C. R. (2011). From explanation to application. *Journal of Applied Communication Research, 39*(2), 214–222.

Berger, C. R., & Bradac, J. J. (1982). *Language and social knowledge: Uncertainty in interpersonal relations.* London: Arnold.

Berger, C. R., & Calabrese, R. J. (1975). Some explorations in initial interaction and beyond: Toward a developmental theory of interpersonal communication. *Human Communication Research, 1*, 99–112.

Berger, C. R., & Gudykunst, W. B. (1991). Uncertainty and communication. In B. Dervin & M. J. Voight (Eds.), *Progress in communication sciences* (Vol. 10, pp. 21–66). Norwood, NJ: Ablex.

Berger, C. R., & Kellerman, K. (1994). Acquiring social information. In J. A. Daly & J. Weimann (Eds.), *Strategic interpersonal communication* (pp. 1–31). Hillsdale, NJ: Erlbaum.

Berger, C. R., & Roloff, M. E. (1980). Social cognition self-awareness and interpersonal communication. In B. Dervin & M. Voigt (Eds.), *Progress in communication sciences* (Vol. 2, pp. 158–172). Norwood, NJ: Ablex.

Berkowitz, D., & Belgrave, L. L. (2010). "She works hard for the money": Drag queens and the management of their contradictory status of celebrity and marginality. *Journal of Contemporary Ethnography, 39*(2), 159.

Bern-Klug, M. (2009). A framework for categorizing social interactions related to end of life care in nursing homes. *The Gerontologist, 49*(4), 495–507.

Berscheid, E., & Walster, E. H. (1978). *Interpersonal attraction.* Reading, MA: Addison-Wesley.

Beullens, K., Roe, K., & Van den Bulk, J. (2011). The impact of adolescents' news and action movie viewing on risky driving behavior: A longitudinal study. *Human Communication Research, 37*(4), 488–508.

Bienenstock, E. J., & Bianchi, A. J. (2004). Activating performance expectations and status differences through gift exchange: Experimental results. *Social Psychology Quarterly, 67*, 310–318.

Bignell J. (2013). *An introduction to television studies.* New York, NY: Routledge.

Bisel, R. S., & Arterburn, E. N. (2012). Making sense of organizational members' silence: A sensemaking-resource model. *Communication Research Reports, 29*, 217–226.

Bishop, J. W., Scott, K. D., Goldsby, M. G., & Cropanzano, R. (2005). A construct validity study of commitment and perceived support variables: A multifoci approach across different team environments. *Group Organizational Management, 30*, 153–180.

Blackwell, D. M. (2010). Sidelines and separate spaces: Making education anti-racist for students of color. *Race, Ethnicity & Education, 13*(4), 473–494.

Blair-Loy, M., Hochschild, A., Pugh, A. J., Williams, J. C., & Hartman, H. (2015). Stability and transformation in gender, work, and family: Insights from *the second shift* for the next quarter century. *Community, Work & Family, 18*, 435–454.

Blakeslee, S. (2005, June 28). What other people say may change what you see. *New York Times*, p. 11.

Blalock, H. M. (1969). *Theory construction: From verbal to mathematical formulations.* Englewood Cliffs, NJ: Prentice Hall.

Blau, P. M. (1964). *Exchange and power in social life.* New York, NY: Wiley.

Blomme, R. (2012). How managers can conduct planned change in self-organizing systems: Actor network theory as a perspective to manager's actions. *International Journal of Business Administration, 3*, 9–22.

Blumer, H. (1969). *Symbolic interactionism: Perspective and method.* Englewood Cliffs, NJ: Prentice Hall.

Blumler, J. G. (1979). The role of theory in uses and gratifications studies. *Communication Research, 6*, 9–36.

Blumler, J. G. (1985). The social character of media gratifications. In K. E. Rosengren, L. A. Wenner, & P. Palmgreen (Eds.), *Media gratifications research: Current perspectives* (pp. 41–60). Beverly Hills, CA: Sage.

Blumler, J. G., & McQuail, D. (1969). *Television in politics: Its uses and influence.* Chicago, IL: University of Chicago Press.

Bodie, G. D., & Jones, S. M. (2012). The nature of supportive listening II: The role of verbal person centeredness and nonverbal immediacy. *Western Journal of Communication, 76*(3), 250–269.

Bolkan, S., & Goodboy, A. K. (2011). Leadership in the classroom: The use of charismatic leadership as a deterrent to student resistance strategies. *Journal of Classroom Interaction, 46*, 4–10.

Bolkan, S., Goodboy, A. K., & Bachman, G. F. (2012). Antecedents of consumer repatronage intentions and negative word-of-mouth behaviors following an organizational failure: A test of investment model predictions. *Journal of Applied Communication Research, 40*(1), 107–125.

Book discussion on *Technopoly*. Retrieved from https://www.c-span.org/video/?31627-1/technopoly

Book, P. L. (1996). How does the family narrative influence the individual's ability to communicate about death? *Omega, 33,* 323–341.

Booth-Butterfield, M., Booth-Butterfield, S., & Koester, J. (1988). The function of uncertainty reduction in alleviating primary tension in small groups. *Communication Research Reports, 5,* 146–153.

Booth-Butterfield, M., & Jordan, F. (1989). Communication adaptation among racially homogeneous and heterogeneous groups. *Southern Communication Journal, 54,* 253–272.

Bormann, E. G. (1996). Symbolic convergence theory and communication in group decision making. In R. Y. Hirokawa & M. S. Poole (Eds.), *Communication and group decision making* (pp. 81–113). Thousand Oaks, CA: Sage.

Borrowman, S., & Kmetz, M. (2011). Divided we stand: Beyond Burkean identification. *Rhetoric Review, 30*(3), 275–292.

Bostrom, R. N. (2003). Theories, data, and communication research. *Communication Monographs, 70,* 275–294.

Bostrom, R. N. (2004). Empiricism, paradigms, and data. *Communication Monographs, 71,* 343–351.

Boulding, K. (1990). *Three faces of power.* Newbury Park, CA: Sage.

Bourhis, R. Y., & Giles, H. (1977). The language of intergroup distinctiveness. In H. Giles (Ed.), *Language, ethnicity and intergroup relations* (pp. 119–135). London: Academic Press.

Bourhis, R. Y., Sioufi, R., & Sachdev, I. (2012). Ethnolinguistic interaction and multilingual communication. In H. Giles (Ed.), *The handbook of intergroup communication* (pp. 100–115). New York, NY: Routledge.

Boyle, M. P., Schmierbach, M., Armstrong, C. L., McLeod, D. M., Shah, D. V., & Pan, Z. (2004). Information seeking and emotional reactions to the September 11 terrorist attacks. *Journalism & Mass Communication Quarterly, 81,* 155–167.

Boysen, G. A. (2008). Revenge and student evaluations of teaching. *Teaching of Psychology, 35,* 218–222.

Braithwaite, D. O., & Baxter, L. A. (1995). "I do" again: The relational dialectics of renewing marriage vows. *Journal of Social and Personal Relationships, 12,* 177–198.

Braithwaite, D. O., Toller, P. W., Daas, K. L., Durham, W. T., & Jones, A. C. (2008). Centered but not caught in the middle: Stepchildren's perceptions of dialectical contradictions in the communication of co-parents. *Journal of Applied Communication Research, 36,* 33–55.

Brann, M., & Mattson, M. (2004). Reframing communication during gynecological exams: A feminist virtue ethic of care perspective. In P. M. Buzzanell, H. Sterk, & L. H. Turner (Eds.), *Gender in applied communication contexts* (pp. 147–168). Thousand Oaks, CA: Sage.

Brasfield, R. (2007). Rereading *Sex and the City:* Exposing the hegemonic feminist narrative. *Journal of Popular Film and Television, 34,* 130–139.

Brashers, D. E. (2001). Communication and uncertainty management. *Journal of Communication, 3,* 477–497.

Bremer, M. (2012). *Organizational culture.* Netherlands: Kikker Group.

Brenders, D. A. (1987). Fallacies in the coordinated management of meaning: A philosophy of language critique of the hierarchical organization of coherent conversation and related theory. *Quarterly Journal of Speech, 73,* 329–348.

Breuer, J., Kowert, R., Festl, R., & Thorsten, Q. (2015). Sexist games=sexist gamers? A longitudinal study on the relationship between video game use and sexist attitudes. *Cyberpsychology, Behavior, and Social Networking, 18,* 197–202.

Brewer, P. R., & Ley, B. L. (2010). Media use and public perceptions of DNA evidence. *Science Communication, 32,* 93–117.

Briefing paper: Social media and public opinion. Retrieved from http://www.langerresearch.com/uploads/Langer_Research_Briefing_Paper-Social_Media_and_Public_Opinion_Oct2012_update.pdf

Broadus, J. (2012). *On the preparation and delivery of sermons.* Mulberry, IN: Southern Grace Publishers.

Brody, H. (2012). From an ethics of rationing to an ethics of waste avoidance. *New England Journal of Medicine, 366,* 1949–1951.

Broger, D. (2011). *Structuration theory and organization research.* Unpublished doctoral dissertation. University of St. Gallen, St. Gallen, Switzerland.

Brooks, D. E., & Ward, C. J. (2007). "Crash" course: Assessing students' engagement with pedagogies of diversity. *Journalism & Mass Communication Educator, 62,* 244–262.

Brown, D., Lauricella, S., Douai, A., & Zaidi, A. (2012). Consuming television crime drama: A uses and gratifications approach. *American Communication Journal, 14*(1), 47–61.

Brown, R. (1965). *Social psychology*. New York, NY: Free Press.

Brown, R. D., (2012). *Dying on the job: Murder and mayhem in the American workplace*. Lanham, MD: Rowman & Littlefield.

Brown, P., & Levinson, S. (1978). Universals in language usage: Politeness phenomenon. In E. Goody (Ed.), *Questions and politeness* (pp. 56–89). Cambridge, UK: Cambridge University Press.

Brown, P., & Levinson, S. C. (1987). *Politeness: Some universals in language use*. Cambridge, UK: Cambridge University Press.

Brownstein, A. L., Read, S. J., & Simon, D. (2004). Bias at the racetrack: Effects of individual expertise and task importance on predecision reevaluation of alternatives. *Personality and Social Psychology Bulletin, 30*, 891–909.

Brubaker, J. (2008). The freedom to choose a personal agenda: Removing our reliance on the media agenda. *American Communication Journal, 10*(3), 1–14.

Brummett, B. (1993). Introduction. In B. Brummett (Ed.), *Landmark essays on Kenneth Burke* (pp. xi–xix). Davis, CA: Hermagoras Press.

Bryant, E. M., & Marmo, J. M. (2012). The rules of *Facebook* friendship: A two-stage examination of interaction rules in close, casual, and acquaintance friendships. *Journal of Social and Personal Relationships, 29*, 1013–1025.

Bryant, E. M., Marmo, J., & Ramirez, A. (2011) A functional approach to social networking sites. In K. Wright & L. Webb (Eds.), *Computer-mediated communication in personal relationships* (pp. 3–20). New York, NY: Peter Lang.

Bryant, J., & Miron, D. (2004). Theory and research in mass communication. *Journal of Communication, 54*, 662–704.

Bryant, L. E. (2003). *Stepchildren's perceptions of the contradictions in communication with stepfamilies formed post bereavement*. Unpublished doctoral dissertation, University of Nebraska, Lincoln, NE.

Budd, M., Entman, R. M., & Steinman, C. (1990). The affirmative character of U.S. cultural studies. *Critical Studies in Mass Communication, 7*, 169–184.

Budd, M., & Steinman, C. (1992). Cultural studies and the politics of encoding research. In S. A. Deetz (Ed.), *Communication yearbook 15* (pp. 251–262). Newbury Park, CA: Sage

Buffington, D., & Fraley, T. (2008). Skill in black and white: Negotiating media images of race in a sporting context. *Journal of Communication Inquiry, 32*, 292–310.

Bugeja, M. (2005). *Interpersonal divide: The search for community in a technological age*. New York, NY: Oxford University Press.

Buldioski, D. (2012). The electronic storyteller. Retrieved from http://www.youtube.com/watch?v=toc5KHWZx4A

Bullingham, L., & Vasconcelos, A. C. (2013). 'The presentation of self in the online world': Goffman and the study of online identities. *Journal of Information Science, 39*, 1–29.

Bunz, U., & Campbell, S. W. (2004). Politeness accommodation in electronic mail. *Communication Research Reports, 21*, 11–25.

Burgess, E. W., & Locke, H. J. (1953). *The family: From institution to companionship*, 2nd ed. New York, NY: American Book Company.

Burgoon, J. K. (1978). A communication model of personal space violations: Explication and an initial test. *Human Communication Research, 4*, 129–142.

Burgoon, J. K. (1994). Nonverbal signals. In M. L. Knapp & G. R. Miller (Eds.), *Handbook of interpersonal communication* (pp. 229–285). Newbury Park, CA: Sage.

Burgoon, J. K., Coker, D. A., & Coker, R. A. (1986). Communicative effects of gaze behavior: A test of two contrasting explanations. *Human Communication Research, 12*, 495–524.

Burgoon, J. K., Dillman, L., & Stern, L. A. (1993). Adaption in dyadic interaction: Defining and operationalizing patterns of reciprocity and compensation. *Communication Theory, 3*, 295–316.

Burgoon, J. K., & Hale, J. L. (1988). Nonverbal expectancy violations: Model elaboration and application to immediacy behaviors. *Communication Monographs, 55*, 58–79.

Burgoon, J. K., & Jones, S. B. (1976). Toward a theory of personal space expectations and their violations. *Human Communication Research, 2*, 131–146.

Burgoon, J. K., & Walther, J. B. (1990). Nonverbal expectancies and the evaluative consequences of violations. *Human Communication Research, 17*, 232–265.

Burke, K. (1945). *A grammar of motives*. New York, NY: Prentice Hall.

Burke, K. (1950). *A rhetoric of motives*. New York, NY: Prentice Hall.

Burke, K. (1965). *Permanence and change*. Indianapolis, IN: Bobbs-Merrill.

Burke, K. (1966). *Language as symbolic action: Essays on life, literature, and method*. Berkeley, CA: University of California Press.

Burke, K. (1968). Dramatism. In D. L. Sills (Ed.), *The international encyclopedia of the social sciences*, *7* (pp. 445–452). New York, NY: Macmillan/Free Press.

Burke, K. (2007). On persuasion, identification, and dialectical symbols. *Philosophy and Rhetoric*, *39*, 333–339.

Burnett, A., Mattern, J. L., Herakova, L. L., Kahl, D. H., Tobola, C., & Bornsen, S. E. (2009). Communicating /muting date rape: A co-cultural theoretical analysis of communication factors related to rape culture on a college campus. *Journal of Applied Communication Research*, *37*(4), 465–485.

Burns, M. E. (2009). Gold medal storytelling: NBC's hegemonic use of Olympic athlete narratives. *Journal of the Communication, Speech & Theatre Association of North Dakota*, *22*, 19–29.

Bute, J. J., & Jensen, R. E. (2011). Narrative sensemaking and time lapse: Interviews with low-income women about sex education. *Communication Monographs*, *78*(2), 212–232.

Bute, J. J., & Vik, T. A. (2010). Privacy management as unfinished business: Shifting boundaries in the context of infertility. *Communication Studies*, *61*(1), 1–20.

Buzzanell, P. M. (2004). Revisiting sexual harassment in academe: Using feminist ethical and sensemaking approaches to analyze macrodiscourses and micropractices of sexual harassment. In P. M. Buzzanell, H. Sterk, & L. H. Turner (Eds.), *Gender in applied communication contexts* (pp. 25–46). Thousand Oaks, CA: Sage.

Buzzanell, P. M., Burrell, N. A., Stafford, R. S., & Berkowitz, S. (1996). When I call you up and you're not there: Application of communication accommodation theory to telephone answering machine messages. *Western Journal of Communication*, *60*, 310–336.

Buzzanell, P. M., & Turner, L. H. (2003). Emotion work revealed by job loss discourse: Backgrounding-foregrounding of feelings, construction of normalcy, and (re)instituting of traditional masculinities. *Journal of Applied Communication Research*, *31*, 27–57.

Buzzanell, P. M., & Turner, L. H. (2012). Effective family communication and job loss: Crafting the narrative for family crisis. In F. C. Dickson & L. M. Webb (Eds.), *Communication for families in crisis: Theories, research, strategies* (pp. 281–306). New York, NY: Peter Lang.

Calzo, J. P., & Ward, L. M. (2009). Media exposure and viewers' attitudes toward homosexuality: Evidence for mainstreaming or resonance? *Journal of Broadcasting & Electronic Media*, *53*(2), 280–299.

Campbell, D. T. (1965). Variation and selective retention in socio-cultural evolution. In H. R. Barringer, G. I. Blanksten, & R. W. Mack (Eds.), *Social change in developing areas* (pp. 19–49). Cambridge, MA: Schenkman.

Career guide to the safety profession. Retrieved from http://www.com.edu/gcsi/docs/careergd.pdf

Carey, J. W. (1975). A cultural approach to communication. *Communication*, *2*, 1–22.

Carey, J. W. (1989). *Communication as culture*. Boston, MA: Unwin Hyman.

Carey, J. W. (1998). Marshall McLuhan: Genealogy and legacy. *Canadian Journal of Communication*, *23*, 13–21.

Carlson, J. M. (1983). Crime show viewing by pre-adults: The impact on attitudes toward civil liberties. *Communication Research*, *10*, 529–552.

Carr, K., & Wang, T. R. (2012). "Forgiveness isn't a simple process: It's a vast undertaking": Negotiating and communicating forgiveness in nonvoluntary family relationships. *Journal of Family Communication*, *12*(1), 40–56.

Casteleyn, J., Mottart, A., & Rutten, K. (2009). How to use Facebook in your market research. *International Journal of Market Research*, *51*(4), 439–447.

Chafetz, J. S. (1997). Feminist theory and sociology: Underutilized contributions for main stream theory. *Annual Review of Sociology*, *23*, 97–120.

Chen, K. (2011). *A test of the spiral of silence theory on young adults' use of social networking sites for political purposes*. Unpublished doctoral dissertation. Iowa State University, Ames, IA.

Chen, Y. W. (2006). *The Twain have met! Investigating crucial indicators for intercultural friendship levels between international students from four East Asian countries and U.S. Americans*. Paper presented at the annual meeting of the International Communication Association, Singapore.

Chen, Y. & Nakazawa, M. (2012). Measuring patterns of self-disclosure in intercultural friendship: Adjusting differential item functioning using multiple-indicators, multiple-causes models. *Journal of Intercultural Communication Research*, *41*, 131–151.

Cheney, G., Munshi, D., May, S., & Ortiz, S. (Eds.). (2010). *Handbook of communication ethics*. New York, NY: Routledge.

Chesebro, J. W. (1993). Preface. In J. W. Chesebro (Ed.), *Extensions of the Burkeian system* (pp. vii–xxi). Tuscaloosa, AL: University of Alabama Press.

Chia, S. C., & Lee, W. (2008). Pluralistic ignorance about sex: The direct and the indirect effects of media consumption on college students' misperception of sex-related peer norms. *International Journal of Public Opinion Research, 20*, 53–73.

Child, J. T., Pearson, J. C., & Nagao, M. (2006). Elusive family problems reported by Japanese college students: An examination of theme variation and methodology. *Journal of Intercultural Communication Research, 35*, 45–59.

Child, J. T., Pearson, J. C., & Petronio, S. (2009). Blogging, communication, and privacy management: Development of the blogging privacy management measure. *Journal of the American Society for Information Science & Technology, 60*(10), 2079–2094.

Cho, H., Rivera-Sánchez, M., & Lim, S. S. (2009). A multinational study on online privacy: Global concerns and local responses. *New Media & Society, 11*(3), 395–416.

Chopra, R. (2001). Retrieving the father: Gender studies, "father love" and the discourse of mothering. *Women's Studies International Forum, 24*, 445–455.

Chory-Assad, R. M., & Tamborini, R. (2003). Television exposure and the public's perceptions of physicians. *Journal of Broadcasting & Electronic Media, 47*(2), 197–215.

Cirksena, K., & Cuklanz, L. (1992). Male is to female as _____ is to: A guided tour of five feminist frameworks for communication studies. In L. Rakow (Ed.), *Women making meaning: New feminist directions in communication* (pp. 18–44). New York, NY: Routledge.

Clair, R. P. (1993). The use of framing devices to sequester organizational narratives: Hegemony and harassment. *Communication Monographs, 60*, 113–136.

Clark, G. (2004). *Rhetorical landscapes in America: Variations on a theme from Kenneth Burke.* Columbia, SC: University of South Carolina Press.

Clason, M. (2008). *Constructions of masculinity and femininity and their impact on sexual harassment in the workplace.* Unpublished dissertation, Marquette University, Milwaukee, WI.

Clawson, R., & Oxley, Z. (2017). *Public opinion: Democratic ideals, democratic practice.* Thousand Oaks, CA: CQ Press.

Cohen, B. (1963). *The press and foreign policy.* Princeton, NJ: Princeton University Press.

Cohen, E. (2007). *Expectancy violations in relationships with friends and media figures.* Paper presented at the annual meeting of the International Communication Association, San Francisco, CA.

Cohen, E. L. (2010). Expectancy violations in relationships with friends and media figures. *Communication Research Reports, 27*, 97–111.

Cohen, L. J., & DeBenedet, A. T. (2012, July 17). Penn State cover-up: Groupthink in action. *Time, 180.*

Coleman, R., & McCombs, M. (2007). The young and agenda-less? Exploring age-related differences in agenda setting on the youngest generation, baby boomers, and the civic generation. *Journalism & Mass Communication Quarterly, 84*(3), 495–508.

Coleman, R., & Wu, H. D. (2010). Proposing emotion as a dimension of affective agenda setting: Separating affect into two components and comparing their second-level effects. *Journalism & Mass Communication Quarterly, 87*(2), 315–327.

Collier, M. J. (1998). Researching cultural identity: Reconciling interpretive and postcolonial perspectives. In D. V. Tanno & A. Gonzalez (Eds.), *Communication and identity across cultures* (pp. 122–147). Thousand Oaks, CA: Sage.

Collins, P. H. (1986). Learning from the outsider within: The sociological significance of black feminist thought. *Social Problems, 33,* 14–32.

Collins, P. H. (1989). A comparison of two works on Black family life. *Signs, 14*, 875–884.

Collins, P. H. (1991). *Black feminist thought: Knowledge, consciousness, and the politics of empowerment.* New York, NY: Routledge.

Collins, P. H. (2000). The power of self-definition. In P. H. Collins (Ed.), *Black feminist thought: Knowledge, consciousness, and the politics of empowerment* (pp. 105–132). New York, NY: Routledge.

Condit, C. M. (1992). Post-Burke: Transcending the substance of dramatism. *Quarterly Journal of Speech, 78*, 349–355.

Conquergood, D. (1992). Life in Big Red: Struggles and accommodations in a Chicago polyethnic tenement. In L. Lamphere (Ed.), *Structuring diversity: Ethnographic perspectives on the new immigration* (pp. 95–144). Chicago, IL: University of Chicago Press.

Conquergood, D. (1994). Homeboys and hoods: Gang communication and cultural space. In L. R. Frey (Ed.), *Group communication in context: Studies of natural groups* (pp. 23–55). Hillsdale, NJ: Erlbaum.

Conrad, C., & Macom, E. A. (1995). Revisiting Kenneth Burke: Dramatism/logology and the problem of agency. *Southern Communication Journal, 61*, 11–28.

Cook, K. S., & Rice, E. (2003). Social exchange theory. In J. Delamater (Ed.), *Handbook of social psychology* (pp. 53–76). New York, NY: Kluwer Academic/Plenum.

Cooley, C. H. (1972). *Human nature and social order*. Glencoe, IL: Free Press.

Coontz, S. (1988). *The social origins of private life*. New York, NY: Verso.

Cooper, J. M. (1996). An Aristotelian theory of the emotions. In A. O. Rorty (Ed.), *Essays on Aristotle's Rhetoric* (pp. 238–257). Berkeley, CA: University of California Press.

Cooper, L. (1932). *The rhetoric of Aristotle*. New York, NY: Appleton-Century-Crofts.

Cooper, J., & Fazio, R. H. (1984). A new look at dissonance theory. In L. Berkowitz (Ed.), *Advances in experimental social psychology* (pp. 229–266). Orlando, FL: Academic Press.

Cooper, J., & Stone, J. (2000). Cognitive dissonance and the social group. In D. J. Terry & M. A. Hogg (Eds.), *Attitudes, behavior, and social context: The role of norms and group membership* (pp. 227–244). Mahwah, NJ: Erlbaum.

Cottrell, N. B., Wack, D. L., Sekerak, G. J., & Rittle, H. (1968). Social facilitation of dominant responses by the presence of an audience and the mere presence of others. *Journal of Personality and Social Psychology, 9*, 245–250.

Coupland, D. (2010). *Marshall McLuhan: You know nothing of my work!* New York, NY: Atlas & Company.

Coupland, N., Coupland, J., Giles, H., & Henwood, K. (1988). Accommodating the elderly: Invoking and extending a theory. *Language in Society, 17*, 1–41.

Cox, E. M., & Ebbers, L. H. (2010). Exploring the persistence of adult women at a Midwest community college. *Community College Journal of Research & Practice, 34*(4), 337–359.

Cox, S. A., & Kramer, M. W. (1995). Communication during employee dismissals: Social exchange principles and group influences on employee exit. *Management Communication Quarterly, 9*, 156–190.

Craig, R. T. (1999). Communication theory as a field. *Communication Theory, 9*, 119–161.

Craig, R. T. (2007). Communication theory as a field. In R. T. Craig & H. L. Muller (Eds.), *Theorizing communication: Readings across traditions* (pp. 63–98). Thousand Oaks, CA: Sage.

Craig, R. T., & Muller, H. L. (2007). *Theorizing communication: Readings across traditions*. Thousand Oaks, CA: Sage.

Creede, C., Fisher-Yoshida, B., & Gallegos, P. V. (Eds.). (2012). *The reflective, facilitative, and interpretive practice of the Coordinated Management of Meaning: Making lives and making meaning*. Madison, NJ: Farleigh Dickinson University Press.

Cronen, V. E. (1995a). Coordinated management of meaning: The consequentiality of communication and the recapturing of experience. In S. J. Sigman (Ed.), *The consequentiality of communication* (pp. 17–66). Hillsdale, NJ: Erlbaum.

Cronen, V. E. (1995b). Practical theory and the tasks ahead for social approaches to communication. In W. Leeds-Hurwitz (Ed.), *Social approaches to communication* (pp. 217–242). New York, NY: Guilford Press.

Cronen, V. E., & Pearce, W. B. (1981). Logical force in interpersonal communication: A new concept of the "necessity" in social behaviors. *Communication, 6*, 5–67.

Cronen, V. E., Pearce, W. B., & Harris, L. M. (1982). The Coordinated Management of Meaning: A theory of communication. In F. E. X. Dance (Ed.), *Human communication theory* (pp. 67–89). New York, NY: Harper & Row.

Cronen, V. E., Pearce, W. B., & Snavely, L. M. (1979). A theory of rule-structure and types of episodes, and a study of perceived enmeshment in undesired repetitive patterns (URPs). In D. Nimmo (Ed.), *Communication yearbook 3* (pp. 225–239). New Brunswick, NJ: Transaction Books.

Croucher, S. M., Holody, K. J., Hicks, M. V., Oommen, D., & DeMaris, A. (2011). An examination of conflict style preferences in India. *International Journal of Conflict Management, 22*, 10–34.

Csikszentmihalyi, M. (1991). Reflections on the "Spiral of Silence." In J. A. Anderson (Ed.), *Communication yearbook 14* (pp. 294–298). Newbury Park, CA: Sage.

Cuddon, J. A. (2013). *Dictionary of literary terms and literary theory*. Hoboken, NJ: Wiley-Blackwell.

Culnan, M. J. & Markus, M. L. (1987). Information technologies. In F. M. Jablin, L. Putnam, K. H. Roberts, & L. W. Porter (Eds.), *Handbook of organizational communication: An interdisciplinary perspective* (pp. 420–443). Newbury Park, CA: Sage.

Cupach, W. R., & Spitzberg, B. H. (2011). *The dark side of close relationships II*. New York, NY: Routledge.

Cushman, D. P., & Cahn, D. D. (1985). *Communication in interpersonal relationships*. Albany, NY: SUNY Press.

Cushman, D. P., & Pearce, W. B. (1977). Generality and necessity in three types of human communication theory: Special attention to rules theory. In B. Ruben (Ed.), *Communication yearbook 1* (pp. 173–182). New Brunswick, NJ: Transaction Books.

Cushman, D., & Whiting, G. C. (1972). An approach to communication theory: Toward consensus on rules. *The Journal of Communication, 22*, 217–238.

Cultural Environment Movement. (1996). Viewers' declaration of independence. *Cultural environment monitor, 1*, 1.

Cupach, W. R., & Metts, S. (1994). *Facework*. Thousand Oaks, CA: Sage.

Currier, J. M., & Holland, J. M. (2012). Examining the role of combat loss among Vietnam veterans. *Journal of Traumatic Stress, 25*, 102–105.

Daas, K. L. (2011). The pieties of death: A Burkean analysis of the Tri-State crematory case. *Texas Speech Communication Journal, 36*(1), 82–93.

Daft, R. L. & Lengel, R. H. (1986). Organizational information requirements, media richness and structural design. *Management Science, 32*, 554–571.

Dainton, M., & Aylor, B. (2001). A relational uncertainty analysis of jealousy, trust, and maintenance in long-distance versus geographically close relationships. *Communication Quarterly, 49*, 172–188.

Dainton, M., & Zelley, E. D. (2014). *Applying communication theory for professional life*. Thousand Oaks, CA: Sage.

Dance, F. E. X. (1967). Toward a theory of human communication. In F. E. X. Dance (Ed.), *Human communication theory* (pp. 288–309). New York, NY: Holt.

Daniels, T. D., Spiker, B. D., & Papa, M. J. (2008). *Perspectives on organizational communication*. Boston, MA: McGraw-Hill.

Darwin, C. (1948). *The origin of species*. New York, NY: Random House.

Davis, A. J. (2012). *Defining mixed race on television: Defining Barack Obama and Saturday Night Live*. Unpublished Master's thesis. California State University, Sacramento, CA.

Davis, J. (2010). Architecture of the personal interactive homepage: Constructing the self through MySpace. *New Media & Society, 12*(7), 1103–1119.

D'Angelo, J., & Van Der Heide, B. (2013). The formation of physician impressions in online communities:

Negativity, positivity, and nonnormativity effects. *Communication Research, 41*, 49–72.

DeAndrea, D. C., & Walther, J. B. (2011). Attributions for inconsistencies between online and offline self-presentations. *Communication Research, 38*, 805–825.

Dearing, J. W., & Rogers, E. M. (1996). *Agenda-setting*. Thousand Oaks, CA: Sage.

DeFrancisco, V. (1991). The sounds of silence: How men silence women in marital relationships. *Discourse and Society, 2*, 355–370.

DeHart, P. (2012). *Laws common and unwritten: On the natural law and the possibility of civic cooperation for the common good*. APSA 2012 Annual Meeting Paper. Retrieved from http://ssrn.com/abstract=2110682

Delaney, T. (2008). *Simpsonology*. Amherst, NY: Prometheus Books.

Delisay, F. (2012). The spiral of silence and conflict avoidance: Examining antecedents of opinion expression concerning the U.S. military buildup in the Pacific Island of Guam. *Communication Quarterly, 60*, 481–503.

Dennis, A. C., & Wood, J. T. (2012). "We're not going to have this conversation, but you get it": Black mother–daughter communication about sexual relations. *Women's Studies in Communication, 35*(2), 204–223.

deSousa, R. (2011). Local perspectives on empowerment and responsibility in the new public health. *Health Communication, 26*(1), 25–36.

DeWitt, L. (2006). Face-Negotiation theory. *North Dakota Speech and Theatre Journal, 19*, 38–42.

DeWitt, D. M., & DeWitt, L. J. (2012). Case of high school hazing: Applying restorative justice to promote organizational learning. *NASSP Bulletin, 96*, 13–22.

Deyo, J., Walt, P., & Davis, L. (2011). Rapidly recognizing relationships: Observing speed dating in the south. *Qualitative Research Reports in Communication, 12*(1), 71–78.

de Zúñiga, H. G., Jung, N., & Valenzuela, S. (2012). Social media use for news and individuals' social capital, civic engagement and political participation. *Journal of Computer-Mediated Communication, 17*, 319–336.

Dijkstra, A. (2009). Disengagement beliefs in smokers: Do they influence the effects of a tailored persuasive message advocating smoking cessation? *Psychology & Health, 24*(7), 791–804.

Dillow, M. R., Malachowski, C. C., Brann, M., & Weber, K. D. (2011). An experimental examination of the effects of communicative infidelity motives on communication and relational outcomes in romantic relationships. *Western Journal of Communication, 75*(5), 473–499.

Dimmick, J., Chen, Y., & Li, Z. (2004). Competition between the Internet and traditional news media: The gratification-opportunities niche dimension. *The Journal of Media Economics, 17*, 19–33.

Dimmick, J., Sikand, J., & Patterson, S. J. (1994). The gratifications of the household telephone: Sociability, instrumentality, and reassurance. *Communication Reports, 21*, 643–663.

Dindia, K. (2003). Definitions and perspectives on relational maintenance communication. In D. J. Canary & M. Dainton (Eds.), *Maintaining relationships through communication: Relational, contextual, and cultural variations* (pp. 1–30). Mahwah, NJ: Erlbaum.

DiVerniero, R. A., & Hosek, A. M. (2012). Students' perceptions and communicative management of instructors' online self-disclosure. *Communication Quarterly, 59*, 428–449.

Dobkin, B. A., & Pace, R. C. (2006). *Communication in a changing world.* New York, NY: McGraw-Hill.

Doherty, W. J., Boss, P. G., LaRossa, R., Schumm, W. R., & Steinmetz, S. K. (1993). Family theory and methods. In P. G. Boss, W. J. Doherty, R. LaRossa, W. R. Schumm, & S. K. Steinmetz (Eds.), *Sourcebook of family theories and methods: A contextual approach* (pp. 313–341). New York, NY: Plenum.

Domenici, K., & Littlejohn, S. W. (2006). *Facework: Bridging theory and practice.* Thousand Oaks, CA: Sage.

Donnelly, J. H., & Ivancevich, J. M. (1970). Post-purchase reinforcement and back-out behavior. *Journal of Marketing Research, 7*, 399–400.

Donovan-Kicken, E., Tollison, A. C., & Goins, E. S. (2011). A grounded theory of control over communication among individuals with cancer. *Journal of Applied Communication Research, 39*(3), 310–330.

Donsbach, W. (Ed.). (2013). *The spiral of silence: New perspectives on communication and public opinion.* New York, NY: Routledge.

Donsbach, W., Salmon, C. T., & Tsfati, Y. (2013). *The spiral of silence: New perspectives on communication and public opinion.* New York, NY: Taylor & Francis.

Dougherty, D. S. (2001). Sexual harassment as [dys]functional process: A feminist standpoint analysis. *Journal of Applied Communication Research, 29*, 372–391.

Dougherty, D. S., & Krone, K. J. (2000). Overcoming the dichotomy: Cultivating standpoints in organizations through research. *Women's Studies in Communication, 23*, 16–40.

Dow, B. J. (1990). Hegemony, feminist criticism and *The Mary Tyler Moore Show. Critical Studies in Mass Communication, 7*, 261–274.

Dragojevic, M., Giles, H., & Watson, B. M. (2012). Language ideologies and language attitudes. In H. Giles & B. M. Watson (Eds.), *The social meanings of language, dialect and accent: International perspectives on speech styles* (pp. 1–25). New York, NY: Peter Lang.

Dray, W. (1957). *Laws and explanation in history.* London: Oxford University Press.

Dresner, E. (2006). Middle region phenomena and globalization. *The International Communication Gazette, 68*, 363–378.

Drum, K. (2011). On the importance of public opinion. *Mother Jones, 36*, 3.

Dubbelman, T. (2011). Playing the hero: How games take the concept of storytelling from representation to presentation. *Journal of Media Practice, 12*(2), 157–172.

Duck, S. (1994). *Meaningful relationships.* Thousand Oaks, CA: Sage.

duGay, P., Hall, S., Janes, L., Mackay, H., & Negus, K. (1997). *Doing cultural studies: The story of the Sony Walkman.* London: Sage/The Open University.

Dunbar, N. E., & Segrin, C. (2011). Clothing and teacher credibility: An application of Expectancy Violations Theory. *ISRN Education,* 2012.

Dunleavy, K. N., & Martin, M. M. (2010). Instructors' and students' perspectives of student nagging: Frequency, appropriateness, and effectiveness. *Communication Research Reports, 27*(4), 310–319.

Eckstein, N. J., & Turman, P. D. (2002). "Children are to be seen and not heard": Silencing students' religious voices in the university classroom. *Journal of Communication and Religion, 25*, 166–192.

Edmonds-Cady, C. (2009). Getting to the grassroots: Feminist standpoints within the welfare rights movement. *Journal of Sociology & Social Welfare, 36*(2), 11–33.

Edsall, R. (2007). Cultural factors in digital cartographic design: Implications for communication to diverse users. *Cartography and Geographic Information Science, 34*, 121–129.

Eilders, C., & Porten-Cheen, P. (2015). The Spiral of Silence revisited. In G. Vowe & P. Henn (Eds.), *Political communication in the online world* (pp. 88–102). New York, NY: Routledge.

Eisenberg, E. M. (2007). *Strategic ambiguities: Essays on communication, organization, and identity.* Thousand Oaks, CA: Sage.

Eisenberg, E. M., & Goodall, H. L. (2004). *Organizational communication: Balancing creativity and constraint.* Boston, MA: Bedford/St. Martin's.

Eisenberg, E. M., Goodall, H. L., & Tretheway, A. (2010). *Organizational communication: Balancing creativity and constraint.* New York, NY: Bedford/St. Martin's.

Elgin, S. (1988). *A first dictionary and grammar of Laadan,* 2nd ed. Madison, WI: Society for the Furtherance and Study of Fantasy and Science Fiction.

Elkin, R. A., & Leippe, M. R. (1986). Physiological arousal, dissonance, and attitude change: Evidence for a dissonance-arousal link and a don't remind me effect. *Journal of Abnormal and Social Psychology, 51,* 55–65.

Elkins, J. R. (2001). Narrative theory and literary criticism. Retrieved from www.wvu.edu/lawfac/jelkins/lawyerslit/theories.html

Ellemers, N., & Haslam, S. A. (2012). Social Identity theory. In P. van Lange, A. Kruglanski, & T. Higgins (Eds.), *Handbook of theories of social psychology* (pp. 379–398). London: Sage.

Ellison, N. B., Heino, R., & Gibbs, J. (2006). Managing impressions online: Self-presentation processes in the online dating environment. *Journal of Computer-Mediated Communication, 11.* Retrieved from http://jcmc.indiana.edu/vol11/issue2/ellison.html

Elmore, C. (2009). Turning points and turnover among female journalists: Communicating resistance and repression. *Women's Studies in Communication, 32*(2), 232–254.

Emmers, T. M., & Canary, D. J. (1996). The effect of uncertainty reduction strategies on young couples' relational repair and intimacy. *Communication Quarterly, 44,* 166–182.

England, P. (1989). A feminist critique of rational-choice theories: Implications for Sociology. *The American Sociologist, 20,* 14–28.

Engleberg, I. N., & Wynn, D. R. (2013). *Working in groups.* Boston, MA: Pearson.

Entman, R. M. (1993). Framing: Toward clarification of a fractured paradigm. *Journal of Communication, 43*(4), 51–58.

Erbert, L. A. (2000). Conflict and dialectics: Perceptions of dialectical contradiction in marital conflict. *Journal of Social and Personal Relationships, 17,* 638–659.

Englehardt, E. E. (2001). *Ethical issues in interpersonal communication.* Fort Worth, TX: Harcourt.

Espinoza, A., Garcia-Fornes, A., & Sierra, C. (2012). Self-disclosure decision making based on intimacy and privacy. *Information Sciences, 211,* 93–11.

Ethics of Isocrates, Aristotle, and Diogenes. Retrieved from http://www.san.beck.org/EC22-Aristotle.html

Eyal, K., & Finnerty, K. (2007). The portrayal of consequences of sexual intercourse on prime-time programming. *Communication Research Reports, 24,* 225–233.

Faber, R. J. (2000). The urge to buy: A uses and gratifications perspective on compulsive buying. In S. Ratneshwar, D. G. Mick, & C. Huffman (Eds.), *The why of consumption* (pp. 177–196). London: Routledge.

Falk, E. (2009). Press, passion, and Portsmouth: Narratives about "crying" on the campaign trail. *Argumentation & Advocacy, 46*(1), 51–63.

Farber, B. A., Shafron, G., Hamandi, J., Wald, E., & Nitzburgh, G. (2012). Children, technology, problems, and preferences. *Journal of Clinical Psychology, 8,* 1225–1229.

Faulkner, S. L. (2015). That baby will cost you: An intended ambivalent pregnancy. *Qualitative Inquiry, 18,* 333–340.

Faulkner, S. L., & Ruby, P. D. (2015). Feminist identity in romantic relationships: A relational dialectics analysis of e-mail discourse as collaborative found poetry. *Women's Studies in Communication, 38,* 206–226.

Ferguson, D. A. (1992). Channel repertoire in the presence of remote control devices, VCRs and cable television. *Journal of Broadcasting & Electronic Media, 36,* 83–91.

Fernback, J. (2007). Beyond the diluted community concept: A symbolic interactionist perspective on online social relations. *New Media & Society, 9,* 49–69.

Ferrara, M. H., & Levine, T. R. (2009). Can't live with them or can't live without them? The effects of betrayal on relational outcomes in college dating relationships. *Communication Quarterly, 57*(2), 187–204.

Festinger, L. (1957). *A theory of cognitive dissonance.* Stanford, CA: Stanford University Press.

Festinger, L., & Carlsmith, J. M. (1959). Cognitive consequences of forced compliance. *Journal of Abnormal and Social Psychology, 58,* 203–210.

Festinger, L., Riecken, H. W., & Schacter, S. (1956). *When prophecy fails.* Minneapolis, MN: University of Minnesota Press.

Ficara, L. C., & Mongeau, P. A. (2000, November). *Relational uncertainty in long-distance college student dating relationships.* Paper presented at the annual meeting of the National Communication Association, Seattle, WA.

Fiese, B. H. (2003). Coherent accounts of coping with a chronic illness: Convergences and divergences in family measurement using a narrative analysis. *Family Process, 42*, 439–451.

Fine, M. G. (2009). Women leaders' discursive constructions of leadership. *Women's Studies in Communication, 32*(2), 180–202.

Finklehor, D., & Ormrod, R. (2000, June). Kidnapping of juveniles: Patterns from NIBRS. *Juvenile Justice Bulletin.* Washington, DC: U.S. Department of Justice, Office of Justice Programs: Office of Juvenile Justice and Delinquency Prevention.

Finn, A. N., & Schrodt, P. (2012). Students' perceived understanding mediates the effects of teacher clarity and nonverbal immediacy on learner empowerment. *Communication Education, 61*, 111–130.

Fischer, C. (2010). Sweet land of . . . conformity. *Boston Globe*, p. K1.

Fisher, R. (2012). *The social psychology of intergroup and international conflict.* New York, NY: Springer.

Fisher, W. R. (1984). Narration as a human communication paradigm: The case of public moral argument. *Communication Monographs, 51*, 1–22.

Fisher, W. R. (1985). The narrative paradigm: An elaboration. *Communication Monographs, 52*, 347–367.

Fisher, W. R. (1987). *Human communication as narration: Toward a philosophy of reason, value, and action.* Columbia, SC: University of South Carolina Press.

Fisher-Yoshida, B. (2012). Coordinated Management of Meaning (CMM) as reflective practice. In C. Creede, B. Fisher-Yoshida, & P. V. Gallegos (Eds.), *The reflective, facilitative, and interpretive practice of the Coordinated Management of Meaning* (pp. 219–240). Madison, NJ: Farleigh Dickinson University Press.

Fiske, S. T., & Taylor, S. E. (1984). *Social cognition.* Reading, MA: Addison-Wesley.

Flaherty, K. E., & Pappas, J. M. (2009). Expanding the sales professional's role: A strategic re-orientation? *Industrial Marketing Management, 38*(7), 806–813.

Flanagin, A. J. (2007). Commercial markets as communication markets: Uncertainty reduction through mediated information exchange in online auctions. *New Media & Society, 9*, 401–423.

Flint, D. J. (2006). Innovation, symbolic interaction and customer valuing: Thoughts stemming from a service-dominant logic of marketing. *Marketing Theory, 6*, 349–362.

Foa, U., & Foa, E. (1974). *Societal structures of the mind.* Springfield, IL: Thomas.

Foa, U. G., & Foa, E. B. (1976). Resource theory of social exchange. In J. W. Thibaut, J. T. Spence, & R. C. Carson (Eds.), *Contemporary topics in social Psychology* (pp. 133–149). Morristown, NJ: General Learning Press.

Fogel, J. M. (2012). *A modern family: The performance of "family" and familialism in contemporary television series.* Unpublished doctoral dissertation. University of Michigan, Ann Arbor, MI.

Ford, L. A., & Crabtree, R. D. (2002). Telling, re-telling and talking about telling: Disclosure and/as surviving incest. *Women's Studies in Communication, 25*, 53–87.

Forsythe, L. (2012). CMM and healthcare qualitative simulation research. In C. Creede, B. Fisher-Yoshida, & P. V. Gallegos (Eds.), *The reflective, facilitative, and interpretive practice of the Coordinated Management of Meaning: Making lives and making meaning* (pp. 95–106). Madison, NJ: Farleigh Dickinson University Press.

Forte, J. A. (2004). Symbolic interactionism and social work: A forgotten legacy, part 2. *Families in Society, 85*, 521–530.

Forte, J. A., Barrett, A. V., & Campbell, M. H. (1996). Patterns of social connectedness and shared grief work: A symbolic interactionist perspective. *Social Work with Groups, 19*, 29–51.

Foss, K., & Foss, S. (1991). *Women speak: The eloquence of women's lives.* Prospect Heights, IL: Waveland Press.

Foss, S., Foss, K., & Trapp, R. (1991). *Contemporary perspectives on rhetoric.* Prospect Heights, IL: Waveland Press.

Fox, C. (2002). Beyond the "tyranny of the real": Revisiting Burke's pentad as research method for professional communication. *Technical Communication Quarterly, 11*, 365–388.

Frankenberg, R. (1993). *White women, race matters: The social construction of Whiteness.* Minneapolis, MN: University of Minnesota Press.

Freeth, R. (2012). We are human too. *Therapy Today, 23*, 7.

French, J. R. & Raven, B. (1959). *The bases of social power.* Ann Arbor, MI: University of Michigan Press.

French, S. L., & Brown, S. C. (2011). It's all your fault: Kenneth Burke, symbolic action, and the assigning of guilt and blame to women. *Southern Communication Journal, 76*(1), 1–16.

Frewin, K., & Tuffin, K. (1998). Police status, conformity and internal pressure: A discursive analysis of police culture. *Discourse & Society, 9*, 173–185.

Frymier, A. B. (2005). Students' classroom communication effectiveness. *Communication Quarterly, 53*, 197–212.

Frymier, A. B., & Houser, M. A. (2002). The teacher-student relationship as an interpersonal relationship. *Communication Education, 49*, 207–219.

Frey, L. R., Botan, C. H., & Kreps, G. L. (2000). *Investigating communication: An introduction to research methods,* 2nd ed. Boston, MA: Allyn & Bacon.

Galanes, G., & Adams, K. (2013). *Effective group discussion: Theory and practice.* Boston, MA: McGraw-Hill.

Gallois, C., & Callan, V. J. (1991). Interethnic accommodation: The role of norms. In H. Giles, J. Coupland, & N. Coupland (Eds.), *Contexts of accommodation: Developments in applied socio-linguistics* (pp. 245–269). Cambridge: Cambridge University Press.

Gallois, C., Ogay, T., & Giles, H. (2005). Communication accommodation theory. In W. Gudykunst (Ed.), *Theorizing about intercultural communication* (pp. 121–148). Thousand Oaks, CA: Sage.

Garber, M. (2011). Webs and whirligigs: Marshall McLuhan in his time and ours. Retrieved from http://ffffound.com/image/cfc6c98c37b262a79c7b436e5c9c08d1dad35835

Garcia-Jimenez, L., & Craig, R. (2010). What kind of difference do we want to make? *Communication Monographs, 77*, 429–431.

Garnett, J., & Kouzmin, A. (2009). Crisis communication post-Katrina: What are we learning. *Public Organizational Review, 9*, 385–398.

Gasiorek, J., & Giles, H. (2012). Effects of inferred motive on evaluations of nonaccommodative communication. *Human Communication Research, 38*, 309–331.

Gaudine, A., & Thorne, L. (2012). Nurses' ethical conflict with hospitals: A longitudinal study of outcomes. *Nursing Ethics, 19*, 727–737.

Gearhart, S., & Zhang, W. (2015). Gay bullying and online opinion expression testing Spiral of Silence in the social media environment. *Social Science Computer Review, 32*, 18–36.

Gecas, V., & Burke, P. J. (1995). Self and identity. In K. S. Cook, G. A. Fine, & J. S. House (Eds.), *Sociological perspectives on social psychology* (pp. 41–67). Boston, MA: Allyn & Bacon.

Geertz, C. (1973). *The interpretation of cultures.* New York, NY: Basic Books.

Geertz, C. (1983). *Local knowledge.* New York, NY: Basic Books.

Gencarelli, T. F. (2006). Neil Postman and the rise of media ecology. In C. M. K. Lum (Ed.), *Perspectives on culture, technology, and communication: The media ecology tradition* (pp. 201–25). Cresskill, NJ: Hampton.

Gendrin, D. M. (2000). Homeless women's inner voices: Friends or foes? In M. J. Hardman & A. Taylor (Eds.), *Hearing many voices* (pp. 203–219). Cresskill, NJ: Hampton Press.

Gerbner, G. (1969). Toward "cultural indicators": The analysis of mass media public message systems. *AV Communication Review, 17*(2), 137–148.

Gerbner, G. (1998). Cultivation analysis: An overview. *Mass Communication and Society, 3/4*, 175–194.

Gerbner, G. (1999). What do we know? In J. Shanahan & M. Morgan (Eds.), *Television and its viewers: Cultivation theory and research* (pp. ix–xiii). Cambridge: Cambridge University Press.

Gerbner, G., & Gross, L. (1972). Living with television: The violence profile. *Journal of Communication, 26*, 173–199.

Gerbner, G., Gross, L., Jackson-Beeck, M., JeffriesFox, S., & Signorielli, N. (1978). Cultural indicators: Violence profile No. 9. *Journal of Communication, 28*, 176–206.

Gerbner, G., Gross, L., Morgan, M., & Signorielli, N. (1982). Charting the mainstream: Television's contributions to political orientations. *Journal of Communication, 32*, 100–127.

Gerbner, G., Gross, L., Morgan, M., & Signorielli, N. (1986). Living with television: The dynamics of the cultivation process. In J. Bryant & D. Zillman (Eds.), *Perspectives on media effects* (pp. 17–40). Hillsdale, NJ: Erlbaum.

Gerbner, G., Gross, L., Morgan, M., & Signorielli, N. (1980). The "mainstreaming" of America: Violence profile no. 11. *Journal of Communication, 30*(3), 10–29.

Gerbner, G., Gross, L., Morgan, M., Signorielli, & Shanahan, J. (2002). Growing up with television: The cultivation perspective. In J. Bryant & D. Zillmann (Eds.), *Media effects: Advances in theory and research* (pp. 17–41). Hillsdale, NJ: Erlbaum.

German, K. M. (2009). Dramatism and dramatistic pentad. In S. W. Littlejohn & K. A. Foss (Eds.), *Encyclopedia of communication theory* (Vol. 1, pp. 320–322). Los Angeles, CA: Sage.

Gibbs, J. L., Ellison, N. B., & Lai, C. H. (2011). First comes love, then comes *Google*: An investigation of uncertainty reduction. *Communication Research, 38*, 70–100.

Giddens, A. (1979). *Central problems in social theory: Action, structure, and contradiction in social analysis.* Berkeley, CA: University of California Press.

Giddens, A. (1984). *The constitution of society: Outline of the theory of structuration.* Berkeley, CA: University of California Press.

Giddens, A. (1980). Classes, capitalism, and the state. *Theory and Society, 9,* 877–890.

Giddens, A. (1993). *New rules of sociological method: A positive critique of interpretive sociologies,* 2nd ed. Cambridge, UK: Polity Press.

Giddens, A. (1994). *Beyond left and right: The future of radical politics.* Cambridge, UK: Polity Press.

Giddens, A. (2003). Risk and responsibility. *The Modern Law Review, 62,* 1–10.

Giles, H. (1973). Accent mobility: A model and some data. *Anthropological Linguistics, 15,* 87–105.

Giles, H. (1980). Accommodation theory: Some new directions. *York Papers in Linguistics, 9,* 30.

Giles, H. (2008). Communication accommodation theory. In L. A. Baxter & D. O. Braithwaite (Eds.), *Engaging theories in interpersonal communication* (pp. 161–174). Los Angeles, CA: Sage.

Giles, H. (2012). Principles of intergroup communication. In H. Giles (Ed.), *The handbook of intergroup communication* (pp. 3–18). New York, NY: Routledge.

Giles, H., Coupland, N., & Coupland, J. (1991). Accommodation theory: Communication, context, and consequence. In H. Giles, J. Coupland, & N. Coupland (Eds.), *Contexts of accommodation: Developments in applied sociolinguistics* (pp. 1–68). Cambridge: Cambridge University Press.

Giles, H., Linz, D., Bonilla, D., & Gomez, M. L. (2012). Police stops and interactions with Latino and White (non-Latino) drivers: Extensive policing and communication accommodation. *Communication Monographs, 79,* 407–427.

Giles, H., Mulac, A., Bradac, J. J., & Johnson, P. (1987). Speech accommodation theory: The first decade and beyond. In M. L. McLaughlin (Ed.), *Communication yearbook 10* (pp. 13–48). Newbury Park, CA: Sage.

Giles, H., & Smith, P. M. (1979). Accommodation theory: Optimal levels of convergence. In H. Giles & R. N. St. Clair (Eds.), *Language and social psychology* (pp. 231–244). Oxford: Blackwell.

Giles, H., & Wiemann, J. (1987). Language, social comparison, and power. In S. Chaffee & C. R. Berger (Eds.),

Handbook of communication science (pp. 350–384). Newbury Park, CA: Sage.

Ginnett, R. (2005). What can leaders to do avoid groupthink? *Leadership in Action, 25,* 13.

Gitlin, T. (1980). *The whole world is watching: Mass media in the making and unmaking of the New Left.* Berkeley, CA: University of California Press.

Givertz, M., & Segrin, C. (2012, May). *The association between over involved parenting and young adults' self-efficacy, psychological entitlement, and family communication.* Paper presented at the annual meeting of the International Communication Association, Phoenix, AZ.

Glascock, J., & Ruggerio, T. E. (2004). Representations of class and gender of primetime Spanish-language television in the United States. *Communication Quarterly, 52,* 390–402.

Glenn, C. L., & Johnson, D. L. (2012). "What they see as acceptable": A co-cultural theoretical analysis of black male students at a predominantly white institution. *Howard Journal of Communications, 23*(4), 351–368.

Glynn, C. J., & McLeod, J. M. (1985). Implications of the spiral of silence for communication and public opinion research. In K. R. Sanders, L. L. Kaid, & D. Nimmo (Eds.), *Political communication yearbook 1984* (pp. 43–65). Carbondale, IL: Southern Illinois University Press.

Glynn, C. J., Hayes, A. F., & Shanahan, J. (1997). Perceived support for one's opinions and willingness to speak out: A meta-analysis of survey studies on the spiral of silence. *Public Opinion Quarterly, 61,* 452–463.

Goffman, E. (1967). *Interaction rituals: Essays on face-to-face interaction.* Garden City, NY: Doubleday.

Goffman, E. (1974). *Frame analysis: An essay on the organization of experience.* New York, NY: Harper & Row.

Goins, M. N. (2011). Playing with dialectics: Black female friendship groups as a homeplace. *Communication Studies, 62*(5), 531–546.

Golden, J. L., Berquist, G., Coleman, W. E., & Sproule, J. M. (2011). *The rhetoric of Western thought,* 10th ed. Dubuque, IA: Kendall-Hunt.

Golish, T. D., & Powell, K. A. (2003). "Ambiguous loss": Managing the dialectics of grief associated with premature birth. *Journal of Social and Personal Relationships, 20,* 309–334.

Gong, G. (2011). When Mississippi Chinese talk. In A. Gonzalez, M. Houston, & V. Chen (Eds.), *Our voices: Essays in culture, ethnicity, and communication* (pp. 104–111). New York, NY: Oxford University Press.

Gonzalez, A., & Gonzalez, J. (2002). The color problem in sillyville: Negotiating white identity in one popular "kid-vid." *Communication Quarterly, 50,* 410–422.

Gonzalez, A., Houston, M., & Chen, V. (Eds.). (2011). *Our voices: Essays in culture, ethnicity, and communication.* New York, NY: Oxford University Press.

Good, J. E. (2009). The cultivation, mainstreaming, and cognitive processing of environmentalists watching television. *Environmental Communication, 3*(3), 279–297.

Goodboy, A. K., & Bolkan, S. (2011). Attachment and the use of negative relational maintenance behaviors in romantic relationships. *Communication Research Reports, 28,* 327–336.

Gordon, G. (1982, January). An end to McLuhanacy. *Educational Technology, 44,* 39–45.

Gordon, T., & Willmarth, S. (2012). *McLuhan for beginners.* Danbury, CT: For Beginners Press.

Gouran, D. S. (1998). The signs of cognitive, affiliative, and egocentric constraints in patterns of interaction in decision-making and problem-solving groups and their potential effects on outcomes. In J. Trent (Ed.), *Communication: Views from the helm for the 21st century* (pp. 98–102). Needham Heights, MA: Allyn & Bacon.

Gouran, D. S., & Hirokawa, R. Y. (1996). Functional theory and communication in decision-making and problem-solving groups. In R. Y. Hirokawa & M. S. Poole (Eds.), *Communication and group decision making* (pp. 55–80). Thousand Oaks, CA: Sage.

Gouran, D. S., Hirokawa, R. Y., & Martz, A. E. (1986). A critical analysis of factors related to decisional processes involved in the *Challenger* disaster. *Central States Speech Journal, 37,* 119–135.

Granberg, E. M. (2011). "Now my old self is thin": Stigma exits after weight loss. *Social Psychology Quarterly, 74*(1), 29–52.

Gray, H. (1989). Television, Black Americans, and the American dream. *Critical Studies in Mass Communication, 6,* 376–386.

Gray, J. B. (2009). The power of storytelling: Using narrative in the healthcare context. *Journal of Communication in Healthcare, 2*(3), 258–273.

Green-Hamann, S., Eichhorn, K. C., & Sherblom, J. C. (2011). An exploration of why people participate in Social Life support groups. *Journal of Computer-Mediated Communication, 16,* 465–491.

Greene, A. (2012). Practical follow-up. *Journal of Participatory Medicine, 4,* 18.

Greene, K., & Kremar, M. (2005). Predicting exposure to and liking of media violence: A uses and gratifications approach. *Communication Studies, 56,* 71–93.

Gross, M., Guerrero, L. K., & Alberts, J. K. (2004). Perceptions of conflict strategies and communication competence in task-oriented dyads. *Journal of Applied Communication Research, 32,* 249–271.

Grossberg, L. (1986). Is there rock after punk? *Critical Studies in Mass Communication, 3,* 50–74.

Grossberg, L (2010). *Cultural studies in the future tense.* Durham, NC: Duke University Press.

Gu, R., Higa, K., & Moodie, D. R. (2012). A study on communication media selection: Comparing the effectiveness of the media richness, social influence, and media fitness. *Journal of Service Science and Management, 4,* 291–299.

Gudykunst, W. B. (1995). Anxiety/uncertainty management (AUM) theory. In R. Wiseman (Ed.), *Intercultural communication theory* (pp. 8–58). Thousand Oaks, CA: Sage.

Gudykunst, W. B., & Hammer, M. R. (1987). The influences of ethnicity, gender, and dyadic composition on uncertainty reduction in initial interactions. *Journal of Black Studies, 18,* 191–214.

Gudykunst, W. B., & Matsumoto, Y. (1996). Cross-cultural variability of communication in personal relationships. In W. B. Gudykunst, S. Ting-Toomey, & T. Nishida (Eds.), *Communication in personal relationships across cultures* (pp. 19–56). Thousand Oaks, CA: Sage.

Gudykunst, W. B., & Nishida, T. (1984). Individual and cultural influence on uncertainty reduction. *Communication Monographs, 51,* 23–36.

Gudykunst, W. B., & Nishida, T. (1986a). Attributional confidence in low- and high-context cultures. *Human Communication Research, 12,* 525–549.

Gudykunst, W. B., & Nishida, T. (1986b). Social penetration in close relationships in Japan and the United States. In R. Bostrom (Ed.), *Communication yearbook 7* (pp. 592–610). Beverly Hills, CA: Sage.

Gudykunst, W. B., Chua, E., & Gray, A. (1987). Cultural dissimilarity and uncertainty reduction processes. In M. McLaughlin (Ed.), *Communication yearbook 10* (pp. 456–469). Newbury Park, CA: Sage.

Gudykunst, W. B., Yang, S. M., & Nishida, T. (1985). A cross-cultural test of uncertainty reduction theory: Comparison of acquaintances, friends, and dating relationships in Japan, Korea, and the United States. *Human Communication Research, 11,* 407–454.

Guerrero, L. K. (2008). Expectancy violation. Retrieved from http://www.communicationencyclopedia.com

Guerrero, L. K., & Bachman, G. F. (2010). Forgiveness and forgiving communication: An expectancy-investment explanation. *Journal of Social and Personal Relationships*, *27*, 801–823.

Gunaratne, S. A. (2010). De-westernizing communication/social science research: Opportunities and limitations. *Media, Culture & Society*, *32*(3), 473–500.

Gibbs, J. L., Ellison, N. B., & Lai, C. (2011). First comes love, then comes *Google*: An investigation of uncertainty reduction strategies and self-disclosure in online dating. *Communication Research*, *38*(1), 70–100.

Giles, H., Willemyns, M., Gallois, C., & Anderson, M. C. (2007). Accommodating a new frontier: The context of law enforcement. In K. Fiedler (Ed.), *Social accommodation* (pp. 129–162). New York, NY: Psychology Press.

Gissel, A. L. (2012). *The effects of email address on norm violations on evaluations of job applicants*. Unpublished doctoral dissertation. North Carolina State University, Raleigh, NC.

Groupthink: A risk to a good leadership team. Retrieved from http://chinabusinessleadership.com/2012/09/11/group-think-a-risk-to-a-good-leadership-team

Guerrero, L. K., & Bachman, G. F. (2008). Communication following relational transgressions in dating relationships: An investment-model explanation. *Southern Communication Journal*, *73*, 4–23.

Guo, L., Chen, Y. N. K., Vu, H., Wang, Q., Aksamit, R., Guzek, D.,…McCombs, M. (2015). Coverage of the Iraq War in the United States, Mainland China, Taiwan and Poland: A transnational network agenda-setting study. *Journalism Studies*, *16*, 343–362.

Ha, L., & Fang, L. (2012). Internet experience and time displacement of traditional news media use: An application of the theory of the niche. *Telematics & Informatics*, *29*(2), 177–186.

Hajek, C., Villagran, M., & Wittenberg-Lyles, E. (2007). The relationships among perceived physician accommodation, perceived outgroup typicality, and patient inclinations toward compliance. *Communication Research Reports*, *24*, 293–302.

Hall, E. T. (1966). *The hidden dimension*. Garden City, NY: Anchor/Doubleday.

Hall, E. T. (1977). *Beyond culture*. Garden City, NY: Anchor/Doubleday.

Hall, E. T. (1992). *An anthropology of everyday life*. New York, NY: Doubleday/Anchor Books.

Hall, S. (1980a). Encoding/decoding. In S. Hall, D. Hobson, A. Lowe, & P. Willis (Eds.), *Culture, media, language* (pp. 128–138). London: Hutchinson.

Hall, S. (1980b). Cultural studies and the centre: Some problematic and problems. In S. Hall, D. Hobson, A. Lowe, & P. Willis (Eds.), *Culture, media, language* (pp. 15–47). London: Hutchinson.

Hall, S. (1981). The whites of their eyes: Racist ideologies and the media. In G. Bridges & R. Brunt (Eds.), *Silver linings: Some strategies for the eighties* (pp. 28–52). London: Lawrence and Wishart.

Hall, S. (1989). Ideology and communication theory. In B. Dervin, L. Grossberg, B. J. O'Keefe, & E. Wartella (Eds.), *Rethinking communication: Paradigm issues* (pp. 40–51). Newbury Park, CA: Sage.

Hall, S. (1992). Cultural studies and its theoretical legacies. In L. Grossberg, C. Nelson, & P. Treichler (Eds.), *Cultural studies* (pp. 277–294). New York, NY: Routledge.

Hall, S. (1997). The problem of ideology: Marxism without guarantees. In S. Hall (Ed.), *Representation: Cultural representations and signifying practices* (pp. 30–46). London: Sage/The Open University.

Hall, S. (2013). The spectacle of the other. In S. Hall, S. Nixon, & J. Evans (Eds.), *Representation: Cultural representations and signifying practices* (pp. 112–144). Thousand Oaks, CA: Sage.

Hamilton, H. E. (1991). Accommodation and mental disability. In H. Giles, J. Coupland, & N. Coupland (Eds.), *Contexts of accommodation* (pp. 157–186). New York, NY: Cambridge University Press.

Haraway, D. (1988). Situated knowledges: The science question in feminism and the privilege of partial perspective. *Signs*, *14*, 575–599.

Harding, S. (1987). Introduction: Is there a feminist method? In Sandra Harding (Ed.), *Feminism and methodology* (pp. 1–14). Bloomington, IN: University of Indiana Press.

Harding, S. (1991). *Whose science, whose knowledge? Thinking from women's lives*. Ithaca, NY: Cornell University Press.

Hargie, O., Tourish, D., & Wilson, N. (2002). Communication audits and the effects of increased information: A follow-up study. *The Journal of Business Communication*, *39*, 414–436.

Haridakis, P. M., & Rubin, A. M. (2005). Third-person effects in the aftermath of terrorism. *Mass Communication and Society*, *8*, 39–59.

Haridakis, P., & Hanson, G. (2009). Social interaction and co-viewing with YouTube: Blending mass communication reception and social connection. *Journal of Broadcasting & Electronic Media, 53*, 317–355.

Harmon-Jones, E. (2009). Cognitive dissonance theory. In S. W. Littlejohn & K. A. Foss (Eds.), *Encyclopedia of communication theory* (Vol. 1, pp. 109–111). Los Angeles, CA: Sage.

Harrigan, M. M. (2009). The contradictions of identity-work for parents of visibly adopted children. *Journal of Social & Personal Relationships, 26*(5), 634–658.

Harrigan, M. M., & Braithwaite, D. O. (2010). Discursive struggles in families formed through visible adoption: An exploration of dialectical unity. *Journal of Applied Communication Research, 38*(2), 127–144.

Harris, M., & Cullen, R. (2008). Renovation as innovation: Transforming a campus symbol and a campus culture. *Perspectives: Policy and Practice in Higher Education, 12*, 4–51.

Hart, R. P. (1997). *Modern rhetorical criticism.* Boston, MA: Allyn & Bacon.

Hartsock, N. (1981). Political change: Two perspectives in power. In C. Bunch (Ed.), *Building feminist theory: Essays from Quest, a feminist quarterly* (pp. 55–70). New York, NY: Longman.

Hartsock, N. (1983). The feminist standpoint: Developing the ground for a specifically feminist historical materialism. In S. Harding & M. B. Hintikka (Eds.), *Discovering reality* (pp. 283–310). Boston, MA: Ridel.

Hartsock, N. C. M. (1997). Standpoint theories for the next century. *Women and Politics, 18*, 93–101.

Harwood, J. (2002). Comunicación intergeneracional entre extraños y entre miembros de la familia [Intergenerational communication between strangers and family members]. *Revista Latinoamericana de Psicologia, 34*, 75–82.

Harwood, J. (2000). Communicative predictors of solidarity in the grandparent-grandchild relationship. *Journal of Social and Personal Relationships, 17*, 743–766.

Harwood, J. (2006). Communication as social identity. In G. Shepherd, J. St. John, & T. Striphas (Eds.), *Communication as...: Perspectives on theory* (pp. 84–90). Thousand Oaks, CA: Sage.

Haase, C. E. (1909). Ideal education for girls. Registrar of Milwaukee Downer College. Records 1852–1964. Milwaukee Manuscript Collection L. University Archives. Golda Meir Library, Research Center, University of Wisconsin, Milwaukee, WI.

Hatch, M. J. (2006). *Organizational theory: Modern, symbolic, and postmodern perspective.* Oxford: Oxford University Press.

Hayden, S. (1994). Interruptions and the construction of reality. In L. H. Turner & H. M. Sterk (Eds.), *Differences that make a difference: Examining the assumptions in gender research* (pp. 99–106). Westport, CT: Bergin & Garvey.

Hechter, M. (2004). From class to culture. *The American Journal of Sociology, 110*, 400–445.

Hehl, J., & McDonald, D. D. (2012). Older adults' pain communication during ambulatory medical visits: An exploration of communication accommodation theory. *Pain Management Nursing, 13*, 186–210.

Heider, F. (1958). *The psychology of interpersonal relations.* New York, NY: Wiley.

Heiss, S. N., & Carmack, H. J. (2012). Knock, knock; who's there? Making sense of organizational entrance through humor. *Management Communication Quarterly, 25*, 106–132.

Hensley, T. R., & Lewis, J. M., (2010) *Kent state and May 4th—A social science perspective.* Kent, OH: Kent State University Press.

Herakova, L. (2009). Identity, communication, inclusion: The Roma and (new) Europe. *Journal of International and Intercultural Communication, 2*(4), 279–297.

Herek, G. M., Janis, I. L., & Huth, P. (1987). Decision making during international crises: Is quality of process related to outcome? *Journal of Conflict Resolution, 31*, 203–226.

Herrington, W. (2012). *Homeless perceptions.* Saarbrücken, Germany: Lambert Academic Publishing.

Herrmann, A. (2007). *Narrative and ethnography as existential phenomenological approaches to organizational sensemaking.* Paper presented at the annual meeting of the International Communication Association, San Francisco, CA.

Herzog, H. (1944). Motivations and gratifications of daily serial listeners. In P. F. Lazarsfeld & F. N. Stanton (Eds.), *Radio Research, 1942–1943.* New York, NY: Duell, Sloan and Pearce.

Higgins, C., & Walker, R. (2012). Ethos, logos, pathos: Strategies of persuasion in social/environmental reports. *Accounting Forum, 36*, 194–208.

Hine, R. (2011). In the margins: The impact of sexualised images on the mental health of ageing women. *Sex Roles, 65*(7), 632–646.

Hirokawa, R. Y., Gouran, D. S., & Martz, A. E. (1988). Understanding the sources of faulty group decision making: A lesson from the *Challenger* disaster. *Small Group Behavior*, 19, 411–433.

Hirschmann, N. J. (1997). Feminist standpoint as postmodern strategy. *Women and Politics*, 18, 73–92.

Hmielowski, J. D., Holbert, R. L., & Lee, J. (2011). Predicting the consumption of political TV satire: Affinity for political humor, *The Daily Show* and *The Colbert Report*. *Communication Monographs*, 78(1), 96–114.

Ho, D. Y. (1976). On the concept of face. *American Journal of Sociology*, 81, 867–884.

Hochschild, A. R., Machung, A. (1989). *The second shift: Working parents and the revolution at home*. New York, NY: Viking Penguin.

Hodge, B. (2003). How the medium is the message in the unconscious of 'America online.' *Visual Communication*, 2, 341–353.

Hoelzl, E., Pollai, M., & Kastner, H. (2011). Hedonic evaluations of cars: Effects of payment mode on prediction and experience. *Psychology & Marketing*, 28(11), 1113–1127.

Hoffman, M. F., & Cowen, R. L. (2010). Be careful what you ask for: Structuration theory and work/life accommodation. *Communication Studies*, 61, 272–303.

Hofstede, G. (1980). *Culture's consequences: International differences in work-related values*. Beverly Hills, CA: Sage.

Hofstede, G. (1991). *Cultures and organizations: Software of the mind*. London: McGraw-Hill.

Hofstede, G. (2001). *Culture's consequences: Comparing values, behaviors, institutions, and organizations across nations*. Thousand Oaks, CA: Sage.

Hogg, M., & Giles, H. (2012). Norm talk and identity in intergroup communication. In H. Giles (Ed.), *The handbook of intergroup communication* (pp. 373–388). New York, NY: Routledge.

Holbert, R. L., LaMarre, H. L., & Landreville, K. D. (2009). Fanning the flames of a partisan divide: Debate viewing, vote choice, and perceptions of vote count accuracy. *Communication Research*, 36(2), 155–177.

Holliday, A. (2013). *Understanding intercultural communication: Negotiating a culture of grammar*. New York, NY: Routledge.

Hollingshead, A. B., Wittenbaum, G. M., Paulus, P. B., Hirokawa, R. Y., Ancona, D. G., Peterson, R. S., Jehn, K. A., & Yoon, K. (2005). A look at groups from the functional perspective. In M. S. Poole & A. B. Hollingshead

(Eds.), *Theories of small groups: Interdisciplinary perspectives* (pp. 21–62). Thousand Oaks, CA: Sage.

Holmgren, A. (2004). Saying, doing and making: Teaching CMM theory. *Human Systems: The Journal of Systemic Consultation and Management*, 15, 89–100.

Hoover, J. D., Hastings, S. O., & Musambira, G. W. (2009). "Opening a gap" in culture: Women's uses of the compassionate friends website. *Women & Language*, 32(1), 82–90.

Hoppe-Nagao, A., & Ting-Toomey, S. (2002). Relational dialectics and management strategies in marital couples. *Southern Communication Journal*, 67, 142–159.

Hopper, R., Knapp, M. L., & Scott, L. (1981). Couples' personal idioms: Exploring intimate talk. *Journal of Communication*, 31, 23–33.

Horan, S. M. (2012). Affection exchange theory and perceptions of relational transgressions. *Western Journal of Communication*, 76, 109–126.

Horowitz, D. (2012). *Consuming pleasures: Intellectuals and popular culture in the post-war world*. Philadelphia, PA: University of Pennsylvania Press.

Houle, K. (2009). Making strange. *Frontiers: A Journal of Women Studies*, 30(1), 172–193.

Houston, M. (1992). The politics of difference: Race, class, and women's communication. In L. F. Rakow (Ed.), *Women making meaning: New feminist directions in communication* (pp. 45–59). New York, NY: Routledge.

Houston, M., & Kramarae, C. (1991). Speaking from silence: Methods of silencing and of resistance. *Discourse and Society*, 2, 387–399.

How people learn about their local community. Retrieved from http://pewInternet.org/Reports/2011/Local-news/Part-1.aspx

Hsu, C. (2004). *Sources of differences in communication apprehension between Chinese in Taiwan and Americans*. Paper presented at the annual meeting of the International Communication Association, New Orleans, LA.

Hsu, C. (2012). The influence of vocal qualities and confirmation of nonnative English-speaking teachers on student receiver apprehension, affective learning, and cognitive learning. *Communication Education*, 61, 4–16.

Huber, J. L. (2010). Singing it out: Riot grrrls, Lilith Fair, and feminism. *Kaleidoscope: A Graduate Journal of Qualitative Communication Research*, 9, 65–85.

Huddy, L. (2012). From group cohesion to political cohesion and commitment. In P. A. Van Lange, A. W. Kruglanski, & T. E. Higgins (Eds.), *Handbook of theories of social psychology* (pp. 379–398). Thousand Oaks, CA: Sage.

Hughes, P. C., & Dickson, F. C. (2006). Relational dynamics in interfaith marriages. In L. H. Turner & R. West (Eds.), *The family communication sourcebook* (pp. 373–388). Thousand, Oaks, CA: Sage.

Hunt, D., Atkin, D., & Krishnan, A. (2012). The influence of computer-mediated communication apprehension on motives for Facebook use. *Journal of Broadcasting & Electronic Media, 56*(2), 187–202.

Hunt, S. B. (2003). An essay on publishing standards for rhetorical criticism. *Communication Studies, 54*, 378–384.

Hutcheson, J. (2012). Achieving a transcendent episode. In C. Creede, B. Fisher-Yoshida, & P. V. Gallegos (Eds.), *The reflective, facilitative, and interpretive practice of the Coordinated Management of Meaning* (pp. 111–123). Madison, NJ: Farleigh Dickinson University Press.

Hyde, M. (2004). Introduction: Rhetorically we dwell. In M. Hyde (Ed.), *The ethos of rhetoric* (pp. xii–xxvii). Columbia, SC: University of South Carolina Press.

Ifert-Johnson, D., Roloff, M. E., & Riffee, M. A. (2004). Politeness theory and refusals of requests: Face threat as a function of expressed obstacles. *Communication Studies, 55*, 227–238.

Ifert-Johnson, D. (2007). Politeness theory and conversational refusals: Associations between various types of face threat and perceived competence. *Western Journal of Communication, 71*, 196–215.

Ifert-Johnson, D., & Lewis, N. (2010). Perceptions of swearing in the work setting: An Expectancy Violations Theory perspective. *Communication Reports, 23*, 106–118.

Ifert-Johnson, D. (2012). Swearing by peers in the work setting: Expectancy violation valence, perceptions of message, and perceptions of speaker. *Communication Studies, 63*, 136–151.

Ifert-Johnson, D. & Acquavella, G. (2012). Organization-public relationship: Satisfaction and intention to retain a relationship with a cell phone service provider. *Southern Communication Journal, 77*, 163–179.

Ichiyama, M. A. (1993). The reflected appraisal process in small-group interaction. *Social Psychology Quarterly, 56*, 87–99.

Imamura, M., Zhang, Y. B., & Harwood, J. (2011). Japanese sojourners' attitudes toward Americans: Exploring the influences of communication accommodation, linguistic competence, and relational solidarity in intergroup conflict. *Journal of Asian Pacific Communication, 21*, 103–120.

Infinedo, P. (2016). Applying uses and gratifications theory and social influence processes to understand students' pervasive adoption of social networking sites: Perspectives from the Americas. *International Journal of Information Management, 36*, 192–206.

Inglis, F. (1993). *Cultural studies*. Cambridge, MA: Basil Blackwell.

Innes, M. (2002). Organizational communication and the symbolic construction of police murder investigations. *British Journal of Sociology, 53*, 67–68.

Innis, H. (1951). *The bias of communication*. Toronto: University of Toronto Press.

Ivy, D. K. (2012). *GenderSpeak: Personal effectiveness in gender communication*. New York, NY: Pearson.

Iyengar, S., & Kinder, D. R. (1987). *News that matters: Television and American opinion*. Chicago, IL: University Press.

James, D., & Drackich, J. (1993). Understanding gender differences in amount of talk. In D. Tannen (Ed.), *Gender and conversational interaction* (pp. 281–312). Oxford: University Press.

Jameson, J. K. (2004). Negotiating autonomy and connection through politeness: A dialectical approach to organizational conflict management. *Western Journal of Communication, 68*, 257–277.

Jandt, F. E. (2012). *An introduction to intercultural communication: Identities in a global communication*. Los Angeles, CA: Sage.

Janis, I. L. (1972). *Victims of groupthink: A psychological study of foreign-policy decisions and fiascoes*. Boston, MA: Houghton Mifflin.

Janis, I. L. (1982). *Groupthink: Psychological studies of policy decisions and fiascoes*. Boston, MA: Houghton Mifflin.

Janis, I. L. (1989). *Crucial decisions: Leadership in policymaking and crisis management*. New York, NY: Free Press.

Janis, I. L., & Gilmore, J. B. (1965). The influence of incentive conditions on the success of role-playing in modifying attitudes. *Journal of Personality and Social Psychology, 1*, 17–27.

Jaworski, A., & Coupland, J. (2005). Othering in gossip: "You go out you have a laugh and you can pull yeah okay but like . . ." *Language in Society, 34*, 667–694.

Jeffres, L. W., Atkin, D. J., & Neuendorf, K. A. (2001). Expanding the range of dependent measures in mainstreaming and cultivation analysis. *Communication Research Reports, 18*, 408–417.

Jenkins, J. J., & Dillon, P. J. (2012). "This is what we're all about": The (re)construction of an oppressive organizational structure. *Southern Communication Journal, 77*, 287–306.

Jensen, K. (2011). A matter of concern: Kenneth Burke, phishing, and the rhetoric of national insecurity. *Rhetoric Review, 30*(2), 170–190.

Jiang, L. C., Bazarova, N. N., & Hancock, J. T. (2011). The disclosure-intimacy link in computer-mediated communication: An attributional extension of the hyperpersonal model. *Human Communication Research, 37*(1), 58–77.

Jin, B., Jin, Y. P., & Hye-Shin, Kim. (2010). What makes online community members commit? A social exchange perspective. *Behaviour & Information Technology, 29*(6), 587–599.

Johnson, K. A. (2011). Citizen journalism, agenda-setting and the 2008 presidential election. *Web Journal of Mass Communication Research, 28*, 23–33.

Johnston, A., Friedman, B., & Peach, S. (2011). Standpoint in political blogs: Voice, authority, and issues. *Women's Studies, 40*(3), 269–298.

Joseph, A. L., & Afifi, T. D. (2010). Military wives' stressful disclosures to their deployed husbands: The role of protective buffering. *Journal of Applied Communication Research, 38*(4), 412–434.

Jourard, S. M. (1971). *The transparent self* (rev. ed.). New York, NY: Van Nostrand.

Kahlor, L., & Eastin, M. S. (2011). Television's role in the culture of violence toward women: A study of television viewing and the cultivation of rape myth acceptance in the United States. *Journal of Broadcasting & Electronic Media, 55*(2), 215–231.

Kalman, Y. M., & Rafaeli, S. (2011). Online pauses and silence: Chronemic expectancy violations in written computer-mediated communication. *Communication Research, 38*(1), 54–69.

Kang, T., & Hoffman, L. H. (2011). Why would you decide to use an online dating site? Factors that lead to online dating. *Communication Research Reports, 28*, 205–213.

Katz, E., Blumler, J. G., & Gurevitch, M. (1974). Utilization of mass communication by the individual. In J. G. Blumler & E. Katz (Eds.), *The uses of mass communication: Current perspectives on gratifications research* (pp. 19–32). Beverly Hills, CA: Sage.

Katz, E., Gurevitch, M., & Haas, H. (1973). On the use of the mass media for important things. *American Sociological Review, 38*, 164–181.

Kaufman, J. M., & Johnson, C. (2004). Stigmatized individuals and the process of identity. *The Sociological Quarterly, 45*, 807–833.

Kaye, B. K., & Johnson, T. J. (2004). A web for all reasons: Uses and gratifications of Internet components for political information. *Telematics and Informatics, 21*, 197–223.

Kellermann, K., & Reynolds, R. (1990). When ignorance is bliss: The role of motivation to reduce uncertainty in uncertainty reduction theory. *Human Communication Research, 17*, 5–35.

Kellner, D., & Hammer, R. (2004). Critical reflections on Mel Gibson's *The Passion of the Christ. Logos, 3*, 3–4.

Kelly, C., & Zak, M. (1999). Narrativity and professional communication: Folktales and community meaning. *Journal of Business and Technical Communication, 13*, 297–317.

Kennedy, G. A. (1991). *Aristotle on Rhetoric: A theory of civil discourse.* New York, NY: Oxford University Press.

Kephart, W. M. (1950). A quantitative analysis of intragroup relations. *American Journal of Sociology, 60*, 544–549.

Kerbrat-Orecchioni, C. (2012). From good manners to facework: Politeness variations and constants in France from the classic age to today. In M. Bax & D. Kadar (Eds.), *Understanding relational (im)politeness: Relational linguistic practices over time and across cultures* (pp. 131–153). Amsterdam, Netherlands: John Benjamins.

Kesebir, S. (2012). The superorganism account of human sociality: How and when human groups are like beehives. *Personality and Social Psychology Review, 16*, 233–261.

Keyton, J. (2005). *Communication and organizational culture.* Thousand Oaks, CA: Sage.

Keyton, J., Ferguson, P., & Rhodes, S. C. (2001). Cultural indicators of sexual harassment. *Southern Communication Journal, 67*, 33–50.

Kim, R. K., & Levine, T. R. (2011). The effect of suspicion on deception detection accuracy: Optimal level or opposing effects. *Communication Reports, 24*, 51–62.

Kim, K-H., & Yun, H. (2007). Crying for me, crying for us: Relational dialectics in a Korean social network site. *Journal of Computer-Mediated Communication, 38*(1), 298–318.

Kim, Sei-Hill (2012). Testing fear of isolation as a causal mechanism: Spiral of silence and genetically modified (GM) foods in South Korea. *International Journal of Public Opinion Research, 24*, 306–324.

Kinefuchi, E., & Orbe, M. P. (2008). Situating oneself in a racialized world: Understanding student reactions to *Crash* through standpoint theory and context-positionality frames. *Journal of International and Intercultural Communication, 1*, 70–90.

Kiousis, S. (2011). Agenda-setting and attitudes. *Journalism Studies, 12*(3), 359–374.

Kirkwood, W. (1992). Narrative and the rhetoric of possibility. *Communication Monographs, 59*, 30–47.

Kirschbaum, K. (2012). Physician communication in the operating room: Expanding application of face-negotiation theory to the health Communication context. *Health Communication, 27*, 292–301.

Kissack, H. (2010). Muted voices: A critical look at email in organizations. *Journal of European Industrial Training, 34*(6), 539–551.

Kissling, E. (1991). Street harassment: The language of sexual terrorism. *Discourse and Society, 2*, 121–135.

Knapp, M. L. (1978). *Nonverbal communication in human interaction.* New York, NY: Holt, Rinehart & Winston.

Knapp, M. L., & Hall, J. A. (2010). *Nonverbal communication in human interaction.* Boston, MA: Cengage /Wadsworth.

Knapp, M. L., Hall, J. A., & Horgan, T. G. (2014). *Nonverbal communication and human interaction.* Boston, MA: Cengage/Wadsworth.

Knapp, M. L., & Vangelisti, A. L. (2009). *Interpersonal communication and human relationships,* 6th ed. Boston, MA: Allyn & Bacon.

Knoble, N. B., & Linville, D. (2012). Outness and relationship satisfaction in same-gender couples. *Journal of Marital and Family Therapy, 38*, 330–339.

Knobloch, L. K. (2008). Uncertainty reduction theory. In L. A. Baxter & D. O. Braithwaite (Eds.), *Engaging theories in interpersonal communication: Multiple perspectives* (pp. 133–144). Thousand Oaks, CA: Sage.

Knobloch, L. K., Miller, L. E., Bond, B. J., & Monnone, S. E. (2007). Relational uncertainty and message processing in marriage. *Communication Monographs, 74*, 154–180.

Knobloch, L. K., Satterlee, K. L., & DiDomenico, S. M. (2010). Relational uncertainty predicting appraisals of face threat in courtship: Integrating uncertainty reduction theory and politeness theory. *Communication Research, 37*(3), 303–334.

Knobloch, L. K., & Solomon, D. H. (2003). Responses to changes in relational uncertainty within dating relationships: Emotions and communication strategies. *Communication Studies, 54*, 282–305.

Knobloch-Westerwick, S., & Meng, J. (2009). Looking the other way: Selective exposure to attitude-consistent and counterattitudinal political information. *Communication Research, 36*(3), 426–448.

Knox, R. E., & Inkster, J. A. (1968). Postdecision dissonance at posttime. *Journal of Personality and Social Psychology, 8*, 310–323.

Koenig-Kellas, J. (2008). Narrative theories. In L. A. Baxter & D. O. Braithwaite (Eds.), *Engaging theories in interpersonal communication: Multiple perspectives* (pp. 241–254). Thousand Oaks, CA: Sage.

Koerber, C. P., & Neck, C. (2003). Groupthink and sports: An application of Whyte's model. *International Journal of Contemporary Hospitality Management, 15*, 20–28.

Koerner, A. (2015). Family communication. In C. Berger (Ed.), *Interpersonal communication* (pp. 419–442). New York, NY: Walter de Gruyter.

Korsch, B. M., Gozzi, E. K., & Francis, V. (1968). Gaps in doctor-patient communication. *Pediatrics, 42*, 855–871.

Kosenko, K. A. (2010). Meanings and dilemmas of sexual safety and communication for transgender individuals. *Health Communication, 25*(2), 131–141.

Kosenko, K. A. (2011). The safer sex communication of transgender adults: Processes and problems. *Journal of Communication, 61*(3), 476–495.

Kramarae, C. (1981). *Women and men speaking: Frameworks for analysis.* Rowley, MA: Newbury House.

Kramarae, C. (2005). Muted group theory and communication: Asking dangerous questions. *Women and Language, 28*(2), 55–61.

Kramarae, C. (2009). Muted group theory. In S. W. Littlejohn & K. A. Foss (Eds.), *Encyclopedia of communication theory* (Vol. 2, pp. 667–669). Los Angeles, CA: Sage.

Kramarae, C., & Treichler, P. (1985). *A feminist dictionary.* Boston, MA: Pandora.

Kramer, M. W. (2004). Toward a communication theory of group dialectics: An ethnographic study of a community theater group. *Communication Monographs, 71*, 311–332.

Kramer, M. W. (2005). Communication and social exchange processes in community theater groups. *Journal of Applied Communication Research, 33,* 159–182.

Kramer, M. W., & Berman, J. E. (2001). Making sense of a university's culture: An examination of undergraduate students' stories. *Southern Communication Journal, 66,* 297–311.

Kubey, R., & Csikszentmihalyi, M. (1990). *Television and the quality of life: How viewing shapes everyday experience.* Hillsdale, NJ: Erlbaum.

Kurtz, H. (1998, August 13). Homicide rate down, except on the evening news. *San Francisco Chronicle,* p. A8.

Kwak, H. (2012). Self-disclosure in online media. *International Journal of Advertising, 31*(3), 485–510.

LaPoire, B. A., & Burgoon, J. K. (1992). A reply from the heart: Who are Sparks and Greene and why are they saying all these horrible things? *Human Communication Research, 18,* 472–482.

Lamoureux, E. L. (1994). Rhetorical dilemmas in Catholic discourse: The case of bishop John J. Meyers. *Communication Studies, 45,* 281–293.

Langellier, K. M., & Peterson, E. E. (2004). *Storytelling in daily life.* Philadelphia, PA: Temple University Press.

LaPoire, B. A., & Burgoon, J. K. (1996). Usefulness of differentiating arousal responses within communication theories: Orienting response or defensive arousal within nonverbal theories of expectancy violation. *Communication Monographs, 63,* 208–230.

LaRose, R., & Eastin, M. S. (2004). A social cognitive theory of Internet uses and gratifications: Toward a new model of media attendance. *Journal of Broadcasting & Electronic Media, 48,* 358–377.

LaRossa, R., & Reitzes, D. C. (1993). Symbolic interactionism and family studies. In P. G. Boss, W. J. Doherty, R. LaRossa, W. R. Schumm, & S. K. Steinmetz (Eds.), *Sourcebook of family theories and methods: A contextual approach* (pp. 135–163). Thousand Oaks, CA: Sage.

Lash, S. (2007). Power after hegemony: Cultural studies in mutation. *Theory, Culture, & Society, 24,* 55–78.

Lasswell, H. D. (1948). The structure and function of communication in society. In L. Bryson (Ed.), *The communication of ideas: A series of addresses* (pp. 215–228). New York, NY: Harper.

Lather, J., & Moyer-Guse, E. (2011). How do we react when our favorite characters are taken away? An examination of a temporary parasocial breakup. *Mass Communication & Society, 14*(2), 196–215.

Lavelle, J. J., Rupp, D. E., & Brockner, J. (2007). Taking a multifoci approach to the study of justice, social exchange, and citizenship behavior: The target similarity model. *Journal of Management, 33,* 841–866.

Lawrence, R. G., & Schafer, M. L. (2012). Debunking Sarah Palin: Mainstream news coverage of "death panels." *Journalism Quarterly, 13,* 766–782.

Lea, M., & Spears R. (1992). Paralanguage and social perception in computer-mediated communication. *Journal of Organizational Computing, 2,* 321–341.

LeBaron, M. (2003). Culture-based negotiation styles. Retrieved from http://www.beyondintractability.org /essay/culture_negotiation

Lee, C., & Niederdeppe, J. (2011). Genre-specific cultivation effects: Lagged associations between overall TV viewing, local TV news viewing, and fatalistic beliefs about cancer prevention. *Communication Research, 38*(6), 731–753.

Lee, F., & DeMarco, D. (2016). Storytelling/narrative theory to address health communication with minority populations. *Applied Nursing Research, 30,* 58–60.

Lee, M. J., Bichard, S. L., Irey, M. S., Walt, H. M., & Carlson, A. J. (2009). Television viewing and ethnic stereotypes: Do college students form stereotypical perceptions of ethnic groups as a result of heavy television consumption? *Howard Journal of Communications, 20*(1), 95–110.

Leeds-Hurwitz, W. (1990). Notes on the history of intercultural communication: The foreign service institute and the mandate for intercultural training. *Quarterly Journal of Speech, 76,* 262–281.

Leinaweaver, J. (2012). On becoming a global human: CMM, international adoption, and the global burden of self. In C. Creede, B. Fisher-Yoshida, & P. V. Gallegos (Eds.), *The reflective, facilitative, and interpretive practice of the Coordinated Management of Meaning* (pp. 173–190). Madison, NJ: Farleigh Dickinson University Press.

Lemin, D. (2010). *Public opinion in the social media era: Toward a new understanding of the spiral of silence.* Ann Arbor, MI: ProQuest Publishing.

Lester, J. (2008). Performing gender in the workplace: Gender socialization, power, and identity among women faculty members. *Community College Review, 35,* 277–305.

Leung, L., & Wei, R. (2000). More than just talk on the move: Uses and gratifications of the cellular phone. *Journalism & Mass Communication Quarterly, 77,* 308–320.

Levine, T. R., Anders, L. N., Banas, J., Baum, K. L., Endo, K., Hu, A. D. S., & Wong, C. H. (2000). Norms, expectations, and deception: A norm violation model of veracity judgments. *Communication Monographs, 67*, 123–137.

Levine, T. R., Sang-Yeon Kim, & Ferrara, M. (2010). Social exchange, uncertainty, and communication content as factors impacting the relational outcomes of betrayal. *Human Communication, 13*(4), 303–318.

Levinson, P. (2000). McLuhan and media ecology. In *Proceedings of the Media Ecology Association,* Vol. 1. Retrieved from http://www.media-ecology.org/publications/MEA_proceedings/v1/McLuhan_and_media_ecology.html

Levinson, P. (2001). *Digital McLuhan: A guide to the information millennium.* London: Routledge.

Lev-On, A. (2012). Communication, community, crisis: Mapping uses and gratifications in the contemporary media environment. *New Media & Society, 14*(1), 98–116.

Levy, M., & Windahl, S. (1985). The concept of audience activity. In P. L. Palmgreen, L. A. Wenner, & K. E. Rosengren (Eds.), *Media gratifications research: Current perspectives* (pp. 109–122). Beverly Hills, CA: Sage.

Lewis, J., & Morgan, M. (2001). He may not be a liberal but he plays one on TV: Imagining the ideology of President Clinton. *The Communication Review, 4*, 327–346.

Leysan Khakimova, L., Zhang, Y., & Hall, J. A. (2012). Conflict management styles: The role of ethnic identity and self-construal among young male Arabs and Americans. *Journal of Intercultural Communication Research, 41*, 37–57.

Lim, J. (2011). First-level and second-level intermedia agenda-setting among major news websites. *Asian Journal of Communication, 21*(2), 167–185.

Lim, S. S., Vadrevu, S., Chan, Y. H., & Basnyat, I. (2012). Facework on Facebook: The online publicness of juvenile delinquents and youths-at-risk. *Journal of Broadcasting & Electronic Media, 56*, 346–361.

Lim, T., & Bowers, J. W. (1991). Facework, solidarity, approbation, and tact. *Human Communication Research, 176*, 415–450.

Lin, C. A., & Salwen, M. B. (1997). Predicting the spiral of silence on a controversial issue. *Howard Journal of Communications, 8*, 129–141.

Linder, E. W. (2012). *Yearbook of Canadian and American churches.* Nashville, TN: Abingdon Press.

Lingle, J. H., & Ostrom, T. M. (1981). Principles of memory and cognition in attitude formation. In R. E. Petty, T. M. Ostrom, & T. C. Brock (Eds.), *Cognitive responses in persuasive communications* (pp. 399–420). New York, NY: McGraw-Hill.

Lipp, D. (2013). *Disney U: How Disney University develops the most engaged, loyal, and customer-centric employees.* New York, NY: McGraw-Hill.

Lippmann, W. (1922). *Public opinion.* New York, NY: Harcourt Brace.

Liska, C., Petrun, E. L., Sellnow, T. L., & Seeger, M. W. (2012). Chaos theory, self-organization, and industrial accidents: Crisis communication in the Kingston coal ash spill. *Southern Communication Journal, 77*(3), 180–197.

Littlejohn, S. W., & Foss, K. A. (2011). Theories of human communication, 10th ed. Long Grove, IL: Waveland Press.

Littlejohn, S., & Foss, K. (2008). *Theories of human communication,* 9th ed. Boston, MA: Cengage/Wadsworth.

Liu, J. (2006). *A cross-national and double-sided test of 'spiral of silence' theory: Culture, governmental form and personality.* Paper presented at the annual meeting of the International Communication Association, San Francisco, CA.

Loehwing, M., & Motter, J. (2012). Cultures of circulation: Utilizing co-cultures and counterpublics in intercultural new media research. *China Media Research, 8*(4), 29–38.

Logan, R. K. (2011). McLuhan misunderstood: Setting the record straight. *International Journal of McLuhan Studies, 1*, 27–47.

Long, E. (1989). Feminism and cultural studies. *Critical Studies in Mass Communication, 6*, 427–435.

Longley, J., & Pruitt, D. G. (1980). Groupthink: A critique of Janis' theory. *Review of Personality and Social Psychology, 1*, 74–93.

Lord, C. (1994). The intention of Aristotle's *Rhetoric.* In E. Schiappa (Ed.), *Landmark essays on classical Greek rhetoric* (pp. 157–168). Davis, CA: Hermagoras Press.

Lovejoy, K., & Saxton, G. D. (2012). Information, community, and action: How nonprofit organizations use social media. *Journal of Computer-Mediated Communication, 17*, 337–353.

Loveland, M. T., & Popescu, D. (2011). Democracy on the web. *Information, Communication & Society, 14*(5), 684–703.

Lucaites, J. L., & Condit, C. M. (1985). Reconstructing narrative theory: A functional perspective. *Journal of Communication, 35,* 9–108.

Lucas, K., & Sherry, J. L. (2004). Sex differences in video game play: A communication-based explanation. *Communication Research, 31,* 499–523.

Lucas, K., & Steimel, S. J. (2009). Creating and responding to the gen(d)eralized other: Women miners' community-constructed identities. *Women's Studies in Communication, 32*(3), 320–347.

Lull, J. (1982). How families select television programs: A mass-observational study. *Journal of Broadcasting, 26,* 801–811.

Lum, C. M. K. (2006). Notes toward an intellectual history of media ecology. In C. M. K. Lum (Ed.), *Perspectives on culture, technology, and communication: The media ecology tradition* (pp. 1–60). Cresskill, NJ: Hampton.

Lusch, R. F., Brown, J. R., & O'Brien, M. (2011). Protecting relational assets: A pre and post field study of a horizontal business combination. *Journal of the Academy of Marketing Science, 39*(2), 175–197.

Lustig, M. & Koester, J. (2013). *Intercultural competence.* New York, NY: Pearson.

Lyman, S. M. (1990). *Civilization: Contents, discontents, malcontents, and other essays in social theory.* Fayetteville, AK: University of Arkansas.

MacCabe, C. (2008). An interview with Stuart Hall, December 2007. *Critical Quarterly, 50,* 12–42.

Macdonald, D. (1967). He has looted all culture. . . . In G. Stearn (Ed.), *McLuhan: Hot and cool* (pp. 56–77). New York, NY: Dial.

MacIntyre, A. (1981). *After virtue: A study in moral theory.* Notre Dame, IN: University of Notre Dame Press.

MacKinnon, B. (2012). *Ethics: Theory and contemporary issues.* Boston, MA: Cengage.

Maier, S. (2010). All the news fit to post? Comparing news content on the web to newspapers, television, and radio. *Journalism & Mass Communication Quarterly, 87*(3), 548–562.

Maity, S. K., Gupta, A., Goyal, P., & Mukherjee, A. (2015). A stratified learning approach for predicting the popularity of Twitter idioms. In *Proceedings of the International Conference on weblogs and social media* (pp. 642–645). Palo Alto, CA: Association for the Advancement of Artificial Intelligence.

Mandziuk, R. M. (2003). Commemorating Sojourner Truth: Negotiating the politics of race and gender in the spaces of public memory. *Western Journal of Communication, 67,* 271–291.

Manwell, L. A. (2010). In denial of democracy: Social psychological implications for public discourse on state crimes against democracy post-9/11. *American Behavioral Scientist, 53*(6), 848–884.

Marchand, M. (1989). *Marshall McLuhan: The medium and the messenger.* New York, NY: Ticknor & Fields.

Markey, P. M., & Markey, C. N. (2007). Romantic ideals, romantic obtainment, and relationship experiences: The complementarity of interpersonal traits among romantic partners. *Journal of Social and Personal Relationships, 24,* 517–533.

Marlow, M. L., & Giles, H. (2013). "I don't know how to speak so I just stay silent": Uncertainty management among Chinese immigrant women seeking health care in the United States. In F. Sharifian & M. Jamarani (Eds.), *Language and intercultural communication in the new era* (pp. 245–262). New York, NY: Routledge.

Marrs, P. (2012). Taming the lizard: Transforming conversations-gone-bad at work. In C. Creede, B. Fisher-Yoshida, & P. V. Gallegos (Eds.), *The reflective, facilitative, and interpretive practice of the Coordinated Management of Meaning* (pp. 77–94). Madison, NJ: Farleigh Dickinson University Press.

Marsh, C. (2006). Aristotelian ethos and the new morality: Implications for media literacy and media ethics. *Journal of Mass Media Ethics, 21,* 338–352.

Martin, J. (2012). "That's how we do things around here": Organizational culture (and change) in libraries. Retrieved from http://www.inthelibrarywiththeleadpipe.org/2012/thats-how-we-do-things-around-here/

Martin, J. N., & Nakayama, T. K. (2011). *Experiencing intercultural communication: An introduction,* 4th ed. New York, NY: McGraw Hill.

Martins, L. L., & Shalley, C. E. (2011). Creativity in virtual work: Effects of demographic differences. *Small Group Research, 42,* 536–561.

Martins, N., & Harrison, K. (2012). Racial and gender differences in the relationship between children's television use and self-esteem: A longitudinal panel study. *Communication Research, 39*(3), 338–357.

Marx, K. (1963). *The communist manifesto of Karl Marx and Friedrich Engels.* New York, NY: Russell & Russell.

Marx, K., & Engels, F. (1848). *The Communist manifesto.* New York, NY: Penguin Books.

Matheson, C. (2001). The Simpsons *and philosophy: The d'oh! of Homer*. Ottawa, IL: Open Court.

Matsumoto, D. R., Frank, M. G., & Hwang, H. S. (2013). *Nonverbal communication: Science and applications*. Thousand Oaks, CA: Sage.

Matz, D. C., & Wood, W. (2005). Cognitive dissonance in groups: The consequences of disagreement. *Journal of Personality and Social Psychology, 88*, 1–22.

May, A., & Tenzek, K. E. (2011). Seeking Mrs. Right: Uncertainty reduction in online surrogacy ads. *Qualitative Research Reports in Communication, 12*(1), 27–33.

May, S. (2012). *Case studies in organizational communication: Ethical perspectives and practices*. Thousand Oaks, CA: Sage.

McAulliff, B. D., & Kovera, M. B. (2012). Do jurors get what they expect? Traditional versus alternative forms of children's testimony. *Psychology, Crime & Law, 18*, 27–47.

McBride, C., & Toller, P. (2011). Negotiation of face between bereaved parents and their social networks. *Southern Communication Journal, 76*, 210–229.

McCartha, M., & Strauman, E. C. (2009). Fallen stars and strategic redemption: A narrative analysis of the *National Enquirer*. *Florida Communication Journal, 37*(2), 71–82.

McClish, G. (2007). A man of feeling, a man of colour: James Forten and the rise of African American deliberative rhetoric. *Rhetorica, 25*, 297–328.

McClure, K. (2009). Resurrecting the Narrative Paradigm: Identification and the case of Young Earth Creationism. *Rhetoric Society Quarterly, 39*(2), 189–211.

McCombs, M. E. (2004). *Setting the agenda: The mass media and public opinion*. Cambridge, UK: Polity.

McCombs, M. E., & Bell, T. (1996). The agenda-setting role of mass communication. In M. B. Salwen & D. W. Stacks (Eds.), *An integrated approach to communication theory and research* (pp. 93–110). Mahwah, NJ: Erlbaum.

McCombs, M. E., & Shaw, D. L. (1972). The agenda-setting function of mass media. *Public Opinion Quarterly, 36*(2), 176–187.

McCombs, M. E., & Shaw, D. L. (1993). The evolution of agenda-setting research: Twenty-five years in the marketplace of ideas. *Journal of Communication, 43*(2), 58–67.

McCombs, M., & Funk, M. (2011). Shaping the agenda of local daily newspapers: A methodology merging the agenda setting and community structure perspectives. *Mass Communication & Society, 14*(6), 905–919.

McDevitt, M., Kiousis, S., & Wahl-Jorgensen, K. (2003). Spiral of moderation: Opinion expression in computer-mediated discussion. *International Journal of Public Opinion Research, 15*, 454–471.

McEwan, T., & Guerrero, L. K. (2012). Maintenance behavior and relationship quality as predictors of perceived availability of resources in newly formed college friendship networks. *Communication Studies, 63*, 421–440.

McGloin, R., & Nowak, K. (2011). *Using Expectancy Violations Theory to explain the effect of avatars on purchase intention and the uncanny valley*. Paper presented at the annual meeting of the International Communication Association, Boston, MA.

McGuire, T. (2010). From emotions to spirituality: "Spiritual labor" as the commodification, codification, and regulation of organizational members' spirituality. *Management Communication Quarterly, 24*(1), 74–103.

McKinney, D. H., & Donaghy, W. C. (1993). Dyad gender structure, uncertainty reduction, and self-disclosure during initial interaction. In P. Kalbfleish (Ed.), *Interpersonal communication: Evolving interpersonal relationships* (pp. 33–50). Hillsdale, NJ: Erlbaum.

McLaughlin, H., Uggen, C., & Blackstone, A. (2012). Sexual harassment, workplace authority, and the paradox of power. *American Sociological Review, 77*, 625–647.

McLaughlin, C., & Vitak, J. (2012). Norm evolution and violation on Facebook. *New Media & Society, 14*, 299–315.

McLuhan, M. (1962). *The Gutenberg galaxy*. New York, NY: Mentor.

McLuhan, M. (1964). *Understanding media*. New York, NY: Mentor.

McLuhan, M., & Fiore, Q. (1967). *The medium is the massage: An inventory of effects*. New York, NY: Bantam Books.

McLuhan, M., & Fiore, Q. (1968). *War and peace in the global village*. New York, NY: Bantam Books.

McLuhan, M., & Fiore, Q. (1996). *The medium is the massage: An inventory of effects*. San Francisco, CA: HardWired.

McLuhan, M., & McLuhan, E. (1988). *Laws of media: The new science*. Toronto: University of Toronto Press.

McLuhan, M., & Nevitt, B. (1972). *Take today: The executive as dropout*. New York, NY: Harper & Row.

McLuhan, M., & Parker, H. (1969). *Counterblast*. New York, NY: Harcourt, Brace & World.

McLuhan's relevance in today's media mess age. *Saturday-Post*. Retrieved from http://www.siliconvalleywatcher.com/mt/archives/2011/07/the_importance_2.php

McMillan, K., & Albrecht, S. (2010). Measuring social exchange constructs in organizations. *Communication Methods and Measures*, 4(3), 201–220.

McPhee, R., Poole, M. S., & Iverson, J. (2014). Structuration theory. In L. L. Putnam & D. Mumby (Eds.), *The SAGE handbook of organizational communication: Advances in theory, research, and methods* (pp. 75–100). Thousand Oaks, CA: Sage.

McPherson, M. B., & Liang, Y. (2007). Students' reactions to teachers' management of compulsive communicators. *Communication Education*, 56, 18–33.

McQuail, D. (1984). With the benefits of hindsight: Reflections on uses and gratifications research. *Critical Studies in Mass Communication*, 1, 177–193.

McQuail, D., Blumler, J. G., & Brown, J. (1972). The television audience: A revised perspective. In D. McQuail (Ed.), *Sociology of mass communication* (pp. 135–165). Harmondsworth, UK: Penguin Books.

Mead, G. H. (1934). *Mind, self and society: From the standpoint of a social behaviorist*. Chicago, IL: University of Chicago Press.

Meisenbach, R. J., Remke, R. V., Buzzanell, P. M., & Liu, M. (2008). "They allowed": Pentadic mapping of women's maternity leave discourse as organizational rhetoric. *Communication Monographs*, 75, 1–24.

Meraz, S. (2011). Using time series analysis to measure intermedia agenda-setting influence in traditional media and political blog networks. *Journalism & Mass Communication Quarterly*, 88(1), 176–194.

Merritt, B. D. (1991). Bill Cosby: TV auteur? *Journal of Popular Culture*, 24, 89–102.

Messersmith, A., Keyton, J., & Bisel, R. B. (2009). Teaching organizational culture: Orientations on discourse and culture. *Communication Teacher*, 23, 81–86.

Metts, S., & Lamb, E. (2006). Methodological approaches to the study of family communication. In L. H. Turner & R. West (Eds.), *The family communication sourcebook* (pp. 83–108). Thousand Oaks, CA: Sage.

Metzger, M. J. (2004). Privacy, trust, and disclosure: Exploring barriers to electronic commerce. *Journal of Computer-Mediated Communication*, 9, 204–223.

Meyer, J. R. (2011). Regretted messages: Cognitive antecedents and post hoc reflection. *Journal of Language & Social Psychology*, 30(4), 376–395.

Meyer, M. D. E. (2003). "It's me. I'm it": Defining adolescent sexual identity through relational dialectics in *Dawson's Creek*. *Communication Quarterly*, 51, 262–280.

Meyrowitz, J. (1985). *No sense of place*. New York, NY: Oxford University Press.

Miceli, M., Near, J., Rehg, M., and Van Scotter, J. (2012). Predicting employee reactions to perceived organizational wrongdoing: Demoralization, proactive personality, and whistle-blowing. *Human Relations*, 65, 923–954.

Miike, Y. (2007). An Asiacentric reflection on Eurocentric bias in communication theory. *Communication Monographs*, 74, 272–278.

Mikucki-Enyart, S. (2011). Parent-in-law privacy management: An examination of the links among relational uncertainty, topic avoidance, in-group status, and in-law satisfaction. *Journal of Family Communication*, 11(4), 237–263.

Milkie, M. A. (1999). Social comparisons, reflected appraisals, and mass media: The impact of pervasive beauty images on Black and White girls' self-concepts. *Social Psychology Quarterly*, 62, 190–210.

Miller, A., & Roberts, S. (2010). Visual agenda-setting and proximity after Hurricane Katrina: A study of those closest to the event. *Visual Communication Quarterly*, 17(1), 31–46.

Miller, G. R. (1981). Tis the season to be jolly: A yule-tide 1980 assessment of communication research. *Human Communication Research*, 7, 371–377.

Miller, G. R., & Steinberg, M. (1975). *Between people: A new analysis of interpersonal communication*. Chicago, IL: Science Research Associates.

Miller, K. (2005). *Communication theories: Perspectives, processes, and contexts*. New York, NY: McGraw-Hill.

Miller, K. (2009). *Organizational communication*. Boston, MA: Sage.

Millhous, L. M. (2004). Projected measures of motivation and media choice. *Communication Research Reports*, 21, 154–163.

Min, S., & Kim, Y. M. (2012). Choosing the right media for mobilization: Issue advocacy groups' media niches in the competitive media environment. *Mass Communication and Society*, 15(2), 225–244.

Minnebo, J., & Eggermont, S. (2007). Watching the young use illicit drugs: Direct experience, exposure to television and the stereotyping of adolescents' substance use. *Young, 15,* 129–144.

Minnebo, J., & Van Acker, A. (2004). Does television influence adolescents' perceptions of and attitudes toward people with mental illness? *Journal of Community Psychology, 32,* 257–275.

Modaff, D. P., Butler, J. A., & DeWine, S. (2011). *Organizational communication: Foundations, challenges and misunderstandings.* Boston, MA: Pearson/Allyn & Bacon.

Molnar, G., & Kelly, J. (2012). *Sport, exercise, and social theory: An introduction.* New York, NY: Routledge.

Monge, P. R. (1973). Theory construction in the study of communication: The system paradigm. *Journal of Communication, 23,* 5–16.

Monge, P. R., & Contractor, N. (2003). *Theories of communication networks.* Oxford: University Press.

Mongeau, P. A., & Henningsen, M. L. (2008). Stage theories of relationship development. In L. A. Baxter & D. O. Braithwaite (Eds.), *Engaging theories in interpersonal communication* (pp. 363–376). Thousand Oaks, CA: Sage.

Mongeau, P. A., Jacobsen, J., & Donnerstein, C. (2007). Defining dates and first date goals: Generalizing from undergraduates to single adults. *Communication Research, 34,* 526–527.

Moniz, R. J. (2011). Communicating who we are: The theory of organizational culture in the workplace. *NASSP Bulletin, 96,* 228–242.

Montgomery, E. (2004). Tortured families: A Coordinated Management of Meaning analysis. *Family Process, 43,* 349–372.

Moody, M. (2011). A rhetorical analysis of the meaning of the "independent woman" in the lyrics and videos of male and female rappers. *American Communication Journal, 13*(1), 43–58.

Moon, D. (2008). Concepts of "culture": Implications for intercultural communication research. In M. K. Asante, Y. Miike, & J. Yin (Eds.), *The global intercultural communication reader* (pp. 11–26). New York, NY: Routledge.

Moon, H., Quigley, N., & Marr, J. C. (2012). How interpersonal motives explain the influence of organizational culture on organizational productivity, creativity, and adaptation: The ambidextrous interpersonal motives (AIM) model of organizational culture. *Organizational Psychology Review, 2,* 109–128.

Moon, S., & Nelson, M. R. (2008). Exploring the influence of media exposure and cultural values on Korean immigrants' advertising evaluations. *International Journal of Advertising, 27,* 299–330.

Moore, J., & Mattson-Lauters, A. (2009). Coordinated management of meaning: Do established rules aid in chat room experiences? *American Communication Journal, 11,* 1–35.

Moran, R. (1996). Artifice and persuasion: The work of metaphor in the *Rhetoric.* In A. O. Rorty (Ed.), *Essays on Aristotle's Rhetoric* (pp. 385–398). Berkeley, CA: University of California Press.

Morgan, M. (1986). Television and the erosion of regional diversity. *Journal of Broadcasting & Electronic Media, 30,* 123–129.

Morgan, M., & Shanahan, J. (2010). The state of cultivation. *Journal of Broadcasting & Electronic Media, 54*(2), 337–355.

Morris, M., & Ogan, C. (1996). The Internet as mass medium. *Journal of Communication, 46,* 39–50.

Morrison, E. W. (2002). Information seeking within organizations. *Human Communication Research, 28,* 229–242.

Morrison, J. C. (2006). Marshall McLuhan: The modern Janus. In C. M. K. Lum (Ed.), *Perspectives on culture, technology, and communication: The media ecology tradition* (pp. 163–200). Cresskill, NJ: Hampton.

Motley, M. T. (1990). On whether one can(not) not communicate: An examination via traditional communication postulates. *Western Journal of Speech Communication, 54,* 1–20.

Mulrine, A. (2008, June 2). To battle groupthink, the Army trains a skeptics corps. *U.S. News & World Report, 30,* 32.

Mumby, D. (2011). *Reframing difference in organizational communication studies: Research, pedagogy, and practice.* Thousand Oaks, CA: Sage.

Mumby, D. K., & May, S. (2005). Introduction: Thinking about engagement. In S. May & D. K. Mumby (Eds.), *Engaging organizational theory & research* (pp. 1–14). Thousand Oaks, CA: Sage.

Muraco, A., & Fredriksen-Goldsen, K. I. (2011). That's what friends do: Informal caregiving for chronically ill lesbian, gay and bisexual elders. *Journal of Social and Personal Relationships, 28,* 1073–1092.

Murdock, G. (1989). Cultural studies: Missing links. *Critical Studies in Mass Communication, 6,* 436–440.

Murray, J. (2003). An other-Burkean frame: Rhetorical criticism and the call of the other. *Communication Studies, 54*, 169–187.

Murray, D. S. (2012). Interactional logics: Moving CMM forward by looking back. In C. Creede, B. Fisher-Yoshida, & P. V. Gallegos (Eds.), *The reflective, facilitative, and interpretive practice of the Coordinated Management of Meaning* (pp. 153–172). Madison, NJ: Farleigh Dickinson University Press.

Muthusamy, S. K., & White, M. A. (2005). Learning and knowledge transfer in strategic alliances: A social exchange view. *Organization Studies, 26*, 415–441.

Mutz, D. C., & Nir, L. (2010). Not necessarily the news: Does fictional television influence real-world policy preferences? *Mass Communication and Society, 13*(2), 196–217.

Myers, S. A., & Anderson, C. M. (2008). *The fundamentals of small group communication.* Thousand Oaks, CA: Sage.

Nakayama, T. K., & Krizek, R. L. (1995). Whiteness: A strategic rhetoric. *Quarterly Journal of Speech, 81*, 291–309.

Neel, J. (1994). *Aristotle's voice: Rhetoric, theory and writing in America.* Carbondale, IL: Southern Illinois University Press.

Neel, J. (2013). *Aristotle's voice: Rhetoric, theory, and writing in America.* Carbondale, IL: Southern Illinois University.

Neff, G., Jordan, T., McVeigh-Schultz, T., & Gillespie, T. (2012). Affordances, technical agency, and the politics of technologies of cultural production. *Journal of Electronic & Broadcasting Media, 56*, 299–313.

Neill, S. (2009). *The alternative channel: How social media is challenging the spiral of silence theory in GLBT communities of color.* Unpublished Master's thesis. American University, Washington, DC.

Nelson, C. (1989). Writing as the accomplice of language: Kenneth Burke and poststructuralism. In H. W. Simons & T. Melia (Eds.), *The legacy of Kenneth Burke* (pp. 156–173). Madison, WI: University of Wisconsin Press.

Neuliep, J. W. (2012). The relationship among intercultural communication apprehension, ethnocentrism, uncertainty reduction, and communication satisfaction during initial intercultural interaction: An extension of anxiety and uncertainty management (AUM) theory. *Journal of Intercultural Communication Research, 41*(1), 1–16.

Neuliep, J. W., & Grohskopf, E. L. (2000). Uncertainty reduction and communication satisfaction during initial interaction: An initial test and replication of a new axiom. *Communication Reports, 13*, 67–77.

Neuwirth, K., Frederick, E., & Mayo, C. (2007). The spiral of silence and fear of isolation. *Journal of Communication, 57*, 450–468.

Newcomb, H. (1978). Assessing the violence profile studies of Gerbner and Gross: A humanistic critique and suggestion. *Communication Research, 5*, 264–283.

Nichols, M. H. (1952). Kenneth Burke and the new rhetoric. *The Quarterly Journal of Speech, 38*, 133–134.

Nichols, W. L. (2012). Deception versus privacy management in discussions of sexual history. *Atlantic Journal of Communication, 20*(2), 101–115.

Nicolini, D. (2013). *Practice theory, work, and organization: An introduction.* New York, NY: Oxford University Press.

Niederdeppe, J., Fowler, E. F., Goldstein, K., & Pribble, J. (2010). Does local television news coverage cultivate fatalistic beliefs about cancer prevention? *Journal of Communication, 60*(2), 230–253.

Nkomo, S. M., & Cox, T. (1996). Diverse identities in organizations. In S. R. Clegg, C. Hardy, & W. R. Nord (Eds.), *Handbook of organizational studies* (pp. 338–356). London: Sage.

Noelle-Neumann, E. (1983). The effect of media on media effects research. *Journal of Communication, 33*, 157–165.

Noelle-Neumann, E. (1984). *The spiral of silence: Public opinion—our social skin.* Chicago, IL: University of Chicago Press.

Noelle-Neumann, E. (1985). The spiral of silence—A response. In K. R. Sanders, L. L. Kaid, & D. D. Nimmo (Eds.), *Political communication year-book, 1984* (pp. 43–65). Carbondale, IL: Southern Illinois University.

Noelle-Neumann, E. (1991). The theory of public opinion: The concept of the spiral of silence. In J. A. Anderson (Ed.), *Communication yearbook 14* (pp. 256–287). Newbury Park, CA: Sage.

Noelle-Neumann, E. (1993). *The spiral of silence: Public opinion—our social skin*, 2nd ed. Chicago, IL: University of Chicago Press.

Noelle-Neumann, E., & Petersen, T. (2004). The spiral of silence and the social nature of man. In L. L. Kaid (Ed.), *Handbook of political communication* (pp. 339–356). Mahwah, NJ: Erlbaum.

Nomai, A. J., & Dionisopoulos, G. N. (2002). Framing the Cubas narrative: The American Dream and the capitalist reality. *Communication Studies, 53*, 97–111.

Northup, T. (2010). Is everyone a little bit racist? Exploring cultivation using implicit and explicit measures. *Southwestern Mass Communication Journal, 26*(1), 29–41.

Norwood, K. M., & Baxter, L. A. (2011). 'Dear birth mother': Addressivity and meaning-making in online adoption-seeking letters. *Journal of Family Communication, 11*(3), 198–217.

O'Brien Hallstein, D. L. (1999). A postmodern caring: Feminist standpoint theories, revisioned caring and communication ethics. *Western Journal of Communication, 63*, 32–56.

O'Brien Hallstein, D. L. (2000). Where standpoint stands now: An introduction and commentary. *Women's Studies in Communication, 23*, 1–15.

O'Leary, C. M. (1997). Counteridentification or counterhegemony? Transforming feminist standpoint theory. *Women and Politics, 18*, 45–72.

O'Neill, B. S., & Arendt, L. A. (2008). Psychological climate and work attitudes: The importance of telling the right story. *Journal of Leadership & Organizational Studies, 14*, 353–370.

Oetzel, J. G., Ting-Toomey, S., Yokochi, Y., Masumoto, T., & Takai, J. (2000). A typology of facework behaviors in conflicts with best friends and relative strangers. *Communication Quarterly, 48*, 397–419.

Oetzel, J., Ting-Toomey, S., Chew-Sanchez, M. I., Harris, R., Wilcox, R., & Stumpf, S. (2003). Face and facework in conflicts with parents and siblings: A cross-cultural comparison of Germans, Japanese, Mexicans, and U.S. Americans. *Journal of Family Communication, 3*, 67–93.

Olsen, T. (1978). *Silences*. New York, NY: Delacorte Press.

On the importance of public opinion. Retrieved from http://www.motherjones.com/kevin-drum/2011/03/importance-public-opinion

Ono, K. A. (2011). Critical: A finer edge. *Communication & Critical/Cultural Studies, 8*(1), 93–96.

Orbe, M. P. (1998). *Constructing co-cultural theory: An explication of culture, power, and communication.* Thousand Oaks, CA: Sage.

Orbe, M. P. (2005). Continuing the legacy of theorizing from the margins: Conceptualizations of co-cultural theory. *Women and Language, 28*(2), 65–66.

Ortiz, M., & Behm-Morawitz, E. (2015). Latinos' perceptions of intergroup relations in the United States: The cultivation of group-based attitudes and beliefs from English- and Spanish-language television. *Journal of Social Issues, 71*, 90–105.

Ott, B. (2003). "I'm Bart Simpson, who the hell are you?" A study in postmodern identity (re)construction. *Journal of Popular Culture, 37*, 56–82.

Out at the *New York Times*: Gays, lesbians, AIDS, and homophobia inside America's paper of record. Retrieved from http://www.huffingtonpost.com/2012/11/28/new-york-times-gays-lesbians-aids-homophobia_n_2200684.html

Owlett, J. S., Richards, K., Wilson, S. R., DeFreese, J. D., & Roberts, F. (2015). Privacy management in the military family during deployment: Adolescents' perspectives. *Journal of Family Communication, 15*, 141–158.

Pacanowsky, M. E. (1983). A small town cop. In L. L. Putnam & M. E. Pacanowsky (Eds.), *Communication and organizations: An interpretive approach* (pp. 261–282). Beverly Hills, CA: Sage.

Pacanowsky, M. E. (1989). Creating and narrating organizational realities. In B. Dervin, L. Grossberg, B. J. O'Keefe, & E. Wartella (Eds.), *Rethinking communication* (pp. 250–257). Newbury Park, CA: Sage.

Pacanowsky, M. E., & O'Donnell-Trujillo, N. (1982). Communication and organizational cultures. *Western Journal of Speech Communication, 46*, 115–130.

Pacanowsky, M. E., & O'Donnell-Trujillo, N. (1983). Organizational communication as cultural performance. *Communication Monographs, 50*, 127–147.

Pacanowsky, M. E., & O'Donnell-Trujillo, N. (1990). Communication and organizational cultures. In S. R. Corman, S. P. Banks, C. R. Bantz, & M. E. Mayer (Eds.), *Foundations of organizational communication: A reader* (pp. 142–153). New York, NY: Longman.

Pachirat, T. (2013). *Ethnography and interpretation.* New York, NY: Routledge.

Pais, S. (1997). Asian Indian families in America. In M. K. DeGenova (Ed.), *Families in cultural context* (pp. 173–190). Mountain View, CA: Mayfield.

Palmieri, C., Prestano, K., Gandley, R., Overton, E., & Zhang, Q. (2012). The Facebook phenomenon: Online self-disclosure and uncertainty reduction. *China Media Research, 8*(1), 48–53.

Papa, M. J., Daniels, T. D., & Spiker, B. K. (2008). *Organizational communication: Perspectives and trends.* Thousand Oaks, CA: Sage.

Papacharissi, Z., & Rubin, A. M. (2000). Predictors of Internet use. *Journal of Broadcasting & Electronic Media, 44*, 175–196.

Parker, B. J., & Plank, R. E. (2000). A uses and gratifications perspective on the Internet as a new information source. *American Business Review, 18*, 43.

Parkes, D. (2011) *Making dialogic or relational conversations in formal workplace mentoring relationships.* Unpublished doctoral dissertation. Fielding Graduate University, Santa Barbara, CA.

Parks, M., & Adelman, M. (1983). Communication networks and the development of romantic relationships: An expansion of uncertainty reduction theory. *Human Communication Research, 10,* 55–80.

Patton, T. O. (2004). Reflections of a Black woman professor: Racism and sexism in academia. *Howard Journal of Communications, 15,* 185–200.

Pearce, K. (2012). Living into very bad news: The use of CMM as spiritual practice. In C. Creede, B. Fisher-Yoshida, & P. V. Gallegos (Eds.), *The reflective, facilitative, and interpretive practice of the Coordinated Management of Meaning* (pp. 277–294). Madison, NJ: Farleigh Dickinson University Press.

Pearce, W. B. (1989). *Communication and the human condition.* Carbondale, IL: Southern Illinois University Press.

Pearce, W. B. (1994). *Interpersonal communication: Making social worlds.* New York, NY: HarperCollins.

Pearce, W. B. (1995). A sailing guide for social constructionists. In W. Leeds-Hurwitz (Ed.), *Social approaches to communication* (pp. 88–112). New York, NY: Guilford Press.

Pearce, W. B. (2005). The Coordinated Management of Meaning (CMM). In W. B. Gudykunst (Ed.), *Theorizing about intercultural communication* (pp. 35–54). Thousand Oaks, CA: Sage Publications.

Pearce, W. B. (2012). Evolution and transformation: A brief history of CMM and a meditation on what using does to us. In C. Creede, B. Fisher-Yoshida, & P. V. Gallegos (Eds.), *The reflective, facilitative, and interpretive practice of the Coordinated Management of Meaning* (pp. 1–22). Madison, NJ: Farleigh Dickinson University Press.

Pearce, W. B. (2007). *Making social worlds: A communication perspective.* Malden, MA: Blackwell.

Pearce, W. B., & Conklin, F. (1979). A model of hierarchical meanings in coherent conversation and a study of indirect responses. *Communication Monographs, 46,* 75–87.

Pearce, W. B., & Cronen, V. E. (1980). *Communication, action, and meaning: The creation of social realities.* New York, NY: Praeger.

Pearce, W. B., Cronen, V. E., & Conklin, F. (1979). On what to look at when analyzing communication: A hierarchical model of actors' meanings. *Communication, 4,* 195–220.

Pearson, J. C. (1985, October). *Innovation in teaching gender and communication: Excluding and including women and men.* Paper presented at the annual meeting of the Organization for the Study of Communication, Language, and Gender, Lincoln, NE.

Pearson, J. C., & VanHorn, S. B. (2004). Communication and gender identity: A retrospective analysis. *Communication Quarterly, 52,* 284–299.

Pearson, J. C., West, R., & Turner, L. H. (1995). *Gender and communication,* 3rd ed. Madison, WI: Brown & Benchmark.

Perloff, R. M. (1993). *The dynamics of persuasion.* Hillsdale, NJ: Erlbaum.

Perse, E. M., & Courtright, J. A. (1993). Normative images of communication media: Mass and interpersonal channels in the new media environment. *Human Communication Research, 19,* 485–503.

Perse, E. M., & Greenberg-Dunn, D. (1998). The utility of home computers and media use: Implications of multimedia and connectivity. *Journal of Broadcasting & Electronic Media, 42,* 435.

Petersen, T. (2012). The enduring appeal of an unwieldy theory. *International Journal of Public Opinion Research, 24,* 263–268.

Peterson, I. (2002, August 14). Questions about germ scientist after Princeton anthrax finding. *New York Times,* p. A21.

Petronio, S. (1991). Communication boundary management: A theoretical model of managing disclosure of private information between married couples. *Communication Theory, 1,* 311–335.

Petronio, S. (2000). The boundaries of privacy: Praxis of everyday life. In S. Petronio (Ed.), *Balancing the secrets of private disclosures* (pp. 37–49). Mahwah, NJ: Erlbaum.

Petronio, S. (2002). *Boundaries of privacy: Dialectics of disclosure.* Albany, NY: SUNY Press.

Petronio, S. (2004). Road to developing communication privacy management theory: Narrative in progress, please stand by. *Journal of Family Communication, 4,* 193–207.

Petronio, S. (2010). Communication privacy management theory: What do we know about family privacy regulation? *Journal of Family Theory & Review, 2,* 175–196.

Petronio, S., & Martin, J. N. (1986). Ramifications of revealing private information: A gender gap. *Journal of Clinical Psychology, 42,* 499–506.

S., & Sargent, J. (2011). Disclosure predica-
...s arising during the course of patient care: Nurses'
...vacy management. *Health Communication*, *26*(3),
255–266.

Petronio, S., Martin, J. N., & Littlefield, R. (1984). Pre-
requisite conditions for self-disclosing: A gender issue.
Communication Monographs, *51*, 268–273.

Philipsen, G. (1995). The Coordinated Management of
Meaning theory of Pearce, Cronen, and associates. In
D. Cushman & B. Kovacic (Eds.), *Watershed traditions
in human communication theory* (pp. 13–43). Albany,
NY: SUNY Press.

Placone, R. A., & Tumolo, M. (2011). Interrupting the
machine: Cynic comedy in the "Rally for Sanity and/
or Fear." *Journal of Contemporary Rhetoric*, *1*(1),
10–21.

Planalp, S. (1987). Interplay between relational knowledge
and events. In R. Burnett, P. McGhee, & D. Clarke
(Eds.), *Accounting for relationships: Social representations of interpersonal links* (pp. 173–191). London:
Methuen.

Planalp, S., & Honeycutt, J. M. (1985). Events that increase
uncertainty reduction in personal relationships. *Human
Communication Research*, *11*, 593–604.

Planalp, S., & Rivers, M. (1988). *Changes in knowledge
of relationships*. Paper presented at the annual meeting
of the International Communication Association, New
Orleans, LA.

Planalp, S., Rutherford, D. K., & Honeycutt, J. M. (1988).
Events that increase uncertainty in personal relationships
II: Replication and extension. *Human Communication
Research*, *14*, 516–547.

Poe, P. Z. (2012). Direct-to-consumer drug advertising
and "Health media filters": A qualitative study of older
adult women's responses to DTC ads. *Atlantic Journal
of Communication*, *20*(3), 185–199.

Polkosky, M. D. (2008). Machines as mediators: The
challenge of technology for interpersonal theory and
research. In E. A. Konijn, S. Utz, M. Tanis, & S. B.
Barnes (Eds.), *Mediated interpersonal communication*
(pp. 34–57). New York, NY: Routledge.

Poole, M. S. (1983). Review of *Communication, action
and meaning: The creation of social realities*. *Quarterly
Journal of Speech*, *69*, 223–224.

Poole, M. S. (1990). Do we have any theories of group
communication? *Communication Studies*, *41*, 237–
247.

Poole, M. S. (2007). Generalization in process theories of
communication. *Communication Methods and Measures*, *1*, 1–10.

Poole, M. S., & DeSanctis, G. (1990). Understanding the
use of group decision support systems: The theory
of adaptive structuration. In J. Fulk & C. Steinfield
(Eds.), *Organizations and communication technology*
(pp. 175–195). Thousand Oaks, CA: Sage.

Poole, M. S., & McPhee, R. D. (2005). Structuration theory. In S. May & D. K. Mumby (Eds.), *Engaging organizational theory & research* (pp. 171–195). Norwood,
NJ: Ablex.

Poole, M. S., Seibold, D. R., & McPhee, R. D. (1986). A
structurational approach to theory-building in group
decision-making research. In R. Y. Hirokawa & M.
S. Poole (Eds.), *Communication and group decision-
making* (pp. 237–264). Beverly Hills, CA: Sage.

Poole, M. S., Seibold, D. R., & McPhee, R. D. (1996). The
structuration of group decisions. In R. Hirokawa &
M. S. Poole (Eds.), *Communication and group decision
making* (pp. 114–146). Thousand Oaks, CA: Sage.

Popper, K. (1976). The myth of the framework. *Boston
Studies in the Philosophy of Science*, *245*, 35–62.

Postman, N. (1971). *Teaching as a subversive activity*. New
York, NY: Delta.

Postman, N. (1992). *Technopoly: The surrender of culture
to technology*. New York, NY: Knopf.

Potter, W. J. (1991). The relationships between first and
second order measures of cultivation. *Human Communication Research*, *18*, 92–113.

Potter, W. J. (1993). Cultivation theory and research: A
conceptual critique. *Human Communication Research*,
19, 564–601.

Practical followup. Retrieved from http://www.jopm.org
/opinion/editorials/2012/08/29/practical-followup

Preston, E. H. (1990). Pornography and the construction of
gender. In N. Signorielli & M. Morgan (Eds.), *Cultivation analysis: New directions in media effects research*
(pp. 107–122). Newbury Park, CA: Sage.

Prichard, P. (1987). The making of McPaper: The inside story of USA Today. Washington, DC: Andrews
McMeel Publishing.

Przybylski, A. K., & Weinstein, N. (2012). Can you connect
with me now? How the presence of mobile communication technology influences face-to-face conversation
quality. *Journal of Social and Personal Relationships*,
29, 1–10.

Punyanunt-Carter, N. (2007). Using attachment theory to study communication motives in father-daughter relationships. *Communication Research Reports, 24*, 311–318.

Quick, B. L. (2009). The effects of viewing *Grey's Anatomy* on perceptions of doctors and patient satisfaction. *Journal of Broadcasting & Electronic Media, 53*(1), 38–55.

Quinlan, M. M., Bates, B. R., Webb, J. B. (2012). Michelle Obama "got back": (Re)defining (Counter) stereotypes of Black females. *Women & Language, 35*(1), 119–126.

Radway, J. (1984). *Reading the romance: Women, patriarchy, and popular literature.* Chapel Hill, NC: University of North Carolina Press.

Radway, J. (1986). Identifying ideological seams: Mass culture, analytical methods, and political practice. *Communication, 9*, 93–123.

Ragas, M. W., & Kiousis, S. (2010). Intermedia agenda-setting and political activism: MoveOn.org and the 2008 presidential election. *Mass Communication & Society, 13*(5), 560–583.

Ramirez, A., Jr., & Walther, J. B. (2009). Information seeking and interpersonal outcomes using the Internet. In T. D. Afifi & W. A. Afifi (Eds.), *Uncertainty, information management, and disclosure decisions: Theories and applications* (pp. 67–84). New York, NY: Routledge.

Ramirez, A., Jr., Walther, J. B., Burgoon, J. K., & Sunnafrank, M. (2002). Information seeking strategies, uncertainty, and computer-mediated communication: Toward a conceptual model. *Human Communication Research, 28*, 213–228.

Ramirez A., Jr., & Wang, Z. (2008). When online meets offline: An Expectancy Violations Theory perspective on modality switching. *Journal of Communication, 58*, 20–39.

Ramsey, M. C., Venette, S. J., & Rabalais, N. (2011). The perceived paranormal and source credibility: The effects of narrative suggestions on paranormal belief. *Atlantic Journal of Communication, 19*(2), 79–96.

Raschick, M., & Ingersoll-Dayton, B. (2004). The costs and rewards of caregiving among aging spouses and adult children. *Family Relations, 53*, 317–325.

Raven, B. H. (1993). The bases of power: Origins and recent developments. *Journal of Social Issues, 49*, 227–251.

Rawlins, W. K. (1992). *Friendship matters: Communication, dialectics, and the life course.* New York, NY: Aldine De Gruyter.

Rawlins, W. K. (2009). *The compass of friendship: Narratives, identities, and dialogues.* Thousand Oaks, CA: Sage.

Ray, T. (2012). To de-westernize, yes, but with a critical edge: A response to Gunaratne and others. *Media, Culture & Society, 34*, 238–249.

Real, M. R. (1996). *Exploring media culture.* Thousand Oaks, CA: Sage.

Reimer, V., & Ahmed, R. (2012). "Feeling good never looked better": Examining stereotypical representations of women in Special K advertisements. In T. Carilli & J. Campbell (Eds.), *Challenging images of women in the media* (pp. 3–16). Lanham, MD: Lexington Books.

Reimer, B., & Rosengren, K. E. (1990). Cultivated viewers and readers: A life-style perspective. In N. Signorielli & M. Morgan (Eds.), *Cultivation analysis: New directions in media effects research* (pp. 181–206). Newbury Park, CA: Sage.

Reitzes, D. C., DePadilla, L., Sterk, C. E., & Elifson, K. W. (2010). A symbolic interaction approach to cigarette smoking: Smoking frequency and the desire to quit smoking. *Sociological Focus, 43*(3), 193–213.

Reuther, C., & Fairhurst, G. T. (2000). Chaos theory and the glass ceiling. In P. Buzzanell (Ed.), *Rethinking organization and managerial communication from feminist perspectives* (pp. 236–253). Thousand Oaks, CA: Sage.

Reynolds, P. D. (2007). *A primer in theory construction: An A&B classics edition.* Boston, MA: Allyn & Bacon.

Reynolds, P. D. (2016). *A primer in theory construction.* New York, NY: Routledge.

Reynolds, T. (2002). Rethinking a Black feminist standpoint. *Ethnic and Racial Studies, 25*, 591–606.

Rhys, W. R., & Bywater, I. (1954). *Rhetoric.* New York, NY: Modern Library.

Richards, I. A. (1936). *The philosophy of rhetoric.* New York, NY: Oxford University Press.

Richardson, B. K., & Taylor, J. (2009). Sexual harassment at the intersection of race and gender: A theoretical model of the sexual harassment experiences of women of color. *Western Journal of Communication, 73*(3), 248–272.

., V. P., McCroskey, J. C., & Hickson, M. L. ,8). *Nonverbal behavior in interpersonal relations.* ,oston, MA: Allyn & Bacon.

.chmond, V. P., Smith, R. S., Heisel, A. D., & McCroskey, J. C. (2001). Nonverbal immediacy in the physician-patient relationship. *Communication Research Reports, 18*, 211–216.

Riddle, K. (2010). Always on my mind: Exploring how frequent, recent, and vivid television portrayals are used in the formation of social reality judgments. *Media Psychology, 13*(2), 155–179.

Riddle, K., Potter, W. J., Metzger, M. J., Nabi, R. L., & Linz, D. G. (2011). Beyond cultivation: Exploring the effects of frequency, recency, and vivid autobiographical memories for violent media. *Media Psychology, 14*(2), 168–191.

Roberts, K. C. (2004). Texturing the narrative paradigm: Folklore and communication. *Communication Quarterly, 52*, 129–142.

Robinson, L. (2007). The cyberself: The selfing project goes online, symbolic interaction in the digital age. *New Media & Society, 9*(1), 93–110.

Roethlisberger, F. L., & Dickson, W. (1939). *Management and the worker.* New York, NY: Wiley.

Roffers, M. (2002). Personal communication, Milwaukee, WI.

Rogelberg, S. G., Rhodes-Shanock, L. R., & Scott, C. W. (2012). Wasted time and money in meetings: Increasing return on investment. *Small Group Research, 43*, 236–245.

Rogers, E. M., & Dearing, J. W. (1988). Agenda-setting research: Where has it been? Where is it going? In J. A. Anderson (Ed.), *Communication yearbook 11* (pp. 555–594). Newbury Park, CA: Sage.

Rogers, L. E., & Escudero, V. (2004). Theoretical foundations. In L. E. Rogers & V. Escudero (Eds.), *Relational communication: An interactional perspective to the study of process and form.* Mahwah, NJ: Erlbaum.

Rogerson, K., & Roselle, L. (Eds.). (2016). *Routledge studies in global information, politics, and society.* New York, NY: Routledge.

Rogerson-Revell, P. (2010). "Can you spell that for us non-native speakers?" Accommodation strategies in international business meetings. *Journal of Business Communication, 47*, 432–454.

Roloff, M. (2009). Social exchange theory. In S. W. Littlejohn & K. A. Foss (Eds.), *Encyclopedia of communication theory* (Vol. 2, pp. 894–896). Los Angeles, CA: Sage.

Roloff, M. E. (1981). *Interpersonal communication: The social exchange approach.* Beverly Hills, CA: Sage.

Romo, L. K. (2011). Money talks: Revealing and concealing financial information in families. *Journal of Family Communication, 11*(4), 264–281.

Romo, L. K. (2012). "Above the influence": How college students communicate about the healthy deviance of alcohol abstinence. *Health Communication, 27*(7), 672–681.

Rorty, A. O. (1996). Structuring rhetoric. In A. O. Rorty (Ed.), *Aristotle's rhetoric* (pp. 1–33). Berkeley, CA: University of California Press.

Rose, J. (2011). Diverse perspectives on the groupthink theory—A literary review. *Emerging Leadership Journeys, 4*, 37–57.

Rose, R., Suppiah, W., Uli, J., & Othman, J. (2006). A face concern approach to conflict management—A Malaysian perspective. *Journal of Social Sciences, 2*, 121–126.

Rosenberg, J., & Egbert, N. (2011). Online impression management: Personality traits and concerns for secondary goals as predictors of self-presentation tactics on Facebook. *Journal of Computer-Mediated Communication, 17*, 1–18.

Rosenthal, R., & Jacobson, L. (1968). *Pygmalion in the classroom: Teacher expectation and pupils' intellectual development.* New York, NY: Holt, Rinehart & Winston.

Rothwell, J. D. (2012). *In mixed company: Communication in groups and teams.* Boston, MA: Cengage/Wadsworth.

Rothwell, J. D. (2013). *In mixed company: Communicating in small groups.* Boston, MA: Cengage.

Rowland, R. C. (1987). Narrative: Mode of discourse or paradigm? *Communication Monographs, 54*, 264–275.

Rowland, R. C. (1989). On limiting the narrative paradigm: Three case studies. *Communication Monographs, 56*, 39–53.

Rubin, A. M. (1981). An examination of television viewing motives. *Communication Research, 8*, 141–165.

Rubin, A. M. (1994). Uses, gratification and media effects research. In J. Bryant & D. Zillman (Eds.), *Media effects: Advances in theory and research* (pp. 281–301). Hillsdale, NJ: Erlbaum.

Rubin, A. M., & Step, M. M. (2000). Impact of motivation, attraction, and parasocial interaction on talk radio listening. *Journal of Broadcasting & Electronic Media, 44*, 635–654.

Rubin, L. (1998, March). *Friends and kin.* Speech presented at the conference on Successful Relating in Couples, in Families, between Friends, and at Work, Tucson, AZ.

Ruddick, S. (1989). *Maternal thinking: Towards a politics of peace.* Boston, MA: Beacon Press.

Rudra, K., Chakraborty, A., Sethi, M., Das, S., Ganguly, N., & Ghosh, S. (2015). #FewThingsAboutIdioms: Understanding idioms and its users in the Twitter online social network. In T. Cao (Ed.), *Advances in knowledge discovery and data mining* (pp. 108–121). Rotterdam, Netherlands: Springer.

Ruggiero, T. E. (2000). Uses and gratifications theory in the 21st century. *Mass Communication & Society, 3*, 3–37.

Russ, T. L. (2012). The relationship between communication apprehension and learning preferences in an organizational setting. *Journal of Business Communication, 49*, 312–331.

Rutenberg, J., & Zeleny, J. (2008, May 15). The politics of the lapel, when it comes to Obama. *New York Times,* p. A27.

Ryan, E. E. (1984). *Aristotle's theory of rhetorical argumentation.* Montreal: Les Editions Ballarmin.

Ryan, K. M. (2007). *He's a rebel: A discourse analysis of Nike's Bode Miller Olympic advertising campaign.* Paper presented at the annual meeting of the International Communication Association, San Francisco, CA.

Ryan, E. B., MacLean, M., & Orange, J. B. (1994). Inappropriate accommodation in communication to elders: Inferences about nonverbal correlates. *International Journal of Aging and Human Development, 39,* 273–291.

Rydell, R. J., Hugenberg, K., & McConnell, A. R. (2006). Resistance can be good or bad: How theories of resistance and dissonance affect attitude certainty. *Personality and Social Psychology Bulletin, 32*, 740–750.

Rydell, R. J., McConnell, A. R., & Mackie, D. M. (2008). Consequences of discrepant explicit and implicit attitudes: Cognitive dissonance and increased information processing. *Journal of Experimental Social Psychology, 44*, 1526–1532.

Sabatelli, R. M., & Shehan, C. L. (1993). Exchange and resource theories. In P. G. Boss, W. J. Doherty, R. LaRossa, W. R. Schumm, & S. K. Steinmetz (Eds.), *Sourcebook of family theories and methods: A contextual approach* (pp. 385–411). New York, NY: Plenum.

Sahlstein, E., Maguire, K. C., & Timmerman, L. (2009). Contradictions and praxis contextualized by wartime deployment: Wives' perspectives revealed through relational dialectics. *Communication Monographs, 76*(4), 421–442.

Salem, P. (2007). Making sense of knowledge management. *RCA Vestnik (Russian Communication Association), 1*, 47–68.

Salmon, C. T., & Kline, F. G. (1985). The spiral of silence ten years later: An examination and evaluation. In K. Sanders, L. L. Kaid, & D. Nimmo (Eds.), *Political communication yearbook 1984* (pp. 3–29). Carbondale, IL: Southern Illinois University Press.

Salmon, G., & Faris, J. (2006). Multi-agency collaboration, multiple levels of meaning: Social constructionism and the CMM model as tools to further our understanding. *Journal of Family Therapy, 28*, 272–292.

Samovar, L. A., & Porter, R. E. (1995). *Communication between cultures,* 3rd ed. Belmont, CA: Wadsworth.

Samovar, L. A., Porter, R. E., McDaniel, E. R., Roy, C. S. (2013). *Communication between cultures.* Boston, MA: Cengage/Wadsworth.

Sanker, D. (2012). *Collaborate: The art of we.* San Francisco, CA: Jossey-Bass.

Sapir, E. (1921). *Language: An introduction to the study of speech.* New York, NY: Harcourt, Brace & World.

Satir, V. (1988). *The new peoplemaking.* Mountain View, CA: Science and Behavior Books.

Sawyer, K. (2012). Extending sociocultural theory to group creativity. *Vocations and Learning, 5*, 59–75.

Schell, J. (1982). *The fate of the earth.* New York, NY: Avon Books.

Schoebi, D., Perrez, M., Bradbury, T. N. (2012). Expectancy effects on marital interaction: Rejection sensitivity as a critical moderator. *Journal of Family Psychology, 26*, 709–718.

Schramm, W. L. (1954). *The process and effects of mass communication.* Urbana, IL: University of Illinois Press.

Schultz, B. G. (1996). *Communicating in the small group,* 2nd ed. New York, NY: HarperCollins.

Schulz, A., & Roessler, P. (2012). The spiral of silence and the Internet: Selection of online content and the perception of the public opinion climate in computer-mediated communication environments. *International Journal of Public Opinion Research, 24*, 346–367.

Schwartz, J. (2005, April 4). Some at NASA say its culture is changing, but others say problems still run deep. *New York Times*, pp. 1–3.

J., & Wald, M. L. (2003, March 9). 'Group- ˌ is 30 years old, and still going strong. *New York ˌmes,* pp. 4–5.

ˌibold, D. R., & Myers, K. K. (2005). Communication as structuring. In G. J. Shepherd, J. St. John, & T. Striphas (Eds.), *Communication as . . . Perspectives on theory* (pp. 143–152). Thousand Oaks, CA: Sage.

Seibold, D., & Myers, R. (2007). Group argument. *Small Group Research Journal, 38,* 312–336.

Selby, G. (2000). The limits of accommodation: Frederick Douglas and the Garrisonian abolitionists. *Southern Communication Journal, 66,* 52–66.

Semlak, J. L., & Pearson, J. C. (2011). Big Macs/Peanut butter and jelly: An exploration of dialectical contradictions experienced by the sandwich generation. *Communication Research Reports, 28*(4), 296–307.

Sevenans, J., Walgrave, S., & Vos, D. (2015). Political elites' media responsiveness and their individual political goals: A study of national politicians in Belgium. *Research & Politics, 2,* 1–7.

Shanahan, J., & Jones, V. (1999). Cultivation and social control. In D. Demers & K. Viswanath (Eds.), *Mass media, social control and social change* (pp. 35–61). Ames, IA: Iowa State Press.

Shanahan, J., & Morgan, M. (1999). *Television and its viewers: Cultivation theory and research.* Cambridge: Cambridge University Press.

Shannon, C., & Weaver, W. (1949). *The mathematical theory of communication.* Urbana, IL: University of Illinois Press.

 Shaw, M. E. (1981). *Group dynamics: The psychology of small group behavior.* New York, NY: McGraw-Hill.

Sheckels, T. F. (2009). The rhetorical success of Thabo Mbeki's 1996 "I am an African" address. *Communication Quarterly, 57*(3), 319–333.

Sheriff, R. E. (2000). Exposing silence as cultural censorship: A Brazilian case. *American Anthropologist, 102,* 114–132.

Sherry, J. L. (2010). The value of communication science. *Journal of Applied Communication Research, 38*(3), 302–306.

Sherry, J. L., Lucas, K., Rechtsteiner, S., Brooks, C., & Wilson, B. (2001, May). *Video game uses and gratifications as predictors of use and game preference.* Paper presented at the annual meeting of the International Communication Association, Washington, DC.

Shimanoff, S. (1980). *Communication rules: Theory and research.* Beverly Hills, CA: Sage.

Shimanoff, S. (2009). Facework theories. In S. W. Littlejohn & K. A Foss (Eds.), *Encyclopedia of communication theory* (pp. 374–377). Thousand Oaks, CA: Sage.

Shin, D. (2011). Understanding e-book users: Uses and gratification expectancy model. *New Media & Society, 13*(2), 260–278.

Shinnar, R. S., Young, C. A., & Meana, M. (2004). The motivations for and outcomes of employee referrals. *Journal of Business Psychology, 19,* 271–283.

Short, J. A., Williams, E., & Christie, B. (1976). *The social psychology of telecommunications.* London: Wiley.

Shutiva, C. (2011). Native American culture and communication through humor. In A. Gonzalez, M. Huston, & V. Chen (Eds.), *Our voices: Essays in culture, ethnicity, and communication* (pp. 188–203). New York, NY: Oxford.

Sicafuse, L. L. & Miller, M. K. (2010). Social psychological influences on the popularity of amber alerts. *Criminal Justice and Behavior, 37*(11), 1237.

Signorielli, N. (1990). Television's mean and dangerous worlds: A continuation of the cultural indicators perspective. In N. Signorielli & M. Morgan (Eds.), *Cultivation analysis: New directions in media effects research* (pp. 85–106). Newbury Park, CA: Sage.

Simmons, V. N., Webb, M. S., & Brandon, T. H. (2004). College-student smoking: An initial test of an experiential dissonance-enhancing intervention. *Addictive Behaviors, 29,* 1129–1141.

Simpson, C. (1996). Elisabeth Noelle-Neumann's "spiral of silence" and the historical context of communication theory. *Journal of Communication, 46,* 149–173.

Small, T. A. (2011). What's the hashtag? A content analysis of Canadian politics on Twitter. *Information, Communication and Society, 14,* 872–895.

Smith, P. (2011). *The renewal of cultural studies.* Philadelphia, PA: Temple University Press.

Smudde, P. M. (2004). Implications on the practice and study of Kenneth Burke's idea of a "public relations counsel with a heart." *Communication Quarterly, 52,* 420–432.

Snyder, J. L., & Cistulli, M. D. (2011). The relationship between workplace e-mail privacy and psychological contract violation, and their influence on trust in top management and affective commitment. *Communication Research Reports, 28*(2), 121–129.

Snyder, M. (1979). Self-monitoring processes. In L. Berkowitz (Ed.), *Advances in experimental social psychology* (pp. 86–131). New York, NY: Academic Press.

Soar, M. (2000). Encoding advertisements: Ideology and meaning in advertising production. *Mass Communication & Society, 3*, 415–437.

Sonja Utz, Camiel J. Beukeboom, Walther, J. B., DeAndrea, D. C., & Tong, S. T. (2010). Computer-mediated communication versus vocal communication in the attenuation of pre-interaction impressions. *Media Psychology, 13*, 364–386.

Sosulski, M. R. (2009). Developing a standpoint practice method with cases: Authority, subjectivity, reflection. *Affilia: Journal of Women & Social Work, 24*(3), 226–243.

Sparks, G. G., & Greene, J. O. (1992). On the validity of nonverbal indicators as measures of physiological arousal: A response to Burgoon, Kelley, Newton, and Keeley-Dyreson. *Human Communication Research, 18*, 445–471.

Sparks, G. G., & Ogles, R. M. (1990). The difference between fear of victimization and probability of being victimized: Implication for cultivation. *Journal of Broadcasting & Electronic Media, 34*, 351–358.

Speer, R. B., Giles, H., & Denes, A. (2013). Investigating stepparent-stepchild interactions: The role of communication accommodation. *Journal of Family Communication, 13*, 218–241.

Spencer, A. T., Croucher, S. M., & McKee, C. (2012). Barack Obama: Examining the climate of opinion of spiral of silence. *Journal of Communication, Speech & Theater Association of North Dakota, 24*, 27–34.

Stafford, L. (2008). Social exchange theories. In L. A. Baxter & D. O. Braithwaite (Eds.), *Engaging theories in interpersonal communication: Multiple perspectives* (pp. 377–389). Thousand Oaks, CA: Sage.

Stanley, J. (2011). The ways of silencing. *The New York Times online*. Retrieved from http://opinionator.blogs.nytimes.com/2011/06/25/the-ways-of-silencing/. Accessed on November 3, 2011.

Stapleton, K., & Wilson, J. (2009). Discourse and dissonance: Making sense of socio-political change in Northern Ireland. *Journal of Pragmatics, 41*(7), 1358–1375.

Steele, C. M. (1988). The psychology of self-affirmation: Sustaining the integrity of the self. In L. Berkowitz (Ed.), *Advances in experimental social psychology* (Vol. 21, pp. 261–302). San Diego, CA: Academic Press.

Steele, C. M., Spencer, S. J., & Lynch, M. (1993). Self-image, resilience, and dissonance: The role of affirmational resources. *Journal of Personality and Social Psychology, 64*, 885–896.

Stein, I. F. (2012). Levels of contact in professional coach-client communication. In C. Creede, B. Fisher-Yoshida, & P. V. Gallegos (Eds.), *The reflective, facilitative, and interpretive practice of the Coordinated Management of Meaning* (pp. 65–76). Madison, NJ: Farleigh Dickinson University Press.

Steiner, L. (1988, August). *Oppositional decoding as an act of resistance*. Paper presented at the annual meeting of the Association for Education in Journalism and Mass Communication, Norman, OK.

Steiner, M. A. (2009). Reconceptualizing Christian public engagement: "Faithful Witness" and the American evangelical tradition. *Journal of Communication & Religion, 32*(2), 289–318.

Sternberg, J. (2011). President's address: Space, place, and the media ecology association. *Proceedings of the Media Ecology Association, 11*, 107–112.

Stewart, J. B. (2012). *Tangled webs: How false statements are undermining America: From Martha Stewart to Bernie Madoff*. New York, NY: Penguin.

Stockstill, C. J., & Roach, D. (2007). Communication apprehension in high school athletes. *Texas Speech Communication Journal, 32*, 53–64.

Stones, R. (2005). *Structuration theory*. New York, NY: Palgrave MacMillan.

Stoycheff, E. (2016). Under surveillance examining Facebook's Spiral of Silence effects in the wake of NSA internet monitoring. *Journalism & Mass Communication Quarterly, 93*, 296–311.

Strate, L. (2004). A media ecology review. *Communication Research Trends, 23*, 1–48.

Strate, L., & Wachtel, E. (2005). *The legacy of McLuhan*. Cresskill, NJ: Hampton Press.

Street, R. L. (1991). Information-giving in medical consultations: The influence of patients' communicative styles and personal characteristics. *Social Science and Medicine, 32*, 541–548.

Street, R. L., & Giles, H. (1982). Speech accommodation theory: A social cognitive approach to language and speech behavior. In M. E. Roloff & C. R. Berger (Eds.), *Social cognition and communication* (pp. 193–226). Beverly Hills, CA: Sage.

Strine, M. S. (1992). Understanding how things work: Sexual harassment and academic culture. *Journal of Applied Communication Research, 20*, 391–400.

Strömbäck, J., & Kiousis, S. (2010). A new look at agenda-setting effects—Comparing the predictive power of overall political news consumption and specific news onsumption across different media channels ...edia types. *Journal of Communication, 60*(2), ..–292.

...oud, S. R. (2001). Technology and mythic narrative: *The Matrix* as technological hero-quest. *Western Journal of Communication, 65*, 416–441.

Such, J. M., Espinoza, A., Garcia-Fornes, A., & Sierra, C. (2012). Self-disclosure decision making based on intimacy and privacy. *Information Sciences, 211*, 93–111.

Sullivan, P. A., & Turner, L. H. (2009). Heaping hostility on Hillary: Isms in the 2008 presidential race. In E. L. Kirby & M. C. McBride (Eds.), *Gender actualized: Cases in communicatively constructing realities* (pp. 25–32). Dubuque, IA: Kendall Hunt.

Sun, C. F., & Scharrer, E. (2004). Staying true to Disney: College students' resistance to criticism of *The Little Mermaid. The Communication Review, 7*, 35–55.

Sunnafrank, M. (1986). Predicted outcome value during initial interactions: A reformulation of uncertainty reduction theory. *Human Communication Research, 13*, 191–210.

Surber, J. P. (1998). *Culture and critique: An introduction to the critical discourses of cultural studies.* Boulder, CO: Westview Press.

Suter, E. A. (2008). Discursive negotiation of family identity: A study of U.S. families with adopted children from China. *Journal of Family Communication, 8*, 126–147.

't Hart, P. (1990). *Groupthink in government: A study of small groups and policy failure.* Amsterdam: Swets and Zeitlinger.

't Hart, P. (1998). Preventing groupthink revisited: Evaluating and reforming groups in government. *Organizational Behavior and Human Decision Processes, 73*, 306–313.

Tajeddin, G., Safayeni, F. Connelly, C. E., & Tasa, T. (2012). The influence of emergent expertise on group decision processes. *Small Group Research, 43*, 50–74.

Tajfel, H., & Turner, J. C. (1986). The social identity theory of intergroup behavior. In S. Worchel & W. Austin (Eds.), *The psychology of intergroup relations* (pp. 7–24). Chicago, IL: Nelson Hall.

Takeshita, T. (2006). Current critical problems in agenda-setting research. *International Journal of Public Opinion Research, 18*(3), 11–32.

Tan, A. S. (1982). Television use and social stereotypes. *Journalism Quarterly, 59*, 119–122.

Tan, Y., & Weaver, D. H. (2010). Media bias, public opinion, and policy liberalism from 1956 to 2004: A second -level agenda-setting study. *Mass Communication and Society, 13*(4), 412–434.

Tang, J. H., & Wang, C. C. (2012). Self-disclosure among bloggers: Re-examination of social penetration theory. *Cyberpsychology, Behavior, and Social Networking, 15*(5), 245–250.

Tanno, D. V., & Gonzalez, A. (1998). Sites of identity in communication and culture. In D. V. Tanno & A. Gonzalez (Eds.), *Communication and identity across cultures* (pp. 3–7). Thousand Oaks, CA: Sage.

Taylor, A., & Hardman, M. J. (2000). Introduction: The meaning of voice. In A. Taylor & M. J. Hardman (Eds.), *Hearing many voices* (pp. 1–27). Cresskill, NJ: Hampton Press.

Taylor, D. A., & Altman, I. (1987). Communication in interpersonal relationships: Social penetration processes. In M. E. Roloff & G. R. Miller (Eds.), *Interpersonal processes: New directions in communication research* (pp. 257–277). Newbury Park, CA: Sage.

Taylor, J. R., & Van Every, E. J. (2000). *The emergent organization: Communication as its site and surface.* Mahwah, NJ: Erlbaum.

Tell, D. (2010). Stanton's "Solitude of Self" as public confession. *Communication Studies, 61*(2), 172–183.

Templin, P. (2012). A failure of culture. *Industrial Engineer, 44*, 1.

Terrell, M. (2011, September 20). The bytes and the bees: Love can transcend anything (even Facebook). *USA Today*, p. 4A.

Thaler, P. (2006). The legacy of Neil Postman, and the coming of age of media ecology. *Review of Communication, 6*, 369–373.

Thatcher, M. S. (2011). Negotiating the tension between the discourses of Christianity and spiritual pluralism in Alcoholics Anonymous. *Journal of Applied Communication Research, 39*(4), 389–405.

The critical role of teams. Retrieved from http://www .kenblanchard.com/img/pub/pdf_critical_role_teams.pdf

The Neil Postman Information Page. Retrieved from http:// neilpostman.org

Theiss, J. A., & Solomon, D. H. (2006). A relational turbulence model of communication about irritations in romantic relationships. *Communication Research, 33*, 391–418.

Theye, K. (2008). Shoot, I'm sorry: An examination of narrative functions and effectiveness within Dick Cheney's hunting accident apologia. *Southern Communication Journal, 73*, 160–177.

Thibaut, J., & Kelley, H. (1959). *The social psychology of groups*. New York, NY: Wiley.

Thompson, J., Petronio, S., & Braithwaite, D. O. (2012). An examination of privacy rules for academic advisors and college student-athletes: A communication privacy management perspective. *Communication Studies*, *63*(1), 54–76.

Tidwell, L. C., & Walther, J. B. (2002). Computer-mediated communication effects on disclosure, impressions, and interpersonal evaluations: Getting to know one another a bit at a time. *Human Communication Research*, *28*, 317–348.

Tilley, E. (2010). Ethics and gender at the point of decision making: An exploration of intervention and kinship. *Prism*, *7*(4). Retrieved from http://www.prismjournal.org/fileadmin/Praxis/Files/Gender/Tilley.pdf

Timmer, S. G., Sedlar, G., & Urquiza, A. J. (2004). Challenging children in kin versus nonkin foster care: Perceived costs and benefits to caregivers. *Child Maltreatment*, *9*, 251–262.

Ting-Toomey, S. (1988). Intercultural conflict styles: A face negotiation theory. In Y. Y. Kim & W. B. Gudykunst (Eds.), *Theories in intercultural communication* (pp. 213–238). Newbury Park, CA: Sage.

Ting-Toomey, S. (1991). Intimacy expression in three cultures: France, Japan, and the United States. *International Journal of Intercultural Relations*, *15*, 29–46.

Ting-Toomey, S. (1993). Communicative resourcefulness: An identity negotiation perspective. In R. Wiseman & J. Koester (Eds.), *Intercultural communication competence* (pp. 72–111). Newbury Park, CA: Sage.

Ting-Toomey, S. (1994a). Face and facework: An introduction. In S. Ting-Toomey (Ed.), *The challenge of facework* (pp. 1–14). Albany, NY: SUNY Press.

Ting-Toomey, S. (1994b). Managing intercultural conflicts effectively. In L. A. Samovar & R. E. Porter (Eds.), *Intercultural communication: A reader* (pp. 360–372). Belmont, CA: Wadsworth.

Ting-Toomey, S. (2004). Translating conflict face-negotiation theory into practice. In D. Landis, J. Bennett, & M. Bennett (Eds.), *Handbook of intercultural training* (pp. 215–240). Thousand Oaks, CA: Sage.

Ting-Toomey, S. (2007). Intercultural conflict training: Theory-practice approaches and research challenges. *Journal of Intercultural Communication Research*, *36*, 255–271.

Ting-Toomey, S. (2009). Intercultural conflict competence as a facet of intercultural competence development: Multiple conceptual approaches. In D. Deardoff (Ed.), *Sage handbook of intercultural competence* (pp. 100–121). Thousand Oaks, CA: Sage.

Ting-Toomey, S. (2010). Applying dimensional values in understanding intercultural communication. *Communication Monographs*, *77*, 169–180.

Ting-Toomey, S., & Chung, L. C. (2005). *Understanding intercultural communication*. Los Angeles, CA: Roxbury.

Ting-Toomey, S., & Cocroft, B. A. (1994). Face and facework: Theoretical and research interests. In S. Ting-Toomey (Ed.), *The challenge of facework* (pp. 307–340). Albany, NY: SUNY.

Ting-Toomey, S., & Cole, M. (1990). Intergroup diplomatic communication: A face-negotiation perspective. In F. Korzenny & S. Ting-Toomey (Eds.), *Communication for peace: Diplomacy and negotiation* (pp. 77–95). Newbury Park, CA: Sage.

Ting-Toomey, S., & Oetzel, J. (2001). *Managing intercultural conflict effectively*. Thousand Oaks, CA: Sage.

Ting-Toomey, S., Gao, G., Trubisky, P., Yang, Z., Kim, H. S., Lin, S., & Nishida, T. (1991). Culture, face maintenance, and styles of handling interpersonal conflict: A study in five cultures. *The International Journal of Conflict Management*, *2*, 275–296.

Toller, P. W. (2005). Negotiation of dialectical contradictions by parents who have experienced the death of a child. *Journal of Applied Communication Research*, *33*, 46–66.

Toller, P. W., & Braithwaite, D. O. (2009). Grieving together and apart: Bereaved parents' contradictions of marital interaction. *Journal of Applied Communication Research*, *37*(3), 257–277.

Toma, C., & Hancock, J. T. (2011). A new twist on love's labor: Self-presentation in online dating profiles. In K. Wright & L. Webb (Eds.), *Computer-mediated communication in personal relationships* (pp. 21–40). New York, NY: Peter Lang.

Tong, S. T., & Walther, J. B. (2011). Just say "No Thanks": Romantic rejection in computer-mediated communication. *Journal of Social and Personal Relationships*, *28*, 488–506.

Turnage, A. K. (2007). Email flaming behaviors and organizational conflict. *Journal of Computer-Mediated Communication*, *13*, 43–59.

Turow, J. (2013). *Media today: Mass communication in a converging world*. New York, NY: Routledge.

s. (2009). *How to love the recession: Seven ...eps to find new customers in tough times and ...cally steal the ones your competitors ignored.* Minneapolis, MN: S2 Enterprises Press.

Waldron, V. R., & Lavitt, M. R. (2009). "Welfare-to-work": Assessing communication competencies and client outcomes in a job training program. *Southern Communication Journal, 75,* 1–15.

Walker, L. (1984). *The battered woman syndrome.* New York, NY: Springer.

Walther, J. B., Anderson, D. K., & Park, D. W. (1994). Interpersonal effects in computer-mediated communication: A meta-analysis of social and antisocial communication. *Communication Research, 21,* 460–487.

Walther, J. B., Van Der Heide, B., Kim, S., Westerman, D., & Tong, S. (2008). The role of friends' appearance and behavior on evaluations of individuals on Facebook: Are we known by the company we keep? *Human Communication Research, 34,* 28–49.

Watzlawick, P., Beavin, J. B., & Jackson, D. D. (1967). *Pragmatics of human communication: A study of interactional patterns, pathologies, and paradoxes.* New York, NY: W.W. Norton.

Weaver, D. H., Graber, D. A., McCombs, M. E., & Eyal, C. H. (1981). *Media agenda-setting in a presidential campaign. Issues, images and interest.* New York, NY: Praeger.

White, N., & Lauritsen, J. L. (2012). *Violent crimes against youth—1994-2010.* Washington, DC: U.S. Department of Justice.

Whorf, B. L. (1956). *Language, thought, and reality.* Cambridge, MA: MIT Press.

Wiggins, B. E., & Bowers, G. B. (2014). Memes as genre: A structurational analysis of the memescape. *New Media & Society, 17,* 1886–1906.

Wilson, B. J., Martins, N., & Marske, A. L. (2007). Children's and parents' fright reactions to kidnapping stories in the news. *Communication Monographs, 74,* 46–74.

Winzenburg, S. (2012). In the Facebook era, students tell you everything. *Chronicle of Higher Education, 58,* A26.

Wolf, M. A., Meyer, T. P., & White, C. (2009). A rules-based study of television's role in the construction of social reality. *Journal of Broadcasting & Electronic Media, 43,* 813–829.

Wood, J. T. (1992). *Spinning the symbolic web: Human communication as symbolic interaction.* Amsterdam, Netherlands: Ablex Publishing.

Wood, J. T. (2004). Monsters and victims: Male felons' accounts of intimate partner violence. *Journal of Social and Personal Relationships, 21,* 555–576.

Wood, J. T. (2008). Critical feminist theories. In L. A. Baxter & D. O. Braithwaite (Eds.), *Engaging theories in interpersonal communication* (pp. 323–334). Thousand Oaks, CA: Sage.

Worchel, S., Rothgerber, H., Day, E. A., Hart, D., & Butemeyer, J. (1998). Social identity and individual productivity within groups. *British Journal of Social Psychology, 37,* 389–413.

Zeng, L. (2011). More than audio on the go: Uses and gratifications of MP3 players. *Communication Research Reports, 28,* 97–108.

Zhang, P., & McLuhan, E. (2016). The interological turn in media ecology. *Canadian Journal of Communication, 41,* 207–225.

Zhou, S., Kim, Y., & Kim, Y. (2015). *Theoretical and methodological trends of Agenda Setting Theory: A thematic meta-analysis of the last five decades.* Paper presented at the annual meeting of the Association for Education in Journalism and Mass Communication, San Francisco, CA.

Name Index

Miron, D., 416
Misra, T. A., 108
Mitchell, W., 253
Miyata, K., 385
Modaff, D. P., 258, 259, 262, 264, 276, 499
Molnar, G., 434
Monge, P. R., 51, 54, 157
Mongeau, P. A., 146, 147, 172, 184
Montgomery, B., 187–190, 192, 193, 199–202, 215
Montgomery, E., 102
Moodie, D. R., 222
Moody, G. D., 132
Moody, M., 506
Moon, D., 425
Moon, H., 275
Moon, S., 492
Moore, J., 102, 201
Morgan, M., 398, 404, 406, 409, 412, 413, 415, 416, 418, 434
Morreale, S. P., 286
Morrison, E. W., 150
Morrison, J., 445
Morrison, J. C., 438
Morrissey, M. E., 38
Mueller, A., 120
Mukherjee, A., 184
Mulac, A., 478
Mulkens, S., 131
Muller, H., 43
Muller, H. L., 25, 26
Mulrine, A., 251
Mulwo, A. K., 508
Mumby, D., 258
Munshi, D., 14
Munz, D. C., 185
Muraco, A., 33
Murdock, G., 425
Murray, D. S., 97, 99, 102
Murray, J., 334, 335
Musambira, G. W., 506
Muthusamy, S. K., 168
Mutz, D. C., 417
Myers, K. K., 256
Myers, R., 257, 258
Myers, S. A., 4, 242

Nabi, R. L., 408
Nagao, M., 473
Nakayama, T., 7, 50
Nakazawa, M., 32
Nangabo, D., 496, 498
Nayeem, N., 37

Near, J., 36
Neck, C., 253
Neel, J., 310, 321
Negus, K., 425
Neill, S., 370
Nelissen, S., 53
Nelson, C., 327
Nelson, M. R., 492
Neuendorf, K., 417, 418
Neuliep, J., 142, 146, 148, 471
Nevitt, B., 445
Newcomb, H., 413, 416, 417
Nichols, M. H., 3, 328, 333
Nichols, W. L., 216
Nicolini, D., 260
Nieminen, M., 401
Nir, L., 417
Nishida, T., 149, 467
Noelle-Neumann, E., 369–378, 380, 384–385
Northrup, T., 404
Norwood, K., 196, 200
Norwood, K. M., 187
Nowak, K., 132
Nussman, J., 339

Oakley, J., 322
Obama, B., 39, 251, 348, 355, 367, 373, 423, 485
O'Boyle, N., 201
O'Brien Hallstein, D. L., 513, 520
Obstfeld, D., 300
O'Connor, J., 479
Oda, T., 62
O'Dea, J., 454
O'Donnell, V., 431
O'Donnell-Trujillo, N., 272–281, 280, 286
Oetzel, J., 461, 470, 473
Offenbecher, W., 401
Ogawa, Y., 385
Ogay, T., 491
O'Leary, C., 522
O'Leary, C. M., 524
Oles-Asevedo, D., 330
Oliver, C., 86
Olsen, T., 502
Olson, L. N., 197
O'Neill, B. S., 105
Ono, K., 47, 48
Oosthuizen, I., 286
Orange, J. B., 486
Orbe, M., 485, 498, 514, 522
Ormrod, R., 408

Ortiz, E., 14
Ortiz, M., 417
Orwell, G., 238
Ostrom, T. M., 111
Othman, J., 473
Ott, B., 430
Overton, E., 147, 175
Owlett, J. S., 216
Oxley, Z., 361, 372

Pacanowsky, M., 272–281, 286
Pace, R., 25
Pachirat, T., 279
Pais, S., 486
Palitza, K., 428
Palmieri, C., 147, 175
Papa, M. J., 302
Papadouka, M. E., 367
Park, D. W., 220
Park, R. E., 357
Parker, B. J. 401
Parker, H., 445
Parkes, D., 102
Parks, M., 146, 221, 230
Pascale, R., 159
Pask, E. B., 60
Peach, S., 511
Pearce, C., 53
Pearce, W. B., 52, 83–93, 95, 96, 98–102
Pearson, J. C., 190, 209, 473, 500
Pederson, J. R., 197
Pemberton, A., 131
Pena, J., 232
Penney, J., 7
Perloff, R. M., 118
Perrault, E. K., 153
Perrez, M., 132
Perse, E., 399, 401
Peter, J., 148
Petersen, T., 372, 383
Peterson, I., 405
Petronio, S., 204–209, 211, 212, 214–216
Petrun, E. L., 43
Pettey, G., 60
Philipsen, G., 85, 87, 95
Phillips, C., 339
Planalp, S., 146
Plank, R. E., 401
Poe, P., 70
Pollai, M., 118
Poole, M. S., 33, 100, 258, 262, 264, 268, 269

Shannon, C. E., 136
Shaw, A., 506
Shaw, D., 355, 358
Shaw, D. L., 356
Shaw, M., 242
Shaw, M. E., 33
Sheckels, T., 329
Sheehan, B., 382
Shehan, C., 157, 167, 168
Sherblom, J. C., 224
Sheriff, R., 503–504
Shimanoff, S., 52, 473
Shin, D., 383
Shockley-Zalabak, P. S., 286
Short, J. A., 222
Shrank, W. H., 33
Shulman, H., 233
Shutiva, C., 39, 486
Sicafuse, L. L., 81
Sidelinger, R. J., 131, 168
Sierra, C., 176
Signorielli, N., 406, 407, 409, 412
Silk, K. J., 153
Sillars, A., 473
Silverman, D., 60
Simmons, V., 114
Simon, D., 114
Simons, H., 334
Simpson, A., 355
Simpson, C., 385
Simpson, O. J., 318
Sioufi, R., 482
Skewes, E., 416
Sloan, W. D., 46
Small, T., 7
Smith, P., 80
Smith, P. B., 149
Smith, P. M., 480, 483
Smith, R. A., 185
Smyth, R., 168
Snack, J., 267
Snavely, L., 98
Snedaker, K., 508
Snyder, M., 168
Soar, M., 434
Sohn, Y., 112
Soliz, J., 478, 483
Solomon, D. H., 37, 105, 138, 147
Southwell, B., 367
Sparks, G. G., 131, 442
Sparrow, R., 322
Spears, R., 228
Speer, R. B., 488
Spencer, A. T., 377
Spencer, S. J., 116

Spitzberg, B. H., 491
Sproule, J. M., 310
Stacks, D., 44, 46
Stafford, L., 156, 157
Stafford, R. S., 492
Stanley, J., 519
Starcher, S., 216
Steele, C., 116
Steimel, S. J., 70
Stein, I., 90
Steinberg, M., 145
Steiner, L., 433
Steiner, M. A., 330
Steinman, C., 433
Step, M., 393
Stephens, N., 438–439
Stern, L., 491
Sternberg, J., 450
Stewart, J. B., 318
Stewart, M., 318
Stock, Y., 225
Stockstill, C. J., 37
Stokes, A., 389, 399
Stone, J., 117
Stones, R., 268
Stoycheff, E., 385
Strate, L., 451, 454
Strauman, E. C., 344
Street, R., 32, 484, 487–488
Strine, M., 505
Stroh, D. P., 54
Stroud, S. R., 38
Such, J. M., 176
Sunnafrank, M., 148, 151
Sunstein, C., 238
Suppiah, R. W., 473
Surber, J. P., 434
Sutcliffe, K. M., 299–300
Suter, E. A., 39, 351

't Hart, O., 250, 251
Tajeddin, G., 34
Tajfel, H., 479
Takai, J., 461
Takeshita, T., 366
Tamburrini, N., 492
Tang, J. H., 186
Tanno, D., 464
Tasa, T., 34
Tate, A., 367
Taylor, A., 302, 495, 496
Taylor, D. A., 170, 171, 173, 174, 177, 178, 180, 182, 183, 184, 185
Taylor, J., 517
Taylor, M. F., 75

Taylor, S., 105
Templin, P., 285
Tenzek, K. E., 147
Thatcher, M. S., 201
Theiss, J. A., 37
Theye, K., 339, 350
Thibault, J., 155, 157, 164, 177
Thomas, L. J., 201
Thomas-Maddox, C., 58
Thompson, J., 216
Thorne, L., 286
Thorsten, Q., 417
Tidwell, L. C., 147, 232
Tilley, E., 508
Tilly, C., 156
Timmer, S. G., 168
Timmerman, L., 192
Tindale, C., 311
Ting-Toomey, S., 194, 459–463, 465–471, 473
Titsworth, S., 4
Toller, P., 194, 197
Toma, C., 225
Tomasulo, D., 107
Tong, S. T., 223, 225, 226, 227, 230
Torcello, L., 19
Toulmin, S., 343
Tourish, D., 150
Tracy, K., 462, 465, 473
Tracy, S., 263
Trahan, D. P., 185
Treadwell, D. T., 46
Treichler, P., 506
Trenholm, S., 5
Tretheway, A., 285
Trevino, A. J., 156
Triandis, H., 466
Trimble, M., 517
Triolo, P. K., 289
Trubisky, P., 467
Trussell, N., 163
Tsfati, Y., 370, 386
Tuffin, K., 285
Turkle, S., 38, 444, 454
Turnage, A. K., 38
Turner, C., 265
Turner, J., 479
Turner, J. C., 479
Turner, J. H., 44, 114, 116, 146, 480
Turner, L. H., 32, 121, 171, 185, 464, 500
Turow, J., 391

Uli, J., 473
Ulmer, R., 303

Subject Index

division of labor, 499–500, 521
domestic violence, 503
dominant group, 498, 501, 514
dominant-hegemonic position, 432
dominant position, 432
dominating (DO) style, 470
double agency, 195
double-interact loops, 297–298
drama, 325–326
Dramatism, 324–337
    assumptions of, 326–328
    critique of, 333–336
    at a glance, 326
    guilt/redemption, 329–331
    heurism, 336
    identification, 328–329
    integration of, 333
    as new rhetoric, 328–332
    parsimony, 334
    pentad, 331–332
    in popular press, 332
    scope of, 333–334
    substance, 328–329
    utility of, 334–336
dramatistic ratios, 332
drive reduction, 158
driverless automobiles, 450
dual climates of opinion, 379
dualisms, 524
dualistic approach, 188, 189
duality of structure, 263–266
duration, 295–296
dyadic uniqueness, 183

ecology, 438
effect, 51
effective matrix, 164
effort, 297
electronic era, 443–444
electronic interdependence, 441
electronic media, 441, 444
Emory University, 18
emotions, SI Theory and, 81
empirical approach, 47, 48
enactment, 299–300
enculturation performances, 281,
    283–284
enhancement, 448
enmeshment, 91
Enron, 15
entertainment, ethics, 16, 17
entry phase, 139
environment, 8
environmental advocates, 380
epideictic rhetoric, 317, 318–319

episode relationships, 92
episodes, 90–91
epistemology, 48, 49, 50, 516
epochs, 441
equifinality, 55–56
equilibrium, 216
equivocality, 293–294
    enactment, 299–300
    principles of, 298–299
    reducing, 299–301
    retention, 300–301
    selection, 300
essentialism, 522
ethics
    business and industry, 15–16
    communication and, 14–20
    defined, 14
    entertainment, 16, 17
    higher education, 16, 17–18
    medicine, 16, 18
    politics, 16, 19
    religious, 16–17
    technology, 16, 19
ethnography, 279–281
ethos, 310, 311
Eurocentrism, 44, 50
evaluation, 481
evolutionary theory, 291–292
EVT. *See* Expectancy Violations
    Theory (EVT)
exit phase, 139
expectancies, 124–125
Expectancy Violations Theory
    (EVT), 119–132
    arousal, 127
    assumptions of, 124–127
    communicator reward valence,
        129–130
    critique of, 130–132
    at a glance, 124
    heurism of, 131–132
    integration of, 130
    in practice, 121
    proxemics, 121–123
    scope of, 131
    territoriality, 123–124
    testability of, 131
    threat threshold, 127–128
    utility of, 131
    violation valence, 128–129
expectations
    culture and, 125–126
    interactional, 125
    pre-interactional, 125
expert power, 266

explanation, 136
exploratory affective exchange
    stage, 181
external noise, 10
external stress, 245
extractive strategy, 148

face, 461–462
    negative, 462
    politeness theory and, 462–463
    positive, 462
Facebook, 40, 216, 225
Facebook Addiction Disorder
    (FAD), 40
face concern, 462
face management, 469–470
face need, 462
Face-Negotiation Theory (FNT),
    459–475
    assumptions of, 464–466
    conflict, 465
    conflict management across
        cultures, 470–472
    critique of, 472–474
    face, 461–462
    face management, 469–470
    face-saving, 465–466
    facework, 463–464
    at a glance, 463
    heurism of, 473
    individualistic and collectivistic
        cultures, 466–469
    integration of, 472
    logical consistency of,
        472–473
    politeness theory, 462–463
    self-identity, 464–465
face restoration, 466
face-saving, 465–466
face-threatening acts (FTAs), 465
face-to-face (FtF) communication,
    219–220, 224
facework, 463–464
FAD, 40
faith, ethics and, 16–17
false consciousness, 427
family conflict, as unwanted
    repetitive pattern, 99
fate control, 163
The Fate of the Earth (Schell),
    347
Fate of the Earth (Schell), 347
feedback, 11, 12, 55, 229–230,
    297–298
feminism, 512

homeostatic, 55
homogeneity, 242, 245
Homo narrans, 342
honesty, 183–184
hot media, 445–447
Hovland, Carl, 28
hubris, 244
Hudson, Rock, 21
human choice, 207
human nature, assumptions
about, 158
Hurricane Katrina, 249, 361
hyperpersonal effect, 227
hyperpersonal model, 227
hyperpersonal perspective,
227–231, 233
channel management, 229
feedback, 229–230
idealization of the sender, 228
selective self-representation,
227–228
warranting, 230–231
hypotheses, 52

I, 78–79
ice age analogy, 409
ideal self, 220
identification, 328–329
ideology, 48, 424–425
idioms, 182
illusion of invulnerability, 246–247
illusion of unanimity, 248
imperviousness to influence, 396–397
implicit theorists, 43
importance, 109
impression management, 116,
220–221, 224–225, 230–231
indirect stereotyping, 485–486
individual
in organizations, 277
in society, 79
society and, 75
individual communicator factors,
125
Individual Differences Perspective,
388
individualism, 92, 466–469, 468–469
inductive logic, 59
Industrial Revolution, 499
industry, ethics and, 15–16
information, organizing, 288–289
information environment, 294–295
information seeking, online, 148
information-seeking behavior,
141, 144

in-groups, 479
Initial Interaction Theory. *See*
Uncertainty Reduction Theory
(URT)
Innis, Harold Adams, 439
insults, 90
integrating (IN) style, 470
integration, 198, 199
intentionality, 396
interactional dialectics, 195,
196, 198
interactional expectations, 125
interactional model of
communication, 10–12
Interaction Theory. *See* Uncertainty
Reduction Theory (URT)
interactive strategies, 144–145
interdependence, 54
intergroup overaccommodation, 489
intermedia influence, 364–365
internal stress, 245
Internet
as enhancement, 448
free speech and, 19
obsolescence and, 448
reversal by, 450
in Russia, 378
Uses and Gratification Theory
and, 397–399
interpersonal communication,
31–33, 223–224
interpersonal conflict, 470
interpersonal meaning, 88
interpretive approach, 47, 48
intimacy, 183–184
intimate distance, 122
intrapersonal communication, 30–32
introduction, 314
invention, 312–313
invulnerability, 246–247
Iowa School, 70–71
irrelevant relationship, 106
ISIS, 249
isolation, 374–375

James, William, 70
Jeanne Clery Act, 17
Jefferson, Thomas, 249
Johnson, Lyndon, 406
joy and grief dialectic, 197
Judeo-Christian ethics, 16–17
judicial rhetoric, 318

Kennedy, John F., 447
Kennedy, Ted, 335

knowledge, 516, 517
knowledge gathering, 516
Kopechne, Mary Jo, 335
Kuhn, Manford, 70–71

labels, 78
labor, sexual division of, 499–500,
521
lack of decision-making procedures,
244–245
lack of impartial leadership, 244
language, 27, 76, 327
effects of, 481–482
Lasswell, Harold D., 357
last-minute swing, 380
laws of media, 447–450
leadership, lack of impartial, 244
legitimate power, 266
Lewinsky, Monica, 330
lien, 461
life experiences, 22
life scripts, 91–92
liking, 483
Limbaugh, Rush, 446
limited effects, 388
linear model of communication,
9–10
Lippmann, Walter, 357
listening, ethics of, 20
literate era, 443
"living system" metaphor, 289
logic
deductive, 59
of good reasons, 347
inductive, 59
logical consistency, 56, 58
of Communication
Accommodation Theory, 491
of Communication Privacy
Management Theory,
215–216
of Cultivation Theory, 416–417
of Cultural Studies, 433–434
of Face-Negotiation Theory,
472–473
of Narrative Paradigm, 349–350
of Organizational Culture Theory,
285
of Organizational Information
Theory, 302
of Rhetorical Theory, 320–321
of Spiral of Science Theory,
384–385
of Uses and Gratification Theory,
400–401

utility of, 507–508
women's translation processes, 502–503
mythos, 341

narration, 339, 344–345
narrative, 339
narrative malleability, 339
Narrative Paradigm, 338–352
  assumptions of, 341–344
  critique of, 349–351
  at a glance, 341
  heurism of, 351
  integration of, 348–349
  key concepts, 344–348
  logical consistency of, 349–350
  narration, 344–345
  narrative rationality, 345–348
  in popular press, 348
  vs. rational world paradigm, 342
  scope of, 349
  utility of, 350–351
narrative rationality, 345–348
National Association of Colleges and Employers, 307
National Commission on the Causes and Prevention of Violence, 406
National Safety Management Society, 4
the negative, 330
negative face, 462
negative self-talk, 78
negotiated position, 432
negotiation, culture and, 472
neo-Marxists, 424
networks, 34
neutralizing, 198, 199
New England Journal of Medicine, 18
new media, 37
newspapers, 421
news reporting, 421–422
New York Times, 21
Nichols, Marie Hochmuth, 334
Nixon, Richard, 447
Noelle-Neumann, Elisabeth, 370
  See also Spiral of Silence Theory
noise, 9–10
nominal concepts, 45
nonaccomodation, 487–488
non-intimacy, 173
nonverbal communication, 120, 126–127, 225–226
norms, 482–483

No Sense of Place (Meyrowitz), 451
novelty and predictability, 194–195, 196, 197
numbers, 440

Obama, Barack, 39, 485
obliging (OB) style, 470
observations, 59
obsolescence, 448
Occupy Wall Street, 15, 381–382
OCT. *See* Organizational Culture Theory (OCT)
OIT. *See* Organizational Information Theory (OIT)
onion analogy, 175–176
online information, 210
online relationships, 219–220, 223–225
ontology, 48–50, 516, 517
openness, 54
openness and protection, 194, 196
operationalize, 59
opinion, 372
oppositional position, 432
order, 329–330
organizational communication, 31, 34–36, 288–289
organizational culture, 275–276
  symbols, 277–278
  variety of, 278–279
Organizational Culture Theory (OCT), 272–286
  assumptions of, 276–279
  communicative performance, 281–284
  critique of, 284–286
  cultural metaphor, 275–276
  ethnographic understanding, 279–281
  at a glance, 275
  heurism of, 285–286
  integration of, 284
  logical consistency, 285
  in practice, 282
  symbols, 277–278
  utility of, 285
Organizational Information Theory (OIT), 287–304
  assumptions of, 292–294
  critique of, 302–303
  cycles, 297–298
  General Systems Theory, 290–291
  at a glance, 290
  heurism of, 303

  information environment, 294–295
  integration of, 301–302
  key concepts, 294–298
  logical consistency of, 302
  in popular press, 296
  principles of equivocality, 298–299
  reducing equivocality, 299–301
  rules, 295–297
  theory of sociocultural evolution, 291–292
  utility of, 303
organizational rituals, 282
organizational rules, 296
organizations, self-governing, 296
orientation stage, 180–181
Other-Burkean frame, 335–336
ought self, 220
outcome, 157, 162
out-groups, 479
out-group stereotypes, 247
outsider within, 520
overaccommodation, 488–490
overattribution, 228
overestimation of the group, 246–247

pack journalism, 365
paradigm, 340
paradigm shift, 340
parametric rules, 53
parasocial interaction, 393
Park, Robert E., 357
parsimony, 56, 58
  of Coordinated Management of Meaning, 101
  of Dramatism, 334
  of Relational Dialectics Theory, 201
  of Structuration Theory, 269–270
partial, 520
particular others, 79
passion performances, 281, 282–283
passive strategies, 144
pathos, 311
Paux Christi, 380
Penn State University sexual abuse scandal, 249
pentad, 331–332
pentadic ratios, 332
People for the Ethical Treatment of Animals (PETA), 380
perception, 481
  gender-based differences in, 499

performance
  communicative, 281–284
  defined, 281
  enculturation, 281, 283–284
  passion, 281, 282–283
  political, 281, 283
  ritual, 281, 282
  social, 281, 283
personal boundary, 212
personal distance, 122
personal identity, 389
personal idioms, 182
personal information, online, 210,
    224
personal integrative needs, 390
personal meaning, 87–88
personal phase, 139
personal relationships, 389
personal rituals, 282
personal space, 121
personnel, 296
persuasion, 36
  See also Rhetorical Theory
  Cognitive Dissonance Theory
    and, 113–115
  political, 332
PETA. *See* People for the Ethical
    Treatment of Animals (PETA)
phenomenology, 27–28
physical (external) noise, 10
physical arousal, 127
physician-assisted suicide, 18
physiological noise, 10
Plato, 340
pluralistic ignorance, 376
policy agenda, 361–362
politeness theory, 462–463
political performances, 281, 283
political persuasion, 332
political rhetoric. *See* deliberative
    rhetoric
politics
  ethics, 16, 19
  Mean World Index and, 413
positive face, 462
positivistic (empirical) approach,
    47, 48
post-decision dissonance, 113–114
Postman, Neil, 450–451
power, 163, 261
  coercive, 265
  expert, 266
  legitimate, 266
  media and, 426
  opposition to those in, 511

referent, 266
reward, 264–265
struggle for, 426
types, 264
women and, 265
power differences, 487–488
power relations, 425–426
practical consciousness, 262–263
praxis, 192
predicted outcome value (POV),
    151, 152
prediction, 136
pre-interactional expectations, 125
premature birth, 197
presence and absence dialectic, 197
pressures on dissenters, 248–249
pressure toward uniformity, 248–249
primary territories, 123
priming, 361
print era, 443
Prisoner's Dilemma, 159–160
privacy rule attributes, 212
private boundaries, 210–211
private disclosures, 208–209
private information, 208
  boundary turbulence principle,
    214
  control principle, 209–210
  co-ownership and guardianship
    principle, 212–214
  online, 210
  ownership principle, 209
  rules principle, 211–212
private life, 499
privilege, 61
problem-solving groups, 240
process, 5
productive exchange, 165
promises, 90
Proportional Representation of
    Diversity (PROD) index, 415
proxemics, 121–123
proxemic zones, 121–123
psychological noise, 10
public, 372
public agenda, 361
public and private dialectic, 195, 196
public communication, 31, 36–37
public distance, 123
public image, 175
Public Interest Research Group
    (PIRG), 19
public life, 499
public opinion, 372–373, 376–378
  See also Spiral of Silence Theory

Public Opinion (Lippmann), 357
public speaking, 307
public territories, 123
punctuation, 90
punishment, 158
pure research, 59
purpose, 332
Pygmalion effect, 78

qualitative research, 60–64
quantitative research, 59–60, 62–63
quasi-statistical sense, 375–376

race, 92
race card, 485
radio, 449
rationale, 110
rationality, 159
  narrative, 345–348
rationalization, 159
  collective, 247–248
rational world paradigm, 340, 342,
    343
ratio of the senses, 444
RDT. *See* Relational Dialectics
    Theory (RDT)
reactivity searching, 145
real and ideal dialectic, 195–196
real concepts, 45
receiver, 9, 228
reciprocity, 175
*Reclaiming Conversation: The
    Power of Talk in the Digital
    Age* (Turkle), 454
redemption, 330–331
referent power, 266
reflected appraisals, 78
reflexivity, 262–263
reframing, 198, 199
regulative rules, 98
relational costs/rewards, 177–179
Relational Dialectics Theory (RDT),
    187–203
  assumptions of, 190–191
  autonomy and connection,
    192–193
  beyond basic dialectics, 196–198
  contextual dialectics, 195–196
  core concepts, 191–192
  CPM Theory and, 208
  critique of, 200–201
  at a glance, 189
  heurism of, 201
  integration of, 200
  novelty and predictability, 194–195

openness and protection, 194
parsimony, 201
in popular press, 193
responses to, 198–200
utility of, 201
relational factors, 125
relational uncertainty, 147
relationships, 45–46
consonant, 106
defined, 91
developed, 145–147
development of, 219, 225
dissonant, 106
episode, 92
evaluating a, 161–163
irrelevant, 106
long-distance, 147
nature of, 158
online, 219–220, 223–225
personal, 389
relevance, 363
reliability, 62–63
religion, 381
ethics and, 16–17
research, 21
agenda setting, 356–359
applied, 59
pure, 59
qualitative, 60–64
quantitative, 59–60, 62–63
reliability, 62–63
scientific method, 58–60
theory and, 43
validity, 63
research process, 49–50, 58–64
resonance, 411, 412
resources, 96–97, 264
allocative, 264
authoritative, 264
retention, 300–301
retrieval, 448–449
reversal, 448, 449–450
reward-cost ratio, 177–178
reward power, 264–265
rewards, 156, 158
relational, 177–179
rhetoric, 36–37
defined, 309
deliberative, 317, 319
epideictic, 317, 318–319
forensic, 317, 318
judicial, 318
types of, 317–320
Rhetoric (Aristotle), 206, 306–323
assumptions of, 309–311

canons of, 312–317
Rhetorical Theory, 306–323
arrangement, 313, 314
assumptions of, 309–311
canons, 312–317
critique of, 320–322
delivery, 313, 316–317
at a glance, 308
heurism of, 321–322
integration of, 320
invention, 312–313
logical consistency of,
320–321
memory, 313, 316
in practice, 316
rhetorical tradition, 308–309
style, 313, 315
syllogism, 311–312
test of time of, 322
types of rhetoric, 317–320
rhetorical tradition, 26–27
Rhetoric of Motives (Burke),
328–332
ridicule, 504
ritual, 504
ritual performances, 281, 282
ritual perspective, 405–406
role dialectics, 197
roles, 34
role taking, 77
Romney, Mitt, 485
Rubin, Alan, 393
rule development, 211
rules
constitutive, 97
defined, 295
habitual, 53
organizational, 35, 296
in Organizational Information
Theory, 295–297
parametric, 53
private information, 211–212
regulative, 98
role of, 207–208
in Structuration Theory, 260–261,
263–264
tactical, 53
rules approach, 51, 52–53
ruling class, 515–516
Russian Internet usage, 378
Ryan, Paul, 348

salience, 362
salwar kameez, 486
same-sex marriages, 26–27

Sandberg, Sheryl, 508
Sanders, Bernie, 15
Sandy Hook Elementary/Newtown
shooting, 363, 421
Sapir-Whorf hypothesis, 327
scapegoating, 330
scene, 331
Schramm, Wilbur, 392
scientific method, 58–60
scope, 56, 58
of Communication
Accommodation Theory,
490–491
of Coordinated Management of
Meaning, 100–101
of Dramatism, 333–334
of Expectancy Violations
Theory, 131
of Groupthink, 252
of Narrative Paradigm, 349
of Social Exchange Theory, 167
of Social Information Processing
Theory, 232
of Social Penetration Theory,
184–185
of Structuration Theory, 269
of Symbolic Interaction
Theory, 80
secondary territories, 123
second order effects, 411–412
second shift, 500
segmentation, 198, 199
selection, 198, 199, 300
selective attention, 111
selective exposure, 111
selective interpretation, 111
selective retention, 111
selective self-representation,
227–228
selectivity, 396
self, 77–79
looking-glass self, 77–78
self-appointed mindguards, 248
self-awareness, 23
self-censorship, 248
self-concept, 81
defined, 73
development of, 73–74
as motivation for behavior, 74–75
self-disclosure, 137, 164–165, 174,
176, 208
guidelines for, 177
on social media, 147–148
self-esteem, 32
self-fulfilling prophecy, 74–75, 78